ON ACTIVE SERVICE
IN PEACE AND WAR

HENRY L. STIMSON

PORTRAIT BY KARSH

ON
ACTIVE SERVICE
IN PEACE AND WAR

BY

HENRY L. STIMSON

Secretary of War 1911-13, Secretary of State 1929-33
Secretary of War 1940-45

AND

McGEORGE BUNDY

1971

OCTAGON BOOKS
New York

Reprinted 1971
by arrangement with Harper & Row, Publishers, Incorporated

OCTAGON BOOKS
A DIVISION OF FARRAR, STRAUS & GIROUX, INC.
19 Union Square West
New York, N. Y. 10003

About one fifth of the material in this book was
published serially under the title of *Time of Peril*

LIBRARY OF CONGRESS CATALOG CARD NUMBER: 79-159230

ISBN 0-374-97627-9

Printed in U.S.A. by
NOBLE OFFSET PRINTERS, INC.
NEW YORK 3, N. Y.

THIS   BOOK   IS   DEDICATED

TO

M. W. S.

WHOSE LOVE AND CARE HAVE
MADE   POSSIBLE   BOTH   THE
LIFE AND THIS RECORD OF IT

H. L. S.   McG. B.

TABLE OF CONTENTS

Introduction by Henry L. Stimson   xi

PART I: ON MANY FRONTS

I   Attorney for the Government   3

II   With Roosevelt and Taft   18
1. Running for Governor   2. Secretary of War   3. The Split of 1912

III   Responsible Government   56
1. Framing a Program   2. In Convention Assembled 3. Success, Failure, and Victory   4. Credo of a Progressive Conservative

IV   The World Changes   82
1. War Comes to America   2. Colonel Stimson

V   As Private Citizen   101
1. The League of Nations Fight   2. At the Bar   3. The Peace of Tipitapa

VI   Governor General of the Philippines   117
1. The Background   2. A Happy Year   3. Later Disappointments and Some Hopes

PART II: WITH SPEARS OF STRAW

VII   Constructive Beginnings   155
1. Washington in 1929   2. London in 1930   3. Latin America in 1931

VIII   The Beginnings of Disaster   190
1. Before the Storm   2. Economic Crisis in Europe 3. More about "These Damn Debts"

IX   The Far Eastern Crisis   220
1. A Japanese Decision   2. From Conciliation to Nonrecognition   3. Shanghai   4. The Borah Letter   5. Conclusion and Retrospect

X   The Tragedy of Timidity   264
    1. Disarmament—A Surface Issue   2. The Failure of
    Statesmanship

XI   Out Again   282
    1. The Campaign of 1932   2. Middleman after Election

XII   Toward General War   297
    1. Citizen and Observer   2. 1933–1940—Cast as Cas-
    sandra

Part III: TIME OF PERIL

XIII   Call to Arms   323
    1. Back to Washington   2. The Newcomer   3. The
    Best Staff He Ever Had

XIV   The First Year   345
    1. Men for the New Army   2. Supplies   3. To Britain
    Alone

XV   Valley of Doubt   364
    1. A Difference with the President   2. The Price of
    Indecision

XVI   The War Begins   382
    1. Pearl Harbor   2. Mission of Delay   3. War Secretary

XVII   The Army and Grand Strategy   413
    1. Pearl Harbor to North Africa   2. The Great Decision

XVIII   The Wartime Army   449
    1. Reorganization   2. "Dipping Down"   3. The Place
    of Specialists   4. Student Soldiers   5. The Army and the
    Negro   6. Science and New Weapons

XIX   The Effort for Total Mobilization   470
    1. Military Manpower   2. National Service   3. Labor
    and the War   4. The Army and War Production—A Note
    on Administration   5. Public Relations

XX   The Army and the Navy   503
    1. Stimson and the Admirals   2. Lessons of Antisub-
    marine War   3. Unification and the Future

XXI   The Army and the Grand Alliance   524
       1. Stilwell and China   2. France—Defeat, Darlan, De
       Gaulle, and Deliverance   3. FDR and Military Govern-
       ment   4. A Word from Hindsight

XXII   The Beginnings of Peace   565
       1. A Shift in Emphasis   2. The Morgenthau Plan
       3. The Crime of Aggressive War   4. Planning for Recon-
       struction   5. A Strong America   6. Bases and Big Powers
       7. The Emergent Russian Problem

XXIII The Atomic Bomb and the Surrender of Japan   612
       1. Making a Bomb   2. The Achievement of Surrender

XXIV   The Bomb and Peace with Russia   634

XXV   The Last Month   656
       1. Judgment of the Army   2. The Chief of Staff   3. The
       Commander in Chief   4. The End

       Afterword by Henry L. Stimson   671

       A Note of Explanation and Acknowledgment
            by McGeorge Bundy   673

       Brief Chronology of World War II   679

       Index   685

INTRODUCTION

THIS book contains an account of the years of my public service—my actions, motives, and estimates of results—from my point of view. The writing of the book has been the work of Mr. McGeorge Bundy. Its style and composition are his; but, where he writes of what I have thought and felt, he does so after we have worked together for eighteen months in an earnest effort to make an accurate and balanced account. We have aimed to present not only my past experience but my present opinions as clearly and as honestly as we can. The result is a record which I believe fully reflects my best judgment of what my public life has been. I am profoundly grateful to him for having made possible this record upon questions which are vital to me and on which I have spent most of my active life.

This book is intended to be a "pilot biography"—to be written while my memory of important events is still alive—in order to forestall possible biographies written without the careful aid of my papers or myself. Unfortunately I have lived long enough to know that history is often not what actually happened but what is recorded as such. While it is as accurate as Mr. Bundy and I can make it, we know that even so it contains errors of fact and judgment, and accordingly my executors will be directed to place my diaries and other papers in a depository where, in due time, they will be perfectly accessible to historians and other students, in order that such errors may be corrected in the cold light of history.

Inasmuch as I did not enter into public office until I was over thirty-eight years old and kept no diaries of my previous life, and as the reader may have some interest in the sources from which I came and the formative conditions which developed and influenced me during my early life, it has seemed well that I should add to this introduction a few pages bearing on those factors. It will be necessarily a little longer and I trust a little more illuminating than a transcription of *Who's Who* and will be wholly dependent upon my own memory. When a man reaches my age, there are—for better or worse— few who can either corroborate or contradict him.

My forebears on both sides of my family were nearly all of New England stock, products of the Massachusetts migration during the first half of the seventeenth century. They were sturdy, middle-class people, religious, thrifty, energetic, and long-lived. Almost the only non-English strain was composed of the French Huguenot Boudinots, represented in my great-grandmother, whose stories to me of her childhood talks with George Washington, coupled with the fact that I possessed for some years not only all my grandparents but in addition no less than four great-grandparents, convinced me that man's normal term of life on this earth was at least a hundred years. Soon after the Revolution both sides of the family moved from Massachusetts and took up land in New York, my Stimson ancestor, who had been a soldier in the Continental Army throughout the war, becoming the first settler of Windham in the Catskills, and the ancestors of my mother settling on the Delaware River near Delhi. Both lines contained enough clergymen and deacons to keep up fairly well the moral standards of the stock. From these agrarian surroundings of up-State New York my father's father and my mother's mother, years later, attracted by the great city which was developing at the mouth of the Hudson, moved down to New York to try to find a more interesting and varied life.

I was born in New York City on September 21, 1867. Less than nine years thereafter my young mother died leaving her two children motherless, but the doors of my grandparents' home immediately opened and took us in to the loving care of the large family within.

From then until I was thirteen years old I lived the life of a New York City boy. During the morning I attended New York schools whose curricula were so unsatisfactory that for two years my hard-working father took me entirely out of school and himself gave me the only teaching of that period which stood by me in later years. During the afternoon I had no outdoor place wherein to play except the cobbled streets of the city. There were then in New York no recreation grounds in or out of the schools, and the grassy meadows of Central Park were strictly foreclosed against trespass. Nor were there any rapid transit systems by which to reach the outside country.

But at thirteen there came a great change. My mental and physical horizons broadened before me. My father, dissatisfied with the conditions in New York, placed me in Phillips Academy at Andover, Massachusetts. I was much younger than any other boy in the school but the new surroundings were like heaven to a boy who craved escape from city life. I have heard the discipline of Phillips Academy of those old days described by an alumnus as "perfect freedom, tempered by expulsion." Of the outdoor life of the students that was a fair description. There was football, baseball, skating, bobsledding, and walking over the hills and woodlands of northern Massachusetts within generous limits, quite untrammeled by authority.

But once we entered the classroom it was quite a different matter. Andover fitted a boy for college and it fitted him well. The courses taught were fewer than they are today, but they were taught with extreme thoroughness. And the numbers of each class being large, the mere experience of standing up before a good-sized audience and answering tough problems before a rapid-firing instructor was in itself a stiff discipline to the average boy. To me it opened a new world of effort and competition. It also opened to me a new world of democracy and of companionship with boys from all portions of the United States. At that time Phillips Academy contained about two hundred fifty students, many coming from rural New England, but the remainder from nearly every other state in the Union. A large percentage of them were working their own way in whole or in part.

School life was extremely simple and inexpensive. The cost of tuition was sixty dollars a year. The school possessed no dormitories except the Latin and English Commons, in which nearly a third of the students lived. These consisted of two rows of very cheaply built three-story wooden houses, each house containing rooms for six students. The rental for each student was three dollars a term. There was no sanitation or water except from a single outdoor pump from which each student carried his own requirements, and no heat except that which came from each student's stove. And as the two rows of Commons stood on the northwestern slope of Andover Hill facing the distant New Hampshire hills on the horizon, winter life there was neither soft nor enervating. Some of the remaining students roomed in the houses of instructors but most of them were in boardinghouses approved by the faculty in the town of Andover.

The result for me was association with a very different group of young men from those I had met in New York; they were representatives of homes of many varieties scattered all over the United States—most of them simple homes—but in general the boys were drawn to Andover by the desire to get the teaching given by a school which was known to have represented for over a hundred years the ideals of character and education believed in by the founders of our country.

I was too young to appreciate the full advantages of these new associations at first, but as the years of my course rolled by they were brought home to me, and I can never be sufficiently grateful to the school for the revolution it worked in my own character. In 1905 I was elected a trustee of the school and subsequently the president of the Board of Trustees, a position I held until my resignation in 1947. During these forty-two years the development of the school—its ideals as well as its buildings and surroundings—has been one of the greatest interests of my life.

I was graduated from Andover in 1883 in the Classical Department—a year too young to be admitted to Yale—and spent the intervening year in special tutoring in New York, returning to Andover during the spring term of 1884 and taking up special scientific courses.

In the autumn of 1884 I entered the class of '88 at Yale. That college had not yet fully embarked upon its career as a university. The elective system had only begun. The courses of freshmen and sophomores were still prescribed and consisted largely of Latin, Greek, and mathematics taught rather less effectively than at Andover. Even in junior and senior years, with the exception of "Billy" Sumner's economics and some of the courses in English and history, there was much time lost. There was little opportunity for individual thinking as distinguished from reciting things taught. The chief fruits of my four years at Yale came from the potent democratic class spirit then existing on the Yale campus; and that experience was most important to my life, both in the character developed and in the friendships formed.

When, after my graduation in 1888, I went for two years to the Harvard Law School, I found an atmosphere both inside the halls of the university and outside in its yard which was remarkably different from that in New Haven. In the classrooms of the Law School there was a spirit of independent thinking unlike anything I had met before. It was highly competitive and provocative of individual reasoning. To one who had been accustomed to enter a classroom for the purpose of reciting from memory lessons previously learned from higher authority, this was a sharp surprise. In the Law School classrooms one was obliged to form his own opinions and rules of law by induction from legal decisions stated without comment —and to do it on the floor. The whole atmosphere was electric with the sparks of competitive argument. On the other hand, among the students of the university at large, there was little of the corporate class spirit and democratic energy which was so visible on the Yale campus. The Harvard student, even if he was an undergraduate, seemed to think less in terms of his class and college and more in those of the outside world than his opposite number at Yale. There was also broader and more individualistic thinking open to him. For example, in philosophy he might study under three great teachers—George H. Palmer, William James, and Josiah Royce, and these were available whether he was an undergraduate or in a professional school.

In the retrospect of years it is hard, if not impossible, to balance fairly the benefits to their students accruing sixty years ago from the corporate energy and democratic spirit of Yale as against the courageous individualism and broader philosophy of Harvard. I can only say that I am glad to have had a vision of both of these great institutions, and further, that the teachings of the Harvard Law School created a greater revolution in my power of thinking than any teaching that I got from

Yale, while the faith in mankind that I learned on the campus at New Haven was greater and stronger than any such faith I achieved at Harvard.

In 1885, at the close of my freshman year at Yale, there came to me an unexpected and exceptional opportunity to become acquainted with another very democratic side of American life. My pioneer ancestors had given me a sound body and a love of the outdoors, together with a deep yearning for the loneliness of the wilderness. By a stroke of good fortune I received in 1885 a chance to visit a portion of the western United States while it was yet a frontier, with Indians still restive and wild animals still abundant. The effect on my future life was profound. For over twenty years thereafter I spent a portion of nearly every year in the mountains and forests of the western Rockies or Canada, exploring, hunting, and traveling by horse, foot, or canoe. I came into contact with the simple rough men of the wilderness, both red and white. I witnessed an Indian outbreak in 1887. I came to know the Blackfeet and hunted and climbed with their young men. I became a fair rifleman and canoeman; was at home in forest, prairie or mountains; could pack my own horses, kill my own game, make my own camp, and cook my own meals. There were no guides in those days in the places I visited. With George Bird Grinnell I explored and mapped that portion of Montana now comprising Glacier National Park, and one of the mountains there still bears my name. When I married I obtained a devoted helpmeet who also loved the wilderness and was willing to endure its discomforts and hardships, so our trips were continued until well into middle life.

Looking back, I find it hard to exaggerate the effect of these experiences on my later life. That effect, physical, mental, and moral, was great. Not only is self-confidence gained by such a life, but ethical principles tend to become simpler by the impact of the wilderness and by contact with the men who live in it. Moral problems are divested of the confusion and complications which civilization throws around them. Selfishness cannot be easily concealed, and the importance of courage, truthfulness, and frankness is increased. To a certain extent the effect is similar to the code of honor learned by the soldier in the field.

After the termination of my work at the Harvard Law School in 1890, I lived for three years with my father in New York City. He was the man who of all others had the greatest influence upon the ideals and purposes of my adolescent life. He had been a soldier in the Civil War and had well-nigh paid for that experience with his life. At the close of the war he became a banker and broker in the firm of his father in New York. He married in 1866 and some five years afterward, when my mother's failing health drove the family to Europe, he gave up his business in Wall Street, to which he had never given his heart, and began the study of medicine in Zurich and Paris under Pasteur, completing his course and taking his medical degree on his return at the Bellevue Hospital Medical College. My mother's death was a crushing blow to him and he never remarried but devoted himself with such effort to his profession that he advanced with unusual speed to eminence in the branch of his choice—surgery. He became professor of surgery in the New York University Medical School, and subsequently in the Cornell Medical College from its establishment until the date of his death. He became attending surgeon at the Presbyterian and Bellevue hospitals and finally at the New York Hospital where he remained for twenty-two years until his retirement, carrying in addition to his service at the hospital full responsibility for the heavy service at their emergency branch, the House of Relief in Hudson Street. He was never particularly interested in the development of a lucrative private practice. His heart was in his hospital work. I remember his quoting to me some famous French surgeon who had said that he much preferred the poor for his patients for God was their paymaster. While I was with him he lived frugally, mainly on his salary as a professor and the income from the slender savings of his early years as a young banker. In spite of the bent for mathematics and science which underlay his success in his profession, throughout his life he maintained his love of the classics and of classical and European history, remembering his Latin poetry long after my own memory of it was sadly dimmed. The influence of such a character upon his children was their greatest loadstone and guide. My sister never married and lived with him in a wonderful companionship until his death. My own three years in his house, in close and affectionate contact with him while working my way in the practice of the law downtown, was a period of dominant importance in the shaping of my future life.

On July 6, 1893, I married Miss Mabel Wellington White, the daughter of Mr. and Mrs. Charles A. White of New Haven, Connecticut. That marriage has now lasted for over fifty-four years, during which she has ever been my devoted companion and the greatest happiness in my life.

I was admitted to the bar in New York County in June 1891. Five months afterward I became a clerk in the office of Root & Clarke, and on January 1, 1893, I was admitted to the firm. Mr. Bronson Winthrop, who became my lifelong partner, was admitted to the firm on the same day. On Mr. Clarke's retirement in 1897 the firm's name became Root, Howard, Winthrop & Stimson, and after Mr. Root became Secretary of War in the Cabinet of President McKinley the firm name became Winthrop & Stimson. It so continued until 1927 when it was changed to Winthrop, Stimson, Putnam & Roberts, the name it holds today, when the partners number thirteen and the law clerks in its office thirty-six more. The firm received its character from its original founder, Elihu Root, who was our exemplar of what a high-minded counselor should be, and the memory of whose rectitude, wisdom, and constructive sagacity ever remained before us. Winthrop and I did our utmost to carry on the traditions of the firm which Mr. Root left. The character of the young men who thereafter came into the firm has been a source of high satisfaction in my life. Even now, when I am no longer an active member of the firm, I find my association with its members one of my greatest comforts. During my various excursions into public life I always felt that I remained a lawyer with a law firm waiting as a home behind me, to which I could return on the completion of my public task and where I would always find awaiting me congenial friends and collaborators in the law. This feeling gave me a confidence in the performance of my public duties which was an inestimable encouragement.

The early nineties were times of seething political activity in New York. I came of a Republican family but when President Cleveland raised the issue of reducing the tariff I followed him and voted for him in 1892. But the government of the state and city of New York, at that time under the influence of Tammany Hall, was of such a character as to make the path of a young Democrat difficult to follow. And when Mr. Cleveland's own party rejected his policies; when the membership of the Court of Appeals was sullied by the appointment by Governor Flower to that court of Isaac Maynard in 1893, as a reward for political services; and finally when in 1894 the Lexow investigation revealed a sink of corruption in the New York Police Department, I enrolled myself and worked as a Republican.

The local Republican party in some portions of New York City was not much above Tammany in political righteousness, being more eager to get sops of patronage by trading with the dominant Democrats than to follow Republican principles. But in the center of Manhattan were several Assembly districts where the situation was different and where a Republican ticket with proper effort could be elected. In one of these, the 27th Assembly District, I lived and worked as a Republican. I became the captain of an election district and learned what constant effort was required to persuade the ordinary American citizen in a great city to take the trouble to exercise his duties as a voter. I eventually became the president of my Assembly district club and a member of the Republican County Committee of New York County. We ardent young men had a hard fight, for the Republican organization of the county, as I have just pointed out, was far below in character that which we believed it should be. It seemed to us of little beneficial effect to laboriously bring out voters on election day to vote for a candidate who had been selected and nominated by a corrupt county leader. The primaries in those days were very imperfect. They had no basis in law but were created simply by rules of the Republican organization. We saw ourselves habitually outvoted at conventions by the fraudulent use of this defective machinery. So finally we staged a revolt and when in 1897 we were thus outvoted in a convention in which we believed we really held the majority of votes, we retired from the room, nominated two well-qualified gentlemen as independent candidates for membership in the state Assembly and in the city Board of Aldermen, and successfully carried that ticket to victory at the subsequent election over the candidates of both the Republican machine and the Democratic party. By that demonstration of power we brought the Republican county machine to its knees and the following winter a primary election law, drawn by ourselves, was by the force of public opinion carried through the legislature. That law put an end to the flagrant methods of the preceding years and I believe has been in effect ever since, governing the conduct of primaries and party elections in a way which makes it more possible than before for honest voters, if they are willing to work hard enough, to succeed in preventing machine control. By those early years of hard political work I gained a foothold in my knowledge of the elements of American citizenship. I could talk the language of the trade and meet the professionals in politics on a fair basis.

It was during these years that I met Theodore Roosevelt, who had been a notable and picturesque figure in New York public life ever since the early eighties. His vigorous efforts for a cleanup in our local political life had already made him a marked leader among all the young men who, like myself, had been similarly interested. Our friendship, which began in 1894, lasted until his death in 1919.

In 1894 came the Spanish war; it caught me napping. Until then the United States had passed through a period of profound peace ever since the end of the Civil War. Not only had we been free from strife ourselves, barring occasional small affrays with Indians on our western frontier, but during that time there had been no wars in the outside world of enough importance to attract much popular attention. The century was apparently closing with a growing extension of democracy, freedom, and peace throughout the world. I can remember that that was my feeling. The thought of preparing oneself for possible military service hardly entered my head. So in April, 1898, when the United States declared war upon Spain, I found myself over thirty years of age and entirely untrained and unprepared for military service. I enlisted in Squadron A of the National Guard, one of the troops of which participated in the Puerto Rican campaign. My own troop was not selected and I was relegated to the task of training myself for a possible spread of the war or the coming of some new war, a duty which until then I had wholly failed to recognize. The Spanish war was terminated by armistice in August of the same year. I remained in the squadron for nine years, rising from a private to a first lieutenant. It was a fine organization. It took its work seriously and, there being no state police in New York in those days, participated in not infrequent field service including the maneuvers at Manassas with the Regular Army in 1904. The main result, however, was that my attention was turned to possibilities and duties to which my mind had before been closed.

My close friendship with Mr. Root also brought me near to the Army and the War Department. I followed with great interest his work in reorganizing our military establishment, creating for the first time a General Staff and War College, and laying the foundation for the government of the Philippine Islands. In this way I was unconsciously building up a background of preparation for opportunities which many years later unexpectedly came my way in 1911, 1917, 1928, and 1940.

Despite these various activities, my main occupation during these early years of my life was as a young and active lawyer in New York City. The firm of which I was a member had a wide and varied practice. Mr. Root being a prominent advocate and trial lawyer, my attention had been drawn early in that direction when I acted as his assistant in cases of importance. Even after he left us, my interest in the art and duties of advocacy still remained. I became active in the Association of the Bar of the City of New York and became familiar with its historic traditions of public service. Through many channels I came to learn and understand the noble history of the profession of the law. I came to realize that without a bar trained in the traditions of courage and loyalty our constitutional theories of individual liberty would cease to be a living reality. I learned of the experience of those many countries possessing constitutions and bills of rights similar to our own, whose citizens had nevertheless lost their liberties because they did not possess a bar with sufficient courage and independence to establish those rights by a brave assertion of the writs of habeas corpus and certiorari. So I came to feel that the American lawyer should regard himself as a potential officer of his government and a defender of its laws and constitution. I felt that if the time should ever come when this tradition had faded out and the members of the bar had become merely the servants of business, the future of our liberties would be gloomy indeed.

I became familiar also with the less direct ways in which the practice of the law is conducive to good citizenship and the lawyer is a stabilizing force in the body politic. I came to realize how important was his trained recognition that there are always two sides to a question and his appreciation of the importance of a fair hearing in every controversy. I came to realize the importance played in a democracy by persuasion as distinguished from force or threats and to recognize the importance of the lawyer as a trained advocate of persuasion.

For ten years after our marriage my wife and I lived in rented homes in the city, varying in size and location according to our means. In 1903 we established a home in the country. Although my profession made it necessary for me to spend most of my time in New York City, both she and I were at heart lovers of the country and desired a place where we could at least spend our week ends and which, as we grew older, might become more and more our real domicile. The spot we selected, in West Hills of the Township of Huntington, lies on the summit of the central ridge of Long Island and affords glimpses of the sound on the north and the distant ocean on the south. From this fact we coined the name "Highhold." This has been our home for forty-four years and is the place to which we have retired now that our work in both New York and Washington has ended.

When we purchased our home it was a farm in a purely farming country, six miles away from Huntington, the nearest village. During the passing years the surrounding countryside has gradually filled up with homeseekers from New York. But our modest farmland and woods have remained the same; and even today I can still look from my piazza to the distant rim of the ocean over a stretch of countryside which, to all appearances, is the same as it was forty years ago.

HENRY L. STIMSON

PART ONE

ON MANY FRONTS

CHAPTER I

Attorney for the Government

THEODORE ROOSEVELT, at the end of 1905, was in full course. A year before, he had been triumphantly elected President in his own right; he was now preparing for a good fight with the Fifty-ninth Congress on railroad rates, pure food, and other issues of his Square Deal. His popularity was enormous; his joyous self-confidence was at its peak. In kinetic response to his personal preaching of a new morality, the country was alive to the meaning of righteous government as it had not been for generations.

The President himself carried the banner for new reforms. Meanwhile he faced a problem in consolidating gains already made. His first administration had seen two legal events that opened the door to more aggressive law enforcement: the Supreme Court's antitrust decision in the *Northern Securities* case, and the passage of the Elkins Act of 1903 against railroad rebates. To get the full value of these new opportunities, the President needed lawyers; he had a vigorous and effective Attorney General in W. H. Moody, but among the law officers in the lower echelons of the federal Government there was room for improvement. In over two years no important conviction had been obtained under the Elkins Act, and it was common knowledge that rebates continued. T.R. wanted the legal help of some of "my type of men."

In December, 1905, Stimson was invited to Washington to see the President. His principal previous connection with Theodore Roosevelt had been as a fellow member of the Boone & Crockett Club of New York, and he traveled to the capital with his mind turned to problems of bear hunting. Calling on his former senior partner, Secretary of State Root, he learned what the President wanted, and a few minutes later, sitting in the White House, he was listening to "the most commanding natural leader" he ever knew. The President had a job for him: would he serve as United States Attorney for the Southern District of New York?

The call of Theodore Roosevelt was irresistible, and Stimson at once accepted. The President said he would discuss the matter with the patronage boss of New York, Senator Tom Platt, and see if it could be arranged. There was plenty of time; the term of the present incumbent had still six weeks to run.

On January 11, 1906, having heard nothing further from the White House, Stimson read in the morning papers that his appointment had been announced the day before by the President. Apparently Senator Platt had given his consent, for the appointment was readily confirmed, and on February 1 Stimson took office. It was his first public office; it came unsought, as did every one of his later appointments. And in 1947 it was clear to him that this first decision was the one from which all his later opportunities developed. On February 1, 1906, he crossed forever the river that separates private citizens from public men.

The law of the United States—the federal law—is applied and interpreted by a hierarchy of courts ranging from the Supreme Court in Washington through the Circuit Courts of Appeals to the District Courts. But the law is *enforced* by prosecutors; no judge, however upright, can personally apprehend a lawbreaker. When Stimson became United States Attorney for the Southern District of New York, he became the chief law-enforcement officer of the American national Government in the most populous and important district in the country. At any time such office presents a challenge to the honor and ability of a member of the bar. And it happened that when Stimson took office there were two circumstances which gave the challenge special point.

One was the nature of the laws now requiring enforcement. In older and simpler times the function of the United States Attorney had been one that a good lawyer could faithfully execute with half his time and almost no assistants. It had been

so executed, with distinction, by Elihu Root less than a generation before—it was the first of many parallels between Mr.
Root and his junior partner that both were thirty-eight when
they assumed this office. But now, in 1906, the United States
was asserting its latent strength; its lawyers were expected
to do successful battle with the corporate giants of the time.
No longer would it be the major business of the United States
Attorney to pursue petty smugglers and violators of the postal
laws.

And it happened that in the years since Mr. Root's incum-
bency the office of the federal attorney had become less and
less competent to deal with cases of such magnitude. Until
just before Stimson's appointment the law provided that the
United States Attorney might keep as his reward a generous
proportion of the moneys recovered in customs cases by his
endeavors, so that in Southern New York the job was reported
to be worth $100,000 a year. But the incumbents, though gen-
erally honorable men, had hardly been of the stature to command any such sum in private practice, and it had become the
habit of the Attorney General to retain private lawyers whenever he had a case of unusual importance or difficulty to press
in the lower courts; his official subordinates were considered
no match for the eminent counsel who acted for the defense in
major cases.

Stimson was hired (at $10,000 a year) to do two things—
first, to make war on violators of the federal law, especially
on the new front of great corporate transgression, and second,
to reorganize his office in such fashion that he himself, with
his own official assistants, would try all important cases. Although he began his court battles before his reorganization of
the office was complete, his final successes at the bar depended
in so great a degree upon the men he gathered around him that
we shall do well to look first at this question of building a team.

When Stimson took office, he had eight assistants at an
aggregate salary of $22,000 a year. This total was less than
what he himself had earned in 1905 as a successful but not
particularly outstanding young lawyer. It was therefore not
surprising to him to find that, with two or three exceptions,
the men in his new office were not of very high caliber—com-

petent and ambitious lawyers were not attracted by the Government's salary scale.

It was not easy at first to see what could be done about it. It might be possible to increase appropriations somewhat (and an increase of 50 per cent was in the end obtained), but even a double rate would hardly attract established lawyers earning five or ten times as much as the best offer Stimson could make. Nor was it likely that among New York's practicing attorneys there was much unrecognized and underpaid talent which could be attracted by a government job—at the New York bar real ability was quickly recognized and rewarded.

Or was it? Granted that few good men over thirty-five were earning less than $10,000, what about the men even younger? Stimson's mind turned back to his own years as a junior—he remembered the time in 1893 when a guaranteed salary of $2,000 had permitted him, after five years of waiting, to marry and support his wife. There were underpaid lawyers of high quality in New York, and he knew where to find them; they were the men fresh out of law school who worked as juniors in the big downtown offices. They knew little about prosecution, it was true, but they knew about as much as he did himself—and as much as most lawyers in private practice would know; perhaps indeed they would know more, for the things they had learned about criminal law in classrooms would not have faded from their minds as from those of their seniors. He would raid the law firms—better yet, he would canvass the law schools and offer his jobs to men whose brains were guaranteed by their deans. Perhaps with these bright young men he could stretch his funds a long way; perhaps they would feel, as he did, the challenge of the job and take its opportunities in partial payment.

And that was the way it turned out, although it took months to find and win the men he wanted. He wrote to the law school deans; he talked to his contemporaries to find out if they knew and would recommend to him particularly likely youngsters; he added his own zealous arguments to the general appeal of a chance to fight under the banner of T.R. and reform. When he got through he had a team of assistants tender in years but equal in their combined talents to any office anywhere, public or private. In later years Stimson always claimed for himself the ability to judge and choose men, and he was prepared to rest this claim with a recapitulation of the names of his chief assistants when he was United States Attorney for the Southern District. Felix Frankfurter went on to the United States Supreme Court and Thomas D. Thacher to the highest court of New York State; Winfred Denison's brilliant career was tragically cut short; all of the others became leaders in private practice, their names perhaps not recognized by the general public but known and honored by the bar.[1] And their youth was for Stimson an advantage and a pleasure. They were able, eager, and loyal, and they were happy to be overworked. They would work in the evenings through the week, and come down to Highhold for the week end in relentless zest for the labor of winning cases for the United States. They were gay, too, and in 1947 Stimson remembered with delight the day when he had seen a future Supreme Court Justice in a losing foot race around the fields of Highhold against a future judge in the New York Court of Appeals.

In later years, when the success of his term as United States Attorney was laid at his door in public and private tributes, Stimson always felt that he could properly accept the credit for choosing these young men, but he always added that the direct honor for cases won was mainly theirs: "For the first few months of my administration I was busy explaining the responsibilities, the duties, and high function of that office to all of the young men of the City of New York who would listen to me. The response that I then found . . . was one of the most inspiring lessons in public spirit and optimism that I have had the happiness to experience; and . . . [It is the] devoted work of those men and that spirit brought with the office to which is due whatever credit and whatever success it has attained."[2]

[1] On a loving cup presented to Stimson by his staff when he retired in 1909 the following names appear: D. Frank Lloyd, Henry A. Wise, J. Osgood Nichols, Winfred T. Denison, Goldthwaite H. Dorr, Felix Frankfurter, Hugh Govern, Jr., Francis W. Bird, Emory R. Buckner, William S. Ball, John W. H. Crim, Thomas D. Thacher, Daniel D. Walton, Harold S. Deming, Robert P. Stephenson, Wolcott H. Pitkin, Jr.

[2] Speech as guest of honor at a testimonial dinner of the New York bar, May 20, 1900.

The first great group of cases which Stimson brought to trial were prosecutions for the offense of rebating. The railroad rebate was an extraordinary device; it had played a major role in the development of gigantic near monopolies. The idea was simple: a large corporation shipping its goods by rail could use its bargaining power as a major customer to force reimbursement of a part of the legal shipping rates charged by the railroad, thus obtaining an advantage over competitors. This reimbursement was called a rebate. In particularly flagrant cases like that of the Standard Oil Company, the big shipper received in addition a rebate on the shipping rates paid by his competitors.

Rebates had been criminal for many years before 1903, but the Elkins Act of that year was the first to give effective weapons to Government prosecutors. Under the Elkins Act, the size of permissible fines was greatly increased, and the shipper as well as the railroad could be prosecuted. The power to impose large fines on the offending corporation was most important, for juries were much more willing to penalize the profiting corporations than to put unhappy corporation underlings in jail while the corporate profiteers went untouched. But before February, 1906, there had been no successful prosecution for rebating.

The first evidence for Stimson's own prosecutions came from the offices of William Randolph Hearst late in 1905; Hearst's peculiar compound of policies at this time included a lively opposition to the "Interests," and his reporters were good sleuths. The new United States Attorney followed up Hearst's leads with energy; within five months he had brought seven indictments, and in the following year his office brought fourteen more. By the time he made his first personal report to the Attorney General, in July, 1907, a total of $362,000 had been assessed in fines for rebating, and it had become customary for defendants to plead guilty in order to avoid the painful publicity of trial and certain conviction.

Stimson's most important rebating prosecutions were against the American Sugar Refining Company and railroads from which it had received rebates. These cases were a remarkable illustration to him of the problems involved in prosecuting big corporations. In the first place, the volume and complexity of the evidence was almost overwhelming; it was necessary to unravel the freight transactions in which the rebate was artfully embedded, and then to reconstruct what actually happened in a manner clear and convincing to the jury. This could be done with assurance only after such an amount of study that Stimson and his assistants in the end were more familiar with these transactions than the officers of the offending corporations.

These cases also demonstrated with remarkable clarity both the stubbornness and the eventual weakness of the corporate wrongdoer. The New York Central Railroad and the American Sugar Refining Company had been partners in rebating, as Stimson proved in three successive jury trials. The Railroad carried its case on through the Supreme Court, as if persuaded that such unwonted misfortune in the federal courts must be an accident. The Sugar Company, on the other hand, fought only one case and then surrendered without a trial on the remaining indictments. The eminent lawyer who was counsel for the company came to Stimson's office bearing a white flag: 'Damn it, Stimson, we think you're wrong on the law and wrong on the facts, but we can't stand the publicity.' Yet this same lawyer had no complaint whatever against the fairness and sobriety of the Government's prosecutions. It was not publicity in itself that he feared; it was public proof of guilt.

The victory thus won showed the wisdom of Elihu Root's advice to Stimson after his first successful trial. The way to stop rebating for good, Root said, was to keep on hitting until the railroads and the shippers understood that they could and would be punished in the courts for their offenses. Stimson's successful prosecutions, followed by others in other federal districts, put a stop to rebating as a major corporate practice in a very few years. In one of the later prosecutions a fine of fantastic size was imposed—$29,000,000 assessed by Kenesaw Mountain Landis in Chicago against the Standard Oil Company. Unlike the more modest fines imposed by the judges before whom Stimson argued, this great judgment was promptly reversed by a higher court.

From the standpoint of their broad effect on the conduct of

business, the rebating cases were probably the most important in Stimson's service as United States Attorney. But there were two other main undertakings which were even more demanding in their preparation and presentation, both of them striking examples of the kind of battle for simple morality in high places which was typical of so much of Theodore Roosevelt's era.

One was the prosecution of Charles W. Morse for misusing the funds of the Bank of North America. Morse's activities were a major element in bringing on the financial panic of 1907, and he was an object of public wrath long before any indictment was found. Morse had concealed his misapplication of bank funds by fictitious loans to dummies of no responsibility; the difficulty was to show that what was to all appearances a real loan was in fact a misapplication of the funds of the bank to a speculation by Morse himself and that the form of a loan had been adopted to deceive the bank examiners. Nor was this case made easier by the fact that Morse, the primary culprit, was not himself the president of the bank. The case was more than a year in preparation, and Stimson made every effort to exclude from the trial the sort of atmosphere of indiscriminate vengeance which malefactors of great wealth so easily arouse against themselves. Morse was duly convicted and sentenced to fifteen years in the penitentiary; but it was typical of the plausible deceitfulness of the man that three years later he was pardoned on the ground of ill health—and lived on long enough to have a further brush with the law.

The second big case—or rather set of cases—in the later years was one to which Stimson always referred as "The Case of the Seventeen Holes." This was a case of customs fraud on a grand scale, and it eventually resulted in a recovery by the Government of about $3,500,000 in back duties. The principal defendant was, once again, the American Sugar Refining Company, this time accompanied by other sugar refiners.

The Case of the Seventeen Holes was an astonishing illustration of the level to which business ethics had fallen in this period. As the defense counsel summed it up, "The charge is that over a series of years the American Sugar Refining Company of New York has been systematically, in season and out of season, from 1901 down until the close of 1907, engaged in stealing from the United States."[3] This had been done by fraudulent weighing of sugar for the determination of custom duties, and the method of the fraud gave the case its name. In seventeen large Government scales, through seventeen small holes, the company's checkers had "systematically" and furtively introduced wires by which they distorted the weights recorded by these scales; the result was that the company, "in season and out of season," had paid duty on less sugar than it actually imported.

Stimson spent the better part of two years of his life on these customs cases. The system of the seventeen holes was uncovered by a federal agent named Richard Parr at the end of 1907, but the first good jury evidence of fraud was obtained only after an exhaustive study of the company's records demonstrated a marked and continuing difference between the amount of sugar sold by the company and the amount on which it paid duty. After a year of preparation the first case, a civil suit, was started for recovery of duty on a small number of specified bales of sugar. Stimson's object here was simply to fix the fact of fraud by the corporation, and the verdict for the Government was wholly effective to this end; only $134,000 was recovered by this verdict, but the evidence of corrupt conspiracy was so damning that rather than face further trial, the American Sugar Refining Company promptly paid $2,000,000 in back duties, and over $1,300,000 more was paid by other guilty refiners.

Criminal prosecution of the guilty individuals was more difficult. The evidence available was sufficient for the indictment and conviction of the men on the docks, the tools of the company, and a number of these men were duly tried and sentenced, as were a number of conniving Government employees. It was much harder to bring home the crime to the company's senior officers. But as Stimson reported to the Attorney General, "Our evidence indicates that this company down to minute details, was virtually run by one man," the president; the president died only two weeks after Parr's first

[3] Quoted in the *Outlook*, May 1, 1909.

discovery of fraud and so escaped prosecution, but the next senior officer connected with the operation, the secretary-treasurer of the company, was duly convicted.

Stimson resigned as United States Attorney in April, 1909, but he continued to act as a special assistant to the Attorney General in the customs cases for more than a year thereafter. The sum of what he and his assistants learned was set forth in a report which shows how badly the clean breezes set loose by Theodore Roosevelt had been needed—and it should be noted that the frauds of the customs-house were not a subject of notorious exposés when Stimson entered office; in his first annual report he had treated customs cases as routine affairs deserving little attention. By 1910 both he and the public had learned better:

"The foregoing investigation had made clear to me the following points:

"*First:* That in the administration of the Customs service in this Port, there has been widespread fraud and corruption among both the importers and the Customs officers.

"*Second:* That this is not the result of the malfeasance of any one officer or administration, but is the result of a lax system during the twenty years covered by our investigation, and probably going back very much further, in which not only the administrative officers, but the laws, regulations and traditions of the service were at fault.

"*Third:* That in spite of the abundant resources which have been placed at our disposal, and of our own unceasing efforts for a year, it seems likely that a comparatively small number of the persons legally or morally guilty can be visited with suitable punishment through the process of the criminal law. . . .

"We have found that local politics have continually had a debasing effect upon the Customs service; that the large sugar refiners have been able to exert great political influence upon Customs officers; that some of the local party organizations have been able to exercise a strong influence upon the course of investigations, and even of prosecutions, through their power over investigators and witnesses. We have found instances of Government agents reporting, many years ago, abuses which were left unpunished until our prosecutions. Years ago, the American Sugar Refining Company was caught using light trucks on its scales in the weighing of its sugar. Later, its employees were found tampering with the scale beam. So far as I can find, nothing was done to remedy this, except to supply Government trucks and to board up the scales. Not a man was prosecuted, nor were the employees of the Sugar Company even refused access to the scales."[4]

The frauds themselves were bad, but this callous indifference to the law and the interests of the United States was even worse, and, having gone as far as he could with punishment under the law, Stimson recommended a further course of action, one which was to him a course of last resort, only to be used when there was no longer any possibility of remedy in the courts:

"I believe, therefore, that there is great need in this matter for the 'punishment of publicity.' . . . I believe . . . that a thorough ventilation of the administration of the Custom House would greatly assist the efforts of those officials who are trying now to reform it. It is difficult for a stranger to have any notion of the way in which this system of graft has entered into the conception of all of the subordinates of this service, or how they have stood together in their defense of it. Almost all of the [Government's] weighers have taken money, and even men otherwise right-minded will vigorously defend the ethics of 'house money.' Such a situation needs the tonic of public indignation to set it right.

"For this reason, it is my view that as soon as the executive has finished its work; as soon as all the indictments which can be found through the ordinary resources of the criminal law have been found . . . and before public interest in the scandal has so subsided that the opportunity is lost, a public investigation of the situation should be made, and the facts now held under ban of secrecy made a matter of public record."[4]

It is important to observe that this was emphatically not an effort to influence public opinion *before* indictment and trial. Stimson could fairly claim that he never tried his cases in the press; his steady refusal to encourage headlines before trial

[4] Report to the President, April 20, 1910.

had indeed won him a reputation for chilly austerity among New York reporters. The principle here asserted was the quite different one that known wrongdoing must be stamped as wrong by public opinion; men whose moral sense had been blunted must be made to understand how their actions looked to the people; the hand of the hard-pressed reformer must be upheld by informed opinion. Public reports of known facts were a fully justified and indeed indispensable weapon to this end.

And Stimson's repugnance to sensational reports before trial did not extend to any feeling that proper court proceedings should go unreported. A year before, the first trial and conviction of the American Sugar Refining Company for custom fraud had gone almost completely unnoticed in the press. Stimson would have expected the silent treatment from the *Herald* of James Gordon Bennett; he had prosecuted Bennett for indecency in his personal columns and collected a $25,000 fine. He would have expected it from Joseph Pulitzer's *World*; he had brought an indictment for criminal libel against Pulitzer at T.R.'s request. But the general reticence of the press in the face of a trial whose implications went so deep was extremely disturbing, and he had turned on March 8, 1909, to Editor Roosevelt of the *Outlook* for a redress of the balance. T.R. was delighted to help, and "The Case of the Seventeen Holes" was fully and accurately reported in his weekly on May 1; subsequent developments received generous space in the New York dailies.

Stimson did not keep in close touch with the customs service after 1910, but he always believed that the great fraud trials of 1909 and 1910 marked a turning point in the ethics of federal law enforcement on the docks. And, at least among customs officials, his own fame persisted. He and Mrs. Stimson traveled repeatedly to Europe in later years. On their return to New York they were invariably hustled through the customs with gingerly respect.

On April 1, 1909, Stimson resigned his office. He had served for more than three years, and it was time to return to private practice; although $10,000 a year, in the days before income tax, was a fair salary for a federal officer, it was less than half of what he had earned before, and he was feeling the pinch. And in a sense the most interesting part of his job was done. The office had been reorganized, and a new standard of effectiveness was soundly established. If he were to retain his standing as a member of the New York bar, he must sooner or later return to private practice, and this seemed a suitable time.

On May 20, in a gesture as unusual as it was heart-warming, the leaders of the New York bar tendered to Stimson a dinner, and during the after-dinner speeches they bestowed their praises with a lavish hand. Yet because this was praise from stern judges, and because it came from the men whose good opinion he most coveted, and most of all because it came from men who might have been expected to resent and belittle his activities against great corporations, Stimson believed that parts of these speeches might be taken, with appropriate discount, as a fair summary of his achievement. At the least, they may serve to show how fortunate he had been in winning the kind of reputation he desired:

"Nor is there time to refer to the many important litigated cases which Stimson directed, or in which he was personally engaged. He had to deal with difficult and complicated questions of law and fact. He had to solve the difficult riddles which Congress is constantly framing in the form of statutes. He had to investigate the involved accounts of great railroad systems and complex banking transactions. He had to uncover new and subtle schemes for concealing violations and evasions of the law. He was unaided by senior counsel. Single-handed, he was constantly opposed to the veterans of the bar. And he was almost uniformly successful, not only in obtaining verdicts and judgments, but in holding them. Among his adversaries were Mr. Choate, the leader of the American bar, Judge Wallace, Judge Parker, Judge Choate, Senator Spooner, John E. Parsons, John G. Milburn, Austen Fox, DeLancey Nicoll, John M. Bowers, Wallace Macfarlane, Congressman Littlefield, John B. Stanchfield. . . .

"Above all other considerations, it should be appreciated that in all this conspicuous and successful work, there was no bravado or parade or bombast, no press interviews, no calling the newspapermen together and communicating to them the plans and exploits of his office, no beating of kettledrums, no eager straining after notoriety and applause, no exhibitions of vanity and conceit, no interjection of his own personality; only the plain, quiet, unostentatious, faithful, and impartial performance of his duty as he understood it. Truly may he be said to have redeemed the administration of justice by the federal authorities from the reproach and contempt into which it was falling, and vindicated and upheld the supremacy of the law. He showed how justice could be effectively and impartially administered by gentlemanly and dignified methods."[5]

And from the leading lawyer of New York, Joseph H. Choate, who presided at the dinner, came a still more ringing tribute:

"It has been the good fortune of Mr. Stimson during the last three years to hold that office when it was charged with the severest responsibilities, the most onerous duties, and the most complex difficulties that I think have ever surrounded any law office in the United States. Here center the great interests of the nation, and the cases that have come into his hands for presentation and argument have been of the utmost importance. I have observed with great interest his self-reliance, his courage, his absolutely perfect preparation, and that tenacity of purpose which distinguishes all the great lawyers that I have ever known . . . and you will bear me witness that he has always held his own against [the leaders of the bar] and has never been charged with anything oppressive, or brutal, or cruel, which so often pertains to the office of prosecuting officer."

Stimson's success as United States Attorney is an important factor in his later career; it gave him his first public reputation and opened the door to immediate and striking opportunities. But it is not the cases tried, or the reputation won, that is most important for our purpose. It is rather the effect of his experience on Stimson's own attitudes. This was his first public office, and it was a case of love at first sight, as Mrs. Stimson often smilingly complained in later years. How it struck him is best revealed in the report of his twentieth Yale reunion in 1908. Talking to his classmates, in the intimate

[5] Remarks of William D. Guthrie.

informality of a small group of lifelong friends, he explained
what it meant to him to become attorney for the United States:

"The last two years of my life have represented a complete
change in my professional career. The profession of the law
was never thoroughly satisfactory to me, simply because the
life of the ordinary New York lawyer is primarily and essentially devoted to the making of money—and not always successfully so. There are some opportunities to do good in it. . . .
[But] it has always seemed to me, in the law, from what I have
seen of it, that wherever the public interest has come into conflict with private interests, private interest was more adequately represented than the public interest. Whenever a great
public question has come up, in which there has been a rich
corporation on one side and only the people on the other, it
has seemed to me that the former always had the ablest and
most successful lawyer to defend it, and very often the side of
the people seemed to go almost by default. I have found comparatively few successful lawyers, in modern times, putting
their shoulders to the public wheel. . . . My private practice,
up to the last three years, brought me constantly into contact
with the side of the corporation, and the office I was in constantly represented the larger corporations of New York. And,
therefore, when I was taken, as you might say, by the back of
the neck, and started out without anticipating it and without
expecting it, and turned loose with nothing but my oath of
office to guide me, the first feeling was that I had gotten out
of the dark places where I had been wandering all my life,
and got out where I could see the stars and get my bearings
once more; and there has been, during those two years, a feeling that the work I was doing amounted to a little bit, or
would amount to something if I put my whole heart into it
and did it thoroughly. And it has made a tremendous difference and a tremendous change in the satisfaction of my professional life. There has been an ethical side of it which has
been of more interest to me, and I have felt that I could get a
good deal closer to the problems of life than I ever did before,
and felt that the work was a good deal more worth while. And
one always feels better when he feels that he is working in a
good cause."

CHAPTER II

With Roosevelt and Taft

S TIMSON'S years as United States Attorney made him one of the trusted lieutenants of the Roosevelt administration, and he found the end of T.R.'s term an emotional and somewhat saddening time. He went to Washington for the famous farewell luncheon of the Tennis Cabinet, and when the Colonel sailed for Africa, Stimson was happy to have been chosen to act as his agent at home in a number of small personal matters. The good fight continued, for Stimson at least, in the new administration. For the next year and a half he was largely occupied with the completion of his customs cases, and he received from President Taft and Attorney General Wickersham exactly the same wholehearted support that he had become used to with President Roosevelt and Attorneys General Moody and Bonaparte.

In the three years that followed the inauguration of Mr. Taft, the controlling factor in American political life was the fluctuating relationship between the ex-President and the President. In the end, in 1912, the two men became open enemies, and the Republican party was split down the middle. To Stimson this result was both unnecessary and catastrophic. Throughout the three-year period before the break he was active in politics, and his weight was continuously thrown in favor of party and personal harmony. As a result of the events of those years he was twice selected for important assignments, once by Mr. Roosevelt and once by Mr. Taft. As a loyal admirer of both men, he refused to believe, then or later, that their differences were irreconcilable. Almost until the end, he hoped for peace and party unity. Almost from the beginning, the current ran against his hopes.

In June, 1910, when T.R. returned in triumph from his African expedition and his grand tour of Europe, the situation was already difficult. Mr. Taft had been nominated and elected as the direct heir of Mr. Roosevelt. The comradeship and affection between the two men had been famous for many years, and in T.R.'s Cabinet, Secretary of War Taft had been in many ways an assistant President. In 1908, in their explicit policies and principles, the two men were indistinguishable; as a candidate Mr. Taft repeatedly announced that his whole program and purpose was the consolidation of the Roosevelt policies. But in the first year of his term there arose two serious issues that served to alienate many progressive Republicans who idolized Colonel Roosevelt.

One was the tariff. In later years Stimson came to believe that tariff revision was full of danger for all Republican presidents who dared to face it; with the best will in the world, no Republican seemed able to stave off the logrolling of special interests. In 1909, after pledging his support to tariff reduction, Mr. Taft finally signed the notorious Payne-Aldrich tariff, whose extensive rate increases had been ruthlessly exposed by progressive Senate Republicans. And what happened to Mr. Taft in 1909 was to happen to Mr. Hoover in 1930. Both times it was hoped that this logrolling orgy would be the last one, and both Presidents set much store by their success in setting up executive tariff commissions to establish the basis for a sensible tariff. But both times their hopes proved unfounded. Both times the new and higher tariff promptly became highly unpopular throughout the country, and in both cases the presidents concerned were reduced to defensive claims that the measures might have been worse. The guilt for the tariff increases in fact belonged to Republicans and Democrats, East and West alike, but in both cases these increases became a major cause of dissension within the Republican party, and of organized insurgency against the President.

In 1909 Stimson had no part in the tariff agitation; but in the other main issue between Taft and the Republican progressives he was for a time closely concerned. The famous Ballinger-Pinchot controversy remains today a matter of debate among public men and historians, some holding that Secretary of the Interior Ballinger was greatly wronged, and others that only the prompt and energetic public opposition of Gifford Pinchot and his young friend Louis R. Glavis prevented a disastrous reversal of the conservation policies of Theodore Roosevelt. What is not a matter of doubt is that the controversy made a permanent break between President Taft and the more emotional progressives.

Stimson's own sympathies in the Ballinger-Pinchot affair were with Pinchot, who was a lifelong friend. He was consulted by Pinchot and was instrumental in the selection of Mr. George W. Pepper to represent Pinchot before the congressional committee which ultimately heard the issues between Ballinger and Pinchot. In the early preparation of the case he also met and became friendly with Louis D. Brandeis, who was retained by *Collier's* magazine to show that its accusations against Ballinger were justified. The majority report of the committee cleared Ballinger of malfeasance, but the general public reaction was unfavorable to the Taft administration. Stimson, however, did not share in the antiadministration sentiment thus stirred up.

The Payne-Aldrich tariff and the Ballinger-Pinchot case, in combination with a number of smaller incidents rising out of Mr. Taft's temperamental aversion to Western progressives, had laid the groundwork for a split in the Republican party by the time T.R. arrived from Europe. The ex-President's warm affection for Mr. Taft had already cooled considerably; real or fancied slights were almost inevitable in the changed relationship of the two men. T.R.'s silence about the Taft administration was complete, but he listened, at Oyster Bay, to a series of Republicans of all stripes. His intimate friend Henry Cabot Lodge and his son-in-law Nicholas Longworth came to argue the case of the Republican regulars. Pinchot and James Garfield came to explain to their beloved chief how his policies had been betrayed; Pinchot had already told his story once, in a quick trip to Egypt. And Stimson came—as Root already had in London—to urge the Colonel not to get into the internecine party strife, but to bide his time and avoid a split with Taft. So far as Stimson could see at this time, it was this middle-of-the-road advice that accorded with T.R.'s own views.

Meanwhile there was trouble brewing nearer home, in New York, and this nearer trouble was to bring Theodore Roosevelt and Stimson closer together than ever before.

1. RUNNING FOR GOVERNOR

The Governor of New York in 1910 was Charles Evans Hughes, whose investigation of insurance companies had led to his nomination in 1906. In four years of campaigning and administration Hughes had won a nation-wide reputation as a first-rate leader and executive; he had demonstrated the power of an aggressive governor to force reform by the pressure of public opinion. In so doing, however, he had earned the violent opposition of regular politicians in his own party. In April, 1910, by his acceptance of appointment to the United States Supreme Court, he lost his greatest political weapon, for his approaching withdrawal from New York politics to the Court left him with no chance to use his great popularity as a threat against the machine. At the same time, in an effort to complete his reform program, Hughes was heavily engaged in a battle for the direct primary—a measure feared and hated by machine politicians. At the Harvard Commencement late in June he urged T.R. to pitch in and help. Theodore Roosevelt was not the man to run away from a fight; the direct primary was a cause he believed in, and his support was promptly and publicly given to Hughes's bill. Almost as .promptly the bill was defeated, and T.R. chose to consider that he must fight to the bitter end for a victory over the forces of evil. The scene of battle shifted to the forthcoming September convention of the Republican party at Saratoga, where a platform and a candidate would be adopted for the gubernatorial election in November. At this point Stimson was drawn into the matter. He had been mentioned as a possible candidate for Governor even before Colonel Roosevelt's return, and in the middle of June at Sagamore Hill T.R. himself had remarked to Stimson that he would be the best Governor, though not the best candidate.

July and August Stimson spent on vacation in Europe; when he returned, the Colonel was in the West, making the series of speeches which defined his New Nationalism in terms as terrifying to conservatives as they were heartening to the insurgents. Stimson wrote congratulating his friend and leader on the famous Osawatomie speech, the most terrifying of the lot. At the same time, true to his continuing conviction that a split with Mr. Taft would be catastrophic, he urged the Colonel to speak as warmly as possible about the Washington administration. The reason for this position is important, for it is central to Stimson's political thinking:

"I was much pleased that you enumerated a definite and constructive radical platform at Osawatomie.

"The only thing I wished to say particularly is that it seems to me vitally important that the reform should go in the way of a regeneration of the Republican party and not by the formation of a new party. To me it seems vitally important that the Republican party, which contains, generally speaking, the richer and more intelligent citizens of the country, should take the lead in reform and not drift into a reactionary position. If, instead, the leadership should fall into the hands of either an independent party or a party composed, like the Democrats, largely of foreign elements and the classes which will immediately benefit by the reform, and if the solid business Republicans should drift into new obstruction, I fear the necessary changes could hardly be accomplished without much excitement and possibly violence. . . . I think the attempt to reform the Republican party can be made successful and that that should be the aim. . . . I have heard . . . that even in advocating certain policies supported by Taft you studiously avoid his name. I have denied that there could have been any such purpose. But it seems to me that if you could avoid this criticism it would go a long way in the direction above mentioned. It would emphasize the continuity of the reform inside the Republican party, of which Taft is now the official head."[1] Colonel Roosevelt did not answer this letter directly, but in conversations on Long Island during September Stimson found no reason to believe that his advice was unacceptable.

[1] Letter to Theodore Roosevelt, September 2, 1910.

The immediate problem was in New York. Although Stimson had originally hoped that T.R. would stay out of the battle in the state, he supported Colonel Roosevelt's campaign for election as temporary chairman of the Saratoga convention. The issue in New York was to him essentially the same as in the nation—it was a battle to win the Republican party to the cause of reform. The objection to fighting it in September, 1910, was tactical; Republican machine opposition to the direct primary, together with some unsavory political scandals of the previous winter in Albany, added to the evident trend away from the party in power throughout the country, made a defeat in November seem inevitable—for *any* Republican. This objection did not disturb Stimson for himself—he was not impressed by the talk of his availability as a candidate— but he hated to see the ex-President hazard his great name and invaluable prestige in a losing fight. Only after the Colonel had by his own decision become the leader of the fight did Stimson enlist as his ardent supporter—there was then no other possible course. The object of the battle was now a simple one—to elect Theodore Roosevelt as temporary chairman at Saratoga over the machine candidate, a personally estimable stand-pat conservative who was also the Vice President of the United States. Vice President Sherman was not openly endorsed by President Taft, but there was clearly tension in Washington as the battle developed.

The Saratoga convention was to open on September 27. Well before that date, it became clear to the reformers that Roosevelt was probably going to win his fight; speculation turned to the question of his choice of a candidate for Governor, and Stimson's name came forward more prominently than before—he was known as one of T.R.'s particular protégés in New York. So on September 24 Stimson raised the subject with the Colonel:

"I told him that during the last day or two hints had come to me indicating that the New York [city] leaders felt that I was probably going to be the candidate, and I wanted to warn him particularly against my candidacy as affecting his own prestige and leadership in the country. I said to him, 'If I run and am defeated, as looks now almost certain, it will be made a defeat for you. Our relations have been so close that I will be taken to be your personal candidate, and when I am defeated it will be used to injure your leadership.' He said, 'I have considered all that. So far as my own personal position is concerned I do not care in the least. I should be proud to go down fighting for you. On the other hand, I do realize the disadvantage and the chance for attack which lies in our close association. For that reason I have felt that an upstate man should be chosen. But the trouble is that there is no one who measures up to the situation. We cannot put up a man of whom it will be said that we put him up to be defeated. We believe we are fighting for a big issue, and to do a thing like that would stultify us at once. I am still trying to find a good upstate man.' "[2]

At Saratoga on the twenty-sixth the matter came up again, in a meeting between Colonel Roosevelt, Elihu Root, and Stimson. As Stimson recalled it, "Root said . . . , 'Isn't there some way we can keep Harry out of this? I hate to have him sacrificed.' Roosevelt then said, 'So do I; but I have the feeling that with a good fight a licking won't necessarily hurt him.' Then Root said, 'That might be so if it wasn't too bad a licking; but I am afraid we are in for a terrible licking, and then it will be different. I think the country has made up its mind to change parties. It is like a man in bed. He wants to roll over. He doesn't know why he wants to roll over, but he just does; and he'll do it.' Roosevelt said, 'That's so. I think you are right.' "[3] Either that evening or twenty-four hours later Stimson had a further long talk alone with Root, "discussing the conditions under which it would or would not be my duty to run"; Stimson and Root agreed that if the party leaders on the reform side thought Stimson their best candidate, he should accept the nomination. But his own preference was strongly against running, and he would make no effort whatever to win support. On this understanding Stimson left the matter in the hands of his oldest counselor and guide. On the twenty-seventh T.R. was triumphantly elected

[2] Personal Recollections of the convention and campaign of 1910, probably written about December, 1910.
[3] Personal Recollections of 1910.

as temporary chairman, and that night, in a hotel room very probably smoke-filled, he and his colleagues in the battle against reaction met for several hours; Stimson, waiting outside, went to bed. Some time after midnight he was awakened and told that he was the choice of the reform leaders as candidate for Governor. To put it bluntly, he was T.R.'s handpicked candidate, selected as the best man to run with credit in a losing cause. But it was his cause as well as the Colonel's, and he cheerfully accepted the nomination. Like almost every other candidate in history, he promptly forgot his gloomy forebodings of the week before and set out to win, with the energetic support of the greatest campaigner of the time, his friend and leader Theodore Roosevelt. At the worst, it would be a good fight.

Nothing about the campaign of 1910 in New York was so important for Stimson's life as the simple fact that he did not win. The defeat did not do him any important damage, but victory would almost surely have opened to him a strong possibility of great advancement, even toward the White House. At the least it would have made him a commanding national figure at a very early age. And possibly—this was the thought that struck him with particular force in 1947—his victory, which would have been T.R.'s victory too, might have served to sustain that great leader in his original inclination to work out the New Nationalism *within* the Republican party. But Stimson and Colonel Roosevelt did not win.

The principal and overriding reason for their defeat was that mysterious but evident tendency which Elihu Root had described in September—every so often the people decide to roll over. The political ineptness of Mr. Taft, as shown in the Payne-Aldrich tariff and the Ballinger-Pinchot controversy, certainly contributed; the dubious conduct of the machine Republicans in Albany contributed more; the high cost of living was a major issue, and it was quite useless for Stimson to point out, as he repeatedly did, that the Governor of New York State had no influence whatever on this item. In November, 1910, the people rolled over, and it was small consolation that in New York they rolled less far than in most other states.

The campaign in New York was fought on very few issues. The Republicans fought for a continuation of the Hughes policies and against Tammany control. The Democrats—and many conservative Republicans—fought against T.R. Over and over again they argued that Stimson for Governor in 1910 meant Roosevelt for President in 1912. When they wearied of this chant, the Democrats would unconcernedly blame the Republicans of New York for all the failures of the Taft administration, and then they would discourse on the extravagance of Governor Hughes, promising meanwhile to extend the benefits which Hughes had instituted at some public expense. It was not, on the Democratic side, a brilliant campaign. The Democrats knew perfectly well that they were going to win, and their candidate, an honorable papermaker named John A. Dix, who later proved almost as subservient to Tammany as Stimson foretold in his speeches, conducted a front-porch campaign, safe, dignified, and not talkative.

Meanwhile Stimson was trying to make up by energy what he lacked in experience. He had rung doorbells and helped to organize the vote in a single Assembly district, but a state-wide campaign was wholly new to him, and the arts of the campaign speaker were not his natural forte. Years later Felix Frankfurter, who traveled with Stimson in his special train as brain trust and factotum, could recall the high-pitched but friendly scolding of T.R., 'Darn it, Harry, a campaign speech is a poster, not an etching!' But in four weeks of ceaseless speech-making, six or seven times a day, Stimson gradually improved. If he lacked the explosive and contagious enthusiasm of T.R. and perhaps also the experience and skill of Hughes, he was nevertheless, he always insisted, a reasonably competent campaigner. His principal problem was to prove by personal force that he was not just Theodore Roosevelt's puppet, and he gradually developed a glowing paragraph which seldom failed to win applause. These were the days before the radio, when one good speech with variations would last for most of a campaign, and the following apostrophe, taken from a speech delivered at Amsterdam, is typical of dozens very much like it: "My opponents have been shouting through the state one argument against me . . . they say you must not vote for Stim-

son because he is Roosevelt's man [prolonged applause]. . . .
If they mean when they say that that I admire the standards of
courage and integrity and civic righteousness which Theodore
Roosevelt has shown for thirty years [applause], if they mean
that, why then I am frank to say that I am Roosevelt's man and
I am proud of it [applause]. But if they mean something else,
if they mean something very different, if they mean that if you
should elect me Governor of this state I would administer this
great office according to any other suggestion or any other
dictation than my own will and my own oath of office, why
then I say to you that I am not only not Mr. Roosevelt's man
but I am not any man's man [applause] and I think you will
find that Colonel Roosevelt, from his experience with me as
District Attorney when he was President, will be the first one
to tell you so [applause]."

Many of Stimson's friends argued that Colonel Roosevelt's
energetic help was doing him more harm than good. Stimson
wholly disagreed. It was true that Roosevelt-haters in New
York City were giving their money to the Democrats; it was
true that Stimson's father no longer found it pleasant to visit his
club because so many of the members were rabid about the
socialist Roosevelt and his tool Stimson; it was true that the
daily press of New York City, with two exceptions, was
opposed to Stimson because he was Mr. Roosevelt's friend.
All these considerations together did not outweigh the magic
of T.R.'s appeal to the ordinary voter. Before the Saratoga
convention Stimson heard a wise professional politician estimate that the Republicans would lose in November by 300,000
votes; the difference between this gloomy forecast and the
actual margin of 66,000 he thought mainly attributable to
the campaigning of Theodore Roosevelt.

The real source of damage within the party, as Stimson saw
it, was not Mr. Roosevelt but the regular Republican machine.
The battle of Saratoga ended with a closing of ranks on the
part of such regulars as James Wadsworth and Job Hedges,
but there were others who did not so readily forgive. Stimson's zealous and devoted friends among the younger Republicans did what they could to organize and manage his campaign, but many of the professionals on whom they relied were

cool and distant. And many Republicans in the Washington administration felt that a Stimson victory would be of no value to Mr. Taft. The President himself was cordial in his public support, but he would have been more than human if he had not felt that victory in New York was less important than victory in states where T.R. was not so active.

At the same time, oddly enough, the more ardent progressives were temporarily annoyed at both Stimson and Colonel Roosevelt for compromising with the regulars. The Saratoga platform contained a hearty endorsement of the Taft administration, and both Stimson and the Colonel treated their fight as part of the general Republican cause. Gifford Pinchot's personal loyalty was great enough to bring him to an offer of speech-making support, but he coupled his offer with a warning that he must be free to attack President Taft, and Stimson did not accept his help. So hard it was already, in 1910, even in a state election, to keep party harmony among the deeply divided Republicans.

But it was an energetic campaign, and Stimson enjoyed it. He knew his cause was good; he had nothing to lose; he was proud of both his friends and his enemies. When the election returns rolled in and he realized he was beaten, he found himself undismayed. He promptly congratulated Governor-elect Dix and announced his conviction that the fight for progressive policies had just begun. The defeat of 1910 was a setback, but not a major disaster. The major disaster lay ahead, but the main immediate effect of the campaign on Stimson himself was that it gave him within six months a new and unexpected opportunity for service. In spite of his eloquence, he was marked as "Roosevelt's man," and as such he had acquired a particular value for William Howard Taft.

2. SECRETARY OF WAR

In the spring of 1911 President Taft accepted the resignation of Secretary of War Jacob Dickinson, who wished to give more attention to his private affairs. Casting about for a new Secretary, he was bound to consider the internal condition of the Republican party. He knew that the old personal affection between himself and Theodore Roosevelt was dead; both had done thoughtless things and spoken incautiously among friends, and partisans of both had been unkindly quick to kindle the consuming fires of mutual mistrust. But the end of a friendship was not the same thing as the destruction of the party. T.R. had greatly disturbed the President with his speeches in the summer of 1910, but during the campaign in the autumn he had been less of a maverick, and after the election Oyster Bay became very quiet indeed. The President wanted nothing so much as assurance that Colonel Roosevelt would stay out of the 1912 campaign; one way to attain this result might be to disarm the Colonel's criticism by bringing into the administration some men of his type. When Secretary Ballinger resigned in March, 1911, Mr. Taft appointed Walter L. Fisher, a distinguished conservationist, to be Secretary of the Interior, and in May, against the advice of conservatives in the Cabinet, he offered the job of Secretary of War to Stimson.

"The first intimation that I received that my name was being considered for appointment came through Senator Root. He asked me to meet him uptown in New York; he told me that Mr. Dickinson was about to resign and that my name was under consideration by the President. I think that this was on Monday, May 8th. I asked him his advice and he advised me to accept the appointment. . . . I think on Wednesday night, I received a long-distance message from Hilles, asking if I could meet him the following morning in New York. I met him at the Manhattan Hotel. He told me that Mr. Taft was prepared to offer me the appointment if I would accept. I raised the question of my political sympathies. I told Hilles that Mr. Taft ought to know that in the Pinchot-Ballinger issue I had strongly sympathized with Mr. Pinchot and still did so. Hilles said that he did not think that this would interfere with the appointment as that was over, but that he would talk it over with Mr. Taft. . . . He said 'The President thinks that you are in general sympathy with his attitude which is of a middle-of-the-road progressive, not running to extreme radicalism on one side or to conservatism on the other.' I told him I thought that was true. I further said that before I could answer definitely, I must consult four persons: my wife, my father, my law partner, and Colonel Roosevelt. Mr. Hilles told me that the President was anxious to have the matter settled as soon as possible, and I told him I would communicate with these people as soon as possible. I did this at once, seeing my partner that morning, my wife that evening, and Colonel Roosevelt either that evening or the following evening. My father was at sea and I communicated with him by wireless, receiving finally his reply on Friday evening, May 12th, when I at once telephoned to Washington. My acceptance of the appointment was announced in the papers of Saturday morning, May 13th. Hilles told me over the telephone before final acceptance that he had reported my statement about Pinchot to the President, and he had said that he did not consider that any objection to my appointment."[4]

This consultation with his closest advisers became Stimson's habit in all later personal decisions of this sort. In this case his wife and his father were the two people nearest to him personally; his partner, Bronson Winthrop, was the man whose generous understanding of public service was to make possible repeated absences from the law offices in Liberty Street; and Theodore Roosevelt was the man to whom he owed first loyalty in matters of politics. The first three gave the answer they had given in 1906 and would give again in other cases— he must accept any call to public service which attracted him as an opportunity for accomplishment. The interview with T.R., reaching the same conclusion, had a special significance.

"Mrs. Stimson and I motored over to Sagamore Hill to tell him of Mr. Taft's offer to me of the position of Secretary of War and to ask his advice in regard to it. We found them at home in the evening alone and had one of the most delightful visits that we have ever had with them. Mr. Roosevelt warmly and strongly urged me by all means to accept the position. In everything he said he indicated a warm personal interest in my welfare. Mrs. Stimson evidenced a good deal of reluctance about joining the Taft administration mentioning how difficult it would be for her to feel any great loyalty toward that

[4] Personal Reminiscences, 1911-1912, written March, 1913, hereafter called "Reminiscences, 1911-1912."

administration. Roosevelt at once said that the question of loyalty is settled 'by Harry's doing his best in the War Department so as to help make Mr. Taft's administration a success.' As regards my interest he said that he had regard for my future and that it would be much better for me to be spoken of as ex-Secretary of War than merely as the defeated candidate for Governor.

"I went away with the feeling that I virtually carried his commission to do my best to make Mr. Taft's administration a success.

"I find this statement in a letter from him, dated May 31, about two weeks afterwards:

" 'I am more and more pleased with your having accepted the appointment and Gifford Pinchot and Jim Garfield feel the same way. Both of them are still inclined to be entirely off in matters political but they are nothing like as violent as they were six months ago—one symptom is that they now admit that both you and I have a substratum of decency in our composition.' "[5]

So on May 12, having received the approval of all those whose approval mattered most, Stimson accepted Mr. Taft's offer, and set out to be a loyal member of the Taft administration. This decision he never regretted; it had the effect of placing him in a peculiarly difficult position in the next year, when Mr. Roosevelt and Mr. Taft became open antagonists, and what he suffered in that position we must shortly tell. But it also gave him two years of service with the United States Army, an institution which he devotedly admired, and this was a preparation of enormous value for labors thirty years later. And, of course, it made him a Cabinet officer at the age of forty-three; he would have been chilly indeed if he had not felt as he rode the train to Washington a deep glow of pride and a sense of high challenge.

The United States Army in 1911 was an organization of 4,388 officers and 70,250 enlisted men. About a quarter of this formidable force was on "foreign service" in American possessions—the Philippines, Hawaii, Alaska, the Canal Zone, and

[5] Reminiscences, 1911-1912.

Porto Rico; the rest was scattered in fifty posts within the United States. It was a profoundly peaceful army, in a nation which saw no reason to suppose that there was any probability of war for decades, if ever. The office of Secretary of War had great prestige; it had been occupied in recent years by Elihu Root and President Taft. But it would probably be fair to say that, so far as his strictly military duties were concerned, the Secretary of War was in 1911 by a good deal the least important officer in the Cabinet—except in the opinion of those few who, like Stimson himself, had a lively interest in military affairs.

The men deeply interested in the Army, in 1911, may be divided into two categories—those who lived by it and those who lived for it. This division may not be scientifically exact or even wholly fair, but it accurately reflects the situation as Stimson saw it after a few months of hard work and study. The Army was going through the pangs of a long-delayed modernization, and in almost every issue before the Secretary of War there was a sharp division between men who preferred the old way—the way of traditional powers and privileges— and men whose eyes were fixed on the ideal of a modernized and flexible force, properly designed for the fulfillment of its assignment as the army of a democracy at peace.

The basic instrument for the modernization of the Army, in 1911, was the General Staff, and it was therefore natural that Stimson's first and most important battle should have been for the protection of this body and its authority. The General Staff of the American Army was the creation of Elihu Root, and Stimson always ranked this achievement as one of the two or three most important in all the long and brilliant career of the ablest man he ever knew. The General Staff was a German invention, but Mr. Root's adaptation of it was designed to meet the peculiar problems of the American Army. His General Staff, organized under a Chief of Staff responsible to the Secretary of War and the President, was designed to meet three requirements: civilian control in the executive branch, sound general planning, and constant cross-fertilization between the line of the Army and its high command in Washington. Failure to meet any one of these basic requirements after the Civil War had made the Army a stultified plaything of ambitious generals and their political friends in Congress. By changing the title of the Army's ranking officer from "Commanding General" to "Chief of Staff," Root emphasized the principle of civilian control by the President as Commander in Chief—the "Chief of Staff" held his power as the President's agent, not as an independent commander. By establishing his General Staff free of routine administrative duties Root emphasized its basic function of policy making. By providing for limited terms of service for its members, he insured a constant movement of officers from the Staff to the line and back. He thus struck the first blow in a campaign to end forever the authority of armchair officers who had never commanded troops, but who knew their way around Capitol Hill. Ten years later it fell to Stimson to finish this particular job.

The Chief of Staff of the Army when Stimson became Secretary on May 22, 1911, was Major General Leonard Wood. This remarkable officer Stimson held as the finest soldier of his acquaintance until he met another Chief of Staff thirty years later. Wood had started as an Army surgeon, but his energy and driving zest for command had brought him into the line of the Army. He had commanded the Rough Riders of Theodore Roosevelt, and in Cuba he had won a great reputation as a colonial administrator. Wood was imaginative, relatively young, and as yet unhardened by the bitter disappointments which marked his later career. He and Stimson at once became warm personal friends; they shared an enthusiasm for horses and for hunting; together they inspected Army camps in the West and combined business with pleasure. In Washington they fought together in defense of the General Staff.

Their principal adversary was Major General Fred C. Ainsworth, the Adjutant General. Ainsworth, another doctor, had risen to high office in Washington by reason of his great administrative skill and his even greater skill in dealing with Congressmen. He was a master of paper work and politics, but unfortunately he was greedy for power, and he hated the whole concept of the General Staff, just as he disapproved of all the

ideas for Army reform which attracted the sympathetic support of Stimson and Wood. The Adjutant General in law and
principle was subordinate to the Chief of Staff, but in practice
Ainsworth had been able to preserve his authority under
Wood's predecessors; in some respects, because of his influence
with Congressmen, he had been the most powerful officer in
the War Department. Wood, taking office in 1910, set out to
become master in his own house.

When Stimson arrived in Washington, Wood and Ainsworth were already at loggerheads; as an incident of their
conflict, there was in session a board of officers (headed by
Ainsworth himself) to study the administrative procedures
of the War Department. This apparently harmless subject
was full of explosive possibilities, for Ainsworth regarded
himself as the high priest of Army administration, and any
opinion contrary to his own would not be well received. Late
in 1911, the board of officers reported; the minority report
recommended the abolition of the bimonthly muster roll. This
was a radical recommendation, for the muster roll was the
Army's basic administrative record. But the minority report
was approved by Wood and then by Stimson; they believed
that the new methods would give fully satisfactory results and
save much time. Ainsworth did not agree, and on February
9, 1912, after a six-week delay, he submitted his views to Wood
in a memorandum so grossly insubordinate that as soon as he
read it Stimson realized that the time for drastic action had
come. Once before he had been forced to warn Ainsworth
against insubordination. Now in a bitter outburst against "incompetent amateurs" Ainsworth laid down a challenge which
could not be ignored. The memorandum went so far as to im-
pugn the honor and good faith of any who would tamper with
the muster roll.

"I glanced at it [Ainsworth's memorandum] and at once
seeing its character directed Wood to turn it over to me and
to pay no further attention to it. I told him I would attend to
it myself and for him to keep his mouth shut.

"The only member of the Department whom I consulted
was Crowder, Judge Advocate General. I asked him to read
the memorandum and advise me what disciplinary measures

the law allowed. He came to my house and we discussed it. He suggested two ways of treating it, one by administrative punishment and the other by court-martial. He himself started to recommend the administrative punishment. I told him no, that I intended to court-martial him. . . . I told him I proposed to find out whether the Army was ready to stand for the kind of language that General Ainsworth had used as proper language for a subordinate to use to a superior. I intended to put it up to the general officers of the Army to say whether that was proper or not. I told him also that I preferred to use a big gun rather than a little gun. When I had to deal a blow, I believed in striking hard. He loyally acquiesced in my decision and under my direction at once commenced the formulation of charges and selection of a court. I also consulted the President and Mr. Root. Both concurred with me in thinking that a court-martial should be ordered. The President said to me: 'Stimson, it has fallen to you to do a dirty job which your predecessors ought to have done before you.'

"Root said that when a man pulls your nose there is nothing to be done but to hit him. . . .

"I concluded . . . that a measure of discipline must be taken at once if at all and I therefore relieved Ainsworth as soon as the paper could be prepared.

"As soon as he was relieved, telegrams were sent to a number of retired general officers in various parts of the country, asking them if they would serve on a court-martial which the President was about to call. We had to call upon retired officers because there were no others of rank equal to that of the defendant. Knowing Ainsworth's reputation as a fighter, I rather expected that he would stand trial, although I realized from my previous experience as District Attorney how much greater that responsibility would appear to him than it would to an outsider. I think I had rather brighter hopes than the average officers around me that Ainsworth might lie down, but I recognized that it was a good deal of a gamble.

"Next day we were sitting in Cabinet meeting, when the messenger brought word that Senator Warren wanted to see the President on a very important matter. The President stepped out, was gone a few minutes, and came back and said to me 'Ainsworth wants to retire. How is it? Good riddance?' I said 'Yes, Mr. President, provided it is done at once and provided he apologizes.' He stepped out again and in the interval I got Root on the telephone at the Senate, told him that Ainsworth proposed to surrender and retire and asked his advice as to whether I should accept it. He said, 'By all means; best possible result.'

"The President came back again and said, 'He will get right out but he will not apologize.' I said, 'I think you had better let him get out; we will waive the apology.' I stepped into the President's room with him that time and saw Warren, who had brought the message. I told him that I thought he had done a good piece of work for the Army. He told me that he had had difficulty in getting Ainsworth to agree to retire; that Ainsworth wanted to fight, but that his friends advised him not to run the risk.

"As far as Ainsworth's reputation in the Army was concerned, his retirement under fire greatly injured it. Many officers have since said to me 'Why, we always thought that he was a fighting man, but we have had no use for him since he crawled.' His retirement then simplified matters in the Department. . . . Before I left office in March, 1913, . . . very important reforms in the methods of administration were well under way, reforms which had been perfectly impossible to accomplish when General Ainsworth was present. But more than that, it enabled the department to work as a harmonious team and it dealt a death blow to the idea that any one member of that team could run his office for his own personal advancement."[6]

The relief of Ainsworth was a vital victory for the whole concept of the General Staff. It insured the power of the Chief of Staff against all bureau chiefs, and in this sense it expanded his power far beyond that of the commanding generals of former days. It also asserted and defined the duty of the President and the Secretary of War under the new system—they might have any Chief of Staff they desired, but they must support the officer of their choice. There have been struggles for power and personal feuds in the War Department since 1912, and there are still many matters of tradition over which

[6] Reminiscences, 1911-1912.

the wise man does not ride roughshod, but since the relief of
Ainsworth no important challenge has been given to the final
authority of the Chief of Staff, under the Secretary and the
President. Even the great Pershing, field commander of the
entire fighting Army in 1918, learned that in the making of
long-range decisions he was subordinate to the Chief of Staff
in Washington.

But if the relief of Ainsworth set a fine precedent, and wonderfully clarified the situation inside the War Department,
it did not help Stimson and Wood one bit with their second
great difficulty—relations with Congress. Ainsworth had two
powerful friends in key positions—Representative Hay, Democrat, the chairman of the House Committee on Military Affairs, and Senator Warren, Republican, chairman of the
parallel committee in the Senate. The alliance between Army
bureaucrats and influential Congressmen was useful to both
sides; Ainsworth's promotions had come mainly by congressional fiat, while Army appropriations for post construction,
river and harbor work, and other undertakings could be and
were distributed as political rather than strategic purposes
dictated. Thus the relief of Ainsworth was more than a personal affront to his congressional friends; it was a direct challenge to the whole concept of congressional government—it
asserted the national interest and the authority of the executive branch against the parochial pork barrel and the authority
of Congress. For their audacity in this attack on congressional
power, Stimson and Wood paid the price of constant conflict.
But by continued boldness they were able to hold their own.
When a conference committee of Congress put a rider into
the Army Appropriation Bill which would have disqualified
Wood for service as Chief of Staff, Stimson wrote and President Taft signed a stinging veto, and the country applauded.
The congressional plotters, placed on the defensive—much to
their surprise, for they had not supposed that the President
would run the risk of leaving his soldiers unpaid—were forced
to repass the bill without the offensive clause. In this affair as
in others President Taft showed clearly both his reluctance
to fight and his essential courage in a pinch. He tried hard to
believe that an amended rider would not disqualify Wood, but

Stimson got a direct admission of his purpose from Representative Hay, who was an honest man, and the President at once promised a second veto, even though the support of Senator Warren seemed essential to his success in the approaching Republican Convention at Chicago. He was on solid ground; Warren and Hay yielded, and whatever political advantage there was in the matter accrued to the President. And the Army did not go unpaid, for while the legislators were removing their monkey wrench, they continued by joint resolution the appropriations of the previous year. This experience gave Stimson a lifelong belief that the way to deal with congressional riders is to veto the whole bill and let public opinion take its angry and accurate course.

The issue of authority was thus settled, in principle; in practice, however, substantial power remained with Congress, through its control of appropriations. It was not always necessary for the legislators to resort to flagrantly unjustified riders, and as the administration lacked a disciplined majority—or indeed any majority at all in the House of Representatives— Stimson was not able to secure approval of such ardently advocated reforms as the consolidation of the numerous small posts into a few large ones, strategically located with an eye to climate and training facilities. Nor was he able to prevent a cut in the appropriations for the General Staff, which did not become an unchallenged and fully honored institution until after World War I. Under heavy prodding Congress accepted his principle of an organized reserve, into which all regulars should pass after completing their enlistment, but the principle was so hedged with reservations that after two years only sixteen names appeared on the reserve roster. In summary, Stimson was able to defend the Army against Congress, but not to use the congressional power as an agent of constructive change.

Fortunately there remained a considerable outlet for his energy in the executive authority of the Secretary, and the outstanding advance of his term as Secretary of War was made as a purely executive decision. This was the tactical organization of the Army inside the United States. Prior to 1912, units of infantry, cavalry, artillery, and coast artillery

were commanded by the senior administrative officer of each
area, without any regard for their tactical grouping in the
event of war. This meant that a brigadier general might have
under his command several companies of immovable coast
artillery troops, a battalion or two of infantry, and a cavalry
squadron. Yet these scattered infantry and cavalry units were
the only mobile tactical force in the country, and in the event
of a crisis they would be the field force of the Army. What
Stimson and Wood did has in retrospect the simple logic of
elementary prudence; they ordered a reorganization under
which the command of units corresponded with their probable
tactical employment in the event of emergency—infantry divisions were organized and commanders named. The troops could
not be brought together in one place, for lack of money, but at
least on paper the Army was given an organization suitable for quick action. The result was that in early 1913, when
there was an alarm along the Mexican border, a single order
from Washington was sufficient to concentrate a division of
field service troops at Galveston, Texas. Before the reorganization the same result could have been achieved only by hundreds of orders and the *ad hoc* construction of an entirely new
command. Yet this elementary application of military common
sense was accepted by the line of the Army only after a prolonged and carefully organized series of deliberations, including a conference at Washington of every active general officer
in the Army.

The Army of 1912 was slowly awakening after a slumber
of nearly fifty years which had been only briefly disturbed by
the absurd confusion of the Spanish war. Men like Root and
Stimson, learning to follow the principles and recommendations of a small group of devoted and progressive officers,
found themselves confronted by the vast inertia of somnolent
inbreeding. The Army, as progressive officers understood it,
was a small nucleus of professionals who must be organized
and prepared to do two things: to fight at once in case of war
and—almost more important—to expand indefinitely by en-
rolling citizen soldiers. Wood and Stimson had no patience
with the notion that it took three years to make a soldier—
Wood insisted he could do it in six months, and five years later

he proved his point by producing the magnificent 89th Division of the National Army. What he and Stimson envisioned in 1912 was a small but highly trained Army, concentrated in eight large posts where training in the combined arms could be carried out, with short enlistments and a heavy turnover, so that military skills might be diffused through an increasing proportion of the population. It was from Wood that Stimson first learned to think of the Regular Army as a focus of professional skill from which military training might be given to all the nation's manhood. Wood understood the Army; he also knew how to interpret the Army to civilians, and he knew how to make and honor good civilian soldiers. To the men who thought of the Army as a small and select club, the men who regarded military skill as a sacerdotal secret imparted only at West Point, all of Wood's preaching was dangerous nonsense. The Old Guard of the Army, reinforced by the Old Guard of the Military Affairs Committees, wanted long enlistments, no reserves, no planning, and a welter of small and expensive posts; above all, they wanted not to be disturbed. As he looked back in 1947, amazed that there should have been issues so bitter on points so obvious, and yet remembering the power and skill of the opposition he and Wood had faced, Stimson was at a loss to decide whether he had accomplished wonders or done far, far less than he should. Probably the right answer was a little of both.

Whatever else it was, his service with the Army was great fun. The Regular Army officer, except in his most reactionary form, was a man whom Stimson quickly understood and with whom he felt a natural sympathy. The code of the officer and gentleman was his own code, and he fully shared the enthusiasm of most officers for the out-of-doors. During this first term as Secretary of War he made scores of friends in the Army, and he kept meeting them at later stages of his life. Some were the colleagues of his reforms at this time; others were men who gave him comradeship and guidance in World War I. Still others, like Leonard Wood and Frank R. McCoy, were friends and co-workers not only in 1911 but in many later events. And two of his young aides of the time were men whose later careers he watched with great affection and admiration. Between them Lieutenants George S. Patton and John C. H. Lee carried a total of seven stars in World War II.

The Secretary of War in 1911 was also in effect the Secretary of the Insular Possessions and to a large degree the Secretary of Public Works. Stimson thus found himself responsible for the continued construction of the Panama Canal, the administration of the Philippines and Porto Rico, and for important decisions on harbor development, river engineering, and the use of water power. His responsibility for the possessions need not here detain us; given such administrators as George W. Goethals in Panama and Cameron Forbes in the Philippines, Stimson found it necessary only to be sure that the War Department gave them its full support. In observing their work, and particularly in two visits to the Caribbean and the Canal, he formed lasting opinions about the nature of the American commitment in the areas acquired after the Spanish war; he became a believer, not in manifest destiny, but in American responsibility for the welfare of these new possessions, and fifteen years later he responded quickly to a chance to play his part first in Central America and then in the Philippines. But between 1911 and 1913 these areas were placid, and they posed no major problems.[7]

In the field of public works the situation was different. Here there was posed a neat problem of constitutional law and governmental authority which plainly demonstrated Stimson's basic attitude toward the powers of the National Government. The problem was in the control and regulation of water power in navigable streams, for which Stimson assumed responsibility when he became Secretary of War.

[7] In one issue affecting the Panama Canal, Stimson took a stand which he later regretted. Under the Hay-Pauncefote Treaty with Great Britain, the United States agreed to charge equal tolls on ships of all nations using the Canal. In spite of this agreement, Stimson joined with President Taft and others who argued that it would be legitimate to remit the tolls on American coastwise vessels. The argument was that the right of subsidy was unquestioned, and that remission of tolls was merely a form of subsidy. In later years Stimson found this rather legalistic argument quite insufficient to outweigh the evident fact that remission of tolls seemed a breach of faith to the British and to such Americans as Elihu Root, and he was glad that Woodrow Wilson reversed the position which he had shared as Secretary of War.

The specific issue posed in 1912 was between those who denied any federal power to exact compensation for leases of water-power sites on navigable streams and those, like Stimson, who asserted that the federal power extended to this point and well beyond, under the commerce clause of the Constitution. On one side of the issue were those who genuinely disapproved the notion of federal regulation, and they were joined by the usual corporations whose pocketbook might feel the pinch of any federal supervision. These forces commanded a majority of Congress in opposition to any new assertion of national authority. On the other side were the conservationists —men whose central argument was that water power, as a basic national asset, should not be freely turned over to exploitation by private interests. The issue was first brought to Stimson's attention by friends like Gifford Pinchot well before he became Secretary of War, but it was only after he had been some months in Washington that he began to give the matter close study. This study produced an interesting result.

Abstractly, the position of his conservationist friends was the position Stimson liked. He believed that the national interest in national resources should be asserted. But concretely, he was dealing with a question of constitutional law, and, more important still, with a President who tended to be a strict constructionist. Mr. Taft himself was a believer in conservation, but he was also a careful lawyer with the lawyer's respect for procedure and authority. It thus became necessary for Stimson to prove to the President that the constitutional power over commerce did in fact extend to include charging fees for dam-site leases. In order to accomplish this purpose Stimson collected a large body of information proving that in most cases dams were important not only as they might obstruct navigation, but as they might *assist* it; this point was of critical importance because it gave the Federal Government an interest not only in controlling dam construction but in promoting it, and thus the construction of dams became a legitimate Government function. But if it was proper for the Government to build dams, it was clearly proper for the Government to make any contract it chose with private dam-builders, and therefore it was entirely constitutional for the Government to exact payment for its leases of water-power sites. This rather technical and complex argument was effective with President Taft, and in his veto of the so-called Coosa River Bill (a veto written by Stimson) he asserted very plainly the doctrine of federal authority over water power in navigable streams. A year later, in a notable opinion, the Supreme Court upheld the same doctrine, and on even broader grounds.[8]

The principle thus asserted marked the beginning of an interest in water power and public utilities which Stimson maintained for thirty years. After leaving office in 1913, he continued his work with Pinchot and others for the advancement of the idea of federal control and regulation. At the same time he remained a strong believer in the private operation of public utilities, and after World War I, as lawyer and investor, he had an active part in the building of one of the most successful of all the great private utility companies. Thus in the 1930's when another Roosevelt undertook the great experiment of the Tennessee Valley Authority, Stimson approached the problem with mixed feelings. On the one hand, as a private investor and a believer in private enterprise, he was opposed to Government operation and even questioned the constitutionality of TVA. On the other hand, as a conservationist and a believer in the federal power to build dams and control water power, he was unable to feel that TVA was all wrong, and to one of the lawyers opposing the TVA as unconstitutional he remarked that 'if you are going to defeat this great public undertaking you must find some better argument than the foresight of James Madison.' His basic opposition to TVA was grounded in the belief that Government enterprise could not be kept free of the spoils system and political patronage, but by 1947 it seemed clear that this belief in this case had been unfounded. He remained persuaded that the competition in power rates offered by the TVA, which paid no dividends, no interest charges, and no federal taxes, was unfair, but this was essentially a problem of bookkeeping. In any case TVA was here to stay, and he had learned in 1912 that the principle of planned and co-ordinated river development was a sound one. By 1947 he was prepared to admit—perhaps

[8] *United States* vs. *Chandler-Dunbar Water Power Co. et. al.*, 229 U.S. 53.

even to claim—what he had denied in 1935, that the principle
of TVA, as an adventure in the effective use of national resources, was a direct outgrowth of the position he and other
conservationists had taken back in 1912.

President Taft, as T.R.'s Secretary of War, had been the
roving member of the Cabinet, a sort of political factotum
whom the President used for many jobs outside his Department. This experience guided him in his own Cabinet practice,
and during Stimson's two years in Washington he was often
assigned to jobs which fell outside his departmental domain.
His first service after his appointment—even before he was
sworn in—was the delivery of a speech on the President's
favorite reciprocity agreement with Canada. This was a congenial labor, for it was one of the few chances Stimson ever had
as a Republican spokesman to uphold the principle of tariff
reduction. And indeed most of his work of this kind during his
first ten months was work he liked—he was interested in many
national issues, and in the greatest of all, the fight for unity in
the Republican party, his interest was personal and intense.

Mr. Taft used his Cabinet more freely and fully as a group
of general counselors than did any of the later presidents with
whom Stimson served, possibly excepting Mr. Truman. His
Cabinet meetings were repeatedly the scene of vigorous discussion of major decisions of policy, and in these meetings
Stimson found himself more often than not in a minority. He
and Walter Fisher represented a sort of liberal wing of the
Cabinet, and, although the President always listened with
good will and was himself not basically averse to their ideas,
he generally avoided decisive support of their position.

A typical issue of 1911, and one which assumed a peculiar
and bitter significance because of its connection with Theodore
Roosevelt, was the question of Government policy toward the
trusts. This was a subject to which Stimson had given considerable thought during his work as a Government prosecutor.
He emerged with a dual conviction—first, that effective
federal regulation of large corporations in interstate commerce was absolutely essential, and second, that what Joseph
H. Choate called "government by indictment" was a most
unsatisfactory method of arriving at this goal. Time after time

businessmen of high character and evident good will had come into the United States Attorney's office in New York to plead for a clarification of Government policy; they wished to obey the law, but the very general language of the Sherman anti-trust law made it almost impossible for them to know what was and was not permissible. And Stimson as a district attorney was quite unable to give them any assurance of protection. His own policy was to refrain from antitrust prosecutions unless he had clear evidence of flagrantly unfair practices and purposes, but he could not fix Government policy on combinations in restraint of trade, nor could he bind his successors or his colleagues in other districts. It also became clear to him that the blunt weapon of prosecution was wholly inadequate to protect the *public* interest—it included no provision for a constant flow of accurate information upon which Government policy could be based. Both the public interest and the selfish interest of honorable businessmen required a more careful statement of the law governing competition and a more flexible instrument for federal supervision of business practice.

This position Stimson first urged on the President in early November, 1911, asking him to read a proposed speech on the subject. Mr. Taft "at first said, 'All right, go ahead; it will be all right whatever you say.'"[9] Stimson, however, insisted that the President read his speech with care, and when the President had done so, he asked Stimson not to deliver the speech, at least for the time being.

Once again, Mr. Taft was torn between two counsels—on the one hand were men like Stimson, arguing as Theodore Roosevelt argued; on the other side were such men as Attorney General Wickersham, strong believers in the Sherman Act and in the sufficiency of a policy of energetic prosecution under that law. The President in the end adopted both positions, and in his message to Congress in December, 1911, he combined a defense of the Sherman Act with recommendations along the lines Stimson had advocated, "but these propositions came in the last two pages of the message and were subordinated to about eight or ten pages in defense of the Sherman law . . . and as Root afterwards expressed it to me

[9] Reminiscences, 1911-1912

no one really knows what the President's position on the trust question is."[10]

The President's compromise decision of December had the incidental effect of freeing Stimson to make his long-planned speech. This speech deserves brief quotation because it demonstrates a position which Stimson firmly believed to be the proper Republican doctrine of the time:

"We need not deceive ourselves with the idle dream that our virile American democracy will permit the prices of the things it buys to be controlled by a monopoly which is beyond the reach of the hand of its Government.

"If therefore we are unwilling to accept state regulation of prices, we must accept the only other regulation which is possible—that of competition, actual or potential. . . . The public will have no reason to fear oppressive prices provided the field is kept free for new competing capital to come in whenever the prices in that field are sufficient to tempt it. The avenues by which the new capital can come in must be kept open. The rules of the game must be such as to prevent a new and smaller competitor from being driven out of the field by an older and a larger one. The old rules of fair play in trade under the common law are no longer adequate. The entry of large business into the game has made necessary some changes in rules which were sufficient so long as the size of competitors was approximately equal. . . .

"The various forms of so-called cutthroat competition; boycotting competitors by compelling customers not to trade with them; so-called factors' agreements; interfering with the contracts of competitors by threats or fraud; setting up fictitious independents; favoritism in giving credit; and general discriminations among customers—all of these methods by which can be recognized the illegal purpose of crushing out a competitor and controlling the market heretofore shared with him should be carefully defined and punished.

"This is the first great piece of constructive work that our situation seems to me to require. . . .

"But I believe there is a second and even more important step to be taken. Thus far the function of the Government

[10] Reminiscences, 1911-1912.

which we have discussed has been purely negative; it has merely said 'Thou shalt not.' I believe that the time has come for the exercise of its affirmative powers. . . .

"The criminal provisions of the law should be supplemented by legislation which will establish an administrative bureau for the permanent, continuous, and watchful oversight of corporate business engaged in interstate commerce—legislation which will give stability to such legitimate business and at the same time safeguard the just interests of the public. Such a bureau would become an assistance and safeguard to the honest businessman and yet at the same time make the law vastly more effective against the other kind. It could collect a large amount of information which would be of inestimable service in informing the business community as to what the law meant; at the same time, it could furnish Congress similar information for the purpose of perfecting future legislation, and would bring to the side of the public the tremendous power of publicity. . . .

"It is folly to accuse such a system of being too inquisitorial. That objection generally comes from the men who desire no regulation whatever."[11]

The speech concluded with a statement which represented, in 1911 and in 1947, Stimson's basic view of the problem of government and business:

"We are engaged in learning; and while we are inflexible in our resolution that the interest of the public must dominate the situation, we realize more fully than before that the interest of the public is inextricably bound up in the welfare of our business. The best minds can see only a comparatively short distance into the future and but inadequately understand the great forces of modern society now at work. What we should attempt is to direct these forces toward a just industrial system, leaving full play to individual initiative and full scope for individual reward, but at all hazards to secure social and industrial freedom to the great mass of the people."

This address of December, 1911, is important as a part of Stimson's life and a basic statement of his carefully deliberated opinions. It has interest too in the striking resemblance

[11] Address to the Republican Club of New York City, December 15, 1911.

between Stimson's program and that followed by Woodrow Wilson later in the passage of the Clayton Act and the creation of the Federal Trade Commission. But, as Stimson's own reminiscences remarked in 1913, the speech was of little or no value when delivered. Not only was Mr. Taft preoccupied with the defense of his own antitrust prosecutions, but he and Attorney General Wickersham between them had permitted a suit to be brought whose bill of particulars contained remarks about Theodore Roosevelt which ended forever any chance of a Taft-Roosevelt reconciliation. In an antitrust action against the United States Steel Corporation, the Government claimed that President Roosevelt, in 1907, had been deceived into a wrong approval of the purchase by United States Steel of the Tennessee Coal and Iron Company. T.R. was infuriated; and whatever the rights and wrongs of the situation, it was certainly a most extraordinary charge for the lawyers of any administration to level without warning at an ex-President of their own party. The case was secretly prepared, and Stimson like most other members of the Cabinet remained in complete ignorance of its explosive nature until the fat was in the fire. The steel suit dragged through the courts for nine years, only to be lost in the end by the Government, but the unhappy reference to T.R., in which Mr. Taft himself apparently had no personal part, was a direct forerunner of the final tragic split of the Republican party.

3. THE SPLIT OF 1912

To many of the members of Mr. Taft's Cabinet the final break with Theodore Roosevelt, in February, 1912, was merely the fulfillment of the long expected. To some it was even a desirable ending to an anomalous situation; so long had they feared and mistrusted Colonel Roosevelt that they were delighted to have him in open opposition where they could freely attack him. Even Mr. Taft himself, once as warm as any man in his personal friendship with T.R., felt that in the new position of open hostility there was a genuine mission for him; he could join his own inevitable defeat with the defeat of Rooseveltism.

To Stimson it was entirely different. He had joined the Taft Cabinet on Theodore Roosevelt's express advice; throughout the first ten months of his service he was in constant and friendly correspondence with the Colonel and had been generously helped by both private counsel and public support in the columns of the *Outlook*. When others talked of an inevitable break and announced their certainty that the Colonel would be a candidate against Mr. Taft in 1912, Stimson denied it and denied it again. He knew that T.R. was under heavy pressure from the insurgents, but he could not and would not believe that his friend and personal leader would give in to this pressure and come out in open opposition to the man he had himself made President.

On January 7, 1912, together with Secretary of the Navy Meyer, Stimson went to Oyster Bay. He and Meyer were in roughly the same position—both were devoted personal friends of Mr. Roosevelt; both were bound by official loyalty and genuine respect to President Taft. Deeply disturbed by increasing rumors that the Colonel would be a candidate, they decided to go to see him. They were received with great warmth and remained for three hours, discussing the matter thoroughly. Meyer emphasized the evident fact that only the Democrats could gain from a Taft-Roosevelt split. Stimson placed his appeal on more personal grounds: he feared that the ordinary man, and the historian too, would think it personally unfair for Mr. Roosevelt to run against his old friend Taft—it would seem like turning against his friend in the time of heaviest need. Mr. Roosevelt "started a little when I said this," but "he did not say anything in resentment and seemed to understand the spirit in which I said it." As Stimson recalled it in early 1913, "The underlying basis of the whole conversation was that under no circumstances would he be a candidate for the Presidency," although he would of course not promise to refuse a genuine draft.[12] Stimson and Meyer came away much encouraged and convinced that the Colonel would not betray his own interests and Mr. Taft's by an open break.

During the remainder of January, in frequent conversations

[12] Reminiscences, 1911-1912.

with such friends as Senator Root, Stimson found his confidence in this view gradually fading away. A letter from the Colonel on January 19 gave him serious concern—it seemed to breathe a new spirit of battle; it was not like the man who had remarked on January 7 that "the Presidency could never appeal to him again as it had in the past . . . and that he no longer itched to get his hands on the levers of the great machine again."[13] By early February, Stimson was greatly worried—and he had reason to be, for the evidence now available indicates that Mr. Roosevelt's mind was made up before the end of January. On February 7 Stimson sent a long letter arguing that there was nothing to gain and everything to lose in an open break, both for Colonel Roosevelt personally and for the Republican party. "To that letter I never had any direct reply," but a friendly note on other subjects arrived in the last days of February. By then, however, Theodore Roosevelt was a declared candidate for the Republican nomination.

Stimson was terribly disappointed, but the worst was yet to come. He knew that the coming fight would be bitter; he knew that he himself would be a Taft man; he had no choice, in common decency, and in any case he believed that Theodore Roosevelt was making a campaign on false issues—he saw no such ground as the Colonel claimed for opposing Mr. Taft. But for all that, his friendship for Mr. Roosevelt was one of his most deeply prized possessions. How could he hew to the line of friendship while maintaining his outspoken support of Mr. Taft?

He tried. He was already scheduled to make a speech on March 5 in Chicago. When the news of Mr. Roosevelt's decision came, he inserted in his Chicago speech two brief paragraphs stating his position between Taft and Roosevelt:

"I am for Mr. Taft because I believe that he has faithfully carried out this progressive faith of the Republican party; that his administration stands for orderly, permanent progress in our National Government; and that to refuse him the nomination on the assertions that have been made against him would be a blow to that progress and would put a premium upon hasty and unfounded criticism.

[13] Reminiscences, 1911-1912.

"I entered into public life under the inspiration of Theodore Roosevelt. I am a firm believer in the great national policies for which he has fought. And I now remain his sincere friend. But I believe that those who are forcing him, contrary to his original intention, into the arena against Mr. Taft, are jeopardizing instead of helping the real cause of progress in the nation. The introduction of such a contest at this time, dragging in, as it necessarily will, new and personal issues which are quite foreign to the great progressive policies for which the Republican party stands, cannot fail to weaken whichever candidate is eventually nominated in June."

This statement, carefully designed to avoid angering Mr. Roosevelt, was forwarded by Stimson to him before the speech was delivered; with the advance copy went a letter full of the personal unhappiness Stimson felt: "The past week or so has not been a happy one for me. There is no use pretending that I was not surprised or that I don't feel that you have made a mistake; for I do. . . . You have been right so many times that perhaps you are right now. All the same I have thought all along that Mr. Taft should be renominated, and I think so still; and I am going to say so, publicly, in the speech that I am going to make in Chicago. . . . I am a poor hand at keeping quiet and balancing on a fence. But I feel very much as if the horizon of my little world was swimming a good deal and it is hard to look forward to a time when I am not working or thinking with you. . . ."

The answer that Stimson received showed the Colonel at his best: "Dear Harry: Heavens' sake! You have most often been right; I hope I am right now. I needn't tell you my dear fellow that I don't care a rap about your attitude in favor of Mr. Taft. I have always told you that you would have to be for him. I shan't look at the speech much though I should like to, simply because I haven't time. The newspapers waste their time if they try to tell me that you have said anything against me. . . ."

That is where the story should end, but it does not. When Stimson made his speech Colonel Roosevelt *did* read it; the paragraphs quoted above *did* make him angry, and he said publicly things about Stimson that deeply hurt a devoted friend—things that Stimson heard Roosevelt afterward regretted saying and that need not, therefore, be repeated here. As a result a friendship which had grown warmer and warmer for six years was shattered, and for three years the two men did not meet.

Time after time in those three years Stimson went back over the events described above; he had angered the Colonel by saying he was "forced" into the contest—he might better have said "urged"—but in all conscience there was no insult in what he said, and he could only believe that T.R.'s anger was in some part a recognition of the truth of his remarks. Long as he had hesitated, and much as he had resisted the continuous urgings of his progressive friends, after taking the plunge Mr. Roosevelt had no wish to be reminded that part of him had always opposed the decision. He was a fighter, and in the fight of 1912 he bitterly and quite unfairly attacked many older and closer friends than Stimson. Stimson himself was always most unhappy at what Mr. Roosevelt said of Elihu Root—a man who owed him much, certainly, but to whom he owed much more. Only in this one outburst did T.R. ever attack Stimson; compared with what he said of Mr. Root, this was magnanimous treatment, and Stimson knew it. Political attacks were normal, and expected, in such a situation, even between friends, but those hot and angry personal denunciations by a master of invective were quite different. Colonel Roosevelt made his oldest friends into liars, ingrates, knaves, and thieves, always no doubt sincerely but with a wrathy ferocity that made it quite impossible to smile as if he were a mere Peck's Bad Boy. And, hardest of all for Stimson, these outpourings came from a man whose personal kindliness and compelling charm he had a hundred times experienced, and whose magnificent spirit he knew to be basically undefiled. In his personal denunciation of his friends Theodore Roosevelt was brutally unfair—and to no one more than to himself. Fortunately for Stimson his relationship with Theodore Roosevelt did not end in 1912. Three years later a new common cause brought them together, and when the Colonel died, in 1919, Stimson lost a friend as close as the one he had lost in 1912.

The campaign of 1912 need not detain us here. The Roosevelt hat went into the ring in February; from then on matters went from bad to worse. Mr. Taft won the nomination at a convention at which Elihu Root was chairman; Mr. Roosevelt cried "Theft" and formed the Progressive party. The Republican party was split right down the middle, and Woodrow Wilson was easily elected. Both Mr. Taft and Mr. Roosevelt were far more bitter at each other than at the Democrat Wilson; each found consolation in the defeat of the other. It was an extraordinary campaign in many ways, perhaps most of all for its demonstration of the personal magnetism of Theodore Roosevelt; he became the principal target of both his opponents but with a brand-new party ran second, well ahead of President Taft.

For Stimson it was a wretched campaign. He was treated with perfect sympathy and fairness by the President, and indeed he never admired Mr. Taft more than for his sensitive recognition that Mr. Roosevelt's personal friends, even when repudiated, could not join in any direct attack on their former leader. Stimson tried in the spring to write a speech which would help the President without hurting Mr. Roosevelt. He produced an effort which was of high moral tone but no possible political value. Stimson and Senator Root talked it over. "He liked it very much and fully agreed with what I said, but he agreed with me that it would do no good in the campaign. He said, 'It would not have any more effect than to read the 23rd Psalm.' "[14] Mr. Taft accepted the situation with perfect understanding, and called on Stimson only for formal speeches defending the administration and its policies.

For Stimson himself the campaign of 1912 had an odd result. Until that campaign he had been known as a progressive Republican, and in his own view he remained a progressive even after the split. Yet for the rest of his life he was often tagged as a stand-patter because he remained with President Taft. This he thought as unfair to him as it was to Mr. Taft himself. It was not principle but personality, not purpose but method, that divided Mr. Taft and Mr. Roosevelt. Once the campaign had begun, both sides made issues where none had

[14] Reminiscences, 1911-1912.

been before, and it was true that most of the real reactionaries were with Mr. Taft and almost all the "lunatic fringe" of radicals with T.R. But between the two great men themselves —and to Stimson both were great—there was no such basic division.

Perhaps if Stimson had been a private citizen he would have followed Mr. Roosevelt into the new party. His first personal loyalty would certainly have been to the Colonel. But as it was he had no choice, and no doubts. "One of the main reasons why I had been taken in was on account of my close association with Roosevelt and with a view to conciliating his following. . . . All such hopes had, of course, turned to ashes in the present situation. I had never had any doubts whatever as to the proper course to pursue. In the first place I had not gone in myself with any political commission, but had gone in to make as good a Secretary of War as I could.

"I had gone in with that express commission from Roosevelt. When he now turned against the President I could no more resign than I could openly come out against the President. Either one would have been rank disloyalty to the commission which I had accepted from Mr. Taft and which had been approved in 1911 by Roosevelt.

"Under the circumstances as I confronted them then in the winter and spring of 1912, it would have been just as serious a blow to Mr. Taft to have a member of his Cabinet resign under those circumstances as it would to have me support Roosevelt while in the Cabinet."[15]

The election of 1912 brought an end to a most unhappy period in Stimson's life. The tension lifted, especially at the White House, where Mr. Taft proved himself a good loser, almost happy to be relieved of an office he had never really liked. Stimson finished his term with a burst of renewed activity on the Army reforms he had learned to value so highly. Through letters to friends of his who knew the President-elect, he was able to communicate some of his ideas to Mr. Wilson and he was succeeded by Lindley Garrison, a man with whom he soon established very friendly relations; Garrison quickly grasped the basic principles for which the Army

[15] Reminiscences, 1911-1912.

progressives were working, and the War Department was undisturbed by the change of administration. On March 4 Stimson returned to private life, with no personal regrets whatever.

Service with Mr. Taft had sometimes been difficult, for this President was not a political leader but a judge. Nor had Stimson always agreed with his chief on policy. But in basic honesty and personal courage, Mr. Taft was the equal of any man Stimson ever worked for, and in addition he was kindly, candid, and easy to work with. It was his misfortune that he was not born to like the polemics of political leadership; his instinctive lifelong yearning for the duties of the bench was a better guide than the family ambition which led him to the White House. To Stimson he was and remained for many years afterward a loyal and devoted older friend.

Nor should we end this chapter without recalling that the main business of Stimson's two years, after all, was the Army. For what he learned in those two years, and what he was able to do as his contribution to military reform, he always remained grateful to the man who appointed him. For his later service in the largest assignment he was ever given, these two years were the most important in his early public life.

CHAPTER III

Responsible Government

I. FRAMING A PROGRAM

THE awakening of conscience and complaint that marked American politics from 1890 to 1917 crossed Stimson's life at three points. As a citizen of New York City he had met it as an issue simply of honest and efficient administration— municipal corruption could be beaten by electing a strong and honest mayor. As district attorney charged with the execution of federal laws he had become a sufficient symbol of righteousness to win political attention. The problem was again presented mainly as one of civic virtue—of finding and convicting the wicked. From 1911 to 1915 he was deeply involved in the study of American Government as a whole, and here he faced at close range problems that would not yield to the simple criteria of right and wrong which seemed sufficient for a judgment of Tammany Hall or Charles W. Morse. For if the body politic was diseased, the cure was not obvious and many solutions were being offered.

The theoretically easy and emotionally satisfactory solution to the failures of democracy lay in "more democracy." If government was inefficient or subservient to powerful private interests, turn it back to the people. This solution, which was in direct line with the traditions of Jeffersonian democracy, found its expression in the movement for the direct election of senators and the direct primary and more exuberantly in the campaigns for the initiative, the referendum, and the recall. The initiative was to provide a method of popular legislation by direct individual proposal and public vote; the referendum would permit the people to pass directly on laws suggested

56

either by individuals or by the legislature; the recall would provide a means for the removal of elective officers by a simple popular vote. The people had lost control of their Government because its complexities provided a smoke screen for the manipulations of bosses and private interests; then let the people themselves take charge.

The popular force of these arguments was very strong; the direct primary became a cause to which all parties gave lip service, and the direct election of senators became law as the Seventeenth Amendment in May, 1913. The other measures in the general program of direct government made less headway, but the attitude that inspired them remained.

Other students were in the meantime working out a wholly different set of conclusions. Admittedly government—especially state government—was susceptible of corruption and prone to inefficiency; the ascendancy of the boss and the ordinarily inviolate security of powerful business interests had made good government an uphill fight. But to many it seemed clear that the remedy could not lie in such simple nostrums as those of direct government. After all, the state officers and legislators were all directly elected—somewhere among them lay the power, and as individuals they were directly responsible to the voters. It was not the simple principle of democracy that was here at fault; the worst of these men often gloried in their heavy and unbroken majorities. The answer must lie somewhere else. If they were essentially ineffective and yet continued in office by re-election, it must be that their ineffectiveness had not been made evident to the voter. And to those who reached this conclusion an explanation at once suggested itself as they looked at the existing governments. The difficulty faced by the public was that it was seldom easy to find out what official was responsible for any given success or failure. American Government in the early twentieth century was characterized by divided authority and general impotence; finding the sinner in politics was like finding the little round ball in the old shell game. The finger of blame was pointed by one officeholder at another, right around the circle, as Nast had drawn it a generation before in his famous cartoon of the

Tweed Ring.[1] Nowhere could the voter stop his search and surely know who was his man—his public servants were collectively responsible, of course, but as individuals? He could not say.

The ordinary result of this condition was ordinary corruption, and from the Civil War onward American local politics had been largely a matter of alternating long-term boss control and short-term reformist rebellion. But toward the end of the century the problem was seen to be more serious. The bosses were friends of "the interests"; while "the interests" were themselves more or less invisible, this connection was not in itself widely disturbing. But the imperial achievements and excesses of American capitalists were not so easily camouflaged as the quiet negotiations of insignificant politicians. In the years of Theodore Roosevelt the battle for public regulation was fought and apparently won in the ballot boxes. It seemed to be the public verdict that government must assume the duty of energetic action in the regulation of commerce, industry, and labor. It was this assignment of new duties which brought into the open the basic inefficiency of the state and federal governments.

Responsibility could not be divorced from authority. And as they further studied the history of state government, men began to think that irresponsibility was a direct result of scattered authority and divided power; fear of too much government had led to untrustworthy government. The true remedy for American misgovernment would lie, then, in exactly the opposite direction from that indicated by the advocates of direct democracy. The elected officials must have more power, not less—only so could they be held accountable for success or failure.

It was in this stream of thinking that Stimson had found himself in January, 1911, when at Theodore Roosevelt's request he made a speech to the Republicans of Cleveland, Ohio. In preparing that speech he was for the first time forced to organize his own mind. He had been asked to talk on the progressive

[1] And as Hamilton had foretold when he argued against a divided or plural executive branch in the seventieth article of the *Federalist*. This article became a text which Stimson often quoted in these years.

movement in the party. And he did so, confining his attention to state government. After paying his respects to the general good will of all progressives of all schools, he addressed his attention to the sources of the evils they were attacking:

"I think it is clear that the underlying cause of this movement is the present inefficiency of our state governments. . . . As has been pointed out by Mr. Croly in his brilliant study of this subject,[2] the prevailing form of our present state government took shape during the first half of the last century when the political views of Jefferson and Jackson were current. . . . Fear of such tyranny as some of the Royal Governors exercised over their colonies before the Revolution was allowed to color and influence a situation which was entirely different. They cut the Executive down to a term too short to carry through any constructive policy; they took away his chiefs of departments, and made them either elective or otherwise independent of him; they separated him as far as possible from the representative lawmaking body with which he must work; and in every way they reduced him to a mere ornament of doubtful beauty."

Then he stopped and made a comparison which he was later to use with its cutting edge: "Which one of you businessmen would assume the presidency of a great enterprise under pledge to conduct it to a successful conclusion, if you were limited to one or two years for the task; if you could not choose your own chiefs of departments, or even your legal adviser; were not allowed full control over your other subordinates; and if you were not permitted freely to advise with and consult your executive committee or your board of directors?"

Having appealed to the common sense of his largely Republican audience, he returned to his main theme: "So long as our nation remained young and hopeful, so long as our problems were simple, we could scrape along even with happy-go-lucky inefficiency. And we have done so. For a long time the only result of our faulty organization . . . was to develop a professional political class which ran our government for us. *The boss and his power is the direct outgrowth of depriving the public officer of his power.*

[2] Herbert Croly, *The Promise of American Life*, Macmillan, 1909.

"But this condition of national simplicity remains no longer. The giant growth of our industries, the absorption of our free land, the gradual change of our nation from a farming people to one living largely in cities, with needs far more diversified than those of their fathers, have brought us face to face with the most acute problems of modern democracy. Side by side with our helpless officialdom has grown up the tremendous structure of modern incorporated business. There is nothing inefficient in that development. Its wealth is limitless and increasing, its organization has the perfection of a military machine, its ministers spring to their tasks endowed with the best specialized training that science can give them. The result of contact between the two could have but one issue. So long as they occupy any ground that is common, so long as business has any relations to the public, one or the other must control. And it is not difficult to see, under present conditions, which that one must be."

Business had grown big, but this in itself was no sin. The crime was simply in the failure of government to keep pace—"one or the other must control," and control should rightly belong *only* to government.

"One result of this growth of the power and wealth of business has been a complete change in the attitude of the private citizen towards the Executive. Instead of regarding it as a possible tyrant, as Jefferson did, we now look to executive action to protect the individual citizen against the oppression of this unofficial power of business. When Mr. Jefferson wrote to Archibald Stewart: 'I would rather be exposed to the inconveniences attending too much liberty than those attending too small a degree of it,' he never dreamed that out of too much liberty from official control might develop an unofficial power capable not only of overwhelming the individual citizen but the state government along with him. He never dreamed that the time would come when the net earnings of a single private business association would far exceed the total revenues of the great states of New York and Ohio put together. In other words, the danger feared by Jefferson is now reversed. It is not the people who are in danger from a strong state government. It is the government itself that is in danger from private influence. And the danger is that it will not be strong enough or pure enough to protect the single citizen from the same influence.

"It is to this situation that the progressive movement in the various states addresses itself. This is the main evil to which, in one form or another, the various remedies are being applied. . . ."

This attack on Thomas Jefferson was a congenial labor for Stimson. As he wrote to a friend at the time, "Poor old Jefferson . . . what I have charged up mainly to his account was his fear of any strong Executive, about which he was so fond of talking, and his opposition to any strong government. . . . I have never thought Mr. Jefferson guilty of originating much of any political ideas. His power and his accomplishment was that he popularized ideas originated by others, most of which he very imperfectly understood."

Anyhow Jefferson was certainly no help in the problems which the speaker took up next: "The people in their perplexity are trusting more and more to the Executive; they are trusting less and less to the legislature. They recognize that the Executive has become the representative of the whole state in a sense not hitherto appreciated. They appeal to him for relief from the obstacles which block the free course of representative government."

Governors of strong character, he went on, had been able to push through or slide around the obstacles of the system, but always at great cost of time and energy, and he might have added that states could hardly expect as their normal right such men as the three he mentioned—Charles Hughes, Theodore Roosevelt, and Woodrow Wilson. The conclusions he reached were simple: "We should frankly abandon the theory of the separation of the executive and the legislative functions, and our state constitutions should be changed to accomplish that end. To sum up my analysis, I believe that the causes of our trouble are, in the main, threefold: first, our state Executives are not strong enough or responsive enough to deal with modern conditions; second, our local legislatures, largely owing to the same change in modern conditions, have tended to become less representative of public opinion and more representative of private interest; and third, the theory of separating the Governor from the legislature is a tremendous block to efficiency. These very defects naturally suggest their remedies; and I believe that the true line of progress is to aim to perfect and strengthen our representative system of government, through the Executive, rather than to weaken it or abandon it for any other."

Thus back in 1911 Stimson had laid down the main line of his thinking. The speech was praised by his friends—T.R. was particularly cordial. "I think your speech not only admirable, but one of as wise originality as we have recently seen." The "originality" was largely in detail of organization and Colonel Roosevelt would have been pained to know how much Stimson's general line of attack paralleled that of Woodrow Wilson in New Jersey. The fact of the matter was that Stimson was expressing views which were widely held by writers like Wilson, Herbert Croly, and Henry Jones Ford and certainly shared by many a state Governor. For us the important fact is that, from the preparation of this speech forward, they became Stimson's views, strongly held and zealously advocated.

The ideas of 1911 were reinforced, not weakened, by his experience in the War Department, and he returned to New York with an increased conviction that his basic theories were sound. In a speech delivered in Philadelphia in May, 1913, he extended to the Federal Government his insistence upon a strong Executive, and although he was now cut off from active participation in national politics, the next two years provided in New York State an unusual opportunity for constitutional thinking.

The Republican party in New York, as elsewhere, was split down the middle by the campaign of 1912. To Stimson the principal objective of the moment was to end the split, recreating the progressive Republican party as it had been in the second term of Theodore Roosevelt. To him the Republican party still remained the proper vehicle for progressive policies; he saw it as the descendant of the Federalist party and the historic party of positive government. "Throughout its existence," he wrote to an Ohio Republican, "it has contained within its membership the men who believed that the Government was not a mere organized police force, a sort of necessary evil, but rather an affirmative agency of national progress and social betterment."[3] This, as Stimson well knew, was only a partial statement of the nature of the Republican party; it had also been in some places and at certain times the party of the stand-patters. The present problem, indeed, was to prevent these stand-patters from taking control. Two things were required to remake the party after 1912; one was the reassertion of Republican-Federalist principles in a positive, progressive program, and the other was the elimination of those leaders of the far right who in their opposition to all effective government were at once betraying the true party tradition and lending substance to the complaints of the progressives.

At first in the spring of 1913 it appeared that the principal duty of the Republican party in New York was to clean out its machine leaders and reactionaries, and for several months Stimson and a group of his friends devoted their energies to an abortive effort to unseat the Republican boss, William Barnes, Jr. A Harvard graduate and leading citizen of Albany, Barnes had become, in his effective control of the extremely conservative wing of the party, a symbol of reaction. To Stimson, such leadership seemed intolerable.

But it was a fruitless undertaking. Barnes was lawfully established as state chairman; he would not resign and, lacking an outstanding leader willing to give his full energy to the business of politics, the liberal Republicans were unable to effect their projected "grass roots" rebellion.

When they were forced to leave Barnes in his glory, the attention of the reformers turned from men to ideas and for their ideas they steadily made friends, hammering a detailed and practical program out of the general notions which they and others had brought to the subject of government. Their pressure forced Barnes to give them a hearing in the party. In convention in September, 1913, they made some progress; at a mass meeting under Root in December they made more. And then in the spring of 1914, by one of the curious ironies of

[3] Letter to George W. Wess, December 16, 1913.

politics, Tammany Hall presented the reform Republicans with a great opportunity, for on April 7 in a vote that was evidence of the efficiency of the Democratic machine and the apathy of the rest of the state, there was approved a Democratic proposal for a constitutional convention to be held in the summer of 1915. With this convention as a definite objective, the reform Republicans, of whom Stimson was perhaps the most active, framed a program with which in that summer they took control of the party. In terms of New York State this program spelled out the general principles of responsible government which had increasingly enlisted Stimson's convictions: The Governor should be strong; his executive power should not be hampered by the existence of other elective officials; he should formulate and propose the financial program of the state and be free to bring his measures personally before the legislature.

This program with other measures of less personal interest to Stimson became, though not in binding form, the platform upon which Republican candidates campaigned for election as delegates to the convention, in the election of November, 1914. And to the consternation of Tammany Hall two-thirds of those elected in November were Republicans.

The Progressive or Bull Moose party failed to elect a single delegate. The leadership of the convention would be entirely in the hands of the Grand Old Party; it would now be seen whether in fact the Republicans of New York were a party of progress and reform. Many of his progressive friends were pessimistic, but Stimson was full of hope. It was true that many of the Republican delegates were extremely conservative and that very few of them as yet fully understood the principles for which Stimson and others were working; but in the platform of 1914 and the general attitude of the more interested members of the party, Stimson and his friends thought they saw the beginnings of a movement which might produce substantial fruits in the convention.

Stimson himself was elected as a delegate at large, running third highest of fifteen successful candidates. It was his first and only elective office and its importance in his life runs far beyond its meaning to the voter or the general historian, for in the convention of 1915 the work and thinking of several years came to a focus.

2.   IN CONVENTION ASSEMBLED

The convention which met in Albany on April 6, 1915, contained an extraordinary group of men, old and young.

Easily chief among them was Elihu Root. Having behind him the commanding prestige of a singularly distinguished career, with his brilliance and industry unweakened by his seventy years, he guided the convention throughout its labors. His close attention was given to every amendment passed, and the force of his personal leadership was the great agent of successful compromise and adjustment wherever the issues were complex and major elements divided. Root occupied a position of unique distinction among Republicans. Twenty years before he had been floor leader of an earlier constitutional convention. Throughout the state men now leaders in their own right looked to him for guidance. It was only his earnest advocacy of the cause of responsible government that made possible the construction work of the convention; his voice was persuasive to many who might otherwise have regarded with suspicion and fear the demand for stronger and more active government. Root's interest in the convention had been largely developed by Stimson, and if the latter had done nothing else for the idea of responsible government, he would have been content to stand on his work in winning Root to its support.

Root was not only president of the convention but the leader of the much smaller but still controlling group of men who came to be known by their adversaries as "the federal crowd." These were the Republicans who wanted reform; the four most energetic were Wickersham, Parsons, O'Brian, and Stimson.

George W. Wickersham, floor leader of the Republicans and chairman of the Judiciary Committee, had been President Taft's Attorney General. He was a man of force—perhaps of more force than political experience. In his mistrust of Colonel Roosevelt he seemed a stern conservative, but his anti-

trust prosecutions under Mr. Taft had been extremely energetic. He was as firm in his convictions as he was friendly
and gregarious in social doings, and to the "federal crowd"
he brought industry, intelligence, and the prestige of a distinguished career.

Herbert Parsons was in Stimson's view, then and after, the
ablest younger Republican of New York State. He had been
one of Theodore Roosevelt's principal political advisers for
the state during Roosevelt's Presidency. He had been six
years in Congress. He combined a talent for party work with
the finest personal integrity. More than most of his colleagues
in the party, he had a keen sense of the validity of the new
drives for social legislation, and his influence was thrown
steadily in the direction of humanitarian government. Parsons
was most active in the management of the convention and
became the chairman of the Committee on Industrial Interests
and Relations—in a later day it would have been called the
Labor Committee.

John Lord O'Brian was a forty-year-old progressive Republican from Erie County. He had first become prominent as
an ardent and effective supporter of Governor Hughes. A man
of modesty, with a sensitive intelligence and a lively wit, he
was the leading representative of the younger and more
progressive up-State Republicans.

These men, with Stimson, were Mr. Root's principal lieutenants, but there were others in the convention who were
usually friendly to the reform program—such men as Seth
Low, ex-president of Columbia and former reform Mayor of
New York, and Frederick C. Tanner, the new and youthful
chairman of the Republican State Committee.

These men with a few others formed the nucleus which gave
to the convention a program of revision. It was their task in
committee and on the floor to win support for as many of
their reforms as possible. This task was greatly complicated
by the fact that not all the able leadership was in the camp
of the "federal crowd." On the one hand were the Democrats
and on the other the conservative up-State Republicans, and
there were striking personalities in each group.

The idea of a constitutional convention had been of Democratic origin, but the fifty-two Democrats who came to Albany were no longer very eager for change, for it was clear that change could no longer be of their making. The great party issue was the reapportionment of the legislature to remove certain restrictions on the representation of New York City in the state Senate, and on this issue defeat was certain. No one in the Republican party would vote for a change which might eventually have the effect of increasing Democratic strength at Albany; and even the less partisan Republicans—Stimson and his friends among them—held that it was meet and right that no one city should dominate the councils of the state. To the Democrats all this was pious fraud, made more bitter by the fact that in their view this was the central wrong, to right which they had for two years been urging a convention. Their elder statesmen, Delancey Nicoll and Morgan J. O'Brien, spoke with cool and prayerful logic; their younger leaders, Al Smith and Robert Wagner, used facts and figures, eloquence and emotional appeal, to urge "justice" for the citizens of their city. It was useless. Nor would Stimson, then or later, admit that they were right. In New York State, from the seaboard to the Great Lakes, there was a great variety of people and industries; he did not think they should be subjected to the entire control of the urban masses who lived in a single metropolitan corner, however numerous the latter might be. In any event the Republicans would not stand for change. In a final vote almost purely on party lines they continued the restrictions on New York City which had been written into the constitution in 1894.

To their credit the Democratic leaders after this rebuff continued to take an active and largely constructive part in the convention. Alfred E. Smith was especially conspicuous. He was only forty-one, but for twelve years he had been in the legislature, and he had served as speaker in the Democratic Assembly of 1913. His detailed and sensitive understanding of the affairs of the state was of frequent effect in adjusting general principles of reform to the specific peculiarities of New York, and, in spite of his frankly cordial connection with Tammany, he was in general sympathy with most of the program for responsible government. Stimson, like the rest of the convention, from President Root downward, was much drawn to this knowing, friendly, and constructive critic; he formed for Al Smith a warm respect which later grew to affection.

However it might affect the sensibilities of the Democrats, the issue of reapportionment was essentially not central to the work of the convention, and the most important opposition faced by Root and his friends came not from the Democrats but from a group of men, mainly up-State Republicans, to whom the whole program of responsible government was offensive. Of this group the leaders were two—William Barnes of Albany and Edgar Brackett of Saratoga.

Barnes in 1915 was no longer Republican state chairman, having wisely yielded that office in order not to face a fight over his re-election. He remained, however, the undisturbed satrap of Albany, and, though for unity he had sacrificed much, there was in him more of principle and less of unadulterated bossism than many critics saw—and all that was principle rebelled at the new ideas. He was currently engaged in his celebrated libel suit against Colonel Roosevelt, in which the latter successfully defended, as truth, his assertion that Barnes and Boss Murphy of Tammany were covert allies against popular rights. To the convention Barnes brought the weight of his up-State following and the convictions of a stern conservative.

His assault on the program of the reformers took a form which has become familiar through the years. He offered an amendment, short and simple: "The legislature shall not grant any privilege or immunity to any class of individuals not granted equally to all the members of the State." It is an injustice to summarize his objective bluntly, but so unjustly summarized, his purpose was to prevent all forms of "social legislation"—minimum wage laws, workmen's compensation laws, old-age pensions, and the like. All this he would do in the name of equality, and he described the road to serfdom with energy and conviction: "The principle of equality must suffocate in the atmosphere of legislation for privilege. The sea of experiment on which we are asked to embark offers no possibility of return. It is not within the power of the human mind

having secured largesse—something for nothing—not to develop further demands for acquisition without performance.
. . . The certain destination involved in this kind of legislation will not be the attainment of the socialistic ideal but the tyrannous autocratic state. . . ."

Neither the socialistic ideal nor the tyrannous autocratic state was of great concern to Stimson and his friends as they opposed the Barnes amendment on the floor. Their attention was centered on more immediate problems, and with the energetic assistance of the younger Democrats they attacked Barnes from all directions. His proposal would reduce government to impotence; it would remove from the state all power of control over matters of labor, health, and social reform; it would hamstring government in emergency; it might in the end so undermine the prestige of the state as to expose it to rebellion.

The vehemence of the denunciation was an index of the amendment's importance. It was, for all its innocent appearance, in direct opposition to the central postulate of responsible government, namely, that the inevitable movement of the times had made more and better government a vital necessity. As Stimson had said four years before: "For the very purpose of preserving the old standards of the citizen's rights to his life, his liberty and his pursuit of happiness, it is essential that the arm of the state should be more effective than ever before; . . . and that it should penetrate far more constantly into the citizen's affairs."[4]

All this Barnes denied. The cleavage was clear. One group would entrust wide powers to government as a matter of necessity and right, and on the same grounds the other group would deny such powers. No man could hold to both philosophies, and the vote on the Barnes amendment was perhaps the most significant in the convention. It was beaten more than two to one, but among those who stood firm for *laissez-faire* "equality" were forty Republicans and only five Democrats. The "federal crowd" were in a badly divided party, and the division was one of principle.

Second only to Barnes as a leader of the opposition among

[4] Speech at Cooper Union, May 3, 1911.

Republicans was Brackett of Saratoga—a statesman of the old school, as he was the first to admit. He was capable of impassioned but generally good-humored eloquence on every subject from the health-giving waters of Saratoga Springs to the iniquities of Tammany Hall, but he reserved his finest wit and his sternest oratory for two subjects: the sins of the "federal crowd" and the splendor of the legislative branch. He was openly opposed to giving any member of the executive branch "any power worthy of the name," and he therefore strongly opposed the "short-ballot" proposal of the reformers, under which only the Governor and the Lieutenant Governor would be elective officers, other executive officials being appointed by the Governor himself and responsible directly to him.

In the debate on the short ballot Brackett was apostrophized by the Democrat Delancey Nicoll with the sort of kindly ridicule which Brackett himself often employed: "Although this amendment goes such a very little way, it has excited the most intense antagonism on the part of . . . the delegate from Saratoga, whose oration of great force and length on Saturday morning denounced us all, Democrats and Republicans alike, as being engaged in a conspiracy to steal away the liberties of the people and establish an autocratic and oligarchic form of government. He said . . . that we were pulling the whole temple down and striking a blow at the very foundation of our Republican system. Ah, I must say to my dear old Cincinnatus from Saratoga, the old order of things gives place to the new. . . . If this convention shall pass this amendment I want to say this to my old and venerable friend from Saratoga: Content yourself with the motto of Cato to his son: 'When vice prevails and impious men bear sway, the post of honor is a private station.' Retire, sir, retire, sir . . . lie down to pleasant dreams, dreaming of a heaven where they have elections every day, where even the doorkeeper in the House of the Lord is elected, where no man is ever appointed to office, where all ballots are long and all terms are short, where only the spirits of the Old Guard that never surrender are admitted and where the souls of the ungodly federal crowd are stopped at the gate."

Senator Brackett, with his remarks about the "natural

ferocity" of an ex-Secretary of War and the autocratic pre-
dilections of such politicians by appointment as Root, Wickersham, and Stimson, represented more than himself alone. There
were many like him, up-State legislators who saw no good in
these new-fangled notions from New York City and Washington. Few of them were in the convention, but their weight
outside was greater than it seemed; they were leading citizens
in their counties, and skillful in the matter of votes.

Nevertheless the reform Republicans controlled the convention. They were the chairmen of the major committees.
They were the most zealous in attendance, the most interested,
and the most effective. The house at No. 4 Elk Street where
Stimson, Parsons, O'Brian, and several others lived was a
center of constant activity, and from it there emanated an
atmosphere of energetic optimism. It became known as "the
ice house," for to other delegates there was something a trifle
forbidding about the righteousness and zeal of the "federal
crowd"; and Stimson himself was somewhat amused and not
surprised to find that once more his opponents were calling
him "frosty." In his own recollection later, there seemed a
warmth and sense of comradeship about "the ice house" which
was rare in his political experience. The men who lived there
had ideas, and they believed they had a chance to apply them
practically to the fundamental law of the greatest state in the
Union.

The work of the summer took two major forms—study and
discussion in committee, and debate on the floor of the convention. It was not till August that the committee chairmen began
to bring in their reports. The short ballot might be a familiar
notion to its earnest advocates, from President Wilson down,
but in a committee of practicing politicians no merely evan-
gelical appeal would do. So each of the major measures was
worked out in long sessions, and gradually the weight of informed opinion was brought as far as possible to support the
Root program.

To Stimson all this was highly educational. Legislative
labor of this sort was largely a new experience, and in contending for his program he developed a new respect and liking
for the complex arts of the active member of a lawmaking

body; much that he learned in 1915 was of lasting value, and if it was true, as Senator Brackett maintained, that his inclinations were naturally executive and despotic, he nevertheless learned thoroughly how much of human kindness and persuasion there must always be in carrying an effective majority of any parliamentary assembly.

From committee the successive amendments emerged to the floor and then in long and serious debate each one was fully argued. Stimson was frequently on his feet. He was perhaps not eloquent but he had a firm grasp of the facts and a capacity for organizing them. His major effort was for the executive budget—indeed, he often found himself regarded almost as a man of one idea, so zealous was he in its advocacy.

The particular importance of the executive budget had come home to Stimson during his years in the War Department, where he had been forced to study at firsthand the consequences of haphazard financial methods. He there discovered that routine War Department appropriations were in the hands of seven different committees and subcommittees of Congress and that the authority of the Secretary of War in controlling expenditures in his own Department was negligible. Mr. Taft indeed undertook in 1912 to present for the executive branch a general budget. The opposition majority in Congress ignored it, and it was not merely a matter of partisan disagreement. To the legislative mind it seemed altogether wrong that financial proposals should originate in the executive branch; it seemed a wicked interference with the legislators' prerogative of appropriation.

To Stimson, an executive mind, it seemed that this legislative attitude was based on a misunderstanding. He agreed that control of the purse strings was a legislative prerogative, but he felt that the essence of this prerogative was in the power to control and limit expenditures, not in the power to initiate and promote them. He believed that expenditures should be *proposed* by the men responsible for administration; the only likely source of a general and not a local outlook was in the Executive, who was responsible to all the people. And the only way in which the people could hope to unravel the mysteries of governmental spending was through the existence of a single concentrated financial plan. The proper function of the legislature was to hold down the aggregate of expenditures, and this was the very function least fulfilled when the members of the legislature themselves initiated those expenditures. In the logrolling which inevitably developed among its members when the legislature originated all financial proposals, it was left to the Executive, Governor or President, to control by veto the financial excesses of the lawmaking body. This was a direct reversal of the proper relationship. In a system of government which was manifestly unfitted for the increasing duties of the new century, nothing was more obviously outdated than the Government's disorganized financial methods.

All this and much more Stimson said in his speeches to the convention, and when his amendment was adopted with only four dissenting votes, it was his personal triumph. Under the proposed new article the Governor of New York was to prepare and submit each year a budget covering all the expenses desired for the executive branch. His proposal was to have priority over any other financial legislation, and its items could be reduced but not increased by the legislature. The question of financial responsibility would thus be clearly assigned—to the Governor when he got what he asked for; to the legislature for what it denied him. The major financial problems of the state would appear in a single measure, to be considered as a whole; if the people were ever to have a clear appreciation of the economics of their government, this was the way they might get it.

Long after the constitutional convention of 1915 Stimson retained his special interest in the idea of the executive budget. He followed with care its growing popularity in other states and in the National Government; he assisted in its belated adoption in New York, and he felt some pride in the belief that of all the reforms considered at Albany in 1915 none made more rapid progress to acceptance throughout the country, and none was more generally successful in operation.

In Stimson's 1915 amendment there was one provision which deserves particular attention. Although not generally adopted by those states which later turned to the executive budget, it was always to Stimson one of the most important aspects of his proposed reform. He proposed that the Governor and other officers of the executive branch should appear before the legislature, in person, to explain and defend their requests for funds. This was an effort on his part to strike a blow at the heart of the system of divided government which existed in most American state constitutions and in the Federal Constitution as well. This attack on the separation of the legislative and executive branches was violently opposed by traditionalists and especially by friends of the legislative branch. Yet Stimson always believed that such a procedure would in fact increase the power and dignity of the legislature. He saw it as a means of providing frequent and accurate reports to the lawmakers, without the hullabaloo which too often attached to formal investigations, and he saw it too as a method of insuring careful work by executive officials. He knew, as he told the convention, that his own War Department estimates would have been made with much greater care if he had been under an obligation to defend them personally before Congress.

3. SUCCESS, FAILURE, AND VICTORY

While Stimson worked on his budget amendment, other parts of the reform program were being framed into amendments by other leaders. In the end thirty-three changes in the constitution were accepted by the convention for submission to the voters in a referendum. The central reforms in these amendments, as Stimson saw it, were the executive budget, the shorter ballot, and the reorganization of the executive branch to bring its various departments unmistakably under the Governor's control. Each of these changes was a major step toward increased executive authority, and thus toward responsible government. Second in importance were the "home rule" amendments, designed to free cities and counties from some of the restraints of control by the state legislature; these amendments were designed to have the dual effect of giving to local governments proper authority in their own affairs, while removing from the legislature many of the local problems which distracted its attention from state-wide issues. A somewhat distinct but similar achievement was the reform of the state judiciary, to minimize the "scandal of the law's delays." There were many other changes of detail. To Stimson, when the convention adjourned in September, it seemed that a great constructive work had been done. He believed that the amendments, taken together, would move New York a long step forward on the road to a simplified, efficient, responsible state government, and he looked forward hopefully to victory for the new constitution at the polls in November. If the reforms in many particulars did not go as far as he would have liked, they went a great deal farther than he had believed probable a year before.

And for this result the main credit belonged to one man, Elihu Root. It was the signal accomplishment of Root that by his selfless and self-evident devotion to the improvement of the New York Constitution he set the tone for debates and votes in which thoughts of party were subdued, give-and-take became the rule of action, and neither the best nor the indifferent became the enemy of the good. The sense of high seriousness which animated the convention, and the long thoughts about state government to which its members were aroused, worked through those members far beyond the summer of 1915. Probably the outstanding value of the constitutional convention was its effect upon the younger men who worked there—as Stimson put it, 'it was a great school of government.'

The best teaching is said to be that which has close contact with reality; and in the reality of dealing with such unruly scholars as William Barnes and Edgar Brackett, Root and his followers were forced to adjust their purposes to the available votes. They produced the best constitution the convention would approve, but their thumping majorities were sometimes proof not of sentiment for reform but of concessions to the unenlightened. Thus the short ballot was turned by hard necessity into a less long ballot. The attorney general and the comptroller remained elective, the former as a concession to the lurking popular distrust of any Governor unhampered by an independent legal counselor, the latter simply because the current incumbent was a man with many friends. Stimson, as the agent of the compromise, was left to endure the good-humored jibes of the Democrats and the scandalized complaints of the thoroughgoing reformers. The jibes were natural, but the complaints seemed to him less justified, and throughout the convention and the campaign for its adoption he was considerably annoyed by the noises of disgust from reformers in the outside world which greeted every adjustment of the ideal to the possible. Some of these reformers were his friends, men from whom he had learned much of what he believed, and their failure to make due allowance for the necessities of the situation was disappointing.

This gap between the man of unburdened principle and the man responsible for action was one which Stimson observed many times before and after 1915, and usually his sympathy remained with the practical man. Each case, of course, was subject to a separate judgment. He himself often felt that the bolder policy was the better politics, but his first inclination was always to defer to the judgment of the man on the spot.

Fortunately most of his reforming friends, men like Herbert Croly of the *New Republic*, in the end supported the revised constitution and energetically joined in the battle for its adoption. It was support from conscience, not from feeling, but even such backing was very welcome. For when they returned from Albany, the sponsors of responsible government learned that in persuading the convention they had done little to persuade the voters.

The central difficulty was that Stimson and his friends lacked a mandate. The convention had assembled under laws passed by very different people from those who in the end controlled it, and its positive reforms were not the result of the kind of prolonged public pressure which is generally required for constitutional change. Nor was there time, in the eight weeks between the end of the convention and the state referendum, for the kind of educational campaign which was the only alternative method of obtaining popular support. Such education requires not weeks but years, during which the gradual development of public interest enlists the support of those practical men who wish to ride the tide. In 1915 there was no solid public feeling behind the reformers and a clear field was left for the enemies of any part of the revised constitution to attack it with impunity.

Thus opposition which had been covert at Albany became open and noisy in the campaign. Tammany Hall denounced the new constitution from top to bottom. Samuel Gompers and his American Federation of Labor found in it thirteen fatal flaws. Stimson inclined to believe that for Mr. Gompers the really fatal flaw was in his failure of election as a delegate; however earned, his opposition was violent. Tanner was able to hold the official organizations of the Republican party in line, but individual leaders, especially up-State, did not hide their opposition, as Stimson found when he went campaigning. Where the leaders were friendly, he found large and friendly audiences, but when he arrived at Saratoga to speak at a mass meeting in support of the constitution, he was urbanely introduced by his incorrigible friend Brackett to a hall containing about seven citizens.

The professional politicians were joined in their opposition by many other groups, each with reasons of its own—especially violent opposition came from city employees nervous about the effects of the "home rule" amendments. Much other opposition was on the wholly illogical ground that the convention had omitted some desirable amendment—it was like rejecting a new shirt because you also wanted a new hat.

The mobilization of opposition was made much easier by a tactical error of the reformers. In their anxiety to emphasize the interlocking unity of their amendments, they had bunched all but a few of the changes in a single proposal, to which the voters must say "yes" or "no" as a whole. With no driving affirmative sentiment for the reform program, voters who disliked any single item were tempted to vote "no" on the whole program.

Two other factors worked against Stimson and his friends. Faced with the problem of securing popular support for a general program based on unfamiliar concepts of government, they needed a great teacher—a man who knew how to catch the imagination of the general public and enlist its backing for a cause. Stimson and others earnestly made speeches and wrote letters, but they lacked the ability to set fire to public feeling, and the one man who might have done it for them kept a stony silence down in Oyster Bay. Thus there was no knight in armor. Still more unfortunately, a work which could only succeed if strong public interest should be aroused was undertaken in a year when war had seized the center of the stage. The summer of 1915 was one of increasing tension, as America watched the great battle in Europe, and President Wilson carried on his intricate maneuvers with the Germans. The *Lusitania* had been sunk in May, and after that the war, and its possible effect on America, far outshadowed the problems of state government which had been pushed forward by a small group of men in the face of public apathy.

So on November 2 the proposed new constitution was defeated by a vote of more than two to one. In retrospect it seemed as if there might be more need for explanation of its 400,000 friends than its 900,000 enemies, so great were the forces arrayed against it, but to Stimson at the time the vote was a great disappointment. Still, as the weeks passed and the personal hurt faded, he began to believe that, in the end, the work at Albany would not be wasted, and so it proved.

Thirty years later a look at the Constitution of New York showed the following: a shortened ballot, a reorganized administration, a stronger Governor, a greater measure of home rule for counties and cities, less purely local legislation, and most particularly an executive budget. The similarity with the stillborn product of 1915 was astonishing.·

In much of this later movement Stimson played his part, from the side lines. But the principal agent was Governor Al Smith, who with persistence, good humor, and great skill guided his version of the program, piece by piece, into the fundamental law. So largely has the government of New York thus changed that for a generation now successful administration has been the rule and not the exception in Albany, and so well have the voters liked their governors that not since 1920 has a candidate for re-election been defeated. It might be stretching the facts to say that boss rule has wholly disappeared, but it would certainly be fair to say that now the Governor has become himself the boss, and as he must face the voters at the polls, authority and responsibility are clearly joined.

4. CREDO OF A PROGRESSIVE CONSERVATIVE

The constitutional convention of 1915 was Stimson's last major labor in the field of domestic American affairs, and in concluding this chapter it seems proper to give a general summary of his lifelong opinions on American government.

His basic convictions were two—first that the primary and overriding requirement of all government was that it should not infringe the essential liberties of the individual, and second, that within this limitation government could and must be made a powerful instrument of positive action. The primary and essential liberties of the individual, freedom of speech and of person, were on the whole properly protected by bills of rights in the federal and state constitutions. To Stimson as a lawyer with experience both as a student of the common law and as a public prosecutor, this essential restraint imposed by law on all government was a fundamental principle of any decent society.

But to construe this respect for personal freedom into an assertion that all government was evil seemed to him absurd. The power of government must always be superior to the power of private citizens, and in the industrial civilization of the twentieth century it was the duty of government to provide for the general welfare wherever no private agency could do the job. In a choice, the smallest competent unit of government was always preferable; Stimson preferred the township to the state and the state to the national government. But often there was no choice; national problems must be solved by national authority.

It was the need for more and better action that led Stimson to his program of responsible government. This was essentially an attempt to combine democracy with leadership. The democrats of the nineteenth century had feared government as the tool of despotism and had deliberately made it weak. Stimson and his friends feared weak government as an open invitation to private despotism, and they sought to restore its strength. Stimson himself never feared governmental dictatorship in the United States; he believed that the temper of the nation forbade it; with a certainty far greater than any confidence in the written words of the Constitution, he believed that the United States was and would remain a free country. On the one occasion in his life when a President seemed to be trying to throw aside the restraints of constitutional government, the attempt of Franklin Roosevelt to remake the Supreme Court in his own image, the response of the people confirmed Stimson's confidence. And even in this case there was no immediate question of dictatorship, as he saw it.

The essential safeguard against the abuse of power was the sentiment of the people. Against invasions of basic freedom that sentiment could be enforced and protected through the courts and in Congress; against bad administration or undesirable policies, it could be enforced at the polls. To go farther, as the doctrine of separate powers had done, and make the government weak because all government seemed dangerous, was in Stimson's view a plain abdication of responsibility and an open confession that democracy and effective government could not be combined.

So he turned in the other direction and framed into a concrete program his personal belief in the value of leadership. He would make the Executive strong and leave him free to carry out his program. Given such freedom, the Executive could be held fully responsible for his record, and he could be judged at the polls. The voters would know whom to praise or blame.

Nor did this doctrine imply any contempt for the legislative branch. What Stimson desired was a system in which the Executive and the legislature would be in close and constant contact. He hated the nineteenth-century predominance of the legislature over the Executive, because he believed that it led to weak and ineffective government, but this opposition to what Woodrow Wilson called "Congressional Government" could not fairly be construed as opposition to Congress itself. The Congress to Stimson was a vital instrument of responsible government; its basic function, however, was to legislate and to control appropriations, not to administer. Administration, the exercise of power in action, belonged to the executive branch, and it was this exercise of power which Stimson desired to set free. The President in the nation, and the

Governor in the state, must be the finally responsible political leaders. The constitutional provisions which made it possible for a President to be rendered powerless by legislative opposition he considered clearly wrong. This sort of stalemate, which occurred twice while he was in Republican Cabinets and twice more when he was in private life watching Democratic Cabinets suffer, had no useful purpose whatever; it was a wholly different thing from the legitimate and indeed indispensable labor of an active minority in the legislature.

Thus Stimson believed in strong government. But even this belief was qualified. That the President should have great powers did not mean that these great powers should always be in use. Stimson was emphatically not one of those who believed that the best thing to do with all social and economic problems was to dump them on the federal Executive. If he was a progressive, he was also, he thought, a conservative. He believed in private enterprise and in decentralized authority. He particularly admired the tradition of local self-government. He believed in the rights and responsibilities of rich men as well as poor men. He saw no reason to approve the notion of a nationally planned economy—economic regulation was inevitable and desirable; economic dictatorship was not. He believed himself a democrat, in that he placed his basic reliance on the political wisdom of the entire American people, but he never posed as an egalitarian. He was not disposed to assume that labor was always right as against capital, or that the basic issue was always between the House of Have and the House of Want.

He believed that the Government was the government of the whole nation, and that there was always a policy which was best for all the people, and not good merely for one group as against another. That he or any other man would always find the right policy was too much to ask of mere human beings, but the test of purpose remained. The best political leadership, as he understood it, was that which appealed not to class against class or to interest against interest, but above class and beyond interest to the good of the whole community of free individuals. It was to set the stage for this sort of leadership that he worked for responsible government.

CHAPTER IV

The World Changes

1. WAR COMES TO AMERICA

THERE seems to be little doubt now that August, 1914, marks the end of an era in human affairs. When the great powers of Europe began their general war, the world turned a corner.

From this generalization the United States is not exempt, and it happens that Stimson's life shows forth clearly the nature of the change wrought by the first war. In the years before 1914 and by a carry-over for one year thereafter, his predominant interest was in domestic affairs. From the death of the constitution of 1915 until his retirement in September, 1945, his public activity was almost entirely devoted to issues arising from the fact that the United States is not alone in the world.

It is not easy for those who have grown up since 1914 to understand how little Americans of that time expected any part of what happened in the following years, or how radically the texture of American attitudes was changed by these events. Of course the war was not the only source of change. The vast flow of immigration, the end of the frontier, the surging challenges of industrial development, and many other elements were involved in the changing pattern of American society in the early twentieth century, and there was novelty in the air long before 1914. But it was domestic novelty, and about it there was an air of innocence that did not survive the war. To Stimson, as he looked back in 1947 at the years before 1914, it was not the problems but the serenity of life that stood out. The age of Theodore Roosevelt, for all of its

moral battles, had been a time of hope, not fear, and confidence, not worry; the strenuous life itself was a life of well-
equipped big-game hunting, or else of soldiering which even
at San Juan Hill, its proudest hour, engaged only the young
and adventurous few. War as a desperate and horribly destructive test of the whole fabric of civilization was war unthinkable in 1914.

If younger Americans found it hard in later years to reconstruct a proper image of life before the first war, many of
their elders faced the same problem in reverse. "New occasions
teach new duties," but the lesson is a hard one when the occasion is unwelcome and the duty harsh and deadly. Inexorably the First World War brought the United States into intimate connection with the quarrels of Europe, for the first
time in a century and for the first time ever as an active world
power. Most of Stimson's later public service was devoted to
one aspect or another of this great new relationship.

When the Austrian ultimatum was delivered to the Serbians
Stimson read the news in an afternoon extra as he came from
a political discussion of "responsible government" among Republican leaders. He never forgot his wonder as he read the
newspaper and realized that, if the Austrians meant what they
said, their note spelled war. The fearful fact that an Austro-
Serbian war must also involve Russia, Germany, France, Belgium, and Great Britain he learned more gradually, during
the succeeding days. And as the struggle developed, his attitude toward the American relation to it gradually changed,
as did that of most of his compatriots.

But from the very beginning, Stimson's sympathies were
strongly on the side of the French and the British. He had
lived in Paris as a boy while his father studied medicine under
Pasteur and other Frenchmen; Dr. Stimson had begun his
studies in Berlin and had quickly departed, disgusted by the
martial swagger of the youthful German Empire. Stimson
had thus learned from his father to mistrust the Prussians and
admire the French; to this he had added, from his own experiences in later travels and in Washington, a lively respect
for both Great Britain and France. And the German invasion

of Belgium was so evidently cynical and brutal that it at once hardened his sympathies against the Central Powers.

At the same time, during the first year and more of the war, Stimson had no other thought than that the proper duty of the United States was to remain neutral. Through the winter of 1914-1915, when the war seemed quietly stalemated, American foreign policy was hardly a major issue, to him or to the general public. But even the joint effect of the *Lusitania* sinking and the Bryce "atrocities" report, in the spring of 1915, did not drive Stimson from his belief in neutrality. In a speech delivered at Carnegie Hall on June 14, he shocked many of his friends by the violence with which he denounced Germany, but it was not the basic war purpose of the Germans which he attacked; it was rather the fact that Germany, in her *method* of warmaking, had violated the rights of neutral nations, first in Belgium and now on the high seas. In later years Stimson was to come to the conclusion that the basic wickedness of Imperial Germany, as of her successor the Nazi Reich, lay in her complete acceptance of the use of war as an instrument of expansionist policy, and he was to have a leading role in the assertion and development of the principle that aggressive war is the basic crime among the nations. But in 1915 it was not warmaking, but *illegal* warmaking, that he attacked.

In taking the position that he did, Stimson was of course following the almost unanimous sentiment of the time; it was only as they looked back on World War I that men began to learn that in modern industrial civilization war itself has become the basic crime. Stimson, in June, 1915, aligned himself directly behind President Wilson, who, he said, "has stated and defined those [neutral] rights of our citizens with clearness and precision." He quoted with approval the concluding passage of Wilson's note of May 13, 1915, on the subject of the *Lusitania*: "The Imperial German Government will not expect the Government of the United States to omit any word or any act necessary to the performance of its sacred duty of maintaining the rights of the United States and its citizens and of safeguarding their free exercise and enjoyment." It was only in his parsing of this sentence that Stimson became more explicit than the President, and the following comment had a prophetic accuracy: "Now 'any act' may include force. If the Government of the United States is not to omit 'any act necessary to the performance of its sacred duty,' it stands by this declaration pledged to the use of force if Germany persists in her attacks upon our citizens traveling on the high seas."[1] This was simple logic; as long as President Wilson's notes could restrain the Germans from unrestricted submarine warfare, there was nothing in Mr. Wilson's policy, or in Stimson's, that required American participation in the war. But the moment the Germans definitely adopted as the official policy the method of the *Lusitania* attack, the United States was pledged to fight.

Nor did Stimson in 1915 consider this a narrow ground on which to enter a major war. Much of this speech was devoted to a careful description of the vital importance of the rights of neutrals. "The progress of our race towards civilization has not been along the smooth pathway of logic. We have not succeeded in abolishing war in the name of its inhumanity and in substituting for it a rule of peace and reason. Instead of that, we have struggled along, gradually narrowing and restricting the area of war as we have grown less and less willing to endure its ravages. This may be illogical but man is not always a logical animal. And so we have found that his progress, attained in this halting and stumbling method, has been more effective and permanent than tons of rhetoric and volumes of theory. . . . Now by far the greatest advance which has been thus slowly made in putting brakes on the savagery of war has been in the development of the rights of the neutral. . . . Gradually for the modern world there have been won great areas of neutrality into which the clashes of belligerents are not supposed to enter—buffers of civilization against the shocks of war—ever-widening areas of peace which are full of promise for the ages of the future." Neutral rights must be defended, even at the risk of war.

This was the state of Stimson's mind in 1915, and his position was shared by almost all those who were prepared to oppose Germany at all. It is another measure of the colossal effect of the First World War that for Stimson and many

[1] Speech at Carnegie Hall, June 14, 1915.

others its devastation served to effect a complete reversal of this traditional doctrine of neutrality. In later years Stimson many times argued with force his deep conviction that in modern war there is always one aggressor, and sometimes two, and that there can be no neutrality in the face of aggression. But in 1915 it was not yet known that the wars of the industrial age were terrible and devastating beyond all predecessors, so terrible even in their so-called legal forms that it was necessary to describe as wholly insufficient the historic effort of "gradually narrowing and restricting the area of war" by international law and neutral rights.

Even two years later, in 1917, when unrestricted submarine warfare was resumed, Stimson no longer believed that the rights of neutrals were the fundamental issue. Certainly the submarine attacks were the immediate cause of war, but the basic enemy was Prussianism. Unfortunately nothing in American theory, practice, or attitudes called for war on Prussianism as an enemy in itself, and it seems entirely clear that if the Germans of World War I had respected American rights at sea, the United States would never have entered the war. Stimson for one never in any way publicly advocated entry into the war until the Germans reversed their U-boat policy in January, 1917.

What he did advocate, early and late, and in vigorous opposition to Mr. Wilson, was preparedness. He was fresh from his experience as Secretary of War, and intimately aware of the fantastic weakness of the American Army; he knew that the Army's mobile force was about 24,000 men, and that these men had ammunition enough for about a day and a half of modern battle. He would have been an advocate of military improvements even if there had been no war in Europe. But the European struggle, and particularly the fact that the United States stood pledged to maintain, by force if necessary, her national rights on the seas, made an increased military effort absolutely vital. The great professional leader in this cause was General Wood; Stimson became both an ardent supporter of Wood's efforts and, as an ex-Secretary of War, an active preacher of preparedness in his own right. In 1914 and 1915 he visited Wood's camp at Plattsburg where many civilian leaders were getting a taste of real military training. In 1916 he enrolled at Plattsburg himself and succeeded in shooting so well that the doctors, waiving both his age and his near-blindness in one eye, pronounced him fit for active service.

In his work for preparedness Stimson did not openly criticize President Wilson until the middle of 1916. With the domestic program of the New Freedom he found himself in general sympathy, and he was never eager to criticize any President for actions in the field of foreign affairs. Secretary of War Garrison was a firm believer in better preparation of the Army, and as long as Garrison remained in office Stimson made it his business to support the War Department. He particularly approved of his successor's effort to build a reserve force—a Continental Army—which should avoid the state politics and other weaknesses characterizing the National Guard. Yet Stimson himself went farther. In speeches during 1915 he regularly made clear his personal belief that the basic military strength of the country lay in the obligation of every man to defend his country, and he pointed with admiration to the system of universal military training in effect in democratic—and neutral—Switzerland. In the beginning of 1916, in the speech in which he announced his support of Garrison's Continental Army, he also announced his personal belief that the correct basic method of insuring the national defense, in peace and in war, was "some system of universal liability to military training." This belief he never thereafter abandoned, and in early 1917, as the war crisis approached, he became an ardent advocate of immediate conscription.

It was in the late spring of 1916 that Stimson first became an active public opponent of Mr. Wilson. For this opposition there were three causes. First, he was strongly opposed to the President in the basic matter of his attitude toward the war; though Mr. Wilson had succeeded in putting a temporary stop to unrestricted submarine warfare, such phrases as "too proud to fight" struck no responsive chord in Stimson's mind, and he felt too that even a neutral nation was under obligation to take a moral stand on such an act as the violation of Belgium. Stimson was not neutral in thought, and he saw no reason to be. Secondly, Mr. Wilson was a Democrat, and Stimson was a devotedly loyal Republican. He had given a great deal of time over a period of three years to the work of rebuilding the Republican party, and he believed that this party was the proper one to take the helm in the storms he saw ahead. Finally, and this was the point on which Stimson's personal opposition was strongest, the President had shown himself a very halfhearted believer in preparedness, so slack that Secretary Garrison finally resigned in protest against his policies. The President had deserted Garrison on the issue of the Continental Army and had instead made his peace with the congressional supporters of the National Guard. It was a plain surrender on an issue Stimson considered vital.

Stimson's own candidate in 1916 was Elihu Root. He believed that Mr. Root was by all odds the best qualified individual in the country, and he vigorously rejected arguments that his candidate might not be a good vote getter. He believed that the crisis demanded the best man in the party, and he found that even Mr. Root's opponents could not deny his superb qualifications. But neither the prodigal son T.R. nor most western Republicans were willing to accept Mr. Root, and the nomination went to Charles E. Hughes. Stimson promptly gave his full support to Hughes, and he was both surprised and chagrined when Hughes barely missed victory in November. The Hughes campaign was something of a disappointment to Stimson, who felt that a more vigorous and outright stand would have been more successful, but nothing in the campaign lessened his great admiration for Hughes, and he thought it a very great loss to the people of the United States that Hughes was not their war President in 1917 and after. It was also a great loss to the Republican party, for if Hughes had won, there would almost surely have been no Harding era.

The year 1916 ended with Mr. Wilson's abortive effort to secure peace by mediation. 1917 began with the German decision to resort to total war at sea. Rightly contemptuous of America's military strength, and wrongly supposing that they could force a decision long before American soldiers could become an important obstruction, the German militarists decided for war. Although President Wilson was appalled at the necessity, on April 2 he called for a declaration of war, and on April 6 Congress gave it to him. The country was more than ready for the decision.

The resumption of unrestricted U-boat warfare had been to Stimson as to most Americans a clear signal that war was coming. He had quickly abandoned his earlier reluctance to go on long-distance speaking tours for preparedness, and the declaration of war found him in the middle of a two-week swing through those parts of the Middle West which had been reported least enthusiastic about war. Everywhere Stimson and his colleagues Frederic R. Coudert and Frederick W. Walcott preached the need for conscription at home as the only way of destroying German authority abroad, and they were greeted with great enthusiasm. In these speeches Stimson threw aside his earlier arguments about neutrality and for the first time vigorously discussed the basic issue of the war as he understood it both then and later:

"America is not going to war with Germany merely because, as one of the accidents of the great struggle raging across the water, we have suffered an incidental injury, gross and unbearable as that injury may be. . . . It is because we realize that upon the battlefields of Europe there is at stake the future of the free institutions of the world." The German violations of neutrality were merely the inevitable result of the German theory that all rights belonged to the state. The world was a house divided between those who believed in the individual and democracy and those who believed in the state and autocracy.

Thus the problem of war and peace seemed to Stimson to rise out of a still deeper problem, that of the basic relationship between man and the state. In 1917 it seemed clear that the war was essentially the result of the Prussian doctrine of state supremacy. It was the Prussian logic of the advantage of the stronger which had destroyed the notion of limited war. There were other elements in the war, of course, but Stimson always believed that the essential guilt belonged to Germany.

And in later years, when he saw the rise of militaristic dictatorship in Italy, Japan, and Germany again, he found no reason to change his view that the primary threat to peace is always from those nations which deny individual freedom.

Nations which respected the dignity of the citizen, holding that the rights of man precede the rights of government, seemed not to be disposed toward aggression, whether they were have or have-not nations. But where the state was the object of highest honor and its advantage the only test of justice, war and threats of war seemed to be the normal condition. If the world was to have either freedom or peace, it must destroy autocratic aggression.

This was the issue that Stimson saw in 1917, and he believed that "Into such a struggle a man or nation may well go with lofty faith and burning ardor."

In the grim aftermath of World War I it became fashionable in some circles in the United States to scoff at the fiery idealism with which the country entered that struggle. And probably it is true that, as they thought and spoke in the terms of which Stimson's speech is typical, the American people had little real concept of the difficulty of the mission they had assumed. The glowing hopes of early 1917 did not long survive the armistice; they were based on innocence and ignorance. But it always remained Stimson's view that it was not in the war but in the peace that the tragic error was made. It was right that the United States should make war on German militarism; it was right too that this warmaking should be undertaken in a spirit of exaltation; but it was tragically wrong that the United States should not remain a member of the team after victory, bearing her full share of the joint responsibility for peace.

President Wilson clearly stated in his final address to Congress that the issue of the war was what Stimson had said it was in January, and in his analysis he went one step farther: "Neutrality is no longer feasible or desirable where the peace of the world is involved and the freedom of its peoples. . . . We are at the beginning of an age in which it will be insisted that the same standards of conduct and of responsibility for wrong done shall be observed among nations and their governments that are observed among the individual citizens of civilized states." This was the naked truth, in Stimson's view, and he fully recognized Mr. Wilson's great service after 1917 in spreading this doctrine.

But there was one man who had preached this sermon earlier, when it was unpopular, and in later years Stimson believed that of all Theodore Roosevelt's great services to his country none was greater than his personal crusade in favor of a strong American stand against Germany. Colonel Roosevelt became venomously embittered against Mr. Wilson, and few will deny that this bitterness detracted from the grandeur of his preaching, but on two great issues, as early as 1915, he took stands that Stimson considered wholly right: he was in favor of action against Germany, placing righteousness ahead of peace, and he was in favor of a strong organization of the world's great powers after the war to keep the peace. It was true that even T.R. never publicly asked outright for a declaration of war until after January 31, 1917, and it was true too that his hatred and mistrust of Wilson later led to a disappointing weakening in his support for a League of Nations. But to Stimson he was and remained, in his work as a private citizen in 1915 and 1916, a magnificent leader, and it was with a feeling of homecoming that he accepted the mediation of Robert Bacon and responded to the Colonel's invitation to Oyster Bay at the end of 1915. From that day until the death of Mr. Roosevelt three years later, Stimson's admiration and affection for a great man was renewed in all its earlier force.

In the spring of 1917 it was with an honest sense of dedication that the American people faced the war. They were not, by this time, ignorant of war's meaning, for they been watching the Western Front for more than thirty months. Yet Stimson found, in his western tour, that they responded with enthusiasm to his speeches in favor of universal training, and when he went to Washington on his return Secretary of War Baker thanked him for the speeches and said that he felt the issue was now won.

There was then only one thing for Stimson himself to do, and he did it. On May 31, 1917, he was sworn in as a major in the Army.

2. COLONEL STIMSON

Stimson joined the Army in 1917 for many reasons, but the basic one was that, after preaching preparedness for years and war for months, he could not in conscience remain a civilian. Though in some ways it might be quixotic for a man nearly fifty to become a soldier, it was the only way in which Stimson could feel comfortable in his mind. And of course it was also true that he had envied combat soldiers for many years; he realized that men like Justice Holmes and General Charles F. Adams, whose Civil War reminiscences he had often listened to in Washington, had known a part of life he wished to know. For nearly twenty years he had felt a certain regret that he had not been free to go to the Spanish-American War, and this time, in a much greater contest, he did not propose to be left behind. He heard many leading citizens of New York arguing that for the United States it would be a war of money and supplies, but he wholly disagreed. He himself was urged to accept a flattering offer of civilian work in Washington, but he refused. His proper place was in the Army.

His first hope had been to go as part of the division of volunteers which Theodore Roosevelt planned to raise. He had spent much time in 1916, when the Mexican situation was tense, helping T.R. with lists of officers, and in the spring of 1917 he waited until Colonel Roosevelt's offer was finally rejected by the Government before he felt free to join up on his own. Then he faced a problem; he was forty-nine, and his only field experience had been in very short sessions with the National Guard, for whose training he had as little respect as the sternest professional. How would he equip himself for the battlefield duty which alone would satisfy his desires?

This problem could be solved only in gradual stages, as Stimson discovered after discussing his situation with Army friends. The first step, obviously, was to get into uniform. This was quickly accomplished with the help of his old friend Enoch Crowder. General Crowder, the organizer of the draft, obtained for Stimson a commission as a judge advocate major in the Reserve, with the understanding that he might prepare himself for later service in the field artillery. He was assigned to the War College in Washington, and there he spent the summer of 1917, doing three things. In office hours he worked at the War College as a staff intelligence officer; in the early mornings he drilled with the artillery at Fort Myer; in the evenings, under the direction of another old friend in the Regular Army, he studied the duties of artillery officers. It was a strenuous summer.

But in September he got his chance. The field artillery was expanding rapidly, and in its search for field-grade officers for the new regiments the Army was running short of qualified men. Stimson had not hidden either his ambition or his studies, and as the summer waned he heard that his name was on a list of officers recommended for promotion to lieutenant colonel and assignment to field service in the artillery of the drafted divisions of the National Army. Then he heard that his name had been removed from the list by Secretary of War Baker.

In later years, as the partisan feelings of 1917 and 1918 faded, Stimson came to have great respect for Newton D. Baker, the Cleveland peace lover who became a distinguished Secretary of War. But he had strongly disapproved the decision to reject the Roosevelt volunteers, and in 1917 and for some time after he believed that Baker lacked the force and knowledge for his assignment. It was not pleasant, therefore, to find that this man's decision had barred him from active service. But there was only one thing to do. Stimson obtained his superior's permission and requested an interview with the Secretary of War.

Baker received him openly and cordially. He had removed Stimson's name, he said, because he did not want the Army used as a source of glory for politicians. Stimson replied that he had no political ambitions, that the assignment proposed was one for which he had diligently prepared, and that his military friends had advised him that he could serve the Army best as a tactical staff officer, assisting the commander of a field artillery regiment or brigade. "What is a tactical staff officer?" Baker asked. Stimson explained; Baker said he would reconsider; the interview closed.

As he was leaving the Secretary's office Stimson passed the open door of the office of Major General Hugh L. Scott, the Chief of Staff. Scott had been away; Stimson saw him inside and went in to explain why he had called on the Secretary without Scott's permission. Scott was an old friend and fellow lover of the West. He heard the story; then he made Stimson repeat it while he took notes. Where would he like to be sent? What sort of duty did he desire? What was this list he had been on? Stimson tried to say that he had left his case with Baker. Scott merely repeated his questions. Stimson returned to his office, and within an hour Scott's aide telephoned. He reported that the Secretary of War had approved Stimson's appointment as Lieutenant Colonel, Field Artillery, National Army, and his immediate assignment for duty with troops at Camp Upton, Yaphank, Long Island. On his arrival at Upton Stimson was assigned as second in command of the 305th Regiment, Field Artillery, 77th Division, National Army.

The 305th Field Artillery was the unit of which Stimson always thought first in later years when he looked back at the war. Although he was twice detached from it, suffering the disappointment of leaving it for good just as it was going into its first offensive action, the 305th was his outfit. In two three-month stretches, in the autumn of 1917 and the summer of 1918, he acquired a deep and lasting affection for the unit and all its members. He considered it a remarkable regiment.

Most of the officers were ex-civilians, men much like himself, but all much younger, who had entered officers' training camps before or just after the outbreak of war. Mainly New Yorkers, they were mostly young college graduates. They were enthusiastic, inventive, and impatient to be at the front. Their sense of honor was rigorous, and they were natural leaders; if the method of their selection was perhaps less democratic than methods Stimson was to approve one war later, they nevertheless fully justified their privileges in training and action.

But the real revelation to Stimson was the quailty of the enlisted men of the regiment. The energy and ability of the young officers was no more than he would have expected from what he had seen at Plattsburg, but he was joyfully astonished at the work of the drafted soldiers of New York City and its environs. These men, representing almost every national strain in the American melting pot, had had little experience of heavy physical exertion, and little formal education. As a group they seemed small and underfed. But they had other qualities, the qualities that make for survival in a metropolis.

They were quick, resilient, and endlessly resourceful. They took the Army as it came, and they showed a capacity for pride in their performance that seemed wholly incompatible with their assumed air of urban cynicism. The men and their Plattsburg officers made a wonderful team.

The initial training of the regiment at Upton made heavy demands on both officers and men. The National Army paid the price of unpreparedness. There were no guns for training, no horses to pull them, and no wire communications, until Stimson unearthed a little of all three through grateful clients. There was no artillery range in the crowded area around the camp until he laid it out. Other shortages were filled by other officers who were not of the red-tape and clay-pipe school. The 305th, Stimson was sure, was better at this game than other parts of the division, and the division was better than other divisions. This may have been mere unit pride, but it was a fact that the War Department, having originally planned that the 77th should be a training ground for replacements, changed its plans after watching the division develop. It was the first division of the National Army to enter the line in France.

But before that time Stimson had been detached and sent overseas on his own. In December the division commander offered him a chance to go to France to attend a school at Langres where general staff corps officers were being produced for the new Army. It was a wrench to leave his regiment, but this new assignment was directly in line with his hope to become a tactical staff officer, and he remained fearful that someone in Washington might decide to keep him at home; it seemed well to move toward the sound of the guns. So Christmas, 1917, found him at sea in the war zone; for the first time in twenty-four years of marriage he faced a prolonged separation from his wife. He was to be overseas nine months; the loneliness of those months was beyond anything he had known before or was to know again. An added sadness was the recent death of his father. But Dr. Stimson had visited the front lines himself, bringing antitoxins from America. When he sailed, Lieutenant Colonel Stimson knew that he was carrying on as his father would desire. And Mrs. Stimson's reaction was to make strenuous efforts to persuade her husband that she too should find a way to France.

When he arrived in Paris, Stimson learned that the staff school was not ready for him, and he was attached for a month to the 51st Division of the British Army, for training. This training period with the famous Highland Division was a high point in his Army experience. The 51st had just completed a prolonged and costly fight in the battle of Cambrai. When Stimson arrived, its sector was quiet, and a few days later it was pulled back a few miles, out of the line. But the visiting American found more than enough opportunities to visit the forward areas, with corps or division officers as his guides. Those British officers had an attitude toward both bombing and shellfire which seemed to Stimson unreasonably casual. It was some time before he accustomed himself to the unaffected nonchalance of his colleagues in the face of fire. Granted that the danger was not prohibitive, he never felt it entirely wise to prefer an open road to a muddy trench just because one's boots were clean and the Boche only shelled the road at fixed intervals. But it gave him a taste of fire, and he behaved like a perfect guest; when his British hosts threw aside their helmets just at the moment when they might become useful, he followed suit, and when he was told that three officers were safe walking in an observed field because 'the Boche never wastes shells on less than four,' he tried to believe it.

Whatever their idiosyncrasies, the Scots knew their trade; both as professional training and as an apprenticeship in the battle zone, Stimson's visit was extremely valuable. And as he examined the casualty reports of the division and listened to the details of its magnificent record, he acquired an admiration for the British nation in arms that lasted for the rest of his life.

His class at the staff school finally opened at the end of February. There he found himself among friends; the officers studying at Langres included such old friends as Major George Patton, Herbert Parsons, and Willard Straight. For twelve weeks Stimson worked as a student of staff duties, and worked hard. It was the most rigorous professional training he ever had, and it served him well both in the following months and many years later. After his successful completion of the General Staff course, he always felt able to speak as something more than a mere amateur on military subjects. It was fortunate that he was kept busy, for only hard work and high hopes could keep a man calm during the spring of 1918, as the Germans launched against the British Army the first of their last great attacks.

Graduating from the General Staff College in May, Stimson paid a brief visit to the 26th Division on a quiet sector of the front and then repaired to GHQ at Chaumont to learn his new assignment. He had given much thought to this question himself; should he go at once to duty on a division general staff? Would it not be better to mark himself first as basically a line officer? His Army friends advised the latter course, if he had any voice in the matter, and fortunately he did. General Pershing, at Chaumont, evidently puzzled by the problem of placing an ex-Secretary of War, asked Stimson what he wanted to do, and his face cleared wonderfully when Stimson replied that he would like to rejoin the newly arrived 77th Division. So on the last day of May he went back to his old regiment, now in final training outside Bordeaux at Souge.

The 77th had changed little since the previous autumn; Stimson had greatly gained by his six months of separate service, and he returned with the glamour of a relatively battle-scarred veteran. He had also learned a good deal about artillery and about staff work, and his regimental and divisional commanders made energetic use of his extra knowledge. The last weeks before the division moved forward were very busy ones, but Stimson had the good fortune, as an elderly and presumably trustworthy officer, to be ordered to Paris on division business just in time to see the great Fourth of July parade.

There followed a very crowded week. The 77th was ordered into the line in a quiet sector near Baccarat, at the southern end of the front. Just before the 305th went into position, the major commanding the first battalion was promoted and removed to the division staff. Stimson took over, temporarily, and on July 11 his battalion led the regiment into position. The same day he gave the order which sent off what he believed was the first shell fired against the Germans by the National Army.[2] The 305th had begun to fight.

For the next three weeks he was wonderfully happy. To command first-class troops at the front had been his pre-eminent ambition since the beginning of his service. The Baccarat sector was quiet, so that the hideous side of war was absent. It was a realistic dress rehearsal for the work which all were expecting later. There were one or two alarms and tense moments, but in the main it was a quiet period, and Stimson's most important decision was to disregard a panicky request for fire that would have brought his shells down on American positions. He and his troops kept busy, camouflaging their position, practicing their communication signals, and getting the hang of active service. As they worked, they began to feel that heartening self-confidence that comes to a good unit sometime in its first campaign when the men in it suddenly understand that now they are veterans—now they *know*. For the only thing worse than the fear that fills all battlefields is the fear of fear that fills the hearts of men who have not fought. The 305th was not fully blooded in the Baccarat sector, but it ceased to be a green unit.

And then, on August 2, after only three weeks in the line, Stimson was ordered home. The order was a compliment; he was one of two non-Regular officers among twenty-one selected by name at GHQ for promotion and the command of newly formed artillery regiments. And he left a unit which wanted him back; the division commander placed on record his hope that if Stimson should return to France, he might be given command of a regiment in the 77th. Professionally, it was all very gratifying, and of course it also meant that he would soon be with Mrs. Stimson again. But it was a disappointment nevertheless, and a grave one, for it meant that he must leave his own battalion just as the real fighting was about to begin. If he could have foreseen that the war would end before he could get back, Stimson might perhaps have broken his invariable rule and asked for a change of military orders

---

[2] Boasts of this kind have to be carefully phrased. It was the first shell, not the first shot, and Stimson spoke of the National Army, not the Regulars or the National Guard.

from General Pershing. But in August, 1918, all the Americans in France were talking of the great operations planned for 1919, so Stimson followed orders and hoped for the best. He left his outfit, and his fighting service came to an end.

The remainder of his war service is quickly told. He returned to the States, had a week's leave, and then, on being given his choice of the new regiments, took over the 31st Artillery at Camp Meade. He explained his choice in a letter to Herbert Parsons: "It was well started and nearest to the coast for a return." In September and October Camp Meade was struck by the flu epidemic, and his new regiment suffered more deaths and casualties than artillery troops would ordinarily lose in a major battle. Daily Stimson visited his men in the wards, refusing to use the ghastly white masks that medical personnel were wearing. It was a grim duty, and harder for him than anything he had seen or done at the front.

But the epidemic was short, and even while it raged the unit was busy. To train and lead a regiment was a new and searching test, but these were good troops, and although he could now see the war ending, Stimson kept at it. This time the equipment was at hand—he even had a band. He laid out ranges; he guided his officers; he preached unit pride, and he could feel the regiment begin to come alive. He also had more unusual problems to solve: to fight the fear of flu he dosed his command with an elixir guaranteed harmless by Johns Hopkins and advertised by Stimson as a help against flu—and the sickness rate did go down; he ordered his enthusiastic but somewhat unimaginative band to stop including the dead march in its repertoire of hospital music. In short, he did all the hundred and one things that the colonel of a brand-new unit must do. But probably, if the soldiers of the 31st Artillery remembered Stimson at all, they remembered him for this: after the armistice his was the first regiment in the country to be discharged. On December 9, 1918, he was himself once more a civilian. He later joined the Reserve and became a brigadier general, but he was mustered out as a colonel, and for the rest of his life "Colonel" was a title that his close friends often used.

Stimson's year and a half in the Army marked the fulfillment of a twenty-year hope that if the country should have another war while he was young enough he would be able to go on active service as a soldier. Although he never faced the final test of battle in a great offensive or a last-ditch stand, he saw enough of war and danger to be able to feel certain that he was a good soldier; this knowledge was important to him. And the war taught him many things; most of all, perhaps, it taught him the horror of war, but he also saw at firsthand the color of the courage of British and French and American troops, and he learned as he worked with the men of his own Army that the strength and spirit of America was not confined to any group or class. 'It was my greatest lesson in American democracy.' *

* From my discussions with Mr. Stimson have come many observations and recollections which I have quoted. In order to set off these remembered comments from passages found in contemporary records, I have in these cases used the single and not the double quotation marks. McGeorge Bundy

CHAPTER V

As Private Citizen

1. THE LEAGUE OF NATIONS FIGHT

IN 1919 and 1920 Stimson was a private citizen, but he had an active part in the prolonged struggle over the great national and international problem of those years: the fight for the League of Nations. The rejection of the League was to him the greatest error made by the United States in the twentieth century, and it happened that the difficulties involved in the struggle were to reappear more than ever in the later years of his public service.

Stimson never believed that the great rejection of responsibility which took place in 1920 was either inevitable or due solely to any single group of men. It was a most difficult and complicated subject, and the events which led to the final tragic result were not to be explained by easy phrases. There were times when Stimson inclined to put the weight of responsibility on Woodrow Wilson, and other times when his main annoyance was directed at the Republican "irreconcilables."

The idea of the League and the specific provisions contained in the Covenant were of course the product of many minds in many nations, but to the people of the United States, in 1919, the League was Mr. Wilson's League. In Stimson's view this was a grave misfortune. Many of the men who should have been among the strong supporters of the League of Nations had become, since 1914, bitter enemies of Woodrow Wilson. These men were in such a frame of mind that if the President had presented them with the Kingdom of Heaven they would have found it immoral and un-American.

At the same time, as Stimson saw it, to the degree that the League *was* Mr. Wilson's, it contained certain weaknesses. The President failed to take with him to Paris any leading Republicans—not even Elihu Root, who was pre-eminently fitted to go; he appealed unsuccessfully for a Democratic Congress just two months before he sailed; and when he got to Paris he continuously ignored rising reports of opposition at home.

Further—and to Stimson this was his greatest error of all—Mr. Wilson was persuaded that he must produce a full-fledged Covenant, complete in all its parts and wholly up to date in its assertion of the joint responsibility of all the nations for the maintenance of peace. This was an attitude which rose from the President's own clear understanding of the true meaning of modern war, but to Stimson it always seemed that in his obstinate effort to enact his personal version in a nation which was learning its new lessons slowly and reluctantly, Mr. Wilson showed a terrible lack of appreciation of the political realities of the situation. This was a point which he often discussed with Elihu Root in this period, and it seemed to him then and later to be near the heart of the failure of the United States after World War I.

The great lesson of that war was that the United States could not remain aloof from world affairs and still keep the world "safe for democracy." This much, in 1918, was generally known and understood. What was not understood, because it was unpleasant, was the kind and degree of responsibility which the country must assume. To Mr. Wilson, whose mind was clear and logical in the extreme, the implications of the new doctrine were as easy as any other new concept, and he allowed it to be firmly embedded in the famous Article X of the Covenant, under which member nations undertook "to respect and preserve as against external aggression the territorial integrity and existing political integrity of all members of the League." To such Americans as Elihu Root this provision, unamended, seemed most unwise, for they believed that it committed the United States to more than its people would approve. It seemed very improbable that Americans would honor this obligation in the case of renewed

Balkan struggles, for example, and Mr. Root and Stimson, with many others, argued that a failure to do what was promised would inevitably destroy the whole usefulness of the League. This forecast was confirmed in melancholy fashion by the actions of other nations fifteen years later.

What seemed preferable, to Mr. Root and to his student Stimson, was that the League should have a much more general charter, and that it should be permitted to grow and develop gradually, adding to its formal obligations only as the genuine sentiment of the nations permitted. In this fashion, they believed, the slowly growing spirit of international responsibility might be fostered, unchecked by the disillusionment of broken pledges. To them the central requirement was for a constantly available international meeting-ground. The ancient pride of sovereign nations could not be ended in a day, but if international discussion could become a regular habit, and if the United States, particularly, could learn to consider herself a participant in the world's problems, then the resort to war might not become necessary.

It must not be supposed that either Mr. Root or Stimson objected to Mr. Wilson's basic purpose. They fully agreed with him that a new era was coming in international law and that the old doctrine of neutrality must be abandoned. As Stimson wrote, in February, 1919, in an open letter to Will Hays, the Republican National Chairman, "The time is surely coming when in international law an act of aggression by one nation upon another will be regarded as an offense against the community of nations; just as in the development of municipal law a homicide has become an offense against the state instead of merely a matter of redress by the victim's family. So I feel that one country should take advantage of this time to help move the world along towards that condition of development."

Thus as he faced the problem of the League of Nations and its draft Covenant in March, 1919, Stimson had a double attitude. First and foremost, he was unequivocally in favor of American participation in the League. But secondly, he was opposed to unreserved ratification of the Covenant, and particularly to the acceptance of Article X. And Mr. Wilson and the Senate "irreconcilables" between them blocked the way to ratification of the sort of League he wanted.

Stimson's position was best expressed in the reservations proposed by Elihu Root in June, 1919, and he never retreated from his belief that ratification with the Root reservations would have been the best course. Unfortunately the agent of the Root position in the Senate was Henry Cabot Lodge. Lodge himself was probably not at first an "irreconcilable"; but he was the Senate majority leader, and his principal object in life was to hold the Republican party together. To do this, he moved farther and farther in the direction of such bitter-end opponents of any and all Leagues as William E. Borah, Hiram Johnson, and Frank B. Brandegee. The Root reservations did not reach the Senate floor unchanged. Through the summer of 1919 the Senate Foreign Relations Committee under Lodge sat on the treaty and waited for public support of Mr. Wilson's League to die down. In November, when the mind of the country had been thoroughly confused and Mr. Wilson's health was giving way, Lodge brought to the vote a treaty loaded with his own, the Lodge reservations. There was something in the Lodge reservations for everybody; all of Mr. Root's basic ideas were there, but so were many more, designed partly to appease nationalists and partly to anger Mr. Wilson. To Stimson the Lodge reservations, taken together, were wholly unsatisfactory, "very harsh and unpleasant in tone." (Diary December 3, 1919) His view was the view of many a Republican, and he always believed that if the moderate Republican senators and the President had been able to get together, a satisfactory compromise could have been reached. But there was no outstanding leader to show the way to the Republican moderates, and on his side the ailing Wilson proved more stubborn than ever. The Democrats voted solidly against ratification with the Lodge reservations, and the treaty went unratified.

Throughout 1920 Stimson continued to hope for ratification of one kind or another. And if in 1919 his principal complaint was against Wilson, in 1920 he began to feel that his real enemies were the Republican die-hards. In the preconvention campaign he strongly supported the candidacy of his friend

Leonard Wood, who was in his view the most commanding national leader available. Wood was a believer in a modified League, and he was not the man to sell out to the die-hards. But in the notorious Chicago convention of 1920 the die-hard senators threw the nomination to Warren G. Harding.

Then Stimson, in company with almost all the leaders of his party, made a serious mistake, one which he characterized in 1947 as 'a blunder.' He supported Harding, on the ground that Harding's election would mean ratification with proper reservations as to Article X, and he joined in the signing of the famous Statement of Thirty-one Republicans, which urged the election of Harding as the best way into the League. This statement, partly designed to strengthen Harding's inclination toward the League but mainly written to keep pro-League voters in the Republican party, represented the honest sentiments and hopes of the loyal Republicans who signed it. Events soon proved that these men were deceived and their hopes unfounded. Stimson had his moments of misgiving during the campaign and regularly denounced the Republican "irreconcilables." But in later years the man whose position he admired most in the 1920 campaign was Herbert Parsons, who left the party on the League issue. Parsons and Stimson had worked together in New York in early 1920 to strengthen the pro-League wing of the Republican party; in late 1919 when Parsons first discussed the possibility of a bolt, Stimson had expressed his sympathy. "I told him that . . . if the situation ever came to a point where the Republican party stood for a selfish isolation of America as against a participation in the burdens of the world at the present time by this country, I should certainly vote against the Republican party." (Diary, November 26, 1919) In the campaign of 1920 Stimson and most of his friends were self-deceived. Parsons was not; he saw through the double-talk of Harding and deliberately broke with the Republicans to support Cox. For a man whose whole public career had been built on solid Republicanism and whose experience was largely in the mechanics of party organization and discipline, it was a bold and gallant decision. When Herbert Parsons died, five years later, Stimson wrote of him: "He never performed a greater act of courage or of self-abnegation than in making his decision to leave the party in which he had labored so long and on whose welfare and progress the efforts of his whole life had been expended. His spirit was that of a crusader. Well would it have been for us if more of that spirit had characterized the postwar attitude of us all towards our governmental problems."[1]

Yet from another standpoint, it was probably fortunate for Stimson's later usefulness that he did not follow Parsons in 1920. If he had broken with his party, he would in all probability not have been called back to public service at any time in the following twelve years, and it is not likely that he could ever have made himself a leading Democrat. Parsons himself lost much of his former prestige and influence after 1920, whereas Stimson had the good fortune to be able to work for the principles both believed in, first as a private citizen and later in public life. The problem both men faced in 1920 was one of those trying cases which have no certain answer; no decision in American political life is more difficult than the choice of whether or not to leave one's party. What Stimson regretted, looking back at 1920, was not his decision to remain a Republican; for that there was probably sound justification. What he could not forgive was his honest but wholly mistaken conclusion that Harding's election was desirable from the standpoint of those who believed in the League of Nations. He had signed the letter of the thirty-one in response to the leadership of men like Elihu Root, and in this decision he had distinguished company. But he would have done better not to sign that letter and not to write, as he had, opposing the position taken by Parsons. He would have done better to keep still.

With the election of President Harding, all hope of American participation in the League soon died. In the years that followed, the temper of the American people became constantly more isolationist, and the penalty of this error was visited upon the nation and the world in later events which will occupy the bulk of this book. What killed the League in America? Was it the blindness of its creator or the malevolent skill of its few wholehearted enemies? To Stimson it was always both, but he could see in 1947 what as a loyal Republican

[1] Letter to the New York *Times*, September 23, 1925.

he had missed in 1920, that in the errors of Woodrow Wilson there was always a certain prophetic grandeur. Even if he was wrong on Article X, he was wrong in the right direction. And his stubbornness was the stubbornness of high principle. For the men who hated the very notion of a League Stimson would not speak so kindly. They must have been sincere, but it was a sincerity of purblind and admitted nationalistic selfishness, a sincerity of ignorant refusal to admit that the world changes, a sincerity embittered in almost every case by a hatred of the foreigner. It was the sort of sincerity, in short, from which wars are bred. And it bred one.

2. AT THE BAR

Warren G. Harding was the only President between Theodore Roosevelt and Harry S. Truman under whom Stimson took no federal oath of office. He shared the oblivion which overtook most of the younger eastern Republicans during the early 1920's. He did not feel any grievance on this account, nor was he ever inclined to judge harshly the well-meaning man whom kingmakers had thrust into an office he was wholly unequipped to fill. Toward the men in the Harding administration whose active corruption completed the ten-year decline of his party's standing before the country, he was less charitable, and he was glad that the work of cleaning the stables was in the end largely accomplished by Republican lawyers like Harlan Stone and Owen Roberts, though the initial disclosures of corruption were made by zealous and distinguished Democrats.

Between 1918 and 1927 Stimson held no federal office of any kind, yet he retained his interest in public affairs. He was active in behalf of his favorite reform, the executive budget; both in New York and in Washington he argued and testified for its adoption. As one of the early members of the American Legion he was a stern and outspoken opponent of the bonus. As a New York lawyer he protested when in the red scare of 1920 the New York Assembly refused to seat duly elected Socialist members; this protest contains a principle which seemed to him of some importance in 1947:

"I am one of those who believe that our American system of government is, as a whole, the best that has yet been devised upon this earth, and I have not the slightest sympathy with or faith in the tenets of Socialism. Yet even I can think of some matters in which I believe our government can be improved, and I hope during the remainder of my life to be free to urge upon my fellow citizens the desirability of the changes and reforms that I think desirable to make life in America more just, more fair, and more happy for the average man. If I believe this, what right have I to deny to the man who believes in Socialism or in a soviet government the opportunity of endeavoring to persuade a majority of the inhabitants of America that a government and a society framed according to his beliefs will be best for America—provided always he confines himself to the democratic methods of peaceful persuasion to accomplish his ends?"[2]

Protests of this kind, and action wherever necessary in defense of basic liberties, always seemed to Stimson a duty particularly incumbent on members of the bar. It was as a private lawyer that he wrote this letter, and it was as a private lawyer that he spent the bulk of his time in the years after World War I.

For the first time in more than a decade, his private practice became his primary interest. He returned from the war to find that as the head of the family, after his father's death, he had increased financial responsibilities, and in the following eight years he undertook a series of major cases. He also attended with care and energy to his private investments and became in this period a rich man. After 1928 his private affairs never again became his leading interest, but the financial freedom which he achieved in the postwar decade was sustained and protected for him by devoted friends.

This book is a record of Stimson's public service, and we unfortunately cannot stop to consider the ins and outs of even his major law cases. He defended the makers of cement against an antitrust suit; he handled one side of the celebrated *Southmayd Will* case; he was retained by the bituminous coal operators to file a brief before a Government commission in-

²Letter to the New York *Tribune*, published January 16, 1920.

vestigating the coal industry. Both the cement case and the coal case were affected with a public interest, and in both cases Stimson found his basic opinion reinforced by his experience. The cement case was an excellent illustration of the dangers of "government by indictment"; the cement companies were guilty, under the letter of the law, but what they had done had been part of the war effort, with the direct encouragement of the Government.

The coal brief was a study in industrial strife. The burden of Stimson's argument was that members of the United Mine Workers, under John L. Lewis, had been guilty of outrageous crimes of violence, culminating in the hideous massacre of 1922 at Herrin, Illinois. The self-proclaimed "liberals" who were always ready to do battle against the use of force by owners seemed to Stimson disgracefully quiet in their placid contemplation of such lawlessness as the Herrin affair. At the same time his study of the coal industry and his dealings with the coal operators showed him that on both sides of the fence there was a history of ruthlessness, and in a sense the irresponsibility of capital struck him as the more culpable, because he continued to believe that men of wealth and power had special obligations to the community.

The 1920's are remembered now mainly as a time of false hopes and national complacency. Stimson could not claim, in 1947, that he had foreseen the breakdown that occurred in 1929, or that during the twenties he was fully aware of the degree to which the work of reform remained unfinished. But he thought it wrong to set those years and their achievement entirely to one side. For this was a time of industrial expansion, and of economic development, as well as a time of extravagance and irresponsibility. The country was complacent, yet its accomplishment was not negligible. In these years private philanthropy and private charity flourished as never before, and if the spirit of reform largely vanished from the national scene, it found an outlet in some of the states, where men like Alfred E. Smith were at work, and in many local communities. Stimson himself was active in state reform; Smith consulted him frequently, and he served under Charles E. Hughes on a Commission for Reorganizing the State Departments which did much to bring to life the reforms first put forth in the stillborn constitution of 1915. And in many boards and committees in New York City, Stimson like other citizens tried to do his part in community life. In later years, when young men spoke to him with enthusiasm of the work of the New Deal, he always insisted that the work done in towns and cities, and in the states, was of the greatest importance; he remained always a believer in strong national government, but he also believed in local self-government and in private charity. To these local undertakings he devoted himself in the twenties, as he had done, indeed, in one degree or another all his life, in the time that was left over from his private business.

3.   THE PEACE OF TIPITAPA

Stimson's return to active public service began in 1926. In the spring of that year he undertook an advisory brief for the State Department in the tangled dispute between Chile and Peru over the provinces of Tacna and Arica. The *Tacna-Arica* case need not detain us here; it was a legacy from the war of 1879 between Chile and Peru; Secretary Hughes began, Secretary Kellogg continued, and President Hoover completed a prolonged and complex work of mediation by which the matter was settled. Stimson never had more than a minor part in the affair. Its principal value to him was in its practical confirmation of a view he had long held: the notion of honest elections and plebiscites is not a fruitful one in most Latin American countries in any critical issue, unless those plebiscites and elections are impartially guided by an outside agency. The Tacna-Arica area, in 1926, was under Chilean control, and Stimson after careful study concluded that any plebiscite conducted in an area dominated by Chilean police would have a result hardly likely to satisfy Peru, or even disinterested observers.

After the *Tacna-Arica* case Stimson undertook a semiofficial visit to the Philippines where his old friend Leonard Wood was Governor General. The details of this voyage must wait for another chapter. What is important here is that on his return Stimson had two friendly meetings with President Calvin Coolidge. Mr. Coolidge proved a good listener, and Stimson liked both his caution and his evident intention to say no more than he would do. He was already an admirer of Mr. Coolidge's courage in standing for economy in an extravagant era, and although he never felt that this old-line Yankee was one of the outstanding presidents of his time, he soon found that Mr. Coolidge was a wholly satisfactory chief; he gave his chosen subordinates unreserved confidence, and he never let them down.

His first assignment from President Coolidge came in the spring of 1927, when he was sent as a special emissary to Nicaragua. He was given a full grant of power direct from the President to act for the United States Government in seeking a solution to an intolerable situation. It was a flattering assignment, for the position in Nicaragua was both complex and dangerous. Stimson and his wife spent a month in the little tropical republic, and they both believed, then and later, that hardly any single month in their lives was better spent. Stimson's first book was written as a description of the problem of American policy in Nicaragua and of his own part in the new departure of 1927, and to that book the reader must turn for his detailed view of the matter.[3] Only a bare outline can here be given.

Nicaragua in 1927 was torn by a bitter civil war between the two traditional opposing parties, the Liberals and the Conservatives. The war was a violent expression of the continuing struggle for power between rival oligarchic groups in a country few of whose 700,000 inhabitants were sufficiently educated or alert to be politically important. The methods of the war were typical of civil strife in politically backward countries; the armies on both sides were raised by impressment from the lower classes; the countryside was full of armed deserters; the fields were untilled; the already shaky national economy was being further weakened by the waste of war and civil unrest. In actual combat both armies were brave and bitter, but their courage was not accompanied by generosity toward the vanquished. No prisoners were being taken by either side.

[3] *American Policy in Nicaragua*, Scribner's, 1927.

The American interest in Nicaragua was dual.[4] First, under the Monroe Doctrine and its Roosevelt Corollary, the United States had assumed a special responsibility for the treatment given by her Latin neighbors to foreign nationals and foreign property; the civil strife of 1926 and 1927 produced strong hints from Great Britain and others to the effect that if the Americans would not permit other foreigners to protect themselves, they must provide a satisfactory substitute.

At the same time Nicaragua, strategically located near the Panama Canal, was a country whose independence and integrity must be especially protected by the United States. Thus, lacking any smallest desire to dictate or dominate in the internal affairs of any Latin American country, the American Government since 1912 had felt it necessary to post marines in Nicaragua for the maintenance of civil peace at least in neutral zones where the peculiarly unselective warmaking of the combatants should not penetrate.

In 1925, when a coalition government appeared to be in peaceful and unchallenged control of the country, the American marines, 100 in number, were withdrawn. The coalition government was promptly overthrown by an extremist conservative named Chamorro. Denied recognition by the United States, in accordance with the treaty of 1923, Chamorro was eventually forced to resign. The Civil War of 1926 and 1927 was essentially a war for the succession to Chamorro. The Conservative Diaz, recognized by the United States and most European nations, was opposed by the Liberal Sacasa, who enjoyed the recognition and military aid of revolutionary México. Having at first placed an embargo on all shipments of arms or ammunition to Nicaragua, the United States in early 1927 responded to the Mexican activities by opening to the Conservatives the right of military purchase in the United States. The unhappy war in Nicaragua then acquired a new and sensitive aspect as an issue between the Americans and their Mexican neighbors. Feeling in Latin America was high, and not favorable to Uncle Sam.

To Stimson it seemed clear that the first and great objective

---

[4] For a more detailed discussion of the basis of American policy in Latin America as Stimson understood it see pp. 174-187.

was to end the war as quickly and as fairly as possible. Although the American Government had endorsed Diaz, it was clear that this was not a case in which the right was all on one side. Indeed, it seemed to Stimson as if the Liberals and the Conservatives were essentially very similar, even in their mutual hatred. But his first assignment was to investigate and report, and he accordingly suspended judgment until he should have a chance to see the situation on the ground.

In the first ten days of his visit he conferred at length with the Americans on the spot and with Nicaraguans of all schools of opinion. He talked with President Diaz and with the extreme Conservatives; he talked with the Liberals in their stronghold at León; he held himself open in Managua to visitors who wished to present their views. Three things speedily became clear. First, the civil war was hopelessly stalemated; both sides were incapable of effective offensive action; the Conservative superiority in numbers was matched by the superior military skill of the Liberal general. If the war continued, neither side could win and all Nicaragua must be the loser. Second, the bulk of the people, including even the active Liberals and Conservatives, were heartily sick of war. Stimson learned of this feeling from his own meetings, and he found forceful confirmation in the experiences of Mrs. Stimson, who held a series of meetings with Nicaraguan women. Third, most Nicaraguans, on both sides, would be happy to see the war ended by a promise of mediation and good offices from the United States, and by "good offices" they meant American supervision of a new national election. This faith in American honor was somewhat surprising, although very gratifying, for it had been widely announced that the Liberals, enjoying Mexican support, were an anti-Yankee party. It at once became possible for Stimson to hope that his mission might result in a return of peace. And so it turned out.

The detailed terms of the settlement finally arranged three weeks after Stimson landed need not concern us here. It was provided that Diaz should continue as President until 1928, when the regular scheduled national election would be held under American guarantees of fairness and American control. Meanwhile both sides were disarmed and a general amnesty was proclaimed, and the maintenance of civil order in Nicaragua became the responsibility of a new constabulary trained and initially led by American marines. The war ended and, with the exception of continued guerrilla operations by one of the Liberal leaders who failed to honor his personal pledge, peace came to Nicaragua.

In negotiating this settlement Stimson was again and again reminded of his dictum that trust begets trust. Once he had persuaded the leaders on both sides that his purpose was honorable and his objective the restoration of a fair and independent peace, he found them, almost without exception, frank, moderate and co-operative. He was particularly impressed by the manner and bearing of General Moncada, the Liberal leader. Moncada was the most important single figure involved in the negotiations; it was his decision that would determine whether or not the Liberal army should continue to fight. Stimson's first meeting with him took place in the little town of Tipitapa on May 4; it lasted thirty minutes and resulted in a full agreement. This agreement involved a rather curious condition, one for which Stimson was widely criticized in some circles but of which he always remained extremely proud. Moncada accepted the basic conditions of the peace settlement as given above, but he found the continuance of Diaz through 1928 a stiff pill for himself and a stiffer one for his troops, who after all had been fighting Diaz all winter. He therefore asked for, and Stimson gave him, a letter stating that as a condition to its supervision of elections the United States would insist on the retention of Diaz and on a general disarmament. This letter was in form a threat that if Moncada did not accept, the United States would forcibly support the Diaz Government. But in fact it was merely a method of assisting the statesmanlike labors of Moncada. Stimson would have been extremely embarrassed if Moncada had proved untrustworthy, for he had no authority to pledge his Government to virtual war in Nicaragua; but he followed his policy of trust and good will, and Moncada was as good as his word. He and most of his chieftains accepted the "Peace of Tipitapa," and the bulk of the armies on both sides turned in their weapons to the marines. Only one held out, a man named Sandino who had a long record as a bandit leader in Mexico. Sandino's plainly unprincipled and brutal activities attracted an astonishing amount of uncritical support both in Latin America and in the United States, but his operations were confined to a small and sparsely settled area.

Thus within a month of his arrival Stimson had succeeded in restoring general peace. He had also pledged the United States to a fair and free election, and only the redemption of this pledge could mark a real ending point to his efforts. After his return to the United States he did much work in the preparations for the 1928 elections and was in constant touch with the officer who supervised them, his friend General Frank R. McCoy. Both men bore in mind the vital importance of keeping full control of the voting machinery, and McCoy organized an election of complete probity, in which a full and secret suffrage was maintained. To Stimson's personal satisfaction the Liberal Moncada was elected President. Thus the United States, at some expense and with considerable effort, succeeded in this one war in substituting ballots for bullets. And the warmth of Stimson's reception, after the settlement and before his departure, among all sorts of Nicaraguans clearly indicated to him that, at least among the people most closely concerned, he was regarded as a good and useful friend.

There is much more to the story of American dealings with Nicaragua. It need not be supposed that one or two free and honest elections wholly changed the political conditions and attitudes of that small country, or that the end of civil war brought any quick solution to the problems of poverty and backwardness which have plagued the country for so long. Nor did the American Government quickly find any easy way to combine its respect for the sovereignty of small nations with its overriding concern for the strategic security of the Panama area. But during the years in which Stimson followed it closely the story of American-Nicaraguan relations was constantly more hopeful, and one of his last official acts as Secretary of State in early 1933 was to approve the withdrawal on schedule of the last American marines. The marines had come to save lives in the civil war; they had remained to disarm the contenders, chase bandits, and hold an election,

and they left behind in the end a country peaceful and independent. It was a job well done.

To Stimson himself the big lesson of his Nicaraguan experience was a simple one: if a man was frank and friendly,
and if he treated them as the equals they most certainly were,
he could talk turkey with the politicians and other leaders
of Latin America as he could with his own American colleagues. And they would not let him down.

It happened that the Peace of Tipitapa and the transatlantic
flight of Charles E. Lindbergh took place within a few days
of each other, and Stimson always felt that his work in
Nicaragua was somewhat blanketed from the public by the
extraordinary and consuming interest attaching to Colonel
Lindbergh. But in the Coolidge administration, and particularly at the White House, where the Nicaraguan troubles
had been a severe annoyance, his work was highly approved
and his pledges fully redeemed. Calvin Coolidge was pleased,
and his satisfaction was probably largely responsible for Stimson's return in less than a year to full-time public service as
Governor General of the Philippine Islands.

CHAPTER VI

Governor General of the Philippines

1. THE BACKGROUND

EARLY in February, 1928, Stimson sailed from San Francisco to begin service as Governor General of the Philippine Islands. He had retired for good from his law firm, and now he was embarked with Mrs. Stimson on a journey halfway around the world. It was a strange undertaking for a sixty-year-old New York lawyer, and during the preceding month he had been kept busy acknowledging letters in which congratulations were tempered by a certain tone of condolence, as if to say that this was all very well but did he know what he was letting himself in for? Only a few recognized the feeling with which Stimson himself had accepted the appointment—a feeling that this was to be a last short adventure before his old age, and that it would be a welcome addition to his memories. The Philippines to most Americans were still, in 1928, a far-off unhealthy country, in which one might take a distant, not unkindly interest but to which one would hardly go as a working official. And, indeed, if the appointment to the Philippines had been merely a routine call to public service, Stimson might well have refused, for life at home had become increasingly satisfactory in the years since the war, and Stimson was not insensible to the dangers and difficulties of so great a change in his life. But as it happened, his interest in the Philippines was intense, and he believed that there was offered to him now an unusual opportunity for special service. In order to understand his position, we must briefly consider the history of the Philippine Islands.

The Philippine Islands were named by the Spanish explorer

Villabos in 1543; they were conquered by Spaniards a generation later and for more than three centuries remained under
the Spanish flag. Then in 1898, by the historical accident that
Spain had also kept Cuba, the Philippines passed to American
control. The American reaction to this quirk of fate was
mixed, but the resulting official policy was, in Stimson's view,
excellent. As he later wrote, "What we proposed to do was
stated with wisdom and foresight by our Senate in its resolution of February 14, 1899, when we ratified the treaty with
Spain and took over the Islands. 'Resolved that by the ratification of the treaty of peace with Spain it is not intended to
permanently annex said islands as an integral part of the
United States; but it is the intention of the United States to
establish on said islands a government suitable to the wants
and conditions of the inhabitants of said islands, to prepare
them for local self-government, and in due time to make
such disposition of said islands as will best promote the interests of the citizens of the United States and the inhabitants
of said islands.' "[1] This general policy was defined in greater
detail in the famous letter of instructions to William H. Taft
which was prepared by Secretary Root and signed by President McKinley on April 7, 1900. This letter outlined in some
detail the great principles of individual human rights "which
we deem essential to the rule of freedom." It instructed Taft's
commission to insure the maintenance of these principles at
all costs, bearing in mind, however, "that the government
which they are establishing is designed, not for our satisfaction or the expression of our theoretical views, but for the
happiness, peace, and prosperity of the people of the Philippine Islands, and the measures adopted shall be made to con-
form to their customs, their habits, and even to their prejudices,
to the fullest extent consistent with the accomplishment of
the indispensable requisite of just and effective government."[2]

The policy of McKinley and Root was carried out with unwearied devotion and sympathy by Taft and his successors
for thirteen years. The great political objective of this period
was to educate the Filipinos to a constantly growing measure

[1] "Future Philippine Policy under the Jones Act," *Foreign Affairs*, April, 1927.
[2] *Annual Report of the Secretary of War*, 1900, p. 74.

of democratic self-government, and after the mutually magnanimous conclusion of the Philippine insurrection, in 1902,
the progress made in pursuing this objective was remarkable.
Perhaps no group of white men has ever accomplished so
much with a colonial people as the American officials, educators, and missionaries who went to the Philippines in the
early twentieth century. Taft's dictum that the Philippines
were for the Filipinos became and remained the fixed policy
of the American authorities, and the small colony of Western
businessmen in Manila never found the Governors General
willing to subordinate their mission to commercial interests.

This political policy was gradually matched by economic
concessions culminating in 1913 with the establishment of complete free trade between the Islands and the United States.
Not until later did the profound significance of this step become fully apparent.

In 1913 the Philippines enjoyed a measure of prosperity
and health incomparably greater than any they had dreamed
of fifteen years before. In thousands of schoolhouses an effort
had begun to satisfy the deep thirst of the Filipino people for
education. The health and sanitation of the tropical islands
had been greatly improved—conspicuously, the death rate in
Manila had been cut in half. An equitable system of justice
was in full operation. A constantly growing number of Filipinos were participating in the work of government, both
legislative and administrative, though the final authority in
the Islands remained the American Governor General. The
Americans and the Filipinos had become fast friends.

But though much had been done, a great deal more remained to do, and, as Secretary of War, in 1912, writing with
the knowledge that a new administration was about to take
office, Stimson issued a strong warning against any change in
policy. This warning must be quoted in detail, for it represents very clearly the peculiar difficulty of the American mission to the Philippines as Stimson understood it.

"All this has made for the betterment of the condition and
the hopefulness of the outlook of the individual Filipino. Yet
with all the progress of the decade, our work in the Philippines has but just commenced. Along no line, moral, mental,

or material, can it be counted as completed. With all the remarkable advance in education, there are still over a million Filipino children of school age unreached. With all that has been done in constructing public works, there are still vast regions of the islands cut off from means of communication and transportation and from facilities for moral and mental betterment. In spite of the higher wages and greater freedom now granted to labor, the old system of peonage, ingrained through centuries, is still accepted as their economic lot by the Philippine masses, and would make them only too ready victims for the rich and educated Philippine minority, who still regard the status of peonage as the natural lot of the ignorant masses. And, finally, the success of the constantly increasing native participation in the native government has been accomplished only because every step has been carefully checked and watched by Americans, and probably nothing is more certain than that, without these checks, such progress would have been impossible. Not only this, but the suspension of these checks now would, with almost equal certainty, forbid the eventual establishment of anything like popular self-government in the Islands, and would subject the great mass of people there to the dominance of an oligarchy, and probably an exploiting oligarchy. A complete release from American direction would not merely retard progress along every line noted here, but would inevitably mark the beginning of a period of rapid retrogression. There are few competent students of recent Philippine affairs who do not believe that if American control were now removed from the Islands practically all signs of American accomplishment in the Philippines during the last decade would disappear in the next generation. Until our work in the archipelago is completed, until the Filipinos are prepared not only to preserve but to continue it, abandonment of the Philippines, under whatever guise, would be an abandonment of our responsibility to the Filipino people and of the moral obligations which we have voluntarily assumed before the world."

In the face of this warning, which very possibly they did not read, for it was embedded in the annual report of the Secretary of War, the policy makers of the Wilson administration promptly undertook to execute a program of rapid withdrawal. In this they were carrying out a part of their national platform; they were also in harmony with the advice of leading Filipinos. The Democratic party, partly on partisan grounds and partly in the conviction that there could be no such thing as truly disinterested colonial government, had steadily urged in years of opposition that the United States should get out of the Philippines as quickly as possible. Meanwhile political leaders in the Islands had raised the standard of independence, and their cries were heard with sympathy by many generous-spirited Americans who had more knowledge of the ideals of freedom than of the political realities of the Philippines. Woodrow Wilson, succeeding to the Presidency in 1913, was not only a Democrat but a man whose ignorance of the Philippines was fully matched by a doctrinaire sympathy with brave words everywhere.

It thus happened that between 1913 and 1921, in a period which Stimson wryly called "the Harrison interlude," the Republican policy of slowly expanding self-government under American supervision was abandoned in favor of a policy of rapid "Filipinization," accompanied by an astonishing abdication of the Governor General's supervisory and executive functions. The Governor General, Francis Burton Harrison, succeeded in permanently disbanding the experienced and disinterested cadre of American officials which had played so great a part in raising and maintaining high standards of civil service in the Philippines; Harrison went so far as to turn over to the Filipinos powers specifically reserved to the Governor General by the Jones Act of 1916, a measure sponsored by his own party.

The result of those eight years was the one which Stimson and Americans experienced in Philippine affairs had expected. As Stimson later put it, "The Malay tendency to backslide promptly made itself felt with disastrous consequences. The sanitary service became disorganized with resulting epidemics of smallpox, and cholera, which within a single period of two years carried off over sixty thousand people. The Philippine government was allowed to invest its funds in a national bank, a railroad, cement factory, sugar centrals and other business enterprises substantially all of which were failures. The bank nearly became insolvent, the insular currency dropped to fifteen percent below par and the insular government was wholly unable to live within its revenue."[3]

Shortly after his inauguration in 1921 President Harding sent to the Philippines a mission headed by Leonard Wood, with former Governor General Cameron Forbes as his chief associate. The Wood-Forbes mission was to report whether or not "the Philippine Government is now in a position to warrant its total separation from the United States Government." The mission's report, though moderate in tone, made clear the opinion of the mission that the Philippines were not yet ready for unsupervised self-government. It drew particular attention to the condition of the public service. "It is the general opinion among Filipinos, Americans, and foreigners that the public services are now in many particulars relatively inefficient; that there has occurred a slowing down in the dispatch of business, and a distinct relapse toward the standards and administrative habits of former days. This is due in part to bad example, incompetent direction, to political infection of the services, and above all to lack of competent supervision and inspection. This has been brought about by surrendering, or failing to employ, the executive authority of the Governor General, and has resulted in undue interference and tacit usurpation by the political leaders of the general supervision and control of departments and bureaus of the government vested by law in the Governor General."[4]

Challenged by the condition he had found, General Wood accepted appointment as Governor General, and during the next six years he did his best to restore the earlier high standards of administration in the Islands. "Such a restoration," Stimson reported, "necessarily could be only partial. The 'Big Brother' method was gone forever as the admirable force of American civil servants who had been brought to the Philippines by Governor Taft and his successors during the first

---

[3] "Future Philippine Policy under the Jones Act," *Foreign Affairs*, April, 1927.
[4] Report of the Special Mission to the Philippine Islands, printed as House Document No. 325, 67th Congress, 2nd Session, pp. 22-23.

fifteen years had been dismissed and scattered. But, under the broad powers of supervision and veto granted to the Governor General by Congress in the Jones Act of 1916, Governor Wood has found an instrument for the gradual rehabilitation of the Philippine government. It has been a most difficult and un-grateful task. Powers of supervision over any race or people once abandoned can be re-established only with the utmost difficulty. To any governor not possessing the titanic energy as well as the colonial experience and unfailing patience of Leonard Wood, the task would have been impossible, for in the Philippines this supervisory power of the Governor General must take the place and perform the duty which in Amer-ica is performed by organized public opinion. . . . By the work thus patiently and laboriously performed the damage done by the reckless experiment of the Harrison administra-tion has been practically repaired. The currency has been restored to par. The bank has been saved from insolvency. The government is living within its income. Taxation which is very moderate is being satisfactorily paid. Sanitation has been restored and while eternal vigilance is necessary, that vigilance at present is being maintained. When an epidemic of Asiatic cholera was brought over from China to Manila in the autumn of 1925, it was promptly suppressed by the vigor-ous measures taken by Governor Wood. Education is highly popular and constitutes the largest item of the budget. There is in general throughout the Islands a very evident condition of ease and contentment which strikes the visitor at the present time as in the sharpest possible contrast with the conditions which he sees across the way in China."[5]

Such was the outline of the American connection with the Philippine problem as Stimson understood it in 1926 when with his wife he visited General Wood in Manila. It was a visit which Wood had requested him to make for the purpose of obtaining his advice on some matters of a legal and govern-mental character and during the six weeks of his stay Stimson saw a great deal about the Philippines with which he had only distantly come in contact before. He was more than ever

[5] "First Hand Impressions of the Philippine Problem," *Saturday Evening Post,* March 19, 1927.

gripped by the extraordinary educational venture on which the American Government was then embarked. He also found, with a shock of happy recognition, that the central political problem of the Philippines seemed to be one for which his own political thinking of the previous decade suggested an almost tailor-made solution.

The labors performed by Leonard Wood in the Philippines had not won him the cordial support of Filipino politicians. The reassertion of powers left unused by his predecessor seemed to the Filipinos a clear backward step, and although they could not deny the existence of the abuses which Wood was working to correct, neither pride nor politics made it easy for them to accept his course with equanimity. Thus it happened that during the Wood administration there had developed an impasse, not between Wood and the Filipino people, who were largely indifferent to politics and as a whole respected and admired Wood's Herculean efforts on their behalf, but between Wood and the leaders of the elective legislature. It became the declared policy of these leaders not to co-operate with the Governor General, and as their complaints carried more readily across the water to America than the solid facts about Wood's administration, there was the usual reaction among uncritical liberals at home. Fortunately Wood was firmly supported by President Coolidge, and by the time Stimson arrived on his visit to the Islands the Filipino leaders had begun to moderate their position. But the policy of non-co-operation still persisted, and the Cabinet remained unfilled because the Philippine Senate and the Governor could not agree on appointments.

During his visit Stimson talked and traveled with Wood, observing with keen admiration the vigilance and energy with which the Governor looked after the interests of his people, using his powers of inspection as a constant goad to the lazy and a menace to the faithless.

But he also talked with Filipinos, and particularly with Manuel Quezon and Sergio Osmeña, the two who then shared leadership among the Filipino politicians. Quezon, whom he had known since 1913, was the particular symbol now of opposition to Wood's regime; he had raised with eloquence and vigor the standard of immediate independence. Yet in long talks with Quezon, Stimson became certain that the fiery Filipino was by no means unready to co-operate, under the Jones Act of 1916, so long as he could not have independence. He was even willing to suspend active discussion of independence in return for genuine co-operation in gradually extending Filipino participation in the administration of the Government. Quezon was a politico, but Stimson found that in frank discussion he was both friendly and reasonable.

Osmeña he found even more interesting. The studious and highly intelligent Chinese mestizo, though less eloquent and vigorous than his half-Spanish colleague, had thought deeply on the government of the Philippines. On Osmeña's home island of Cebu Stimson discussed with him at length the notion both men had developed that the solution to the current impasse might lie in an adaptation of Cabinet government. Osmeña emphasized the importance of co-operation with the legislature, while Stimson put his stress on the final responsibility of the Governor General in major matters, but each recognized the validity of the other's position, and when they parted both believed that effective co-operation could be achieved on these general terms.

These conversations with Filipino leaders culminated in a meeting on September 9, 1926, in which Stimson presented a memorandum of his suggestions to Quezon, Osmeña, and Manuel Roxas in the presence of Governor General Wood. In this memorandum he developed in detail a scheme for combining effective executive authority with the beginnings of responsible Cabinet government. He pointed out that such a plan would require a frank recognition by the Filipinos of the American Governor's executive powers under the organic law. It was exactly this recognition which had hitherto been denied to General Wood. At the same time Stimson pointed out that the powers vested in the legislature under the Organic Act made it essential for the two branches to co-operate and, as the best means to this end, he urged that Cabinet appointments by the Governor should be drawn from the party dominant in the legislature. The memorandum further emphasized certain powers which must be reserved to the Governor and concluded: "If this whole program is tried, it must be first broached without any attempt by either side to boast of a victory over the other. The only chance of its success would be from both sides treating it as a fresh start in a sincere effort of co-operation between American and Filipino representatives."

But a fresh start was exactly what could not be expected of either Filipinos or Americans under the administration of General Wood. Both sides, and in Stimson's opinion the Americans more justifiably, were keenly aware of what they considered the bad faith and unsympathetic attitudes of the other. And General Wood was by no means disposed to accept what he considered the alien principle of Cabinet government, no matter what restrictions might be admitted by its advocates. Stimson left the Philippines with the deadlock unbroken but without finding any reason to change his opinion that there remained only personal reasons for its existence.

In public statements both in the Philippines and after his return to the United States, Stimson frankly stated his general views on the Philippine situation. In the Philippines, acting to support his friend Wood, he strongly defended the Wood administration against wild charges of militarism and laid the responsibility for non-co-operation squarely on the Filipino leaders. In his statements in the United States he dealt first with the general question of independence, basing his strong opposition on two general grounds. First, he held that the Philippines without American protection must certainly become a prey to one or another of the expanding and over-populated nations in the Far East. Second, and this was the point that was more dear to him although the one less palatable to Filipino leaders, he argued that the American responsibility within the Philippines would not be fully discharged until there had been widely established in the Islands the attitudes of mind which would permit the unsupervised survival of free democratic institutions.

So far from finding hope of progress in the idea of independence, Stimson argued that discussion of this issue was indeed a serious obstacle to effective political development in the Islands and urged that the United States adopt a fixed policy of maintaining its responsibility in the Philippines while aiming at increasng self-government and ever closer co-operation between the Filipino and American peoples.

In the summer of 1927, having returned to the United States for a badly needed rest, General Wood finally consented to a long-deferred operation and died on the operating table, the victim of his own tenacious courage. Later in the year, while President Coolidge was still considering his choice of a new Governor General, Quezon and Osmeña came to the United States to give their advice in the matter. At the end of November they called on Stimson in New York and strongly urged him to accept appointment as the next Governor. That these two leaders should make such a plea to such a man at such a time was remarkable. In his public statements and in his private conversations Stimson had never concealed three opinions which Filipino leaders could hardly be expected to approve. As part of his conviction that the Philippines were not ready for independence, he had emphasized "the Malay tendency to backslide"; he had warned that political leadership in the Islands was confined to a small group of educated mestizos, who might be expected, if the Islands were turned loose, to govern as an undemocratic oligarchy with small regard for the interests of the great farming masses; finally, he had constantly and vigorously asserted the absolute present necessity of retaining final authority in the hands of an American Governor General. All of these views were well known to Quezon and Osmeña, and yet they promised that if he should come as Governor General he could be assured of their energetic co-operation, and "when I suggested that such co-operation must involve no surrender of American principle, they cordially accepted that limitation."[6]

The position then taken by Quezon and Osmeña, and loyally maintained by them afterwards, could only be explained in terms of their willingness to accept at face value Stimson's assurances that his position, like that of McKinley, Root, Taft,

[6] Annual Report of the Governor General of the Philippine Islands, 1928, printed as House Document No. 133, 71st Congress, 2nd Session, p. 2; hereafter in this chapter this document is called simply "Report."

Forbes, and Wood, was based primarily on a genuine concern for the interests of the Filipino people and no one else. It was this basic Filipino trust in American colonial policy that made the relations of the United States in the Philippines different from those of any other colonial power with any other subject people; and although in their more explosive moments Filipino leaders were capable of vigorous anti-American statements, neither to their own people nor to Americans familiar with the Islands were these statements ever so significant as the basic friendliness which belied them. There can be no understanding of the history of American possession of the Philippine Islands without an appreciation of this fundamental fact.

With the assurance of support from the two outstanding Filipino leaders of the day, Stimson in due course accepted President Coolidge's offer of appointment as Governor General; for he saw every reason to hope that he might become a leading instrument in the realization of the brave hope for a co-operative advance toward self-government which he had outlined a year before. It was an opportunity too great to be missed.

2. A HAPPY YEAR

When the new Governor General and Mrs. Stimson disembarked in Manila on the first of March, 1928, they entered a world so different from the one they had left that in retrospect it often seemed to both of them that their year in the Philippines was a dream. The three thousand islands of the tropical archipelago offered a variety of strange scenic beauty that had already in their earlier visit caught their fascinated admiration. The eleven million people of many different races varied in their nature from the small pure-blooded Spanish colony in Manila to the primitive pagan tribes of the mountains. In the civilization of the Philippines could be found in wonderful admixture the effects of Malay inheritance, Moslem invasion, Spanish occupation, Christian conversion, and American education.

All this had been quite sufficiently exciting to the Stimsons when they came merely as visitors. Now as the Governor General and his lady they were to be the living symbols of the far-off supreme authority of the United States Government. Stimson was now to be the agent of the great republic and upon him would rest the final authority and the final responsibility for government. To eleven million people he was now representative of America and in his every move there would be judged not an individual but the whole of American colonial policy.

And he was not merely representative. It had been the tradition since the days of Taft that Governors General in the Philippines should be left free by Washington to execute their own policies in their own way. President Coolidge, of all the Chief Executives whom Stimson served under, was the most firm in giving to his subordinates both freedom and full support. It was typical of the man to have suggested to Stimson that if a letter of instructions was needed, Stimson should write it himself. There was no letter, and no order of any kind, except to do a good job. For Stimson Mr. Coolidge was a perfect chief.

The first task of the new Governor General was to make effective use of the "co-operation" which he had been promised. On March 2 he talked privately for an hour and a half with Osmeña, the Acting President of the Senate, and Roxas, the Speaker of the House; Senate President Quezon was in the United States under treatment for tuberculosis. This conversation was followed by another the following day, and during the weeks that followed, Osmeña and Roxas were frequent visitors at Malacañan Palace, the Philippine White House.

Though the root of the problem of co-operation lay in attitudes and policies which have already been discussed, it is important to understand the particular facts of the situation faced by Stimson and his Filipino leaders. Under the Jones Law, or Organic Act, of 1916, which had the same standing in Filipino law as the Constitution in the United States, the powers of the Philippine Government were sharply divided into the traditional three areas of legislative, executive, and judicial power. The elected House and Senate[7] held a legislative authority differing from that of their American counterparts

[7] A few seats, less than 10 per cent, were filled by executive appointment to insure representation of the non-Christian tribes.

only in that laws of certain kinds required the approval of the American President, while laws of any kind might be annulled by the American Congress. Neither of these powers was often used, although of course their existence had a substantial effect on the initiative of the Philippine legislature. The significant legislative authority of the Filipinos, however, rested less in their affirmative than in their negative prerogatives. By refusing confirmation to the nominees of the Governor General, the Senate might seriously hamper his work, and both houses possessed the far broader power to refuse new legislation or appropriations. Though somewhat limited by a provision continuing the appropriations of the previous year whenever no appropriation bill should be passed, this control over the law and the purse strings effectively insured to the Filipinos a power of veto over all new projects of the Governor General. And it would be wrong to suppose that the Governor General had any certain escape from this veto to the supreme authority of the American Congress, for in that body his recommendations would be balanced against those of the Filipinos and against other considerations more influential than either. Generally speaking, both the Governor General and the Filipino leaders were well off when ignored by Congress.

The executive power of the Philippine Government belonged to the Governor General under the general supervision of the President of the United States. The provisions of the Jones Law on this point were complete and explicit, so much so that they had been particularly emphasized to Governor General Harrison by Secretary of War Baker at the time of the passage of the act. "All executive functions of the government must be directly under the Governor General or within one of the executive departments under the supervision and control of the Governors General," said the Act. This was the authority which had been partly discarded by Harrison and restored against opposition by Wood.

The Supreme Court of the Philippines, subject to review by the United States Supreme Court, was granted judicial powers like those of its superior. A majority of the Court, in Stimson's time, were Americans, and the appointive power rested with the American President. Judges of lower courts were appointed by the Governor General "by and with the advice and consent of the Philippine Senate."

But while the final authority in the executive and judicial branches rested with Americans, it must be remembered that except at the very top, in the Governor General's office and in the insular Supreme Court, almost all of the officers of these branches were Filipinos. When Stimson arrived in Manila, only the Vice Governor (who was ex officio the Secretary of Public Instruction) and the Auditor, of his official family, were Americans. The men in charge of the remaining executive departments were Filipinos, and their subordinates were Filipinos. The elected Governors of the provinces, except those mainly inhabited by the non-Christian tribes, were Filipinos. So were most of the judges of lower courts and a large minority of the Supreme Court.

There was thus no question of instituting or maintaining an administration of the Islands by Americans. The day-to-day administration now belonged to the Filipinos, and no American could reverse this situation, even if he wanted to. Stimson had around him in 1928 and 1929 not more than half a dozen American assistants of any direct importance to him; these men made up in energy and devotion much of what they lacked in numbers, but they were necessarily auxiliary agents, not leaders in their own right.

Yet there persisted a natural fear among Filipinos that in the exercise of his indisputable final power the Governor General might in effect nullify the Filipinization of the civil service and the executive departments, and it was one of the first fruits of Stimson's cordial relationship with Osmeña and Roxas that he found a way to reassure the public on this point. Being informed by them that Filipinos were nervous about his intentions in dealing with his subordinates, he wrote and made public a letter denying one of the frequent requests he received for intervention. In the course of this letter he remarked that "The Organic law, which forms the basic constitution of our government in the islands, certainly does not contemplate that I should substitute my own personal judgment for the official judgment of the various executive of-

ficers to whom by law the administration of such details . . .
is intrusted in the conduct of the insular government. The
great power of supervision and control over the executive
functions of government which that Organic law imposes
upon me should ordinarily not be invoked to interfere with
the conduct of government by my subordinates, unless they
have been guilty of some misconduct or negligence deserving
of grave reprehension or even removal from office."[8]

Taken by itself, this letter would give an unbalanced view
of Stimson's position. Like almost every aspect of his policy
in the Philippines, the question was two-sided; if it would be
usurpation to butt into the ordinary business of his subordinates, it would be faithless abdication not to maintain and
exercise his duty of "supervision and control," and long before
his arrival in the Philippines Stimson had made it clear that
he favored action to enable the Governor General to carry
out this duty more effectively. He had strongly urged the
prompt enactment of a bill pending in Washington which
would provide the Governor with technical advisers and investigating assistants responsible directly to him and to him
alone. This bill was opposed by Filipino leaders, who feared
that it aimed at the substitution of Americans for Filipinos in
the actual administration of the Islands, and who in any case
did not notably share Stimson's enthusiasm for effective "supervision and control."

The solution of this problem on a mutually satisfactory
basis was in Stimson's view one of the most striking successes
of his year in the Philippines. While the Washington legislation was still awaiting action, and after prolonged conferences and final agreement with Stimson, the Philippine legislature itself passed in August a law (the Belo Act) providing
the Governor General with the necessary money and authority for personal assistants, American or Filipino, and, as Stimson remarked in a public statement, it did so "in a way to
insure the permanence and non-partisan character of the
provision quite as effectively as if it had been furnished by
congressional action." For the act contained a permanent appropriation, any change in which would be subject to a guber-

[8] Report, Appendix A.

natorial veto. For his part, in the same statement Stimson made clear his intention not to interfere with the exercise of administrative duties by his Filipino officials. "The true purpose of the statute is just the opposite, namely, to develop the autonomy of the heads of the departments by placing the Governor General in a position where he can safely intrust ever widening powers of discretion to those department heads with the assurance that he will, nevertheless, be kept in touch with the progress of government and so provided with the information necessary for his action, under the Organic law, in cases of dereliction or neglect of duty on their part."[9]

Parallel with this clarification of the Governor General's position in the executive department was the even more important work of establishing a clear working relationship with the legislature. Here again the question was two-sided. On the one hand, Stimson had no intention of violating the Jones Law by surrendering to the legislators his final responsibility, but at the same time he recognized the force of Quezon's contention that the legislative branch, which contained the active political leaders of the Filipino people, could hardly make progress toward self-government unless it were brought into close connection with the administrative work of government. Otherwise, under the Jones Law, its essential powers would be merely negative and sterile.

In this problem, as in many others, the solution was made easier by the work of Leonard Wood. Under Harrison the Philippine legislature, reaching out for new authority and power, had established a number of government-owned corporations and had placed the voting power of these corporations in the hands of a Board of Control in which the Governor General could be outvoted by his two colleagues, the President of the Senate and the Speaker of the House. These corporations, which included the national bank, were a transparent device for evading the authority of the American executive. Wood had abolished the Board of Control as a violation of the Jones Law, and when Stimson took office an appeal against his assumption of personal authority over the government-owned corporations was awaiting final judgment in the

[9] Public memorandum of August 8, 1928, Report, Appendix C.

United States Supreme Court. The decision handed down on May 14 fully upheld Wood and reasserted in unmistakable terms the authority of the Governor General. Without any action of his own, therefore, and without the unpleasant duty of making a decision, Stimson found his authority strongly reinforced. The government-owned corporations had always been extremely interesting to Filipino politicians, and his undisputed control of them placed him in a strong bargaining position. At the same time he could afford to be generous and make a co-operative gesture. "I let it be known that whereas I proposed to retain and exercise all the powers vested in me by the decision of the Supreme Court, I did not intend to make any immediate or radical change in the management of these corporations and would devote myself to a careful study of their requirements, and that in such action as I eventually took I would endeavor to carry out the legitimate purposes which the Filipinos had in mind in establishing these corporations so far as that could be done without danger to their security or the violation of more fundamental policy."[10]

With his authority firmly established, and his determination to maintain it clear, Stimson proceeded to take three steps, with the concurrence of the Filipino leaders, which established a working machinery for co-operation with the legislature. A favorable opportunity for these moves was created by the insular elections in June. Although Stimson was disappointed at the absence of any "clear-cut normal insular issues between the two principal parties," there was one issue of major importance—that of co-operation or non-co-operation with the new Governor General. "The result of this issue was fortunate for future co-operation. All of the candidates who raised it were defeated. . . ."[11] The Nationalista party, led by Quezon, Osmeña, and Roxas, was returned with handsome majorities in both houses, and when the Eighth Philippine Legislature convened in July, the time was ripe for steps toward formalizing the co-operation which had thus far been maintained by constant conference between Stimson, Osmeña, and Roxas.

[10] Report, p. 6.
[11] Report, p. 5.

First, Stimson appointed a Cabinet from members of the Nationalista party, after discussing his nominees with the party's leaders. It will be remembered that the Islands had been without a Cabinet since Wood's acceptance of the resignations of all but one of his Cabinet in 1923. The re-establishment of that body, and the appointment of men who were of the same party as that which controlled the legislature, "was the principal and most direct step toward securing co-operation between that body and the executive. It postulated that in the performance of their administrative duties they should be a loyal part of an independent executive and yet at the same time in constant touch with the legislature, and therefore sympathetic and responsive to the policies laid down by that body." And in Stimson's time that postulate was thoroughly sustained. "The Secretaries of departments became true and efficient constitutional advisers. . . . I believe that the change wrought by their appointment was little short of revolutionary."[12]

In their conversations of 1926, both Stimson and Osmeña had mentioned with favor the possibility of appointing Cabinet members from the legislature itself, and not merely from the party there dominant. But in 1928 certain legal doubts on both sides prevented such a step, and it therefore became necessary to find another method for the establishment of close relations between the members of the Cabinet and the legislators. The solution found was the amendment of the rules of procedure of the two houses to permit to Cabinet members the privileges of the floor. A plan which Stimson had vainly urged in New York in 1915 thus came to life ten thousand miles away.

The third step in the co-operative machinery, and to Filipinos the most important, was the re-establishment of the Council of State, another organization set up by Harrison and dismantled by Wood. The Council of State was a body consisting of the Governor General, his Cabinet, and the presiding officers and majority floor leaders of the two houses of the legislature. Stimson's Council, unlike Harrison's, was, by the terms of the order creating it, purely advisory. Stimson made this limitation entirely clear to the Filipino leaders before he

[12] Report, pp. 7, 8.

set it up; he did not want them to have any great hopes which might later be jarred. He hoped that the Council of State, like the Cabinet, would lead to increasing participation by Filipinos in the work of government, but he could not permit any such development to undermine his basic powers, and particularly in the three fields of health, finance, and law and order he must retain an untrammeled jurisdiction. These reservations were not of serious present concern to the Filipinos; as Osmeña put it, the legal forms of the Council of State were unimportant, "its political function of co-operation being the important one." (Diary, March 20, 1928)

It would be easy to misunderstand the meaning of these steps toward co-operative government, and there were a few in Manila who did so misunderstand them. On the one hand, Americans who had hoped for a "firmer" policy argued that the new Governor General was undoing the good work of General Wood. On the other hand, a few opposition Filipinos, as Quezon reported with some amusement to Stimson, took to "spreading around the story that I was the ablest and most dangerous Governor-General that was ever in the Islands, and that while I wore an ingratiating smile, I was engaged in destroying their liberties." (Diary, October 17, 1928) But the bulk of the Filipino press and public, along with the majority of Filipino politicians, were as cordial in their support of the new policy as Stimson's superiors in Washington. The American public, too, was pleased, insofar as it considered the Philippine problem at all. Neither Filipinos nor Americans were disturbed by the theoretical incompatibility of keeping final authority while maintaining close co-operation with legislative leaders. In practice no such incompatibility existed.

Probably Stimson's greatest asset in carrying out the above policy was that the Filipinos trusted him. He had gone out of his way to earn their trust, and he described the method he followed in some detail in his report to the President at the end of the year. "In view of misunderstandings of past years, I think it worth while to record certain features in detail for the benefit of American administrators who, like myself, may be without previous experience in the Orient. When I assumed office I was warned that the nature of the oriental was such that it would be dangerous for me to confer with them without the presence of American witnesses. I rejected this advice, feeling that it was better to trust and be betrayed than to make mutual confidence impossible. So far as I am aware, I was not betrayed in a single instance; and the character of our conferences became such that I was frequently made the recipient of confidences by the Filipino leaders which proved of priceless value to my administration. Again, bearing in mind the responsibilities of leadership in political organizations in the United States, I was very careful never to surprise the Filipino leaders of the party organizations with which I was dealing by an executive decision of any importance. Instead I always conferred with them about it beforehand, giving them an opportunity to discuss it and, if finally decided on, to prepare their followers for its announcement. Furthermore, if possible the announcement of such a decision was always made as one in which they had participated or had suggested. In that way many an important executive policy, which inevitably would have been resented by Filipino public opinion had it been deemed to be sole act of an alien executive, was accepted or welcomed as coming also from their own leaders. These precautions may seem trivial and self-evident, but in such a situation as exists in the Philippines I am satisfied that they are vital, and unless they are constantly borne in mind, misunderstandings and suspicions are inevitable."[13]

In Manuel Quezon's autobiography the effect of this policy is clearly described: "Of course we had our disagreements, but we discussed our differences of opinion with perfect sincerity and frankness, and after the discussions were over there was never a bad taste in our mouths. It had been my wont after the departure of Governor-General Stimson to tell everyone of his American successors . . . that no representative of the United States in the Philippines had won my respect and even my personal affection more than did Governor-General Stimson. This, I added, was due to the fact that he never left me in doubt as to what he had in mind whenever he expressed his ideas on any subject. There was never any mental reservation whenever he talked to me, and he therefore made

[13] Report, pp. 2-3.

me feel that he gave me his entire confidence exactly as he would have done it if I had been an American sitting at his council table as the senior member of his official family."[14]

The significant phrase in Quezon's comment is "exactly as ... if I had been an American." Before his term as Governor General, Stimson had himself imperfectly understood the depth of racial feeling in the Philippines, and perhaps more important to his success there than any theory of co-operation was his early appreciation of the importance of avoiding even the appearance of racial snobbery. His conversations with Quezon and Osmeña before taking office had made clear the importance of this matter, and he was thus forewarned. Arriving in the Islands, he was shocked to find that among many Americans the early friendliness nourished by Taft and others had given way to an attitude more like that of the traditional hard-bitten commercial white men in the Far East. Finding that the church of his own denomination excluded Filipinos, Stimson angrily shifted his allegiance to the local Episcopalians, who were still carrying on the great work begun by Bishop Charles H. Brent a generation earlier. And with Mrs. Stimson's spirited help, he set out to demonstrate that Filipinos would be welcome at the social functions of the Palace. The results were prompt and overwhelming. When the Governor General and his lady demonstrated their ability to dance the Philippine *rigodón* at their first ball, the newspapers were filled with flamboyant satisfaction, and Mrs. Stimson's personal triumph was complete when she appeared in the traditional evening dress of the Filipina three months later at a party given by the legislature for the Governor General. There was nothing difficult or dutiful about such gestures— they were indeed very easy and pleasant. But their significance for Stimson's administration can hardly be overestimated. Late in the year of her residence, as she was walking through the Palace with a group of friends, among them Osmeña, Mrs. Stimson was complimented on certain changes she had made in the decoration of the building. "Mrs. Stimson," said Osmeña, "the best improvement that you have made in the Pal-

[14] From *The Good Fight* by Manuel Luis Quezon. Copyright 1946, by: Aurora A. Quezon, Maria Aurora Quezon, Maria Zeneida Quezon, Manuel L. Quezon, Jr. Reprinted by permission of Appleton-Century-Crofts, Inc., publishers.

ace is that you have opened its doors again to the Filipinos."
(Diary, February 21, 1929)

The policy and technique of mutually confident co-operation was in the main a political undertaking, and the purposes
by which Stimson was guided were mainly political. But parallel to the political program, and interlocked with it in his
thinking, was an interest in the economic development of the
Islands, and to many in the Philippines who were not deeply
concerned with the relationship between the Governor General and the Philippine legislature it appeared that the primary interest and purpose of Governor Stimson was economic.
Nor did Stimson object to this opinion. The economics of the
Philippines were the principal subject of his major public addresses throughout his term. If political theory was in the end
more significant to him than economics, he himself emphasized that his great goal of stable self-government was dependent on economic development.

His basic position was stated in his inaugural address on
March 1. "Among the various matters which I deem important, I lay particular stress upon industrial and economic progress. It has often seemed to me that sometimes in our insistence
upon political development we overlook the importance of
the economic foundations which must underlie it and upon
which it necessarily rests. By some of us, industrial development has even been dreaded as if it were inconsistent with the
liberties of a people. As a general proposition, I believe that
no greater error could be made." The speaker continued with
a recital of the development of political freedom in those nations which had developed a "middle artisan class," the industrial guild, and "in later days the trade union." Then Stimson
emphasized that "The world has now reached a stage of progress where government is expected to engage in activities for
the social benefit or protection of the individual, all of which
are expensive and require greater governmental revenues. . . .
All of these services minister to the comfort and welfare of
the individual citizens; some of them, like education, directly
conduce to his ability to govern himself. Some of them are
particularly necessary in the tropics with its constant threat of

epidemic disease. But they all cost money. . . . To support them a community must possess the wealth which comes only with industrial development."

And the passage ended with a flat assertion that political freedom and economic strength were inseparable. "In short, it is the simple truth not only that individual freedom and the practice of self-government are found to be most prevalent and firmly held in those communities and nations which have a highly developed system of industry and commerce as a foundation, but it is also true that only in such communities and nations can the average citizen attain the degree of individual comfort, education, and culture which modern civilization is coming to demand."[15] If he had been a phrasemaker, Stimson might well have used the slogan later developed by Wendell Willkie: "Only the productive can be strong, and only the strong can be free."

Of itself, this doctrine was acceptable enough to the Filipinos, although not many of them seemed fully to grasp the connection between economics and politics; the attitude of leaders with whom he discussed his program was at first that economics was a harmless interest of the Governor's which they were quite willing to indulge. Their faces showed keen interest only as the conversation turned to such matters as the revival of the Council of State. And this apathetic attitude acquired an admixture of suspicion and fear when Stimson began to spell out the practical meaning of his interest in economic development.

For it was a necessary condition of economic growth in the Philippines that large quantities of foreign—presumably American—capital be attracted to the Islands. Without heavy new investment neither the industries nor the agriculture of the Philippines could produce on an expanded scale in competition with other countries. And without revision of the Philippine corporation laws heavy new investment could not be obtained. Thus the program of the Governor General flew squarely in the face of the natural prejudices which the Filipinos shared with most colonial peoples. Hospitality to foreign capital is not a popular policy in most such countries, and

[15] Report, Appendix E.

the inescapable logic which requires foreign investment as the preliminary to economic independence is often obscured by the equally inescapable logic by which *uncontrolled* foreign investment leads to economic slavery. Of nothing in his term as Governor General was Stimson more proud than of his success in winning Filipino approval of a more liberal corporation law.

His preparations were careful. Using the prestige of his own official utterances to emphasize the positive values of economic development, he at the same time firmly insisted that no laws or actions giving capital unfair advantages would ever command his support, and he was believed. The required legislation was prepared not in the Governor General's office but by a committee of "prominent and respected lawyers," both Filipino and American. The detailed economic position of the Islands and their need for capital was expounded in a separate report by a visiting American, Vice President Lyman P. Hammond of the Electric Bond & Share Company. Most important of all, Stimson won the open and fighting support of Quezon, who returned from the United States in August. "After studying carefully the general principles involved in the legislation, he became convinced of their wisdom and threw himself heart and soul into the leadership of the legislative contest." Since the support of Quezon could hardly have been obtained without the previous establishment of political co-operation, it is evident that the economic program was quite as dependent on politics as politics on economic development.

The corporation bills were not passed unamended. One of their outstanding provisions was the repeal of "certain enactments which forbade any investor to be interested in more than one agricultural corporation at a time." These enactments were a part of a deeply cherished Filipino land policy aimed at the prevention of great corporate land holdings. "The average Filipino believes that it is better for his country to be slowly and gradually developed by a population of comparatively small individual landowners than to be more rapidly exploited by a few large corporations which own the land and till it either with tenant farmers or hired employees." If foreign investment could only be obtained by authorizing holding companies which would in effect nullify this land policy, he wanted no part of it. This feeling Stimson at first imperfectly appreciated. But as he studied the problem he was largely converted to the Filipino position. "The existence of this native sentiment has not been generally recognized in the United States, but the events of my own year's experience brought it to my attention as one of the deepest and most controlling currents of public opinion in the Islands and one which it would be folly to disregard or attempt to defy."[16] The corporation bills, as finally passed, contained provisions designed to prevent holding companies from obtaining financial control of the corporations in which they might invest, and Stimson pledged himself to vigilance in recommending further changes should they be necessary to protect the historic land policy of the Islands. And a few months later he officially discouraged a major American rubber company from undertaking any large-scale land purchases.

The prolonged public debate over the corporation bills was in Stimson's view of great educational value. It directed the attention of the Filipinos toward the basic economic realities of their situation, and as by-products of the discussion a number of less important but useful economic measures were passed by the legislature. A good beginning was thus made on a purpose which Stimson ranked far above any merely legislative accomplishment, however necessary, namely, "to transform the attitude of the minds of the whole people on this subject, so that they should recognize that such development might, if intelligently handled, be made an aid, and not an enemy, to their aspirations for freedom."[17]

Stimson had originally intended not to remain as Governor General more than a year, but as 1928 drew to an end, he found himself drawn more and more to a reconsideration of his original plan. His policies of economic development and political co-operation were fairly launched, but both of them still depended in considerable measure on his personal prestige; neither could yet be called a solid tradition. The detailed

[16] Report, p. 4.
[17] Report, p. 9.

application of both was only beginning, and Stimson felt the
urge of the successful builder not to leave his work at a time
when it was progressing so favorably. More than that, he liked
the life of the Governor General. The frequent trips of inspection gave full rein to his hankering for travel and for sport,
while at the same time the viceroyal privileges of the Governor were not unpleasant. Compared to the life of a practicing
New York lawyer, it was not an unduly strenuous existence,
and like most of his predecessors Stimson had been captivated
by the unaffected trust and affection so freely granted
by the Filipino people. The assignment thus combined a more
agreeable life than the one he had left with very much greater
opportunities for usefulness. But events in the United States
intervened to prevent the gratification of his wish. Mr. Herbert Hoover had been elected President and he desired Stimson's presence in his Cabinet in a position far more important
than that of Governor General of the Philippine Islands. At
the end of January, 1929, Stimson accepted appointment as
Mr. Hoover's Secretary of State, and a month later he sailed
from Manila, never to return. His direct connection with the
Philippine Islands thus came to an end just a year after his
arrival in Manila.

His last month in the Islands was at once one of the most
active and one of the most satisfactory in Stimson's entire life.
Against the background of his deep private happiness in the
prospect of four years of service in the highest appointive office in the American Government there unrolled a series of
events which served to cement in lasting form his devoted affection for the Philippine Islands and their people. The news
of his new assignment was greeted with enthusiasm by all sections of Manila opinion; the press and political leaders vied
with one another in expressions of their approval of his work
and their good wishes for his future. In the legislature the
prevalent good feeling took the practical form of rapid approval in a special session (summoned by Stimson before his
appointment) of a series of measures sponsored by the Governor General. The legislature further took the unprecedented
step of inviting the Governor to address it. In this, his last
major public statement, Stimson paid his tribute to Quezon,

Osmeña, and Roxas—"It has been my good fortune to have been in public life at different times and in different capacities and to have met with many men in public life in my own country. Never have I received more loyal friendship, more frank and fair treatment than I have received from the gentlemen who have been the heads of your two houses." He added similar and equally sincere words of praise for the legislature itself, and for his Cabinet—"I will not admit that any Governor General in the whole history of these Islands has ever had as good a Cabinet as I have now." Then he re-emphasized, to loud applause, his conviction that by traveling along the "pathway of economic development" the legislature was "traveling along the road which eventually leads to self-government and freedom." And he ended on a note of personal gratitude: "Now, my friends, it is approaching the time when I must say farewell. I hate to say it. I came here as a stranger to a strange land, and I have found nothing but kindness and friendship. I have not even an uncomfortable memory of that wonderful year. . . . My wife and I have felt the warmth of your affection and we value it more than I can say. I am not going to try to express it. I only wish to say in going that although I shall not be present with you, I shall be your friend at home; and I shall carry away memories which have caused me to feel the greatest possible obligation to the kindness of your people; and I shall not forget it."

On March 3 Stimson sailed from Manila. "The Cabinet and Staff came with Quezon and Roxas to the Palace to say good-by and go with us to the pier. Quezon brought a beautiful silk Governor General's flag made by Filipino ladies, and Roxas a beautiful but enormous Filipino flag also made of silk. . . . Manila certainly did its best to give us a warm send-off. A committee under the chairmanship of Mr. Torres had been appointed and a crowd had already assembled on the grounds of Malacañan. All the whistles blew at two o'clock and again when the ship sailed at four. On our way to the pier the streets were lined with people. The University cadets were in one place and another corps of cadets at another place, while drawn up at the pier was a guard of honor consisting of the entire battalion of the 31st Infantry of the American

Army. At the pier itself, I should conservatively estimate the number of people assembled at ten thousand. They not only crowded the entrance but they crowded the entire length of the pier, which is about twelve hundred feet long. As we walked the length of the pier through the upper gallery, the entire way was lined with constabulary on each side keeping the way open but with the people grouped on each side in rows two or three deep. When we got on board, a great many friends had been permitted to come on and say good-by to us there. The boat pulled out at four o'clock, and as it pulled out the entire pier, both upper and lower, was lined the entire length with friendly brown faces." (Diary, March 7, 1929)

3. LATER DISAPPOINTMENTS AND SOME HOPES

It would be pleasant if the story of Stimson's work in the Philippines could be ended with his triumphant departure from the Islands in 1929. It cannot. The foundation he laid in one year for the development of political and economic autonomy, based though it was on a precedent tradition of thirty years' standing, was in the main discarded in the years that followed. Conditions beyond his control—and beyond the control of anyone in the Philippines, twisted the Philippine policy of the United States away from what Stimson had planned; and the subsequent history of the Islands has not fulfilled the pleasant, peaceful, and progressive prospect that opened before both Filipinos and their American friends in 1929.

The first blow was struck by Americans; the Philippine experiment may be regarded pridefully as an example of American idealism at its practical best, but the end of that experiment was caused by American realism at its impractical worst. It was a small and selfish group of American sugar interests that first disrupted the harmony of 1929.

Warning of this attack came while Stimson was still in the Philippines, in the form of a resolution, introduced in Congress by a Representative Timberlake, which would have restricted the duty-free importation of Philippine sugar. Parallel to the Timberlake Resolution were a number of requests from American trade associations for tariff restrictions on other Philippine products. It thus appeared that American interests seeking tariff protection were determined on ending the free trade between the Philippines and the United States; these were strong interests—they were of the same sort as those which one year later produced the Hawley-Smoot tariff.

The effect in the Philippines was immediate. Free trade with America had existed for fifteen years; in that time insular agriculture, the only large source of export value, had become entirely dependent on the American market. Without free trade the foundations of the Filipino economy would be destroyed, and the final result of the American connection with the Philippines would be disaster. In the face of such a danger it seemed idle to talk of economic development; to the degree that they saw the Timberlake Resolution as a straw in the wind, men hesitated to make new investments. The mere suggestion of a tariff barrier produced, in Stimson's words, a "withering effect" on business confidence.

But even more serious was the withering of political co-operation. Filipino leaders continued to treat Stimson with full and friendly confidence; they knew that he was a vigorous opponent of tariff restriction. But Stimson was not America, and agitation for a tariff was painful evidence that Stimson's policy might not for long be American policy. The economic menace of the tariff restrictions thus reopened for urgent consideration among Filipinos the vexed issue of independence.

Stimson, as we have seen, believed that complete independence from the United States was the wrông final goal for the Philippines; he considered it impractical and unrealistic; he believed it neither useful for the Filipinos nor advantageous to the United States. The Filipinos, in his view, required American support and protection in order to avoid intimidation from large oriental neighbors, while America's political position in the Far East was greatly strengthened by the existence in the Philippines of an outpost of American civilization. Independence he thought a misnomer for the legitimate and natural Filipino aspiration toward full self-government.

In his inaugural address Governor General Stimson, like several of his predecessors, had withdrawn himself completely from any participation in discussion of independence. "It is not within the province of the Governor General to determine the future relations of the inhabitants of these islands to the United States; that duty rests with the government of the United States."[18] By giving the Filipino public the more concrete and significant immediate goals of greater political autonomy and economic development, Stimson largely succeeded in quieting the agitation for independence. Particularly significant was his success with Quezon, who came to recognize that Stimson's method of developing Cabinet government under the Jones Act would offer all the advantages of independence, without its danger.

All this was changed by the tariff agitation in the United States. Stimson at first hoped that the terrible threat of a tariff barrier would dissuade Filipino leaders from their continued public support of "independence"; talking with Quezon "I said that what I would fear was that when the dilemma was presented between tariff against the Philippines on one side and independence on the other, the American Congress remembering the long-continued demands for *immediate independence* by the Filipinos would at the behest of the American special interests give the Filipinos immediate independence and disregard the real harm and cruelty which this would do to them." (Diary, January 6, 1929)

Quezon's first reaction was most surprising and very satisfactory to his friend. "He agreed with me that this was the chief danger and said, and this was the most keenly significant thing that he said, 'If I could get a dominion government with free trade advantages, I would do so at the price of giving up all agitation for independence for thirty years and would not hesitate for a moment. By dominion government I do not mean all of the things which a dominion contains which are unfair to the mother country. England has given Canada many things which are highly unfair to England. I don't ask for those, but if we could get the dominion system, even without those, I would abandon the agitation for independence for thirty years.' " (Diary, January 6, 1929)

But Quezon was not able to hold to this position. The strong

[18] Report, Appendix E.

general reaction of Filipino opinion was directly opposite to Stimson's argument. Ten days later Quezon reported that he had been talking with Filipino businessmen, individuals certain to be damaged by any tariff law. "The consensus of their attitude was 'If we are going to be subject to this kind of attack on our free trade, such as is now going on in the United States, we will be in constant uncertainty and danger. Even if we defeat it now, no Congress can bind its successor and the attack will be renewed. We might as well end it entirely and build up a separate system.'" (Diary, January 16, 1929) And the following day Quezon reported on the feelings of the politicians; he had consulted legislative leaders and the entire Cabinet; "The unanimous opinion expressed was that if they had to choose between free trade and independence, they would take independence." (Diary, January 17, 1929) It was wholly clear that the Filipinos had reacted with angry pride to what they considered a blow below the belt. Quezon said that "He did not think you could keep the Filipinos from agitation if the tariff threat were continued. He said that if they had been under any ordinary Governor General, we would have been flooded already with resolutions for immediate independence from every municipality and barrio in the Islands." With his usual courage Quezon was trying for the time being "to sit on the agitation," but it was a very hot seat.

In his first fifteen months as Secretary of State, Stimson went three times to Capitol Hill to testify on the Philippines. Twice he won his point. In April, 1929, he made a strong appeal against the Timberlake Resolution. In October of the same year he spoke against a bill which would have extended American coastwise shipping restrictions to Philippine waters. In both cases he was sympathetically heard; in both cases the press supported the free-trade position, and the advocates of restriction were beaten. The third time was different. "The opponents of Philippine imports being defeated thus twice in direct attacks lined up behind the independence movement and my next skirmish with them was before the Senate Committee on Insular Affairs. . . . There I had a hopeless fight because that committee was already committed by a large majority to Philippine independence." (Diary, August 28, 1930)

Stimson repeated to the committee all the convictions which we have discussed above but it was an unpleasant session. As the months passed congressional sentiment for independence constantly increased, and Stimson was particularly saddened by the way in which the advocates of independence pushed the Filipino leaders into a corner. "The selfish interests which want to get rid of the Philippines so as to get rid of their competition . . . have got evidently a majority in both houses [of Congress] pretty well pledged for that. The poor Filipinos themselves have at last realized their danger and are almost pathetic in their desire to escape, but of course they are tied hand and foot by their previous slogans and they do not dare to change for fear of political death in the Islands." (Diary, February 10, 1932) In the spring of 1931, Stimson was party to a final effort to kill the slogan value of independence by substituting a program of responsible Cabinet government under the Jones Act. In this move he had the support of Quezon and the War Department, and the devoted and diplomatic assistance of Frank McCoy, but the effort failed. Neither President Hoover nor Governor General Davis really approved the idea, and Quezon was soon driven by circumstances back to the idea of independence. To Stimson one of the most disheartening aspects of the situation was the number of Americans schooled in the old tradition who now threw up their hands and came out in favor of early independence. Even former Governor General Forbes was among those who advised Mr. Hoover to sign the Hare-Hawes-Cutting Act of 1933, which was passed with a whoop over his courageous veto. As Stimson had often prophesied to Quezon and Osmeña, the independence movement in the end persuaded even the good friends of the Filipinos that American protection should be ended.

The Hare-Hawes-Cutting Act had the one redeeming feature that it was subject to Filipino approval, and by the strenuous effort of Quezon that approval was denied. But protected by their "generosity" in offering independence, the tariff interests were now too strong to be completely beaten, and in 1934 Quezon accepted the Tydings-McDuffie Act, which was only slightly modified from its predecessor. Under this act, in 1935, the Philippines Commonwealth Government was established, and the Islands were to become independent in 1946, when they would be faced with the full effect of the American tariff wall.

It is fortunate for the honor of the United States that the story does not end here. The tariff provisions of the Tydings-McDuffie Act were modified a few years later, to permit a progressive imposition of the deadly barrier over a period of twenty years, in the hope that this might give the Filipinos time to develop new markets. And before 1946 arrived, Philippine-American relations were subjected to a sterner test than any in their previous association.

Already in 1935 Filipino leaders were aware that in achieving independence they had achieved too much, even aside from economic questions. In that year Stimson heard reports both from Quezon and from Governor General Murphy about the rising fear of Japanese penetration. Both Murphy and Quezon talked in terms of a "permanent association" between the Philippines and the United States, and Stimson wholly agreed when Murphy emphasized that such a connection must be voluntary on both sides. In his personal opposition to independence he had always insisted that no American could or should stop the Filipinos if their mature judgment was in favor of independence; all he had argued was that the United States must so conduct itself as to give that mature judgment a full and fair opportunity. His favorite phrase was that the time for cave-man methods had ended and that any permanent marriage between the Philippines and the United States must be based on mutual consent. As fear of Japanese expansion increased, it became more and more clear that the Filipinos wanted what Stimson had always told them they wanted—not independence, but self-government under American protection.

When war came, in 1941, and the Filipino people had to choose between Japanese promises and American reality, the American experiment in the Philippines was triumphantly vindicated. In 1941 Stimson was again Secretary of War, and his part in the epic of Bataan and Corregidor will be found in a later chapter. After that campaign, during the years of the Philippine Government's exile, he was in constant contact with his old friends Quezon and Osmeña, and Philippine problems came to his attention as a sort of "counsel for the situation," although the War Department was no longer charged with the responsibility for the Islands. The war served to end discussion of the tired issues of the past. Both sides had come to realize that there must be a continuing connection between the two nations, and both knew too that the old days of paternal Governors General could not be brought back. And the war served a great purpose in reviving the interest of the American people; as they watched with admiration the loyal resistance of the Filipinos, and compared it to the behavior of other colonial peoples, they realized that their agents had done well, and the economic legislation passed after the war, while far from perfect, was very much better than the original Tydings-McDuffie Act.

On July 4, 1946, in accordance with plan, the Philippine Republic was established. For Stimson it was a date marked by both fear and hope. The fears were old ones. Could the Filipinos govern themselves, insuring to themselves the peace and individual liberty which had been enforced so long from above? Would the politicos be able to give honest, democratic government to a nation which had been so short a time exposed to democratic doctrine? Might they not slide back down the hard road up which they had been led, lacking the experience and self-discipline for full self-government? Could they achieve alone the economic growth on which free government must depend? And Stimson had his fears for the United States also. Would she firmly maintain her duty to defend and protect the Philippines? Would her citizens continue to recognize their responsibility for Philippine prosperity and force a lowering of tariff barriers if that should be found necessary? Would able Americans respond to the continuing challenge of the Islands, and go as counselors, expert advisors, and assistants when the call came through, as it would surely do?

Stimson's hopes were simple. For nearly fifty years, sometimes in perfect harmony, more often with natural difficulties, Filipinos and Americans had lived together. In this common experience he had shared enough to know that with all its human failings, it was greatly to the credit of both peoples. The establishment of Philippine independence changed the setting for that old connection, and in settling old difficulties it raised new ones. But the sovereign remedy was still the same —trust and friendship on both sides. It was one of the greatest satisfactions of his life that he had been able to give and receive, in peace and war, such trust and friendship with the Filipino people, and he hoped that other Americans might have a similar satisfaction in the future.

PART TWO

WITH SPEARS OF STRAW

CHAPTER VII

Constructive Beginnings

---

1. WASHINGTON IN 1929

IT DID not seem fitting for the Governor General of the Philippines to take any active part in American politics, and during his year in Manila Stimson was more remote than ever from the Republican activities from which he had withdrawn in 1920. There were Republicans and Democrats in the Philippines, of course, but their interests were mainly insular—they tried to get promises from both parties as to Philippine affairs. The great issue of the 1928 campaign was of little moment to men in the Philippines, for there was no prohibition in Manila. Stimson was pleased by the nomination of Herbert Hoover in June, and delighted by his election in November. His admiration and affection for Al Smith did not extend to Smith's party. But it did not occur to him that the election might concern him personally, except in that Smith would have returned him, cordially but firmly, to private life, while Hoover might let him continue his experiment in responsible government.

He was therefore astonished to learn through a cable from his partner George Roberts, on January 26, 1929, that the President-elect wished to know his feelings about possible appointment in the new Cabinet, perhaps as Attorney General, perhaps as Secretary of State. After taking counsel, as always, with Mrs. Stimson he replied that he thought "Hoover should carefully consider" the dangers of withdrawing him from Manila at a time when tariff agitation had seriously disturbed public opinion in the Philippines. He continued, "If after such consideration he should offer me the State Department, would accept. Would not care to accept Justice, for as you know my interest in legal problems is not so great as twenty years ago." In this refusal to become Attorney General he persisted in the face of a warning from Roberts that Mr. Hoover might not like so blunt an answer. "You may soften my expression but my refusal must be shown to be absolute. It would be wiser for me to go into private life than accept Justice. It requires keen interest in the new problems of a great Department to furnish the driving power necessary to make good. I think that I would have that in the State Department, for I have been thinking about similar problems. In the other Department such tastes and sympathies would be almost entirely lacking. You must have no misunderstanding with Hoover. He is very determined and almost quarreled with me in 1917 when he urged me to become his counsel as Food Director, although I well knew that after my advocacy of the War, I must fight as combatant or lose my self-respect. It would augur ill for our future association if I began by not speaking frankly now." Mr. Hoover did not resent definite answers, and on January 30 Stimson received word that the President-elect had decided to make him Secretary of State. During the next four years Stimson and Mr. Hoover had many disagreements; both were stubborn, and temperamentally they were quite unlike each other. But to Stimson his association with Herbert Hoover became and remained one of the most valued friendships of his life; he never felt any inclination to retract what he had said in his first reply: "I deeply appreciate the confidence shown by Hoover and personal association with him would be most agreeable."

Of all the assignments to which he was called in his years of public service, the appointment to the State Department was the one for the difficulties of which Stimson was least prepared. It was also the one occasion in his life when a call to public service interrupted work which he hated to leave. "This is, of course, a terrific revolution in all my plans. . . . I cannot but feel badly at this interruption of our far-reaching plans, which have just been getting so nicely under way. . . . Certainly American democracy is a terribly wasteful instrument of human endeavor. Now I must go to Washington and face a new problem of organization and learn a new field of endeavor. I feel very ignorant and unqualified for it."[1]

Foreign affairs, in all the years of his life after 1929, were to be Stimson's greatest single interest. His work in the State Department was followed by years of constantly growing tension in world affairs and finally by a great war in which he played an active part. Throughout this period the foreign relations of the United States became constantly more important, until in 1947 it seemed obvious to him that "Foreign affairs are now our most intimate domestic concern." It is therefore of some importance to note that when Stimson became Secretary of State in 1929 he was not at all an expert on American foreign policy. And still less was he thoroughly informed of the problems and attitudes of many other nations. Of continental Europe, particularly, he knew very little beyond what a man might know from casual reading of the newspapers. Yet most newspapers commenting on his appointment seemed to feel that he was well prepared for his new assignment, and if he had looked back over the list of his predecessors, Stimson could not have concluded that his preparation was any feebler than the average.

And in some areas, of course, he had had unusual experience. In the Tacna-Arica and Nicaraguan affairs he had learned something about Latin America. In the Philippines he had learned much about the Far East, and this knowledge he had supplemented by short visits in China and Japan. He knew Great Britain and France. And every country that he had visited had made him more conscious of the interest and importance of foreign relations. It was this rising interest, especially stimulated by his year in the Philippines, that moderated his reluctance to leave Manila and gave him the necessary sense of challenge in the new assignment.

Stimson was held in Manila until late February by the special session of the Philippine legislature. The voyage home was punctuated by brief visits in Hong Kong, Shanghai, and Tokyo. In all three places the new Secretary of State was given a most friendly welcome. On March 26 he reached Washington, and two days later he took the oath of office. "My former

[1] Letter to A. T. Klots, January 31, 1929.

chief, good old Chief Justice Taft, was good enough to come down to the Department and swear me in in the large outer room before a galaxy of newspapermen and photographers who dictated how we should stand, look, and appear in a way I had not been accustomed to in the Philippine Islands." (Diary, August 28, 1930) This was only the first of many differences between the State Department and Malacañan Palace; in the four years that followed Stimson was not once as happy as he had been in Manila.

Yet in the spring of 1929 the foreign relations of the United States, by any standard of later years, were remarkably placid. The world was at peace, and it was more prosperous than at any time since the Great War. The United States was at once withdrawn from the painful daily problems of Europe and amiably interested in the advancement of pacific hopes. This curious combination of irresponsibility with idealism had just found expression in the leading role of the American State Department in constructing the Pact of Paris, the Kellogg-Briand Pact for the renunciation of war. In this treaty, ratified by the American Senate in January, 1929, the nations of the world solemnly declared that "they condemn recourse to war for the solution of international controversies, and renounce it as an instrument of national policy in their relations with one another." The treaty contained no provision for enforcement, and one of its authors, Frank B. Kellogg, had specifically stated that no enforcement was incumbent on the signatories. It was a pact of self-denial, and its weaknesses were soon to become apparent, but in the spring of 1929 it was young and undamaged, and it fairly represented both the profoundly peaceful attitude of the Americans and their gross ignorance of what must be done to keep the peace unbroken.

A Secretary of State of unusual skill and stature, Charles Evans Hughes, had conducted American foreign policy with vigor and distinction during the drab Harding years. In a series of treaties signed under the leadership of Hughes at Washington in 1921-1922, a settlement had been reached in the Pacific and the Far East which seemed to preserve peace with honor, and a bold beginning had been made in the post-war mission of disarmament. Under Hughes and his successor the State Department had begun to turn away from earlier ill-advised adventures in Latin America. The American contribution to reconstruction in Europe seemed to Americans more than generous. And American nonrecognition of the Russian Bolsheviks was generally approved—by Americans. As for the League of Nations, no responsible political leader dared to advocate adherence, but suspicion of the League had begun to decrease, and in dozens of nonpolitical activities individual Americans, and even official observers, were co-operating in its work. But in 1929 there still hung over America the fog of isolationism that had been created when the warm idealism of Wilson crashed against the cold nationalism of Brandegee and Lodge. The country had defied reality in 1920; nine years later there had come no punishment for this folly, and the people were thus more confirmed than ever in their determination to avoid foreign entanglements. Narrowly considered, American foreign relations between 1920 and 1929 had been highly successful. The experience of 1917 had lost its original glamour. More and more men like Stimson, who persisted in the conviction that America had played a necessary and noble part in World War I, found their convictions lightly set aside by younger men. Outright disillusionment with Wilson's great crusade was constantly increasing. The American people were perhaps less prepared than ever before to take a responsible part in the world's affairs.

But the peace they enjoyed was fragile—as fragile as the great stock market boom which Stimson found in full swing when he returned from Manila. Eight months later the bubble of speculative wishes burst, and within two years the whole flimsy fabric of the postwar peace began to come apart. But isolationism and false hopes persisted, and the American Secretary of State suffered accordingly. He was plunged into a desperate world-wide battle for the highest stakes, and his hand, as he later said, was 'a pair of deuces.'

But in the spring of 1929 all this was in the future. To American newspapers, when Stimson took the oath of office, the most interesting and important question about the new Secretary of State was whether he could settle the painful issue of precedence which had arisen between Mrs. Gann, the Vice

President's sister and official hostess, and Mrs. Longworth, the wife of the Speaker of the House. When Stimson solved this problem by passing it on to the diplomatic corps, he was applauded as a Daniel come to judgment. And in a way the solution was symbolic. If the United States could hand its international problems to the League, or to any of the foreigners from whom they came, perhaps the problems might cease to exist. Meanwhile, on with the boom.

And it was only as he looked back later that the tragic folly of these attitudes was wholly clear to Stimson. Of course he had never shared the prevailing horror of foreign entanglements. He entered office as a recognized believer in international co-operation. There were things to be done by such men in 1929, and Stimson went to work without any knowledge of the task that lay ahead. It was only as history unrolled that he learned how his hands were tied from the beginning by the opinions of his countrymen.

When Stimson arrived in Washington, he had three things to do before he could really begin to work. He must find a place to live; he must get himself an Under Secretary of his own choosing, and he must become better acquainted with his new chief, Mr. Hoover. All three of these matters were quickly settled, and each of them in singularly satisfactory form.

The most difficult was finding a house. It was not until midsummer that the Stimsons decided to buy an estate called Woodley. At the time it was an expensive decision, but as it was done by the sale of some wonderfully high-priced stocks which were radically devaluated by the market crash a little later, it was probably a most profitable investment. But the financial advantage was the least of the matter. For most of the sixteen years that followed, Woodley was Stimson's home, and in all Washington there was not a house where he and his wife could have been happier. The old southern colonial building was comfortable and spacious; the grounds were extensive; the view across Rock Creek Valley to the center of the city was peaceful and consoling to them both. It was as near as they could come to Highhold, and when Woodley was given to

Andover, in 1946, the wrench of parting was more severe than either of them would have thought possible when they first moved in.

The search for an Under Secretary had begun even before Stimson returned from the Philippines. The labor of scouting was shared by two old friends, Felix Frankfurter and George Roberts. Men who seemed suitable to both Frankfurter and Roberts were not numerous, but the Harvard Law School did Stimson one more kindness by holding a celebration at which Frankfurter found himself seated next to Joseph P. Cotton. Cotton was an old friend; it was he almost alone who had caught the spirit of the Philippine interlude, writing to congratulate Stimson on his opportunity for adventure. When Stimson learned that Cotton would serve him, he knew that he could find no better man. Everything that Cotton did in the months that followed confirmed this judgment, and his death in March, 1931, was the heaviest personal blow of Stimson's service as Secretary of State. It was also a great loss to the United States, for Cotton was only fifty-six when he died and few men of his generation were more fully equipped for distinguished public service.

To Stimson he was a godsend. Cotton was able, flexible, understanding, kindly, and witty. He was idealistic but not foolish, practical but not cynical, wholly loyal, and completely frank. In many of his qualities he was a most valuable complement to Stimson, who knew that he sometimes seemed stern and aloof to his subordinates. Cotton promptly became Stimson's alter ego—he was what the perfect Chief of Staff is to the Army commander—and something more. While he lived, he was Stimson's chief adviser in every field, and his freewheeling executive in many.

Stimson's first ten days as Secretary of State were spent at the White House as the President's guest. It was a typical gesture of personal kindness, and it allowed the two men to become fully acquainted with each other. For years Stimson had admired Herbert Hoover, but he had never known him well. Now he was astonished by the President's extraordinary grasp of facts. 'He has the greatest capacity for assimilating and organizing information of any man I ever knew.' Mr.

Hoover was very fully informed, so Stimson learned more than he taught, confining his own comments to an ardent advocacy of his Philippine doctrine.

There were two major foreign issues before the American Government in 1929, when these early conversations took place. One was the tariff, and to Stimson's great relief this subject did not fall within the jurisdiction of the State Department. He had seen in 1909 what happens when Republicans revise the tariff and he had shuddered in 1928 when he found that Mr. Hoover as a candidate had promised tariff revision. But it was a settled decision when he reached Washington; a special session of Congress had already been called. He kept out of it.

The other major question was one that Stimson promptly plunged into with enthusiasm. This was the matter of naval disarmament and relations with Great Britain.

2.   LONDON IN 1930

The absorbing interest of Stimson's first sixteen months in the State Department was naval limitation. The preliminary negotiations lasted seven months; detailed preparation for the Conference occupied three more; for three months in early 1930 he was in London attending the prolonged Conference in which his principal hopes were realized; for three months after that his main objective in life was to secure the ratification of the treaty by the Senate. The London Naval Treaty was to him at the time a great forward step, and of his part in it he was proud. He could not know that it was to be the last concrete achievement of the great postwar movement to turn swords into plowshares, and that in a very few years the whole effort of which it was a part would break down. In 1930 the Naval Treaty seemed a monument to the constructive and co-operative statesmanship of the leaders of three great seafaring nations.

The First World War left to the victors overwhelming military strength and a strong disinclination to use it. It produced in all countries, and with particular force in the English-speaking nations, a desire to be rid forever of the heavy burden of preparation for war. The first great result of this sentiment was the series of treaties signed at Washington in the winter of 1921-1922. Spurred on by a magnificent gesture from Secretary of State Hughes on behalf of the United States, the naval powers of the world succeeded in ending an incipient race in battleship building. Warships of more than 10,000 tons were rigidly limited; great building programs were abandoned, and much tonnage was scrapped. More significant still, the Naval Treaty was accompanied by a general political settlement in the Pacific Ocean which appeared to lay the foundation for lasting good relations among the major Pacific powers, and particularly between the United States and Japan.

In the years after 1922, though the Washington treaties retained their force and favor, it became evident that they were incomplete. Competition had been ended in the field of capital ships, but it reappeared in other categories, and particularly in the construction of heavy cruisers of 10,000 tons, with 8-inch guns—so-called Treaty cruisers, whose specifications were determined more by the words of the Washington settlement than by the requirements of naval strategy. This new naval rivalry became the principal immediate obstacle to broader discussions of land and air disarmament. And it assumed particular bitterness in issues between Great Britain and the United States, two nations which on any rational ground should have been delighted to see each other strong. In 1927, in Geneva, irreconcilable differences between the British and the Americans caused a breakdown of naval discussions; in these discussions the Japanese honorably participated as a good neighbor to both parties. During 1928 and early 1929 there was no improvement in the situation, and the American Congress authorized a formidable program for the construction of Treaty cruisers, aimed at the achievement of a nebulous but apparently vital goal called "parity" with Great Britain. Nor did the British Conservative Government find it desirable to withdraw from the very advanced position it had maintained in 1927. Under the pressure of these events, Anglo-American cordiality was severely strained, and in the United States there was a marked revival of the anti-British feeling which has so often accompanied assertions of American nationalism. Jingoes in both nations were noisy.

At the same time cooler heads and preponderant opinion in both countries recognized that neither could gain from a naval impasse. Strong public support awaited leaders who would undertake to set their faces against jingoism and work out an agreement. The signing of the Kellogg Pact in 1928 and its ratification by the United States in early 1929 were evidence of a deep-seated yearning for peace and disarmament; a naval race stimulated mainly by considerations of prestige seemed clearly incompatible with these desires. In response to such sentiments tentative steps toward new Anglo-American negotiations had been made even before Mr. Hoover was inaugurated.

But it was the new President who gave real impetus to the effort to break the deadlock of 1927. Even before Stimson's arrival in Washington Mr. Hoover had begun his four-year campaign for effective disarmament. Mr. Hoover's driving energy was wholly enlisted in the effort to give life and reality to the Kellogg Pact. The pact seemed to him a proper starting point for a new and bolder attack in the problem of armaments. And as the first step in breaking the log jam he wished to end naval disagreements between the United States and Great Britain.

Stimson's approach was somewhat different, but it had exactly the same practical result. He inclined to place primary emphasis on the re-establishment of understanding with Great Britain; returning from the Philippines to the Atlantic coast he had been shocked to find that anti-British sentiment had greatly increased since his departure. Being himself a confirmed believer in the vital importance of firm Anglo-American friendship, he at once determined to make the repair of relations with Great Britain a cardinal objective of his service as Secretary of State. The obvious first step was to reach agreement on naval limitation. That such agreement would also contribute to the general cause of disarmament was important to Stimson, and gratifying; but it was the restoration of understanding with Great Britain that he put first.

Although Mr. Hoover's first steps were taken in March and were promptly followed by co-operative gestures from Great Britain, the Americans decided to await the results of a forthcoming British election before beginning detailed negotiation. It seemed likely that the Conservatives might be defeated in this contest, and experience since the war had clearly demonstrated that the British Labor Party was better able than its rival to make progress toward international agreements of a peaceful sort. Meanwhile, as Ambassador to Great Britain, Mr. Hoover appointed Charles G. Dawes, the retiring Vice President, a man who had won high international standing for his part in adjusting postwar debts and reparations. When the Labor leader Ramsay MacDonald became Prime Minister on June 5, the stage was set for active discussion. Two days later Dawes sailed for London, and during the three months that followed he was the active intermediary for a remarkable negotiation between London and Washington.

The detailed record of this negotiation does not belong in this story. Essentially it was a candid and honorable exchange between Mr. Hoover and Mr. MacDonald. Stimson was delighted to find that both men shared his liking for frankness. Each was unruffled by searching questions; both were prepared to make concessions. Gradually the wide gulf that had separated the two nations at Geneva was narrowed. The great concession was Mr. MacDonald's retreat from the unacceptable British requirement of seventy cruisers to a demand for fifty. On the American side there was perhaps no equivalent concession; since the British had conceded the principle of parity, and since the American cruiser fleet was mostly still on paper, it was the size of the British cruiser requirement that determined the major lines of agreement. When this requirement was materially reduced by MacDonald, it was clear that a settlement was in sight. The remaining differences were largely due to the intransigence of the American Navy's General Board, which held a very high opinion of Washington Treaty cruisers and wished its cruiser fleet to contain a larger number of 8-inch-gunned ships than the British were willing to accept. The British argued, first, that such an advantage would be more than parity because of the great difference in fighting power between 8-inch vessels and the usual 6-inch cruiser, and second, that a heavy American preponderance in 8-inch cruisers would stimulate Japanese building in the same class beyond the point acceptable in the British Pacific dominions.

In October, 1929, when it was clear that Anglo-American disagreement had been so narrowed that a final agreement could easily be reached in conference, Ramsay MacDonald visited the United States. It was the first visit of a British Prime Minister to America, and it was a personal triumph not equaled by a foreign statesman until the arrival of Winston Churchill twelve years later on a very different mission. Mac-Donald's gentle sincerity, and his instinctive eloquence and charm, made him the ideal ambassador of a reconstructed friendship. His visit to Mr. Hoover at the President's Rapidan camp marked a high point in the public popularity of both men. Stimson found himself strongly drawn to this Scotsman, so friendly and understanding, so patently one who loved peace and good will to all men, and his friendship with MacDonald grew stronger with every later meeting. Not a year passed in the seven before MacDonald's death that the two men did not meet, at first mainly on business, and, after Stimson left office, as old friends and joint lovers of the Scottish moors.

As disagreement between Great Britain and the United States had been the main obstacle to any extension of the Washington Treaty, the ending of that disagreement opened the way for a general conference of the major naval powers; accordingly in the autumn of 1929 the British issued invitations to France, Italy, Japan, and the United States for a five-power meeting to be held in London the following January. Stimson was to be the head of the American delegation, and he and Mr. Hoover gave much time and thought to the appointment of its other members.

The result was a delegation which in weight and balance always seemed to Stimson as strong as any sent by the United States to an international conference in his lifetime; it contained two Cabinet officers, two Senators, and three Ambassadors. With Stimson from the Cabinet came Secretary Adams of the Navy Department, a man who combined loyalty to his Department with a keen sense of the proper relation of naval interests to national policy. The two Senators were David Reed, Republican of Pennsylvania, and Joseph T. Robinson, Democrat of Arkansas. Reed was a resolute and skillful negotiator and an experienced student of naval affairs. Robinson was the Senate minority leader, but no narrow partisan; his hearty co-operation in London and his sturdy support of the final treaty were indispensable factors in its eventual ratification. The three Ambassadors were Dawes, whose personal diplomacy had already played a major role in naval discussions, Hugh Gibson, Ambassador to Belgium, perhaps America's outstanding expert in the technicalities of disarmament, and Dwight Morrow, Ambassador to Mexico, a man with a well-earned reputation for diplomacy and insight. It was a strong list, well supported by technical experts and advisers. One of the most rewarding experiences of Stimson's life was the privilege of leading such a group of men. From all of them he received complete co-operation and support; each of them employed his special talents wherever the delegation chairman asked for it, and from all came valuable suggestions as to American policy. Every important decision taken at the Conference by the American delegation was unanimous.

The London Naval Conference was opened by King George V on January 17, 1930, and adjourned the following April 22. It was three times delayed by outside events, one of them a Japanese general election, the other two, Cabinet crises in France. From the point of view of the American delegates, its work fell into three phases: the completion of agreement with Great Britain, the negotiation of a settlement with Japan, and the unsuccessful effort to bring France and Italy into an agreement on vessels of 10,000 tons and less.

Agreement with Great Britain was easy. As soon as the American delegation was able to make a detailed study of the issues which had separated the American Navy's General Board from the last British proposals of the Hoover-MacDonald conversations, it came to a unanimous agreement that insistence on the General Board's position would wreck the Conference for a purely hypothetical advantage, and it reduced the American requirement in 8-inch cruisers from twenty-one to eighteen, asking in return a balancing increase in the American quota of 6-inch ships. From the moment of this decision, which was reached on February 4 and promptly endorsed by Mr. Hoover, there remained only trivial differences between the British and the Americans, and these were easily adjusted in later meetings.

This shift in the American cruiser balance from 8-inch to 6-inch ships was the concession most violently attacked by big-navy men when the treaty came before the Senate for ratification. It would be hard to say whether these American advocates of 8-inch strength or the British who had opposed a twenty-one-ship American fleet of 8-inch vessels were the more eloquent in describing the superiority of the heavier guns to any vessels with smaller weapons. In Stimson's view this eloquence later assumed a comical aspect, for the Washington Treaty 8-inch ships did not turn out to be an outstanding success, in peace or war, while the so-called London cruisers, 6-inch ships of 10,000 tons, proved to be among the most valuable and effective vessels in the American Navy. And this was only the most conspicuous example of the errors of technical judgment which lay behind many of the positions ardently presented as matters of national necessity by the various delegations. It was fortunate for the United States Navy that its chief representative in London, Admiral William V. Pratt, took a different position on cruisers from most of his colleagues. Pratt had been carefully selected for this mission by the administration's civilian leaders, and Stimson found that he thoroughly justified their confidence in his judgment and vision.

Agreement with the Japanese was reached only after prolonged and complex negotiations conducted for the Americans mainly by Senator Reed. The essential difficulty was one of Japanese pride, which had been seriously offended by the Washington ratio of ten-ten-six in battleship strength. The Japanese now wished their proportion to be seven against the ten of the United States and Great Britain, and they particularly wished to achieve this ratio in 8-inch cruisers. This the Americans could not accept without arousing a storm of anti-Japanese resentment at home, and the British were perhaps even more categorical, maintaining that any increase in Japanese heavy cruisers would force additional British building in that category and so destroy the Anglo-American agreement. The Japanese never surrendered the principle for which they were contending, but they finally accepted a compromise skillfully designed by Senator Reed. The Japanese fleet was limited to a strength of six to ten in heavy cruisers, but the Americans agreed not to complete their heavy-cruiser program until after 1936, at which time the expiration of the treaty would permit a reopening of the question. The Japanese achieved their ratio of seven in other categories, and in submarines they were granted parity. To Stimson the outstanding feature of the Japanese negotiations was the frankness and friendliness with which the Japanese delegates advanced their position. From the first preliminary conversations in Washington until the treaty was ratified, Japanese political leaders were continuously fair and conciliatory; they were faced by a noisy big-navy opposition at home, but they spoke of it and dealt with it in the same manner as British and American leaders. Only the heavy-cruiser question might have led to disagreement, and in the face of a firm Anglo-American front the Japanese in the end had to choose between abandoning their demands and accepting the responsibility for failure to reach agreement. The Minseito Cabinet preferred international good will to national pride. Japan sacrificed less in the London Treaty than either of her English-speaking rivals, and she gained greatly in good will among the Western nations.

The third problem—and one to which no solution was found—was to bring France and Italy into the treaty. This was a question which only indirectly affected the Americans; the size of the French and Italian navies was not in itself a matter of concern to the United States; these were European fleets, almost entirely, and there was no American demand for supremacy, or even parity, in European waters. It was only as the French and Italians, building against each other, might arouse the British to expand their requirements that Americans would be affected. Nor was there anything important that the American delegation could do to bring the French and the Italians together. Behind their naval rivalry lay a series of important political differences in the Mediterranean area. At London the French would not abandon their insistence on a cruiser fleet strongly superior to the Italians', and the latter never budged from their claim to parity with France. Even when MacDonald and the British offered political guarantees of the Mediterranean *status quo* which, while not very strong, probably overstepped the majority opinion of the British Parliament, the French were not appeased. Stimson, constantly offering his services as honest broker to both sides, could not remember when he had seen three grimmer and less compromising faces than those of the French leaders as they insisted on their full naval program. And one of these grim faces was that of the great apostle of peace and international friendship, Aristide Briand. No Frenchman could give parity to Italy and survive in political life.

It was during the prolonged attempt to break the Franco-Italian deadlock that Stimson had his first painful experience with those Americans who, as he later put it, were convinced "that the world would overnight become good and clean and peaceful everywhere if only America would lead the way." Believing that the French would give up their extreme demands if the British and the Americans would join in a "consultative pact" against aggression, a number of Americans, newspapermen and private citizens, kept urging "leadership" on the American delegation and on Mr. Hoover, quite oblivious of the fact that no consultative pact which could be ratified in the American Senate would contain anything of the remotest value to France. Stimson was more than willing to join in any consultative agreement that was acceptable to the Senate, and as a private citizen he fully shared the view that it was foolish for America to be frightened by all "entanglements" in Europe, but his main business was to bring home a treaty which could be ratified. If there were to be political guarantees in a settlement, they would have to come from Great Britain, and Stimson did what he could to persuade the British leaders that they would do well to accept the advice of their own Foreign Office in favor of such guarantees. But no American leader could promise any "consultative pact" except one wholly divorced from any responsibility for action, and Briand himself told Stimson that so weak an offer would have no effect whatever on French naval demands.

All that the United States could do was to make its friendly interest in a solution perfectly evident, and this Stimson did. He made it clear in a press statement on March 24 that the United States would be happy to see French demands for security settled by the British and that a pact involving only consultative obligations might then be acceptable to Americans. Further than that he could not go, and indeed messages from home made it appear that even in going so far the American delegation had outrun much senatorial opinion. The American *démarche*, combined with a last effort by Mac-Donald, succeeded in changing the atmosphere of the Conference, and it ended with a far better feeling among the French and Italians than had seemed likely in early March. But no agreement was reached, and in its provisions for the limitation of vessels under 10,000 tons the London Naval Treaty remained a three-power settlement. For two years afterward the French and Italians continued to negotiate for a settlement; in these negotiations the American State Department, and still more the British Foreign Office, took an active and friendly interest. But no agreement was reached; the French continued to insist on superiority, and the Italians clung to parity.

The Franco-Italian disagreement in London was Stimson's introduction to the complexities of postwar Europe. He had of course known that the French were wholly determined to protect the *status quo* of the peace treaties, and that the Italians were deeply dissatisfied with the results of Versailles. But he had not previously understood the full meaning of this cleavage, and the degree to which it dominated the international relations of the two countries. In London, and indeed throughout his term as Secretary of State, it was French intransigence that he found particularly annoying; but he was never able to forget the great part France had played in 1914-1918, and his friendship for the French people, and most of their leaders, never wavered. Reconciliation between France and Italy, however, remained a problem in statesmanship for the leaders of these two countries, not for an American, and it was the common tragedy of the two nations that in this task their leaders failed—and though the French were more at fault in the beginning, it seemed obvious to Stimson that the later and decisive guilt belonged to the Fascist dictator Mussolini.

In its clauses limiting the tonnage of cruisers, destroyers, and submarines, the London Treaty was signed by only three powers, but in other important respects it was a five-power settlement. It provided for the immediate scrapping of nine battleships already earmarked for eventual destruction by the Washington Treaty. It declared a holiday in battleship building until 1936, thus saving the expense of new construction authorized in the Washington Treaty. Most important of all, from Stimson's standpoint, it provided for rules prohibiting unrestricted submarine warfare; this clause, which was the only one in the treaty without a time limit, was ratified by all five nations and later adhered to by every significant naval power in the world. It marked the acceptance by the nations of a rule of international law for which Elihu Root had vainly contended in 1922, and to Stimson at the time it seemed an achievement which in itself justified the Conference. It outlawed the form of war which had been directly responsible for American participation in the Great War. Nothing that happened in World War II was more saddening to Stimson than the promptness with which all belligerents prided themselves on submarine campaigns which flagrantly violated this treaty. But the future was hidden in 1930, and no section of the treaty was more generally approved than its restriction of submarine warfare.

It was as a team that the Americans had labored in London, and on their return to Washington they went to work as a team to secure Senate ratification of their treaty. Mr. Hoover was once more the leader; he insisted on prompt action, and when the Senate adjourned in early July without a vote, he convened a special session. Stimson played his part in public speeches, statements on Capitol Hill, and verbal exchanges with Senator Hiram Johnson. Perhaps most important of all, Senators Reed and Robinson were firm in their insistence that Uncle Sam had not been cheated by the foreigners. The opposition was noisy but hopelessly outnumbered; only the most embittered isolationists and the most violent big-navy men were against ratification. On July 21, after the threat of all-night sessions in the midsummer heat had wilted the opposition, the treaty was ratified by a vote of fifty-eight to nine. It was a great triumph for Mr. Hoover, and a great personal satisfaction to Stimson.

The London Naval Treaty had begun to die even before it expired in December, 1936. By the middle of that year European rivalry had so developed that the British invoked the "escalator clause" of the treaty in order to avoid scrapping vessels previously earmarked for destruction; the British example permitted the Americans and the Japanese to follow suit. And long before 1936 the Japanese had served notice that after that date they would no longer accept naval inferiority to any nation; their insistence on parity, wholly unacceptable to Great Britain and the United States, effectively ended the era of general naval limitation.

The London Treaty thus had a short and far from placid life. But Stimson did not for a moment believe that for that reason it was a failure. In itself the treaty was an important step toward disarmament and lasting peace. In its political effects it was wholly beneficial, serving to end a significant rift between Great Britain and America, while at the same time it improved the political relations between the United States and Japan. It was not the London Treaty that was a failure. The failure was that of the leaders in Japan and on the continent of Europe who so quickly turned away from the peaceful path on which the treaty was a milestone.

Nor can it be argued that the treaty served as a boomerang against the United States by unwisely limiting her naval strength. It was not the treaty, but Congress and the President, supported by the public, that prevented the construction of fighting ships in the years that followed. Long before he left office in 1933 Stimson had become an advocate of increased naval construction; there was plenty of room for it under the London Treaty. But a different course was taken, and even under Franklin Roosevelt, who firmly believed in a stronger Navy, construction was so slow that when the London Treaty expired, in 1936, existing American plans for naval construction aimed to achieve treaty strength only in 1942.

There was folly in the attitudes which forced the London

Treaty to take the shape it did, but Stimson could not feel, looking back, that this was the fault of the American negotiators. The American delegation was sent to London to get parity. A more ridiculous goal can hardly be imagined. On every ground, the United States should have been happy to see the British Navy just as big and strong as the British pocketbook would permit—excepting of course as this size might stimulate rival building. That America should have no other important object than a fleet as big as the British was utter nonsense. But there it was, and Stimson did his best to deal with it. No treaty without parity would have received ten votes in the American Senate, so the American delegation brought back parity. What good it did his country, Stimson was never able to say.

There remained the solid fact of complete naval limitation, binding on three powers whose uncontrolled rivalry had only a year before threatened serious political results. This was the real gain at London, more important by far than the amount of reduction in naval armament which was achieved. This reduction was by no means insignificant, but it was not nearly so great as Mr. Hoover had originally hoped it might be. Among all the principal participants on the American side it was perhaps Stimson who was happiest about the treaty. He had seen it throughout as a method of bringing the British and the Americans together, ending mutual irritation and beginning a closer co-operation in all things. This objective had been attained. Anglo-American relations reached a level of cordiality in the year after the London Conference that was not equaled again until 1940.

3. LATIN AMERICA IN 1931

When Stimson returned in September, 1930, from a vacation after the approval of the naval treaty, he was greeted at once by a problem which occupied a great part of his attention during the six months that followed—the problem of Latin American policy. "Cotton was waiting for me with the question of the recognition of the new revolutionary juntas in Argentina, Peru, and Bolivia." (Diary, September 15, 1930) The Latin

American countries, most of them heavily dependent on the export of one or two major raw materials, were the first to be heavily stricken by the spreading world depression; during 1930 and 1931 there were ten successful revolutions among the twenty republics of Latin America. This instability, combined with a rising tide of boundary disputes and the steady pursuit of certain positive American objectives in Latin America, gave to that area a continuing importance throughout Stimson's term as Secretary of State. After the spring of 1931 still more urgent questions in other parts of the world absorbed the bulk of his time, however, and it will be convenient to treat all of his Latin American activities in this section.

The Latin American policy of the United States in 1929 was in essence what it had always been. It comprised three principles. The first and greatest of these was the Monroe Doctrine, which asserted that the United States could not permit any non-American power to make any of the independent nations of the Americas "subject for future colonization." The Monroe Doctrine did not oppose the *existing* colonial holdings of European powers, but it placed the United States in lasting opposition to any expansion by any European nation in the Americas, even by the expedient of acquiring the colonies of another European nation. Effective at first largely by virtue of the co-operation of Great Britain, the Monroe Doctrine when Stimson took office in 1929 had been American policy for over a century, and for more than twenty years it had been completely unchallenged. It was an axiom of American policy, and it was so accepted by the Eastern Hemisphere. And the United States in the twentieth century was quite able to sustain it alone.

The second great principle of American policy in Latin America was at once more regional and more intense. This was that in the Caribbean Sea and in Central America the United States was bound to especial vigilance by the requirements of her national defense. The Panama Canal, and the Atlantic islands which covered the Canal and the Gulf of Mexico, were vital links in the strategic security of the United States. Thus the general sensitivity of the United States toward European activities in Latin America has always been especially acute in the case of Central American and Caribbean republics. At the same time these were in general the countries least able to maintain internal order and safeguard the legitimate rights and interests of foreign nationals in their territory. When Stimson became Secretary of State, the American Government was directly involved in the internal affairs of no less than three of these countries, while in two more she had certain contractual rights of intervention. All of these complications were the direct result of America's strategic concern for the security of her continental defense; she had intervened because of her overriding national interest and her abnormal sensitivity to the possibility of intervention by other nations acting to safeguard their rights under the sanction of international law.

But this intervention was to some degree in conflict with the third great principle of American policy toward Latin America, which was to respect the independence and integrity of all the nations of the American continent. This principle had been violated in the war of 1848; it had been violated again, perhaps (on this point Stimson was never convinced), when Theodore Roosevelt, in his eagerness to get on with the building of the Panama Canal, "took the Isthmus" from Colombia. It nevertheless remained general American policy to avoid any infringement of the sovereignty of Latin American nations. As Stimson put it in a speech outlining his own attitude toward Latin American affairs, "it is a very conservative statement to say that the general foreign policy of the United States during the past century toward the republics of Latin America has been characterized by a regard for their rights as independent nations which, when compared with current international morality in the other hemisphere, has been as unusual as it has been praiseworthy."[2]

It was the constant endeavor of the American State Department, while Stimson was its Secretary, to bring American policy into the strictest conformity with this third great principle, and to do it in such a way as to satisfy not only Americans, but Latin Americans as well, of the good intentions of

[2] Address to Council of Foreign Relations, February 6, 1931, printed in *Foreign Affairs*, April 1931, and hereafter in this chapter called "Council Speech."

the Northern Colossus. In this purpose the State Department was merely developing a line of policy pursued with particular energy by two earlier Secretaries, Root and Hughes. On their foundations Stimson was able to build, and in Latin America as in naval limitation he had the hearty support of President Hoover. As President-elect, Mr. Hoover had made a highly successful tour of Latin America, constantly asserting his conviction that "we wish for the maintenance of their independence, the growth of their stability, and their prosperity." Stimson was further supported by a distinguished staff of diplomatic assistants. The chiefs of mission in Latin America were mainly career officers, partly because Mr. Hoover was anxious to strengthen the diplomatic service and partly because the men who had earned political rewards were not ordinarily eager to serve in Latin America. The Assistant Secretary in charge of Latin America, Francis White, was an experienced and skillful professional diplomat; he had a thorough knowledge of Latin America and a sound sense of policy. White was appointed before Stimson took office, and he remained through the whole four years of the Hoover administration.

The question of recognition raised by Cotton on September 15 was one which recurred repeatedly in following months as Latin American peoples exercised their predilection for revolution as a means of registering discontent. Throughout this period Stimson and Mr. Hoover steadily adhered to a policy of quickly recognizing each revolutionary government just as soon as it had demonstrated its *de facto* control of the country and had announced its readiness to fulfill its international obligations. This had been the traditional policy of the United States, except during the Wilson administration, and in Stimson's view Wilson's well-intentioned experiment had been far from successful. "The American policy in regard to these matters had been undeviating until Woodrow Wilson came in and it was interesting to get a new view of the dangers which have come from his curious character—a blend of high idealism with absolute inability to foresee the reaction which his views and efforts would produce on other people. Whereas all the rest of the world had heretofore been satisfied to decide questions of recognition upon the outward facts of our relations with other nations, Wilson must needs try to delve into their internal policies and to seek to reform them according to his own views and his own forecast of world movements. The result when he tried it on Mexico in 1914 was simply to set everything at sixes and sevens. Instead of promoting feelings of friendship with Mexico he initiated feelings of hate and hostility towards this country which have lasted until Morrow's ambassadorship." (Diary, September 15, 1930)

Stimson believed that the true line of policy was one announced by an earlier Democrat. "Said Mr. Jefferson in 1792: 'We certainly cannot deny to other nations that principle whereon our own Government is founded, that every nation has a right to govern itself internally under what forms it pleases, and to change these forms at its own will; and externally to transact business with other nations through whatever organ it chooses, whether that be a king, convention, assembly, committee, president, or whatever it be.'[3] Whatever theoretical advantages there might be in the Wilson policy, it was certain to be ineffective in practice. Free constitutional institutions could not be imposed on a sovereign nation by the diplomatic device of nonrecognition. Nonrecognition could only be regarded as a form of intervention, and because of the size and power of the United States, and the degree to which its lead was followed by European countries, such intervention was of more than theoretical importance in Latin America. Stimson set his face against the Wilson theory. "The present administration has declined to follow the policy of Mr. Wilson and has followed consistently the former practice of this Government since the days of Jefferson. As soon as it was reported to us, through our diplomatic representatives, that the new governments in Bolivia, Peru, Argentina, Brazil, and Panama were in control of the administrative machinery of the state, with the apparent general acquiescence of their peoples, and that they were willing and apparently able to discharge their international and conventional obligations, they were recognized by our Government."[4]

[3] Jefferson to Pinckney, *Works*, III, 500, quoted in Council Speech.
[4] Council Speech.

In one section of Latin America, however, Stimson could not follow this traditional policy. In the five republics of Central America (excluding Panama) "An entirely different situation exists from that normally presented." For these little states, under a treaty signed in 1907 and renewed in 1923, had bound themselves not to recognize revolutionary governments in each other's countries until they had been approved in a national election. The State Department under Secretary Hughes had announced its adherence to their principle, and Stimson followed the same policy. The reason for the treaty of 1923 was simply that most of the Central American republics required a special method of discouraging their turbulent citizens from constant rebellion and military uprising, and although the policy of Hughes involved "possible difficulties and dangers of application," Stimson believed in 1931 "that no impartial student can avoid the conclusion that the treaty and the policy which it established have been productive of very great good." It had materially reduced the incidence of bloodshed in the turbulent and immature republics of Central America.

In 1934, when the Central American republics themselves abandoned the treaty of 1923, the United States extended its doctrine of *de facto* recognition to all of Latin America. Stimson by that time was no longer in close touch with Latin American policy, but he believed that the Roosevelt administration did well in avoiding a return to the misplaced morality of Woodrow Wilson.

The policy of promptly recognizing *de facto* governments was one way of avoiding intervention in the internal affairs of Latin American countries. Another method, also contrary to the practice of Mr. Wilson, was to withhold arms and munitions from insurrectionists. Twice in the first two years of Stimson's service the President imposed embargoes on the shipment of arms to revolutionaries. In 1929 the embargo was applied against Mexican rebels; the rebellion failed, and the embargo was generally applauded. In 1930, acting on exactly the same principles, the administration imposed a similar embargo against revolutionaries in Brazil, but this time the rebellion was almost immediately successful, and Stimson was widely criticized, first, for backing the wrong horse, and second, for "taking sides in civil strife." Both criticisms he considered wide of the mark. It was not the object of the United States to pick the winner in Latin American civil conflict, nor was it "taking sides" to withhold munitions from rebels. The American policy, formally embodied in joint resolutions of the Congress in 1912[5] and 1922 and in an inter-American treaty of 1928, was to give its recognition and support to the existing government and to embargo shipments to any rebel group whose formal belligerence had not been recognized.[6] This was a position which Stimson accepted and sustained with great vigor; he had an abiding dislike for the few Americans who chose to make money out of the dirty business of providing weapons for revolutionaries. Both as United States Attorney in New York and as Secretary of War he had "personally witnessed the activities by which some of our munitions manufacturers for sordid gain became a veritable curse to the stability of our neighboring republics"; as United States Attorney, indeed, he had received the formal approval and thanks of Secretary of State Root for his action against the Americans engaged in that sordid traffic.

"With these activities in mind," he continued, "I had little difficulty in reaching the conclusion that those who argued for the liberty of our munitions manufacturers to continue for profit a traffic which was staining with blood the soil of the Central American republics were not the progressives in international law and practice." He preferred the policy of prompt embargo against rebels. "Until belligerency is recognized and until the duty of neutrality arises, all the humane predispositions towards stability of government, the preservation of international amity, and the protection of established intercourse are in favor of the existing government."[7] This policy was one which Stimson had cause to advocate again a few years later on behalf of the mother country of Hispanic America.

[5] In the framing of the resolution of 1912 Stimson shared as Secretary of War.

[6] Unfortunately for Stimson, when he imposed the embargo against the Brazilian rebels, he was not informed of the treaty of 1928. This oversight naturally produced "some rather nasty remarks" when he announced it in Cabinet, though he could properly say in reply that "even without the treaty I had acted rightly, which was a good deal better than if I had acted wrongly in the face of the treaty." (Diary, November 7, 1930)

[7] Council Speech.

A third general Latin American policy of the State Department in the Hoover administration was its refusal to use the authority and weight of the American Government on behalf of the financial interests of private citizens in Latin America. Stimson took his cue here from Elihu Root, whose words he quoted in a speech to the Army War College on January 5, 1931. "He said, 'It has long been the established policy of the United States not to use its Army and Navy for the collection of such debts.' By that he meant the debts owed by a foreign government to American citizens. He went on: 'We have not considered the use of force for such a purpose consistent with that honorable respect for the independent sovereignty of other members of the family of nations which is a most important principle of international law and the chief protection of weak nations against oppression.' That has been, I think, a fair statement of the honorable position of this country in that particular matter." The same point was made with emphasis by Mr. Hoover in his inaugural address. When flagrant injustice was done to American investors, the State Department, under Stimson as under those before and after him, was quite prepared to make diplomatic representations, but the "big stick" was not at the disposal of every citizen who had a claim in Latin America.

This policy had already been followed by the State Department and by Ambassador Morrow in arranging a settlement of long-standing controversies with Mexico in 1928. It was followed by Stimson in 1929 in Cuba, when he refused to support the claim of one Barlow against the Cuban Government. Barlow had friends in the Senate, and the Secretary of State was forced to defend his stand before the Senate Foreign Affairs Committee, but most of the Senators were friendly.

Stimson received a less friendly response in the spring of 1931 when he categorically refused to permit American forces to proceed into the interior of Nicaragua to protect American life and property endangered by raids of the outlaw followers of Sandino. "This Government," he announced, "cannot undertake the general protection of Americans throughout the country with American forces. To do so would lead to difficulties and commitments which this Government does not propose to undertake. . . . Those who remain do so at their own risk. . . ." This blunt announcement was widely criticized as a sudden reversal of the American position in Nicaragua, but Stimson stuck to his guns. And some bluntness was necessary, for "the American interests on the east coast have got to be so that they feel that they have a right to call for troops whenever any danger apprehends. In that way they are a pampered lot of people. . . ." (Diary, April 15, 1931) This was the sort of attitude which could not be permitted to grow unchecked; it flew directly in the face of Stimson's announced intention to withdraw the marines from Nicaragua after the next election in 1932. Each intervention by American troops undermined the slowly growing capacity of the Nicaraguan Government to maintain order with its marine-trained forces. Fortunately, Stimson found that his refusal to protect American business interests in the Nicaraguan interior was well received in Congress.

The Nicaraguan policy announced in April, 1931, was generally maintained both in that country and elsewhere through the next two years. Stimson reluctantly permitted naval vessels to proceed to ports where there was unrest, but he firmly opposed any extended police operations beyond those to which the Government was already committed in Haiti and Nicaragua. Particularly after the beginning of the Far Eastern crisis in 1931 he was opposed to such action. It would be contrary to his whole policy in Latin America, and it would also be used against him in the Far East. When he was asked by a visitor in March, 1932, whether he would land forces if they were needed to protect American interests in Chile and Colombia, "I told him not on your life; that if we landed a single soldier among those South Americans now, it would undo all the labor of three years, and it would put me in absolutely wrong in China, where Japan has done all of this monstrous work under the guise of protecting her nationals with a landing force." (Diary, March 7, 1932)

Perhaps the most striking Latin American policy of the Hoover administration was its deliberate pursuit of nonintervention in the sensitive Central American and Caribbean area. It was here that American policy in the past had given rise to especial fear and suspicion in Latin America. In a radio address on May 5, 1931, on "The Work of the State Department," Stimson pointed out that the development of sound inter-American relations had been retarded "by several historic sore spots which have been obstinately interfering with the growth of good will and friendly relations between us and our neighbors to the south. Bitter memories arising out of former differences with Mexico; the occupation by our forces of Haiti under a treaty with that nation made in 1916; the presence of our marines in Nicaragua, though there at the request of her government and for the purpose of assisting her in the training of her constabulary, have all suffered distortion in South America unwarranted by these events as we understand them. Each has been used by the enemies and critics of the United States as proof positive that we are an imperialistic people prone to use our power in subverting the independence of our neighbors. And these accusations, however unjustifiable, have damaged our good name, our credit, and our trade far beyond the apprehension of our own people."

The Mexican boil had been lanced by Dwight Morrow. It was further salved by prompt American support of the Mexican Government against armed rebellion in 1929. In Cuba Stimson repeatedly refused to intervene under the Platt Amendment; whatever the need for such intervention in the past, he believed that "the situation in Cuba ought to so develop that less and less pressure would be necessary on the part of the United States to keep matters straight." (Diary, September 18, 1930) Stimson believed with Elihu Root that the Platt Amendment was "not intended to produce meddling in the internal affairs of Cuba," and he neither opposed nor gave special support to the government of President Machado.

In Nicaragua the general peace established by Stimson's mission of 1929 continued throughout his term as Secretary of State, punctuated only by sporadic outbreaks from the bandit Sandino; these outbreaks served to prove Sandino a skillful guerrilla, but in their violence and irresponsibility they also helped to destroy his reputation as a great patriot. They did not divert Stimson from a firm determination to get American marines out of Nicaragua, and after the United States had kept its pledge to hold a second fair and free election in 1932, the marines were duly withdrawn.

In Haiti, following the recommendation of a commission led by Cameron Forbes and including as a very active member William Allen White, the State Department undertook the liquidation of the work begun by President Wilson and his Assistant Secretary of the Navy, Franklin Roosevelt.[8] Stimson was more pessimistic about the future of Haiti than about that of his own experiment in Nicaragua, but he was bound to admit in 1932 and early 1933 that the Haitians were doing better than he had expected. The withdrawal planned by the Hoover administration was completed in 1934 by its successor; Mr. Roosevelt accomplished in an executive agreement what Mr. Hoover had tried to do in a treaty that went unratified.

All these actions were examples of a shift in policy which Stimson considered a natural development in maturing American history—the abandonment of the so-called Roosevelt corollary to the Monroe Doctrine. Theodore Roosevelt had believed it necessary, in both international politics and international law, that the American denial of any European right to intervene should imply the duty of the United States to intervene herself whenever a Latin American government was wholly unable to meet its foreign obligations. This was the policy which had brought American marines to Nicaragua, an American-written constitution to Haiti, and American customs collectors to the Dominican Republic. The marines, the constitution, and the collector of customs were all honestly intended to serve the best interests of the country to which they were sent, and they all did good service. But they were American, foreign, Yanqui, and as time passed they aroused more resentment than they did gratitude.· So at the end of the Coolidge administration, in a long memorandum by J. Reuben Clark, the State Department abandoned Theodore Roosevelt's corollary; the memorandum was duly published under Stimson in March, 1930, and Stimson himself asserted the Monroe Doctrine in terms which excluded intervention even

---

[8] In early 1933, when Stimson made his first visit to Franklin Roosevelt, he heard a high-spirited account of his new friend's early work in writing the Constitution of Haiti.

with the best intentions: "The Monroe Doctrine was a declaration of the United States versus Europe—not of the United States versus Latin America."[9] Stimson always believed that the American record in Cuba, Santo Domingo, and Nicaragua was on balance a credit to the United States, but he recognized that the rising nationalism of Latin America, aided and abetted by uninformed and captious criticism in the United States, had made it time to retire.

The American nations are strong on conferences and commissions, and the Hoover administration bore its share of this burden. Mr. Hoover's greatest personal triumph in this field was his settlement of the long-standing Tacna-Arica dispute in which Stimson had been counsel to the State Department three years before. The ugly issues between Colombia and Peru in Leticia, and between Bolivia and Paraguay in the Chaco, had the constant and devoted attention of Francis White, who sought with endless patience and good will to use American good offices to end these disputes, but without success. The Letician affair was finally settled by the League of Nations, but the Chaco became the scene of the first declared war in the Western Hemisphere in the twentieth century. In all these cases the United States was careful to avoid any heavy-handed action, and occasionally Stimson was annoyed by his own restraint. "I am getting quite blue over the bad way in which all Latin America is showing up. It seems as if there is nothing we could count on so far as their having any courage and independence is concerned, and yet if we try to take the lead for them, at once there is a cry against American domination and imperialism." (Diary, November 11, 1932) He had the satisfaction in August, 1932, of seeing the Latin American republics adopt his doctrine of nonrecognition of territorial conquest, but the doctrine did not in the end restrain the Bolivians and Paraguayans from a particularly senseless war.

The Latin American policy of the Hoover administration was overshadowed after the middle of 1931, first by the economic crisis in Europe, and then by the political crisis in Asia. But when Stimson came to the end of his term as Secre-

[9] Council Speech.

tary of State, and cast up his accounts in an article for *Foreign Affairs*,[10] he found that the Latin American policy he had pursued under Mr. Hoover was the best available example of "the fundamental purposes and philosophy of this administration" in foreign affairs. "It has not hesitated to impose upon itself, in the interest of the development of the peace of the world, the same standards which it has insisted upon in respect to the world at large. It has not allowed the preponderance of the material and military power of the United States in this hemisphere to prescribe a different rule of conduct here from that which it has believed to be necessary to the development of peaceful relations elsewhere throughout the world. This has been true in spite of the fact that one of the localities which has called for the exercise of these principles has been the one spot external to our shores which nature has decreed to be most vital to our national safety, not to mention our prosperity, namely, the narrow isthmus of Central America and the islands of the Caribbean Sea commanding the entrance to the Panama Canal, that vital link in our national defense.

"From the beginning, Mr. Hoover's administration has been determined to better the relationship of the Government with our Latin American neighbors. We have sought to make our policy towards them so clear in its implications of justice and good will, in its avoidance of anything which could be even misconstrued into a policy of forceful intervention or a desire for exploitation of those republics and their citizens, as to reassure the most timid or suspicious among them. We have been withdrawing our marines as rapidly as possible from Santo Domingo, Haiti, and Nicaragua, completing in the last-named country, amid the grateful recognition of all its parties, a successful educational experiment in the fundamentals of self-government in the shape of free elections. We have redeclared once again our national policy against the use of military pressure to collect business debts in foreign countries. We have promptly lent friendly assistance permitted by international law to the Mexican Government in

[10] "Bases of American Foreign Policy during the Past Four Years," *Foreign Affairs*, April, 1933.

quelling a military revolt against its authority. We have re-established the sensible practice of our forefathers as to the recognition of new governments in conformity with their rights to regulate their own internal affairs, and, in view of the economic depression and the consequent need for prompt measures of financial stabilization, have accorded to them recognition under this policy with as little delay as possible in order to give them the quickest possible opportunities for recovering their economic poise. We have co-operated with the Latin American states in their efforts to restore peace among their numbers in the Chaco and on the Amazon. We have completed the settlement of Tacna-Arica. And in social and intellectual ways we have endeavored to establish the nations of Latin America as our associates and our friends in intellectual and commercial intercourse. Mr. Hoover, as Presi-dent-elect, visited them in a journey through South America for the very purpose of dissipating the fears and antagonisms which had grown up amongst some of them as to the intentions and policies of this Government. Subsequently, we have enter-tained as national guests the Presidents-elect of Mexico, Brazil, and Colombia. We have enlisted our great institutions in the undertaking of systematic intellectual exchange with them; and together with them the United States has become officially represented in many world conferences upon scien-tific and welfare advancement. These acts have all been de-signed to impress them, as well as the other nations of the world, that the United States is aiming for progress by the creation of good will and human advancement, and not by exploitation."

The London Treaty and Latin American policy were typ-ical constructive undertakings of the sort that Stimson had anticipated when he left Manila in March, 1929. Taken to-gether, they represented a substantial achievement for his first two years. But these two years are separated by the two that followed as light is separated from darkness, and we shall do well to stop here for a last look at the situation of the world as it appeared from the State Department between 1929 and 1931.

These were the last two years of Stimson's life in which he was able to think of peace as reasonably well assured, and international good will as something more than a brave hope. In later years he remained a believer in the ideal of peace and the objective of good will, but after 1931 he faced, with all other men of good will, the lengthening shadow of rising lawlessness among the nations. Even in 1931 the great depression had begun to overturn governments and rekindle ancient grievances, but in the early months of that year it still seemed possible that the postwar settlement might not be seriously shaken.

These two years were years of peace and trust, and Stimson adopted as his guide in foreign policy a principle he always tried to follow in personal relations—the principle that the way to make men trustworthy is to trust them. In this spirit he made one decision for which he was later severely criticized: he closed down the so-called Black Chamber—the State Department's code-cracking office. This act he never regretted. In later years he was to permit and indeed encourage similar labors in another Department, but in later years the situation was different. In 1929 the world was striving with good will for lasting peace, and in this effort all the nations were parties. Stimson, as Secretary of State, was dealing as a gentleman with the gentlemen sent as ambassadors and ministers from friendly nations, and, as he later said, 'Gentlemen do not read each other's mail.'

In a similar spirit, the spirit of peacemaking and mutual good will, Stimson had made one other move which brought him some criticism. In the summer of 1929 a serious issue arose between China and Soviet Russia over their conflicting interests and rights in North Manchuria. In the course of this dispute the Russians sent troops into Chinese territory, and for a time there seemed to be danger of either war or annexation. Stimson, undismayed by the fact that the United States had no diplomatic relations with Soviet Russia, took the lead in organizing an international *démarche* invoking the Kellogg-Briand Pact and pleading with both nations to avoid a breach of the pact, and of the peace. This *démarche* greatly annoyed the Russians, whose self-righteousness in foreign affairs makes that of all other nations seem mild indeed, but it was notable that their troops were quickly withdrawn and a peaceful settlement was reached. The Kellogg-Briand Pact and Stimson's initiative may have had very little to do with this gratifying result, but the fact that the peace was kept seemed encouraging at the time. It was the first invocation of the pact, and from its apparent success believers in the new order of peace took courage.

It was only in 1931 that the weakness of the economic and political underpinnings of the postwar peace began to make itself apparent. Almost overnight, in May, 1931, the whole tenor of the State Department's work and of Stimson's own activities was radically changed.

CHAPTER VIII

The Beginnings of Disaster

I. BEFORE THE STORM

FIVE times in Stimson's life a turning point in the world's affairs coincided with a drastic change in his own personal activity. The first was in 1912, when Theodore Roosevelt with noble motives wrecked the Republican party as Stimson had known it. The second was in 1917, when war came to him as to millions of other Americans. The last two were 1940 and 1945; in the former year a desperate crisis gave him a new opportunity for activity; in the latter decisive victory released him to retirement. The third time was in 1931.

To Arnold Toynbee, writing a few months later of the shrunken hopes and bloated fears resulting from that year's events, 1931 was the *annus terribilis* of the postwar era.[1] In 1931 three terrible facts in deadly series made themselves apparent. First the rising storm of a world-wide depression knocked down the postwar financial system as a willful child knocks down a file of tin soldiers—by toppling the little fellow in the rear rank. Second, in an outburst stimulated by suffering, and deriving strength from the apparent failures of peaceful leadership, the military leaders of Japan undertook a major adventure in aggression. Third, and most terrible of all, it soon became clear that the climate of opinion in America was such that the American Government, in responding to this double challenge, could do no more than dull the

[1] Arnold J. Toynbee, *Survey of International Affairs, 1931*, Oxford University Press, 1932. This annual survey remains the best general work available for the period 1929-1933 and it has been heavily drawn upon in this and following chapters. Stimson himself used it often in later years when he had occasion to consider the events of his service as Secretary of State.

sharpest edges of economic disaster and military aggression. Though the roots of failure were deep in earlier years, and the hope of success not dead for years afterward, it was not hard for Stimson, in 1947, to endorse the view of 1931 that Toynbee had so early taken. It was the year in which the peace of 1919 was challenged and found wanting.

By the nature of his office, Stimson was of all Americans the man most closely and continuously affected by these events. Second only to the President, he was the responsible spokesman and leader of the United States in foreign affairs, and Mr. Hoover in 1931 and afterward was overwhelmingly occupied in his struggle against economic catastrophe at home.

Looking back at this period, Stimson reluctantly concluded that he had salvaged very little from the storm—except perhaps the honor of his country, so far as honor can be saved by words. But he was not disposed to accept the blame for this result; from 1931 to 1933 the American Secretary of State was the servant of events, and not their master. And both in minor victories and in major defeats Stimson, as he looked back in 1947, found the American record far from barren; he felt that at least the State Department had fought on the right side. And in those two crowded, bitter, almost disheartening years he saw many lessons that he was eager in 1947 to share with others.

In order to make clear the nature of his experience and the setting in which he worked, we must begin with a summary of his position in the early months of 1931, just before the storm broke.

The winter and spring of 1931 were months of change in the senior staff of the State Department. It was as if Stimson, knowing there was trouble ahead, had reorganized his Department in preparation. But one change was no part of any plan. On March 10, after a prolonged and gallant struggle, Under Secretary Cotton died. This was an irreparable loss. Joe Cotton had possessed exactly the kind of courage that Stimson needed in his first assistant—the courage to talk back, and the courage to support his chief even when it was politic to stand aloof. With Cotton in the State Department, Stimson had been able to stay three months in London at the Naval Conference with complete certainty that a first-rate man was boldly and responsibly doing what he believed Stimson would want done. After Cotton's death, when he was again abroad on major missions, Stimson was never able to feel this sort of confidence in the Acting Secretary. William R. Castle, the man who replaced Cotton, was not Stimson's choice; though he had ability and wide experience, he did not share Stimson's basic attitudes as Cotton had. The selection of Castle was a mistake which Stimson often regretted. The two men were not fitted to make a team. And although the choice was one strongly urged by the President, Stimson could not on that account acquit himself of an administrative blunder. All he could claim was that he learned from his mistake, and twelve years later a relatively innocuous—and probably inadvertent—piece of interference in departmental assignments from a different President produced an instant offer of resignation. From his experience in the State Department Stimson developed a rule which he later applied with complete fidelity. He would freely recognize the right of the President to veto any proposed appointments to major positions, but he would vigorously oppose any attempt to select his subordinates for him.

Fortunately, during this same period in the State Department Stimson was acquiring a group of other assistants who served him with distinction in the following years. The first step had been taken the previous November, with the appointment of Allen T. Klots as special assistant to the Secretary. Klots was the son of a Yale classmate, and for nearly thirty years he and Stimson had been extremely close to each other. Klots had made a distinguished record in college, in war, and in Winthrop & Stimson. He served Stimson in Washington as the young lawyer serves a senior counsel—his assignments were as varied as Stimson's own.

A second major new assistant was James Grafton Rogers, appointed in February to fill a position long vacant as Assistant Secretary of State. Rogers was a Westerner, the only one who ever served on any of Stimson's administrative staffs. His origin was a political advantage, but it was for himself that

Stimson valued him. He had great energy and ability, and his gusty wit was a major source of relief from the dismal burden of State Department duties. Rogers became Stimson's constant adviser, at first largely on legal questions and later on matters of major policy. More than any other individual, he took the place of Cotton.

Two more important additions were made in April and May. Cotton's death had left the Department without a senior officer experienced in economic matters. To remedy this weakness Stimson appointed Harvey H. Bundy, a Boston lawyer with experience in finance, as Assistant Secretary, and Herbert Feis, a distinguished New York economist, as Economic Adviser to the Secretary. He never regretted either appointment. Bundy was assigned at first to the complicated questions of policy involved in defaulted foreign loans of American private investors and later to the broader problems of war debts. Feis became Stimson's primary source of economic counsel in all phases of foreign affairs—he was the only man appointed by Stimson who was retained in office by the next administration.

With these four appointments Stimson rounded out the team with which he served through his last two testing years as Secretary of State. The new men ably supplemented those whom he had with him already. Captain Eugene Regnier, who had been with him in the Philippines, remained at his side as the perfect aide, and something more. In the complex problems of entertainment and protocol which are inevitable in the State Department he was invaluable, and his intimate counsel was important in wider fields. Assistant Secretary White remained in charge of Latin America, and the administrative direction of the Department and the foreign service continued to rest in the experienced and skillful hands of Assistant Secretary Wilbur J. Carr.

Under Castle in policy and Carr in administration, the State Department's career officers at home and abroad executed their regular assignments with their accustomed skill and devotion. It is the habit of many Americans to assume that their foreign service does not match that of other nations. Stimson by 1931 was persuaded that this view was wholly wrong, and the events of the next two years reinforced him in the conviction that American professional diplomats were at least as good as any in the world—their difficulty was that their country seldom supported them with effective policies.

In his last two years Stimson relied heavily on this powerful and well-balanced team, and it was not the fault of his associates that he never was able to look back at the State Department with the same sense of reminiscent satisfaction that he felt when he recalled the Federal Building in New York, or Malacañan Palace, or, later, the Pentagon Building. The team was a good one, but it was forced to fight a losing battle.

It was characteristic of the period that Stimson's State Department assistants were assembled with far greater difficulty than any of his other staffs, with the possible exception of his small group of American advisers in the Philippines. The difficulty in the Philippines was natural and understandable; the tradition of colonial service was never very strong in the United States, and 1928 was not a year in which many Americans were eager to travel 8,000 miles to participate in an uncertain experiment. But Stimson was surprised and a little disappointed to find that many first-rate men would not come even as far as Washington to serve as his major assistants. There was no dearth of men who wanted to be Assistant Secretary of State; but, in one of Stimson's favorite phrases, the men who made themselves applicants were usually men who were thinking 'what the job would do for them,' and he was hunting for men whose first interest was 'what they could do for the job.' Bundy and Feis were appointed only after other men more familiar to Stimson had regretfully refused to serve. It was true that 1931 was a year in which many an outstanding younger man in the business or professional world of New York was hard pressed to protect his family and his career, and Stimson never presumed to judge any individual's decision. But taken together, the series of refusals he received was indicative of the preoccupation of able men in 1931 with their own affairs; the needs of the nation, and the world, were given second rank. The usual reluctance of private citizens of standing and ability to become entangled with government was intensified in 1931 by the economic depression and the evident difficulties faced by an administration which lacked congressional support. And as he pleaded with the men he wanted, Stimson had neither the crusading spirit of Theodore Roosevelt's day nor the overriding appeal of national defense to assist him. Yet events were to demonstrate that there were few periods in which the American State Department had greater need for talented officers than 1931 and 1932, and although Stimson in the end obtained men whom he would not for a moment have traded off for others, it was only after prolonged labor and much lost time that he got them. If it had not been for the devoted and constant searches of Frankfurter, Roberts, and Klots, he might have had to wait indefinitely.

And he was saddened to observe in 1947, as the war atmosphere died away, that his successors in Cabinet office were having similar trouble. The labor of disinterested Government service, and the financial sacrifice which it involved, seemed to fall upon a relatively small group of men. To Stimson this was doubly unfortunate—it meant that many able men never gave any return of public service to their country; it also meant that men who ought to be permitted respite in private life, for the pursuit of their chosen profession and the repair of finances damaged by Government salaries, were overworked and penalized by their own conscientious response to calls for help.

If the depression was a contributing difficulty in Stimson's search for able subordinates, it was an even greater element in his relationship with Mr. Hoover. To Stimson it always seemed that there were few loyalties more binding than that of a Cabinet officer to his chief, and that no obligation was more compelling than that of respect for the President of the United States. It is therefore somewhat difficult to report clearly and properly the deep divisions of both principle and attitude which developed in the last two years of the Hoover administration between the President and his Secretary of State. The matter is not made easier by the fact that Stimson's personal admiration and affection for Herbert Hoover were never greater than in 1947. Mr. Hoover was to him one of the great Americans of his time, and one of the most unjustly maligned. It was of the greatest importance to him, therefore, that no words of his should be taken as a new source for unfair criticism.

At the same time Mr. Hoover and Stimson always did each

other the honor of frankness, and their differences were candidly recognized by both men. Both understood that Mr. Hoover's views would always be controlling, and neither allowed differences of opinion to do more than cause occasional very short-lived outbursts of temper. No record of Stimson's service as Secretary of State would be remotely accurate without a frank recognition of their differences, and no statement of Stimson's opinions would be fair to Mr. Hoover if it were to give the impression that he shared them all.

Temperamentally Stimson and Mr. Hoover were wholly different. One was by nature and training an advocate and a fighter; the other was an organizer and planner. Mr. Hoover liked to calculate his moves as he would the building of a bridge, while Stimson preferred to choose his main objective and then charge ahead without worrying, confident that aggressive executive leadership would win followers. Neither method was entitled to any special credit over the other, and successful presidents have used both. But Mr. Hoover and Stimson were unusually one-sided in their respective preferences. To Stimson Mr. Hoover's habit of considering his problem from all angles often seemed to be nothing but a preference for "seeing the dark side first"; he constantly felt that Mr. Hoover gave himself unnecessary trouble by his willingness to fret over hostile criticism. "I do wish he could shield himself against listening to so much rumor and criticism. If he would only walk out his own way and not worry over what his enemies say, it would make matters so much easier. . . . He generally comes out right, but he wastes an enormous amount of nerve tissue and anxiety on these interruptions." (Diary, December 4, 1930) In Stimson's view, this concern over what others thought tended to deprive Mr. Hoover of the greatest asset of an American President—the right of leadership.

And there was a further difference in temperament, important beyond its appearance. Mr. Hoover was a worker, capable of more intense and prolonged intellectual effort than any other man Stimson ever met; his cure for all his troubles as President was more and harder work. Stimson was not made that way; his strength depended on regular rest, substantial vacations, and constant physical exercise, nor did he accept as suitable exercise Mr. Hoover's game of medicine ball—it seemed to him as dull as weight lifting, and about as refreshing. More and more after the middle of 1930 Stimson found himself oppressed by the official atmosphere of Washington. It was not just the depression—it was the way the administration allowed itself to become absorbed in a fog of gloom. Mr. Hoover was fighting hard in a great battle, but there was no zest anywhere.

Stimson found ways to escape from this atmosphere. Without escape he could not have lasted out his term. After 1929 he had some weeks of real vacation each summer, and in Washington he was able to get much refreshment from horseback riding and deck tennis. And he found encouragement and lightness of spirit in one further quarter—occasional visits to Mr. Justice Oliver Wendell Holmes. Justice Holmes had precisely the spirit which Stimson missed in his official work. The diary entry of November 1, 1930, contains a delighted four-page entry on a visit to Holmes, of which the following are extracts:

"Then after I had a ride on horseback, I dropped in to see Justice Holmes. I felt that I needed something to cure my staleness. It has been dreadfully dull and stale, nothing but work . . . and the ever present feeling of gloom that pervades everything connected with the administration. I really never knew such unenlivened occasions as our Cabinet meetings. When I sat down today and tried to think it over, I don't remember that there has ever been a joke cracked in a single meeting of the last year and a half, nothing but steady, serious grind. . . . I am afraid I am too much of a loafer and enjoy my recreation too much to be able to stand this thing perpetually.

"With the staleness arising from the situation, I went to Justice Holmes to liven me up, and I had the most delightful talk that I have enjoyed for a month of Sundays. Holmes is the last of the old Roosevelt familiars, who is alive and in this town, and it was a joy to talk with him. He is ninety years old and gives no sign of it in his liveliness and vigor. He still swears like a trooper, enjoys a joke and makes plenty of them, full of the life and vigor that he used to have. . . . He told me that he had been having a rather unsuccessful summer so far as self-improvement was concerned. . . . He said 'the fact of the matter is that I am at last getting a little old.' I told him that was nonsense while he was thinking of self-improvement.

"I told him about Mr. Root's experience at his reunion, when he told me that if he found anybody who looked decrepit, with a long white beard and white hair, going around bent over a stick, you may be sure that that man had lived in the country all his life without any strain; that he was probably a college professor, and that he had led a perfectly blameless life, following every hygienic rule. While on the other hand, when he found one of his classmates who was vigorous, keen, and interested in everything going around, you can bet that he had lived in the city and had violated every rule of health all his life. Justice Holmes laughed and said, 'Good Lord, that's just it. I remember now a time many years ago, the last time I went to the reunion of the Class of '61, and I went into the room and looked around and said, "Good Lord, are these my contemporaries?"' and he said, 'I fled and took refuge in the Porcellian Club.'

"He told me that he had been trying to keep up his reading of philosophy. . . . He said, 'You know I can't take man quite so seriously as these other fellows do. It seems to me that he can't quite occupy the attention of God that they all think he does. I can't believe that if a comet, for instance, should hit the earth and knock it to smithereens that it would make such a very great difference to the universe.' And then he talked of his old arguments with Josiah Royce. He laughed and laughed over them. He said that the trouble with Royce was that whenever he, Holmes, got him cornered, he would take refuge in saying, 'Well, I am in the bosom of God'; while Holmes would reply, 'Nonsense, you are just in a rathole that I have cornered you in.' I told him that I remembered Royce as having written a book entitled, *The Religious Aspect of Philosophy*, and I heard the story that when old Professor Shaler met Royce the first time after he had read it and Royce asked him how he had liked the book, Shaler said that it had the wrong title, it ought to be called, *The Irreligious Aspect of Philosophy.* . . . Altogether we had a wonderful half-hour's talk. When I went away, he looked at my riding clothes and said, 'Good Lord, how I envy you. You know I never rode a horse except during the Civil War while I was on the Staff, and I had to ride then for the sake of my position.'

"I came away completely cheered up with my horizon all changed, and it has given me a pretty clear idea of what I needed, which is a little more recreation and change from the unvarying attitude of grind and business that I get in the administration. How I wish that I could cheer up the . . . President and make him feel the importance of a little brightness and recreation in his own work. But after all I suppose he would reply and say that he gets his recreation in his own way, and that my way would not suit him at all. I came home and had dinner with Mabel. . . . We spent the evening reading together, and then, for the first time in some days, I got a good long night's sleep."

In addition to differences of temperament, there were major latent differences of policy between Mr. Hoover and Stimson. In 1929 and 1930 these were concealed; they did not affect the major problems of those years—in Latin American affairs and naval limitation the two men were almost always in cordial and complete agreement. But in the later years nearly every major issue produced an important cleavage. The basic difference was one between two men who were both deeply devoted to peace, but in such opposite ways that in the end, when the troubles of their time in office ripened into World War II, Stimson was one of the earliest and most ardent advocates of the necessity of American action to prevent victory by the aggressor, while Mr. Hoover, until Pearl Harbor, was convinced that the United States could and should remain aloof. This basic difference expressed itself in many forms; it was at the root of disagreements over war debts, the Far East, disarmament, and "foreign entanglements."

The story of Stimson's last two years in office is in very large degree the story of his efforts to combine loyalty to Mr. Hoover with the advancement of policies which only too often went against the grain of the President's deepest convictions.

In every case of direct conflict, Stimson followed Mr. Hoover's wishes, and time and again he acted as public advocate for courses which his own fundamental principles could hardly have justified. Occasionally he was even persuaded, by forces which every lawyer loyal to his clients will understand, into a genuine belief in policies that later seemed to him insufficient and even wrong. It is not surprising that under such conflicting pressures he should have found these years the least happy of his public career.

But in some degree these differences with Mr. Hoover were merely the reflection of a still greater difficulty—the attitude of the people of the United States. Often the President's restraining hand was the result less of his personal convictions than of his necessary awareness of the state of public opinion, to which as an elected official seeking re-election he was necessarily more sensitive than Stimson, just as in his preoccupation with domestic troubles he was perhaps less struck than Stimson by the magnitude of the world's crisis. Mr. Hoover was a non-interventionist always, but he was never a full-blown isolationist; this could not be said of public opinion in America in the early 1930's. Stimson often repeated in later years a remark made to him by Ogden Mills in 1932—that never in history had the American people been so profoundly isolationist. Not merely were they thoroughly disillusioned about Europe and the Europeans, but they were completely occupied by pressing domestic troubles in which no foreign policy seemed to be important or even relevant. To a greater degree even than in 1923, when George Harvey coined the phrase, the policy of the ordinary American, as distinct from that of his State Department, was "to have no foreign policy."

It was on such a people, with such leaders, that the storm of world catastrophe broke in May, 1931, when a bank in Austria failed.

2. ECONOMIC CRISIS IN EUROPE

This book is clearly not the place for a detailed analysis of the causes of the world-wide economic depression which began in 1929 and dominated world affairs in 1931 and 1932. A catastrophe compounded of so many elements, and subject to so many partisan explanations, cannot be analyzed in a few pages—and certainly not here. Stimson was never an expert in economics; he took his advice in this field from men whose judgment he had learned to trust, and he almost always avoided categorical conclusions about the course of economic affairs. His diary in the State Department years is crowded with reports of what other men thought about the depression—what caused it and how long it would last—but it contains almost no expression of definite opinions of his own.

But as it presented itself in the late spring and summer of 1931, the international depression was no longer merely economic; it had begun to produce results which were of major importance politically. It is usual to date this *political* crisis from the collapse of the Credit-Anstalt, the largest bank in Austria, in May, 1931. In the European financial system of the time, weakened by the declining capital values and the increasingly immobile assets characteristic of depressions, the failure of the Credit-Anstalt was the blow which precipitated a general financial panic. Throughout Central Europe, and particularly in Austria and Germany, there began a vast international run on the banks. Creditors outside these countries, fearful of a total loss of their assets, were wholly undeterred by the ordinary measures designed to restrict such credit transactions. A discount rate of 6 or 7 per cent was negligible when measured against the threat of total loss.

Withdrawals of credit from Germany began in May and became torrential in the early weeks of June. It was apparent that unless something was done quickly, Germany would once more slide down the inclined plane of inflation to financial ruin. Such an event, at such a time, would have had the most serious effects on the political stability of Europe, almost certainly producing an upheaval within Germany and a repudiation or indefinite postponement of all foreign payments. Even the most isolationist of Americans could not view such a prospect with equanimity, for American banks and financial interests throughout the country were heavily involved in large credits to Germany which had been advanced during the boom years; any general German collapse would have violent economic repercussions at home, and not on banks alone.

It was in these circumstances that Mr. Hoover, on June 20, announced his famous plan for a one-year moratorium on all intergovernmental debts. The immediate purpose of this proposal was to strengthen Germany's credit position by relieving her of reparation payments; its broader purpose was to give the whole Western world a "shot in the arm." It was the boldest and most constructive step taken by the United States in its dealings with Europe since 1918. Tragically, it was not nearly enough.

Debts between governments in 1931 were of two major kinds —both resulting from the First World War. On the one hand there were the reparations owed by Germany to the victorious Allied and Associated Powers; in those reparations the United States had refused to share. The amount of the reparations and the time schedule of their payment had been the subject of repeated international discussions in the 1920's; in these discussions a notable part had been played by Americans like Charles G. Dawes and Owen D. Young, whose names had been given to successive plans for payment. But these Americans had participated solely as private citizens; the American Government had from the beginning refused to take any official part in the discussions of reparations. So strong was this feeling that one of Stimson's first official actions as Secretary of State had been to sign and send off a message written by others which he later recognized to be quite ungracious in its expressions of the danger of official entanglement in Young's work. It was American policy to regard reparations almost as "tainted gold."

The other half of the burden of intergovernmental debts was regarded by the United States in a wholly different light. The "war debts" were owed mainly by Allied nations and mainly to the United States. They had arisen from loans made by the American Government after its entry into the war, and from further loans made for reconstruction in the immediate postwar years. The total amount loaned was about ten billion dollars. The amount of these debts had been considerably reduced by negotiations between 1923 and 1926; the American

Government, adhering to its view that all war debts were normal obligations of a debtor to a creditor, had negotiated settlements based on the "capacity to pay" of each debtor government.

In addition to these two major elements in the structure of intergovernmental debts, there were very considerable payments due to Great Britain and France, who had been bankers for the Allied nations before the American entry into the war and middlemen in the flow of credits even after 1917. There were other smaller debts between other nations. But the main current of international payments under the agreements effective in 1931 was from Germany in reparations to the European Allies, and from these nations in debt payments to the United States. In June, 1931, the schedule for the following year involved net payments by Germany of something under four hundred million dollars. Nearly two-thirds of this flow of payments would go through to the United States in payments of interest and principal on the war debts. Two-thirds of the remainder would wind up in France, which was the only other substantial net creditor. Economically, the significant course of intergovernmental debt payments was from Germany to the United States and France. Other nations were either insignificant or, as in the case of Great Britain, merely way-stations on the road—the British would receive from France and Germany almost exactly what they would pay to the United States.

It was generally agreed in international financial circles, in the spring of 1931, that the continuance unaltered of reparation and debt payments on the scheduled scale would be impossible. The nations were thus confronted with the possibility of a repetition of the political crisis of 1923, when German failure to make reparation payments had resulted in French occupation of the Ruhr. Or alternatively, if the Germans did continue to make such payments as were unconditionally required, it was quite likely that they would be bankrupted. Nor was Germany the only country in financial difficulty. However much the American Government might insist that reparations and war debts had no connection with each other, no nation in debt to the United States was likely to keep up its payments if the compensating flow of reparations from Germany should cease. A general default of intergovernmental debts seriously threatened. Such a default would undermine every tendency toward recovery and accentuate every force making for deeper depression.

The plan unfolded by President Hoover to Stimson and to Mellon and Mills of the Treasury in early June had the directness and simplicity of high politics. The United States, as the largest creditor, would propose a holiday on all payments of intergovernmental debts. The debts would simply be forgotten for a year, perhaps two. Stimson listened with delight while Mr. Hoover propounded a doctrine which he had always liked: "It involved a bold emphatic proposition to assume leadership himself, and I, myself, felt more glad than I could say that he was at last turning that way. . . . He told me that he always believed in going out to meet a situation rather than to let it come. . . . Altogether it was one of the most satisfactory talks I have had with him in a long time." (Diary, June 5, 1931)

The two weeks that followed were among the most crowded and exciting of any in Stimson's life. "We have all been saying to each other that the situation is quite like war." (Diary, June 15, 1931) The front was in Central Europe, and with each day that passed the news was worse and the need for action more apparent. This was fortunate, for during the days between June 5 and June 18 Mr. Hoover exhibited every day his capacity for "seeing the dark side." Though the proposal for a moratorium was his own, and its eventual execution was to be his personal triumph, he daily found more reasons for expecting failure in his plan. On June 8 he was worried because a moratorium might appear to connect war debts with reparations, and he and Stimson had an argument about it, the latter urging that "even legally, in domestic law, as soon as a man became insolvent he and his creditors could not make independent arrangements about their debts." Mr. Hoover believed that "we could never explain the matter to our own people if we allowed the two things to get connected; that it would drag us into the European mess and he would never consent to it. . . . At times our argument got quite tense, but finally we came down to our usual terms . . . and we both agreed to think further over it."

In the following days other fears beset the President. He seemed receptive to pessimistic estimates, and Stimson was able to endure the gloomy atmosphere only because he knew that "the responsibility which lay on the President was terrible," that he "was following his usual psychological reaction to a proposition like this," and that "when he finally does make up his mind and does act, he turns to it with great courage."

This estimate, written on June 13, was borne out in what followed. The evening of June 18 was the gloomiest of all at the White House. Stimson and Mills went to the President to make a final presentation of the case for a moratorium. Mills did most of the talking. "The President was tired and . . . he went through all the blackest surmises. . . . It was like sitting in a bath of ink to sit in his room. . . . But I think he is moving at last."

And he was. That same evening Mr. Hoover made his final decision, secured by telephone the support of thirty leading members of the House and Senate, and on the following morning at Cabinet meeting he was at his best, active, clear-sighted, and full of new strength.

Now it was time for Stimson to begin his major diplomatic duty in connection with the moratorium. The key to the success of the scheme was the attitude of the French. The American proposal would be acceptable in America only if it covered *all* intergovernmental loans; the American concession must therefore be matched on a smaller scale by the French. But Mr. Hoover's proposal could not be discussed with the French until he had reached his final decision. Stimson had worried Mr. Hoover by discussing the possibility of an American move even with Ramsay MacDonald in a personal telephone conversation. Nor was joint action with France any part of the American plan, for reparations were a touchy subject among the politicians of Paris; they might not readily consent to a plan which departed somewhat from the Young Plan, and both Mr. Hoover and Stimson were certain that any moratorium would lose its strength and psychological value if subjected to diplomatic bargaining and public speculation before it was announced as a complete and definite proposal.

But the two men nevertheless had no intention of taking the French by surprise. On the afternoon of June 19 Stimson explained Mr. Hoover's plan in detail to the French Ambassador. The American decision was less than twenty-four hours old. In view of the later French attitude, Ambassador Claudel's reaction is interesting. "He said that it was wonderful, that he had no idea the President could go so far." (Diary, June 19, 1931) He further promised to urge his Government to support the plan.

Unfortunately the timing of this interview, though quick, was not quick enough. Mr. Hoover's hand was forced by rumors leaking from Congressmen, and he had to make a public announcement of his plan before the French had had a chance to digest it. On June 20 the proposal was announced from the White House; there followed a rather cautious French response, and two weeks of chilly negotiations were necessary before the French would consent to give up the "unconditional" reparation payments of the Young Plan.

Stimson and Mr. Hoover were criticized in some circles for this untidy aspect of a proposal which in every other respect was a remarkable success. Looking back at it, Stimson could not agree that the fault was his or the President's. Even if the French had had a few more days' notice, he did not believe that they would have been more cordial. Only prior negotiation could have produced that result, and prior negotiation was impossible; it would have caused still more financial unrest in Europe. As Ramsay MacDonald put it to the German Chancellor in early June and to Stimson later that summer, consultation about the moratorium would have been "fatal" to the financial situation. More serious still—and this was the point which Mr. Hoover was forced to bear in mind as he dealt with a politically hostile Congress—negotiations with France would have given free rein to assertions at home that Uncle Sam was being played for a sucker, and the general public support that the President obtained in the United States by making his proposal unilaterally American would have evaporated in a heated atmosphere of charge and counter-charge.

This was a clear instance of the sort of international problem which Stimson had already faced in his work for naval limitation and was to meet again repeatedly in the following months. Time after time the issues which divided the statesmen of the great powers were those on which they themselves would have been happy to reach agreement—and would have found agreement easy—if they had not feared a hostile verdict from public opinion at home. The leaders of France were fully aware of the need for a moratorium; they also understood the importance of quick and unanimous agreement on a plan. But they could not meet Mr. Hoover openly and generously lest they appear to be neglecting issues for which the French Army had been mobilized only eight years before. That the French reaction was not even more bitter than it was Stimson attributed to the "skill and force" with which Premier Pierre Laval held out against extremists, but even Laval was not publicly enthusiastic about the moratorium. What the French Government won for France in the two weeks of negotiation which followed was negligible in fact, but in emotion it was all-important; by their truculence the French leaders aligned themselves with the aggrieved nationalism of their people. The constant repetition of this tragic compulsion to follow the worse course while seeing and approving the better was to bring eventual downfall to all the efforts of the postwar statesmen.

Stimson felt that this French delay in accepting Mr. Hoover's proposal was a matter of major importance. He had pointed out to Claudel in their first interview that everything depended on the psychological effect of the plan; this in turn depended on prompt and generous-spirited approval from France, as the second of creditor nations. The initial effect of Mr. Hoover's announcement was electric; in the United States, in Great Britain, in Germany, the people took hope from his boldness. Withdrawals of credit from Germany ceased; men wrote of the "turning of the tide"; stock prices rose on the world's exchanges. But when no friendly voice was raised in France, spirits sagged, and by the time an agreement had been haggled out, on July 6, the first flush of hope had begun to pale. Of course Stimson could not make the French solely responsible for this unhappy result; there were financial weaknesses in Germany that even a suspension of reparations could not wholly eliminate. But to say that the French attitude was hardly helpful seemed to him to be putting it mildly.

The moratorium remained in Stimson's view one of the best things Mr. Hoover ever did. It definitely shut off the possibility of an immediate major political crisis in Germany. Time was provided for a new study of reparations, and it became possible to apply more orthodox financial remedies to the crisis in Central Europe. If the moratorium did not stimulate the recovery for which Stimson had hoped, it most certainly prevented an immediate and desperate breakdown. And Stimson particularly liked it because it was an example of the bold executive leadership which he considered the central requirement of effective democratic government. Mr. Hoover did what cautious counsels of political prudence forbade, and by so doing he won a major political victory at home and abroad.

Yet the fact remained that the relief afforded by the moratorium was insufficient; within a month further emergency measures were necessary to save Germany. The causes of the world depression were deeper than anything governments were equipped to handle, and the pillars of orthodox international economics continued to collapse one by one. Perhaps the most shocking single event was the departure of Great Britain from the gold standard in September, but this was only one of a long series of happenings which showed clearly that the economic structure of postwar Europe and America was unsound. But these events cannot concern us here; we must return to the story of Stimson's own small part in the struggle.

Long before the crisis which led to the moratorium he had made plans for a summer expedition to Europe. His original purpose was to familiarize himself with the leading men and problems of the European scene. Before, during, and after his service as Secretary of State he remained a strong believer in the value of personal meetings among international leaders. His departure was briefly delayed by the hectic work surrounding the announcement of the Hoover moratorium, but even before the French were brought into line he was on his way, acting on the advice of Ramsay MacDonald and others that any prolonged delay in his departure would give cause for pessimism about the Franco-American negotiations—and in any event Mr. Hoover had taken personal charge of the dealings with the difficult French.

In Italy, his first stop, Stimson was able to pursue his purpose of discussing the general problems of Europe, but when he arrived in Paris the immediate financial crisis of Germany was once more in the front pages; the moratorium, weakened by French delay, had not succeeded for long in stopping private creditors from withdrawing their German assets. He was at once assigned to represent his country in a full-dress international meeting organized by Mr. Hoover. This meeting assembled first in Paris and then in London as the French displayed astonishing pettiness about the time and place at which they would agree to help Germany. Although the Hoover moratorium had so angered the French that Stimson was pointedly snubbed on his arrival, he found himself able to win both French and British support for a stand-still agreement, under which the governments and central banks of the three countries agreed to throw their weight against further liquidation of short-term credits to Germany. This negotiation, which Stimson always considered one of the neatest and most successful of his career, served to end the immediate crisis. The problem of long-range assistance to Germany was turned over to the bankers. It was a characteristic of this period that the fundamental powers of international trade and finance rested less with governments than with private interests or autonomous central banks. This was particularly true of the United States, and if it had not been for the constant and intelligent co-operation which he received from George L. Harrison of the New York Federal Reserve Bank, Stimson would have found it very difficult to play any useful role at all in financial matters.[2]

[2] Harrison became a good friend in this period, and during World War II he was one of Stimson's ablest associates, advising first on problems of wartime finance and later on the uniquely significant question posed by the successful development of the atom bomb.

His experiences in working out the stand-still agreement, and elsewhere in Europe in 1931, had one important incidental result for Stimson. They taught him how to deal with the press. From the very beginning of his term he had found press relations difficult. The ordinary State Department reporter of the time seemed to him irresponsible and often untrustworthy, and at the London Conference he had been greatly annoyed by the zeal with which reporters for newspapers hostile to naval limitation tried to embarrass the American delegation. The result of his annoyance had been a stiff attitude toward all newspapers, and the result of this in turn was that he received a very bad press. This bad press reached a climax in July, 1931, during the London meeting on debts, when Stimson and Castle misunderstood each other over the transatlantic telephone, with the result that the reporters in Washington and London received two different accounts of what was going on. In the face of an outburst of anger from the American reporters in London, Stimson made a clean breast of the story and learned at once, to his great satisfaction, that not all newspapermen are scoundrels. The top-notch correspondents to whom he thus explained the background of the unfortunate incident proved both friendly and forgiving. This experience led him, on his return to Washington, to institute a regular weekly press meeting at Woodley to which he invited, not the journeymen who covered his Department for routine news, but the senior Washington correspondents. These men, with very few exceptions, proved trustworthy and helpful in their attitudes; what was said off the record stayed off the record, and Stimson found himself able to talk freely on the basic policies and purposes which surrounded his day-to-day actions.

The State Department is never likely to have perfect press relations; it is in the difficult position of always having a world-wide audience of foreign diplomats who weigh its every word. Furthermore it must often frame its policy slowly and deliberately while pressing issues fill the headlines. Later, as Secretary of War, Stimson was always a step ahead of the press; he had the war news before they did. In the State Department this situation was often reversed; foreign correspondents could break their stories more quickly, if less accurately, than foreign service officers abroad. But the Woodley conferences proved a great help in 1931 and after; from their beginning Stimson dated the start of a marked improvement in his relation with the press, which can be a powerful assistant to policy, as well as a most annoying opponent.

3. MORE ABOUT "THESE DAMN DEBTS"

The original hope of Stimson and Mills had been that the Hoover moratorium might extend for two years, and if they had had time to look back during 1932 and 1933, they would often have regretted that political considerations forced the President to limit his proposal to one year. For during the last year of the Hoover administration, as men tried to frame a policy for the period after the Hoover year expired, the wretched war debts became an apple of discord in personal, national, and international affairs.

The beginnings were hopeful. In October, 1931, President Hoover and Premier Laval of France agreed that during the period of depression further adjustments of intergovernmental debts might be necessary. The announcement of this agreement was applauded in Europe as proof that the United States was prepared to recognize the connection between reparations and debts. The Europeans refused to be discouraged, either by official warning that the Hoover-Laval statement referred only to emergency depression measures, or by the truculent reluctance with which Congress in December approved the moratorium, adding to its approval a resolution opposing any reduction or cancellation of war debts.

In June, 1932, after a delay caused by elections in France and Germany (the French swung left and the Germans ominously right), the nations concerned with reparations met at Lausanne, Switzerland, to discuss the future of these payments. By this time it was generally agreed that Germany neither could nor would continue reparations payments on anything like the former scale, and after two weeks of negotiation ably led by Ramsay MacDonald (with the assistance of Edouard Herriot of France) an agreement was reached which reduced the obligations of Germany by 90 per cent and ended all strictly "reparations" payments entirely. It was a typical irony of postwar Europe that what had been refused to the German moderates Stresemann and Bruening should now be granted to the nationalist, Von Papen, but in this case the change of policy was an accident of timing, not a concession to truculence. In any event the settlement of Lausanne was generally regarded in Europe as a splendid step forward, for even in the Allied nations reparations had come to be regarded as nothing better than a source of trouble.

But the Lausanne agreement had a joker in it. To Europeans, overreading the Hoover-Laval agreement of the previous October, it seemed obvious that a reduction in reparations must be accompanied by a corresponding reduction in war debts. The economic arguments against reparations, as a permanent barrier to thriving trade, applied with equal force to war debts. And, of course, it would be quite impossible from the standpoint of internal politics to give up reparations without some compensation in debt reduction. For this reason the creditors on reparation accounts concluded at Lausanne a gentlemen's agreement under which they promised each other not to ratify the Lausanne reparation settlement until satisfactory arrangements had been made by all of them with their own creditors, meaning of course the United States.

The report of this gentlemen's agreement leaked out unofficially, in a manner very badly calculated from the point of view of its effect on American opinion. It looked to Americans like a conspiracy against the United States. News of the agreement touched off a discussion between Stimson and Mr. Hoover which showed clearly that the two men were in entire disagreement on the whole question of war debts. Stimson believed that the Lausanne settlement, with or without the gentlemen's agreement, "might really be the beginning of a recovery" and that it must be supported by the United States without fear or rancor. Mr. Hoover did not agree. He had proposed his moratorium purely as a depression measure and to him the gentlemen's agreement looked like the opening step in an attempt at permanent reduction of the war debts—

which indeed it was, as Stimson was quite willing to grant. "He told me that he entirely differed with me, in fundamentals, that we really had no common ground; that he thought that the debts to us could and should be paid; and that the European nations were all in an iniquitous combine against us. I replied that if he felt that way we were indeed on such different ground that I couldn't give him much good advice, and that I ought not to be his adviser." (Diary, July 11, 1932) When the steam had been blown off, both men recovered their good humor, but the difference was apparent. Mr. Hoover thought the war debts could be paid; Stimson did not. The particular issue at this meeting was whether Mr. Hoover should make a statement in effect denouncing the gentlemen's agreement. After three days of debate a compromise solution was reached. The President wrote an open letter to Senator Borah praising the reparation settlement but warning that the United States would not yield to any foreign combination in restraint of payments on the war debts. Then the question was dropped, by the consent of all concerned, at home and abroad, until after the American election in November, when it reappeared with a bang.

The Hoover moratorium had expired in June. In December the resumption of major debt payments was scheduled to begin. Through the summer the world waited, and while it waited, opinion hardened on both sides of the Atlantic. Stimson had noticed evidence during the Lausanne meeting of the degree to which British and French opinion misunderstood the American attitude toward war debts, and he had warned the British Ambassador against thinking that the American position could be stormed by a *fait accompli*. But he had not been able to prevent the gentlemen's agreement, which was wholly natural in its purpose and wholly inflammatory in its effect. In November he found that the situation had grown worse; the people of Great Britain and France had come to think of the war debts as a millstone hung around their necks by the shortsighted—and self-destructive—greed of Uncle Shylock. No statesman in either country could have any other public purpose than cancellation. Stimson did not object to this purpose—by this time he was himself basically a "cancellationist"—but the tone of European statements and opinion was not perfectly calculated to win support from the American people.

And if the atmosphere abroad was not perfect, the feeling at home was desperately bad. For a dozen years, in accordance with the assertions of Democrats and Republicans alike, the American people had been convinced that war debts were a moral and economic obligation as binding as any debt in personal affairs. This position had been reasserted by both candidates in the presidential campaign. The American people, and still more the American Congress, were wholly unprepared to face the economic facts of life; only among economists, bankers, and confirmed believers in international co-operation was there any important sentiment for cancellation. Yet this small group had been joined by the unpredictable individualist Borah, in midsummer, in a speech which seemed to Stimson "temperate, brave, and well-balanced." "Of course he is cautious about some things, but compared with anyone else at either end of Pennsylvania Avenue, it is magnificent." (Diary, July 24, 1932)

Mr. Hoover was no cancellationist, never had been, and never would be. More than that, attempts to connect debts with reparations except in time of economic emergency seemed to him wholly wrong, and it was manifest that the British and French intended to make such attempts. Mr. Hoover preferred to connect debts with disarmament, arguing that instead of welshing on their legal obligations the European debtors should make some effort to cut the burden of their armaments. This position, though eminently logical and morally right in the minds of many Americans, was perfectly designed to annoy the Europeans.

As Stimson saw it, Mr. Hoover might be on strong ground legally, but both economically and politically he was wrong. Economically, the payment of war debts had been a most doubtful blessing to the United States, serving merely to unbalance further an exchange system in which American exports were being strangled by American hostility to imports, and giving rise to a series of credit operations abroad which were of the most unfortunate character. Intergovernmental debts were all dominated by the problem of transfer of payments, a question almost always ignored by heated opponents of cancellation; no amount of disarmament, for example, seemed likely to make dollar payments very much easier. In Stimson's view, the economics of the situation were plainly in favor of cancellation. It would certainly have a considerable reviving effect on world trade, and even a very small gain of this sort would more than balance the payments lost by the United States.

Politically the advantage of cancellation was even greater— it would restore an atmosphere of good feeling and confidence between the United States and western Europe, and this at a time when such good feeling was desperately needed.

The student of Stimson's public activity as Secretary of State will find no statement of this position in the records, and many at least obliquely contradicting it, for he was only the agent of the President and during November and December he executed the policy laid down by Mr. Hoover. The difficulties of this position he described in a diary entry on November 23. "Of course, from the very beginning of this thing I have been fighting a minority battle. I can see all the benefits of the good will that we have been laboring so hard for the past three years to build up tumbling in fragments around us, and I have been trying to make it as easy as possible [for the European debtors]. But my zone of operations has been a very narrow one, for the President has been perfectly set in his policy, and all that I have been able to do is to try to smooth down affairs here and there and to guide the thing into as easy channels as possible. On that point Mills, too, has been against me. He sees only the clear mathematical and legal relations of the two nations, and he has been fighting, of course, for his Treasury. But with our discussions with Great Britain, we have to depart from the legal situation which surrounds a regular loan. The whole idea of taking a position which was taken at Lausanne in regard to reparations, a revision of debts which would bear in mind and help the economic situation, quite apart from the legal situation, has been excluded by the President's position. His position has been based upon the position of the country ever since 1922, and probably no other position was tenable in view of the attitude of Congress. But there is another side, and we all have to come to it sooner or later. The quicker we get these damn debts out of the way in some settlement, in which I hope we may be able to get some quid pro quo for our concessions, the better off we will be."

Compared to Congress, of course, Mr. Hoover was a model of restraint and broad-mindedness, and in dealing with Congressmen he regularly emphasized the genuine difficulties of foreign nations. Mr. Hoover was also quite prepared to discuss debt revision with the Europeans, but he was never able to put aside his desire to state and restate a position that left little room for negotiation—as long as the matter was considered in its purely legal aspect, there could be no "Lausanne settlement" of the war debts; the grounds for such a settlement were not in law, but in policy. What Stimson wanted, and what Mr. Hoover refused, was bold American leadership to get the "damn debts" out of the way. But Mr. Hoover refused, not because he feared to lead, but because he did not agree with Stimson, as the following diary entry makes clear. "I cautioned him that while I was trying to get all the quid pro quo for the debts that I could, I didn't expect that we were going to save much of the debt. Then he wanted to know if I knew that I was ten millions of miles away from his position. He believed that debts were merely a chip on the current of ordinary prosperity. This discouraged me a good deal. I am not an economist, but I know mighty well that if the nations that were receiving reparations could not hold them, we shall not be able to save much of our debts. . . . When I see France, who has a large stake in Europe and who is right next to Germany, give up her war reparations to an extent per capita nearly equivalent to our war debts . . . in spite of all the feeling in France arising out of the war on behalf of those reparations, and in spite of the fact that she has the right to invade Germany to save them, it seems preposterous to think that we should be able to keep our debts when we are three thousand miles away from them and without an army and have no intention or desire to have a war quarrel with either France or Britain." (Diary, December 4, 1932)

So Stimson continued in his small minority, with the friendly company of Borah and the bankers and economists. And he continued to play his role in the singularly complex negotiations which preceded the debt-payment deadline on December 15. It was a hectic period, and there were diplomatic errors on all sides—Stimson made one when he softened a note to Great Britain while leaving a similar note to France in its original stiff form. There were reasons for the mistake, and good ones, but it was nevertheless, as the diary remarked, "unworkmanlike." The debts were too touchy a subject for such errors to be cheap, and yet it was their very touchiness that made errors difficult to avoid. Matters were not simplified, of course, by the fact that Mr. Hoover was now a lameduck President, and President-elect Franklin Roosevelt seemed less co-operative to administration leaders than he seemed to himself. The President was powerless to suspend the payments, as requested by the debtor nations, and unwilling to recommend suspension to a hostile Congress; Mr. Roosevelt held aloof. Matters slid toward an impasse of default from Europe and public resentment at home. Then surprisingly, on December 15 the British courageously paid in full what they owed, and so did several other nations, following their lead. But the French defaulted, and they had company. To Stimson's deep regret, no voice had been raised by the administration to soften the official attitude of America or to battle the illogical sentiment of a nationalistic people. Looking across the Atlantic he found in Edouard Herriot the real hero of the episode. For Herriot, the French Premier, had dared to oppose his people in the interests of international understanding. "He insisted upon payment in the face of the most terribly opposed public opinion and a very adverse Parliament. They finally voted it down and him out of office. But he is much bigger today than anyone on our side of the Atlantic." (Diary, December 15, 1932)

The Hoover administration's direct activity on debts was wound up on December 19 by a final statement from the President. Stimson worked closely with Mr. Hoover on this message, and the pressure had sufficiently lightened so that the President could joke about his friend the Secretary of State as "our friend who was for protecting every country but his own." For his part Stimson was delighted to see Mr. Hoover in good cheer, and he felt that the message to Congress was a good one; although it repeated views Stimson did not share, it was frank and explicit in recommending early and fair-minded negotiation with the debtor nations. Here the matter ended, except for further efforts to help the President-elect which at last resulted in a joint communiqué on January 20, 1933, to the effect that Mr. Roosevelt would be glad to talk with a British representative as soon as he was President.

The later history of the war debts is briefly told. In June, 1933, no further agreement having been reached, the British and several other countries made a "token" payment which temporarily satisfied opinion in both countries; France and most of her friends continued to default. In December, 1933, the same process was repeated. Desultory discussions between the new administration and the debtors revealed no basis for agreement, and in 1934 the United States Congress passed and Mr. Roosevelt signed the Johnson Act, which ended token payments as a device for avoiding default and banned loan flotations by all defaulting countries. Except from Finland, no further war-debt payments of any kind were ever received. The history of the war debts thus ended in mutual ill will between the United States and her debtors.

And as he looked back in 1947, it was the very existence of the war debts, and not any later error in dealing with them, that seemed to Stimson to have been fatal.

Supposing that Mr. Hoover had believed with Stimson in quick cancellation, and supposing that he had chosen to fight on that ground, probably little but glory could have been won, for Congress would almost surely have blocked the effort—it was probably too late, in November, 1932, to educate the American people. Even Franklin Roosevelt, who was almost surely in agreement with Stimson, and politically much stronger than Mr. Hoover, never chose to fight for reduction of the war debts.

The original and fatal error, as Stimson saw it, was the

notion that huge, interest-bearing loans made in emergency conditions for emergency purposes could *ever* be repaid by one government to another. It simply could not be done, politically. And when to the political difficulty there was added the peculiar tariff policy of the American nation, the assurance of default became doubly sure. Debts incurred in a common struggle will never be repaid to a country which hates imports. And any pretense that they will be so paid can only be a source of mutual ill will, increasing by compound interest at a very high rate against a later reckoning. Stimson saw personally the poison spread by the debt question in 1932 and it made him a lasting enemy to any repetition of the financing error of World War I. In the early twenties he had taken the orthodox view that the debts could and should be paid like any other financial obligation. He had had to learn by experience, but the experience was a searing one.

It was because the learning was so bitter that he felt the story worth retelling in 1947. For in that year the American people were once more forced to face the necessity of advancing funds to their European neighbors. The creation of "war debts" had been avoided during World War II by the wonderful engine of Lend-Lease, but in the postwar period there seemed to be a return to the idea of loans, on the theory that money advanced after victory should properly be repaid. A glance at the experience after World War I confirmed Stimson in his view that this distinction was dangerous nonsense. In very large part the "war debts" rancorously repudiated after 1931 were debts arising from postwar "reconstruction." From any practical standpoint there was no distinction between money used to fight a war and money used to recover from its worst ravages. However impolitic it might be to say it, Stimson was wholly convinced in 1947 that, if the United States wished to avoid later bitter disillusionment, it must make its advances to Europe for postwar reconstruction with the same free hand and the same absence of demand for repayment that characterized the wartime operations of Lend-Lease. America's reward must be in world recovery, and not in small debt payments grinding to an embittering halt after ten or twenty years.

CHAPTER IX

The Far Eastern Crisis

---

1. A JAPANESE DECISION

O N THE night of September 18, 1931, military forces of the Japanese Empire occupied strategic cities and towns in South Manchuria. In the eighteen months that followed, the heaviest and most important burden of the American Secretary of State was the handling of the resulting international crisis. This was the beginning of what the Japanese chose to call "the Manchurian Incident"; to Stimson it was always something more. In the title of a book written in 1936 he called it *The Far Eastern Crisis*; this book, published by Harper for the Council on Foreign Relations, contains a more detailed record of Stimson's part in the affair than can be given here. The account in this chapter is designed to present the facts merely in outline; its conclusions will be modified from those of the earlier book as 1947 is different from 1936. What required circumspection then can be discussed more freely now; what was an unfinished history ten years ago is now a played-out tragedy.

The Japanese militarists who planned and executed the Manchurian operations of September, 1931, will probably be regarded by history as the first active aggressors of World War II. There is a direct and significant interconnection between their actions and those others, in Ethiopia, the Rhineland, Spain, China, Austria, Czechoslovakia, and Albania, which culminated in general war in Europe. And it needs no argument to show that the vast struggle in the Pacific which broke out at Pearl Harbor on December 7, 1941, was merely the logical result of the events which began in Manchuria.

The road to World War II is now clearly visible; it has run its terrible course from the railway tracks near Mukden to the operations of two bombers over Hiroshima and Nagasaki.

It was in this focus that Stimson reconsidered, in 1947, his part in the Manchurian affair. Whatever he had done in that connection, and whatever others had done, must now be studied as part of a long sequence of events which had ended in a great war.

Though it was a minor episode compared to the events which followed it, the Far Eastern crisis of 1931-1933 presented as complex a problem to peace-loving statesmen as anything that happened later on the road to world-wide war. As the first attempt to deal with aggression, it had perhaps a special significance; it certainly presented special difficulties. To Stimson, in 1947, the Manchurian affair was no longer of very great interest in itself. But as a lesson in world politics it remained an extraordinarily instructive story. It was not a story with a simple moral; indeed, one reason for Stimson in particular to reconsider the case was that in the years after 1933 there had grown up among many Americans a legend that if he had not been blocked by the wicked British, Stimson would easily have brought the wicked Japanese to terms by bold and energetic action in 1932. It was not as simple as that.

The situation precipitated by Japanese military action in September, 1931, had a history behind it only less complex than the history to which it opened the door. Manchuria was an area in which for half a century the interests of three major nations had been in conflict, and by 1931 the intentions and aspirations of two of these nations had so far developed in mutual opposition that military operations were a painfully natural development.

Shortly stated, the issue in Manchuria was between the Chinese aspiration toward complete national independence and the Japanese conviction that security of basic Japanese interests required the maintenance of extensive economic and political rights in Manchuria. To a certain degree—and it is impossible to be more precise—special Japanese rights in Manchuria were sanctified by treaty. Since the Treaties of Portsmouth and Peking, of 1905, China had recognized certain rights of the Japanese as successors to czarist Russia in South Manchuria. Exactly what these rights involved in practice, and how far they were extended by later agreements, were matters of dispute long before 1931. It was still less clear how their existence could be permanently reconciled with the universally recognized juridical sovereignty of China throughout Manchuria. And the steady increase of Chinese nationalism, extending itself into Manchuria during the 1920's, made these questions constantly more urgent. During the first three decades of the twentieth century, some thirty millions of Chinese poured northward into Manchuria, where they continued to think of themselves as Chinese in Chinese territory. The few hundred thousand Japanese in the area were a mere handful, sufficient only to act as a continual goad to rising Chinese pride.

But the years before 1931 saw no change whatever in the determination of the Japanese to maintain the special position in Manchuria for which they had so greatly sacrificed in their war against Russia in 1904-1905. Around the Japanese-owned railways, and other material holdings, there had grown up a cluster of "vital interests," partly strategic and partly economic—all the more important for the difficulty of defining them—and the whole had become embedded in the national consciousness of a people singularly sensitive to considerations of imperial pride and place.

Thus far the Japanese people were united. A peculiar and vitally important Japanese interest existed in Manchuria. But from 1905 onward there was "a very deep and fundamental cleavage in Japanese political thought as to the *method* by which that interest should be supported and enforced."[1] It was this cleavage which dominated Stimson's early thinking about the Manchurian crisis, and the success with which one side forced its own solution is the primary active cause for the decline and fall of the peace of the Pacific. Determined aggression will always result in war. We have therefore to consider more closely the nature of the Japanese problem.

Emerging from feudal isolation in the middle of the nineteenth century, Japan had with astonishing swiftness adopted

[1] *Far Eastern Crisis*, p. 27.

many of the economic and political customs of the West. She
had developed a dynamic and expanding capitalist economy;
with it she had so far shifted her methods of government that
the Japanese could show political institutions to parallel most
of those of the Western democracies—the legislative assembly,
the responsible Cabinet, the diplomat in Western clothes
speaking the Western idiom. The westernized Japanese, capitalist, engineer, politician, or educator, was received as a
colleague and an equal by his fellows in Europe and the
United States.

But the westernization of Japan was only partial; it did not
wholly supplant the ancient ways. There remained an Emperor
whose person was deified and whose final authority was never
openly denied; if he was in many ways a constitutional monarch, that was not by any constitution but by his divine, and
flexible, choice. Nor were his ministers fully masters in his
house, for military leaders retained their right of direct access
to the Emperor, and many a Japanese officer considered that
no delegation of responsibility and initiative to the Prime
Minister exceeded that implicitly granted to the Emperor's
loyal generals and admirals. Nor did these men admit that
their differences with the civilian elements must be settled by
any appeal to an electorate. Neither side, indeed, was basically
democratic; the instinct for authority remained almost unweakened, and the contest for power in Japan was between
rival groups of leaders near the throne. And the soldier retained the prestige of seven centuries of power, so that only the
most liberal and outspoken ever openly attacked "the military
mind."

In dealing with Manchuria, all Japanese insisted on the
maintenance of special privileges. The cleavage was between
two lines of policy which bore the euphemistic names of
"friendship" and "positive." The "friendship" policy, while
renouncing none of the contractual rights maintained by the
Japanese, aimed at a pacific settlement with China; its great
exponent, Baron Shidehara, was less interested in the military
position of Japan in Manchuria than in the sound development of Japanese economic interests in that area. Shidehara
was Foreign Minister in 1931.

The "positive" policy, on the other hand, rested ultimately on force, and it was not limited by merely economic objectives. To Baron Tanaka, for example, the development of Japanese hegemony in Manchuria was only a stage in the indefinite expansion of the new Japanese Empire; advocates of the "positive" policy were outspoken in their assertion that Japanese rights in Manchuria must be forcefully maintained.

In the perspective of 1947 it is easy to argue that in the contest for power in Japan decisive authority always rested with the militarists and that any less aggressive attitude was merely a passing phase. The emotions generated in the struggle to defeat Japan are still in the foreground, and the peculiar hostility felt by Americans for the Japanese enemy has not yet wholly disappeared. But no judgment of Japan can be based entirely on the events from 1931 to 1945, terrible as they are; to assume that militarism was always dominant in modern Japan is to be left with no explanation for the remarkably restrained behavior of the Japanese Government in the 1920's.

The contest for power between the militarists and the moderates was constant in twentieth-century Japan. In the waging of the Russian war of 1904 the military were dominant. In reviving a country almost prostrated by that contest the moderates took the lead. The expansion of Japan during the First World War was largely military in its origins. When the militarists were in some degree discredited by the failure of their aggressive ventures between 1915 and 1922, the moderates took control. The general Far Eastern settlement of 1922, embodied in treaties and agreements signed at Washington, was a model of friendly conciliation and was accompanied by acts of withdrawal by Japan which no militaristic government would have permitted. During the decade before September 18, 1931, Japanese foreign policy was restrained and peaceable. "Instead of seeking markets by force, she had been following the entirely opposite plan of 'commercial expansion and political good neighborliness.' . . . She had followed this course patiently and in the face of considerable difficulty and provocation." As late as 1930, against the violent objection of the military party, the Japanese Government had ratified the London Naval Treaty. But it was perhaps significant of the rising tension in Japan that this success was followed by the assassination of the senior responsible moderate statesman, Premier Hamaguchi.

What happened in September, 1931, was that the military party, acting on its own initiative, undertook to reverse the "friendship" policy, aiming not merely at a "positive" solution of the Manchurian problem but at a complete reorientation of Japanese foreign policy, away from the conciliatory methods and economic objectives of Shidehara, toward a program of active imperialism. The full explanation of this decision has not yet been written, but elements of its causes were clear even in 1931. The situation in Manchuria, so full of long-term dangers to the Japanese, had become inflamed as a result of anti-Korean demonstrations by the Chinese, and still more by the murder of a Japanese Army officer by Chinese soldiers. There was thus in Japan, partly natural and partly manufactured, a strong public sentiment for firm action. Nor had the Chinese, in negotiations with Baron Shidehara over the vexed issue of railway development, shown any desire to accommodate even the moderate Japanese.

At the same time, in the much broader field of foreign commerce as a whole, the policy of Shidehara was being discredited by the brutal fact of the world depression. Between 1929 and 1931 Japanese foreign trade, an item of primary importance in Japanese economy, was cut in half. And Japanese commercial enterprise was meeting such new and powerful obstacles as the American Hawley-Smoot tariff. As other nations attempted to escape from the depression by limiting their markets, Japanese opinion naturally shifted away from its earlier acceptance of a policy of peaceful trade. And the alternative eagerly and persuasively offered by a strong and active party was that of forceful expansion. The first step taken by the military was to present the Japanese people, and the world, with a *fait accompli* in South Manchuria.

This Japanese *démarche*, if it had occurred two generations earlier, would have had relatively little meaning for the United States. But in the forty years before 1931 the United States had become a world power, and in the Far East both her commercial and her political interests were considerable.

Toward Japan the United States had always been friendly, although in both nations there were groups who argued that the two peoples were natural enemies; toward China, the Americans had assumed a position of unusual importance. In a spirit of what Stimson called farsighted self-interest, the United States had been the leader in developing the principle of the Open Door in China, under which it was agreed that the territorial integrity of China, and free access of commerce, were to be respected by all nations. The principle of the Open Door had been enlarged and made law in the Nine-Power Treaty signed as part of the Washington settlement of 1922. The signatories of that treaty included the United States, Japan, Great Britain, and all the other major nations holding territory in the Pacific except Soviet Russia. And in addition to this formal interest in the integrity of China, there had developed by 1931 an extensive interconnection between Americans and China in the form of missionary and educational undertaking. China was an important friend of the United States.

And above and beyond any specific local interest of the United States in Manchuria there was in 1931 another major American concern which was bound to be seriously affected by the Japanese advance. This was the American interest in world peace, formalized in the Kellogg-Briand Pact, to which China, Japan, the United States, and every other major nation had adhered. The peace of 1931 was a peace based on treaties; the central treaty was the treaty renouncing war, and in the world of 1931 it was no longer possible for any country to pretend that war abroad had no meaning at home.

So the United States was interested when Japanese troops moved out of their railway zone on the night of September 18.

2. FROM CONCILIATION TO NONRECOGNITION

The first requirement of the American Government as it considered the situation in Manchuria on September 19 and after was facts. Accurate information is the raw material of policy. It was therefore fortunate that the representatives of the United States in the Far East during this period, and particularly the men who were in or near Manchuria, were un-usually competent. Throughout the crisis Stimson and his State Department advisers "were habitually placed in the po-sition of having in our hands earlier and more accurate infor-mation than almost any other country."[2]

Reports from the Far East quickly made it clear that the Japanese movement in Manchuria was essentially an act of aggression, and that insofar as it represented the deliberate action of the Japanese Government it was a flagrant violation of the Kellogg Pact, the Nine-Power Treaty, and the Cove-nant of the League of Nations. As Stimson put it on Septem-ber 22, "It is apparent that the Japanese military have initi-ated a widely extended movement of aggression only after careful preparation with a strategic goal in mind."

This was the fact; but it was a fact with a double meaning. As an act of aggression, it was a most serious attack on the en-tire fabric of world peace. "If the military party should suc-ceed in having its way, . . . the damage to the new structure of international society provided by the post-war treaties would be incalculable."[3] On the other hand, as an action evidently undertaken without the approval of the Japanese Premier and Foreign Minister, it remained possible that it was legally less aggression than mutiny. To Stimson and all his advisers it seemed clear that the best hope for an honorable settlement was in the liberal leaders of Japan itself. "The evidence in our hands pointed to the wisdom of giving Shidehara and the Foreign Office an opportunity, free from anything approach-ing a threat or even public criticism, to get control of the situa-tion."[4] This must be done without any surrender of American treaty rights or any approval of the use of force. "My problem is to let the Japanese know that we are watching them and at the same time do it in a way which will help Shidehara who is on the right side, and not play into the hands of any nationalist agitators." (Diary, September 23, 1931)

For the next two months, with gradually decreasing hopes of success, the State Department followed this line. The

[2] *Far Eastern Crisis*, p. 7.
[3] *Far Eastern Crisis*, p. 37.
[4] *Far Eastern Crisis*, p. 34.

method employed was to avoid any public statement critical
of the Japanese, while at the same time using diplomatic channels for the delivery of messages expressing the strong American interest in a peaceful settlement and the deep American
concern at the increasing aggressiveness of the Japanese Government. Stimson was on terms of cordial personal friendship
with the Japanese Ambassador, Katsuji Debuchi; he was certain that Debuchi was a strong supporter of Shidehara's conciliatory policy (this was by no means true of all members of
the Japanese foreign service—the cleavage in Japan was not
one in which all civilians were on one side and all soldiers on
the other). In a series of conferences with Debuchi, Stimson
constantly reiterated his desire not to embarrass Shidehara,
while at the same time he insisted that the American Government could not be unconcerned by such outrages as the Japanese bombings of the Chinese city of Chinchow, on October
8. Other more formal messages were delivered by American
diplomatic officers in Tokyo. Perhaps the strongest was one
delivered by Ambassador Cameron Forbes on November 27,
in protest against apparent Japanese preparations to proceed
with a military occupation of Chinchow, which by then was
the last remaining outpost of Chinese authority in South Manchuria. Stimson reminded Baron Shidehara that only three
days before he had informed Stimson that the highest military
authorities had promised not to advance against Chinchow;
Stimson imparted a sting to his message by pointing out that
American policy had been partly based on confidence in
Shidehara's word. Whether as a result of this message or not,
the withdrawal of the Japanese expeditionary force against
Chinchow began on the following day. Stimson always inclined to take the credit for this withdrawal, but he was forced
to admit that, even if it was his doing, it was the only concrete
result of his appeals. Baron Shidehara and the moderates were
struggling to regain the authority they had lost by the *fait
accompli*; but each new report of Japanese advances in Manchuria, and each new evidence of a stiff tone in official Foreign Office papers showed that they were fighting a losing
battle. The harrowing fact remained that there was nothing
their friends in other countries could do to help them. Any at-

tack by foreigners—and particularly by Americans—on Japanese militarism would merely "play into the hands of any nationalist agitators." Of these there were plenty; one of them was the official spokesman of the Japanese Foreign Office, a man named Shiratori, who delighted in chauvinistic comment on Stimson's statements whether these were public or private.

Meanwhile the main center of discussion of the situation on Manchuria was Geneva. Both the Assembly and the Council[5] of the League of Nations were in session on September 19, and both China and Japan were members of the League—both, indeed, members of the Council. On September 21 the Chinese representative appealed to the Council of the League. Jurisdiction of the controversy thus passed promptly and properly to the League of Nations, of which the United States was not a member.

"We were not a member of the League. Yet we were greatly interested in the matter over which it had thus assumed jurisdiction. By virtue of our propinquity and of our historic interest in the opening up of both China and Japan to the modern world we had in some ways a greater direct interest than any other nation in the world. Furthermore, we were vitally concerned not only in the preservation of peace on this particular occasion, but also in the precedent which a breach of it might have on the post-war treaties."[6] It was at once apparent, therefore, that the State Department must carefully consider its proper course in assisting the League to handle the controversy successfully. Here again Stimson was fortunate in having two able foreign-service officers on the spot—Hugh Wilson, the American Minister to Switzerland, and Prentiss Gilbert, the Consul General in Geneva; in his dealings with the League he also made use of Charles G. Dawes, Ambassador to Great Britain, a man whose high standing in Europe gave his actions unusual weight.

It was evident that the League was the proper agent for handling the situation. Not only was it to the League that China had appealed, but the League, representing sixty-odd

[5] The reader who has forgotten or never knew the League of Nations will find an adequate parallel to these bodies in the General Assembly and the Security Council of the United Nations.
[6] *Far Eastern Crisis*, p. 39.

nations, would be able to act with the authority of world opinion, whereas any independent action by the United States would be merely the action of a single nation susceptible to the charge of self-interest. Furthermore, the League had machinery for handling such controversies, although some of it had never been used, while the treaties under which the United States was an interested party offered no such ready advantages. For these reasons—and also because he had adopted an attitude of watchful waiting while Shidehara tried to get control of his countrymen—Stimson was content at first to leave the leadership in formulating policy to the League.

At the same time it was of great importance that the United States should not act to embarrass the League. "Our policy should be to co-operate and support and so far as possible to avoid clashing with League policy."[7]

The complex and fluctuating course of American co-operation with the League during the autumn of 1931 cannot here be described in detail. Neither the Americans nor the members of the League had any previous experience in collaboration on so touchy a subject as a threat to world peace, and there was misunderstanding and error on both sides. The Americans were frequently nervous lest they offend American public opinion or seem to be instigators of a policy hostile to Japan; the Europeans were often upset by the necessarily tentative and incomplete co-operation of the American representatives, who after all could never act as ordinary members of the Council. But in spite of these minor difficulties, the American effort to co-operate with the League was in general successful, for the major League powers fully shared the American view that every effort should be made to achieve a settlement by conciliatory methods, but without surrendering the obvious rights of China. And although Stimson was criticized in some quarters for the caution with which he conducted his "co-operation," he thought it fair to note that for an American Secretary of State to deal with the League at all was a long step forward. To himself he seemed adventurous.

The Council of the League in September and October contented itself with two hortatory resolutions; faced in Novem-

[7] *Far Eastern Crisis*, p. 41.

ber at Paris with continued Japanese advances in Manchuria, the Council was beginning to consider more energetic action when the Japanese for the first time expressed their willingness to let the League send to Manchuria an impartial Commission of Enquiry. This sudden reversal, coming at a time when disapproval of Japan had reached a new high, acted as a remarkable damper on Western resentment and led to the appointment of the Lytton Commission, complete with an American representative. The unanimous resolution of December 10, establishing the commission, contained a repetition and extension of earlier adjurations in favor of suspending military action and withdrawing troops. But these appeals were as quickly set at naught as those in the earlier resolutions. Japanese aggression continued. On December 11, the moderate Minseito Cabinet fell, and was succeeded by a Seiyukai Cabinet friendly to the "positive" policy in Manchuria. On January 2 the military forces of the Empire occupied Chinchow and destroyed the last remnant of Chinese authority in Manchuria. With the occupation of Chinchow, Stimson's attempts at conciliation by restraint were ended for good, and a wholly new phase of American policy began.

In 1947, reconsidering this first phase of the Manchurian affair, Stimson found it difficult to recapture the atmosphere which had made him so patient in the face of repeated acts of aggression. His original decision to support Shidehara by patience and reticence he thought sound enough, and he would do it again. This was certainly the best chance of success in maintaining peace under law. But perhaps he had clung too long to this hope. Once or twice Western representation had delayed Japanese advances, but throughout this period there was not a single authenticated instance of Japanese withdrawal from any position once effectively taken, and there were scores of reports of Japanese efforts to reinforce the military occupation with a subservient civil administration. These facts were only rendered more significant by constantly misleading Japanese assurances and constantly violated Japanese promises. More than that, the Japanese Foreign Office continued to expand its requirements for any settlement. All this was clear to Stimson. Although clothed in diplomatic language his messages to the Japanese Government in this period were not soft, and his diary entries were still less so. It remains a fact that the American policy of conciliation was often regarded as too kindly to the Japanese and that, in spite of every effort to maintain close co-ordination with the League, American influence was a somewhat restraining factor in discussions of collective action. In the main, these impressions were the result of exaggerated reports of isolated incidents, coupled with repeated efforts by the Japanese to create the impression of a cleavage between the United States and the League. But it was nevertheless true that the United States did not in this period step out boldly against aggression.

The fact was, as he could clearly see in 1947, that Stimson clung for almost three months to his hopes of a change in the Japanese position for the excellent reason that any other course would lead to extremely unsatisfactory results. It was not easy to reach as a final conclusion, one on which policy must be based, the view he expressed in his diary on November 19, that the whole course of Japanese action since September 18 had been one of flagrant aggression, that "whenever they stopped, it was because there were no more forces of Chang's to attack," and that the attack on Tsitsihar, then just completed, was "a flagrant violation of the spirit and probably the letter of all the treaties." For if this were so, and if further it were true, as Stimson stated in the same entry, that "the Japanese Government which we have been dealing with is no longer in control," and that "the situation is in the hands of mad dogs," then what would the American Government do about it, and what would happen to the peace of the Far East?

These were questions debated with increasing urgency in the State Department through the autumn of 1931. Each new Japanese aggression stimulated discussion. Thus on October 9, after the bombing of Chinchow, Stimson brought the matter up in Cabinet. In this meeting Mr. Hoover expressed the tentative view that the baby must not be deposited on the Americans by the League, a position in which Stimson concurred, and he also warned against getting "into a humiliating position, in case Japan refused to do anything about what he called our scraps of paper or paper treaties." This also was a point that Stimson appreciated, but the diary entry continued with a further comment: "The question of the 'scraps of paper' is a pretty crucial one. We have nothing but 'scraps of paper.' This fight has come on in the worst part of the world for peace treaties. The peace treaties of modern Europe made out by the Western nations of the world no more fit the three great races of Russia, Japan, and China, who are meeting in Manchuria, than, as I put it to the Cabinet, a stovepipe hat would fit an African savage. Nevertheless they are parties to these treaties and the whole world looks on to see whether the treaties are good for anything or not, and if we lie down and treat them like scraps of paper nothing will happen, and in the future the peace movement will receive a blow that it will not recover from for a long time."

Such a course was unthinkable. Whatever they might be to other statesmen or to other nations, the treaties were not scraps of paper to Stimson. Respect for treaties was the very foundation of peace. Yet what could he do? The treaties to which the American Government was a party, unlike the Covenant of the League, were treaties without teeth. More important still, since the basic requirement of policy is that it must be supported by public approval and executive leadership, the American Government was without teeth. Mr. Hoover was a profoundly peaceable man. Outraged as he was by Japanese aggression, he was opposed, in every fiber of his being, to any action which might lead to American participation in the struggles of the Far East. In this view he had the support of the American people.

Stimson could not deny that anything more than verbal action to check Japanese aggression might well lead to war. He was himself at first opposed to any American use of economic sanctions on exactly that ground, and on November 19, 1931, he so instructed Ambassador Dawes when the question was raised in the League. The American Government would be delighted if the League would impose sanctions, and would do nothing to interfere with such action, but it would not impose sanctions of its own. This was hardly a noble position, and Stimson was not proud of his part in it. But it was fair to say that the League's interest in sanctions was at no time more than spasmodic. The feeling which had led Dawes to ask for a statement of the American position did not long endure. Like the Americans, the people of Europe were for "letting George do it," and only the smaller powers, those not likely to be named as George, were constantly in favor of economic sanctions.

If it would not condone the tearing up of the treaties, and if it would not take any economic or military action to defend them, what *would* the American Government do? It was this question which produced the famous nonrecognition doctrine as the only available answer. It is first mentioned in Stimson's diary as a suggestion made by Mr. Hoover on November 9. "He . . . thinks his main weapon is to give an announcement that if the treaty is made under military pressure we will not recognize it or avow it." In other words, no fruits of aggression would be admitted as legal by the American Government.

Nonrecognition was a moral weapon, a moral sanction. It was designed originally less as a method of bringing the Japanese to reason than as a method of reasserting the American conviction that no good whatever could come from the breach of treaties. Insofar as it was designed to serve American interests in the Far East, it was aimed rather more at China than at Japan. Stimson was keenly aware of the special relationship between the United States and China which had been developed by generations of missionaries and educators, and by John Hay's Open Door policy; he knew "the incalculable harm which would be done immediately to American prestige in China and ultimately to the material interests of America and her people in that region, if after having for many years assisted by public and private effort in the education and development of China towards the ideals of modern Christian civilization, and having taken the lead in the movement which secured the covenant of all the great powers, including ourselves, 'to respect her sovereignty, her independence and her territorial and administrative integrity,' we should now cynically abandon her to her fate when this same covenant was violated."[8] The United States might not be able to prevent

[8] *Far Eastern Crisis*, p. 90.

aggression against China, but she must certainly make her opinion of it clear.

Quite aside from the specific issue in the Far East, the nonrecognition doctrine was designed by its sponsors as the best available method of reinforcing the treaty structure, and particularly the Kellogg Pact. If the fruits of aggression should be recognized, the whole theory of the Kellogg Pact would be repudiated, and the world would be at once returned to the point of recognizing war as a legitimate instrument of national policy. Nonrecognition might not prevent aggression, but recognition would give it outright approval.

Finally, the nonrecognition doctrine was designed to give expression to the deep and genuine feeling of the American people, and their Government, that what the Japanese were doing in Manchuria was terribly wrong. Not to have made some clear public statement embodying this feeling would have been to deny and stifle a genuine sentiment of the public.

Thus, by what Stimson called "a natural and almost inevitable sequence," the State Department came to its note of January 7. Delivered to both China and Japan, it read as follows:

"With the recent military operations about Chinchow, the last remaining administrative authority of the Government of the Chinese Republic in South Manchuria, as it existed prior to September 18th, 1931, has been destroyed. The American Government continues confident that the work of the neutral commission recently authorized by the Council of the League of Nations will facilitate an ultimate solution of the difficulties now existing between China and Japan. But in view of the present situation and of its own rights and obligations therein, the American Government deems it to be its duty to notify both the Imperial Japanese Government and the Government of the Chinese Republic that it cannot admit the legality of any situation *de facto* nor does it intend to recognize any treaty or agreement entered into between those Governments, or agents thereof, which may impair the treaty rights of the United States or its citizens in China, including those which relate to the sovereignty, the independence, or the territorial and administrative integrity of the Republic of

China, or to the international policy relative to China, commonly known as the open door policy; and that it does not intend to recognize any situation, treaty or agreement which may be brought about by means contrary to the covenants and obligations of the Pact of Paris of August 27, 1928, to which Treaty both China and Japan, as well as the United States, are parties."

With the publication of this note the United States, with Stimson as its spokesman, stepped to the forefront of the nations opposing aggression, and from this time onward, until his retirement from office fourteen months later, Stimson was the outstanding advocate of collective condemnation of Japan. The fact that the note was addressed to both parties to the controversy was a concession to the existence of a Commission of Enquiry holding the dispute *sub judice*. Both in China and in Japan it was understood that the note was aimed at Japanese militarism. The rumors of a more forthright American policy which had begun to circulate in December were fully confirmed. Stimson had succeeded in doing what he set out to do—the long series of notes to and from Japan which had begun the previous September was wound up "with a snap."

And shortly afterward, in accordance with a plan long maturing, the American Government made public the diplomatic correspondence to which this note was the .climax. Stimson here turned to his advantage a Senate Resolution sponsored by a man who was no friend to his policy, Hiram Johnson. Johnson asked for the State Department's correspondence on Manchuria, hoping to uncover sinister and secret collaboration with the wicked League of Nations. What he received was a set of documents which showed no such evil activity but which *did* show that for three months the State Department had been maintaining an attitude of courteous but firm opposition to the operations of the Japanese Army, and that for three months the Japanese had been giving assurances which were promptly violated. The State Department and its Secretary received strong public support in a line of policy more affirmative, both in its use of international negotiations and in its assertion of international interests, than anything done in the preceding decade.

The doctrine of nonrecognition fully safeguarded the moral position of the United States, so far as this could be done without warlike action. In a still greater purpose, however, it was not successful. It did not win the prompt adherence of any other major power. While the first object of the note was simply to bring the American position in balance with the facts of the situation, and thus to reassert American principles and reassure friends of America in China, there was a further hope in the minds of its sponsors. They believed that much might be accomplished in moderating the appetites of the Japanese if it could be clearly demonstrated that the united opinion of the world was definitely and strongly opposed to their course. They therefore hoped that the note of January 7 might be quickly imitated by other great nations. Since it was deliberately designed "to record the final decision of an influential government which had made earnest and patient efforts for a peaceful solution," it could not be subjected to the delays of prior consultation with a view to joint action. Its usefulness in securing international support of its position must lie rather in "the setting up of 'a standard to which the wise and honest may repair,' leaving 'the event in the hand of God.' "[9] Nobody repaired.

Two days before delivering the note to China and Japan Stimson explained his intentions and expressed his hopes to the Ambassadors of Great Britain, France, and several smaller nations which had signed the Nine-Power Treaty. He then waited for results. The first and most disappointing reaction was that of the British Government. Co-operation with Great Britain was in many ways the touchstone of Stimson's foreign policy. Co-operation with Great Britain in the Far East was of particular importance. The two great previous achievements of the United States in Far Eastern affairs, the establishment of the Open Door policy and the negotiation of the Washington Treaties of 1922, had been very largely dependent on British co-operation. John Hay had had the help of Lord Salisbury; Charles Evans Hughes had had the help of Lord Balfour. Stimson waited now for the help of Sir John Simon, and he waited in vain. The response of the British Govern-

[9] *Far Eastern Crisis*, p. 98.

ment, so far from supporting his position, was a plain rebuff. Choosing to maintain their confidence in Japanese assurances about the Open Door, "His Majesty's Government have not considered it necessary to address any formal note to the Japanese Government on the lines of the American Government's note, but the Japanese Ambassador in London has been requested to obtain confirmation of these assurances from his Government." Assurances being the Japanese Government's strong suit, the desired promises were promptly forthcoming.

In later years apologists for British foreign policy in the Manchurian affair were never able to find any satisfactory explanation of this Foreign Office statement. It was even more astonishing in what it did not say than in what it did. As the Englishman Arnold Toynbee put it, "The most conspicuous feature in this communiqué was its silence in regard to all the vital issues—the sovereignty, independence and integrity of China, the violation of the Nine-Power Treaty and the Kellogg Pact, and the assertion of the principle of the non-recognition of the illegal results of force which had just been raised in the American note which was manifestly the most important state paper relating to the Sino-Japanese conflict that had yet seen the light."[10]

What the British would not do the French would not do, nor the Dutch nor the Italians. The American Government stood alone. It seems a fair conjecture that this new form of splendid isolation was partly responsible for the cool cheek of the Japanese reply on January 16, which firmly reasserted Japan's intention to defend the sanctity of treaties and thanked the United States for its eagerness to "support Japan's efforts" to this end. The message continued with a statement of the Japanese position which in effect asserted that the breakup of China was so far advanced as to justify Japan in breaking it up a little further; the Japanese said that this situation must "modify" the application of treaties guaranteeing the territorial and administrative integrity of China. In 1936, as he reconsidered this note, Stimson found in it more than an echo of a leading editorial published by the *Times* of London on January 11, in which it was remarked, "Nor does it seem to be the immediate business of the Foreign Office to defend the

[10] Toynbee, *Survey of International Affairs*, Oxford, 1932, p. 542.

'administrative integrity' of China until that integrity is something more than an ideal."[11] Both the *Times* and the Japanese were eager to forget that it was precisely because of the unsettled state of China in 1922 that the Nine-Power Treaty had sought to safeguard the ideal of administrative integrity.

Thus the prompt success of the declaration of nonrecognition at home and in China was not matched elsewhere. The moral position of the United States was secure, but in ordinary diplomatic terms she had hardly been very successful. "In the middle of January Japan's aggression in Manchuria had achieved complete military and diplomatic success. . . . Her government had successfully resisted attempts of the other nations of the world to intervene with any effectiveness; had delayed and thwarted the efforts of the Council of the League under Article XI, and finally had seen a wedge of differing policies driven between Great Britain and the United States, the two principal nations interested in these international efforts. China was completely discouraged; the other nations baffled and pessimistic. The collective peace machinery had received a blow which made it look entirely ineffective."[12]

3. SHANGHAI

On the evening of January 28, 1932, a Japanese admiral named Shiozawa, commander of Japanese forces in the International Settlement at Shanghai, ordered his marines to advance into Chinese territory. The marines were resisted by determined and skillful infantry of the Chinese Nineteenth Route Army. The admiral replied with a bombing attack on the helpless civilians in the area where fighting was taking place. "It was an act of inexcusable cruelty and has stained the Japanese record at Shanghai for all time. . . . Thousands of helpless civilians met their death and two hundred fifty thousand helpless refugees passed from the ruins of Chapei into the International Settlement. But it was as useless as it was cruel and utterly failed to shake the steady defense of the Chinese troops."[13]

[11] *Far Eastern Crisis*, p. 103.
[12] *Far Eastern Crisis*, p. 110.
[13] *Far Eastern Crisis*, pp. 124-125.

The Japanese attack in Shanghai was the explosive upshot of an energetic and successful boycott of Japanese trade and traders organized by the Chinese in retaliation for the occupation of Manchuria. Economic boycott is seldom wholly peaceful, and there had been cases of unpunished violence against individual Japanese. But once again, as in Manchuria, the Japanese reply was one, not of negotiation, but of unrestrained force.

The fighting whose first night was signalized by such unexpected Chinese resistance and such uncalled for Japanese brutality continued for more than a month, and until they were finally outflanked by a vastly better-equipped force, the Chinese infantry stubbornly held the positions they had defended on the first night. Constant reinforcements from Japan were thrown into a series of frontal attacks, and incidents of brutal and pointless bombing recurred. The issue shifted from one of economics to one of face, and as Japanese embarrassment increased, so did the pride and confidence of all China.

The Shanghai incident produced an international effect quite different from that of the Manchurian occupation. In the first place, this time there was active fighting, and both the Chinese underdog and the Japanese aggressor behaved in such fashion as to arouse strong world sympathy for China. In Manchuria the Chinese had usually refused to contest the Japanese advance; peace-loving Westerners might praise this Chinese restraint, but it was nevertheless somewhat difficult to argue for rights which could be so lightly abandoned by their owners. As history repeatedly demonstrated in the following decade, the world, and particularly the American people, prefers its underdogs to fight for their rights. The Nineteenth Route Army won more sympathy for China than all the eloquence of her protests against the occupation of Manchuria. In this feeling Stimson heartily joined, and he became an avid student of the military operations at Shanghai.

While the Chinese gained by fighting, the Japanese lost. The arrogance of Admiral Shiozawa and the brutality of the Chapei bombing, combined with the ordinary unpopularity of the angry bully, made the Japanese position before the world far less attractive than it had been in Manchuria, where the use of force had been very limited and the case for Japanese rights less clearly false. What had happened in Manchuria, though it eventually became clear enough, was much less fully reported, and much less understood by world opinion, than the events at Shanghai, which involved continuous front-page news, ably reported by both newspapermen and ordinary Westerners on the spot. Shanghai was a part of the accessible Orient in a way that Mukden was not.

Finally, the operations at Shanghai awoke the British Foreign Office. Traditionally the British interest in Manchuria was negligible—and accordingly neglected; traditionally the British interest in Shanghai was intense. Fighting in Shanghai might at any time overrun the fragile defenses of the International Settlement, with very serious results for British property and British subjects. More important still, Shanghai was the focal point of extensive British interests in the Yangtze Valley. Any assertion of a special or exclusive Japanese interest in the Shanghai area would seriously disturb the British.

Thus it happened that in dealing with the situation in Shanghai Stimson and the State Department were in a very much stronger position than they had been in Manchuria. The Japanese were embarrassed by a military check; the Chinese were heartened by gallant resistance; the British were aroused by a clear threat to their interests; public opinion in America was strongly engaged for China and against Japan.

Stimson's problem was to make the most of these advantages in forwarding his own policy of firm respect for treaties and moral condemnation of aggression.

His first decision was to aim at a close and constant cooperation with the British Foreign Office. On January 25, when the situation in Shanghai was becoming critical, Stimson held a series of discussions with his advisers and with the President. "My proposition was to find out what the British would do with reference to two steps, first, to serve notice on Japan to show our alertness to the situation and how big we thought our interests were there and calling their attention to the fact that there was no excuse for their landing troops in the International Settlement; and second, to move some of the

Asiatic Squadron up there provided the British would do the same." (Diary, January 25, 1932) With the President's approval, Stimson on the same day called in the British Ambassador and explained his objectives in detail.

The British reaction to Stimson's inquiry was cordial. The British made Stimson's views about the International Settlement their own, and with the bombing of Chapei the Foreign Office became fully aroused. Sir John Simon dispatched a sharp protest to Tokyo, and in his eagerness to maintain solidarity vis-à-vis Japan, Stimson followed suit, although he was growing tired of diplomatic representations. A plan for a joint appeal to the Japanese Emperor was briefly discussed and reluctantly abandoned. As the fighting spread at Shanghai, the two nations agreed on substantial additions to their naval forces there. The transatlantic telephone was heavily used, and by the last day in January both sides were congratulating themselves and each other that the great objective of a common front had been achieved; in addition the British particularly were working to keep this common front reinforced by the co-operation of other Western powers. For the first time since September 18, the Japanese faced united diplomatic opposition. Although there were some minor difficulties, this front was successfully maintained throughout the Shanghai affair.

Acting in combination, the active resistance of the Chinese and the diplomatic unity of the Western powers succeeded in producing at Shanghai a result quite different from that in Manchuria. Although the Chinese were eventually dislodged from Chapei, the final withdrawal of the Japanese from all areas outside the International Settlement was peacefully effected at the end of May. Japanese face had been partially protected, but the Chinese boycott continued. In their defeat the Chinese had won a moral victory which reminded Stimson of the victory in defeat that Americans had won at Bunker Hill in 1775. And the Japanese, in a remarkable Foreign Office statement, announced that their withdrawal was designed to end "world-wide odium" which the Shanghai incident had brought upon Japan. It was a striking victory for world opinion, and to Stimson it was always a proof of the power of true Anglo-American co-operation.

4. THE BORAH LETTER

As a bloody sequel to Manchuria, Shanghai provided a flaming lesson to the West on the nature of the Far Eastern crisis, and during February and March there occurred a series of events in Western diplomacy which showed how deeply Shanghai had affected the situation. The first problem of the American Government was to examine once more its own policy and purposes. On January 7 the United States had announced a policy of nonrecognition. Was this a sufficient expression of the American position? Was that all the United States would do? The question was discussed at length in Cabinet meetings on the twenty-sixth and twenty-ninth of January. The three principal participants in the discussion were the President, Stimson, and Secretary of War Patrick Hurley. On the twenty-sixth, after Stimson had briefly stated that the situation was serious, Hurley opened the discussion, making the argument that notes and diplomatic representations were not going to do much good unless backed by force, since in his view the Japanese, in Shanghai as in Manchuria, were executing steps in a far-flung plan of imperial expansion which could be blocked only by war. If the United States was not prepared to fight, according to Hurley's argument, she would do better not to waste breath in protests which would be ignored. Was she interested in driving the matter to a showdown?

Only the President could answer this question, and Mr. Hoover's answer was a categorical negative. In his view the integrity of China could be forcefully defended by the Chinese themselves. He agreed with Hurley's analysis of the intentions of Japan, but he also believed that by their mere size and persistence, the 450 million Chinese would eventually frustrate the Japanese grand design. In any event, it was not a proper area or occasion for a war by the United States. "He pointed out strongly the folly of getting into a war with Japan on this subject; that such a war could not be localized or kept in bounds, and that it would mean the landing of forces in the Far East which we had no reason or sense in doing. He said he would fight for Continental United States as far as anybody, but he would not fight for Asia." (Diary, January 26, 1932)

The President however did not at all agree with Hurley about notes and remonstrances. He believed that the Kellogg Pact could become a great moral force against aggression, and he thought that the doctrine of nonrecognition of January 7 was a splendid first step in mobilizing opinion behind the principle of the pact. "He said that he thought that that note would take rank with the greatest papers of this country, and that that was the safe course for us to follow now rather than by getting into a war in China." (Diary, January 26, 1932)

Since Mr. Hoover was the President, and since he believed that any policy of embargo or sanctions might lead to war, his position effectively blocked any governmental support for economic sanctions. This was a point which Stimson had argued with Mr. Hoover several times. The President was always willing to listen, but he was never persuaded. On February 20 he "said he hoped that his mind was not closed on anything, but he admitted that it was as much closed as possible on the question of calling an embargo." He believed that the enforcement of the treaties to which the United States and Japan were parties was a moral obligation to be met by moral pressures.

In taking this position Mr. Hoover was squarely in line with the whole tradition of American foreign policy in the Far East. Even Theodore Roosevelt had always insisted that American interests in the Orient were not worth a war. It was true that the Nine-Power Treaty and the Kellogg Pact had altered the legal and moral position, but, in believing that these alterations did not carry with them an obligation to use force against Japanese aggression, Mr. Hoover was traveling in company with most of his countrymen. As Stimson had himself stated back in November, "The policy of imposing sanctions of force, which Hurley suggested as the only thing possible, had been rejected by America in its rejection of the League of Nations; and America had deliberately chosen to rest solely upon treaties with the sanction of public opinion alone; that this was not the choice of this administration, but a deliberate choice of the country long before we came in." (Diary, November 14, 1931)

Debarred from any advocacy of sanctions, Stimson in early

1932 was hard put to it to find a policy which would be effective. He was finally driven to a double course: a bluff of force and a strong restatement of principles. The bluff was not a very good one; the statement of principles he considered one of the best things he ever did. Let us look first at the bluff.

Words alone were unlikely to be effective in blocking the Japanese. It was necessary that they have some ground for concern about the attitude of the Government which spoke the words. Thus far Hurley was clearly right. Even if the United States was unwilling to impose sanctions and still more unwilling to fight for the "peace of the Pacific," might it not be possible to bluff the Japanese? As Stimson put it to Mr. Hoover after the Cabinet meeting of January 26, "The only difference I could see between his point and mine was the reliance which I felt we could put upon America's strength both economically and militarily. I quoted Roosevelt's saying, 'Speak softly and carry a big stick!' . . . I was against putting any threat into words. I thought we had a right to rely upon the unconscious elements of our great size and military strength; that I knew Japan was afraid of that, and I was willing to let her be afraid of that without telling her that we were not going to use it against her."

This was a view that Mr. Hoover did not fully accept. He was so much a man of peace that he did not like the notion of even unspoken threats of war. Sensitive to criticism from men who shared his Quaker convictions, he was frequently eager to make it perfectly clear that no economic or warlike measures would be taken by his administration against Japan. It was typical of his loyalty to Stimson that he held back from any such statement throughout the winter of 1932, in deference to his Secretary of State's urgent pleading. He further accepted Stimson's suggestion that the American Fleet be left at Hawaii, where it arrived in mid-February by pure coincidence, in maneuvers planned and publicly announced the previous summer. The fleet duly remained in Hawaii instead of returning to its usual west coast bases, and it was probably useful in restraining the more flagrantly headlong Japanese militarists.

But the policy of bluff on which Stimson was forced to rely

was not an easy one to execute, for it was a bluff that could not be expressed. The American Government could not intimate by word or deed that it favored sanctions; any such intimation was barred by Mr. Hoover's position. Stimson even felt it necessary to deny reports circulated privately in Geneva that the American Government was coming round to support of sanctions. All that was possible was to keep silent on future intentions, and the silence was not very impressive. And when friendly governments attempted to sound out the American position, the bluff became still weaker.

The policy of bluff followed in the winter of 1932 was certainly more effective than any public announcement that the United States was opposed to sanctions, but that is about all that can be said for it, and it may be doubted whether Japanese leaders were much surprised when in May Mr. Hoover insisted on a public statement opposing sanctions by the then Acting Secretary of State.

Yet in spite of this basic weakness in his position, Stimson remained throughout the Shanghai incident the leader of opinion against Japan. For by a restatement and elaboration of the basic position of the United States, toward the end of February, he set the tone for the only affirmative action taken by the League. This was accomplished in a public letter to Senator Borah which was in many ways the most significant state paper Stimson ever wrote.

The Borah letter had many causes. The first was the state of American opinion.

In February and March Stimson was backed by a public sentiment against Japan stronger than anything he had behind him before or after. American admiration of China was strongly reinforced by the exploits of the Nineteenth Route Army. Even the dreaded word "sanctions" was now openly noised abroad, and a Committee of Citizens led by such men as Newton D. Baker and A. Lawrence Lowell began to advocate the imposition of a trade embargo against Japan. This committee represented only a small minority in the country, but the indignation to which it appealed was general.

As he considered the feeling of his countrymen, Stimson became more and more convinced of his duty to give official expression to the historic policy and present opinion of his nation. He remembered his own annoyance at President Wilson's hands-off attitude toward the violation of Belgium in 1914. Here was a case of aggression nearly six months old, at least as serious as the German attack on Belgium, and one which furthermore directly violated treaties to which the United States was a party. "As I reflected upon it, it seemed to me that in future years I should not like to face a verdict of history to the effect that a government to which I had belonged had failed to express itself adequately upon such a situation."[14]

A second reason for clear public protest was the importance of remaining loyal to traditional American policy in China. During early February there were intimations from Tokyo that the Japanese no longer considered the Nine-Power Treaty applicable and that China should now be permanently dismembered and her major commercial areas controlled by foreigners. Both Japan and China must be shown how far this or any similar suggestion was from American policy.

Third, and perhaps most important, it seemed time for a new move in the continuing campaign to mobilize world opinion. Secretary Hurley's warning that public opinion would not do the job would certainly prove correct unless the moral disapproval of the United States should be reinforced by that of other major nations.

The obvious ground for a new statement was the Nine-Power Treaty. The first article of that treaty was precisely applicable to the situation in Manchuria; "no human language" could be more clear than its statement of the obligation of its signatories "(1) to respect the sovereignty, the independence and the territorial and administrative integrity of China and (2) to provide the fullest and most unembarrassed opportunity to China to develop and maintain for herself an effective and stable government."

And the obvious partner for a new *démarche* was Great Britain. It was on Mr. Hoover's suggestion that Stimson presented his new plan to the British Ambassador on February 9 and discussed it in detail with Sir John Simon in five transatlantic telephone calls during the following week, trying to

[14] *Far Eastern Crisis*, p. 157.

persuade the British that the interests of both nations would be served by a joint reassertion of the Nine-Power Treaty. These conversations were friendly enough, and Sir John approved of Stimson's plan in principle. In practice, however, he held back. There were various reasons for his reluctance to accept Stimson's suggestion—some good and some less good. Among the good ones were Britain's membership in the League, where measures indicating adherence to the nonrecognition doctrine were pending; it was reasonable that the British should pace their actions to those of the League. Among the bad ones were Sir John's inability to take Chinese territorial and administrative integrity very seriously and his feeling that the question of Shanghai, as a direct threat to Western interests, should be considered separately from that of Manchuria, which he thought a dangerous subject in view of Japanese feelings. Such a separation seemed to Stimson wholly wrong—it would have been a tacit admission that aggression in Manchuria was less reprehensible than aggression in an area where there were extensive British interests.

On February 16 the League appeal was duly passed by twelve members of the Council not party to the Far Eastern struggle. Although very politely worded, this appeal to Japan implied support of the nonrecognition doctrine and called Japan's attention to her obligation under the Nine-Power Treaty. In the days that followed, Stimson finally became convinced that the British Government felt reluctant to join in his *démarche*. He was not especially annoyed at this situation. For a time he considered abandoning the idea of a new American statement, since it would be dangerous to make an official appeal or representation to Japan and find that it went unsupported by other signatories to the same treaty.

Then on February 21 he decided on the Borah letter. The Japanese had launched a major attack the day before and public feeling both at home and abroad was at a new high. It would not do to let this moment pass without an American statement. At the same time, although he had failed to budge Mr. Hoover in his opposition to an embargo, Stimson had the President's strong support for a further effort to mobilize world opinion. In order to avoid or at least minimize diplomatic knifing, Stimson decided to cast his statement in the form of an open letter to Senator Borah; he recalled that Theodore Roosevelt had often used this technique in similar circumstances. On the evening of Washington's Birthday and the morning of February 23, with the help of Rogers, Klots, and Stanley Hornbeck,[15] the letter was written. It was at once approved by the President and by Borah, and on the morning of the twenty-fourth it was published.

The letter to Borah, as Stimson later wrote, "was intended for the perusal of at least five unnamed addressees." It was designed to encourage China, enlighten the American public, exhort the League, stir up the British, and warn Japan. It aimed to do all these things within the framework of a general exposition of the basic attitude of the United States toward the Far East. The reader who bears these purposes in mind will have no difficulty in understanding what lay behind each section of the letter, and it is therefore printed below, without comment:

February 23, 1932.

My dear Senator Borah:

You have asked my opinion whether, as has been sometimes recently suggested, present conditions in China have in any way indicated that the so-called Nine-Power Treaty has become inapplicable or ineffective or rightly in need of modification, and if so, what I considered should be the policy of this Government.

That policy, enunciated by John Hay in 1899, brought to an end the struggle among various powers for so-called spheres of interest in China which was threatening the dismemberment of that empire. To accomplish this Mr. Hay invoked two principles: (1) equality of commercial opportunity among all nations in dealing with China, and (2) as necessary to that equality the preservation of China's territorial and administrative integrity. These principles were not new in the foreign

---

[15] Hornbeck was the chief of the State Department's Division of Far Eastern Affairs throughout this period, and in the course of the crisis he became one of Stimson's most trusted advisers.

policy of America. They had been the principles upon which it rested in its dealings with other nations for many years. In the case of China they were invoked to save a situation which not only threatened the future development and sovereignty of that great Asiatic people, but also threatened to create dangerous and constantly increasing rivalries between the other nations of the world. War had already taken place between Japan and China. At the close of that war three other nations intervened to prevent Japan from obtaining some of the results of that war claimed by her. Other nations sought and had obtained spheres of interest. Partly as a result of these actions a serious uprising had broken out in China which endangered the legations of all of the powers at Peking. While the attack on those legations was in progress, Mr. Hay made an announcement in respect to this policy as the principle upon which the powers should act in the settlement of the rebellion. He said:

"The policy of the Government of the United States is to seek a solution which may bring about permanent safety and peace to China, preserve Chinese territorial and administrative entity, protect all rights guaranteed to friendly powers by treaty and international law, and safeguard for the world the principle of equal and impartial trade with all parts of the Chinese Empire."

He was successful in obtaining the assent of the other powers to the policy thus announced.

In taking these steps Mr. Hay acted with the cordial support of the British Government. In responding to Mr. Hay's announcement, above set forth, Lord Salisbury, the British Prime Minister, expressed himself "most emphatically as concurring in the policy of the United States."

For twenty years thereafter the "open door" policy rested upon the informal commitments thus made by the various powers. But in the winter of 1921 to 1922, at a conference participated in by all of the principal powers which had interests in the Pacific, the policy was crystallized into the so-called Nine-Power Treaty, which gave definition and precision to the principles upon which the policy rested. In the first article of that treaty, the contracting powers, other than China, agreed:

"1. To respect the sovereignty, the independence and the territorial and administrative integrity of China.

"2. To provide the fullest and most unembarrassed opportunity to China to develop and maintain for herself an effective and stable government.

"3. To use their influence for the purpose of effectually establishing and maintaining the principle of equal opportunity for the commerce and industry of all nations throughout the territory of China.

"4. To refrain from taking advantage of conditions in China in order to seek special rights or privileges which would abridge the rights of subjects or citizens of friendly states, and from countenancing action inimical to the security of such states."

This treaty thus represents a carefully developed and matured international policy intended, on the one hand, to assure to all of the contracting parties their rights and interests in and with regard to China, and on the other hand, to assure to the people of China the fullest opportunity to develop without molestation their sovereignty and independence according to the modern and enlightened standards believed to obtain among the peoples of this earth. At the time this treaty was signed, it was known that China was engaged in an attempt to develop the free institutions of a self-governing republic after her recent revolution from an autocratic form of government; that she would require many years of both economic and political effort to that end; and that her progress would necessarily be slow. The treaty was thus a covenant of self-denial among the signatory powers in deliberate renunciation of any policy of aggression which might tend to interfere with that development. It was believed—and the whole history of the development of the "open door" policy reveals that faith— that only by such a process, under the protection of such an agreement, could the fullest interests not only of China but of all nations which have intercourse with her best be served.

During the course of the discussions which resulted in the treaty, the chairman of the British Delegation, Lord Balfour, had stated that—

"The British Empire Delegation understood that there was no representative of any power around the table who thought that the old practice of 'spheres of interest' was either advocated by any government or would be tolerable to this conference. So far as the British Government were concerned, they had, in the most formal manner, publicly announced that they regarded this practice as utterly inappropriate to the existing situation."

At the same time the representative of Japan, Baron Shidehara, announced the position of his Government as follows:

"No one denies to China her sacred right to govern herself. No one stands in the way of China to work out her own great national destiny. . . ."

It must be remembered also that this treaty was one of several treaties and agreements entered into at the Washington Conference by the various powers concerned, all of which were interrelated and interdependent. No one of these treaties can be disregarded without disturbing the general understanding and equilibrium which were intended to be accomplished and effected by the group of agreements arrived at in their entirety. The Washington Conference was essentially a disarmament conference, aimed to promote the possibility of peace in the world not only through the cessation of competition in naval armament but also by the solution of various other disturbing problems which threatened the peace of the world, particularly in the Far East. These problems were all interrelated. The willingness of the American Government to surrender its then commanding lead in battleship construction and to leave its positions at Guam and in the Philippines without further fortifications was predicated upon, among other things, the self-denying covenants contained in the Nine-Power Treaty, which assured the nations of the world not only of equal opportunity for their Eastern trade but also against the military aggrandizement of any other power at the expense of China. One cannot discuss the possibility of modifying or abrogating those provisions of the Nine-Power Treaty without considering at the same time the other promises upon which they were really dependent.

Six years later the policy of self-denial against aggression by a stronger against a weaker power, upon which the Nine-Power Treaty had been based, received a powerful reinforcement by the execution by substantially all the nations of the world of the Pact of Paris, the so-called Kellogg-Briand Pact. These two treaties represent independent but harmonious steps taken for the purpose of aligning the conscience and public opinion of the world in favor of a system of orderly development by the law of nations including the settlement of all controversies by methods of justice and peace instead of by arbitrary force. The program for the protection of China from outside aggression is an essential part of any such development. The signatories and adherents of the Nine-Power Treaty rightly felt that the orderly and peaceful development of the 400,000,000 of people inhabiting China was necessary to the peaceful welfare of the entire world and that no program for the welfare of the world as a whole could afford to neglect the welfare and protection of China.

The recent events which have taken place in China, especially the hostilities which having been begun in Manchuria have latterly been extended to Shanghai, far from indicating the advisability of any modification of the treaties we have been discussing, have tended to bring home the vital importance of the faithful observance of the covenants therein to all of the nations interested in the Far East. It is not necessary in that connection to inquire into the causes of the controversy or attempt to apportion the blame between the two nations which are unhappily involved; for regardless of cause or responsibility, it is clear beyond peradventure that a situation has developed which cannot, under any circumstances, be reconciled with the obligations of the covenants of these two treaties, and that if the treaties had been faithfully observed such a situation could not have arisen. The signatories of the Nine-Power Treaty and of the Kellogg-Briand Pact who are not parties to that conflict are not likely to see any reason for modifying the terms of those treaties. To them the real value of the faithful performance of the treaties has been brought sharply home by the perils and losses to which their nationals have been subjected in Shanghai.

That is the view of this Government. We see no reason for abandoning the enlightened principles which are embodied in these treaties. We believe that this situation would have been avoided had these covenants been faithfully observed, and no evidence has come to us to indicate that a due compliance with them would have interfered with the adequate protection of the legitimate rights in China of the signatories of those treaties and their nationals.

On January 7th last, upon the instruction of the President, this Government formally notified Japan and China that it would not recognize any situation, treaty or agreement entered into by those Governments in violation of the covenants of these treaties, which affected the rights of our Government or its citizens in China. If a similar decision should be reached and a similar position taken by the other governments of the world, a caveat will be placed upon such action which, we believe, will effectively bar the legality hereafter of any title or right sought to be obtained by pressure or treaty violation, and which, as has been shown by history in the past, will eventually lead to the restoration to China of rights and titles of which she may have been deprived.

In the past our Government, as one of the leading powers on the Pacific Ocean, has rested its policy upon an abiding faith in the future of the people of China and upon the ultimate success in dealing with them of the principles of fair play, patience, and mutual good will. We appreciate the immensity of the task which lies before her statesmen in the development of her country and its Government. The delays in her progress, the instability of her attempts to secure a responsible government, were foreseen by Messrs. Hay and Hughes and their contemporaries and were the very obstacles which the policy of the "open door" was designed to meet. We concur with those statesmen, representing all the nations in the Washington Conference, who decided that China was entitled to the time necessary to accomplish her development. We are prepared to make that our policy for the future.

Very sincerely yours,

HENRY L. STIMSON

The Honorable William E. Borah
United States Senate

The Borah letter was published only one day after a Japanese statement which openly repudiated the whole idea of a

strong and independent China. In answer to the League appeal
of February 16, it was announced that "the Japanese Government do not and cannot consider that China is an 'organized
people' within the meaning of the Covenant of the League of
Nations. China has, it is true, been treated in the past by common consent as if the expression connoted an organized
people. But fictions cannot last forever. . . ."

Thus the lines were drawn. On the one hand stood the
United States, insistent on the maintenance of China's independence and integrity. On the other was Japan, impatient
of the "fictions" of the Nine-Power Treaty and determined
to impose a unilateral solution on the ground that "she believes
that she is naturally and necessarily in a far better position to
appreciate the facts than any distant power can possibly be."
To the man with eyes to see and ears to hear, these words from
these nations, if adhered to, could only mean that in the long
run war was inevitable. As Stimson put it in his diary on
March 9, 1932, "At present it seems to me that if Japan keeps
up this attitude in which she now is, we are shaping up an
issue between the two great theories of civilization and economic methods. It looks a little as if Japan had made up her
mind that industrialization and foreign trade will not be
enough for her if she cannot hold it, and is yielding to the
temptation and thinking that she can make markets for herself in China by force, which means that she must permanently
exploit China and impose the suzerainty of a dominant race
upon another race." This would not work; in the long run
China, "the better race," would frustrate Japan. "But in the
meanwhile, there will be presented a very sharp issue with our
policy in the Pacific as exemplified by a long line of steps
which we have taken beginning in 1844 and leading up to the
'Open Door' and the Nine-Power Pact. During the course
of that rivalry it is, in my opinion, almost impossible that there
should not be an armed clash between two such different
civilizations."

Through the decade that followed the dreaded contest came
ever nearer. American diplomacy was sometimes strong and
sometimes gentle in the execution of Pacific policy, but the
basic American stand for treaty rights and a strong China was

never deserted. And though there were ups and downs in Japanese diplomacy too, the general trend was toward constant expansion of the claims of 1931 and 1932. Japan knew better than the West what was right for China; Japan was the proper and natural leader of the new East Asia; Japan would deal with reality while the Americans mouthed their principles. Through this rising stream of aggressive self-justification there ran the increasingly blunt repudiation of the Nine-Power Treaty. First it was unrealistic; later it was obsolete; in the final Japanese statement of December 7, 1941, it was described as "the chief factor responsible for the present predicament of East Asia." A careful reading of the diplomatic negotiations that preceded Pearl Harbor can lead to no conclusion but that it was American support of China—American refusal to repudiate the principles of Hay, Hughes, Stimson, and Hull—which proved the final cause of the breakdown of negotiations and the beginning of war. If at any time the United States had been willing to concede to Japan a free hand in China, there would have been no war in the Pacific. The lines of division laid down so clearly in February, 1932, led straight to Pearl Harbor.

5. CONCLUSION AND RETROSPECT

In the winter of 1932 Stimson's forecast of war was only the expression of the personal fears of an individual. In his official capacity he was armed with "spears of straw and swords of ice,"[16] and he was forced to proceed with a line of policy which seems in retrospect to have been very weak. The Borah letter, with its implication that continued aggression in the Far East might involve a forceful reassertion of powers which had been abandoned in 1922, was the strongest statement Stimson made during the Manchurian crisis, and its implied threat was at no time developed into action.

But at least it stood as a clear statement of American policy and a definite warning that the United States understood and thoroughly disapproved the course of the Japanese. It cer-

---

[16] An old Chinese saying which Stimson picked up from the perceptive French poet and ambassador, Claudel.

tainly compared favorably with the position taken in the following week by the British Government. On February 29, pressed in the House of Commons for a statement on the reaction of His Majesty's Government to the Borah letter, Anthony Eden, Sir John Simon's Under Secretary, said, "We should certainly not agree to seeing the terms of the Nine-Power Treaty flouted, but in face of the assurance given by the Japanese Government I can see no justification for our assuming that anything of the kind is likely to take place." Mr. Eden apparently did not agree with the Borah letter that the treaty had *already* been flouted, and his statement must have been consoling to the Japanese Foreign Office; His Majesty's Government was still receptive to assurances.

But Sir John Simon was not prepared to abandon entirely his Shanghai-born co-operation with the United States. Having stood aside while Stimson warned the Japanese that they were violating the Nine-Power Treaty, he now offered some amends. He was not prepared to admit that the Japanese were behaving badly, but he would agree to go on record that bad behavior was not to be recognized. On March 11, 1932, the Assembly of the League of Nations adopted without dissent the doctrine of nonrecognition. The initiative in this move came from Sir John Simon. Stimson promptly expressed his satisfaction that so far at least the lead of the United States had been followed.

It was now more clear than ever that moral condemnation was to be the main weapon of the Western nations against aggression. On a trip to Geneva in April and early May, Stimson was able to explore at firsthand the opinions and attitudes of the leading statesmen of Europe. Although his mission was nominally concerned with disarmament, his principal interest was the treatment of the Far Eastern crisis; and in conversations with Ramsay MacDonald, Sir John Simon, Tardieu of France, Matsudaira of Japan, and many others, he was able at once to communicate the American attitude and to understand more clearly than he had before the feelings of his colleagues abroad. What he learned was not encouraging.

From the beginning the nonrecognition doctrine had been

a compromise result of two conflicting attitudes. One was the view of which Stimson was the leader—that a united moral judgment against Japanese aggression was the necessary beginning in preserving the peace treaties. In Stimson's thinking through the winter of 1932, nonrecognition had been regarded less as a sufficient step than as a necessary first step. But in the opinion of Mr. Hoover it was not a minimum but a maximum measure. Although the President once or twice suggested the further step of joint withdrawal of ambassadors and ministers from Tokyo, he regarded moral pressure as the only pressure which would be justified in dealing with oriental affairs and he firmly opposed the suggestion of any economic or military action; just as strongly he opposed any economic or military threat. Stimson found in Europe that it was Mr. Hoover's view and not his own that was widely accepted among the diplomats of the major European powers. His own attitude was echoed only among representatives of the smaller nations.

There was no choice as to what he should do next. The country was opposed to sanctions; the President was opposed to sanctions; the major European nations, partly because of a covert friendship for Japan and partly for the simple reason that Asia was no great concern of theirs, were opposed to sanctions. Only the power of moral judgment remained. Perhaps that would be sufficient; in any case the only course for a man who was a soldier and not a critic by temperament was to make the best of his bad situation. Stimson set himself at Geneva and through the remainder of his service as Secretary of State to the purpose of obtaining and maintaining a world judgment against Japan. At the best this policy might in fact deter the Japanese. At the worst it would lay a firm foundation of principle upon which the Western nations and China could stand in a later reckoning.

During the summer of 1932 the situation in the Far East remained relatively quiet. The Japanese had erected a puppet government in Manchukuo. That government began to take over certain international functions of tax and tariff which could not be recognized by governments supporting the nonrecognition doctrine, and Stimson protested. Further Japanese expansion in North China was undertaken and Stimson protested. But the State Department, like the League of Nations, was waiting for the report of the Lytton Commission and while it waited the Japanese continued undisturbed on their way. Reports from the Embassy in Tokyo made it clear that they had no intention of changing their course in response to any form of pressure from the West. Meanwhile in August Stimson was able to take one further step in the development of his campaign for collective moral pressure.

On August 8, 1932, he spoke before the Council of Foreign Relations on "The Pact of Paris—Three Years of Development." In this speech he developed in detail his conviction that the pact marked a new era in international relations, that it made war "an illegal thing," and that it thus wholly altered the old concept of neutrality, conferring new rights and duties on neutral nations. "Hereafter when two nations engage in armed conflict either one or both of them must be wrongdoers —violators of this general treaty law. We no longer draw a circle about them and treat them with the punctilios of the duelist's code. Instead we denounce them as lawbreakers."

He went on to argue that this proper and necessary act of denunciation was in itself a powerful engine of peace. "The Kellogg-Briand Pact provides for no sanctions of force. . . . Instead it rests upon the sanction of public opinion which can be made one of the most potent sanctions of the world. . . . Public opinion is the sanction which lies behind all international intercourse in time of peace. Its efficacy depends upon the will of the people of the world to make it effective. If they desire to make it effective, it will be irresistible. Those critics who scoff at it have not accurately appraised the evolution in world opinion since the Great War."

Though this statement was extreme, it was one which a man might fairly make in trying to give life to the only force available to him. Certainly public opinion would never become a successful sanction unless men believed in it.

To get complete acceptance of a moral sanction was not easy. Enveloped in the pacifistic atmosphere of the twenties, a great many Americans—and many men in other countries too— believed that military or economic pressure was itself immoral.

Though Stimson did not himself accept this position, he was bound to admit its force and acknowledge that the Kellogg Pact would not have had general support if it had included stronger sanctions than that of public opinion. "Any other course, through the possibility of entangling the signatories in international politics, would have confused the broad simple aim of the treaty and prevented the development of that public opinion upon which it most surely relies."

Public opinion was Stimson's only weapon in 1932. Through that year and for a long time after he did his utmost to make it effective. But it was a vain hope, as he always feared it would be. And in this respect his advocacy had been harmful: if people were taught that public opinion was "irresistible," they might the more easily excuse themselves from using stronger weapons. This was a mistake which Stimson himself never made, but he was afraid, in 1947, that in his attempt to make the best of what he had, he had perhaps given aid and comfort to the very irresponsibility he hated. Such were the difficulties of arousing Americans to action without frightening them into a deeper isolation than ever.

This speech of August 8 said pitiably little, in the light of later events, but its statement of the meaning and danger of aggression was exact, and its assertion of the doctrine that war was illegal was received with clamorous disfavor in Japan. The galled jade winced.

The Lytton Commission report was signed early in September and made public at the beginning of October, 1932. It was a masterful summary of events in Manchuria and a decisive judgment against Japan on all major issues. For the student of the origins and meaning of the Manchurian incident it remains today the basic document. Its arraignment of Japan was unanswerable. Stimson devoted his energies in the months that followed to securing its adoption by the League of Nations. When his advice was asked by some of the members of the League he suggested that the Assembly act like a judge receiving the report of a master in chancery; it should adopt the report as its findings and judgment. There can be no doubt that American diplomatic pressure toward this end was both necessary and effective, for other great powers, and particularly Great Britain, continued to edge away from any decisive judgment against Japan; and Sir John Simon in December, 1932, made a speech to the Assembly which could only be taken as an attempt to conciliate Japanese opinion by emphasizing out of all proportion those small sections of the Lytton Commission report upon which a defense for Japan might be based. At last, after months of debate and delay, the League of Nations on February 24, with Japan alone dissenting, adopted a report accepting in full the findings of the Lytton Commission and refusing to recognize the puppet regime in Manchuria. As it had done seventeen months before, the League recommended the evacuation of Japanese troops from all positions outside the railway zone and the re-establishment of a genuinely Chinese regime in Manchuria. On the following day Stimson completed his record of co-operation with the League by a formal statement expressing general approval of all its findings and firm support of the doctrine of nonrecognition. One month later the Japanese gave notice of withdrawal from the League of Nations. A year and a half of debate, conciliation, warning, investigation, and judgment had ended with no greater material result than the nonrecognition of a conquest whose fruits the Japanese Government continued to enjoy unmolested.

In assessing the accomplishment of peace-loving statesmen throughout the world in dealing with the crisis of aggression in Manchuria, it is not easy to come to any final judgment on responsibilities, successes, and failures. It is a fact that aggression was not prevented. If the Japanese had been content with their Manchurian conquest, they might have remained at peace with the world as they had done after the similar conquest of Korea, and the nonrecognition doctrine must in time have become merely a dead letter. The brave hopes for moral condemnation as a policy effective in itself can find little justification in subsequent history. It was hard for Stimson in 1947 to recapture the atmosphere of the opinion, in which he and General McCoy had agreed early in 1933, that "the policy of careful, nonirritating but firm assistance in lining up the powers against Japan is the one that is going to win out, and the moral pressure upon Japan is going to be really more effective than the economic pressure which she is up against in having bitten off more than she can chew." (Diary, January 14, 1933) He had made a mistake which he clearly described fourteen years later. "What happened after World War I was that we lacked the courage to enforce the authoritative decision of the international world. We agreed with the Kellogg Pact that aggressive war must end. We renounced it and we condemned those who might use it. But it was a moral condemnation only. We thus did not reach the second half of the question—what will you do to an aggressor when you catch him? If we *had* reached it, we should easily have found the right answer, but that answer escaped us for it implied a duty to catch the criminal and such a choice meant war. . . . Our offense was thus that of the man who passed by on the other side."[17] Seen in the retrospect of 1947, therefore, the doctrine of nonrecognition and moral condemnation was wholly inadequate.

But from another point of view Stimson's success in securing a unanimous judgment against Japan and a nearly unanimous adoption of the nonrecognition doctrine seemed to him perhaps the greatest constructive achievement of his public life. The United States, with him as spokesman, had taken a leading position in organizing the opinion of the world, and by this leadership there had been secured a united front against approval of conquest by military force. This united front did not prevent aggression or punish it or even act as an effective discouragement to further aggressors. But it prevented any acquiescence by peace-loving powers in a return to the jungle law of international diplomacy before the First World War. If it were true, as Stimson believed in March, 1932, that Japanese aggression must inevitably lead to war, it was also true that the doctrine of nonrecognition laid the cornerstone for a righteous stand on principles of law and order by the nations which in the end combined to win the Second World War. The doctrine of nonrecognition was not so much wrong as insufficient, and its insufficiency was plainly recognized by Stimson long before the outbreak of the war.

And of course from another aspect it seemed to Stimson in

[17] "The Nuremberg Trial," *Foreign Affairs*, January, 1947.

1947 that too harsh a judgment against the doctrine of moral condemnation would be unjustified by the events of 1931 to 1933. The effectiveness of any sanction, moral, economic, or military, rested on the unity and will with which it was executed. The moral condemnation of Japan in 1933 was not truly united or genuine. It was never in the minds of many of the statesmen who supported it anything better than a lightning rod for the resentment of the people of the world. The righteous anger which moved Stimson was not shared, to put it mildly, by Sir John Simon. It was not accidental that Stimson's name alone became pre-eminently known and hated by the militarists of Japan. Whether the Japanese could have been brought to reason if Stimson had had an "opposite number" of his own opinion and temper in the British Foreign Office, he could not say. Perhaps no moral judgment, however swift or united, would have been effective, and before any larger measures could have been adopted both the people and the President of the United States would have had to change their positions, and so would the Prime Minister of Great Britain.

As a test of the League of Nations, the Manchurian crisis was not wholly fair; it involved a distant land in a part of the world with which the Western nations that dominated the League were little concerned; it occurred in a time of general European crisis; it deeply affected a nonmember, the United States; the member of the League most closely affected was led in foreign affairs by a statesman undisturbed by the abstract noun *aggression*. Stimson always believed that in the face of those obstacles the League performed surprisingly well.

His own feeling was that the final failure lay as much in his own country as anywhere. For in the end the basic deterrent to aggression is the willingness of the nations to take action against the aggressor. No more than any other nation was the United States prepared for action in 1932. The moral sense of the nation was sound, and in the end, the United States redeemed by force the principles of the Borah letter. But it was a slow awakening, and if the Japanese had been able to take China as easily as they took Manchuria, it might never have come at all. Fortunately it did not work out that way.

CHAPTER X

The Tragedy of Timidity

1. DISARMAMENT—A SURFACE ISSUE

THE American economic folly of which the war debts were the most striking example was fully matched in the political field by the extraordinary retreat from responsibility which took place after the repudiation of Mr. Wilson's League. Stimson never shared the view of some Frenchmen that this withdrawal was the only major cause of the failure of Versailles; the tragedy of the postwar decades, as he saw it, was that not one but *every* great power was guilty of incredible folly. But it was certainly his belief that the American contribution to failure was as great as that of any other nation. When they rejected the peace treaty in 1919, the Americans became the first to reject the burden of the peacemaker, and the foreign policy of the United States for twenty years after that decision was hobbled and ineffective.

The political history of postwar Europe can easily be read as a series of great hopes meanly lost. It was this reading certainly that seemed accurate to Stimson as he looked back fifteen years later at the two critical years with which he was personally familiar—1931 and 1932. Although there were other crises in other years, it seemed to him quite possible that the later historian would decide that the central turning point—the moment at which the balance shifted from the building of peace to the vain effort to prevent war—was the moment in early 1933 when the political feebleness of the democracies was rewarded by the appointment of Adolf Hitler as Chancellor of the German Reich. Perhaps the events of 1931 and 1932 were already beyond the control of the statesmen then charged with affairs. Yet as Stimson looked back it was a matter of no great difficulty to see what should have been done. More astonishing still, it had been perfectly easy even in 1931 to see what was needed—and the responsible statesmen in private conversations repeatedly told each other the answer. But it happened that each man was at his best in giving advice, not in taking it.

A major focus of European negotiations in 1931 and 1932 was the question of disarmament. This was the honorable legacy of the peace settlement; it had been the intention of the victorious statesmen so to organize Europe that the need for armies and navies would gradually diminish and eventually disappear. There was an assurance of this intention in the Versailles Treaty, a fact which the disarmed Germans never permitted their conquerors to forget. During the 1920's the discussions of disarmament were dilatory and inconclusive, reviving when men like MacDonald, Briand, and Stresemann were in office and dying down when more conservative leaders had control. But by 1931 the hope of tax relief and the shining vision of swords beaten into plowshares—or, in a later metaphor even less scientific, guns churned into butter—had been so long held out to the world that further delay would have been confession of failure. It is a frequent characteristic of diplomacy that it objects much less to failure than it does to the confession thereof, and therefore it was agreed that a full-dress World Disarmament Conference should be held at Geneva in the spring of 1932. The discovery of a political leader in a major country who honestly and confidently expected great results from this conference would not, in 1931, have been an easy task.

Yet there remained some statesmen, and a multitude of private citizens, who believed that effective reduction in armaments was so logical and so desirable, and so certain to contribute to prosperity and peace, that only selfishness and stupidity could stand in its way. They believed that a frontal attack on the problem might overwhelm the resistance of narrow nationalism, and they welcomed the Disarmament Conference as a chance for launching such an attack.

To Stimson this view never seemed realistic; his own conviction was that armaments were less a cause than a result of international insecurity, and he was not optimistic about the prospects for disarmament unless and until the major political difficulties of Europe should have been materially eased. The crux of the Disarmament Conference would be land armaments—air forces were still a somewhat secondary element, and naval strength had been limited at the London Conference almost beyond the point of political practicability. Land armaments were almost wholly a European problem—a problem affecting the relations of France and Italy, Italy and Yugoslavia, central Europe and Russia, and, most important of all, Germany and France. The principal concessions in any land disarmament would have to come from the French, possessors of the strongest and best-equipped army on the continent. What prospect there was that France would agree to disarm until some at least of the reasons for which she kept an army were liquidated, Stimson was never able to see. And since the United States was in 1931 neither a factor of any weight whatever in land armaments themselves nor, in her own view, a party to the issues which lay behind the existence of large armies in Europe, Stimson was not eager to take the lead in urging prompt and plentiful disarmament. To do so, he felt, would merely obscure the realities of the situation, and without any compensating result. His position was clearly stated in January, 1931, in a note to the British Ambassador refusing to have the United States assume the main burden of preparation for the Conference.

"We feel that it will be difficult at best to produce a successful result in the Conference, but it will be wholly impossible unless the representatives of the leading Powers in Europe are willing themselves to meet or arrange a series of conversations beforehand for the purpose of preparation. Thus far there has been no intimation whatever of willingness on the part of France, Italy and Germany, the three Powers most directly interested in land disarmament, to get together and grapple with the fundamental questions which lie at the bottom of such disarmament. This was the course which the British Government and the American Government pursued in the preparation for the London Naval Conference where the issues were much simpler and fewer, and we feel that except for that previous preparation we might easily have failed in the Naval Conference. This kind of preparation cannot be done by third persons, but only by the great Powers themselves as principals. . . ."[1]

And when in 1931, in fulfillment of his fears, the Europeans made no progress toward the solution of the political difficulties, Stimson became gloomy about the prospects of success in disarmament. At the end of the year he refused a request from a friend to make a speech about the coming Conference; "I told him that under the situation I did not think that any member of the Government could make a real statement without dashing the hopes of the world, the situation being that for a year we had been doing all we could to get the nations who had the future of that conference in their hands to lay the foundations for a successful conference and they hadn't done it." (Diary, November 13, 1931)

Thus in Stimson's view the problem of disarmament was secondary to political questions. The limiting factors on all his work for naval restrictions had been political; either the responsible statesmen themselves feared further limitations because they feared other nations, or, as so often in the case of Americans, they were limited by what they thought—or knew—their people would not accept.

Land disarmament was surrounded by similar difficulties, European in origin. And so Stimson's main effort for disarmament in 1931 and 1932 was a double one: first, to persuade the Europeans to take another and less narrow look at their political difficulties, and second, to exert the limited strength of his personal diplomacy in helping them to come closer together. So far as time and his abilities permitted, he played the role of honest broker, never suggesting a specific solution but always endeavoring to show the Germans, the French, and the Italians how their attitudes would seem to the man on the other side. It was a small service, but it was one in which he learned a good deal about Europe and her political leaders These labors were carried out partly in Washington but prin-

[1] *Foreign Relations of the United States,* 1931, I, 482.

cipally in two visits to Europe, one in the summer of 1931 and the second nine months later, to Geneva in the opening days of the Disarmament Conference.

2. THE FAILURE OF STATESMANSHIP

The personalities and problems of Europe in 1931 and 1932 were less significant for themselves than for the way in which they illustrated the sort of diplomatic impasse into which nations and leaders may work themselves when under the influence of nationalism.

In Italy were Benito Mussolini and Count Dino Grandi, his youthful Foreign Minister. It seemed ironical, looking back, but in this period Mussolini was one of the most ardent and least inconsistent advocates of disarmament in all Europe. When Stimson met him, he at first played his role as Duce rather stiffly. "He would turn to Vitetti [the interpreter] and say something in Italian and Vitetti would say in invariably the same formula, 'The Chief of the Government says so and so and so and so.' So the interview was decidedly formal, more or less like Alice in Wonderland in that pose. I felt a little as if he might say 'Off with his head' like the Queen of Hearts."[2] But Mussolini was not then, as Stimson saw him, what he later became, and he was capable of a less rigid attitude. A few days later he took the Stimsons for a motorboat ride; "he showed his attractive side and we both liked him very much." On the question of disarmament he was emphatic that "Italy stood for disarmament and peace," and he suited his actions, in this period, to those words and not to his others about martial glory. Disarmament would of course have increased the relative strength of Italy, so he was surrendering very little. But his conduct of negotiations for arms limitation was less fraudulent than the maneuverings of communist Russia and, later, of Hitlerite Germany. He was assisted by a Foreign Minister who was too good and wise a man to be tolerated when Mussolini shifted his ground. None of the ministers with whom Stimson talked in Europe had a clearer understanding of the major problems of the continent than Dino Grandi. At

[2] Memorandum of interview with Mussolini, July 9, 1931.

London in 1930 Grandi had been inexperienced and not very useful; a year later he had greatly matured—he was candid but tactful and extremely friendly. It was on his initiative and as a result of his diplomatic skill that later in 1931 there was proposed and accepted a one-year truce on all naval construction—this was useful to Italy of course, for she was poor, but it was useful to the rest of the world as well.

Mussolini and Grandi together gave Stimson a clear picture of Italian policy in this period. Italy was for peace and disarmament; Italy feared and opposed "French hegemony" in Europe; Italy stood for "a balance of power," "side by side" with Great Britain; Italy was friendly to Weimar Germany. Stimson warned Grandi "that they should nevertheless be careful that their theory of the balance of power did not lead to another alignment of two groups of nations . . . for that would be the surest way of bringing about competition and ultimate war."[3] There is no record of what Grandi said in reply to this warning.

From an American standpoint, the Italians in 1931 and 1932 were of all the great Continental powers the least difficult. Relations between the two countries were good. Fascism, as Stimson pointed out to Grandi, was a form of government foreign to the American spirit. Grandi explained that he had become a Fascist in the early twenties because he saw the whole framework of society collapsing under attack from the left. Stimson replied that Americans could understand from their frontier experience that in a time of lawlessness there might be need for vigilantes, but the persistence of arbitrary power was something else again. It held the seeds of grave danger, not to Italy alone, but to her neighbors. Grandi did not disagree; he hoped the regime would become less rigid now that real civic danger had disappeared. The grim future of fascism was hidden from both men.

It was not until 1935 that Mussolini deserted the ranks of the peacemakers, and not until 1940 that he crossed his Rubicon and stabbed the French nation in the back. This early Mussolini seemed to Stimson worthy of remembrance in 1947, for whatever his excesses and his absurdities as Italian dictator, he

[3] Memorandum of conversation with Grandi, July 12, 1931.

was in those years, in his foreign policy, a sound and useful leader, no more aggressive in his nationalism than many a democratic statesman. The corruption of mind and spirit which led to his later criminal aggression may have been implicit in his career and course when Stimson knew him. If so, it escaped the observation of the traveling American.

The Germans of 1931 were equally interesting, more complex, and vastly more important. Beaten in 1918 and stripped on the east of much territory which was clearly German in its population and tradition, the Germany of 1931 had a grievance, and in the view of the Americans and the British, people and leaders alike, much of the German grievance was well founded. At least since 1923, Germany had borne herself before the world as a good loser; she had initiated and signed the Locarno Pact, joined the League, and paid her reparations until further payment would have meant general ruin. Later disclosures were to cast a doubt on some at least of this German virtue, but the sentiment of the ordinary American—and Stimson's sentiment—in the summer of 1931 was that the Weimar Republic deserved the assistance and support of all who loved peace, if only to preserve it as a guardian against that other Germany which few—and certainly not Stimson—had forgotten.

The two leading figures in German when Stimson came to visit were President von Hindenburg and Chancellor Heinrich Bruening; with these men Stimson talked as a soldier. President von Hindenburg was a man who had gained great status in the eyes of the English-speaking nations since the war, and Stimson's meeting with him measured up to high expectations. The interview was confined to generalities; Stimson refused to argue the question of war guilt which Hindenburg vigorously raised—he was defending the German Army, however, and not the German Government. Hindenburg seemed to be determined to persist in his guidance of the republic along peaceful paths, and Stimson was severely shocked the next year when he turned Germany over to Von Papen and then to Hitler. He always believed that these terrible steps were the result not of Prussian calculation but of simple senility and ignorant fear.

Stimson and Bruening found that they had been opposite each other in the same sector of the lines in 1918; it was not hard for both to agree that war is a poor method for the settlement of disputes. Bruening was prepared to admit some, though not all, of Stimson's strictures against Prussian militarism; he was clearly not a militarist himself. He was under heavy pressure from the extremes of left and right, and Stimson was struck by a phenomenon which later became painfully familiar: extremism begets extremism. In Bruening's effort to stabilize the German Republic his equal enemies were the Nazis and the Communists, and on the whole it was the latter who were more powerful in 1931. Different though they might be, the Communists and the Nazis were united in preferring civil war to the success of parliamentary democracy. Stimson somewhat discounted Bruening's description of the menace of communism, but he was quite persuaded that the Communists in Weimar Germany were not an imaginary danger.

The foreign policy of Bruening's government was the result of its internal strains. Having won widespread support in their demand for a relaxation of the Versailles Treaty, and possessing an unbreakable case in logic and sentiment for further disarmament by the victorious powers, the Germans were beginning to lose patience, and there were already signs of the recrudescence of a more truculent attitude. Stimson expressed himself forcefully against such a turn of policy. Referring to the specific issue of disarmament, he urged Bruening not to impair his "unimpeachable case before the moral opinion of the world" by any "folly in the building of pocket battleships," and that for Germany "defenselessness was the best protection in my opinion and would sooner or later force the [other] countries to reason."[4] The answer of Bruening to this counsel is not recorded.

To Stimson in 1931 it seemed as if all Germans, and their leaders particularly, were gripped by fear—fear of financial collapse, fear of revolution, fear of giving offense to the naïve and innocent but very powerful Americans, fear of the imperialistic French. Nowhere in Germany was there a leader who would stand up and assert, within the framework of

[4] Memorandum of conversation with Bruening, July 23, 1931.

democracy, that the Weimar Republic proposed to endure and prosper. Bruening had personal courage but he seemed to lack confidence, and Stimson's diary records an effort to give warning of the danger, once again from soldier to soldier. "I told him that I thought of this proposition: 'Suppose it was 1918 and you were commanding a machine-gun patrol on a dark night against a powerful enemy. Rumors began to come in that the outpost on your right was driven back and the outpost on your left was captured and your ammunition was running low. Would you tell all those rumors to your men?' He said of course not. I then said, 'Why don't you behave that way now? That is the way for Germany to treat the present crisis.' "[5] Perhaps the situation was beyond the repair of leadership, even then, and Stimson was not prepared to judge adversely a man who behaved throughout with the personal dignity and moral fiber shown by Bruening. But he missed in Germany the sort of voice that Americans were used to hearing in times of crisis. Perhaps that sort of voice could not be heard or understood in Germany; he did not know.

In any event, the key to disarmament, and the key to the political adjustment from which disarmament might come, lay less in Germany than in France, and it was the French attitudes that were most difficult and distressing to Americans in 1931 and 1932. The policy of France was security—not peace, or disarmament, or virtue, or friendship, but security. At its most intransigent this policy involved a rigid insistence upon every last provision of the Versailles Treaty; at its most reasonable, it was concerned only with the prevention of a third German war of aggression. In 1931 the economic depression had increased the relative strength of France by striking at the financial stability of Austria, Germany, and England. The French had then alienated other nations by using this new economic power as a weapon of diplomacy. In 1931, as for a decade past, the French seemed poor winners to the Anglo-Saxons, unforgiving and suspicious toward their defeated enemies, demanding and even hostile toward their allies. Some Frenchmen were more co-operative than others; it was one thing to face Poincaré or Tardieu, and quite another

[5] Memorandum of conversation with Bruening, July 26, 1931.

to deal with Briand and Herriot. But as a nation, the French were determined not to be caught out by a new outbreak of nationalism in Germany; to the Anglo-Saxons they also seemed determined to pursue a line of policy perfectly designed to develop exactly the sort of Germany they most feared.

It happened that Stimson's visit to France in 1931 occurred during a period of financial crisis, and he was unable to talk much of general European problems. It was not a good time for candid and searching discussion in any case, for the French had been annoyed by the Hoover moratorium and the visiting American Secretary of State was pointedly snubbed. It was not until later in the year that he was able to explore French attitudes in detail; in October Premier Laval arrived in Washington for conversations looking toward a better understanding between the two countries.

Of all of Stimson's foreign friends as Secretary of State, the man whose later career most severely shocked him was Pierre Laval. It was not easy to look back fairly at the Laval of 1931 and 1932, across years in which he recorded himself as a villain like Iago, glorying in unrepentant treason. Yet it is written in Stimson's diary, as a careful and sober judgment of Laval in July, 1931, that he showed himself "an able, forceful man and I think also a sincere man. In his talks with me he was extremely frank and . . . manifested the utmost friendliness." In Washington he showed to even better advantage. To his candor he added good humor and tact, and when Senator Borah, with his usual disregard for the diplomatic comfort of the State Department, chose the occasion of Laval's visit to let fly with a speech denouncing France and all her works, it was Laval's calmness and good sense which permitted Stimson to bring the two men together for a conversation that was amiable and witty on both sides.

But Laval was not prepared to shift the policy of France. He knew and admitted that parts of the Versailles Treaty were nonsense. He said that "its effect upon Central Europe was an absurdity, but it was a political impossibility now to change it." In fact from the French point of view any changes at all in the Versailles Treaty were politically impossible, and Laval suggested that all talk of revision be temporarily abandoned, "that we obtain a political moratorium, perhaps for ten years, and that possibly in that time French minds would cool down and possibly some solution could be made then." Stimson replied, after emphasizing his belief that German opinion was reconciled to the French boundaries of 1918, though not to the eastern settlement, that "to me the political moratorium without an adjustment was an immoral suggestion, and it also flew in the face of history. I referred to the oscillations of history back and forth between Germany and France, and pointed out that the Versailles Treaty froze an extreme oscilla-tion which was unfavorable to Germany at the farthest point o. unfavorability. . . . Any attempt to perpetuate such an oscil-lation would meet with failure. I frankly referred to the his-tory of 1806 after the battle of Jena. France had never been so strong nor Germany so prostrate. Yet in eight years had come the battle of Leipzig and the overthrow of France."[6] There is no record that Laval replied to this comment.

Thus in his conversations with the leaders of Europe Stimson had been able to give them all frank and friendly advice which seemed to him sound and persuasive even after fifteen years. The Italians gained nothing by their opposition to France; the Germans of the Weimar Republic gained nothing by their impatience and their lack of confidence; the French lost to force a hundred times what they might have freely con-ceded to argument. And it seemed clear to him that the French particularly had still held it in their power, in 1931, to extend the necessary hand of reconciliation to a relatively peaceful Germany. What Laval had called a political impossibility was in fact the only course available to France under the conditions of 1931, if she wished to preserve the friendship not only of Germany but of Great Britain and the United States.

If our analysis could end here, American readers might escape with the comfortable feeling that an American Secre-tary of State had duly fulfilled his traditional function of benignly disseminating good advice to blind and selfish foreigners. But the main purpose of what has been written above is merely to set the background for another failure,

---

[6] Memorandum of conversation with Laval, October 23, 1931.

one which in some ways underlay all the others, a failure on the part of the United States of America.

To each of the nations of Europe Stimson was able to give a warning that that nation's policy was incomplete. It need not be supposed that the Europeans were unable to reciprocate. Pierre Laval, for example, talked with Mr. Hoover and Stimson about disarmament. France, he remarked, insisted on security —it was the French way of saying what Stimson himself often said, that political settlement must come before any general abandonment of arms. But arms were not in the French view the only source of security; if the integrity of France—and other countries—could be adequately guaranteed by other means, France would find it easier to disarm. And what Laval asked of the United States was not very much—not an alliance, not a promise to join in resisting aggression, not even a commitment to maintain benevolent neutrality. What Laval asked was what Briand had asked before him, but unlike Briand, Laval connected his request with disarmament. He asked a consultative pact—a promise to consult with France in the event of a breach of the Kellogg Pact. He said that such a promise "would be taken in France as a great gesture which would help very much the possibility of any disarmament." But when Laval turned to Mr. Hoover to ask what he thought of this idea, "the President replied at once that he thought it was a political impossibility." There were undertones of calculation in what Laval suggested; the consultative pact might have meant more to Frenchmen than it seemed to, and it might have committed the United States to more than consultation—this was an old and well-worn issue by 1931. But the phrasing of Stimson's record is striking. Laval had asked of the United States a concession that must have seemed to him small indeed compared to Stimson's suggesting that he consent to revision of the Versailles Treaty. He had received from the American President the same helpless reply that he had himself given earlier—it was a "political impossibility." And Mr. Hoover had spoken "at once," with the certainty of intimate knowledge.

Perhaps no major nation was ever asked for a smaller contribution to peace and disarmament. In the light of what had happened in 1917 and what happened again in 1941, the American refusal to "consult" with other nations in the event of threatened war seems nothing short of madness. Whatever the occult and dangerous implication of consultation, whatever the possible entanglement involved in an agreement to talk, it seemed flatly incredible that the American people could so far have forgotten the realities of life as to believe that those dangers could outweigh the other danger—general war. Yet there it was; a consultative pact was indeed a "political impossibility," as Mr. Hoover said, and as Stimson himself had said in London a year before. Anything, of whatever nature, which implied the slightest responsibility for European peace, was anathema to the American people and doubly damned in the eyes of their watchdogs in the American Senate.

The full meaning of this American position can only be understood if we consider briefly how it appeared to Europeans. To see the European view in its full fury, it is necessary to turn to French writers of the twenties and thirties, from the ancient volcano Clemenceau on down, but Stimson's diary contains an adequate summary from a cooler source: his counselor of forty years, Elihu Root. "He was getting afraid [that] the nations of Europe were crystallizing this hostility against us, and he summed up this as the various counts of their indictment against us. First, that we had made a lot of money out of the war and then insisted upon a rigid payment of the debts which they owed us when they were poor and hard up. Second, that the League of Nations was their engine to preserve peace and, although we had designed it, we had refused to join it. Third, the same way with the World Court. It was our baby but we refused to join it. It was another engine of peace, which we had turned our back on. Fourth, that we insisted upon retaining the doctrine of neutrality and would thus, in case of any new war, make ourselves the arsenal for the combatants and also make money out of it, and thereby would make it impossible to carry out any arrangement for peace which the European nations might have succeeded in making, like the question of embargo against an aggressor." (Diary, December 12, 1930) Mr. Root had a fifth point on the technicalities of disarmament, and Stimson defended the American stand on this last point.

The first point, about money-making and war debts, was framed in somewhat prejudicial language, but it undoubtedly represented a widely held opinion. And counts two, three, and four of Mr. Root's indictment were unanswerable, as Stimson saw it. The American nation had fought a war to "make the world safe for democracy" and had then proceeded to reject all responsibility for maintaining any safety whatever. To the French particularly, feeling as they did that Germany was an enduring menace, and that the American desertion had shifted to France the burden of maintaining law and order, it seemed as if the United States was the primary responsible party in the breakdown of the Versailles settlement. If the Americans were annoyed when France stubbornly refused to make concessions to the Weimar Republic, the French were infuriated when the faithless and irresponsible Americans righteously demanded that France should disarm.

The feeling between France and the United States was duplicated with some modifications between France and Great Britain. The United Kingdom too, in 1931, was unwilling to give further guarantees to the French. The British position was much less culpable than the American, of course, because Great Britain was already committed in large measure by the League Covenant and Locarno. But, the question of blame apart, the situation was the same.

Indeed all the major powers by 1931 had entrenched themselves in self-righteous attitudes which pointed the finger of responsibility at someone else. Each one was in large measure right. More than that, the cooler statesmen of each nation knew what concession, in abstract fairness, their own countries should make. Only they knew too—or thought they knew—that these concessions were "political impossibilities."

This was the situation that Stimson had seen at firsthand, and had lived with for almost a year, when he remarked to Bruening in Geneva, on April 17, 1932, "that the situation in the world seemed to me like the unfolding of a great Greek tragedy, where we could see the march of events and know what ought to be done, but [seemed] to be powerless to prevent its marching to its grim conclusion."

The unrolling of a Greek tragedy may in the end purge the emotions of the beholder, but its working out is seldom pleasant for the protagonists. It was probably fortunate for Stimson, therefore, that he was constitutionally unfitted to play a consciously tragic role. All his life he had been a man of action, and in 1931 and 1932 he made virtues of necessities in most of what he did in foreign relations. Reduced to the role of honest broker, he told himself and others that this was a useful activity, and even in 1947 he remained persuaded that it was the best he could do, given the circumstances. In minor matters, furthermore, it produced visible results—the standstill agreement of July, 1931, was a small thing, but Stimson was proud of his part in it. Similarly his work at Geneva, in 1932, produced no disarmament, but he believed that it improved the atmosphere. Compared to what it might have been if the American nation had chosen otherwise, the influence of an American Secretary of State was small, but it was much greater than nothing at all.

Fortunately for his peace of mind in 1947, the record of his service as Secretary of State did not indicate that he had been wholly converted to false hopes. He had done what he could to help Europe keep her peace, within the boundaries of existing American opinion. But he had also done what he could to enlarge those boundaries, although in this area the powers of a Secretary of State are limited. His fight for the World Court was a typical part of this second battle; a more striking and personal effort is to be found in a speech on the Kellogg Pact delivered on August 8, 1932, before the Council on Foreign Relations. The bulk of this speech was devoted to a study of the pact as it had been applied to the Far East, but it contained a paragraph which was designed to give to the leaders of France some part at least of what they had been asking for.

"Another consequence which follows this development of the Briand-Kellogg Treaty . . . is that consultation between the signatories of the pact when faced with the threat of its violation becomes inevitable. Any effective invocation of the power of world opinion postulates discussion and consultation. As long as the signatories of the pact support the policy which the American Government has endeavored to establish during the past three years of arousing a united and living spirit of public opinion as a sanction of the pact . . . consultations will take place as an incident to the unification of that opinion. The course which was followed in the Sino-Japanese controversy last winter shows how naturally and inevitably consultation was resorted to in this effort to mobilize the public opinion of the world."

This assurance was strictly limited to consultation for the exercise of moral suasion by involving "the power of world opinion"; compared to the sort of consultative pact the French would have liked, it offered perhaps very little. But it offered more than Americans had felt free to give before, and it was reinforced by the fact that Stimson was able to point out that "each of the platforms recently adopted by the two great party conventions at Chicago contains planks endorsing the principle of consultation." This result had been achieved by earnest and nonpartisan negotiations in which Stimson had played a major role, and the principle as he expressed it in the speech of August 8 was one which he had worked out in long deliberation over the problem of widening the American zone of influence without overstepping what the people and the President as their agent would permit. It seemed to him worthy of notice that the principle of consultation marked a position so advanced that even under Franklin Roosevelt it was allowed to lapse.

But for any useful effect on disarmament, it was already too late. Already in August, 1932, it seemed clear that the race against time in Germany was being lost. Bruening had fallen in May; by August Von Papen's government had huffily withdrawn from the Disarmament Conference. By September Stimson was so seriously concerned by the behavior of the German Government that on September 8, a day of ambassadorial calls on the Secretary, "when the German came in, I gave him the devil." The "old Prussian spirit" was abroad again, and the postwar period was ending in failure. Stimson's concession to France, like Herriot's concession to Germany, had been too little and too late. If circumstance and national attitudes were more at fault than individuals, the failure nevertheless remained.

Stimson was not content, in 1947, to rest on his picture of a Greek tragedy, drawn in 1932. Greek tragedy is the tragedy of the inevitable, and the tragedy of the early 1930's was to Stimson always rather a tragedy of foolish nations and inadequate statesmen. The besetting sin of the nations was nationalism; that of the statesmen was timidity. The four critically important powers in the last great attempt to achieve disarmament and a true sense of peace were Germany, France, Great Britain, and the United States. Each of them had it in its power, single-handed, to break the log jam and insure success. Germany could have done it by accepting her inferiority in arms; France could have done it by voluntarily reducing her land army; Great Britain could have done it by giving the French an unconditional guarantee of alliance against aggression; the United States by a much smaller offer to France could have achieved the same result. Each of the four nations later took, voluntarily or involuntarily, exactly the course which in 1932 was inconceivable to each of them, and did so in circumstances vastly more unpleasant than those of 1932.

But nationalism was a sentiment too deep-rooted for its unhappy aspects to be exorcised in a day, and Stimson never wondered that no nation stepped out boldly to cut by a single stroke the Gordian knot of disarmament. Such strokes are rare. What did seem to him disappointing was that he and his colleagues had been unable to perform the ordinary task of statesmanship; they had not found a way to *untie* the knot. What could have been done in one big stroke by one nation could also have been done in a large number of little steps, all four powers contributing in reasonable proportion. The goal of statesmanship in 1931 was stable peace. To reach that goal the statesmen were required to make some inroads on the territory held by nationalism. But they were not without weapons; the peoples who were so full of national pride were also full of a deep yearning for peace. Surely it was the function of statesmanship to show these peoples that peace depended in some part upon the doing of things that nationalism denounced.

Surely it was the duty of the democratic leaders to fight and educate, and not to surrender to the simple formula of "political impossibility."

Some of the responsible statesmen were as narrow as any of their nations; some were embittered by real or fancied hurts from other lands. But taken together, especially when their expert advisers are included, they knew what should be done.

Stimson could not avoid the conclusion that the tragedy of 1932 in the politics of Europe was a tragedy not of Greek inevitability, nor even of the vast human error of nationalistic pride. It was a tragedy of the timidity of statesmanship. He was prepared in 1947 to stand by an outburst recorded on November 30, 1932, in protest against financial troubles; it was an outburst of general applicability, and it fitted with particular force the political failure in Europe: "I broke out and said that I was living in a world where all my troubles came from the same thing, not only in finance but in all matters, where we are constantly shut in by the timidity of governments making certain great decisions, for fear that some administration will be overthrown. . . . I said that the time had come when somebody has got to show some guts."

CHAPTER XI

Out Again

I. THE CAMPAIGN OF 1932

FAR-REACHING political failure in Europe and unblocked aggression in Asia might be the principal concerns of the American State Department in 1932, but for the American people and most of the administration in Washington the important question of the year was the Presidential election. Gradually during the summer and autumn of the year Stimson himself was drawn into the campaign, until in October and early November it was his absorbing task. It was not a pleasant campaign or an easy one; from the beginning defeat was so clearly probable that it was uphill work all the way.

The primary and overriding issue of the campaign, of course, was the depression. The Republicans could not escape from the fact that they had promised prosperity in 1928 and had instead held the Presidency through three years of deepening depression. As Stimson said in a campaign speech, "It is a natural trait of human nature in a democracy to visit upon its officials the responsibility for the consequences when matters go wrong." This broad basic reaction against Mr. Hoover was inescapable.

There was a further difficulty in the pernicious skill with which the Democratic National Committee had spent time and money to blacken the President's reputation. This campaign of defamation, continuous through Mr. Hoover's term, was as unscrupulous as it was clever; it was perhaps equaled only by the attacks made on Franklin Roosevelt by Republican agents in later years. But unlike Mr. Roosevelt, President

Hoover lacked zest for the manipulation of opinion. He was shy and sensitive personally; and he regarded his office with such respect that he considered political polemics improper. He worked at his job with an intensity and devotion unequaled in Stimson's experience, but he seemed unable to present himself to the people as a confident, fighting, democratic leader. In the battle of opinion he was almost from the beginning placed on the defensive.

Nor was his position made easier by the existence of a hostile Congress. The election of 1930 had put the opposition in control of both houses, and Mr. Hoover found himself the victim of what Stimson considered the most unfortunate single aspect of the American constitutional system. Like Mr. Taft and Mr. Wilson before him, he learned that failures resulting from an impasse between President and Congress are usually held against the President.

And finally, Mr. Hoover was up against a candidate who had already demonstrated phenomenal power as a vote getter in two elections in New York and who was to prove himself, in four successive Presidential contests, the greatest campaigner in American political history.

To Stimson the basic issue of the campaign was not the depression but the principles of President Hoover. He believed that the President had labored with great skill and energy to meet the depression with sound and constructive remedies, and that he had shown both courage and wisdom in resisting the "treasury raids" projected by Democratic leaders in Congress. He was in full agreement with Mr. Hoover's insistence that the leadership of the Federal Government must be used to reinforce and not to undermine the functions of state and local government. He fully agreed with the President's doctrine of a balanced budget, local relief, and sound money. He knew that Mr. Hoover had no intention whatever of permitting unnecessary human suffering in the depression, but he shared his conviction that federal action to relieve this suffering must be a last and not a first resort. As he listened to the President's acceptance speech on August 11, 1932, he was convinced that it was "a great state document." "The contrast between this tangible evidence of a faithful President who had worked to the limit for the people during this depression, on the one side, and the untried rather flippant young man who is trying to take his place, on the other, became so evident to me that it seemed as if really the American people and their power of choice were on trial rather than the two candidates." (Diary, August 11, 1932)

Since this was Stimson's feeling, he was naturally eager to give his full support to Mr. Hoover's campaign; he had, however, one reservation, which involved him in the unpleasant duty of seeming to disappoint the President in his time of greatest need. Stimson did not wish to attack the Democratic candidate; he considered such partisan polemics improper in a Secretary of State, and he further believed that the proper strategy of Mr. Hoover's campaign was the positive assertion of achievement and purpose. It was, therefore, a "dreadful shock" when he was told by the President that "somebody from New York ought to make a speech attacking the Roosevelt administration and showing that he was a failure as an administrator, and that I was the best one to do it. . . . For two years I have been making up my mind as firmly as possible that I would not go into this campaign on an attacking basis, or one which would drag me into personalities. Two years ago . . . I was dragged into an attack on Roosevelt in the [gubernatorial] campaign, and I have regretted it ever since. I told all this to the President and frankly told him I wouldn't do it. I told him my métier was to make a constructive speech about him and not Roosevelt. . . . It meant that I was turning down the first request he had made of me in regard to the campaign and it made me feel very badly." (Diary, September 6, 1932)

The pressure for an attack on the Democratic candidate continued, however, and in the end Stimson felt it necessary to recede somewhat from his initial position. He refrained from any direct attack on Roosevelt, but he made speeches contrasting the two candidates in a manner very favorable to Mr. Hoover. Even this he thought a mistake, not because he did not prefer the President to his opponent, but because "to use the great office of Secretary of State to launch a purely personal attack on Roosevelt is quite inconsistent with my dignity and that of the office."

What Stimson much preferred, and undertook with zest, was the task of presenting his personal picture of Mr. Hoover. He believed that the President, cooped up in the White House with his hundreds of pressing duties, had never been really understood by the people. So in his first major campaign speech Stimson's most powerful paragraphs were devoted to a description of the great qualities of his chief:

"I cannot close without trying to give you at least an impression of the personal character of his leadership. I have stood beside him for over three years and have witnessed it at short range. Mr. Hoover is no perfunctory leader. . . . His is a keen and ever-ready power of analysis, his a well-poised and balanced intelligence. Behind those qualities is the most unceasing mental energy with which I have ever come in contact. And again, behind that, although they are shy and never paraded in official discussions, lies the guidance of the human sympathies of one of the most sensitive and tender natures which has ever wielded such official power. . . . The foreign policy of the United States has received the constant benefit of his own wide experience in and knowledge of the affairs of other nations, as well as of the remarkable personal powers to which I have alluded. . . ."[1]

This was an estimate made in the heat of a campaign, but as a statement of Mr. Hoover's personal qualities Stimson in 1947 thought it precise. It was one of the misfortunes of politics that those great qualities were not adequately understood and recognized by many Americans. "The campaign is no longer a campaign of principles. It is a campaign on the President's personality, and the only person who can speak effectively is the President. He has been suffering from the fact that he has stayed in Washington so long that the people have lost touch with him, and he has become a shadow. . . . I have said this to him again and again and again." (Diary October 4, 1932) When Mr. Hoover did at last take his case to the country in a series of fighting speeches, Stimson found their effect "magical," though probably "too late."

[1] Radio address from the Union League Club, Philadelphia, October 1, 1932.

While his estimate of Mr. Hoover's character seemed to him to stand up under the passage of time, Stimson could not say as much for some of his other campaign utterances. He was aware of the way in which a political campaign engages the partisan enthusiasm of speechmakers, but he was nevertheless astonished and pained to find that in 1932 he had been able to make a vigorous defense of the Hawley-Smoot tariff and a strong attack on Democratic low-tariff policy. Loyalty to Mr. Hoover, combined with the campaigner's desire to make the best of everything, excused in his eyes a number of other arguments used in 1932, but to defend the tariff was going a bit far for one of his basic beliefs. He could not attack it, but he might properly have kept still. 'A man's campaign speeches,' he remarked when he looked back at 1932, 'are no proper subject for the study of a friendly biographer.'

Except for the tariff, problems of foreign policy fortunately did not become important campaign issues. There was a short flurry among ardent politicians over the State Department's firmness in opposing the resurgent nationalism of Germany; the "German vote" was regarded as dangerous. But Stimson stood his ground and the President did not interfere. The war debts did not become an urgent subject, though both parties took stands that seemed narrow and unrealistic to Stimson. Everyone was in favor of disarmament, and the administration's stand on Manchuria seemed to be accepted as a source of some political strength. The campaign was fought on domestic issues—on Mr. Hoover's record and on prohibition.

This last topic was one which concerned Stimson as much as any on the political scene. Though he was a personal abstainer for most of his life, he did not believe in national prohibition. But he had rigorously obeyed the law during the dry years, and he thought that outright repeal of the Eighteenth Amendment was of itself no solution to the problem of liquor. To escape from the speak-easy in order to return to the saloon seemed to him not very helpful, and he therefore believed that the Federal Government—as the only effective agency—should retain the power of regulating the liquor trade. This position was essentially the same as that adopted by the Republican party in an effort to satisfy both the drys and the wets, so Stimson was able to give his genuine support to a plank that many regarded as a flagrant straddle. He spoke in defense of the Republican position in a full-length address broadcast from Washington on October 29, and he continued to believe even after repeal that the last word in liquor control had not been spoken. Ideally the problem belonged to the several states, but in 1947 the situation on many state and county lines, wet on one side and dry on the other, seemed to demonstrate that unregulated local option had its grave drawbacks. But the basic difficulty in the liquor problem, during and after prohibition, as Stimson saw it, was the difficulty of persuading Americans as a people to regulate by moderate and not by extreme controls. The fanatical drys and liquor excesses remained inextricably linked in many parts of the country.

As the campaign progressed Stimson experienced the alternations of gloom and fleeting hopes which are the lot of party leaders in a losing contest. By the eve of election he was persuaded that all was lost, and he was also persuaded that this was a most terrible prospect. He believed that the "people of sobriety and intelligence and responsibility" were on Mr. Hoover's side, but he knew that "the immense undercurrent is against us." And in his really unhappy moments, he was capable of such an outburst as this: "The people of the country are in a humor where they don't want to hear any reason. . . . They want a change, and I think they are going to get it, but if they do get it, in less than a year they will be the sickest country that ever walked the face of this earth or else I miss my guess." (Diary, September 22, 1932)

On November 8, in a landslide which left Mr. Hoover the winner in only six states, the people of the United States got their change. And so did Stimson, for with the announcement of the verdict he threw aside his cares and fears like a worn-out mantle. The campaign had been disheartening, but it was over. There was no need for second-guessing on the Republican effort, for "the result is so overwhelming that it removes all of the personal responsibility from it." As for the new administration which had seemed so dangerous, "the one problem that comes up in my mind is the problem of co-operation for the future in order that the nation shall not lose by the transition." (Diary, November 8, 1932)

2. MIDDLEMAN AFTER ELECTION

Compared to the months before the election, the four months between the defeat of Mr. Hoover and the inauguration of Mr. Roosevelt were for Stimson lighthearted and easy. They were months full of complex and unpleasant problems, but at the end of them freedom beckoned, and Stimson was to find much satisfaction in the treatment he received from Republicans and Democrats alike during the interim period.

The change in his mental attitude was recorded at length on November 9:

"I had a good sleep and awoke the morning after the election feeling a greater sense of freedom than I have for four years. In spite of another very rainy day, Woodley never seemed more attractive than it does this morning, on Wednesday, November 9th. Of course my future is all up in the air, I don't know what I shall do. I have been out of my profession now for five years. I am sixty-five years old, and I don't feel very much like going back into the harness again to the life of drudgery that I had before. But I think I shall have to make some reconnection with my profession, because otherwise I shall be completely lost. The great problem is to find out how to do it, and at the same time keep open the chances for capitalizing to the usefulness of the country the experience I have had for the last four years in this very responsible post. Of course my own party is now in opposition, or will be after the fourth of March, and the chances are that the situation will be very different from what it is now. But, fortunately, I have been in a post which has been the most nonpartisan post in the Cabinet and have just as many good friends among the Democrats as among the Republicans, and I trust no enemies; and it may be possible to be useful in some now unforeseen way. At the same time I have taken an active part in the campaign and have made some vigorous speeches against Roosevelt, which cannot make him feel very friendly towards me. So that the

result is that I am in the lap of the gods, and only the future
will tell what we can do.

"The first problem is to make sure that whoever comes in
as Secretary of State after me shall have a fair chance to understand the policies we have been working out during this time,
and, as far as possible, not do something to reverse them unnecessarily. That is what we will have to do this winter in
trying to smooth out the difficulties."

The first efforts of co-operation with the President-elect
were not encouraging. The war debts, necessarily shelved during the campaign, returned at once to make trouble, not only
between Stimson and Mr. Hoover, as we have seen, but between
the President and the President-elect, and this latter difficulty
seemed to involve real personal animus on both sides. Mr.
Hoover asked for Mr. Roosevelt's help in developing a policy
which would reach fruition only after the inauguration; Mr.
Roosevelt argued that he could not intervene in the question,
since all authority and responsibility rested with the men actually holding office. In this case Stimson believed that Mr.
Hoover's stand was a good deal better than his antagonist's,
but he also believed that neither of the two men was at his
best in dealing with the other. This mutual distrust was to persist for twelve years more, and after 1940, when he had come
to feel the same loyalty and affection toward Franklin Roosevelt that he had for Herbert Hoover, Stimson many times
regretted it; it seemed absurd that an ancient grudge should
keep a man of the stature of Mr. Hoover on the side lines at
a time when the country needed every able public servant it
could get.

The war debt negotiations between Mr. Hoover and Mr.
Roosevelt reached an apparent impasse on December 21. On
December 22 Stimson received a telephone message from his
friend Professor Felix Frankfurter. "Frankfurter called me
up from Albany. He was at the Executive Mansion spending
the night with Roosevelt. He said that in the middle of their
conversation, which lasted about two hours, Roosevelt suddenly out of a clear sky said, 'Why doesn't Harry Stimson come
up here and talk with me and settle this damn thing that
nobody else seems to be able to?' And on that basis Frankfurter

called me up. He said that if I would call up Roosevelt and ask him if something couldn't be done, he would invite me up there the day after Christmas to spend the night and we could talk it over. Frankfurter and I had quite a long talk over the telephone. He thinks that there has been a terrible misunderstanding. He said that Roosevelt feels very badly that all cooperative efforts had been broken off. I told him that that was the way we felt down here and that we had gotten the impression that Roosevelt had his own plans and didn't want any cooperation. Altogether it was a funny occurrence. I told Frankfurter that I would think it over. He is to be in New York tomorrow, and I told him I would telephone him there. Frankfurter told me that Roosevelt apparently had no acrimony against me at all even on the subject of my 1930 speech, which Frankfurter had specifically asked about, and Frankfurter told me that he had used the same words about me that had been reported to me by some of the newspapermen, namely, that I didn't play politics."

On the following day Stimson reported this message to the President. "He was against it I could see from the first. He asked me to tell Mills about it, and then Mills was to come in and talk with him about it, which we did. He by that time was crystallized very strongly against going near Roosevelt. He said that the only way that he would reopen the gate was to have Roosevelt send down two or three people of proper eminence to talk with Mills and myself. . . . He was much influenced by the fact that every time he had had any personal interviews with Roosevelt, there has been unfavorable propaganda evidently coming from Roosevelt through the press afterwards. Mills coincided with his views. I did not press the invitation at all. I simply told them the facts, because I was in a position where I could not press it, but I made very clear what I thought of Frankfurter and his personal devotion to me, and Mills coincided in my good opinion of Frankfurter."

So Stimson called Frankfurter and "told him that I could not meet Roosevelt. I told him that I was much gratified that Roosevelt wanted to meet me and had such a pleasant opinion of me but that I could not see at present that it would do any good. We had quite a long talk together. Frankfurter said that he hoped that it would not prevent a meeting later. I said no, that I hoped that might be open, but at present it was shut off."

But a channel of communication was now open. On the twenty-third, even before he called Frankfurter, Stimson had received a four-point message from Mr. Roosevelt by way of Frankfurter and Herbert Feis. The messages related to minor matters, but they were friendly and co-operative in tone.

On the twenty-fourth Frankfurter called again "with a new message from Roosevelt." The President-elect hoped that Stimson would be able to see him in New York in the first two weeks of January. If that was impossible he would stop over in Washington for twenty-four hours to see Stimson, on his way to Warm Springs. "It is renewed evidence on his part of a strong desire to see me, which puts up the responsibility to me very strongly for my answer. I feel very strongly that I should grant the request and so does Rogers and everybody else I have talked with. I told him I could not do so until the President gets back. When he does, I hope he will be more cheerful and rested than he was on Friday; and I shall then put it up to him very strongly, for it is to me incomprehensible that we should take a position which would deprive the incoming President of the United States of important information about foreign affairs, which he wishes apparently to get from me. . . . I can see countless matters in which it will be important for me to have an interview with him in regard to such matters as Manchuria, the conferences and situations in Europe, about which I personally know so much and he so little, that I think it is most important for the United States and her foreign policy during the next four years that we should give this man as fair a chance as possible. It would be the very narrowest and worst position in the world to take to try to prevent his getting such information in order to preserve the tactical position which we have obtained from his mistake hitherto in the way in which he has sought these conferences." (Diary, December 24, 1932)

Mr. Hoover did not return to Washington until after the New Year. Meanwhile Frankfurter came down to the State Department and gave Stimson his view of Mr. Roosevelt. "It was a much more attractive picture than we have been getting from the other side," and it reinforced Stimson in his desire to meet Mr. Roosevelt's request.

On January 3 Stimson had a long talk with Mr. Hoover. "I told him that when a man in America, who had been elected the President of the United States, was going to have the welfare of our country in his hands for four years, if he lived, wanted to gain information about his job, and particularly our foreign relations, it was a very ticklish responsibility to refuse to give it to him. I said even supposing he was as bad as Hoover thought he was it was more dangerous to give him this grievance, I thought, than anything he could do in the way of treachery. In the beginning I told Hoover that I was sufficiently interested in his (Hoover's) policy to want to do anything I could to perpetuate it, and I was sufficiently interested, as he was, in the welfare of the country to do my best to try and make the next administration a success in recovery, if possible. The President thought possibly I might have some influence on him and he agreed to think it over."

And the next day the President "finally yielded and said that he was willing to have me go up there, provided that Roosevelt would ask him first. He is very doubtful about the possibility of success, but he was willing to have me try it. I told him of course I would not think of going up without him, the President, being consulted and asked. I don't want anything to be done which would seem to be putting him to one side. I told this to Frankfurter and he thought that he could handle it all right with Roosevelt." Mr. Roosevelt quickly agreed to send the necessary letter to the President and so, at long last, it was agreed that Stimson should go and see the President-elect. It would be his first meeting with Franklin Roosevelt.

On Monday, January 9, Stimson went to Hyde Park and talked for six hours with Mr. Roosevelt, "there being no others present at any time." "The Governor did everything he could to make the interview pleasant, and his hospitality was very agreeable. . . . We both spoke with the utmost freedom and informality." The two men talked about every major aspect of current foreign policy, and on balance Stimson found that they were in very substantial agreement, although Mr. Roosevelt seemed rather to underestimate the difficulties involved in disarmament, war debts, and the coming world economic conference. The most important point to Stimson was Mr. Roosevelt's quick understanding and general approval of his Manchurian policy. Stimson warned him that the League was approaching a final judgment and that the outgoing administration might have to make a further statement; Mr. Roosevelt promptly agreed and promised that he would do nothing to weaken Stimson's stand. The following week the President-elect went even farther in a public statement in support of the administration's Far Eastern policy. "It was a very good and timely statement and made me feel better than I have for a long time." (Diary, January 17, 1933) In a second meeting in Washington on January 19 Mr. Roosevelt remarked "that 'We are getting so that we do pretty good teamwork, don't we?' I laughed and said 'Yes.' "

And the new relationship between Mr. Roosevelt and Stimson opened the way to new discussions of the problem of war debts. Stimson now found himself acting as Mr. Hoover's liaison officer with Mr. Roosevelt. It proved possible to bring Mr. Hoover and Mr. Roosevelt together again at the White House and an agreement was reached on the procedure to be followed in opening discussions with the British. The discussion showed Mr. Roosevelt's continued belief in his own powers of personal negotiation and Stimson once more felt that the outgoing administration had far more understanding of the problem than Mr. Roosevelt and his leading adviser, Moley. But at least a joint press communiqué was agreed on, and Stimson was also authorized to open the way for Mr. Roosevelt's personal discussion with the British. From the day of this meeting the initiative passed to the man who alone could carry it through, and Stimson confined himself to the dual task of facilitating Mr. Roosevelt's discussion with Sir Ronald Lindsay and conducting necessary State Department action on the debts in such a way as not to embarrass the incoming President. This was a ticklish task, for Mr. Hoover was preoccupied with the task of defending and reinforcing his own record on debts, and the defense of one policy was not easy to reconcile with the beginning of a somewhat different one.

Through the remainder of January and well into February Stimson was in touch with Mr. Roosevelt as occasion demanded. The President-elect was punctilious in securing State Department approval before he undertook any meetings with foreign diplomats. Meanwhile Stimson began to wonder when Mr. Roosevelt would get around to choosing his successor so that detailed arrangements could be made for a smooth transition. In a telephone talk on February 3 he pressed this question with Mr. Roosevelt, urging that without prompt announcement of "the people that we should deal with" it would be hard to get things straight before March 4, and that it would be asking a good deal to expect the outgoing officials to stay very long after that date. Mr. Roosevelt saw the point, but on February 20 he still had not announced his choice of a Secretary of State, although rumors were becoming active and accurate, as Stimson pointed out in a conversation with Mr. Roosevelt on that day; "I then told him that everybody else seemed to know that Hull had been appointed Secretary of State except myself." The President-elect said that Hull was indeed his choice, and two days later the appointment was announced.

The day Cordell Hull's appointment was announced Stimson wrote him a letter of congratulation and received a most cordial reply. Three days later Senator Hull came to the Department and the two men had the first of a regular series of increasingly friendly meetings which lasted without any break in mutual regard for the next twelve years, until age and health separated them. Stimson was at first a little fearful that Hull might be too gentle and slow to be master in his own house under a President who clearly intended to keep a personal eye on foreign affairs. This was an opinion which he thoroughly revised in later years. Hull had his troubles with President Roosevelt—as which of those who worked for that extraordinary man did not?—but Stimson knew him and honored him as a distinguished Secretary of State in a time far more difficult than even the trying years of 1931 and 1932.

In this first talk and others extending through March 8, Stimson and Hull discussed at length all the current problems of the State Department. On no point was there important disagreement, and Stimson was particularly pleased by his successor's evident approval of his Far Eastern policy and his clear intention to support and advance the career officers of the Department.

Thus the big job which Stimson had seen ahead on November 9 seemed fairly well in hand as March 4 approached. And he had established friendly personal relations with the two men who would now be primarily responsible for American foreign affairs. It was a good ending.

In other ways, too, his term was ending well. The press and the public seemed to feel more kindly toward him now than at any time before; the reporters in Washington who had found him chilly and unhelpful in 1929 and 1930 now seemed to feel that he was a fairly decent fellow, and their warmth was the more gratifying because it was unaccustomed. Within the State Department Stimson felt that he was leaving not just faithful assistants but a number of personal friends, and among his chief associates, the men who would be leaving office with him, he had added, in Rogers and Bundy, two new and dear friends. It was quite without any regret, and with a real sense of satisfaction, therefore, that he made ready for his exit.

It was only as he considered the approaching change in the White House that he felt nervous. He had now met Mr. Roosevelt and found him both quick and friendly; he believed further that foreign affairs were safe in his hands. But it was not so clear that all would go well in domestic matters. Mr. Roosevelt had some strange advisers, and his way of doing business had already struck Stimson as "slapdash." Nor had his co-operation in foreign affairs been matched in the far more urgent and dangerous matter of the banking crisis. Stimson heard that some of Mr. Roosevelt's friends were deliberately planning to let the crisis become even more acute until after the inauguration.

As he looked from Franklin Roosevelt to Herbert Hoover in March, 1933, therefore, Stimson found himself unhappy over the approaching change. He was also sorry to see his relationship with Mr. Hoover coming to an end. He had had serious differences with the President, but never any reason to regret his service under a man whose burden had been much greater than his own. On March 2 Stimson stopped at the

White House to have "a word or two of good-by," knowing that he would probably not have the chance in the last crowded hours. He told Mr. Hoover, "I was getting the jitters whenever I thought of how I should feel when I saw the last of him disappearing out of sight on his way to California. . . . I told him that I hoped that, in spite of the fact that we had scrapped a good deal on some points, he did not feel that I did not thoroughly trust him and have confidence in him. He smiled and said that he had been a pretty hard man to deal with these last two years; that he had the jitters himself. We had a nice, frank, confidential talk. I came away feeling as I always do when I have such a talk with him."

On Inauguration Day Stimson went through the usual ceremonies. By afternoon he was out of office and a free man. In the evening he and Mrs. Stimson went out to dinner with their closest State Department friends and associates in a farewell party, and "we had really the best time we have had in Washington. . . . After dinner we talked a little about the crisis but not very long and then when the ladies came down we gathered around the piano and had singing until after midnight . . . the spirit was perfectly lovely and we enjoyed it more than anything that had happened to us here."

CHAPTER XII

Toward General War

I. CITIZEN AND OBSERVER

IN STIMSON'S private life the years from 1933 to 1940 were uneventful. During the first two years after leaving the State Department he returned to his law office in New York but continued to spend part of the winters in Washington at Woodley. Generally speaking, it was a period at first of rest and then of resumed private labor. The first year was not strenuous. In 1935 and 1936 he was occupied in the preparation of *The Far Eastern Crisis.* In 1937 he was elected to serve for two years as president of the New York Bar Association. From 1938 until he was called back to Washington in 1940 he was occupied with the largest single law case of his career. Almost every summer he and Mrs. Stimson went to Scotland, passing through England on their way and thus keeping closely in touch with the current of English opinion. This current was somewhat discouraging, but Stimson persisted in his deep conviction that Great Britain and the United States must reconstruct the understanding which had been damaged first by the Manchurian affair and second by the war debt question.

During the years that he spent in Washington, Stimson was several times a visitor at the White House. He later became a strong opponent of the New Deal, but in the earlier years he found Mr. Roosevelt always willing to hear his views and criticisms in friendly fashion.

Stimson found Mr. Roosevelt's basic view of foreign affairs the same as his own He approved of the President's recognition of Russia and of his policy of building up the fleet; he felt that both were useful complements to the continued firmness of the American stand in the Far East. He found that Mr. Roosevelt was sympathetic to his views on the Philippines. If the President perhaps did not share Stimson's special enthusiasm for a development toward dominion government, he was nevertheless clearly opposed to any irresponsible and faithless abandonment of the Islands, and his weight was always thrown against the effort to strangle Philippine trade with the United States.

With Secretary Hull, Stimson also had regular meetings. He found himself unexpectedly drawn in as a friend and counselor to the new Secretary in the summer of 1933 at the London Economic Conference. When Stimson arrived in London on vacation, this meeting had just been severely affected by one of Mr. Roosevelt's sudden and casual shifts in attitude. Both the tone of his notorious message of July 3 and the operations of his personal diplomat Raymond Moley served to make Secretary Hull's task vastly more difficult. The atmosphere of diplomatic London was sizzling when Stimson arrived, and it was with some difficulty that he held aloof from the charges and countercharges that were privately circulated by very high personages in Great Britain after this affair.

Early in 1934 Stimson had his chance to strike a blow for Hull's dearest policy, and at the same time to give support to a principle which was important to him. For over forty years, since the time in 1892 when he voted for Grover Cleveland, Stimson had been at heart a low-tariff man. His views were by no means radical; he believed that to a certain degree tariff protection was probably a necessary adjunct to the high standard of American living. At the same time he was convinced that by the exigencies of congressional tariff making the American tariff had become a hodgepodge of excessive rates designed mainly to protect inefficient and wholly uneconomic industries. And after his experiences in the State Department he was, emotionally, a stern enemy of the whole concept of economic isolation which lay behind the pressure for higher tariffs. Granting that free trade in the classical sense was no longer possible in an era of managed currency, government controls, and rigid economies, he nevertheless believed that for the

United States, a creditor nation, greater imports were an imperative necessity. Whatever might have been the earlier wisdom of high tariffs, and whatever might be right for other nations, the American tariff must now come down. In the year after leaving the State Department Stimson had occasion to give close attention to the tariff problem. He was particularly impressed by a little book from the pen of Henry Wallace called *America Must Choose* in which the Secretary of Agriculture argued with force and clarity for lower tariffs to permit greater agricultural exports. So in April, 1934, when the first Reciprocal Trade Agreement Bill was before the Senate, Stimson was eager to help, and on receiving Hull's assurance that his support was welcome, he made a radio speech strongly supporting this Democratic measure.

The main argument of this speech was simply for increased foreign trade. Stimson drew on Wallace's book for his contention that without a healthy foreign trade the United States must slip toward a controlled economy. "Mr. Wallace frankly points out the dangers and difficulties which will lie before us if we adopt the former course—the compulsory government control of production and marketing . . .; the suppression of our hereditary initiative and love of freedom; and, worst of all, the stifling of individual free thought and speech which is a necessary accompaniment of the process if we carry national planning to its full conclusion. I am very glad that he frankly announces his own distaste and opposition to such a process and that he evidently believes that we should try as far as possible to follow the other course—that of trying to restore our international trade."[1]

The speech continued with a description of the increasing restrictions placed on foreign trade by foreign nations and then took a course directly in line with Stimson's whole philosophy of government: The power to meet the situation must be given to the Executive. The proposed bill would in effect give to the President authority to make limited changes in the American tariff. "I think that some such legislation should be promptly passed to meet the emergency which confronts us.

[1] Radio address, April 29, 1934.

I am not impressed with the objection that it would give undue or dictatorial powers to our Executive."

Carefully hedged as it was, this speech was not in its direct statement a low-tariff document. In its political effect, however, it was exactly that, as the reaction of its audience demonstrated. Stimson was surprised and pleased with its reception, which was friendly in all quarters but one. "I took a little care of the publicity and it went off with a pretty good bang. The *Times* and *Tribune* [of New York] printed it in full and it obtained great publicity all over the country. The Republicans on the whole were very angry of course for it contravened their rather stupid policy of indiscriminate opposition. This was a time when an opportunity was presented to assist the policy of the conservative advisers of the President and to oppose that of the radicals, and I felt that it was very important to take it. . . . I received a great many letters of commendation and almost no public criticism. . . . Of course Hull and the members of the Department were thoroughly delighted and Hull again and again thanked me for it. The President himself told me that he thought I was the chief influence in securing the probable passage of the bill." (Diary, May 18, 1934) Mr. Roosevelt was not a man who ever sacrificed his friendly feelings to strict accuracy, and Stimson never believed himself the father, or even the midwife, of the Trade Agreements Act. But he was always glad that he had done what he could to help.

Through the succeeding years he became more and more convinced that the path on which Cordell Hull set out in 1934 was the only one which gave any promise of a stable foreign commerce in a prosperous America; tariff reduction, with or without equivalent concessions from other nations, was the only sensible course for the United States.

In 1936 the Republican insistence on a high tariff so disgusted him that in spite of his growing disapproval of the New Deal he took no active part whatever in the campaign. In 1947, when the Republicans in Congress once more demonstrated their continued subservience to the selfish pressure groups which produce tariff barriers, he was more angry still, for the Second World War and its aftermath had made the economic impossibility and blind folly of such a program more evident than ever. He did not know when his party—and many Democrats too—would understand that America must learn to like heavy imports, but he was certain that the longer their ignorance continued, the more painful the resulting lesson would be.

Whatever else it did, Stimson's advocacy of the Trade Agreements Act endeared him to Mr. Roosevelt. A few weeks after making his speech he was called to the White House for lunch, and he had a talk with the President which lasted an hour and a half and was the friendliest he had ever had. It was at this meeting that he discovered how closely Mr. Roosevelt's view of Japan coincided with his own, and he heard from the President an extraordinary but impressive tale of the long-term ambitions of the Japanese as they had been explained to young Franklin Roosevelt by a Japanese friend at Harvard in 1902. "This young Japanese boy had told him of the making in 1889 of the one-hundred-year Japanese plan for the Japanese dynasty, which involved the following steps in the following order:

"1. An official war with China to show that they could fight and could beat China.

"2. The absorption of Korea.

"3. A defensive war against Russia.

"4. The taking of Manchuria.

"5. Taking of Jehol.

"6. The establishment of a virtual protectorate over northern China from the Wall to the Yangtze.

"7. Encircling movement in Mongolia and the establishment of the Japanese influence through instructors as far as Tibet, thus establishing a precautionary threat against Russia on one side and India on the other.

"8. The acquisition of all the islands of the Pacific including Hawaii.

"9. Eventually the acquisition of Australia and New Zealand.

"10. Establishment of Japanese—(using a word indicating a rather fatherly control, which the President said he could not quite remember) over all of the yellow races, including the Malays. In this way the young man said they would have a definite point of threat against Europe.

"When young Roosevelt asked him what they were going to do to the United States, he said that the United States need not have any fear; that all they would do in the new hemisphere would be to establish outposts, one probably in Mexico and another perhaps in Peru; otherwise they would leave us alone. But we must remember that they were a temperate zone people and they must have Australia and New Zealand to expand in. The President commented in how many particulars this plan revealed to him by the young Jap, who was a high-class member of the Samurai caste in Japan, had been confirmed by subsequent events—this having been told to Roosevelt several years before the Russo-Japanese War." (Diary, May 17, 1934) Nothing that happened in the next seven years weakened the aptness of this strange and well-remembered conversation in Cambridge.

This talk with Mr. Roosevelt covered many phases of American policy, foreign and domestic; its entire tone was symbolized in a couple of sentences of mutually satisfactory reminiscence: "I reminded him that his magnanimity towards me had enabled us to work out this working relation which we had and, to explain what I meant, I recalled that I had treated him pretty roughly in 1930. He laughed and said, 'Yes, and I made an utterly unfair answer to you.' He met me fully in the spirit in which I was speaking and said that he felt that my action with him in January, 1933, had helped stave over a very difficult situation." (Diary, May 17, 1934)

Stimson and Mr. Roosevelt had one further talk later in 1934; after that they did not meet again until 1940, although they exchanged several letters. For this there were a number of reasons. One was that this later talk produced a misunderstanding, minor in itself, which for a time clouded Stimson's confidence in the President. Another, probably more important, was Stimson's growing absorption in his New York practice. A third was his increasing opposition to the trend of the New Deal. A fourth was that after 1934, bowing to the overwhelming opinion of his countrymen, Mr. Roosevelt for some years pursued a policy in foreign affairs which seemed to Stimson not sufficiently positive or active. But throughout this period Stimson never forgot that Franklin Roosevelt was a man he knew and liked, and not a bogey, and Mr. Roosevelt for his part sent regular messages of personal cordiality and friendship.

Opposition to the New Deal came naturally to Stimson. He had been a progressive in 1911, but by 1935 he was clearly a conservative, at least in the terms of the 1930's. He was not a New Deal hater; he recognized that much of the New Deal program and more of its motives were admirable. But he was against TVA as government in business; he was against the heavily unbalanced budgets as dangerous to the government's financial stability; he strongly deprecated Mr. Roosevelt's appeals to class feeling; he believed that the Wagner Act was a wholly unbalanced and unfair piece of legislation.

But the one undertaking of the New Deal which aroused him to open and immediate opposition was the Supreme Court Bill of 1937. This he denounced early and vigorously, and he actively participated in the effort which defeated it. In 1935 when the NRA was invalidated and Mr. Roosevelt made his famous remark about the Court and the horse-and-buggy age, Stimson had written him a long and careful letter combining sympathy with a warning against any head-on attack on the Court. He had received in return a most friendly answer, in which Mr. Roosevelt said that the truth was probably halfway between them. The administration's effort in 1937, however, was neither temperate nor intelligent, and in Stimson's view it was a direct assault on the Constitution. He believed that Mr. Roosevelt had no real or justifiable grievance against the Court; he was absolutely certain that the President's way of seeking redress was wholly wrong. His attitude is perhaps best expressed not in his public statements but in a diary entry of a conversation with Hull, whom he continued throughout the period to see at regular intervals: "Before I left I told him very frankly of my shock at the President's Supreme Court proposal. I reminded him that I had supported his work throughout even at the cost of differing from my party and that I had also tried to assist the President when he had asked me in foreign affairs, to all of which Mr. Hull assented. When I said, 'But I cannot tell you how shocked I have been at recent events,' a look of pain came over his face; he raised his hands in deprecation and said, 'I understand, I understand. You mean the Supreme Court and the sitdown strikes.' I said I didn't feel so shocked at the sitdown strikes for that may be for all I know a difficult and involved matter for the government to handle and I realize that it must be difficult, but the other is a straight plain constitutional issue. I said, 'I never expected to live to see a President of the United States try to pack the Supreme Court.' I went on: 'Furthermore in this position at the beginning of the depression I watched many dictatorships come and the steps by which they came. I do not think that the President has any intention of making himself a dictator but I can only say that anyone who had such an intention would follow exactly this course.' " (Diary, April 7, 1937)

This was the high point of Stimson's opposition to the Roosevelt administration. In 1938 he argued strongly for changes in the Wagner Act; this led to his first campaign activity since 1932—he supported his old friend John Lord O'Brian against his old acquaintance Robert Wagner. In 1939, when the administration had begun to catch up with him in foreign policy, he combined his support of Mr. Roosevelt's firm stand against isolationism with a comment which accurately summarizes his general view of the New Deal:

"National strength is not promoted by an extravagance which comes dangerously near the impairment of our national credit. It is not promoted by discouraging the business welfare of the country upon which depends the economic power of the nation. It is not promoted by novel and haphazard experiments with the nation's finance. National unity is not promoted by appeals to class spirit. Nor is it promoted by methods which tend to disrupt the patriotism of either party or the effective co-operation of the two, upon which the co-ordinate working of the American Government depends."[2]

But the tariff, the New Deal, the law, and even the delights of private life were all secondary, in these seven years, to Stimson's constant and intense concern with international political affairs. This was the subject on which he wrote and

[2] Letter to the New York *Times*, March 6, 1939.

spoke most often, the subject on which he constantly sought expert opinion, the subject on which he was most disturbed about the attitude of his countrymen, and, in the end, the subject whose unrolling course returned him to public life.

2. 1933-1940—CAST AS CASSANDRA

The Second World War casts a long shadow backward over the history of the years before its outbreak, and in writing of Stimson's service as Secretary of State from the vantage point of 1947 it has seemed proper to focus attention on those events and actions which now appear as natural forerunners of war. In any retrospective view it is clear that two of the great turning points of the years between wars were the invasion of Manchuria by Japan and the accession of Adolf Hitler. Stimson's connection with both these events has been described, and the description has been set in the dark colors appropriate to the occasion. The failure was evident at the time, and profoundly depressing.

What was not evident—and this point must here be emphasized—was the degree and extent of the failure. There was no sense of general frustration in Stimson's mind as he left the State Department and no certain foreboding of inevitable war. He had no foreknowledge of the series of additional errors and failures which were to bring not merely war but imminent danger of the overthrow of Western civilization. Nor did he at first fully appreciate the diabolical intensity of the forces set free in the new Germany and the new Japan.

It thus happened that in writing of his experience as Secretary of State, and trying to assess the future, between 1933 and 1936, Stimson permitted himself a cautious optimism which was not borne out by events. Both the optimism and the unfulfilled conditions on which it was based deserve attention.

The central effort of Stimson's service as Secretary of State had been to break down the barriers to American co-operation with the rest of the world. "I believe," he wrote in his last weeks in office, "that important foundations of progress have been laid, upon which it will be possible for an enduring structure to be erected by the labors of our successors."[3] His political co-operation with the League, his principle of consultation in the face of a breach of the peace, his earnest effort to mobilize and enforce the sanction of public opinion, feeble though they might seem in contemplation of the great world war which followed, did not seem weak to him, and he was sure that they represented a step in the right direction.

Similarly he believed and repeatedly argued that the League of Nations had been astonishingly successful in view of the difficulties it had faced. Granted that it had not guaranteed peace, it was at least an agency with the proper machinery for such a guarantee, and it had provided the enduring forum and meeting ground the absence of which Sir Edward Grey had considered a primary cause of war in 1914. Granted that it had not applied against Japan the machinery of economic sanctions with which it was provided, it was at least promoting "to a high degree" the "growth and organization of an intelligent public opinion of the world," which was clearly the "first step in developing the machinery of war prevention." Writing in 1934 Stimson argued that "lack of sympathy and cynicism of attitude" toward such efforts would be inexcusable. And the lectures from which those quotations are taken were frankly designed to "offset the pessimism, not to say panic, which we have so commonly expressed as to recent occurrences in Central Europe."[4]

For Stimson greatly underestimated the Nazis during their first three years in power. He did not believe that Hitler would last—after the purge of June 30, 1934, he expressed the view that "Nazism in Germany was on the toboggan" (Diary, July 24, 1934)—and throughout this period he was convinced that economics forbade the persistence of a rearming dictatorship, sharing the view so widely held that Germany's dependence for economic well-being on other nations "offers a fairly safe guarantee against unrestrained violence against her neighbors on the part of Germany."[5]

A somewhat similar hopefulness characterized Stimson's

[3] *Foreign Affairs*, April, 1933.
[4] *Democracy and Nationalism*, Stafford Little Lectures at Princeton University, Princeton, 1934.
[5] *Democracy and Nationalism*, p. 42.

thinking about Japan in this period. Although Manchuria was still occupied, and Japanese tentacles were already reaching out toward other parts of China, he did not believe that either Japan or Germany was wholly lost to liberalism and continued to hope that the passage of time and the continuing pressure of world opinion would bring reversals of the trend in both countries.

These, then, were Stimson's hopes in the first years after his service as Secretary of State. To some degree, it seems clear, they were based on a serious misreading of the strength and menace of modern militaristic dictatorship. But in far greater measure Stimson's error in foresight was due to his failure to anticipate the extraordinary weakness and cowardice which were to be displayed by all the nonaggressive nations, his own included, in dealing with the rise of aggressive states. When he foretold the speedy collapse of Hitlerism, it did not occur to him that Western statesmen would actively connive at the penetration and destruction of one nation after another, and when he hoped for a victory of moderation in Japan, he did not anticipate that his own countrymen would for three years assist in nourishing the Japanese war machine. As these failures became apparent, and particularly as it became clear that the American people were shifting their course toward an isolationism more binding and complete than ever before, Stimson ceased to be a cautious optimist and assumed instead the unhappy and temperamentally ill-fitting role of Cassandra.

The five years of Anglo-French folly which preceded the outbreak of war in September, 1939, need not here be discussed. Stimson watched the course of events, from the betrayal of Ethiopia through the absurd "nonintervention" in Spain, on to the final moral abdication at Munich, in mounting apprehension and dismay, but he spoke no word of these views in public; he agreed with a friend in October, 1938, "in feeling (as Americans whose country would not help out in the situation) a great disinclination to criticize those who had the responsibility." (Diary, October 24, 1938) His public statements and personal efforts were directed toward his own countrymen, in an effort first to stem and then to reverse a rising tide of isolationism. This he undertook in a series of speeches and statements beginning in 1935, in which he steadily developed his basic assertion that the nation could not successfully—or peacefully—set the pursuit of peace ahead of the pursuit of righteousness. In these speeches and statements was Stimson's stand against the danger he had warned of even in his deliberately optimistic assessment of April, 1934, in the last paragraph of the last lecture: "The United States is in its ultimate resources the world's most powerful nation today. It is the nation most safely protected from outside aggression by its geographical position. Its people have taken historic pride in their championships of peace and justice. We are the people, therefore, who can most easily and safely give sympathy, encouragement and help to the world in its vital struggle to protect our common civilization against war. On the other hand, should we refuse to assume even that measure of responsibility, should we insist upon our government retiring into isolation and turning its back upon all efforts for peace in other portions of the world, we must face the fact that the peace machinery will be infinitely weakened and that mankind will be periodically faced with wars which may be as disastrous to us and to our own civilization as to that of the rest of the world."[6] We have seen that in 1931 and 1932 the diplomacy of America was, in all conscience, quite sufficiently hamstrung by American isolationism. In the years from 1935 to 1939 Stimson was forced to watch a demonstration of still greater and more damaging folly. But he did not watch in silence.

In the early 1930's many Americans were persuaded by a new school of writers that in 1917 they had gone to war not because of unrestricted submarine warfare, and still less because Imperial Germany threatened the world's freedom, but because of the munitions makers, the bankers, and the sly propagandists of England and France. In these years still more Americans became convinced by the same writers that, whatever the reason for American participation in the First World War, it had been a ghastly mistake; in a reaction against the uncritical idealism with which they had at first draped their cru-

[6] *Democracy and Nationalism*, p. 86.

sade, the American people turned to an attitude of blanket repudiation of all war for any purpose. This was the time in which men who a few years later would be doing manful service in the great effort to arouse the country to a clear and present danger were too often found among those who had helped forge the chains of a neutrality designed to keep the country out of the First World War—and most imperfectly designed at that.

The first result of the new attitude was a changed view of neutrality; in the belief that it was trade with belligerents which had dragged America into the earlier war, Congress undertook to legislate a prohibition on such trade. The first such legislation was passed in the summer of 1935; it was renewed and extended in 1936 and 1937; it still remained in force in 1939 when war came. Stimson's opposition began before the first joint resolution was passed, and increased in vigor and outspokenness as the menace of aggression steadily grew.

On April 25, 1935, he discussed the concept of neutrality before the American Society of International Law. He repudiated both the traditional neutrality which would trade with all belligerents and the new "isolation" which would trade with none. He argued that war itself was the central evil, and that once "a serious war" had begun, the United States would suffer heavily whether it went in or not. "It is more important to prevent war anywhere than to steer our course after war has come"; "manifestly war can only be prevented by co-operation"; "there is no place of human activities where the maxim 'an ounce of prevention is worth a pound of cure' is so true as it is in the realm of international relations." And finally, "Neutrality offers no certain road for keeping out of war. The only certain way to keep out of a great war is to prevent that war from taking place, and the only hope of preventing war or even seriously restricting it is by the earnest, intelligent, and unselfish co-operation of the nations of the world toward that end. Until America is willing with sympathy and intelligence to do her part in such an endeavor, the life of our whole modern civilization may be at the mercy of the next war."

It will bring into relief the degree to which American

opinion had hardened, ever since 1933, if we note that the positive acts of co-operation for which Stimson argued in this speech were no more than a restatement of his own doctrine of consultation, set forth in August, 1932, and of the assurance given by Norman Davis at Geneva in 1933 that the United States would do nothing to interfere with collective action by the League of Nations against a nation which Americans agreed was aggressive. No such restatement of executive policy was forthcoming, either at this time or for nearly four years afterward. The Davis statement had been the highest point of American postwar co-operation; it was not favorably received in Congress, and until late in 1938 the President and Secretary Hull, whatever their private sentiments, felt unable to play any part in the European struggle for collective security.

Later in 1935, when Italy invaded Ethiopia, Stimson was reluctantly driven to a direct appeal for more energetic Presidential leadership. Contemplating this colonial war of aggression, Congress had passed a "Neutrality Act" which required an embargo on the export of arms to declared belligerents. It at once became apparent, in Stimson's view, that the attempt to legislate peace was a clumsy failure. In this case, as he pointed out in a letter to the New York *Times* and a radio broadcast, the failure lay mainly in the narrowness of the legislation, which gave the President no power to prevent the shipment of oil and other munitions. The United States thus lacked authority for effective co-operation with the League powers in their attempt to impose economic sanctions.

But Stimson's main argument this time was addressed to the Chief Executive. He pointed out that not a word had been said by the administration as to the issues here involved— the moral issue between an aggressor and its victim, the political issue between collective security and international anarchy. Here Stimson saw a clear duty of leadership; he believed that if the President should make his appeal on basic moral and political grounds he would be able to enforce a general voluntary trade embargo against Italy. "The public opinion of America is not indifferent to moral issues. The great masses of our countrymen do not wish to drift into a position of blocking the efforts of other nations to stamp out war. The

only person who can effectively rouse and marshal moral opinion is the President of the United States, and when he tries
to do so I have no doubt of his eventual success. The most
adventurous of our traders would promptly realize the folly
of expecting protection in their dangerous adventure if the
Commander in Chief of our American Army and Navy made
clear to them the implications of this war. Such an announcement from America would by its encouragement of the earnest
efforts of the nations of the world in their struggle for peace
go a long distance toward insuring the eventual success of that
struggle."[7]

Stimson's next attack on the prevailing attitude was delivered in October, 1937, when Japan began her war in China.
The Japanese, he argued, were encouraged by events in the
rest of the world. "The Fascist dictators of Italy and Germany
have boldly and successfully carried through coups invoking in
Ethiopia, the Rhineland, and Spain acts of treaty violation
and indefensible aggression. On the other hand, the peaceful
democracies of the world . . . have yielded to these lawless
acts of the dictators with a lack of their customary spirit. . . .
In America, occupying the most safe and defensible position
in the world, there has been no excuse except faulty reasoning
for the wave of ostrich-like isolationism which has swept over
us and by its erroneous form of neutrality legislation has
threatened to bring upon us in the future the very dangers of
war which we now are seeking to avoid."[8]

The Japanese attack, he continued, raised questions of the
most urgent character, and after a careful disclaimer of any
intent to make more difficult the trying task of the State Department, he gave his general view of the proper American
course. Granting that American military action in Asia was
probably "impossible" and certainly "abhorrent to our people," and insisting, as he always had and would, that the final
destiny of China must depend on China herself, he nevertheless argued that the United States was not bound to "a passive
and shameful acquiescence in the wrong that is now being
done." For a simple weapon of great strength was ready at

[7] Address delivered over the Columbia Broadcasting System, October 23, 1935.
[8] Letter to the New York *Times*, October 6, 1937.

hand, and in language as diplomatic as it was clear Stimson came out flatly in favor of a trade embargo against Japan, pointing out her complete dependence on the American and British markets, particularly the former. His position was set forth in paragraphs that stated his basic attitude on aggression with the clarity which was now permitted to him as a private citizen.

"The present situation brings out . . . the deep-seated error which has pervaded recent American thinking on international matters. I have heard Theodore Roosevelt say that he put peace above everything except righteousness. Where the two came into conflict he supported righteousness. In our recent efforts to avoid war we have reversed this principle and are trying to put peace above righteousness. We have thereby gone far toward killing the influence of our country in the progress of the world. At the same time, instead of protecting, we have endangered our own peace.

"Our recent neutrality legislation attempts to impose a dead level of neutral conduct on the part of our Government between right and wrong, between an aggressor and its victim, between a breaker of the law of nations and the nations who are endeavoring to uphold the law. It won't work. Such a policy of amoral drift by such a safe and powerful nation as our own will only set back the hands of progress. It will not save us from entanglement. It will even make entanglement more certain. History has already amply shown this last fact."

If the Japanese wished to fight a nation which acted by economic measures to obstruct aggression, Stimson was prepared to face the consequences. But he expected no such result, in 1937.

The proposal of an embargo fell on ears not less deaf than those of the Hoover administration had been in 1932 and 1933. Only the day before Stimson's letter Mr. Roosevelt had delivered his famous Chicago speech denouncing the peace-breakers and intimating his belief in a "quarantine" of aggressors. From this speech Stimson at once took hope, but in the months that followed Mr. Roosevelt seemed to conclude that the country was not ready for strong medicine, and the speech remained an isolated episode in a continuing pattern of inaction.

In Congress, indeed, the legislative peacemaking of the ostrich era was capped by the attempt at the turn of the year to enact the so-called "Ludlow Resolution for a National Referendum on a Declaration of War," under which any declaration of war, except in reply to a direct attack, would have had to be subjected to a national referendum before it could be executed. This remarkable proposal seemed to Stimson a final blow at the authority and discretion of the Government in foreign affairs, and he wrote a full and detailed analysis of its failings in a letter published by the New York *Times* on December 21, 1937. This was to him a congressional abdication of all responsibility for foreign affairs; in addition it would certainly strike all aggressors and potential aggressors as a further demonstration that American foreign policy was in the end dependent on a political campaign. The Ludlow Resolution never passed, but at one time it seemed very likely to succeed. For Stimson this was the high point in the prewar self-deception of the American people.

In 1938, Stimson made no major public statement on foreign affairs. His stand was clear, and in any case he was heavily occupied in the largest single lawsuit of his career. He was equally busy in the following year, but the pressure and tempo of events was such that he felt driven to put aside his law three times in the first four months of 1939.

His first statement was on the war in Spain. It was a closely reasoned legal argument for the enforcement of the well-established rule of international law that 'we should furnish arms to the government that had been recognized as legal, and to no other.' In the case of Spain this was the Loyalist government. This was a statement which Stimson was sorry he had not made sooner. He had made no secret of his sympathy with the Loyalist side, but he had held back from direct opposition to the policy of the administration. By January, 1939, it was too late for any statement to be of much use, for the Republican government was at last being overcome by the superior force of fascist intervention. Stimson was not a left-winger, but he believed and repeatedly argued that "the Fascist was incomparably more dangerous to us; more active in their proselytizing, more outrageous and intolerant of international law and methods." And of course, in the case of Spain, it remained a clear and simple fact that the Republicans were the legal and elected government, recognized as such by the United States; nor were the Spanish Loyalists in any sense a purely communist government.

In 1939 general war was imminent, and in 1939 Franklin Roosevelt began his long battle to turn the American people toward the enemy. In March and April of that year Stimson delivered two statements in support of the President's campaign to bring pressure against aggression by methods "short of war, but stronger and more effective than mere words." One was an appeal for modification of the Neutrality Act. The arguments Stimson used in this statement were similar to those already discussed. The other was a letter to the *Times* in which Stimson developed for the first time the basic conviction which dominated his thinking for the next six years.

By now he had long since discarded his hope of 1934 that the Nazi revolution might break down of its own weight. It was clear that Hitler had been permitted to gain strength and pass from one success to another until, in company with his Italian and Japanese colleagues, he represented an overwhelming threat to Western civilization. This letter called in effect for a direct military understanding among the United States, Great Britain, and France, for use in the event of war; Stimson also paid his respects to the faint remaining hope of peace by urging that if anything could stop the Nazis, it would be the spectacle of united and determined democratic opposition. But the heart of the letter is its statement of the basic issues; this was the foundation of belief on which Stimson's whole course of action in the following years was based:

"Fascism . . . is a radical attempt to reverse entirely the long evolution out of which our democracies of Europe and America have grown, and . . . it constitutes probably the most serious attack on their underlying principles which those principles have ever met.

"We know now that the inhabitants of those countries from childhood up, by means of meticulous and absolute government control and by the skillful use of modern engines and methods of mass propaganda, are being taught to reject freedom; to scorn the principles of government by discussion and persuasion instead of force, and to despise the neighboring nations which practice such principles. We now know that those fascist nations have created a skillful technique for foreign aggression and that they are in fact girded under virtual martial law for threats and, if necessary, for acts of force upon their neighbors. . . .

"Furthermore, fascism has involved a serious moral deterioration; an increasing and callous disregard of the most formal and explicit international obligations and pledges; extreme brutality toward helpless groups of people; the complete destruction within their jurisdiction of that individual freedom of speech, of thought, and of the person which has been the priceless goal of many centuries of struggle and the most distinctive crown of our modern civilization. . . .

"It strongly suggests that in our modern interdependent world Lincoln's saying holds true, that a house so divided against itself cannot permanently stand. Today the neighbors of a fascist nation are compelled to live in anticipation of immediate forceful attack. Such a situation is obviously the reversal of all civilized international society as we have known it in the past. . . .

"There is a flood of reaction and violence overrunning the world today. Our faith is that this is temporary; that the great progress of many long centuries will not be permanently lost but that after the social and economic dislocations caused by the Great War are readjusted the progress in freedom and in the humanities will be resumed. In the meanwhile and until the present violence has spent its force that flood must be held back from overwhelming us. . . . .

"I am unalterably opposed to the doctrine preached in many quarters that our Government and our people must treat the nations on both sides of this great issue with perfect impartiality; that, for example, we must sell to a nation which has violated its treaties with us as well as trampled upon the humanities of our civilization the very instruments with which to continue its wrongdoing quite as freely as we sell to its victim the instruments for its self-defense.

"I am opposed to such doctrine because I am confident that we are confronting an organized attack upon the very basis of our civilization and because I know that this civilization was only achieved by the development of what we call law and the humanities; by the respect for justice and fair play to all men; by the principle of the sovereignty of reason rather than force and by the Christian principle of the equal value of all human personalities.

"Such a civilization can only be preserved if we keep alive in our people their faith in these underlying principles. And I see no surer way of destroying their faith than by teaching them that in such a conflict as is now going on in the world neither they nor their government shall discriminate between right and wrong, between an aggressor and his victim, between an upholder of law and a violator thereof. . . .

"We cannot ignore the fact that at almost any moment an armed attack may be aimed by the fascist group of powers against the vital safety of one of the two peace-loving nations upon which today rests in large part the safety of our own civilization—Great Britain and France.

"Such an attack would almost inevitably involve both of those nations and from present appearances would be co-operated in by all three of the fascist powers. In that event only one course could be depended on ultimately to save the present hard-earned civilization upon which our own national welfare rests."[9]

Thus in 1939 Stimson foresaw that if war came it would become the duty of America to prevent a fascist victory. How much that duty would require, and how deeply he himself would be concerned with it, he had of course no way of knowing.

Meanwhile the year wore on from spring to summer, and in Europe the air grew tense with impending crisis. Stimson canceled his plans for a European vacation. In August the German dictator brought off his deal with Moscow, and as August turned to September the Second World War began.

The coming of war in 1939, not for the first or last time in Stimson's life, was a relief. It seemed to mark the end of the hopeless years of concession and appeasement. He shared the

[9] Letter to New York *Times*, March 6, 1939.

prevailing opinion of the Western democratic world, that Britain and France would win their war. His confidence in the French Army was strong, and he approved the strategy of delay and attrition that was adopted by the Allies in the first months after the conquest of Poland. He was deeply angered by talk of a "phony" war.

This misplaced confidence did not blind him to the great issues that still hung in the balance, and he lent his weight to the administration in the fight to repeal the arms embargo, in September and October. His position was best stated in a radio speech of October 5. The embargo legislation had been a wanton encouragement of aggression; its repeal would be morally and materially a forward step. Britain and France were fighting our battle, and any help to them was the best way of avoiding war in the future. Thus far it was much the same argument that others used, but we may note that Stimson denied that the central issue was "how to keep the United States out of war." The "ultimate end" was rather the safety of the nation. "A time might well come when the only way to preserve the security of the people of the United States would be to fight for that security."

Through the winter of 1939-1940 Stimson, with the rest of the world, watched and waited. Like most Americans he disapproved of the Soviet attack on Finland, and he acted as a personal liaison between Mr. Hoover and the State Department in the work of the former for Finnish relief. He continued his activity in support of an embargo against Japan, which still seemed unwise to the administration. But his mind was on the Western Front.

The explosion of Nazi power into Denmark, Norway, Belgium, Holland, Luxembourg, and France made the spring of 1940 a nightmare that none who lived through it can ever forget. It became clear that the Nazi war machine had been tragically underestimated, and it also appeared that not one of the invaded nations was as strong as had been thought. In a short ten-week period the whole aspect of the war was changed, and Great Britain was left alone, as the last outpost of freedom in Europe.

The effect in the United States was immediate. On the one

hand there developed a nearly unanimous determination to double and redouble American military strength, and enormous appropriations were hurriedly passed by Congress. On the other hand the great debate on foreign policy was renewed with greater violence than ever. Those who felt that the battle against Hitler was an American one argued that now more than ever the British needed help; their opponents reiterated the view that Europe's internecine strife was no concern of the United States.

In this atmosphere Stimson went to New Haven for the Yale Commencement of June, 1940. After addressing the alumni on the subject of compulsory military training, he retired from the Commencement celebrations to prepare a radio speech which he delivered on the following night, June 18. This speech fully set forth his principles and policies in the face of the crisis; he later felt that its delivery, putting him squarely on record before he accepted public office, was one of the most fortunate accidents of his life. As an advocate of this policy he entered the Cabinet, and his position was always well known to those who dealt with him; he was thus spared the constant pressure to trim and hedge which beset the other members of the Government.

"The United States today," he began, "faces probably the greatest crisis in its history." Civilization had developed on the basis of certain principles and "today there has come a reversal of all these principles, both international and domestic, on the part of a group of powerful governments." He restated more strongly than ever his conviction that the world was a house divided, and that a totalitarian victory would mean the end of freedom throughout the world, for individuals as for nations.

Against this background Stimson sketched his view of the existing military situation. He found "an appalling prospect." Only one force remained between the Nazis and the Western Hemisphere—the British Fleet. The British Fleet, therefore, must be sustained; if it should be lost, America, almost unarmed, must stand alone against the world. But if the British Fleet should stand unconquered, supported by American aid and reinforced by air power, which must also be based largely on American production, defeat might be prevented; the Nazis might be held. America must therefore support the British Navy, and it followed that she must support and encourage the people of Great Britain. So Stimson came to his recommendations:

"First, we should repeal the provisions of our ill-starred so-called neutrality venture which have acted as a shackle to our true interests for over five years.

"Second, we should throw open all of our ports to the British and French naval and merchant marine for all repairs and refueling and other naval services.

"Third, we should accelerate by every means in our power the sending of planes and other munitions to Britain and France[10] on a scale which would be effective; sending them if necessary in our own ships and under convoy.

"Fourth, we should refrain from being fooled by the evident bluff of Hitler's so-called fifth-column movements in South America. On the face of them, they are attempts to frighten us from sending help where it will be most effective.

"Fifth, in order to assist the home front of Britain's defense we should open our lands as a refuge for the children and old people of Britain whose liability to suffering from air raids in Great Britain is a constant inducement to surrender to terms which she would otherwise resist. [This last phrase, as Stimson later recognized, was a quite unwarranted underestimate of British courage.]

"Sixth, we should, every one of us, combat the defeatist arguments which are being made in this country as to the unconquerable power of Germany. I believe that if we use our brains and curb our prejudices we can, by keeping command of the sea, beat her again as we did in 1918.

"Finally, we should at once adopt a system of universal compulsory training and service which would not only be the most potent evidence that we are in earnest, but which is at the present moment imperative if we are to have men ready to operate the planes and other munitions, the creation of which Congress has just authorized by a practically unanimous vote.

"In these ways, and with the old American spirit of courage

[10] France did not capitulate until four days later.

and leadership behind them, I believe we should find our people ready to take their proper part in this threatened world and to carry through to victory, freedom, and reconstruction."

Short of a direct declaration of war, it would have been hard to frame a more complete program of resistance to the Nazis. And a declaration of war, then and for months thereafter, was not in Stimson's mind. It could not be, because in years of dealing with foreign affairs he had learned the necessity for pitching policy to opinion.

As it was, he had stepped well out in front of the President and most other leaders in the debate—at least ahead of their published opinions. In the newspapers the next morning he found himself on the one hand a hero and on the other a villain. But he did not have much time to consider these reactions, for on the afternoon of June 19 he received a telephone call from the White House.

PART THREE
TIME OF PERIL

CHAPTER XIII

Call to Arms

---

1. BACK TO WASHINGTON

I N HIS New York office, on June 19, 1940, Stimson received
a telephone call from the White House. "I was called up
by the President who offered me the position of Secretary of
War. He told me that Knox had already agreed to accept the
position of Secretary of the Navy. The President said he was
very anxious to have me accept because everybody was running around at loose ends in Washington and he thought I
would be a stabilizing factor in whom both the Army and the
public would have confidence." To say that Stimson was surprised would be putting it mildly. He had known that Mr.
Roosevelt was considering the appointment of one or two
Republicans and that Frank Knox was among those being
considered. Like everyone else, he knew that the Secretary of
War, Woodring, was at odds with both the President and
large parts of the Army. He did not suspect, however, that
these troubles might affect him. Some weeks before, he had
heard from Grenville Clark that his name had been suggested
for the job. Clark had coupled it with that of Judge Robert
P. Patterson as Assistant Secretary. He knew too that this
suggestion had reached the President. But that the President
should have listened to it, and acted on it, was astonishing. His
first reaction was to point out that he was approaching his
seventy-third birthday. The President said he already knew
that, and added that Stimson would be free to appoint his own
Assistant Secretary. Patterson's name was mentioned and approved by both men. Stimson then asked for a few hours in
which to consult his wife and his professional associates.

"I then discussed it with Bronson Winthrop, George Roberts [two of his partners] and Mabel. They all advised me to accept. About seven P.M. I telephoned the President and asked him three questions: (1) Whether he had seen my radio speech and whether it would be embarrassing to him. He replied that he had already read it and was in full accord with it. (2) I asked him whether he knew that I was in favor of general compulsory military service, and he said he did and gave me to understand that he was in sympathy with me. (3) I asked him whether Knox had accepted and he said he had.

"I then accepted." (Diary, June 25, 1940)

Stimson was inclined later to think this diary entry a trifle laconic; conversation with Franklin Roosevelt was seldom so stern and simple. It nevertheless contained the meat of what was said on both sides. Neither man mentioned any political aspect of the appointment. The only bargain struck on either side was an agreement that Stimson would be free to appoint Patterson as his own principal assistant. It was understood on both sides, then and later, that politics was not relevant; it was equally understood that Stimson was to be the undisputed head of his own Department. These understandings remained unbroken to the end.

The appointment of Stimson and Knox was announced on June 20, and Stimson speedily learned that he was a highly controversial figure. The chairman of the Republican National Committee read him out of the party, and Republican pique was general. The Republicans were about to begin their convention, and their minds were so firmly fixed on politics that they insisted on describing the President's maneuver as a political dodge. This was probably true, in part; Stimson was not inclined to deny that Franklin Roosevelt was a talented politician. But it did not seem to him that the Republican outburst was a skillful riposte. There was little political advantage in the repudiation of two stanch Republicans merely because in a time of crisis they had been willing to take office. In effect, the Republican outcry was a kindness to the President; it turned over to him what credit there might be in rising above party prejudice. To Stimson personally it mattered very little; few of the present spokesmen of the party

were his friends, and from those Republicans who were close
to him he had many letters of approval and congratulation.
Should this outburst mean that his party intended in the crisis
to take a generally obstructionist position, it would be a grave
disappointment, but his familiarity with the atmosphere of
conventions led him to postpone any such gloomy conclusion.
His party had been caught off balance, and some unfortunate
statements had been made; perhaps there was nothing more to
it—perhaps the sentiment of the Republican rank and file was
more accurately represented by young Harold Stassen, the
Republican keynoter, who rejected efforts to make him denounce Knox and Stimson, choosing instead to argue that the
President in his hour of need was forced to turn to the Grand
Old Party for help.

The immediate problem now was in the Senate, where his
nomination must be confirmed. On July 2 Stimson appeared
before the Committee on Military Affairs, to which his name
had been referred. This was a new experience. Four times
before his name had been submitted to the Senate, and by four
different presidents. In none of these earlier cases had his
fitness been seriously questioned. This seemed an odd time to
begin. His first reaction was one of annoyance; his second was
more pugnacious—if these people wanted to heckle him, he
would find it pleasant to hit back. His third thought, and the
controlling one, was that he must so conduct himself as not to
embarrass his new chief, while at the same time clearly stating
his understanding of the responsibility for which he had been
named.

So in his opening statement to the committee he reviewed
his position. "The purpose of our military policy is . . . to protect from attack the territory and rights of the United States.
. . . No one wishes to send American troops beyond our borders
unless the protection of the United States makes such action
absolutely necessary. On the other hand I do not believe that
the United States can be safely protected by a purely passive
or defensive defense. I do not believe that we shall be safe
from invasion if we sit down and wait for the enemy to attack
our shores."

This last point he developed in detail. He related it to the

Monroe Doctrine, and pointed out how modern warfare had forced an extension of our line of defense "far out into the Atlantic Ocean." This ocean and the bases controlling it were now gravely menaced. The menace came from potential enemies of a character unique in history. Not only were they engaged in systematic aggression, but once successful they need fear no rebellion. "Genghis Khan and Attila the Hun did not possess tanks, airplanes, or modern guns, nor could they enforce their rules on their victims by a carefully organized secret police like the Gestapo. . . . The modern conqueror, when once he gets into power, will last for a long time. . . . I feel that we are faced with an unprecedented peril."

The existence of this peril was no pleasure to Stimson; he had not conjured it up as a source of excitement for his declining years. Yet some such idea seemed to be in the minds of those who were calling him a warmonger, so he continued on a more personal note. "I am one of those many people who after the great war labored earnestly for disarmament and for the establishment among the nations of a system which should be based upon a reign of law rather than of force, and I regard it as a world tragedy that all such efforts should have resulted in failure; but the facts have to be faced today."

As a beginning in facing the facts, the President had recommended and the Congress had authorized great appropriations for increased military strength. This was a good start, but only a start. Other things than money were needed. Stimson emphasized two—time and spirit. Time could be gained only if the British fleet were sustained. Spirit could best be developed by "establishing a system of selective compulsory training and service." Such a system was in any case essential, because recruiting had already failed; but what Stimson emphasized was its value to the morale of the nation. A country in peril must be united in knowing its danger and working for its safety.

As for the New Haven speech, it had been made by a private citizen. "When you are a private citizen you can speak upon matters which are of concern to the whole Government. When you are the Secretary of War your duty is to confine yourself to preparing the national defense of the United States so that it will be ready to be used when the President and the Congress . . . say the word, and that is the extent of your duty." He was not a stranger to public office; he understood its responsibilities, and the importance of "prudence and care." Still there was nothing to be taken back in the New Haven speech; it might not fit precisely with the requirements of the moment as seen from an official position, but "everything that I have said or advocated has been said in the interest of the defense of the United States, and that alone. I have had no other motive for what I have been talking about, and it is the same one I will represent here if I am confirmed by you gentlemen as Secretary of War—the defense of the United States."

This statement of his position did not satisfy all the members of the committee. For nearly two hours they questioned him, with the extensive assistance of two Senators not members of the committee, Vandenberg and Taft. The majority of the committee were sympathetic; their few questions were simple and friendly. But a few were less gentle. Fortunately the crowd at the hearing was mainly friendly, and for Stimson it was warm work but not unpleasant.

Was he a member of Winthrop, Stimson, Putnam & Roberts? No. Well, he was listed as counsel. "That is a euphemistic term for a gentleman who sits in an office without sharing the profits." (Laughter.) Did this firm have any clients with international investments? He didn't think so, but he didn't know, because he wasn't a partner. Did he have any such clients himself? "I do not." Had he been present at a secret meeting of eighteen prominent bankers to organize the Committee to Defend America by Aiding the Allies? He had, but it was not a secret meeting; it had been held openly in one of the largest clubs in New York; not all of those present had been bankers, and the purpose of the meeting had been to meet Mr. William Allen White.

This was foolishness, but some of the questions were more serious. Stimson refused to be drawn into a discussion of his predecessor Woodring; he refused to say that he would never approve the transfer of American arms to other nations; he firmly denied that this position was the same as approval of "stripping our own defenses for the sake of trying to stop Hitler 3,000 miles away."

As for his relations to the President, of course they had had differences on domestic issues. No, this did not mean that they could not co-operate for national defense. He explained to the committee exactly how he had been appointed; the whole thing had no relation to politics. He was out of politics now. He retained his convictions, but he had a right to subordinate their expression to the paramount duty he had accepted from the President; his position was the same as that of any officer of the United States Army.

In the same way he refused to be drawn into discussion of matters that were properly the business of the President or the Secretary of State. He was unwilling to discuss the detailed present application of policies he had advocated in 1939. The more he was quoted the better his prophecies seemed, but he must repeat that the Secretary of War does not make policy in foreign affairs. "Policy is determined by other branches of the Government, and it is his duty to prepare for the troubles that may be brought about by their determinations." (Laughter.)

Senator Vandenberg was courteous and his questions were fair. Would the policies advocated in the New Haven speech amount to acts of war? Stimson refused a direct answer; he preferred to call them legitimate acts of self-defense in an emergency in which traditional concepts of neutrality no longer applied. He further pointed out that as Secretary of War these would not be his problems to decide. The Vandenberg questions were the most interesting and sensible that he was asked by any opposition Senator, however, and on his return to New York after the hearing he sent a written statement to the committee and to Senator Vandenberg pointing out that many close students of international law felt that the whole theory of neutrality vis-à-vis an aggressor had disappeared with the Kellogg-Briand Pact, so that any of the acts advocated in his New Haven speech would be fully legal under international law.

After Vandenberg came Taft; only the day before, both these gentlemen had seen their ambitions thwarted by the nomination of a dark horse to be Republican candidate for President, and Stimson allowed himself the small satisfaction of asking the chairman if he also had Wendell Willkie around. But to Taft this was no laughing matter. Neither was it to Stimson; he sought no conflict with the son of his old friend and chief, and the only regret he carried away from the hearing was that the questions put to him by Robert Taft should have been so pointedly unfriendly. Here was no effort to find out what he really thought; it was a debater's attempt to make him say things he did not mean, and it was not worthy of a son of William Taft. And the worst of it was that Senator Taft, driven by his own bitter convictions, could see no unfairness in what he was doing.

First Taft remarked that Stimson had presented a novel view of the functions of a Cabinet officer. How could he argue that his general views were not relevant to his work as Secretary of War? His views and advice, as given to the President, would be just as important as the administration of the War Department. How could he immunize his views? Taft here made a fair point; Stimson's opening statement was too strong in its insistence that a Secretary of War should confine himself to preparing the national defense. Although he would not have the responsibility for foreign affairs, he would certainly be an adviser. Stimson acknowledged his error, admitting that he could not immunize himself; it was for that reason, he said, that he had been so frank with the committee.

The discussion then turned back to the New Haven speech. Stimson remarked that since making the speech he had learned that the time for providing bases to the British fleet had probably not come; Great Britain's position was not quite as desperate as he had thought, and she could still use her own bases. "Then," said Senator Taft, "as I understand you, you are in favor of joining in the war just as soon as you figure that the British have no longer a chance."

"That is not quite a fair way of putting it. So long as there is a chance of preserving their fleet and so long as it is evident that without our doing that [providing bases] . . . , they would not be preserved, then I think that we ought to do it."

And then Taft tried to force other conclusions. Would Stimson favor giving credits to the British if they ran out of money? Would he go to war to prevent the defeat of England? It was not the questions but the manner of their asking that was offensive. Each time Taft tried to frame a conclusion and put it in Stimson's mouth. And each time Stimson refused to eat; Taft had so framed the question as to leave out an essential condition. The question of credits to the British would depend on the circumstances at the time, and so, much more, would the question of war. The essential element every time would be what were the best interests of the United States, and you could not tell in advance how events might affect those interests. "Until you put in all of those conditions, you have got to refrain from asking dogmatic questions and I have to refrain from answering such questions."

This was not Stimson's first brush with the isolationist mind, nor was it to be his last; this time he was especially hampered by the necessity of confining his remarks to lines which would not embarrass President Roosevelt and Secretary Hull, and of course it was just that embarrassment which Taft was eager to produce. That the Senator should try to gain his end by a cross-examination so narrow and mistrusting deeply disappointed Stimson. He was not personally damaged; he felt afterward that he had more than held his own. But this readiness, in a great national emergency, to seize every opportunity of embarrassing the administration seemed to him a fantastic distortion of partisan duty. He had been questioned for two hours, and not a word had been said about his competence to direct the Army; the whole discussion had turned on other subjects. This was to be the attitude of the isolationists for the next eighteen months whenever he went to the Capitol. In the Congress were some of the ablest and most farsighted men in the country, and with their help the essential measures were passed, but the hearings and debates also became a sounding board for the hopelessly twisted views of a small group of men who, in the name of peace, would have kept America from acting to delay or block the greatest aggression in history.

From the hearing Stimson went back to New York to complete the windup of his personal affairs. On July 8 he returned to Washington, moving into Woodley. It was good to be back in the house which, next only to Highhold, was his home.

That same day he had a long talk with General Marshall, the

second since his nomination had been announced. George C. Marshall was an officer Stimson had known for over twenty years. His name had appeared on lists of especially qualified officers collected by Stimson for Theodore Roosevelt in 1916 when the latter had hoped to raise a division. When Stimson was himself a soldier in 1918, he had met Marshall at the Staff College in Langres and had been so much impressed that ten years later he had tried unsuccessfully to persuade Marshall to go as his aide to the Philippines. Now he began to know and appreciate still better the quality of the Chief of Staff. He soon understood that the greatest problem a Secretary of War can have would never face him while Marshall was alive and well. He would not have to search the Army for a good top soldier. The right man was already there. Only once in the next five years did it occur to Stimson that he might need a new man, and that was when he was urging the appointment of General Marshall to what he then considered a still more difficult and critical position.

It was only too clear that there was much to be done in the War Department: an enormous program of rearmament was only at its beginning; an equally great expansion of the Army's numbers was but sketchily charted; no trusted staff of civilian assistants was at hand; and meanwhile the last bastion of freedom in Europe was in deadly danger. But when Stimson's nomination was confirmed on July 9, by a vote of fifty-six to twenty-eight, he already felt that there were better days ahead. He was at work again, under a chief whom he was able to admire and like as a man, even as he respected him for his office. He was in charge of the United States Army, which for thirty years he had known and loved and trusted. And he had a good Chief of Staff. No man, he later said, could have asked more of fortune in a time of national peril.

2. THE NEWCOMER

When he was sworn in at the White House on July 10, 1940, Stimson entered an administration which had been in undisputed control of the national government for over seven years. At first he felt some of the sensations of a college freshman, and the kindness and co-operation which he found among his new colleagues were heartening. It was immediately clear that there was no division in Franklin Roosevelt's Cabinet on the central issue—the whole administration knew that the nation was in danger. Stimson had been appointed to take charge of the Army, and he was welcome. With Secretary Hull he had right at the start "the longest, most intimate and confidential talk I have ever had with him," and it was perhaps indicative of their new relationship that "for the first time he went into domestic politics as well as foreign affairs." (Diary, July 16, 1940) Stimson had his differences of opinion with Cordell Hull, then and later, but from his side at least there was never any lack of trust and affection for a man whose position in the government was a good deal more difficult than his own.

A more surprising but equally gratifying cordiality was shown to Stimson on his arrival by Secretary Morgenthau. The Secretary of the Treasury had been closely concerned with many of the problems now entrusted to Stimson; his Department had been drawn into military matters as a result of Mr. Roosevelt's lack of confidence in Stimson's predecessor. To Stimson now Morgenthau gave friendly and tactful help in learning the ropes. Much later, when Stimson was forced to disagree radically with Morgenthau in certain subjects, he remembered the kindness the latter had shown him when he most needed it.

The new Secretary of the Navy, Frank Knox, was an acquaintance of nearly thirty years' standing. He had come to Stimson's office in the War Department at the end of 1911 bearing the best possible introduction, a short note from T.R. at Sagamore Hill with the familiar and compelling recommendation, "He is just our type!" The record which Knox later made as a liberal Republican had won Stimson's respect, and in the spring of 1940 his voice, raised from Chicago in energetic advocacy of help to Britain and an end to partisan squabbles, had been even more impressive; in May and early June the two men had begun a correspondence full of the urgency both felt. In Washington Knox at once became to Stimson a friend in all things, and a partner in most.

As the months passed Stimson gradually became a well-established and familiar member of the government. Mr. Roosevelt's was an administration whose inherently disorderly nature he never learned to love, but for its individual members he soon came to have respect, and with most of them he established relations of friendly confidence. They were certainly not the collection of dangerous and unprincipled power seekers that he had heard denounced in New York for seven years. If as a group they had a failing, it was in their constant readiness for internecine strife, but for this they were perhaps less to blame than their chief, who not infrequently placed his bets on two subordinates at once. To Stimson the whole notion of such conflict was abhorrent, and he found that if he earnestly avoided battle he could generally disarm the advancing enemy. Much of the trouble grew out of the clashes of subordinates whose loyalty was not to the administration as a whole but to some part of it, and in these cases it was a sound rule to smoke a pipe of peace with the rival chieftain rather than to scamper to the White House with some one-sided grievance. Thus it became his practice to keep his troubles away from the President as much as possible, and he found that with men like Hull, Morgenthau, Knox, Ickes, and Jackson he could usually reach a friendly answer to the questions noisily raised by subordinates. There were cases, later on, when no such answer could be found, and more than once Stimson found himself fully engaged in the unpleasant task of winning Presidential support for his position against that of a colleague, but such battles were never of his own choosing.

Although he thus established effective working relations with its leaders, Stimson never became one of the special intimates of the administration, and he occasionally felt that the President listened too much to men who were not his direct constitutional advisers. Fortunately, the principal adviser of this kind was Harry Hopkins, a man for whom Stimson quickly developed the greatest respect, and with whom he established a relation of such close mutual confidence that he was often able to present the position of the War Department more effectively through Hopkins than he could in direct conversation with the President. Hopkins was an extraordinary figure; he possessed a mind of unusual quickness and flexibility, and a sure judgment of both men and affairs; his special value to the President lay in his combination of complete loyalty and a sensitive understanding of Mr. Roosevelt's complex nature. During Stimson's years in Washington, the great influence of Hopkins was time and again exerted on behalf of the War Department. "The more I think of it, the more I think it is a godsend that he should be at the White House." (Diary, March 5, 1941)

Another White House "godsend" was Major General Edwin M. Watson, called "Pa" by half official Washington. Watson's extraordinary personal friendliness and conviviality covered a discerning mind and a strong heart and, like Hopkins, Watson loved his chief too well to withhold frank advice and counsel. To Stimson he was invariably a sympathetic and knowing helper.

No discussion of Stimson's relationship to the administration would be complete without one further name, that of Mr. Justice Frankfurter. Without the least deviation from his fastidious devotion to the high traditions of the Supreme Court, Felix Frankfurter made himself a continual source of comfort and help to Stimson. Although he never heard a word of it from Frankfurter, Stimson believed that his own presence in Washington was in some degree the result of Frankfurter's close relationship to the President. In any event, he found Frankfurter always the most devoted of friends and the most zealous of private helpers, and the Justice's long and intimate knowledge of the Roosevelt administration was placed entirely at his disposal. Time after time, when critical issues developed, Stimson turned to Frankfurter; sometimes he heard from Frankfurter even before he had turned. It is not fitting that the activities of a Justice still serving on the Court should be discussed in detail, and Mr. Justice Frankfurter will not be mentioned again; there was in his relationship with Stimson nothing, of course, that even remotely touched upon his duties as a Justice, while there was much that added to the country's debt to a distinguished American.

And as time passed, Stimson fully clarified his purpose and his position in the eyes of the professional politicians and

Congress. After the first loud objections to his appointment, on the ground that it was the product of a devious political mind, there was not much noise until just after the election, when there were rumors that now the superannuated Republican stopgap would resign, his function fulfilled. "Of course it is not a pleasant matter and troubled . . . me . . . a good deal, so I decided to take it up with the President after the Cabinet meeting. I did so and he was very nice about it and I found out from him then that he had already this morning taken the matter up at his press conference. The question had been asked him on the subject and he had stigmatized it 'off the record' as a lie, and 'on the record' that it was only imaginary." (Diary, November 8, 1940) Stimson never knew whether the President had originally intended that he should stay indefinitely as Secretary of War, but this interview in November was typical of the response he met from the White House on the two or three later occasions when he was concerned about his usefulness to his chief. On the whole it seemed likely that the President thought about the matter as little as Stimson himself. The latter had believed in the beginning that he would be in Washington perhaps a year or eighteen months, until the War Department was fully abreast of its duties and the work had become routine. No such time ever developed, and by the spring of 1941 he no longer thought of any early end to his labors. He and Knox had established themselves as permanent members of the administration.

As doubts about his permanence died down, he found himself in an unusual position, politically. He owed nothing to anybody except the President who had appointed him, and the President demanded absolutely none of the usual political support and assistance. This independence Stimson demonstrated in the campaign of 1940 by maintaining a silence so complete that, as he remarked to a friend, 'no one but my Maker knows how I am going to vote.' The diary entry of October 27 explains this decision. "I shall not take any part in the campaign. I think that is more in accord with the job that I have taken and the way in which it was offered me and the way in which I have accepted it. I think it would probably be better for the President as well as myself if I remain as I have been—a Republican doing nonpartisan work for a Democratic President because it related to international affairs in which I agreed and sympathized with his policies. To go actively into the campaign would arouse great antagonism from a great many people on immaterial issues and would prevent me from doing the service that I want to do for the country and for the cause of national defense. Having made that decision I felt better and enjoyed my ride. . . ." As a matter of fact Stimson voted for Roosevelt; it was a natural decision, and perhaps many men guessed Stimson's mind, but he spoke no public word whatever, and his reasons for his vote, like his reasons for silence, were confided only to the diary: "Roosevelt has won another sweeping victory. . . . It is a tremendous relief to have this thing over and I think that from the standpoint of immediate events in the war, particularly during the coming spring and summer, the election will be very salutary to the cause of stopping Hitler." (Diary, November 6, 1940)

This decision to remain completely out of politics Stimson considered one of the wisest he ever made. By it he and his Department avoided any responsibility for any part of the President's record except as it concerned the national defense; he also avoided antagonism from the Republican side which would have been inevitable if he had thrown his weight publicly against the Republican candidate. He was thus able to maintain his position before Republicans in Congress as counsel for the situation. "Jim Wadsworth [Congressman James W. Wadsworth of New York, Stimson's old friend] came in to see me and I had a long talk with him. . . . He was very much impressed with the seriousness of the [international] situation and told me so. His advice was that I should get in touch with the Republicans so far as I could of the Congress. . . . He said ——— was an honest man and that he trusted me, which I was very much surprised at and I told Wadsworth so. Wadsworth repeated it as being true of practically all of the Republicans." (Diary, January 24, 1941)

At the same time, taking their cue from the President, the Democrats maintained a continuously friendly attitude toward Stimson, accepting with good will his insistence that the War Department could not permit political considerations to control its decisions. He, for his part, maintained cordial relations with the Democratic leaders and, as always in his political life, found that once the central issue of partisan opposition is removed, there are few roses so sweet as those that grow over the party wall. The following diary entry is typical; just before the 1940 election he learned that "a mistake had been uncovered in the Adjutant General's Department in regard to Senator Pat Harrison's request for establishing a C.C.C. camp distribution system at McComb, Mississippi, instead of across the river in Louisiana. The Department had reported that it couldn't be done as cheaply in Mississippi as Louisiana. I was rather distressed at this because we have been obliged to refuse already one or two other requests of Harrison's who has always been a faithful and loyal helper in military matters. This seemed to me a request that we ought to be able to grant. It now appeared by telephone . . . that the Adjutant General was mistaken and that it could be granted more cheaply for McComb than for Louisiana, and I told Brooks at once to telegraph Harrison and his committee who were coming up to see me about it, that they needn't come and the request was granted. When I arrived back in Washington . . . I found a very grateful telegram from him." (Diary, November 2, 1940)

Only once in this period did Stimson have a painful reminder of the baneful influence of politics. The diary entry speaks for itself. "Bob Patterson has been making a number of appointments in the Procurement Branch of the office— this time of young lawyers to help out. All his appointments are good, chosen purely from a professional standpoint and men of high character. But among them he selected Henry Parkman, Jr., of Massachusetts, to be one of the attorneys of the Department and Parkman was the Republican candidate in Massachusetts last fall for Senator against Senator Walsh. Consequently when I got back to the Department yesterday I was met with a terrific telegram from Walsh, professing to be astounded at such an appointment; claiming that Parkman had conducted a very low campaign against him; stating that he was personally obnoxious to himself (Walsh) and demanding that I reconsider the appointment. This made a tough situation, for Walsh is quite capable of doing much harm to the Department's work up on the Hill and undoubtedly may try to do so. I had a talk with Patterson . . . and of course he was pretty stiff about not yielding, but unfortunately he has not got as much experience as I have had with the difficulties of such a situation with a hostile Senator. I talked with Parkman whom I had not met before but who was a very fine-looking fellow and evidently a good man and he was considerate enough to suggest that he had better withdraw. I told him not to do so for a while—that I felt very badly about it and that I would talk with Walsh and see first what could be done. Unfortunately Walsh was not in Washington, so . . . I called him on the long-distance telephone at Clinton, Massachusetts, and he nearly blew me off the end of the telephone, he was so angry and bitter. He is evidently making it a party matter, as the Democratic chairman has also written to Roosevelt about it. Of course it was not a party matter, but the trouble is no one will believe it. No one will believe that we did not both know that he was a Republican candidate for Senator, although as a matter of fact I had never heard of him. . . . It is pretty hard to have such a thing happen, making the possibility of such a critical mess to the Department. It brings out the delicacy of the situation in which I am, in a Democratic Cabinet, and the good luck I have had thus far in avoiding trouble all through the political campaign. I am very anxious not to spoil all matters now by this kind of a row which may spread in all directions. On the other hand, it is very hard to sacrifice Parkman, although he was very nice about it, and his withdrawal will not really be commensurate with the harm that may be done to the Department." (Diary, December 11, 1940)

The core of the difficulty here was in the fact that Walsh, a vindictive man, was no friend to the President; he was also an isolationist. As a veteran Democrat quite prepared to cause maximum embarrassment to the administration in its policy toward the world crisis, he was extremely dangerous. Stimson reached his decision that same night. "I spent considerable time in my bed last night thinking the thing out and finally came to the conclusion that it was my duty toward the job and toward the President not to allow this row with Walsh to come up in the Department, particularly because I did not want to have him raise the issue that he surely would raise of the President's conduct of the war, now, prematurely, before the President has chosen his own ground." Stimson asked a close friend who also knew Parkman to explain the situation to the latter, and "Parkman came back and positively refused to run the risk of embarrassing us and declined to take the job. He behaved very finely about it. I felt very badly and told him so." (Diary, December 12, 1940) This surrender to Walsh was a bitter decision; Stimson took great satisfaction in Henry Parkman's later distinguished service as an officer who rose to the grade of brigadier general, and he was delighted when Walsh was finally retired from public life by another soldier in 1946.

In a sense, of course, it was politically unwise for Patterson to have appointed Parkman in the first place, but it was this kind of political unwisdom that Stimson loved in Patterson; his rugged integrity was in the end an asset that far outweighed the occasional difficulties it caused. The real significance of the Parkman case was that it stood almost alone. In only one other case throughout the war did Stimson have to withdraw an intended appointment to his Department, and in this instance the veto came from the President, probably as a result of misinformation given him by others. Stimson, however, did not go out of his way to appoint the avowed enemies of powerful Senators, and in all important cases he cleared his appointments with the White House.

It was Walsh's isolationism that made him dangerous, and throughout the war Stimson was to find his principal political difficulties with those in both parties whose objective was to discredit the administration's foreign policy. Thus his real opponents were the President's opponents, too, and his position in this respect was like that of any ordinary Cabinet member. With these opponents there could be no real peace or mutual trust, but it was important to fight them only on the central front.

The success with which the War Department kept itself aloof from politics was strikingly demonstrated much later, in 1944, when the Congress entrusted the supervision of voting in the armed forces to a three-man commission consisting of the Secretary of War, the Secretary of the Navy, and the chairman of the Maritime Commission, Admiral Land. Stimson observed with some amusement that two members of the original commission were Republicans, while the third was a professional sailor. There was a mild flurry at the White House over the composition of the staff which Stimson established in the War Department to manage his share of the soldier voting; the officer in charge of the work was Colonel Robert Cutler, and although he had been politically active only as corporation counsel to a Democratic mayor of Boston, he was a registered Republican. But Mr. Roosevelt was less disturbed than his professional Democratic advisers, and Cutler remained on the job, with a Democrat added to his staff in order to disarm criticism. Both in the War Ballot Commission and in the Army, soldier voting was so smoothly and fairly handled that Stimson felt a deep personal debt to Cutler. No job entrusted to his supervision during the entire war had held more explosive possibilities, and none was accomplished with less friction.

3. THE BEST STAFF HE EVER HAD

It is a sound rule for a newcomer in any organization to learn his own particular job before he makes much noise. Stimson's attention, in the early summer of 1940, was directed mainly at his own Department. There was much to be done. The first task, and perhaps the most important, was to restore the unity and morale of the Department. The civilian chiefs of the service departments, Stimson once remarked, may not be able to do very much good, but they certainly have it in their power to do a vast deal of harm. They necessarily outrank any and all military men, and when their power is misused, or when they are at odds with one another, the results within the service are distressing. Some such situation seemed to have arisen in the months before Stimson's arrival, and his first job was to re-establish a proper mutual confidence between the Secretary, the Assistant Secretary, and the Army.

As for his own relationship to the Army, Stimson could only say that the problem never came up. He had the very great—and unusual—advantage of extensive experience with military men, and from his first day in office he found no cause to complain of any lack of loyal support. In his first message to the Army, on July 19, he remarked on the "good spirit of co-operation" he had already found, and this was not wishful thinking. If the Cabinet had shown him the cordiality of sympathetic strangers, the Army seemed to meet him as an old friend. To those who disliked soldiers, this friendship might give the appearance that one more civilian had been captured and tamed by the ferocious militarists. To Stimson it was encouraging assurance that an essential condition of his effectiveness had been fulfilled.

Just as important as his own relationship with the Army was the development of a staff of assistants who would work in the same spirit. The most important single accomplishment of Stimson's first year in office was his success in assembling a team of civilian associates which he later believed to be the best he ever had, in any office. Even if it had been possible to make the War Department a one-man show, Stimson's whole experience of administration was against such a course. At the same time he was not temperamentally fitted for service as a figurehead. He therefore required as his principal assistants men who could combine intelligence and initiative with flawless loyalty to him as chief, and such men are more easily described than found. During his first months in Washington he was greatly helped by Arthur E. Palmer, a young lawyer from his New York firm, but Palmer was too young to be happy out of uniform, and only Patterson of all his civilian assistants was with Stimson from the beginning to the end.

In accordance with the original understanding between the President and Stimson, Patterson was appointed and confirmed as Assistant Secretary of War and was at work by the end of July. His arrival ended for good the division between the Secretary and the Assistant Secretary which had been conspicuous in the early months of 1940. He at once assumed

direct responsibility for the vast Army program of procurement, and throughout the five years that followed he relieved
Stimson of all but occasional labors in this great field.

Probably no man in the administration was more ruthlessly
determined to fulfill his assignment than Patterson; he proposed to let nothing block him in his effort to equip the armies
of the anti-Axis world. He had known war at very close range
in 1918; he was at war from 1940 onward, and he had a fierce
hatred of all delay and any compromise; his only test of any
measure was whether it would help to win, and for any group
or individual who blinked at sacrifice he had only scorn. He
himself was so zealous to fight that only Stimson's personal
plea prevented him from resigning his office in 1944 to take
a commission as an infantry officer again. Patterson was a
fighter, and although he was perhaps not always perfect in
his choice of a battleground, his instinct in the choice of
enemies was unerring.

The next great find was John J. McCloy, a man whose
record so distinguished him that Stimson's principal difficulty
was to retain his services for the War Department. He first
came to Washington at Stimson's personal request to advise
the War Department in its counterintelligence work; after
years of work as a lawyer investigating the Black Tom case
he had a wide knowledge of German subversive methods.
Stimson's early high opinion of him was reinforced by every
report received on his work, and in October, 1940, he was
appointed as a special assistant. So varied were his labors and
so catholic his interests that they defy summary. For five years
McCloy was the man who handled everything that no one
else happened to be handling. He became Stimson's principal
adviser in the battle for the Lend-Lease Act and it was his
skillful preparation that cleared the way for the War Department's successful assumption of the whole military burden of
lend-lease procurement. Later he was Stimson's chief adviser
on matters connected with international relations and his
agent in supervising the great work of military government.
He was equally good in a complicated interdepartmental negotiation or in dealing with Congress. His energy was enormous, and his optimism almost unquenchable. He became so

knowing in the ways of Washington that Stimson sometimes wondered whether anyone in the administration ever acted without "having a word with McCloy"; when occasionally he was the first to give McCloy important news he would remark that his assistant must be weakening.

The third of the Secretary's principal subordinates was Robert A. Lovett, who arrived in November, 1940, to be Stimson's air assistant. For this duty he was conspicuously suited. His enthusiasm for airplanes had made him a naval pilot of distinguished skill in World War I, and in the years between wars he maintained his keen interest in the subject. In 1940 when he came to Washington he had just completed, as a private citizen, a careful survey of the whole problem of air power and aircraft production in the United States. He thus brought to his job the understanding and enthusiasm which were indispensable to a civilian dealing with the Army Air Forces, while at the same time his sensitive intelligence enabled him to maintain cordial relations with the non-fliers of the Department. Lovett possessed incisive judgment and a pertinent wit. He served Stimson in all matters affecting the Air Forces as Patterson served in procurement and supply. Both were in a high degree autonomous officers; both combined initiative with loyalty.

By April, 1941, these three men were in the jobs they were to hold throughout the war. In December, 1940, Patterson had been appointed to the newly created office of Under Secretary, and in April McCloy succeeded him as Assistant Secretary, while at the same time Lovett was appointed to the long-vacant position of Assistant Secretary for Air.

In the same month Stimson acquired a fourth assistant in Harvey H. Bundy, who had served with him before as Assistant Secretary of State from 1931 to 1933. With the title of Special Assistant to the Secretary, Bundy became "my closest personal assistant." A man of unusual tact and discretion, Bundy handled many of Stimson's troubling problems of administration and correspondence and served as his filter for all sorts of men and problems. He also became the Secretary's personal agent in dealings with scientists and educators, two groups whose importance was as great as it was unfamiliar in the great new army of machines and civilian soldiers.

These four men were the "sixty-minute players" in a team to which many others were added for special purposes at different times. Their characteristics as individuals are perhaps less important than the things they had in common. All were men in the prime of life, the forties and fifties, but all were so much younger than Stimson that none ever called him by his first name. All four had been conspicuously successful in private life, three as lawyers and one as a banker; all of them came to Washington at serious financial sacrifice. None of them had ever been politically active, and none had any consuming political ambition. All four were men of absolute integrity, and none was small-minded about credit for his labors. All but one were Republicans, but not one of them ever aroused partisan opposition. They were civilians, but they earned the unreserved confidence of the Army. All of them were wholehearted in their loyalty, but none interpreted loyalty as merely a duty to say yes, and Stimson often trusted their judgment against his own, especially when he was angry. In later chapters their names will be often mentioned, and even when they are not mentioned the reader must bear in mind that very little of what Stimson did was done without their advice and help.

And with these men Stimson established a relationship that was in many ways closer than anything he had known before in public office. These were men who knew how to laugh with him at trying events; nor were they put off or dismayed by his occasional thunderous anger. They could complain about him to Mrs. Stimson as a bad-tempered tyrant who "roared like a lion," but such complaints were registered in his presence with the teasing smile of members of the family. And as he looked back in 1947, he felt a deep and affectionate nostalgia for the days when he had shared Patterson's wrath at incompetence, laughed at the zealous omniscience of his heavenly twain McCloy and Lovett, fumed at Bundy's constant advice not to act on impulse, and lectured them all over the interoffice "squawk box" in tones they all proclaimed as unintelligible.

CHAPTER XIV

The First Year

1. MEN FOR THE NEW ARMY

DURING the months in which he was feeling his way toward full membership in the administration, and well before he had obtained the help of most of the civilian assistants upon whom he later so heavily relied, Stimson was fully engaged in the urgent immediate task of raising an army.

At New Haven in June, in his talks with the President, before his appointment, and at the Senate hearing on his confirmation, he had emphasized his conviction that a selective service bill should be enacted at once. Such a bill was pending before Congress when he took office, and his energies, through July and August of 1940, were largely devoted to the struggle for its enactment.

The principal difficulty was not in the opposition of those groups which always oppose conscription but rather in the widespread feeling among its supporters that no act so controversial could be passed in an election year. Even the Army, which of course supported the bill as essential to an effective mobilization of manpower, was at first pessimistic. The soldiers had been outcasts for so long that they were afraid to count on early acceptance of the novel principle of compulsory peacetime service. Nor could they be of any great assistance in winning support for such a measure; it was better that the "militarists" should remain in the background.

The Burke-Wadsworth Bill was thus not, in its origin, a War Department bill, though it was based in large part on joint Army-Navy staff studies. It was introduced by two farsighted members of Congress; it had been framed by a small group of well-informed private citizens in the Military Training Camps Association. Without this private initiative, and particularly without the indefatigable and intelligent work of Grenville Clark, Stimson was convinced that there would have been no Selective Service Act in 1940.[1]

Stimson's own principal labors in support of the measure were two. First, with General Marshall he determined the position of the War Department, which was essentially that any workable bill would be satisfactory to the Army. As for the necessity of such a bill, the War Department's figures spoke for themselves. The Army had in May been authorized to expand its regular strength to 375,000. The rate of recruiting indicated that by the volunteer system even this small figure could be achieved only very slowly. If Congress wanted an army large enough to defend the country, it must provide for compulsory service. This was the lesson of every previous emergency in American history. Stimson repeated to the House Committee on Military Affairs convictions which he had held for over twenty-five years. Selective Service was the only fair, efficient, and democratic way to raise an army.

His second task was that of insuring active Presidential support of the bill. Here he found himself engaged in a form of sport which had become familiar in the seven years of the New Deal. Franklin Roosevelt was firmly convinced of the need for selective service, and in the end his support was decisive in securing passage of a satisfactory act, but his watchful waiting, on this and many other later issues, was as tantalizing to Stimson as it was to many other men whose policies he in the end supported. In this case, however, 'he came down firmly on the right side every time we asked him to,' and at least once his statement preceded Stimson's request. The effect each time was immediate, and Stimson learned a lesson about the power of Mr. Roosevelt's leadership which he did not forget.

With the help of evident public approval throughout the country, the supporters of compulsory training were able to

---

[1] There might also have been no Stimson as Secretary of War in that year; it was Clark's fight for Selective Service that led him to take the initiative which resulted in the suggestion of Stimson's name to Mr. Roosevelt.

defeat all efforts at delay and all vitiating amendments, and on September 16 the President signed the Selective Service Act of 1940. In retrospect Stimson saw this act as one of the two or three most important accomplishments of the American people in the whole period before the outbreak of active war. It made possible a program of training which fully occupied the Army's resources through the next year; the invaluable months before the shooting began were thus not wasted. And as an unprecedented departure from American peacetime traditions, it demonstrated clearly the readiness of the American people to pay the cost of defense in terms more significant than dollars.

Together with the Joint Resolution of August 27, 1940, which authorized the President to call out the National Guard and the Organized Reserves, the Selective Service Act laid the necessary legislative foundation for a new army of 1,400,000 men. In view of the pressure under which the Army was forced to work, its preparations for housing and training these men seemed excellent to Stimson, and he said so firmly on October 17 when the question appeared briefly in the Presidential campaign.

A more difficult task was the organization of the Selective Service System. Here, too, the Army was prepared. The results of fourteen years of study were incorporated in the Department's plans, and with the advice of Major Lewis B. Hershey, Stimson and the President found it surprisingly easy to organize the great machine which was to serve so well for the duration. The administration of the draft, from the beginning, was a triumph of decentralization; throughout the war it maintained its reputation for fairness, and this reputation rested principally on the character and ability of the thousands of men who served on the local boards. To Stimson this was another proof of the competence of the Army; the methods of 1940 were built on the War Department's study of the magnificent achievement of General Crowder in 1917. President Roosevelt insisted on the appointment of a civilian director, and after some delay Clarence Dykstra was selected, but the success of the draft was not the work of any one man— it was the natural result of many years of careful thought in the War Department. It was a deep personal satisfaction to Stimson to watch the President learning that his fears of a militaristic administration of the draft were unfounded, and the appointment of General Hershey to replace Dykstra when the latter resigned in the middle of 1941 seemed to him a proper recognition of the trustworthiness of the military.

The beginning of the draft, for the sixteen million registrants, was the drawing of numbers on October 29. The same occasion marked for Stimson the ending of four months of arduous argument and preparation. "We had a very impressive ceremony. . . . The President first made an admirable speech on the purposes and methods and democratic nature of the draft. Then I was blindfolded and drew the first capsule. . . . This drawing took place, as will be noted, before election, although everybody was hinting around a little while ago that it would not be done until after election. It thus was a brave decision on the part of the President to let it come now, when there is a very bitter campaign being made against it. . . . In my opinion he showed good statesmanship when he accepted the issue and his technique in bringing it on in this public manner and the solemn nature of the occasion and the character of the speech which he made . . . served to change the event of the draft into a great asset in his favor." (Diary, October 29, 1940)

With manpower for the new army assured, the War Department tackled the equally important problem of leadership. It was apparent that large numbers of additional officers would be required.

Where should they be obtained? Grenville Clark, and many others who had studied the problem, strongly urged that in addition to promotion from the ranks the War Department should go straight to the civilian world, organizing training camps for citizen volunteers on the lines of those which Stimson himself had so much admired in 1916-1917. This solution also appealed to the President, who, however, left the final determination to the War Department.

General Marshall took a different view. Given a Selective Service System, he believed that for the first time in its history the Army would now be in a position to draw its officers from its own ranks. With a large pool of National Guard and Reserve officers to draw on, the Army had no immediate need for more officers; its problem was rather to insure the effective training of those it had. In March, 1941, the matter came to a head.

The issue here was a broader one than any of the participants then realized, and in retrospect Stimson believed that the solution reached was a better one than any of them anticipated. After much discussion it was agreed that there should be no separate "Plattsburg camps"; the Army would instead enlarge its already projected program for training officers from the ranks. As a concession to men not yet subject to draft who might be particularly qualified as leaders, it would offer a special arrangement later known as the Volunteer Officer Candidate program, but even this concession was later withdrawn. In the great task of finding junior officers the Army thus limited itself mainly to its own men, and from this decision grew the Officer Candidate Schools. This was the fair and democratic way to form an officer corps. It also turned out to be the efficient way.

A Secretary of War does not see much of lieutenants, however hard he may try, and Stimson was in no position to offer any final judgment on the quality of the junior leaders thus developed. The Army's insistence on finding its officers among its enlisted men was not duplicated during the war by either the Navy or the Air Forces (in the latter case for what seemed to Stimson sufficient reasons), and Stimson feared that perhaps the Army had lost many fine youngsters who were not reluctant to take the short cut to commissioned responsibility offered by other services. On the other hand, the principle established by the Army was right, and the record of the Officer Candidate Schools was a proud one. These schools were a new development in American military experience, and Stimson did not doubt that many mistakes were made, but he felt sure that the Army of the future would build its leadership on the principles thus boldly and successfully followed throughout Word War II.

Although the Officer Candidate Schools became the source

of most of the Army's new officers, there were of course many specialized skills for which the War Department had to go directly to civil life. The most obvious such cases were doctors, dentists, and chaplains. For other cases, less obvious, Stimson on October 14, 1940, laid down his policy in a "memorandum of suggestions." Commissions direct from civil life were not to be given to men otherwise liable to service under the draft; "all political or personal considerations should be rigidly excluded"; and "commissions should only be given where the individual has special qualifications for the service he is expected to perform."

At first Stimson tried to enforce this ruling by requiring his personal approval for all appointments from civil life. As the Army expanded, such personal supervision became impossible, and the job was turned over to a board of officers under General Malin Craig, who had been Marshall's predecessor as Chief of Staff. General Craig's firm but fair-minded application of Stimson's policy was a great protection to the Army. War generates many pressures, but perhaps none more insistent than that of the enormous number of men who are convinced that they can be useful only as commissioned officers.

This difficulty of course made itself felt also in lower echelons. Replying to one eager mother whose favorite private soldier had not yet been handed his marshal's baton, Stimson remarked that the only course which would satisfy everyone would be to abolish the rank of private.

Quite as important as the procurement of capable junior officers was the selection of their seniors. The policy pursued in promotion of officers was the work of General Marshall. Stimson's only concern was with promotions to general officer's rank, and even here the framing of the lists was a job for the soldiers. The Secretary was in complete sympathy with the Chief of Staff's insistence on selective advancement of the ablest men, regardless of age, and after careful study of Marshall's first list with his old friend Frank R. McCoy, "We both decided that it was an outstanding departmental paper and that the recommendations contained in it were very admirable and clear. Marshall had had the courage and breadth of view to disregard the ordinary official records of officers in certain cases where it was important to do so, and to appoint several men whom McCoy and I knew to be good war men and yet who might not have had as good a record on paper." (Diary, September 21, 1940)

Stimson approved the list, and the President signed it, unchanged; this became the almost invariable practice, although on a later list, in October, Stimson felt it necessary to reinforce Marshall's recommendation for the promotion of George S. Patton to major general, having heard that this name was doubtfully viewed in the White House.

The obverse of promotion was the unpleasant task of weeding out incompetents. At lower echelons this work was slow in development; eventually it was handled by reclassification boards. Complaints against reclassification from influential quarters forced Stimson in 1944 to make a personal investigation of the process of reclassification; he found as he had expected that the rights of officers subjected to this process were almost too carefully safeguarded and flatly refused to intervene. At higher levels he followed the same policy, pointing out to the friends of officers removed from high positions or retired from the Army that any interference from the Secretary's office would be prejudicial to good order and discipline.

This firmness was particularly necessary in the case of senior officers of the National Guard. Stimson had himself been a Guardsman, but partly for that reason he understood how little the training of the Guard had equipped many of its officers for modern field service, and he therefore fully supported General Marshall in the fairly drastic reorganization which was required in making effective fighting units of the Guard divisions.

2. SUPPLIES

The number of men in the United States Government whose central interest was preparation for war, in the summer of 1940, was not very great. Stimson and Judge Patterson were two of them, and in the uphill battle which they fought for the Army's equipment they soon learned all the good reasons why this or that part of their program must be delayed. The basic difficulty was a simple one—the country as a whole was not ready to make any serious sacrifices for national de ense; nothing that was done in production before Pearl Harbor involved the same degree of sacrifice as the nation's decision to raise an army by selective service, but each man squealed as he was hurt. This was true of management and of labor, and it was true of many branches of the Government. The tensions developed during the years of the New Deal were not the perfect background for the labors of Dr. Win-the-War—especially since that doctor could not yet be called by his right name. The President himself had set the tone for this period by a remark that no one need be "discomboomerated" by the crisis.

The one thing upon which the whole country was agreed was that the services must have enough money. At no time in the whole period of the war emergency did Stimson ever have to worry about funds; the appropriations of Congress were always prompt and generous. The pinch came in getting money turned into weapons. Right at the start, Stimson found his temper sorely tried by six weeks of delay in passing a tax law under which contracts could be speedily signed. The issue was a simple one. The existing tax laws made no provision for the special circumstances of defense production, in which large plants must be built which would have almost no value after the emergency had ended. No businessman wanted to be saddled with such white elephants, and it was generally agreed that the law must be changed to permit contractors to write off such construction expenses within a five-year period. The administration insisted, however, that such relief must be accompanied by a stringent excess-profits tax. To all this Stimson agreed, in principle. He was not eager to see business making unnatural profits out of national defense. At the same time the essential thing was speed, and while he did not venture to determine who was right in the mutual recriminations between the Treasury and Congress, it seemed to him clear that neither side was sufficiently concerned with getting the bill passed. Businessmen must be prevented from making excessive profits, but they were not going to sign contracts until they had a bill protecting them against large losses, and too many men in Washington refused to face that simple fact. "The whole thing is a great clash between two big theories and interests. If you are going to try to go to war, or to prepare for war, in a capitalist country, you have got to let business make money out of the process or business won't work, and there are a great many people in Congress who think that they can tax business out of all proportion and still have business-men work diligently and quickly. That is not human nature." (Diary, August 26, 1940)

The War Department had its troubles with more than one company which was slow, or inefficient, or selfish, and Stimson himself had a stiff verbal engagement through the press with certain airplane makers who seemed to think the expansion of civil airlines more important than the growth of the Army Air Forces, but on the whole he was not inclined to blame businessmen for their reluctance to enter defense work without some protection. After World War I he had himself defended companies harried by the Harding administration for having done in wartime what the Wilson administration asked them to do. As for profits, it was obvious that if the government must guarantee against loss, it must also prevent excessive gain, and in the machinery for contract renegotiation as it finally developed Stimson was satisfied that in general this goal was achieved.

A striking example of this reluctance of businessmen to enter the uncertain field of defense production was the manufacture of powder. In the summer of 1940 powder was the most critical shortage of all, but Stimson was forced to make personal pleas to such companies as Du Pont before they would return to the work they had been so unfairly damned for doing in the previous war. One thing was absolutely clear: whoever started America toward war in 1940, it was most certainly not the munitions makers; they went about their work efficiently when called upon, but they did not push.

The most difficult problem in production, during Stimson's first year in the War Department, was inside the Government, in the organization of an effective team of leaders. The War Department itself had much to learn; the mixed atmosphere of the nation did not permit the application of its carefully deliberated plans for mobilization, and the insistent demand was for men who could throw away the book and get results in the face of unexpected handicaps and obstacles. Patterson was such a man, and so was Colonel Brehon Somervell, who in December took charge of the great task of camp construction. Stimson was further greatly assisted by Robert Proctor, a lawyer from Boston whose volunteer services expedited the signing of airplane contracts in the summer of 1940. The regular officers charged with procurement were diligent, but too few of them were men of drive and imagination. Nothing was to be gained by putting unknown hopefuls in their places, however, and Stimson and Patterson for a time did their best with what they had. For the moment the Army was not the critical point in the problem. Even unimaginative officers had more demands than industry could fill. The real confusion in the Government was in the great field of industrial mobilization. Who was to do the job that had been done under Bernard Baruch in 1918?

Franklin Roosevelt experimented with solutions to this problem for nearly four years; his first effort was the appointment of the National Defense Advisory Commission, in June, 1940. This was a committee of seven. In Stimson's view it was just six men too many, but in William S. Knudsen the President found a man who understood production; from the beginning Knudsen was "a tower of strength" in the practical matter of translating a military demand into an operating production line.

There were other problems involved in industrial mobilization, however, and it was not long before the NDAC began to show its inadequacies. Seven advisers could not make decisions. What was needed was a single head, as Stimson, Knox, Patterson, and Forrestal agreed in a long conference on December 17. After discussion with Morgenthau and Jesse Jones, and after the agreement of both William Green and Sidney Hillman had been secured, they went to the President on December 18 to suggest that Knudsen be made the one responsible director of war production. As a concession to the President's fear that such a "czar" might trespass on the legitimate functions of the War and Navy Departments, they further suggested that Stimson and Knox should serve as advisers to Knudsen. From this recommendation developed the Office of Production Management, OPM, to which the President appointed Knudsen as director, Hillman as associate director, and Stimson and Knox as members of the board. The attempt to get a single head had failed, but the new arrangement was certainly an improvement. Stimson's major contribution to its work was his personal intervention to insure the appointment of John Lord O'Brian as general counsel. O'Brian held this position in successive reorganizations throughout the war, and it would be difficult to overestimate the value of his service to his country.

3. TO BRITAIN ALONE

However urgent the work of raising and arming her own military forces, the attention of America in 1940 and early 1941 was mainly centered on Great Britain. In Stimson's office visitors from England were always welcome, and he followed with anxious care the course of the air and sea battle. On two matters his informants all agreed. The British were wholly determined to fight to the end, and to do it successfully they needed all the help they could get. It was the policy of the American Government to provide this help, but it was easier to announce such a policy than to execute it.

The main difficulty, of course, was that America simply did not have much to give; by the standards that were to become familiar in the later years of the war, she had nothing. In 1940 planes were counted one at a time, and even the very few on hand were not battle-tested. The same thing was true of all modern weapons. This brutal fact was too painful to be properly accepted, and during the next two years Stimson had many a bitter hour with Allied leaders who could not believe that the American larder was bare. The President himself was an occasional offender; in his eagerness to help an ally he sometimes gave assurances that could not be fulfilled. It was not easy for anyone to possess his soul in patience during the long months that separated vast programs from finished weapons.

In 1940 the only weapons available in the United States in any quantity were surplus stocks from the last war. Even these were not readily transferable, but in the emergency just after Dunkirk the President and General Marshall succeeded in getting to the British a very substantial number of infantry weapons; this was done by selling them to the United States Steel Export Company, which in turn resold them to the British. The subterfuge was obvious, and unconcealed, but in the emotional reaction to the situation in June, 1940, it was generally approved. And the weapons were, in fact, surplus— there remained enough of these old Enfields and outdated machine guns to equip an army twice the size of anything contemplated in 1940.

A much more complicated question was presented in early August. Ever since May the British had been asking for destroyers. The American Navy had about two hundred old four-stackers in cold storage. They were, however, a part of the Navy's wartime force, and if the United States should be drawn into the struggle they would certainly be used. To the American people, furthermore, ships of the Navy have a special sentimental value. And again, Congress had on June 28 passed a bill providing that no material belonging to the American Government should be delivered to foreign forces unless the Army's Chief of Staff or the Chief of Naval Operations certified that such material was surplus. It was not readily apparent how Admiral Stark could give any such certificates for his destroyers. Finally, there was an old statute apparently forbidding the transfer of naval vessels to a belligerent.

The famous "destroyer deal" by which this log jam was broken was the personal triumph of President Roosevelt. To Stimson this was the President at his best. The obvious answer was that the British should give some *quid pro quo*, and such a suggestion was made by the British on August 5. But it was the President himself, on August 13, in a meeting with Morgenthau, Stimson, Knox, and Welles, who drafted the essential principles of the agreement which was finally reached. In return for fifty destroyers, the British were asked to give the United States the right to fortify and defend certain British held bases in the Atlantic. Such a trade would strengthen both nations, and in the larger sense each would be further strengthened by the increased power of the other. If it was the American interest that the British should master the Nazi submarine, it was clearly the British interest that America should be strong in the Atlantic.

To the successful completion of the President's plan Stimson gave his full support. He strongly urged that there was no need to take the plan to Congress; this was, broadly speaking, an exercise of the traditional power of the Executive in foreign affairs, and it met the requirements of the act of June 28, for surely Admiral Stark's conscience must be clear as he surveyed the stature of American naval strength before and after the agreement. As for the statutes on the transfer of naval vessels, Stimson endorsed the Attorney General's decision that these statutes were designed to meet wholly different circumstances—such cases as that of the *Alabama*, in the Civil War; they would not apply to the present case. Stimson further argued against a State Department view that the agreement should include a specific pledge not to surrender the British Fleet. The Churchill government had already made its position eloquently clear, and to require further pledges would be merely an indication of mistrust. As a Republican, Stimson was in frequent communication with William Allen White, who was finally able to assure him that the Republican candidate, Wendell Willkie, would in general support the plan.

Not all of the President's advisers were so bold. At a meeting of these advisers (at which the President was not present) on August 21, "there was some timidity evident in regard to boldly confronting the situation which existed, and there were suggestions from some of them that it would be better to try to transfer the destroyers to Canada rather than to Great Britain. This suggestion gained enough support to arouse me to strongly make a statement to the contrary. I said that no one would believe that to be the fact; that it was not fact, and that it would simply add a discreditable subterfuge to the situation. I pointed out that today the newspapers had been discussing the fact that the British fleet of destroyers had already been reduced to only sixty vessels and that they had been clamoring for help on this point and that if we should send away from this country an almost equal fleet of fifty destroyers which would subsequently turn up in Great Britain, no one on earth would believe that it had not been intended for Great Britain. I pointed out that Canada had neither the need nor the men to man them and that they would be manned by British seamen anyhow. My statement put an end to the Canadian suggestion, but the fact that it should actually have been put forward was an evidence of how technical stupidity can get into these pleasant people." (Diary, August 21, 1940)

As announced on September 3, the destroyer deal transferred fifty American destroyers to Great Britain, in exchange for a ninety-nine-year lease on bases in six British possessions in the Western Hemisphere. Two additional leases, in Newfoundland and Bermuda, were freely granted. This represented a concession to the Prime Minister's desire that the element of trade be entirely removed from the transaction; unfortunately the element of trade was exactly what was necessary to make the transaction legal under the shackling American statutes. The agreement was met with strong and general approval by the country; the professional isolationists were reduced to unhappy grumbling about "ignoring Congress," for even on the very narrow ground on which these gentlemen chose to consider the security of their country, it was clear that the President had made a good bargain.

To Stimson the whole affair was enormously encouraging. It was clear proof that the Commander in Chief understood high politics; it established a new degree of mutual confidence and friendship among the British, the Americans, and the Canadians; its solid success at the bar of public opinion confirmed his view that the American people were ready for leadership. At a meeting with the President and Prime Minister King of Canada, on August 17, he summed up his feelings. He reminded the others of Franklin's famous remark at the end of the American Constitutional Convention, that for a long time he had wondered about a carved image of the sun which decorated the chair of George Washington, and that now he was persuaded that it was a rising, not a setting, sun. "I said I felt that way about this meeting. I felt that it was very possibly the turning point in the tide of the war, and that from now on we could hope for better things."

Through sheer inadvertence the final agreement, as published, omitted a part of the American obligation—250,000 Enfield rifles with 30,000,000 rounds of ammunition, and 5 B-17 bombers. This was highly embarrassing, but Stimson could see no other course than a frank admission of the error. At a meeting called by the President, "I did my best to point out that I felt that we were committed to the British for it, and that to go back on that commitment would do a great deal of harm to our good name. But the others thought that due consideration could be given in the shape of another transaction which would satisfy the British just as well or better than the flying fortresses, and they persuaded the President to that effect." (Diary, September 13, 1940) A compensating transaction was finally arranged, but it involved a good deal of complicated reasoning, and Stimson was pleasantly surprised by the good temper shown by the British in the face of this American reluctance to admit publicly a simple error.

The destroyer deal was heartening and dramatic, but it unfortunately did not end the problem of aid to Britain. Throughout the summer and autumn of 1940 Stimson was engaged in almost daily labors to speed up the production and transfer of military supplies. Energetic efforts were made to harmonize British and American requirements and types of weapons. British missionaries came in and out of the Secretary's office, and over the weeks a close and intelligent co-operation developed. The Treasury Department under Morgenthau was particularly zealous and effective in finding ways to finance these transactions. But more and more both sides found themselves blocked. The British were running out of dollar exchange and the hands of the Americans were tied by statute; General Marshall with his usual courage was willing to sign the necessary certificate whenever there was any reasonable argument to support it, but there were many laws which left no such loophole and many cases where no honest man could sign. "It is really preposterous to have Congress attempt to tie the hands of the Commander in Chief in such petty respects as they have done recently in this legislation. The chief hold of the Congress on the Executive is their ability to vote or to refuse to vote supplies for an Army and their right to raise and support armies in the Constitution. The more I run over the experiences of this summer, the more I feel that that ought to be substantially the only check; that these other little petty annoying checks placed upon the Commander in Chief do an immense amount more harm than good and they restrict the power of the Commander in Chief in ways in which Congress cannot possibly wisely interfere. They don't know enough." (Diary, September 9, 1940)

On December 17 the President announced his determination to insure all-out aid to Great Britain. On December 29 he presented his case to the people in the "arsenal of democracy" speech. At the start of the new session of Congress there began the great debate which continued for two months, ending with the passage of the Lend-Lease Act, which gave the President the power to "manufacture . . . or procure . . . any defense article for the government of any country whose defense the President deems vital to the defense of the United States," and "to sell, transfer title to, exchange, lease, lend, or otherwise dispose of, to any such government any defense article." In Stimson's view this was one of the most important legislative achievements of the entire war. It was another great Rooseveltian triumph. At one stroke it smashed two bottlenecks: it provided for the financing of the British supply program, and at the same time it gave to the American Government badly needed authority over the whole field of military supplies. It was also a firm declaration of the American intention to block the Nazis; Stimson called it a "declaration of economic war."

Unlike the Selective Service Act, Lend-Lease was in its concept and origin a specifically "administration" measure; it was as members of a united team that the Administration leaders most closely concerned planned their statements to the congressional committees considering the bill. Leaving finance to Morgenthau and foreign policy to Hull, Stimson, as head of the department which would be most directly affected in the execution of any lend-lease program, centered his argument on the practical benefits which would result from passage of the bill.

In prolonged sessions with the House and Senate committees he emphasized that the bill would bring order out of the chaos then surrounding the procurement of munitions for friendly nations. For a dozen different purchasing missions of varying types and sizes it would substitute the trained and experienced military procurement officers of the United States Government. More important, it would permit the American Government to exercise a centralized and effective control over the distribution of weapons produced in the United States, for all such weapons would remain in American hands until they were complete and ready to use. There would be none of the difficulty previously caused by the fact that the same factory often was at work on orders for two or more independent governments.

Most important of all, Lend-Lease was a delegation of power, in the great tradition, to the one man to whom power must always be given in a national emergency—the President. Here Stimson clashed head on with more than one member of his own party, for the Republicans had taken up the chant of "dictatorship." Over and over again he emphasized his conviction that the only sound general principle was to trust the President. "My opinion—and it is one of long standing, and it has come from observation of various men who have held the Presidency during the period of my lifetime, whom I have had the privilege and the honor of observing at close range— my opinion is this: I have been impressed always with the tremendously sobering influence that the terrific responsibility of the Presidency will impose upon any man, and particularly in foreign relations. . . . That has applied to all of the gentlemen whom . . . I have had the opportunity of observing closely. . . . I feel that there is no one else, no other possible person in any official position who can be trusted to make conservatively and cautiously such a tremendous decision as the decisions which would have to be made in a great emergency involving a possible war. . . ."[2]

[2] Hearings on HR 1776, before the House Committee on Foreign Affairs, January 17, 1941.

Five times in the winter of 1941 Stimson went to Capitol Hill to testify in support of the Lend-Lease Act and its first appropriation bill. Five times he found himself involved in warm debate with men who feared the policy proposed and hated its proposer, Mr. Roosevelt. Each time he listened to another set of questions from the well-worn grab bag of isolationism; he had heard them all six months before when he first came to Washington. The answers were still the same. Yes, the United States was in peril; no, he did not think the President was likely to give our Navy away; yes, the Government would administer the act with due regard for the defense of the United States; the whole proposal was in fact designed to do nothing else than improve the security of the United States; no, he did not think it was a breach of neutrality; there was no obligation to be neutral in the face of aggression. It makes a weary tale in the retelling, but the questions were pointed, and so were the answers. Everything that Stimson had said before about the nature of the world crisis he now said again. And each day as he came away worn by the effort of debate he was heartened by the thought that this was a worth-while battle.

The Lend-Lease Act, substantially unweakened by amendment, was signed by the President on March 11, 1941. Congress retained the two controls appropriate to the legislative branch—it reserved the right of appropriation for the program, and it required regular reports. The first seven billions were appropriated shortly after. The administration had made its preparations, and the first supplies were transferred on the same day the bill was passed. Thus the War Department, "in addition to its other duties," became a service of supply to Allied armies everywhere. After the first labors of organization were complete, Stimson turned the job over to Under Secretary Patterson, and the work went ahead like any other program of procurement.

The great labors performed in the administration of Lend-Lease are no part of Stimson's life, and although he came frequently in contact with broad problems of allocation of weapons, this responsibility too was generally in other hands. Throughout the war he never wavered in his belief that the act was a constantly growing force for victory, and in its continued success he read a solid confirmation of his claim that the wise law is the law which gives power to the Executive. At his flexible discretion the President was able to direct where it was most needed the output of the "arsenal of democracy."

As the years passed, the Lend-Lease Act increased in favor in the eyes of Congress. Three times in the war Stimson went up to the Capitol to express his firm conviction that the act should be continued. Each time he found a milder and more friendly audience, until in 1945 he felt as if he must have come to his own funeral, so generous were the praises lavished on his "judgment" and "leadership" four years back. And for his part, as the years passed and the act was constantly renewed, he felt no anger or surprise that he had been so sharply quizzed in 1941. For truly this was a new departure, and in the broad view it was not the fight over the Lend-Lease Act but its eventual successful passage that deserved to be remembered in the record of the Seventy-seventh Congress.

CHAPTER XV

Valley of Doubt

---

1. A DIFFERENCE WITH THE PRESIDENT

THE Roosevelt administration in 1941 was conducting a struggle on two great fronts. One was the crisis in Europe, with its looming counterpart in the Far East; the other was the battleground of American opinion. During the months that followed the passage of the Lend-Lease Act, the tactics of combat on this second battleground became a point of significant divergence between Stimson and his chief.

To the President and all his leading advisers it was clear that the United States must take an ever increasing part in the resistance of the world against German and Japanese aggression. This could only be done with the approval and support of the bulk of the nation, and perhaps no nation of basically sound spirit has ever been more at a disadvantage in adjusting its thinking to a great crisis than the United States before Pearl Harbor. For the cheap and unworthy beliefs into which it was beguiled in the years between 1918 and 1939 the country paid a great penalty, and the full price has perhaps not even yet been exacted. For twenty years the people of the United States had turned their backs to the rest of the world; complacently they had listened to those who argued that their country could be an island to itself; by an overwhelming majority they had enforced a policy of isolation; it was their pressure that had produced legislation designed on the extraordinary theory that a single nation can keep itself out of war by passing laws. As the storm began to rise in 1931, Americans were indignant, as any decent people must be when they see aggression; they were indignant and inactive. Even in 1939 most of them believed that this war was not theirs. It is therefore not strange that in 1940 and 1941 the nation, turning at last to face the facts of life with action, kept thinking in terms of "measures short of war."

American thinking was thus confused, but Americans have no cause to be ashamed of the basic reason for the confusion, which was nothing more nor less than their hatred of war. Many much less noble feelings were involved in the complex emotional reaction called isolationism, but the ordinary American, the man in the great majority who detested the Nazi system and devoutly hoped for its defeat, held back from urging full participation in the struggle for the simple reason that he hated war. It was to this decent feeling that the more rabid isolationist leaders made indecent appeals, and to this decent feeling President Roosevelt deferred in constantly asserting that he was not advocating war, nor leading his country into an inevitable conflict.

Perhaps no public figure in the country had a clearer record of opposition to the whole cast of thinking that dominated the country between the two world wars than Stimson. He constantly denied that war could be avoided by isolation, and never doubted that the final issue of policy was always one of right and wrong, not peace and war. Yet even Stimson did not publicly preach to the American people the necessity of fighting; any such outright appeal would at once have lost him his hearers; always his statements were framed to preach rather the absolute necessity of preventing a Nazi triumph. Although constantly pressed for such an admission by isolationist members of Congress, Stimson never allowed himself to say that the final result of President Roosevelt's policy would be war.

When he first took office in 1940, and for several months afterward, Stimson himself did not honestly believe that war was the probable *immediate* outcome of the policy of helping the British. A declaration of war was certainly not imminent, nor even remotely possible in view of the temper of the people at the time. And of course the country had almost no weapons or troops. As he gradually became convinced that war was inevitable, he was bound to silence by the requirement of loyalty to his chief.

It was after the election, as the year was ending, that Stimson first noted in his diary his feeling that in the end the United States must fight. On December 16 after a meeting with Knox, General Marshall, and Admiral Stark he noted that "there was a basic agreement among us all. That in itself was very encouraging. All four agreed that this emergency could hardly be passed over without this country being drawn into the war eventually." (Diary, December 16, 1940) This belief Stimson continued to hold, ever more strongly, for the next twelve months. But in this period his thinking passed through several distinct stages.

In the first stage, which lasted more or less through the passage of the Lend-Lease Act, he believed that the President was leading the country into active measures just as fast as it was willing to go. He fully approved of the President's radio address of December 29, in which Mr. Roosevelt made entirely clear his decision not to permit the defeat of Great Britain.

Although Stimson felt certain that young Americans would not permanently be willing to remain "toolmakers for other nations which fight" when they had once appreciated the issue "between right and wrong," he admitted that the time was not ripe for the final step. "That cannot yet be broached but it will come in time I feel certain and the President went as far as he could at the present time." (Diary, December 29, 1940)

The second stage of Stimson's thinking is more complicated; it lasted from April, 1941, until the autumn. During this period it was his strong belief that the situation required more energetic and explicit leadership than President Roosevelt considered wise. There were two central reasons for this feeling. First, he was convinced that if the policy of sustaining Great Britain was to succeed, America must throw the major part of her naval strength into the Atlantic battle. There was no other way to insure the safe delivery of the lend-lease supplies which the nation had decided to send to the British; second, Stimson's whole concept of the duty of the Chief Executive centered on his obligation to act as the leader, and not merely the representative, of public opinion. Of the power of forthright leadership he had a higher opinion than the President. It will be helpful to consider each of these points in some detail.

The winter of 1940-1941 was a period of relative quiet in the European war; the principal objective of both sides was to prepare for the great campaigns anticipated in the following spring and summer. It was expected by the British and American leaders that Hitler would then make a final great effort to conquer the British Isles. Accordingly their major purpose was to insure the defense of the British home islands. The bulk of the burden fell to the British themselves; the task of the Americans was to help insure the safe delivery of a maximum volume of supplies of all kinds. But the constantly increasing rate of successful submarine attacks made it seem clear to Stimson, Marshall, and Knox, even in December, that the Royal Navy must have the assistance of American naval units in defending the Atlantic highway. No halfway measures would do. On December 19, "we had about the longest [Cabinet] meeting yet. The President brought up the question of the sinkings on the oceans of the traffic with Great Britain. The list of these sinkings is terrific, over four million tons so far—a terrific loss to civilization and to commerce, all over the world—and it is now very clear that England will not be able to hold out very much longer against it unless some defense is found. The President discussed various measures of getting new ships, taking the ships that were interned belonging to foreign nations on one side—building new ones on the other. I finally told him the story of my leaky bathtub . . . I told him that I thought it was a pretty high price to put so much new water into the bathtub instead of plugging the leaks, meaning by that that I thought we ought to forcibly stop the German submarines by our intervention. Well, he said he hadn't quite reached that yet." (Diary, December 19, 1940)

Through the winter Stimson's belief in the need for convoys grew constantly stronger, as did that of his military advisers and of the Navy Department. Toward the end of March, in a meeting with Knox, "We both agreed that the crisis is coming very soon and that convoying is the only solution and that it must come practically at once." (Diary, March 24, 1941)

The following day a meeting was held with the senior British officers in Washington. "They agreed, each one of them, that they could not, with present naval forces, assume the entire escort duty that is required to protect the convoys of munitions to Great Britain." (Diary, March 25, 1941)

The President was not less aware than Stimson and Knox of the vital importance of assisting the British in the Atlantic, but his approach to the problem was different. April 10 "was a very long day, mostly spent at the White House. . . . The President had evidently been thinking out things as far as he could to see how far he could go toward the direction [of] protection of the British Transport line. He made up his mind that it was too dangerous to ask the Congress for the power to convoy. He thought that if such a resolution was pressed now it would probably be defeated. On this point I am rather inclined to differ with him, provided that he took the lead vigorously and showed the reasons for it. Nevertheless, he had made a decision and it was an honest one. Therefore he is trying to see how far over in the direction of Great Britain we could get and how would be the best way to do it. We had the atlas out and by drawing a line midway between the westernmost bulge of Africa and the easternmost bulge of Brazil, we found that the median line between the two continents was at about longitude line 25. . . . His plan is then that we shall patrol the high seas west of this median line, all the way down as far as we can furnish the force to do it, and that the British will swing their convoys over westward to the west side of this line, so that they will be within our area. Then by the use of patrol planes and patrol vessels we can patrol and follow the convoys and notify them of any German raiders or German submarines that we may see and give them a chance to escape." (Diary, April 10, 1941)

When it came to the announcement of this patrol system, the President, in agreement with the majority of the Cabinet, chose to portray it as a principally defensive move. In a conference with Stimson and Knox on April 24, "He kept reverting to the fact that the force in the Atlantic was merely going to be a patrol to watch for any aggressor and to report that to America. I answered there, with a smile on my face, saying,

'But you are not going to report the presence of the German Fleet to the Americas. You are going to report it to the British Fleet.' I wanted him to be honest with himself. To me it seems a clearly hostile act to the Germans, and I am prepared to take the responsibility of it. He seems to be trying to hide it into the character of a purely reconnaissance action which it really is not." (Diary, April 24, 1941)

The patrol system proved no final answer to the requirements of the Atlantic, and gradually through the summer and autumn the President was driven to continuously stronger measures, acting each time considerably later than Stimson thought right. This divergence between the President and his Secretary of War on the method of entering the Atlantic contest is a clear specific instance of their general disagreement on the second great issue that occupied Stimson's mind at the time: *the President's duty to lead*.

Stimson had the highest respect for Franklin Roosevelt's political acumen, and at no time was he prepared to assert categorically that the President's method was wrong; all he could say was that it was emphatically not the method he himself would have chosen, and that in his opinion the President would have been an even greater politician if he had been a less artful one. This difference between the two men was basic to their natures. In this particular instance it will perhaps never be possible to say with certainty which was right; our task here is merely to present the issue as Stimson saw it.

The central point was stated to the President by Stimson in a private meeting on April 22. "I warned him in the beginning that I was going to speak very frankly and I hoped that he wouldn't feel that I did not have the real loyalty and affection for him that I did have. He reassured me on that point and then I went over the whole situation of the deterioration in the American political situation toward the war that has taken place since nothing happened immediately after the [Lend-Lease] victory. I cautioned him on the necessity of his taking the lead and that without a lead on his part it was useless to expect the people would voluntarily take the initiative in letting him know whether or not they would follow him if he did take the lead." (Diary, April 22, 1941)

Stimson was certain that if the President were himself to go to the country and say frankly that force was needed and he wanted the country's approval in using it, he would be supported. In contrast to this policy, the President's method seemed to him to be one of cautious waiting for circumstance to get the fight started for him. The President was determined to avoid a setback at the hands of the isolationists, and he seriously feared that any overboldness on his part would lead to such a defeat.

On May 6 Stimson delivered a radio address, the text of which had been seen and passed by the President, expressing his own general view of the crisis, so far as loyalty to the President permitted. He came out flatly for active naval assistance to the British, pointing out that any other course would mean the annulment of the objectives of the Lend-Lease Act. And in the last two paragraphs he stated as clearly as he dared his conviction that war was coming.

". . . I am not one of those who think that the priceless freedom of our country can be saved without sacrifice. It can not. That has not been the way by which during millions of years humanity has slowly and painfully toiled upwards towards a better and more humane civilization. The men who suffered at Valley Forge and won at Yorktown gave more than money to the cause of freedom.

"Today a small group of evil leaders have taught the young men of Germany that the freedom of other men and nations must be destroyed. Today those young men are ready to die for that perverted conviction. Unless we on our side are ready to sacrifice and, if need be, die for the conviction that the freedom of America must be saved, it will not be saved. Only by a readiness for the same sacrifice can that freedom be preserved."

There was no bitterness in Stimson's disagreement with the President. One day at a Cabinet meeting, "the President talked a little about his program of patrol and what he was planning to do, . . . and after narrating what had been done he said, 'Well, it's a step forward.' I at once said to him, 'Well, I hope you will keep on walking, Mr. President. Keep on walking.'

The whole Cabinet burst into a roar of laughter which was joined in by the President." (Diary, April 25, 1941)

Although it was one of the strongest, along with a speech by Secretary Knox, Stimson's speech of May 6 was only one of many by administration leaders in this period. Stimson was interested to discover that he and Knox were not the only members of the Cabinet who were disturbed at the President's apparent failure to follow up more rapidly his victory in the Lend-Lease Act. Jackson and Ickes were also worried. The President had his more cautious advisers, however, notably in the State Department. In Mr. Roosevelt's preparations for his own radio speech of May 27, he faced the contrasting advice of two camps, and although the final speech was much stronger than Stimson had feared it might be, it was not nearly so strong as he had hoped. The President firmly asserted the doctrine of the freedom of the seas, and made it clear that he intended to use "all additional measures necessary" to assure the delivery of supplies to Great Britain. He also declared an "unlimited national emergency," thus giving the administration somewhat broader powers in dealing with the crisis. But when, on the following day in his press conference, he allowed himself to say that this bold and vigorous speech did not mean that he planned to institute convoys, Stimson was deeply discouraged. He had himself urged a very different course; in a letter of May 24 to the President he had suggested that the President ask Congress for power "to use naval, air, and military forces of the United States" in the Atlantic battle.

Throughout June Stimson's anxiety increased, and in the first few days of July it reached its climax. On July 2 he made his only wholly pessimistic diary entry in five years. The Nazi attack on Russia had begun and was going altogether too well; meanwhile America seemed to have lost her way. "Altogether, tonight I feel more up against it than ever before. It is a problem whether this country has it in itself to meet such an emergency. Whether we are really powerful enough and sincere enough and devoted enough to meet the Germans is getting to be more and more of a real problem." (Diary, July 2, 1941)

The next day he wrote the following letter and memorandum to the President, who at the time was considering his message to Congress on the occupation of Iceland.

July 3, 1941

My Dear Mr. President:

My thoughts are deeply with you during these critical days. When the time comes for you to speak, my view is that you should speak to the Congress not by message but face to face and do it with personal and disarming frankness. You are such a master of such intercourse that I hesitate even to suggest the points that you should cover.

The main thing it seems to me is to point out how you have done your best to serve the cause of peace and how events have proved too strong for you. That in my opinion is the most appealing and persuasive line and the one which will produce the following of the whole nation. It is the course which all of your constituents have themselves been obliged to follow.

I enclose merely a memorandum of some of the points to be covered, making no attempt at phraseology.

Faithfully yours,

HENRY L. STIMSON

The President,
Hyde Park, New York

MEMORANDUM FOR ADDRESS TO CONGRESS

"I have sincerely hoped that we should not be drawn into this war. I have earnestly tried to avoid the use of force. I have labored with all my strength to secure a national defense, both naval and military, for this nation which would be sufficient to protect it when fighting alone against any combination of nations that might attack it. But my hope is becoming dim. The effort to avoid the use of force is proving ineffective. Our national defense is as yet far from complete. It has now become abundantly clear that, unless we add our every effort, physical and spiritual as well as material, to the efforts of those free nations who are still fighting for freedom in this world, we shall ourselves be brought to a situation where we shall be fighting alone at an enormously greater danger than we should encounter today with their aid."

The attitude suggested in this memorandum was rejected by the President, although the advice of such men as Stimson and Hopkins was again effective in offsetting more cautious counsel from other sources. In a meeting at the White House on July 6, Stimson told the President's advisers that "the President must be frank. Whether or not he was going to ask the Congress for action, he must in any event tell them exactly what he is doing and what he intends to do." (Diary, July 6, 1941) The President's message of July 7 did at least frankly state that he had moved American forces into Iceland and proposed to defend the sea communications between the United States and that island. In comparison with Stimson's own long draft, prepared on July 5 at Mr. Roosevelt's request, the President's message lacked emphasis on the central and controlling fact that Iceland was important principally as a way station on the North Atlantic route from America to Great Britain. It also omitted any intimation of war as imminent. The President was still content to build his case mainly on the defense of the Western Hemisphere, believing that this was a more palatable argument to the people, and one less subject to violent attack from the isolationists.

This effort in July was Stimson's last active attempt to bring the President to his way of thinking. It was clear that Mr. Roosevelt did not agree with him, and Stimson was inclined to believe after July that the President was so far committed to his own more gradual course that nothing could change him.

Moreover, as the summer wore on, the kind of lifting leadership which Stimson desired became less possible. 'The chance for a trumpet call for a battle to save freedom throughout the world had been sunk in a quibble over the extent of defense and the limits of the Western Hemisphere.' Meanwhile, what words might have accomplished earlier was being achieved by events; one of our patrolling destroyers was attacked, and the President publicly announced that the fleet would shoot on sight Axis vessels in the western Atlantic. While the President accomplished his object of having the war come to him, it should be observed that by this policy he in effect surrendered the initiative to the Nazis. By waiting for Nazi attacks on American vessels the President left it to them to choose their time to fight.

Looking back on this period Stimson could not avoid a comparison between Franklin Roosevelt and his distinguished cousin Theodore. From what he knew of both men, he was forced to believe that in the crisis of 1941 T.R. would have done a better and more clean-cut job than was actually done. Equally with his cousin he would have appreciated the true meaning of the Nazi threat, and there can be no higher praise, for no statesman in the world saw and described the Nazi menace more truly than Franklin Roosevelt. T.R.'s advantage would have been in his natural boldness, his firm conviction that where he led, men would follow. He would, Stimson felt sure, have been able to brush aside the contemptible little group of men who wailed of "warmongers," and in the blunt strokes of a poster painter he would have demonstrated the duty of Americans in a world issue. Franklin Roosevelt was not made that way. With unequaled political skill he could pave the way for any given specific step, but in so doing he was likely to tie his own hands for the future, using honeyed and consoling words that would return to plague him later.

The frame of mind of the American people under this treatment was graphically shown in a Gallup Poll at the end of April, 1941. To three questions the public gave three remarkable answers. Of those expressing an opinion, (1) nearly three-fourths would favor entering the war "if it appeared certain that there was no other way to defeat Germany and Italy," (2) four-fifths thought the United States would sooner or later enter the war, (3) four-fifths were opposed to immediate entry into the war.

The most striking fact about this result was that in the considered view of the leaders of the American Government, and also by facts publicly known, it was already clear that "there was no other way to defeat Germany and Italy" than by American entry into the war. The trouble was that no one in authority had said so.

In Stimson's view these answers exactly reflected the leadership of the President. The first answer showed how far he and others had succeeded in giving the American people a clear understanding of the fascist danger. The second answer reflected a somewhat fatalistic expectation that just as America had participated in every general European conflict for over two hundred years, she would probably get into this one too. The third answer, showing opposition to immediate entry, was the direct result of the fact that no responsible leader, and particularly not the President, had explicitly stated that that was necessary; on the contrary, the President in particular had repeatedly said that it was *not* necessary.

To Stimson it always seemed that the President directed his arguments altogether too much toward his vocal but small isolationist opposition, and not toward the people as a whole. By his continuous assertion that war was *not* a likely result of his policy, he permitted the American people to think themselves into a self-contradictory frame of mind. As Stimson constantly pointed out at the time, only the President could take the lead in a warlike policy. Only he had the right and duty to lead his people in this issue.

If Mr. Roosevelt had been himself a believer in neutrality, as McKinley had been in 1898 or Wilson for so long in 1916, it would have been natural that effective pressure for action should develop in private places. But as the proclaimed and acknowledged champion of the anti-Axis cause, he was necessarily its spearhead in policy, and without word from him the American people could not be expected to consider all-out action necessary.

There are those who will maintain that this explanation of Stimson's feelings merely confirms their view that Franklin Roosevelt dishonestly pulled the American people into a war they never should have fought.[1] Nothing could be farther from Stimson's own position, and it should be emphasized that if this charge is to be leveled against Mr. Roosevelt, it

---

[1] Quite aside from all other evidence, any argument that the American people were duped is of course wholly refuted by the Gallup Poll quoted above.

must in some degree be leveled at Stimson too. For the difference of policy between him and the President was one of degree, not of kind. Stimson saw war coming in December, 1940; it was not until April, 1941, that he began to feel that the President could successfully preach war to the people—there are always times, in politics, when it is impossible to speak with entire frankness about the future, as all but the most self-righteous will admit. *The essential difference between Stimson and the President was in the value they set on candor as a political weapon.* And as Stimson himself fully recognized, it was a good deal easier to advocate his policy, as Secretary of War, than to carry it out, as President. Certainly the consequences of failure in a bold course would have been extremely serious—no one can say whether the United States could have surmounted the reaction in feeling which would have set in if any proposal by the President had been roundly beaten in Congress or thoroughly disapproved by the people. On the other hand, it was equally true that the impasse into which America had thought herself in 1941 might have continued indefinitely if that had been the will of the Axis, and if this had happened, the President would have had to shoulder a large share of the blame. It did not happen, and all that America lost by her failure to enter the war earlier was time. But time in war means treasure and lives, and through the summer of 1941 Stimson was constantly faced with concrete examples of the losses incurred by delay.

2. THE PRICE OF INDECISION

The Secretary of War was not the only one who suffered from the difficulties of the strange condition, neither peaceful nor wholly warlike, in which the United States found herself in the latter half of 1941. The entire Army suffered, and it was not surprising that during those months there was a problem of "morale" among the troops. The men drafted in the first year of Selective Service faced many discouragements that the later millions did not know in nearly the same degree. Equipment was extremely scanty, and training programs were incomplete. But most of all, the new Army faced the problem that no one could tell it in clear and compelling terms exactly what it was training for, and the bulk of the selectees came to regard their year of service as something to be finished as quickly and painlessly as possible. The act required that they train for twelve months; they would do it, and then go home.

Probably no obviously necessary measure ever passed Congress by so close a margin as the bill to extend the term of service for selectees which was enacted in August, 1941. When Stimson first discussed this bill with leaders of Congress, they were almost unanimous in their assertion that it could never pass. They turned out to be wrong, by a margin of one vote; for this the country could thank George Marshall, who undertook the main burden of advocating and explaining the bill. Without it, the Army would by December 7 have been largely disorganized by discharges and plans for discharges—the meaning of such a disorganization can best be understood by recalling what happened to the American Army when it began to restore its soldiers to civilian life in 1945.

What made this measure so distasteful to Congressmen was that it seemed to involve an unexpected change in a contract between the selectees and the government. The original act clearly stated that the twelve-month term of service could be extended "whenever the Congress has declared that the national interest is imperiled," but this clause had not been emphasized at the time, and Congressmen did not wish to take the onus of making the required declaration. In fact many of them hoped by inaction to force the President to do by trickery what they themselves refused to do openly. On August 7, Representative Walter G. Andrews, of New York, came to see Stimson. Andrews, "a very good man," and a supporter of the bill for extension, "fished out an opinion which he said the opponents were relying on which held that technically, although not morally, the President would have the power to extend the term of service of each man himself after his one year expired by passing him into the Reserve and then calling him out from the Reserve. This is one of those finespun technical interpretations which possibly is legally correct (I think I can say probably) and yet which is contrary to the intention of the Congress at the time when the statutes last summer were made and I am sure it would arouse great resentment against the President if he followed that. Yet that is just what these cowards in the Congress are trying to do. They want to avoid the responsibility themselves . . . and to throw it on the President and then, if he should take this interpretation, they would be the first ones to jump on him as violating the real purpose of the law." (Diary, August 7, 1941) Stimson himself had felt on several occasions that Mr. Roosevelt might well be more frank with Congress than he was, but certainly in the face of this sort of pusillanimous hostility it was not easy for the President to be trustful.

The battle over this bill involved Stimson in a particularly unpleasant clash with Senator Burton K. Wheeler, the man who had described the Lend-Lease Act as a measure designed to plow under every fourth American boy. Under Wheeler's frank, a million antiwar postcards were sent out in July, containing material designed to show the folly of the President's policy. Some of these cards were delivered to soldiers, and in their anger Stimson and the President decided that the former should make a strong statement. Stimson told his press conference that "this comes very near the line of subversive activities against the United States—if not treason." To this accusation Wheeler hotly replied, and he was able to demonstrate that no copies of his card had been sent intentionally to any soldiers. Against the advice of most of his staff Stimson decided to apologize. It was not a pleasant decision, for the extraordinary bitterness of Wheeler's whole course in 1941 had reached one of its highest points in his attack on Stimson. After making the apology "my mind felt very much better," and the surprised and friendly reaction to his statement in the press confirmed his feeling that he had done the right thing. Even Wheeler seemed to think the apology creditable.

As finally passed, the Draft Extension Act provided for the retention in service of all selectees, National Guardsmen, and Reserves for an additional period of not more than eighteen months beyond the year originally specified. On August 15, the day after its passage, Stimson delivered a radio address to the Army in an effort to explain the reasons for the bill. So far as he could, he rehearsed the nature of the danger facing the country. As it was still the government's policy to discuss the peril in terms of defense, his speech was probably not very effective in its purpose, and although it was sound enough, Stimson thought it "poor" and "defensive" when he read it over after the war. But in 1941 nothing short of a radical change in the country's thinking could fully have reconciled drafted soldiers to an extension of their term of involuntary service. The reports of low morale were disturbing, but the root of the difficulty could not be removed by any action of the War Department. "The trouble has come from the fact that we have [been] trying to train an army for war without any declaration of war by Congress and with the country not facing the danger before it." (Diary, September 15, 1941)

The aspect of morale usually regarded by the public as most important was the provision of adequate facilities for the relaxation and recreation of the soldier off duty. The importance of this undertaking Stimson never denied, and particularly in 1941, while the country was at peace, he pressed for speed and co-ordination in its handling. In Frederick Osborn he found an able and imaginative administrator for these matters, and Osborn's services to the Army constantly expanded in scope throughout the war. But nothing in Stimson's nature or experience led him to believe that the morale of an army could be measured by the number of its recreation halls and canteens. In his report for 1941 to the President he called attention to this curious but widely held delusion, which seemed to him wholly at variance with the best American tradition. ". . . At the same time that we leave no stone unturned for the protection and welfare of our soldiers, we must not forget that it is not the American ideal to bribe our young men into the patriotic service of their country by thoughts of comfort and amusement. Moving pictures and soda water fountains have their places, but endurance of hardship, sacrifice, competition, and the knowledge that he is strong and able to inflict blows and overcome obstacles are the factors that in the last analysis give the soldier his morale. And such is the growing morale of our present Army."

Thus Stimson emphasized, in the autumn of 1941, the one finally critical element in the morale of the individual soldier.

It is his skill and self-confidence as a fighting man that is central, not his comforts. His morale depends finally on his military training and his confidence in his military leaders. And in 14,000 miles of inspections Stimson had already seen enough to be sure that in this most important single matter the Army was sound as ever. In maneuvers in Tennessee and New York, Washington and North Carolina he had seen the new divisions, and many of the new commanders. The new Army was starting right, and public disturbance over the morale of the troops never concerned Stimson as much as critics thought it should; he remained certain that as soon as it was in action, the Army would have no basic problem of morale. To one worried friend he remarked that the day would come when the country would draw its own strength of heart from the spirit of the armed forces, and in the years that followed he found this prophecy constantly confirmed.

The national indecision which produced anxiety in Stimson and a serious problem of morale in the Army had its effect too in the field of production. In three areas Stimson and Patterson found themselves at a disadvantage in their constant campaign for more and better equipment.

The first was the government itself. Even within the Army it required civilian insistence to insure that procurement should be based on a more generous objective than merely the exact tables of equipment of projected units. In the Government as a whole the President continued in his refusal to appoint a single executive head for all production and procurement problems. Severely hampered by limitations on his authority, Knudsen was not able to instill in all his manufacturers the necessary sense of urgency. In September the President superimposed on his existing creation an agency called SPAB, the Supply, Priorities, and Allocations Board, with Donald Nelson as executive director. At the time this seemed a step forward, since it did at least give a single agency more power than Knudsen and his competitors in other places had had, but it soon proved to be only one more unsatisfactory makeshift.

Manufacturers remained cautious—not all of them, of

course, but many. Neither industry nor government was ready for a thoroughgoing conversion from peace to war; it continued to be the general practice merely to add military production to the ordinary civilian business of the country, and only the partial attention of such great industries as those making automobiles and rubber and electric machines was given to military production.

The third and as usual the most explosive source of difficulty was labor. Stimson's general view of the labor problem in a time of national emergency is discussed in a later chapter. It is enough here to remark that a united and patriotic response by workingmen depends on the same factors as the attitude of soldiers, government officials, and businessmen, and during the six months before Pearl Harbor there were more strikes and labor stoppages than there would have been if the country had been actively in the war; the climactic event in this period was a coal strike led by John L. Lewis in November, at a time when every standard of good sense and loyalty demanded full production in the mines. Stimson believed in firmness in dealing with strikes that affected the national defense—in this respect he found the President overcautious; but actually the basic difficulty was the absence of the war spirit.

On August 19, in a talk with Harry Hopkins, Stimson summarized his feelings on the American production program. "Hopkins asserted that the United States was not producing munitions as rapidly as it could. I said that was undoubtedly true but that it was making them as rapidly as I thought they could be made in the light of (1) the fact that there was no objective like a war to stimulate production; (2) the complexity of the organization which did not have any single responsible head; and (3) the 'persuasive' handling of labor. I enumerated the different strikes that were now retarding production. I told him that until those three items were changed he could not expect full production." (Diary, August 19, 1941)

CHAPTER XVI

The War Begins

I. PEARL HARBOR

THE Japanese attack on Pearl Harbor which ended the months of indecision has been the subject of more comment and investigation than any other military action in American history. The extraordinary damage there inflicted by the Japanese, at negligible cost to themselves, made the attack a shocking blow not only at American power but at American pride as well. Stimson was as much dismayed as anyone by the incompetence of the American defense at Pearl Harbor, but he also felt that in the hue and cry over the opening engagement of the war insufficient attention was given to the series of events which preceded it. The problem faced by the United States in the Pacific during 1941 was one of unusual complexity, and in the policy pursued by the American Government there was much that deserved close study, for the Pacific crisis was typical of the difficulties faced by a democracy in dealing with dictatorial aggression. The principal responsibility for the execution of American policy in this period rested with President Roosevelt and Secretary Hull. The position we have now to make clear is Stimson's own, and as such it will vary in some particulars from that of the responsible officers, but these very differences may serve to illustrate the nature of the problem presented to the administration.

The primary and overriding principle of American foreign policy when Stimson entered the Roosevelt Cabinet was unyielding opposition to aggression. It was this single, simple, solid rule that was the final touchstone of policy, however much it might be necessary to give or take in specific instances. We have already seen that by December, 1940, Stimson and others in the Government were persuaded that in the end this principle must lead to war. The world was a house divided, and the stand taken by America must in the end be forcefully upheld.

The second great general principle was that the decisive theater of the world conflict was in Europe. In June, 1941, the already dominant importance of this theater was increased by the German attack on Soviet Russia. If the Germans should quickly conquer Russia they would be vastly strengthened. It was the estimate of War Department Intelligence officers, at first, that the campaign could last only one to three months. On the other hand, if the Nazis should be stopped by the Russians and eventually defeated by a coalition of anti-Nazi powers, the world-wide conspiracy of aggression would be fatally weakened. Throughout 1941, therefore, the principal efforts of the American Government were directed toward the support of those resisting aggression in Europe, and with this policy Stimson heartily agreed. His only serious differences with the President arose out of his conviction that America was destined to play a major fighting role in the war. On this ground, from September onward, he strongly urged the claims of the American Air Forces to a larger share in the American output of military aircraft. Admitting that planes allotted to the United States might not be immediately useful in combat, he argued that "it is better for her [Britain] to have in the world a potent, well-armed, friendly American air force than a few additional planes."[1]

It was against the background of these two major American postulates that the Japanese crisis developed. The exact course of that development it was impossible to foretell because the problem of Japan was necessarily subordinate to the larger questions of aggression in general and Nazi Germany in particular. At different times there existed in the Government a number of different views as to the proper line of policy toward the Japanese.

When he arrived in Washington in 1940, Stimson found

[1] Memorandum to the President, October 21, 1941.

the administration engaged in a line of policy well described by the President as "babying them along." Making no secret of its view that the Japanese militarists were morally no better than the Nazis, and refusing absolutely to modify its cordial relations with China, the American Government was nevertheless still permitting the export of war materials to Japan, although finished munitions were under a "moral embargo" which had been established in 1938 and 1939. Both the President and the State Department were somewhat sensitive to criticism of this policy, since they were as well aware as their critics of the wickedness of the Japanese. Their object was simply to prevent the development of a war crisis in the Pacific at a time when the United States was both unprepared and preoccupied by the Nazis.

Since 1937, when the Japanese attacked China, Stimson had been urging, as a private citizen, an embargo on all American trade with Japan, and this attitude he carried with him into the Cabinet. Recognizing the peril of a premature showdown with Japan, he nevertheless believed that the effect of an embargo would be to check and weaken the Japanese, rather than to drive them into open war. His basic feeling, until more than a year after he entered the administration, was that the Japanese would not willingly take the suicidal step of making war on the United States. The folly of such a course had been convincingly described to him by trustworthy Japanese at the London Naval Conference ten years earlier, and although he did not trust the Japanese leaders of 1940 and 1941 any more than he trusted Hitler, he did not accurately appreciate their lack of prudence.

He therefore argued that the best possibility of a successful diplomatic adjustment with Japan lay in a policy of the utmost firmness. In October, 1940, the embargo on exports to Japan was materially extended, and in support of a still more vigorous policy Stimson wrote a memorandum pointing out how Japan had yielded before to American firmness, in her withdrawal from Shantung and Siberia in 1919 and her acceptance of naval inferiority in 1921. The moral of these events, he wrote, was that "Japan has historically shown that she can misinterpret a pacifistic policy of the United States for weakness. She has also historically shown that when the United States indicates by clear language and bold actions that she intends to carry out a clear and affirmative policy in the Far East, Japan will yield to that policy even though it conflicts with her own Asiatic policy and conceived interests. For the United States now to indicate either by soft words or inconsistent actions that she has no such clear and definite policy towards the Far East will only encourage Japan to bolder action." (Memorandum, October 2, 1940) The theory of this memorandum was not borne out by events. When the United States at last became genuinely firm, the Japanese did not yield; whether they would have yielded if Stimson's policy had been tried earlier it is impossible to say. In retrospect he was inclined to think that even by 1940 it was too late to dissuade them, by any line of diplomacy. To be certainly effective a firm policy would have had to begin much earlier, and such a course would have involved military preparations that would hardly have been greeted with favor by the American people.

The line of policy suggested by Stimson and others was predicated on the assumption that the Japanese, however wicked their intentions, would have the good sense not to get involved in war with the United States. The line of policy of the President and Mr. Hull was based rather on the importance of avoiding such a war, and on the admittedly faint hope that Japanese expansion could at least be restrained by some sort of diplomatic *modus vivendi*; Secretary Hull even dared to believe in the possibility of a complete reversal of Japanese policy; to strengthen this possibility he constantly pointed out to the Japanese the advantages to be gained by a realignment in the Pacific under which the Japanese would discard their expansionist dreams in favor of co-operative participation in a general development of peaceful trade. In such hopes Stimson was unable to join; his own attempts at persuasion had failed in far more hopeful circumstances in 1931, and he feared that the attempt to win the Japanese now could only lead to a further misunderstanding of American intentions. It is only fair to add that Hull himself put the possibility of success at one in ten.

In May, 1941, there arose an issue of grand strategy which clearly illustrated the divergence of opinion on Japan within the Government. This was the question of the movement of the United States Fleet from Hawaii to the Atlantic. With their eyes firmly fixed on the all-important struggle to keep open the Atlantic sea lane to Britain, Stimson, Knox, and Marshall became convinced that the bulk of the fleet should be moved to the Atlantic. This proposal was opposed by the State Department, and not viewed with any great sympathy by the admirals of the Navy. On the side of those urging the move it was argued that the European theater was the only one of decisive importance; that the fleet at Hawaii was no real threat to Japan since the Japanese clearly understood that we should never use it offensively without ample warning; that it had little or no defensive value there, since it was powerless to protect the Philippines, while the defense of Hawaii itself against invasion could easily be secured by land and air forces; that, so far from encouraging the Japanese in their expansion, the use of the fleet in the Atlantic would be a clear sign of the American intention to take active measures against aggression, since the Atlantic was the only ocean in which the American Navy could at the time find active employment. To put the fleet into action would prove the United States to be in earnest.

In opposition to the proposal were two major arguments. Hull insisted that the faint chance of an honorable diplomatic settlement with the Japanese was worth pursuing; he believed that any such chance would vanish with the removal from the Pacific of America's principal striking force. Further, he and his advisers believed that the disappearance of the American fleet from the Pacific would be taken by the Japanese as a go-ahead signal for their southward expansion; from such expansion there might well result a situation in which the United States would be forced to fight. In these opinions the Navy under Admiral Stark concurred, at least to some degree; the Pacific Ocean had for years been the Navy's assumed area of combat.

It is worth noting that in this disagreement both sides believed that the Japanese had no present intention of attacking the United States; the central disagreement was on the degree

of restraint imposed on her other ambitions by the United
States Fleet at Hawaii. In the light of later events it may be
argued either that the Japanese laid their basic plans without
any fear of the fleet or that they regarded its neutralization as
an essential prerequisite to their general attack. Certainly its
presence did not in the end deter them, but it may be considered doubtful whether its active employment against the
Nazis would have been any greater deterrent. So far as Stimson individually is concerned, the core of his position was
simply that in the fight against the Nazis no handy weapon
should be left inactive; his preoccupation with Europe made
him more disposed than ever to minimize the danger from
Japan. He simply could not believe that she would dare to
attack southward so long as both the British Empire and the
United States remained major unbeaten naval powers, and in
this, of course, he was wrong—he had been more nearly right
in 1932, when he had foreseen war as the inevitable final
result of Japanese militarism.

The result of the disagreement within the Government was
compromise; the President decided that three battleships and
an appropriate supporting force should be transferred to the
Atlantic. It does not seem that anyone was wholly pleased by
this arrangement, which, however, had the quite fortuitous
effect of reducing by three the number of capital vessels available as Japanese targets on December 7. The President considered the subject closed, and Stimson swallowed his disappointment.

During July and August, 1941, the whole attitude of the
American Government toward Japan was changed. The advance of the Japanese into southern Indo-China, at a time
when conversations looking toward better relations were being
conducted by Hull with the Japanese Ambassador, made it
finally clear that Japan intended to expand her holdings in
southeast Asia whenever and wherever such expansion was
feasible. An abrupt end was put to a line of American policy
which Stimson at the time considered akin to the "appeasement" of Neville Chamberlain. On July 26, by freezing Japanese assets, the President completed the embargo he had been
constructing so cautiously and gradually for three years. On

August 12, after a wholly unsatisfactory exchange of notes between the President and the Japanese, Hull made it plain to Stimson and Knox that the situation in the Pacific might at any time develop into a military and not a diplomatic problem.

By a curious coincidence there occurred in this same month of August an important change in the thinking of the General Staff with regard to the defense of the Philippine Islands. For twenty years it had been considered that strategically the Philippines were an unprotected pawn, certain to be easily captured by the Japanese in the early stages of any war between the United States and Japan. Now it began to seem possible to establish in the Philippines a force not only sufficient to hold the Islands but also, and more important, strong enough to make it foolhardy for the Japanese to carry their expansion southward through the China Sea. For this change of view there were two leading causes. One was the contagious optimism of General Douglas MacArthur, who in July had been recalled to active duty in the United States Army after five years of service in building and training the new Philippine Army. MacArthur knew the current situation in the Philippines better than any other American officer, and he was surprisingly hopeful about the capabilities of his forces.

The second reason for the new view of the Philippines was the sudden and startling success of American Flying Fortresses in operations from the British Isles. Stimson found his military advisers swinging to the belief that with an adequate force of these heavy bombers the Philippines could become a self-sustaining fortress capable of blockading the China Sea by air power. The supposed advantage of this new weapon was that it could be delivered in force to the Philippines in spite of Japanese control of the surrounding areas.

Both the optimism of General MacArthur and the establishment of an effective force of B-17's were conditional upon time. Thus the new hope for a strong Philippine defense had the effect of making the War Department a strong proponent of maximum delay in bringing the Japanese crisis to a climax. Where before Stimson and Marshall had relied on the general Japanese unwillingness to start a war with the English-speaking powers, they now hoped to have the much stronger reliance of an effective military force on the spot. In their eyes the Philippines suddenly acquired a wholly new importance and were given the highest priority on all kinds of military equipment. As to how much time would be needed, estimates varied. On October 6 Stimson told Hull that "we needed three months to secure our position."

As it turned out, the State Department was able to get only two months of delay after this October conversation, but Stimson considered that Hull did all that he possibly could, and he was at no time critical of the State Department's inability to string out the negotiations any further. The defense of the Philippines was important, but it was certainly less important than the maintenance intact of basic principles of American policy in respect to China, and Stimson was certain that nothing short of an important compromise of these principles could have delayed the Japanese attack.

In the detailed negotiations of October and November Stimson had no active part. The beginnings of effective reinforcement of the Philippines rekindled briefly his hope that Japan might be persuaded not to force the issue; this new and concrete threat might do what a merely potential threat had failed to do. But in the latter part of November even this cautious hope began to disappear; it became apparent that a showdown could not be long delayed.

On November 26 Hull restated to the Japanese the basic American principles for peace in the Pacific. So deep was the gulf between these principles and the evidently fixed intentions of the Japanese Government that on the following morning Hull told Stimson, "I have washed my hands of it, and it is now in the hands of you and Knox—the Army and the Navy." (Diary, November 27, 1941) On the same day the War and Navy Departments sent war warnings to all United States forces in the Pacific.

During the following days it was learned that a large Japanese force was proceeding southward by sea from Shanghai. News of this force strengthened the conviction of the American Government that the next Japanese move would be an extension southward of the venture already begun in Indo-

China. The target of the force might be Thailand, Singapore, Malaya, the Philippines, or the Dutch East Indies. In any of these cases except an attack on the Philippines it would be necessary for the United States to make a decision as to whether or not to join in resistance to the Japanese advance. The whole Cabinet shared the President's view that the country would support a decision in favor of war.

Thus during the first week of December the attention of the American Government was directed at the Southwest Pacific, and the problems faced by the administration seemed to be two: first, to make it clear to the Japanese that aggression beyond a designated point in that area would mean war with the United States, and second, in the event of such aggression, to insure the support of the American people for a decision to fight Japan. It was still considered unlikely that the Japanese would begin their next set of moves by an open attack on the United States, and it seemed even less probable that any such attack would be directed at the United States Fleet in Hawaii.

The administration paid the Japanese the compliment of assuming that they would take the course best calculated to embarrass their potential enemies. It seemed obvious that by limiting their overt attack to such areas as Thailand or the Dutch East Indies or even Singapore they could insure a serious division of opinion among Americans. Although Mr. Roosevelt and his advisers hoped and believed that the country could be persuaded to fight in such a case, they knew that it would reproduce in the Pacific, and in waters half a world distant from the United States, the same questions that had been presented by Nazi aggression in Europe. There could be no assurance that what had been debated indecisively for eighteen months in one case would be determined overnight in the other. In Stimson's opinion the Japanese aggressors made a serious miscalculation when in this crisis of 1941 they did not try to divide their foes by piecemeal attacks on one of them at a time.

On December 7, at 2:00 P.M., "the President called me up on the telephone and in a rather excited voice to ask me 'Have you heard the news?' I said, 'Well, I have heard the telegrams which have been coming in about the Japanese advances in the

Gulf of Siam.' He said, 'Oh no. I don't mean that. They have attacked Hawaii. They are now bombing Hawaii.' Well, that was an excitement indeed." (Diary, December 7, 1941)

When Stimson recovered from his astonishment at the Japanese choice of the greatest American base as a point of attack, he was filled with confident hope of a major victory; it seemed to him probable that the alerted forces at Hawaii could cause very heavy damage to the attacking Japanese. It was not until evening that he learned how great a tactical success the Japanese had achieved in their strategic folly. The military party in Japan had undertaken a war which could have only one final result, but they had certainly made a good beginning.

The disaster at Pearl Harbor raised questions of responsibility, and even guilt, which occupied the attention of a half-dozen boards and committees during and after the war. That so great and unexpected a defeat should be investigated seemed to Stimson entirely natural and proper, but he was frequently irritated by the strange conclusions reached by some of the investigators. The Army's own Pearl Harbor Board so far misconceived the nature of military responsibility that it pointed a finger of blame at General Marshall himself, on the curious theory that the Chief of Staff is directly at fault whenever one of his subordinate staff officers fails to do a thorough job. Only General Marshall himself was seriously upset by this preposterous charge, but Stimson regarded it as outrageous that the reputation of the Army's finest soldier should be unnecessarily subjected to attack, and the answers which Stimson himself was forced to prepare for this and other accusations seemed to him hardly the best conceivable wartime employment of a Cabinet officer's energy.

His own view of Pearl Harbor was fully set forth during these investigations and need not be repeated here in detail. He was satisfied that the major responsibility for the catastrophe rested on the two officers commanding on the spot— Admiral Kimmel and General Short. It was true that the War and Navy Departments were not fully efficient in evaluating the information available to them, and of course it was also true that no one in Washington had correctly assessed

392 ON ACTIVE SERVICE

Japanese intentions and capabilities. Stimson like everyone else was painfully surprised by the skill and boldness displayed by all branches of the Japanese war machine from December 7 onward. Further, Washington had not adequately appreciated the importance of keeping its field commanders fully informed. "The novelty of the imminence of war and the fact that our outpost commanders were untried in their positions now indicate that more details and repeated emphasis would have been a safer policy."[2] In so far as these later views were not matched by foresight in 1941, Stimson along with his associates missed a chance to mitigate or prevent the Pearl Harbor disaster. The men in Washington did not foresee this attack, and they did not take the additional actions suggested by a retrospective view. But the basic fact remained: the officers commanding at Hawaii had been alerted like other outpost commanders; unlike other outpost commanders they proved on December 7 to be far from alert. It did not excuse them that Washington did not anticipate that they would be attacked. Washington's belief was based, among other things, on its quite natural assumption that they would be alert. It was on this assumption that Stimson and others based their initial satisfaction with the news that the Japanese had dared to attack Pearl Harbor. "The outpost commander," Stimson pointed out to the Joint Committee of Congress, "is like a sentinel on duty in the face of the enemy. His fundamental duties are clear and precise. . . . It is not the duty of the outpost commander to speculate or rely on the possibilities of the enemy attacking at some other outpost instead of his own. It is his duty to meet him at his post at any time and to make the best possible fight that can be made against him with the weapons with which he has been supplied."[2] In this duty the commanders in Hawaii failed.

Much of the discussion of Pearl Harbor was confused and embittered by a preposterous effort to demonstrate that President Roosevelt and his advisers had for some unfathomable but nefarious reason "planned it that way." There was also a marked disposition to believe that men friendly to the President were hiding something of crucial importance. Stimson

[2] Statement to the Joint Committee of Congress. March 21, 1946.

for one submitted without reservation every relevant passage from his private diary, and in addition wrote two long statements. In the end the prolonged and exhaustive investigation by a Joint Committee of Congress produced a majority report which Stimson considered both fair and intelligent. While it gave him, with the President and other high officials, a general approval for discharging their responsibilities with "distinction, ability, and foresight," it by no means exonerated War Department officials, and the responsibility which it inferentially placed on him, as head of the War Department, he was quite willing to accept. The twisted and malicious views of the minority report he considered sufficiently answered by the majority.

Even on December 7, in the midst of the first overwhelming reports of disaster, Stimson never doubted that the central importance of the Pearl Harbor attack lay not in the tactical victory carried off by the Japanese but in the simple fact that the months of hesitation and relative inaction were ended at a stroke. No single blow could have been better calculated to put an end to American indecision. "When the news first came that Japan had attacked us, my first feeling was of relief that the indecision was over and that a crisis had come in a way which would unite all our people. This continued to be my dominant feeling in spite of the news of catastrophes which quickly developed. For I feel that this country united has practically nothing to fear, while the apathy and divisions stirred up by unpatriotic men have been hitherto very discouraging." (Diary, December 7, 1941)

In the attack on Pearl Harbor a curtain of fire was lowered over the problems and anxieties of the preceding months. No longer would the secret war plans of the Army's General Staff be freely published by a major newspaper—as the Chicago *Tribune* had done three days before Pearl Harbor; no longer would it be a question whether Congress would permit American vessels to carry arms to Britain—by a narrow margin, in mid-November, the Neutrality Act had been amended to permit such action; no longer would the administration be faced with the awful task of producing on a wartime scale with a peacetime attitude; no longer would there be any foolish doubts about the morale of the American armed forces; no longer would the loud and bitter voices of a small minority be raised in horror at every forward step to block aggression. The die was cast, and Stimson knew that America at war would have unity, courage, strength, and will.

In the four years that followed he suffered often from the cares of wartime office, and over every day was cast the growing shadow of the casualty lists. But to a man whose temperament was that of a soldier, these things were easier to bear than the fearful former sight of America half-asleep. On December 7, 1941, for the first time in more than twenty years, the United States of America was placed in a position to take unified action for the peace and security of herself and the world. The Japanese attack at Pearl Harbor restored to America the freedom of action she had lost by many cunning bonds of her own citizens' contriving. The self-imprisoned giant was set free.

2. MISSION OF DELAY

"All students of history know that every war has three periods . . . the period of the 'onset,' the period of the 'drag' (when the war begins to weigh on the nations involved), and the 'finish.' During the first period it is inevitable that the free government, the government which depends on the consent of the people, . . . should be at a distinct disadvantage." Thus Stimson to his press conference on December 11, 1941. The American people and their leaders were suddenly face to face with the humiliating fact of defeat, and the testing prospect of still further unavoidable reverses. The galvanic awakening of the nation after Pearl Harbor made final victory seem certain, but the "distinct disadvantage" of the present could not be removed overnight.

It quickly became apparent that the skill and boldness shown by the Japanese at Pearl Harbor were not a single isolated phenomenon. At Guam and Wake, Singapore and Hong Kong the enemy victories began. On December 10 came the first landing in the Philippines, to be followed in twelve days by a much larger landing, in the classically anticipated area of the

Lingayen Gulf. Everywhere the enemy's advance was unex-
pectedly successful, and with the destruction of the *Prince of
Wales* and the *Repulse*—again on December 10—it became
apparent that in their technique as well as their power the
Japanese were for the time being masters of the Southwest
Pacific.

For Stimson as Secretary of War the point of focal interest
was the Philippines. It was quickly apparent that the hopes
of the previous autumn could not be realized; there would
be no successful defense of the Philippines by air power.
The preparations had not been completed; the Japanese were
too strong; most important of all, there had been no adequate
realization of the degree to which air power is dependent on
other things than unsupported airplanes. American planes by
scores were lost on the ground, in the Philippines as in Hawaii.
Nor could there be any major reinforcement through the air,
which, like the sea, came swiftly under Japanese control. Thus
the defense of the Philippines became once more the desperate
and losing struggle which had been forecast in the planning
of earlier years.

Thus coldly stated, the problem was one which the American
high command might have been expected to accept regretfully
as insoluble, writing off the Philippines and preparing to
defend the defensible. This point of view was not absent from
the General Staff, and it was forcefully urged by some naval
leaders. But neither strategically nor politically was the problem so simple as it appeared. Strategically it was of very great
importance that the Army in the Philippines should prolong
its resistance to the limit. Politically it was still more important
that this defense be supported as strongly as possible, for neither
the Filipino people nor the rest of the Far Eastern world could
be expected to have a high opinion of the United States if she
adopted a policy of "scuttle." On these grounds Stimson and
Marshall reacted strongly against any defeatist attitude. They
argued "that we could not give up the Philippines in that way;
that we must make every effort at whatever risk to keep Mac-
Arthur's line open and that otherwise we would paralyze the
activities of everybody in the Far East." (Diary, December
14, 1941) Taking his troubles to the White House, Stimson

found to his "great joy" that the President fully agreed with him and Marshall "as against the Navy"; Mr. Roosevelt called in the Acting Secretary of the Navy (Knox was in Hawaii) and "told him his position—told him that he was bound to help the Philippines and that the Navy had got to help in it." (Diary, December 14, 1941)

This difference of opinion with the Navy (which largely disappeared after the appointment of Admiral King as Naval Commander in Chief) was less a matter of strategy than one of attitude. Stimson fully understood that the fleet after Pearl Harbor was in no condition to mount any major counter-offensive, and he admitted too the Navy's right of decision as to acceptable and unacceptable risks for its carriers and remaining battleships. What he and the President opposed was the Navy's apparent lack of aggressive spirit. Frank Knox was a fighter, and his spirit was not broken by the disaster at Pearl Harbor, but the naval high command as a whole was shaken and nervous. The issue was really a broader one than the defense of the Philippines; it was the basic and critical issue between what Stimson called an "aggressive defense" and a "defensive defense." He summarized the matter in his diary after a discussion with McCloy, Lovett, and Bundy on December 17. "I laid before them the issue which was now pending before us, namely as to whether we should make every effort possible in the Far East or whether, like the Navy, we should treat that as doomed and let it go. We all agreed that the first course was the one to follow; that we have a very good chance of making a successful defense, taking the southwestern Pacific as a whole. If we are driven out of the Philippines and Singapore, we can still fall back on the Netherlands East Indies and Australia; and with the cooperation of China—if we can keep that going—we can strike good counterblows at Japan. While if we yielded to the defeatist theory, it would have not only the disastrous effect on our material policy of letting Japan get strongly ensconced in the southwestern Pacific which would be a terribly hard job to get her out of, but it would psychologically do even more in the discouragement of China and in fact all of the four powers who are now fighting very well together. Also it would have a very bad effect on Russia. So this theory goes. It has been accepted by the President, and the Army is taking steps to make a solid base at Port Darwin in Australia." (Diary, December 17, 1941)

Events were to prove that even the aggressive defense adopted by the President and his advisers succeeded only in holding Australia and a small foothold in New Guinea. The attempt to reinforce the Philippines, although undertaken with the firmness and conviction described above, was a failure. The Japanese sea and air blockade was almost complete, and although blockade running was energetically organized, very little reached General MacArthur. Only by submarine could a tenuous connection be maintained. The securing of delay, and the maintenance of American honor in the Philippines, thus fell to the gallant and isolated Philippine and American forces under President Quezon and General MacArthur.

Through December and January Stimson watched with a full heart the skillful and vastly courageous operations of MacArthur's forces. Hopelessly outnumbered, and under-equipped as no American Army force would be again, they exacted losses from the enemy that left no doubt in any mind of the quality of the American soldier. Even more heartening was the overwhelming proof of the loyalty of the Filipinos. By the Japanese attack forty years of American trusteeship were put to the acid test of courage, and the test was triumphantly passed. But even these great considerations were over-shadowed by the need for facing "the agonizing experience of seeing the doomed garrison gradually pulled down." (Diary, January 2, 1942)

And what was "agonizing" for Stimson and others in Washington must necessarily be still more trying for Quezon and MacArthur in the Philippines. These two men were in the battle; they could see, as Washington could not, the tragic sufferings of soldiers and civilians alike under the invasion; they could not see, as Washington could, that it was not for lack of effort that the Philippines were not reinforced. Message after message came from them asking for help, and words seemed to be the only answer. Finally, on February 8, Quezon, with the unanimous approval of his Cabinet, sent a message to the President proposing that the Philippines receive immediate and unconditional independence from the United States, and that they be forthwith neutralized by agreement between Japan and the United States; all troops were to be withdrawn and the Philippine Army disbanded. Quezon's message also contained strictures against the American failure to reinforce the Philippines, in terms as unfair as they were wholly understandable. With his message came one from High Commissioner Sayre stating that, "If the premise of President Quezon is correct that American help cannot or will not arrive here in time to be availing," Sayre would support his proposal. General MacArthur, in forwarding these two messages, added his own. After describing in detail the extremely precarious position of his command, he warned that, "Since I have no air or sea protection you must be prepared at any time to figure on the complete destruction of this command. You must determine whether the mission of delay would be better furthered by the temporizing plan of Quezon or by my continued battle effort. The temper of the Filipinos is one of almost violent resentment against the United States. Every one of them expected help and when it has not been forthcoming they believe they have been betrayed in favor of others. . . . So far as the military angle is concerned, the problem presents itself as to whether the plan of President Quezon might offer the best possible solution of what is about to be a disastrous debacle. It would not affect the ultimate situation in the Philippines for that would be determined by the results in other theatres. If the Japanese Government rejects President Quezon's proposition it would psychologically strengthen our hold because of their Prime Minister's public statement offering independence. If it accepts it, we lose no military advantage because we would still secure at least equal delay. Please instruct me."

Arriving in the War Department, these messages were a serious shock to Marshall and Stimson. Quezon's message seemed to assume that the Japanese were in fact attacking the United States but not the Philippines, and that the Filipino people had no interest in the war, a position which Quezon himself had repeatedly repudiated in public, and to which he could only have been driven by the pressure of his wholly distorted view of the American attitude toward supporting the Philippine campaign. Worse than that, Commissioner Sayre and General MacArthur appeared to have made no effort to dissuade Quezon from his position and had even given it some support in their messages. To Stimson and Marshall it seemed obvious that any such proposal as Quezon's would simply play into the hands of the Japanese. It would completely destroy the historic friendship between the Philippines and the United States. It involved an acceptance of the entirely disproved notion that the Japanese could be trusted to keep an agreement for "neutralization," and worst of all it would treat the "two great powers," Japan and America, as equally guilty of the destruction of the Philippines. "It was a wholly unreal message, taking no account [of] what the war was for or what the well known characteristics of Japan towards conquered people were." (Diary, February 9, 1942)

Stimson and Marshall took the messages to the President at once; "Sumner Welles was present, Cordell Hull being sick. The President read the message and then asked Marshall what we proposed doing about it. Marshall said that I could state our views better than he could and I then gave my views in full and as carefully as I could. In order to be more sure of no interruption, I arose from my seat and gave my views standing as if before the court. The President listened very attentively and, when I got through, he said he agreed with us. Sumner Welles . . . said that he agreed fully." Marshall and Stimson returned to the War Department, where the soldier drafted a reply to MacArthur while the civilian answered Quezon. "We barely finished by two-thirty when we went back again to the White House and there met Welles again, and also this time Stark and King. We spent an hour or more going over the drafts which of course were rather rough. The President was very quick and helpful in his suggestions and by four o'clock we had them completed and took them back to the Department to have written out for sending. It had been a pretty hard day, for the taking of the decision which we reached was a difficult one, consigning as it did a brave garrison to a fight to the finish and at the same time trying to send to Quezon a message which would put our attitude to the

Philippines upon a correct and elevated basis." (Diary, February 9, 1942)

Out of this day's work came the following radiogram to the Philippines.

MESSAGE SENT TO GENERAL MACARTHUR

February 9, 1942

"In the second section of this message I am making, through you, an immediate reply to President Quezon's proposals of February eight. My reply must emphatically deny the possibility of this Government's agreement to the political aspects of President Quezon's proposal. I authorize you to arrange for the capitulation of the Filipino elements of the defending forces, when and if in your opinion that course appears necessary and always having in mind that the Filipino troops are in the service of the United States. Details of all necessary arrangements will be left in your hands, including plans for segregation of forces and the withdrawal, if your judgment so dictates, of American elements to Fort Mills. The timing also will be left to you.

"American forces will continue to keep our flag flying in the Philippines so long as there remains any possibility of resistance. I have made these decisions in complete understanding of your military estimate that accompanied President Quezon's message to me. The duty and the necessity of resisting Japanese aggression to the last transcends in importance any other obligation now facing us in the Philippines.

"There has been gradually welded into a common front a globe encircling opposition to the predatory powers that are seeking the destruction of individual liberty and freedom of government. We cannot afford to have this line broken in any particular theater. As the most powerful member of this coalition we cannot display weakness in fact or in spirit anywhere. It is mandatory that there be established once and for all in the minds of all peoples complete evidence that the American determination and indomitable will to win carries on down to the last unit.

"I therefore give you this most difficult mission in full understanding of the desperate situation to which you may shortly be reduced. The service that you and the American members of your command can render to your country in the titanic struggle now developing is beyond all possibility of appraisement. I particularly request that you proceed rapidly to the organization of your forces and your defenses so as to make your resistance as effective as circumstances will permit and as prolonged as humanly possible.

"If the evacuation of President Quezon and his Cabinet appears reasonably safe they would be honored and greatly welcomed in the United States. They should come here via Australia. This applies also to the High Commissioner. Mrs. Sayre and your family should be given this opportunity if you consider it advisable. You yourself however must determine action to be taken in view of circumstances.

"Please inform Sayre of this message to you and to Quezon.

"Submit by radio the essentials of your plans in accordance with these instructions.

"Second section of message.

"Please convey the following message to President Quezon:

"I have just received your message sent through General MacArthur. From my message to you of January thirty, you must realize that I am not lacking in understanding of or sympathy with the situation of yourself and the Commonwealth Government today. The immediate crisis certainly seems desperate but such crises and their treatment must be judged by a more accurate measure than the anxieties and sufferings of the present, however acute. For over forty years the American government has been carrying out to the people of the Philippines a pledge to help them successfully, however long it might take, in their aspirations to become a self governing and independent people with individual freedom and economic strength which that lofty aim makes requisite. You yourself have participated in and are familiar with the many carefully planned steps by which that pledge of self government has been carried out and also the steps by which the economic independence of your islands is to be made effective. May I remind you now that in the loftiness of its aim and the fidelity with which it has been executed, this program of the United States towards another people has been unique in the history of the family of nations. In the Tydings McDuffie Act of one nine three four, to which you refer, the Congress of the United States finally fixed the year one nine four six as the date in which the Philippine Islands established by that Act should finally reach the goal of its hopes for political and economic independence.

"By a malign conspiracy of a few depraved but powerful governments this hope is now being frustrated and delayed. An organized attack upon individual freedom and governmental independence throughout the entire world, beginning in Europe, has now spread and been carried to the southwestern Pacific by Japan. The basic principles which have guided the United States in its conduct toward the Philippines have been violated in the rape of Czechoslovakia, Poland, Holland, Belgium, Luxembourg, Denmark, Norway, Albania, Greece, Yugoslavia, Manchukuo, China, Thailand and finally the Philippines. Could the people of any of these nations honestly look forward to true restoration of their independent sovereignty under the dominance of Germany, Italy, or Japan? You refer in your telegram to the announcement by the Japanese Prime Minister of Japan's willingness to grant to the Philippines her independence. I only have to refer you to the present condition of Korea, Manchukuo, North China, Indo China, and all other countries which have fallen under the brutal sway of the Japanese government, to point out the hollow duplicity of such an announcement. The present sufferings of the Filipino people, cruel as they may be, are infinitely less than the sufferings and permanent enslavement which will inevitably follow acceptance of Japanese promises. In any event is it longer possible for any reasonable person to rely upon Japanese offer or promise?

"The United States today is engaged with all its resources and in company with the governments of twenty-six other nations in an effort to defeat the aggression of Japan and its Axis partners. This effort will never be abandoned until the complete and thorough overthrow of the entire Axis system and the governments which maintain it. We are engaged now in laying the foundations in the southwest Pacific of a development in air, naval, and military power which shall become sufficient to meet and overthrow the widely extended and arrogant attempts of the Japanese. Military and naval operations call for recognition of realities. What we are doing there constitutes the best and surest help that we can render to the Philippines at this time.

"By the terms of our pledge to the Philippines implicit in our forty years of conduct towards your people and expressly recognized in the terms of the Tydings McDuffie Act, we have undertaken to protect you to the uttermost of our power until the time of your ultimate independence had arrived. Our soldiers in the Philippines are now engaged in fulfilling that purpose. The honor of the United States is pledged to its fulfillment. We propose that it be carried out regardless of its cost. Those Americans who are fighting now will continue to fight until the bitter end. Filipino soldiers have been rendering voluntary and gallant service in defense of their own homeland.

"So long as the flag of the United States flies on Filipino soil as a pledge of our duty to your people, it will be defended by our own men to the death. Whatever happens to the present American garrison we shall not relax our efforts until the forces which we are now marshaling outside the Philippine Islands return to the Philippines and drive the last remnant of the invaders from your soil."

FRANKLIN D. ROOSEVELT.

Thus the order was given, with its reasons, for the continuance of a battle which in the end accomplished all that was desired by the writers of this message. The response from Quezon was prompt and definite. In his autobiography he has described the effect of the President's message as "overwhelming"; he answered at once that he fully understood the reasons for the President's decision and would abide by it. General MacArthur replied with even greater firmness that he would resist to the end, and that he had not the least intention of surrendering Filipino elements of his command. "I count on them equally with the Americans to hold fast to the end," said

his message. As for evacuation, his family would remain with
him, and it was not safe that Quezon should leave, as his health
would not permit the trials of the necessary voyage. Later, at
the direct order of the President (an order fully approved by
Stimson and Marshall), MacArthur, with his family, would
leave the Philippines, to undertake the great task of leading
the Allied forces north from Australia, and Quezon too would
be persuaded to take his government into temporary exile. But
the spirit of resistance symbolized by the two leaders would
endure, in the Philippines and in history.

In this interchange of messages there were many of the
complex elements that lay at the heart of World War II. Here
was the leader of a colonial people, after two months of gallant
resistance to aggression, driven in his resentment of what
seemed a policy of nonsupport to repudiate the role of willing
sacrifice. His American commander, unable to understand
the failure of his government to give him needed help, was
balancing the alternative of resistance against what he himself called a "temporizing plan." Both of these men had already
amply proved their skill and courage; both had repeatedly
demonstrated their devotion to the common cause of the free
world. Yet neither appeared to appreciate the moral abdication involved in the proposal of a neutralized Philippines.

To the men in Washington the proper reply seemed clear,
but to make it was a test of their own resolution. Not for the
first or last time, Stimson and Marshall took courage from
each other and found themselves fully supported by the President. The central problem here was moral, far transcending in
its meaning any question of the "mission of delay." It was a
part of the necessary tragedy of war that this moral issue must
be met by a command to other men to die. Noble Romans
might find such orders easy, but the men who met in the White
House that day were ordinary Americans in their feelings
about human life. To give the order was a matter of duty, but
it was in its loyal execution that the true glory would be
found. And so on February 13 Stimson sent General Mac-
Arthur his final message in acknowledgment of the replies
received from the Philippines: "The superb courage and

fidelity of you and Quezon are fully recognized by the President and every one of us."

The decision of December, reiterated in the radiograms of February, reached its appointed ending in the final surrender of the battered remnants of the American and Filipino forces on Corregidor in early May. There followed three more years of suffering for the survivors and for all who honored their achievement. The best statement of the service of these men to America, the Philippines, and themselves was made by General Wainwright in his last message from the Rock: "We have done our best, both here and on Bataan, and although beaten we are still unashamed."[3]

The advance of the Japanese suffered serious delay only in the Philippines. Singapore fell on February 15; in April the Japanese easily took Batavia, capital of the Netherlands East Indies. Stimson like other Americans could only watch in gloomy frustration while the Japanese filled the vacuum created by their initial victories of sea and air. It was fortunate that the decision to reinforce Australia had been taken in December, for the distance of that continent, and American unfamiliarity with wartime logistics, made the execution of that decision painfully slow. One shipment of light bombers was anxiously watched by Stimson and Marshall as it arrived in December in Brisbane. Six weeks later they were still waiting in vain for word that the planes were ready to fight.

Meanwhile Stimson's own attention was turned to problems of defense closer at home. The losses at Pearl Harbor temporarily so weakened the Navy that the defense of the west coast became an Army assignment, and in December the War Department executed an unprecedented deployment of troops to protect that area. In May, when the Japanese Fleet disappeared eastward on a combat mission, Marshall made a swift and skillful personal inspection of the western defenses, for he joined in Stimson's belief that the famous Doolittle raid—a pet project of the President, and a remarkable psychological victory in a period when such victories were valuable—might provoke retaliation governed more by pride than by strategy.

[3] Biennial report of the Chief of Staff, July 1, 1943, p. 12.

At the same time, mindful of its duty to be prepared for any emergency, the War Department ordered the evacuation of more than a hundred thousand persons of Japanese origin from strategic areas on the west coast. This decision was widely criticized as an unconstitutional invasion of the rights of individuals many of whom were American citizens, but it was eventually approved by the Supreme Court as a legitimate exercise of the war powers of the President. What critics ignored was the situation that led to the evacuation. Japanese raids on the west coast seemed not only possible but probable in the first months of the war, and it was quite impossible to be sure that the raiders would not receive important help from individuals of Japanese origin. More than that, anti-Japanese feeling on the west coast had reached a level which endangered the lives of all such individuals; incidents of extra-legal violence were increasingly frequent. So, with the President's approval, Stimson ordered and McCloy supervised a general evacuation of Japanese and Japanese-Americans from strategic coastal areas, and they believed in 1947 that the eventual result of this evacuation, in the resettlement of a conspicuous minority in many dispersed communities throughout the country, was to produce a distinctly healthier atmosphere for both Japanese and Americans.

It remained a fact that to loyal citizens this forced evacuation was a personal injustice, and Stimson fully appreciated their feelings. He and McCloy were strong advocates of the later formation of combat units of Japanese-American troops; the magnificent record of the 442nd Combat Team justified their advocacy. By their superb courage and devotion to duty, the men of that force won for all Japanese-Americans a clear right to the gratitude and comradeship of their American countrymen.

While the attention of the War Department was necessarily focused in large measure on the threat to the west coast, there were in the early months of 1942 other areas almost equally menaced. Stimson himself was principally interested in the Panama Canal. An attack in California might be extremely disturbing to Californians, and a failure to repel it would be intolerable, but if the Japanese were interested in securing important results, the best target in the Western Hemisphere was the

Canal. A breach in the Gatun Lake Dam or Locks would put the Canal out of service for an estimated two years, and on an inspection trip to Panama in March Stimson found that the officers in charge of the defenses believed that such damage could be effectively prevented only by intercepting enemy aircraft carriers before they had discharged their planes. In retrospect he believed that the Canal would have been a better target than Pearl Harbor for the initial Japanese attack. Even in March, after three months of energetic and able preparation, the Canal defenses were far from perfect, and on his return to Washington he was able to give a considerable stimulus to the varied elements of the new defense system, which was based on a constant patrol of radar-equipped long-range planes, together with an inner patrol and a modern aircraft warning service. Radar equipment and technique were the central requirements, and in his work to supply both to Panama Stimson learned how important it was that the two go together.

One vital element in the defense of the Canal had already been provided shortly after December 7. The attack at Pearl Harbor emphasized again the importance of unity of command; all the armed forces in any one area must have a single commander. Stimson was ashamed that the lesson had to be so painfully learned; for months he had read it in the experience of the British in North Africa, Crete, and Greece. Incautiously he had assumed that it was equally well learned by others, but even after Pearl Harbor it was only by the force and tact of General Marshall that unity of command was quickly established in all the outposts, and even then there were compromises—as in the Atlantic approaches to the Canal, where the naval commander was independent of General Andrews at Panama.

Neither the west coast nor Panama was ever attacked by the Japanese (if we except a brief shelling by a single submarine off California, and the remarkable wind-blown fire bombs of the last year of the war). In the naval victories of the Coral Sea and Midway, the onset was ended. At Guadalcanal in August the initiative passed to the Americans, and in September and October General MacArthur reversed the enemy advance in New Guinea. But months before these events the emphasis in Stimson's thinking had shifted. Having been among the first to insist on the establishment of an effective line of resistance in the Pacific, he became, in February and March, one of the earliest to emphasize that the Pacific theater was and must remain secondary. But this attitude was the result of his thinking on larger matters of strategy, and it may well be left to a later chapter.

3. WAR SECRETARY

The existence of a state of war radically revises the functions of a Secretary of War. In time of peace he is ordinarily one of the most independent and least noticed of Cabinet officers; once or twice a year he takes the stage to make his plea for funds; occasionally the public will be somewhat surprised to discover that he has other than military functions. In a time of approaching crisis he becomes somewhat more important; he must tell what his Department needs, always in terms of defense, and his counsel will have weight in diplomatic problems. In wartime all this changes; suddenly his branch of the Government becomes central. This shift will please some and annoy others of his colleagues, but it is inevitable. He finds himself in constant contact with the President, whose function as Commander in Chief takes precedence over all his other responsibilities; the nature of this relationship depends entirely on the individuals concerned, for it has no constitutional rule, and no set tradition. Only a part of the Secretary's duties concerns directly military questions, for in wartime the demands of the Army enter into every aspect of national life. Furthermore the enhanced prestige of the War Department will often operate to draw its officials into activities which even in wartime are no central part of their business, and frequently the men who mutter most about "military dominance" will be among the first to seek military support when they think they can get it; others, reluctant to accept the responsibility for unpopular decisions, will secure War Department approval for their action and then let it be understood that they have acted only under military pressure.

Within the Army, war brings more changes still. In the making of a citizen army the central issue is leadership; of such leadership war is the final test. But this leadership must be military; the confidence of the Army and the country must be confidence in soldiers. If the generals are successful, they will receive the credit they deserve, and they will receive in addition an uncritical emotional support that has no counterpart in peacetime democratic life. If they fail or seem to fail they will be quickly forgotten, but the fear their failure makes will spread to the whole military establishment. The pearl of highest price for a democracy at war is well-placed confidence in its military leadership. It thus becomes the duty of the Secretary of War to support, protect, and defend his generals. Those who fail must be quietly removed; those who succeed must be publicly acclaimed; those who come under attack, even when the attack is justified, must, if they are skillful fighting officers, be sustained and encouraged—for the first-rate field commander cannot be replaced by formal requisition. A rule which is sound for all administration everywhere thus becomes vital in an army at war. You discipline and reprimand in private; you praise and promote in public; and *you back your subordinates.* The function of the civilian Secretary is dual: as a responsible public official, it is his duty to insure that the Army serves the broad public interest; as the Army's chief it is his duty to act as the defender of the Army against its enemies and detractors.

These, then, were the duties to which Stimson addressed himself after Pearl Harbor. The core of the high command in the War Department did not change between December 7, 1941, and August 15, 1945. To Stimson's staff were added, from time to time, civilians of special qualifications who became members of his small personal circle of assistants. In the General Staff officers came and went, but the atmosphere of that body remained an atmosphere inspired by George Marshall. The unity and harmony at the top remained unbroken, and it was a team of men whose single object was to win the war. The proper record of the men who served there can be written only in terms of the whole accomplishment, and the whole accomplishment cannot yet be assessed as history. In the chapters that follow there will be many a story only half-told, for the decisions and policies in which Stimson had a part have not yet been fully connected in the records with their results. And it is not always easy to be sure— even with the aid of diaries and recollection—whether an idea or a decision started in Stimson's mind or in Marshall's, or in the civil or the military staff. The story that follows is personal, and not official, but the distinction is arbitrary in the extreme. At no other time in his life was Stimson so thoroughly surrounded by loyal, understanding, and able men as during the forty-four months of World War II.

The worst mistake of all would be to assume that in what follows there is any adequate record of the labors of the War Department high command. If there is a man whose personal history parallels that whole vast record it is General Marshall and not Stimson, but probably there is not such a man. For where there is mutual confidence, there can be decentralization, and where there is initiative, decentralization will produce programs and policies and results which no higher commander need expect to find in his biography. In a sense it was Stimson's greatest administrative success that he kept his desk free for those problems which, by their importance or peculiarity, only he could undertake.

This was a necessity for more than one reason. Stimson's mind was so constructed that it could hold only one major problem at a time. He disliked interruptions; he liked thoroughness. Traits of this kind do not grow weaker as a man grows older; if Stimson had not trusted those around him he must inevitably have become a dangerous bottleneck. His value to the War Department must come from the application of his principles and experience to major matters. His friend Grenville Clark used to tell him that he could do his job in four hours a day; this was an optimistic estimate, but the principle was correct.

Neither custom nor statute is based on this theory of a Cabinet officer's functions, and many a man has been buried by the mass of detailed work which will cross a government official's desk if he lets it. From the ordinary details Stimson was protected by the devoted skill of John W. Martyn, the

War Department's senior civil servant. With almost flawless discrimination Martyn separated the wheat from the chaff, calling to Stimson's attention only what it was necessary that he handle. From the thousands of signatures required by law he was relieved by a machine which reproduced his signature in lifelike form. For the mass of visitors who were certain that their business could only be handled by the Secretary of War in person there were two techniques. If possible, they were kept away; if not, then Stimson would hear them briefly and sympathetically, delivering them as quickly as possible into the hands of the appropriate subordinate. If they were then disappointed in their quest, he had still been polite; it was a technique that Stimson would have liked to be able to teach to Franklin Roosevelt, whose natural good will often took the shape of quick and unredeemable promises.

Stimson's concern for his private affairs was cut to a minimum by the painstaking work of his old law firm, the insight and experience of his personal secretary, Elizabeth Neary, and the loyal help of his successive military aides. Most of all, he had the care and support of Mrs. Stimson.

The work that remained was not light. Each day he rose at six-thirty, had a short walk before breakfast, and dictated for an hour or more before proceeding to the Department. There he remained through the day until the late afternoon, returning when he could for a game of deck tennis around five-thirty. In the evening he was usually alone with Mrs. Stimson, reading the "easier" official papers, or at dinner with one of his small circle of close friends; but often when problems were pressing the evening too was given to work.

Washington was a city whose climate he considered designed for the destruction of the sanity of government officials, and he found two ways of escape. He could fly to Highhold for the week end; the small problems of a farm in wartime were a welcome relaxation, and in the intimacy of home he could talk with old friends like a soldier on leave from the front. Or he could go on an inspection trip. Stimson believed that the visits of a Secretary of War were on the whole encouraging to the troops, though this belief was somewhat shaken by the evident disappointment of a group of lieutenants in Newfoundland who had been expecting Hedy Lamarr. In any case he was certain that they were encouraging to him. On four overseas tours and frequent journeys to camps and airfields in the United States he invariably found new strength, and often new ideas, for the work in Washington.

A similar source of encouragement was available in Washington, in the constant stream of men from the war theaters. These were always welcome visitors in the Secretary's office; liaison officers, foreign emissaries, and returning troop leaders he eagerly questioned, and in their answers there was a directness of contact that the daily cables could not give him. In the generally high quality of the officers fresh from the wars there was renewed assurance that the war was in safe hands; it was heartening to find that the major general of 1943 had fulfilled the promise of the major of 1940.

There is terror in the very name of war, and the responsibilities of wartime leadership are wearing beyond the knowledge of those who have not carried them. But in righteous war there is also strength for the spirit, and it comes mainly from the front lines backward. In the needs of the men who were fighting, the undying challenge of their death, and the constant proof of their quality as men and soldiers there was an ever growing source of inspiration for all at home. And this inspiration was greater for Stimson than for the ordinary citizen, for he was closer to the Army, more directly aware of its work, and accountable for its support. In the force of this feeling is not merely the explanation of his continued strength to serve but also the motivation for many of the policies and purposes which we are about to discuss.

CHAPTER XVII

The Army and Grand Strategy

1. PEARL HARBOR TO NORTH AFRICA

IMMEDIATELY after Pearl Harbor it became necessary for the United States and Great Britain to concert their strategy. In the week before Christmas, 1941, Winston Churchill and his principal military advisers arrived in Washington for the first of the great wartime meetings with the President and American advisers.

The most important single accomplishment of this meeting was that it laid the groundwork for the establishment of an effectively unified Allied high command. The Combined Chiefs of Staff, set up in Washington in early 1942, rapidly became a fully developed instrument for the co-ordination of land, sea, and air warfare in a world-wide war. Its seven members, four Americans and three Britons, gradually developed an authority and influence exceeded only by the decisive meetings between the President and the Prime Minister. For their success there were several causes, but in Stimson's mind these could in the main be reduced to two. One was the inflexible determination of Mr. Roosevelt and Mr. Churchill to fight the war as a unified team. The other was the organizing genius and diplomatic skill of George Marshall. It was Marshall who insisted that the Combined Chiefs should in fact be chiefs, and not merely elders of the council; the British members were the direct representatives of the military chiefs of the British armed forces, while the American members were themselves the responsible leaders of the services which they represented. It was Marshall too who guided the development of the staff work of the Combined Chiefs, insisting on a continuous record of consideration and decision and directive. Finally, it was Marshall, with the particular assistance and support of an equally disinterested and farsighted soldier-statesman, Field Marshal Sir John Dill, who made it possible for the Combined Chiefs to act not as a mere collecting point for the inevitable rivalries between services and nations but as an executive committee for the prosecution of a global war.

Marshall was also the primary agent in the establishment and operation of the strictly American counterpart to the Combined Chiefs; in spite of the urging of Stimson and others, the President for some time hesitated to approve an executive agency of this type for co-ordinating the American military effort; he was particularly doubtful about the wisdom of appointing any officer as Chief of Staff to himself. Marshall combined his advocacy of such an appointment with a refusal to accept it for himself, arguing that it would only be acceptable to the Navy if an admiral received the appointment. The Joint Chiefs of Staff, when finally organized, included four officers: the President's Chief of Staff and the senior officers of the Army, Navy, and Army Air Forces; these were the same men who served as American members of the Combined Chiefs, and they exercised direct supervision over the American share of the Allied military effort. The Joint Chiefs became the President's direct military advisers.

As it became gradually more effective, this formal organization of the staffs had, in Stimson's view, a most salutary effect on the President's weakness for snap decisions; it thus offset a characteristic which might otherwise have been a serious handicap to his basically sound strategic instincts. Both in the December meeting of 1941 and in the following June the President made suggestions to the Prime Minister which if seriously pursued must have disrupted the American military effort. Mr. Roosevelt was fond of "trial balloons," and perhaps Stimson's fear of this technique was due largely to its complete dissimilarity from his own method of thought, but he nevertheless felt certain that both Mr. Roosevelt and Mr. Churchill were men whose great talents required the balancing restraint of carefully organized staff advice.

Stimson, as Secretary of War, was neither a professional

soldier nor the finally responsible political leader, and the organization which made the Chiefs of Staff directly responsible to the President left him with no formal responsibility in matters of military strategy. This arrangement might have disturbed him seriously if he had not continued to enjoy a relationship of complete mutual confidence with the President and with Generals Marshall and Arnold. He continued to be called in, as the advocate of the War Department and as a constitutionally recognized adviser to the President, and he thus became an active participant in the two years of Anglo-American discussion over the grand strategy of their European campaigns.

The detailed discussions in the meeting of December, 1941, were largely devoted to the problems of the Pacific, where the situation was immediately critical, but even in the face of the Japanese advance there was no deviation from the principle already accepted by both sides before Pearl Harbor—only the European theater was decisive. In the language of a memorandum prepared by Stimson and used by the President as the agenda for the first general meeting of the conference, "Our joint war plans have recognized the North Atlantic as our principal theatre of operations should America become involved in the war. Therefore it should now be given primary consideration and carefully reviewed in order to see whether our position there is safe." The first essential was "the preservation of our communications across the North Atlantic with our fortress in the British Isles covering the British Fleet." It was accordingly decided that an immediate beginning should be made in the establishment of an American force in Great Britain.

By itself the decision of December was not definitive, since the general agreement on the central importance of Great Britain did not include any strategic plan for the use of that fortress as a base for offensive operations. In the middle of February Stimson began to feel that the absence of such a plan was a serious weakness; without it there was no firm commitment that could prevent a series of diversionary shipments of troops and supplies to other areas more immediately threatened. In March his fears were strikingly confirmed by the arrival in Washington of a gloomy message from Mr. Churchill suggesting increased American commitments in non-European areas of the globe, to meet the Axis threat developing in Africa, southeastern Europe, and the Far East. At a White House meeting Stimson argued that the proper policy was that of avoiding such dispersion, and instead, "sending an overwhelming force to the British Isles and threatening an attack on the Germans in France; that this was the proper and orthodox line of our help in the war as it had always been recognized and that it would now have the effect of giving Hitler two fronts to fight on if it could be done in time while the Russians were still in. It would also heavily stimulate British sagging morale." (Diary, March 5, 1942) Stimson found on the following day that his view was fully confirmed by the detailed military analysis of the War Plans Division under Brigadier General Eisenhower, and the same general position was taken by all the President's advisers, the Navy accepting primary responsibility for the necessary labors in the Pacific. On March 8 the President replied to the Prime Minister proposing as a general rule that the British alone should assume the responsibility for the Middle East, the Americans the responsibility for the Pacific, while both nations jointly should operate in the critical Atlantic theater. At the same time it was decided that the American planners should prepare in detail a plan for invading Europe across the English Channel.

On March 25, "At one o'clock we lunched with the President in the Cabinet room. Knox, King, Harry Hopkins and Arnold, Marshall and I were there. The subject of discussion was the Joint Planners' report. The President started out and disappointed, and at first staggered, me by a résumé of what he thought the situation was, in which he looked like he was going off on the wildest kind of dispersion debauch; but, after he had toyed a while with the Middle East and the Mediterranean basin, which last he seemed to be quite charmed with, Marshall and I edged the discussion over into the Atlantic and held him there. Marshall made a very fine presentation. . . .

Towards the end of the meeting when the President suggested that the subject be now turned over to the Combined Chiefs of Staff organization (British and American), Hopkins took up the ball and made a strong plea that it should not go to that organization at all where it would simply be pulled to pieces and emasculated; but, as soon as the Joint American Army and Navy Chiefs of Staff had perfected it, someone (and he meant Marshall as he had told me before) should take it directly over to Churchill, Pound, Portal, and Brooke, who are the highest British authorities, and get it through them directly. This stopped the President's suggestion and we came away with his mandate to put this in shape if possible over this week end." (Diary, March 25, 1942)

Stimson's own strong distaste for the "charming" Mediterranean basin no doubt contributed to his alarm at the President's interest in it. In any case, this meeting made it clear that although Mr. Roosevelt had agreed to support the idea of a trans-Channel attack, the concept was not yet his own. Two days later, with the warm approval of Hopkins and Marshall, Stimson wrote the President a letter designed to persuade him to take a firm and final position.

Confidential

March 27, 1942

Dear Mr. President:

John Sherman said in 1877, "The only way to resume specie payments is to resume." Similarly, the only way to get the initiative in this war is to take it.

My advice is: As soon as your Chiefs of Staff have completed the plans for the northern offensive to your satisfaction, you should send them by a most trusted messenger and advocate to Churchill and his War Council as the American plan which you propose and intend to go ahead with if accepted by Britain. You should not submit it to the secondary British Chiefs of Staff here for amendment. They know about it and, if they have comment, they can send their comment independently to Great Britain.

And then having done that, you should lean with all your

strength on the ruthless rearrangement of shipping allotments and the preparation of landing gear for the ultimate invasion. That latter work is now going on at a rather dilettante pace. It should be pushed with the fever of war action, aimed at a definite date of completion not later than September. The rate of construction of a number of landing barges should not be allowed to lose the crisis of the World War. And yet that is the only objection to the offensive that, after talks with British critics here, I have heard made.

If such decisive action is once taken by you, further successful dispersion of our strength will automatically be terminated. We shall have an affirmative answer against which to measure all such demands; while, on the other hand, so long as we remain without our own plan of offensive, our forces will inevitably be dispersed and wasted.

Faithfully yours,

HENRY L. STIMSON
Secretary of War.

The President,
Hyde Park, New York

The plan for which Stimson and Marshall were arguing went under the code name of BOLERO. It contemplated a maximum build-up of American strength in Great Britain, looking toward a full-scale invasion in the spring of 1943, with fifty divisions, 60 per cent of them American, on the continent of Europe by the end of that summer. In the event of a desperate crisis on the Russian front in 1942, it also included the alternative possibility of a much smaller "beachhead" invasion in the autumn of that year, but this alternative, known as SLEDGE-HAMMER, was conceded to be less desirable. Concern over the plan SLEDGEHAMMER was in the end the cause of the abandonment of BOLERO; to Stimson, SLEDGEHAMMER's possible dangers did not seem so important. His objective was to secure a decision to invade Europe from the British base at the earliest practicable moment; only developing events could show whether that moment would be in 1942 or 1943.

On April 1 the President accepted the BOLERO plan and dispatched Hopkins and Marshall to London to secure the approval of the British. The emissaries were in the main successful and returned to Washington with an agreement to proceed on the basis of BOLERO. Stimson was delighted. But the agreement held for less than two months.

BOLERO was the brain child of the United States Army; the President and the Prime Minister had accepted it, but neither of the two had been fully and finally persuaded. Stimson never knew which of them was responsible for the Washington meetings in June at which the whole question was reopened. The initiative for the meeting came from Mr. Churchill, but he might well have acted on the basis of an indication that the President was not completely certain about the wisdom of BOLERO. Mr Roosevelt continued to lean toward an operation in North Africa, known in this period as GYMNAST, and on June 17 he reopened the subject with his advisers. "The President sprung on us a proposition which worried me very much. It looked as if he was going to jump the traces [after] all that we have been doing in regard to BOLERO and to imperil really our strategy of the whole situation. He wants to take up the case of GYMNAST again, thinking that he can bring additional pressure to save Russia. The only hope I have about it at all is that I think he may be doing it in his foxy way to forestall trouble that is now on the ocean coming towards us in the shape of a new British visitor. But he met with a rather robust opposition for the GYMNAST proposition. Marshall had a paper already prepared against it for he had a premonition of what was coming. I spoke very vigorously against it." The Navy was noncommittal but not nearly so vigorous in opposition as Stimson would have liked. "Altogether it was a disappointing afternoon." (Diary, June 17, 1942)

In the following two days Stimson prepared his brief in defense of BOLERO. The Prime Minister and his team had arrived, and it was evident that they were discussing new diversions. All of Stimson's experience as an advocate, and all of his conviction that the war would be won only by a cross-Channel campaign went into a letter written on June 19 and dispatched to the President with the unanimous endorsement of General Marshall and his staff.

Personal and Secret

June 19, 1942

Dear Mr. President:

While your military advisers are working out the logistics of the problem which you presented to us on Wednesday, may I very briefly recall to your memory the sequence of events which led to and the background which surrounds this problem. I hope it may be helpful to you.

1. Up to the time when America entered the war, the British Empire had, by force of circumstances, been fighting a series of uphill defensive campaigns with insufficient resources and almost hopeless logistics. The entry of Japan into the war and the naval disasters at Pearl Harbor and the Malay Peninsula imposed new defensive campaigns in the theatres of the Far East.

2. After the discussions with Mr. Churchill's party here last December the need for a carefully planned offensive became very evident. Russia had successfully fought off the entire German Army for six months. Winter had begun and the shaken and battered German Army would be helpless to renew its offensive for nearly six months more. The one thing Hitler rightly dreaded was a second front. In establishing such a front lay the best hope of keeping the Russian Army in the war and thus ultimately defeating Hitler. To apply the rapidly developing manpower and industrial strength of America promptly to the opening of such a front was manifestly the only way it could be accomplished.

3. But the effective application of America's strength required prompt, rapid and safe transportation overseas. The allied naval power controlled the seas by only a narrow margin. With one exception the Axis Powers controlled every feasible landing spot in Europe. By fortunate coincidence one of the shortest routes to Europe from America led through the only safe base not yet controlled by our enemies, the British Isles.

4. Out of these factors originated the BOLERO plan. The British Isles constituted the one spot (a) where we could safely and easily land our ground forces without the aid of carrier-based air cover. (b) through which we could without the aid of ships fly both bomber and fighting planes from America to Europe. (c) where we could safely and without interruption develop an adequate base for invading armies of great strength. Any other base in western Europe or north-west Africa could be obtained only by a risky attack and the long delay of development and fortification. (d) where we could safely develop air superiority over our chief enemy in northern France and force him either to fight us on equal terms or leave a bridgehead to France undefended.

5. The psychological advantages of BOLERO also were manifest. The menace of the establishment of American military power in the British Isles would be immediately evident to Hitler. It at once tended to remove the possibility of a successful invasion of Britain, Hitler's chief and last weapon. It awoke in every German mind the recollections of 1917 and 1918.

6. A steady, rapid, and unrelenting prosecution of the BOLERO plan was thus manifestly the surest road, first to the shaking of Hitler's anti-Russian campaign of '42, and second, to the ultimate defeat of his armies and the victorious termination of the war. Geographically and historically BOLERO was the easiest road to the center of our chief enemy's heart. The base was sure. The water barrier of the Channel under the support of Britain-based air power is far easier than either the Mediterranean or the Atlantic. The subsequent over-land route into Germany is easier than any alternate. Over the Low Countries has run the historic path of armies between Germany and France.

7. Since the BOLERO plan was adopted, subsequent events have tended to facilitate our position and justify its wisdom. (a) The greatest danger to America's prosecution of the BOLERO plan lay in the Pacific from Japan where our then inferiority in aircraft carriers subjected us to the dangers of enemy raids which might seriously cripple the vital airplane production upon which a prompt BOLERO offensive primarily

rests. The recent victory in the mid-Pacific [at Midway] has greatly alleviated that danger. Our rear in the west is now at least temporarily safe. (b) The psychological pressure of our preparation for BOLERO is already becoming manifest. There are unmistakable signs of uneasiness in Germany as well as increasing unrest in the subject populations of France, Holland, Czechoslavakia, Yugoslavia, Poland and Norway. This restlessness patently is encouraged by the growing American threat to Germany.

8. Under these circumstances an immense burden of proof rests upon any proposition which may impose the slightest risk of weakening BOLERO. Every day brings us further evidence of the great importance of unremittingly pressing forward that plan. When one is engaged in a tug of war, it is highly risky to spit on one's hands even for the purpose of getting a better grip. No new plan should even be whispered to friend or enemy unless it was so sure of immediate success and so manifestly helpful to BOLERO that it could not possibly be taken as evidence of doubt or vacillation in the prosecution of BOLERO. Enemies would be prompt to jump at one or the other of these conclusions.

9. While I have no intention of intruding on any discussion of logistics by the staff, one or two possible contingencies have occurred to me which would bear upon the wisdom of now embarking upon another trans-Atlantic expedition such as GYMNAST. (a) Assume the worst contingency possible; Assume a prompt victory over Russia which left a large German force free for other enterprises. It is conceivable that Germany might then make a surprise attempt at the invasion of Britain. She would have the force to attempt it. She may well have available the equipment for both air-borne and water-borne invasion. One of our most reliable military attachés believes emphatically that this is her plan—a surprise air-borne invasion from beyond the German boundaries producing a confusion in Britain which would be immediately followed up by an invasion by sea. Our observers in Britain have frequently advised us of their concern as to the inadequacy of British defenses against such an attempt. Obviously in case of such an attempt it would be imperative for us to push our

forces into Britain at top speed and by means of shipping additional to that already allocated to the project. In case a large percentage of allied commercial shipping had been tied up with an expedition to GYMNAST, such additional reenforcement of Britain would be impossible. (b) On the other hand, if German invasion of Russia is prolonged, even if it is slowly successful, the increasing involvement of Germany in the east tends to make increasingly easy an Allied invasion into France and the acquisition of safe bases therein against Germany. (c) Thus German success against Russia, whether fast or slow, would seem to make requisite not a diversion from BOLERO but an increase in BOLERO as rapidly as possible. (d) Furthermore, BOLERO is one overseas project which brings no further strain upon our aircraft carrier forces. GYMNAST would necessarily bring such a strain and risk. It could not fail to diminish the superiority over Japan which we now precariously hold in the Pacific.

10. To my mind BOLERO in inception and in its present development is an essentially American project, brought into this war as the vitalizing contribution of our fresh and unwearied leaders and forces. My own view is that it would be a mistake to hazard it by any additional expeditionary proposal as yet brought to my attention.

Faithfully yours,

HENRY L. STIMSON
Secretary of War.

The President,
The White House.

On June 21 there was "a good deal of pow-wow and a rumpus up at the White House." Stimson was not there, but he got a full report from Marshall. It appeared that the Prime Minister, who had never really liked BOLERO, was particularly disturbed by some casual remarks the President had made to Lord Mountbatten some time earlier about the possibility of having to make a "sacrifice" cross-Channel landing in 1942 to help the Russians. "According to Marshall, Churchill started out with a terrific attack on BOLERO as we had expected. . . . The President, however, stood pretty firm. I found out afterwards through Harry Hopkins that he [the President] showed my letter, with which Harry said he had been much pleased, to the Prime Minister. I had not anticipated that because I said some very plain things in it about the British. Finally, with the aid of Marshall who came into the conversation as a reserve after lunch, the storm was broken and, according to Harry Hopkins, Marshall made a very powerful argument for BOLERO, disposing of all the clouds that had been woven about it by the Mountbatten incident. At any rate towards the end it was agreed that we should go ahead full blast on BOLERO until the first of September. At that time the Prime Minister wanted to have a résumé of the situation to see whether a real attack could be made [in 1942] without the danger of disaster. If not, why then we could reconsider the rest of the field. At any rate that seems to have been the substance so far." (Diary, June 21, 1942) This was still the decision when the Prime Minister returned in haste to Great Britain as a result of unexpected British reverses in the Near East, where the fall of Tobruk on June 21 had shifted the attention of the Washington meeting from grand strategy to immediate repair work.

On July 10, "Marshall told me of a new and rather staggering crisis that is coming up in our war strategy. A telegram has come from Great Britain indicating that the British war Cabinet are weakening and going back on BOLERO and are seeking to revive GYMNAST—in other words, they are seeking now to reverse the decision which was so laboriously accomplished when Mr. Churchill was here a short time ago. This would be simply another way of diverting our strength into a channel in which we cannot effectively use it, namely the Middle East. I found Marshall very stirred up and emphatic over it. He is very naturally tired of these constant decisions which do not stay made. This is the third time this question will have been brought up by the persistent British and he proposed a showdown which I cordially endorsed. As the British won't go through with what they agreed to, we will turn our backs on them and take up the war with Japan." (Diary, July 10, 1942)

Although this drastic threat was designed mainly as a plan to bring the British into agreement with BOLERO, Stimson in retrospect was not altogether pleased with his part in it; he thought it a rather hasty proposal which showed how sorely the patience of the Americans had been tried by constant appeals for reconsideration. Although the bluff was supported by the British Chiefs of Staff in Washington, who had been converted to BOLERO, it did not appeal to the President. "The President asserted that he himself was absolutely sound on BOLERO which must go ahead unremittingly, but he did not like the manner of the memorandum [a further paper from Marshall, King, and Arnold] in regard to the Pacific, saying that was a little like 'taking up your dishes and going away.' I told him that I appreciated the truth in that but it was absolutely essential to use it as a threat of our sincerity in regard to BOLERO if we expected to get through the hides of the British and he agreed to that." (Diary, July 15, 1942)

Mr. Roosevelt was not persuaded, and the bluff was never tried. It would not have worked in any case, for there was no real intention of carrying it out, and Stimson supposed that the British knew this as well as he did. Furthermore, Stimson knew that the President had a lingering predilection for the Mediterranean, and the Prime Minister had shown on his last visit that he too knew the President's feeling; back on June 21 he "had taken up GYMNAST, knowing full well I am sure that it was the President's great secret baby." In spite of Mr. Roosevelt's renewed assurances of his support for BOLERO, therefore, it was with considerable concern that Stimson watched Hopkins, Marshall, and King leave for London to undertake a final series of discussions on Anglo-American strategy for 1942. He was not surprised—although very deeply disappointed—when these discussions resulted in a decision to launch a North African attack in the autumn. GYMNAST, rebaptized TORCH, replaced BOLERO.

The TORCH decision was the result of two absolutely definite and final rulings, one by the British, and the other by the President. Mr. Churchill and his advisers categorically refused to accept the notion of a cross-Channel invasion in 1942. Mr. Roosevelt categorically insisted that there must be *some* operation in 1942. The only operation that satisfied both of these conditions was TORCH. Stimson admitted that there was considerable force in both of these rulings. His own interest in BOLERO had never blinded him to the dangers of SLEDGE-HAMMER, the 1942 version of that operation. On the other hand, he could understand that for many reasons it was important that American troops should come to grips with the German enemy somewhere, as soon as possible.

But in July, 1942, neither of these considerations seemed to him as important as the fact that TORCH would obviously force an indefinite postponement of effective action in the only decisive theater outside Russia, and he pushed his disagreement with the President to the limits prescribed by loyalty. Again and again he emphasized the unwelcome fact that TORCH destroyed BOLERO even for 1943. The July agreement paid lip service to the build-up in Britain, but an operation in execution will always take priority over one merely in contemplation, especially when the one in contemplation is not viewed with a friendly eye by one-half of the team.

Stimson's disapproval of TORCH was fully shared by the War Department staff, but after a final protest to the President on July 24, during which the two men offered to bet each other about the wisdom of the operation, Stimson limited himself to extracting a promise from Marshall that he would make a stand against the final execution of the operation if at any time "it seemed clearly headed for disaster." (Diary, August 10, 1942) This time never came, for with his usual skill and energy Marshall organized the Army's part of the operation to a point at which he was himself prepared to endorse it. TORCH had what BOLERO had never had, the enthusiastic support of the highest authorities, and it was therefore possible to give it priorities and exclusive rights with the kind of ruthlessness that Stimson had so ardently and fruitlessly urged for BOLERO.

Confessing his doubts only to Marshall, Stimson too gave his full support to the prosecution of TORCH. "We are embarked on a risky undertaking but it is not at all hopeless and, the Commander in Chief having made the decision, we must do our best to make it a success." (Diary, September 17, 1942)

He was particularly delighted with the selection of his old friend George Patton to command the Casablanca landing force; Patton's realistic appreciation of the dangers ahead was matched by his burning determination to overcome them. The work of the General Staff in preparation Stimson considered admirable; so far as possible the dangers he foresaw were minimized. But, as he had feared, the necessary shipping and air support for TORCH were obtained at the expense of the BOLERO build-up in Great Britain.

In October and November there occurred two great and unforeseen events which still further reduced the dangers of TORCH. One was the successful Russian stand at Stalingrad. The shift of the Russians from the defense to a massive counterattack, in the following weeks, finally banished the specter of a German victory in Russia, which had haunted the council table of the Western Allies for a year and a half. At the same time, in the battle of Alamein, the British Eighth Army achieved a definitive victory over the Afrika Korps. To these two major areas Hitler was forced to give new attention, and the prospect of a counterattack through Spain against TORCH was diminished. Stimson nevertheless continued to be greatly concerned with the dangers of such a riposte to the North African attack, and through the early weeks of the invasion he lent his weight to the provision of adequate protective forces opposite Gibraltar. But the attack through Spain did not develop. Providential and unexpected good weather at Casablanca speeded that critical landing, and the heavy submarine and air losses which had been anticipated did not occur. Stimson always considered TORCH the luckiest Allied operation of the war, but he was prepared to admit that those who had advocated the operation could not be expected to see it in that light; the President had won his bet.

The tactical success of TORCH does not of itself dispose of the broader questions of strategy which lay behind the difference between the War Department and the President. The great commitment in North Africa led inexorably to later operations in the Mediterranean theater which were certainly a great contribution to victory; equally certainly these operations were unimportant in comparison with the land and air offensive finally launched from Great Britain. If Stimson or Marshall had been Commander in Chief, the invasion of France would in all probability have been launched in 1943, one year earlier than it actually occurred. Would the war have been ended sooner? This is a problem in a dozen unknowns. No certain answer is possible, and the matter is here left open. All that Stimson could say was that if he were faced with the problems of 1942, he would argue again as he had then.

2. THE GREAT DECISION

As the North African campaign progressed, the joint operations of the British and American forces led to increasing daily co-operation and understanding in the higher echelons, but the basic differences in strategy remained. At Casablanca in January, 1943, the British again refused to go ahead with any cross-Channel operation in the coming year, and it was therefore agreed that the next great move would be to Sicily, in a campaign whose name was HUSKY. In May, at Washington, there was made the first of three binding decisions to launch a cross-Channel invasion in 1944. For the first time the President himself took the stand for which Stimson had argued a year before—he insisted that the first problem was to plan the landing in northern France; when that had been done, it would be possible to see what supplies and troops were available for other operations. The Prime Minister finally accepted this position, although part of his price was that General Marshall should be assigned to him for a tour of North Africa —ruefully Marshall remarked that he seemed to be merely a piece of baggage useful as a trading point. Stimson suspected that his wily English friend, knowing that in Marshall he faced the most powerful single advocate of the Channel attack, was hoping to convert him to the Mediterranean, but he knew that the Prime Minister was also indulging his great respect and affection for General Marshall. And he was not surprised to find that Marshall returned safe, and unconverted, to the Pentagon.

Thus in midsummer, 1943, it was understood that there should be a cross-Channel attack in 1944. A staff was at work in London planning this attack, which was to have a British supreme commander. Meanwhile the invasion of Sicily had begun on July 10, and the question of further Mediterranean operations was still under debate. This was the situation when Stimson arrived in England, on the first of his three wartime visits to the European theater. What happened there is best described in his report of August 4, 1943, to the President. This report records Stimson's side of a prolonged debate with Mr. Churchill, from which he returned to Washington with more definite ideas than ever about the necessity of fighting hard for a cross-Channel invasion in 1944. The term used at the time by Stimson for this invasion was ROUNDHAMMER. (Its official name had become OVERLORD, but Stimson preferred not to mention this new name in his reports. OVERLORD was the final name for the invasion when executed.) The report to Mr. Roosevelt was outspoken, and it must be remembered that this paper, like all of Stimson's comments in this period, was predicated on the assumption that differences with the British were differences between friends.

"My principal objective had been to visit troops. But when I reached London the P.M. virtually took possession of my movements for the first week and I found myself launched in the discussion of subjects and with people which I had not expected. These unexpected subjects were so important that I devoted the bulk of my time to their consideration and altered my trip accordingly.

"Although I have known the P.M. for many years and had talked freely with him, I have never had such a series of important and confidential discussions as this time. He was extremely kind and, although we discussed subjects on which we differed with extreme frankness, I think the result was to achieve a relation between us of greater mutual respect and friendship than ever before. I know that was the case on my side. Although I differed with him with the utmost freedom and outspokenness, he never took offense and seemed to respect my position. At the end I felt that I had achieved a better understanding with him than ever before. . . .

"I told him that the American people did not hate the Italians but took them rather as a joke as fighters; that only by an intellectual effort had they been convinced that Germany was their most dangerous enemy and should be disposed of before Japan; that the enemy whom the American people really hated, if they hated anyone, was Japan which had dealt them a foul blow. After setting out all the details upon which my conclusion was predicated, I asserted that it was my considered opinion that, if we allow ourselves to become so entangled with matters of the Balkans, Greece, and the Middle East that we could not fulfill our purpose of ROUNDHAMMER in 1944, that situation would be a serious blow to the prestige of the President's war policy and therefore to the interests of the United States.

"The P.M. apparently had not had that matter presented to him in that light before. He had no answer to it except that any such blow could be cured by victories. I answered that that would not be so if the victories were such that the people were not interested in and could not see any really strategic importance for them. Towards the end he confined his position to favoring a march on Rome with its prestige and the possibility of knocking Italy out of the war. Eden on the other hand continued to contend for carrying the war into the Balkans and Greece. At the end the P.M. reaffirmed his fidelity to the pledge of ROUNDHAMMER 'unless his military advisers could present him with some better opportunity' not yet disclosed. . . .

"On Thursday, July 15th, I called at the office which had been set up to prepare plans for ROUNDHAMMER under Lt. Gen. Morgan of the British Army as Chief of Staff and Maj. Gen. Ray W. Barker of the U.S.A. as his deputy. . . . I was much impressed with General Morgan's directness and sincerity. He gave us his mature opinion on the operation, with carefully stated provisos, to the effect that he believed that with the present allocated forces it could be successfully accomplished. He was very frank, however, in stating his fear of delays which might be caused by getting too deep into commitments in the Mediterranean. . . . Barker who explained the details of the plan to us shared the same fear. In other words, they both felt that the plan was sound and safe but there might be a subsequent yielding to temptation to

undertake new activities which would interfere with the long
stage of preparation in the false hope that such interference
could be atoned for by subsequent speeding up.

"During the fortnight that I spent in England I found the
same fear pervaded our own officers who were engaged in
ROUNDHAMMER preparations. . . . They were all confident that
the plan was feasible. On one particular danger which the
P.M. had frequently urged upon me, namely the fear of a
successful German counterattack after the landing had been
made, the airmen were confident that they could by their
overwhelming superiority in the air block the advances of the
German reinforcements and thus defeat the counterattack.
The matter had been carefully studied by them. They told me
that their confidence was shared by the officers of the RAF. . . .

"I saw the P.M. again at a dinner given by Devers on
Wednesday where I sat beside him, and again on Saturday I
was with him nearly all day when he took me to Dover with
a smaller family party in his special train. . . . During the
trip back he brought me with evident delight a telegram which
he had just received from the Combined Chiefs of Staff in
Washington, telling him that General Marshall had proposed
that a study be made of the operation known as AVALANCHE.
[This was the landing executed in the following September
at Salerno on the west coast of Italy near Naples.] He took
this as an endorsement by Marshall of his whole Italian policy
and was greatly delighted. I pointed out to him that it probably meant that Marshall had proposed this as a short cut
intended to hasten the completion of the Italian adventure
so that there would be no danger of clashing with the preparations for ROUNDHAMMER. . . .

"On Monday, July 19, I talked over the new telephone with
Marshall and found that my assumption of Marshall's position was correct and that he had only suggested AVALANCHE so
as to leave more time for ROUNDHAMMER and to obviate the
danger of a long slow progress 'up the leg' [of Italy] which
might eliminate ROUNDHAMMER altogether. I told him also
of my talks with the P.M. and with the other military men,
including particularly Morgan, and at the close of my statement he suggested to me that I should go as promptly as possi-

ble to Africa to see Eisenhower, where I should be able to round out what I had gotten in London with the views of the people in Africa. He said, 'Then you will have all sides and I think it is very important for you to go and to go quickly.' Information which I subsequently received from the P.M. as to his proposed early visit to America caused me to understand why Marshall urged haste. . . .

"I told the P.M. of my talk with Marshall and his confirmation of my interpretation of his support of AVALANCHE, namely that he favored it only for the purpose of expediting the march up the peninsula and that he was still as firmly in favor of ROUNDHAMMER as ever. I pointed out to the P.M. that Marshall's view as to ROUNDHAMMER had always been supported by the whole Operations Division of the American General Staff. I also told him of my talk with Generals Morgan and Barker and of their full support of the ROUNDHAMMER proposition.

"He at once broke out into a new attack upon ROUNDHAMMER. The check received by the British attack at Catania, Sicily, during the past few days had evidently alarmed him. He referred to it and praised the superlative fighting ability of the Germans. He said that if he had fifty thousand men ashore on the French Channel coast, he would not have an easy moment because he would feel that the Germans could rush up sufficient forces to drive them back into the sea. He repeated assertions he had made to me in previous conversations as to the disastrous effect of having the Channel full of corpses of defeated allies. This stirred me up and for a few minutes we had it hammer and tongs. I directly charged him that he was not in favor of the ROUNDHAMMER operation and that such statements as he made were 'like hitting us in the eye' in respect to a project which we had all deliberately adopted and in which we were comrades. . . . On this he said that, while he admitted that if he was C-in-C he would not set up the ROUNDHAMMER operation, yet having made his pledge he would go through with it loyally. I then told him that, while I did not at all question the sincerity of his promise to go with us, I was afraid he did not make sufficient allowance for the necessary long-distance planning and I feared that fatal curtailments might be made impulsively in the vain hope that those curtailments could be later repaid. I stressed the dangers of too great entanglement in an Italian expedition and the loss of time to ROUNDHAMMER which it would involve. He then told me that he was not insisting on going further than Rome unless we should by good luck obtain a complete Italian capitulation throwing open the whole of Italy as far as the north boundary. He asserted that he was not in favor of entering the Balkans with troops but merely wished to supply them with munitions and supplies. He told me that they were now doing magnificently when only being supplied ten tons a month. (*Note:* In these limitations he thus took a more conservative position than Eden had taken at the dinner on July 12.)

"When I parted with him, I felt that, if pressed by us, he would sincerely go ahead with the ROUNDHAMMER commitment but that he was looking so constantly and vigorously for an easy way of ending the war without a trans-Channel assault that, if we expected to be ready for a ROUNDHAMMER which would be early enough in 1944 to avoid the dangers of bad weather, we must be constantly on the lookout against Mediterranean diversions. I think it was at this meeting that he told me of his intention of coming to America and that he expected to come in the first half of August. I then understood what Marshall had meant in his telephone message as to the promptness on my part and I thereafter aimed my movements so as to be able to return to America in time to report to the President before such meeting."

From England Stimson flew to Africa to consult General Eisenhower, so as to have a clear understanding of the present potentialities of the Mediterranean theater. There he found that Eisenhower, in agreement with American officers in London and Washington, was in favor of a limited attack on Italy, having for its main object the capture of air bases in the Foggia area which were vitally needed for the prosecution of the air offensive against Germany; the air forces based in Great Britain were finding themselves severely limited by their distance from southeastern Germany and by the adverse weather conditions of the British Isles. In Stimson's report on this view he concluded:

"Such a project if feasible would not only not impair ROUNDHAMMER but it would greatly aid and facilitate it and would have the maximum advantage in effect upon Germany both psychologically and materially.

"This conception of the American staff of an Italian operation is entirely different from the conception put forward at times to me by the P.M. and Eden and also made by certain others, notably General Smuts in a letter to the P.M. This last, which for brevity I will call the British conception, is not put forward as an aid to ROUNDHAMMER but as a substitute to supplant it. It contemplates an invasion from the south—in the direction of the Balkans and Greece or possibly towards southern France though this last suggestion has not been pressed. Such a southern invasion and the ROUNDHAMMER invasion cannot be both maintained. On the contrary, if they are both held in contemplation, they will be in constant interference and will tend to neutralize each other. For example, under the American conception it is absolutely essential to have a speedy daring operation which will not draw upon or interfere with the mounting of ROUNDHAMMER. A slow progressive infiltration of the Italian boot from the bottom, time consuming and costly, would be sure to make ROUNDHAMMER impossible.

"The main thing therefore to keep constantly in mind is that the Italian effort must be strictly confined to the objective of securing bases for an air attack and there must be no further diversions of forces or matériel which will interfere with the coincident mounting of the ROUNDHAMMER project."

This memorandum of August 4 was sent to Harry Hopkins for delivery to the President at Shangri-La, Mr. Roosevelt's place of escape from Washington. Stimson went to Highhold for three days of rest. The President sent him a message that he had read it and "would see me as soon as he returned to Washington." Back at the Pentagon, Stimson received word "that he would see me tomorrow, Tuesday, at lunch. In order to prepare for my talk with him I invited Harry Hopkins over to lunch and talked over with him my memorandum, which he had read and also my conclusion. . . . I was very much interested to find as I went over with Harry Hopkins the suggestions in my own mind that he agreed with every step and with my final conclusion." (Diary, August 9, 1943)

The diary entry for the next day is as follows:

"Last night was the hottest night that I can ever recall in Woodley and I did not sleep very well as a consequence, particularly as I was tired with the hard day.

"Nevertheless I got up and dictated immediately after breakfast a proposed report of my conclusions on the events stated in the memorandum which I had already sent to the President. I decided that it would be better to present them to the President in writing. The decisions that I have recommended are among the most serious that I have had to make since I have been in this Department and I have found that a good written report gets further and lasts longer than a verbal conference with the President. It was hard work grinding my mind down to the summary of such important matters when I was feeling as tired as I was this morning. Nevertheless I managed to do it."

Later in the morning, when these recommendations had been typed as a letter to the President, "I read them over and signed it. Then I called in Marshall and let him read them, telling him that that was going to be my report to the President and I wanted him to know what I was going to say in case he had any serious objections to it. He said he had none but he did not want to have it appear that I had consulted him about it. I told him that for that very reason I had signed the paper before I showed it to him or anyone else and that I proposed to send it in unless there was some vital objection which I had been unable to conjure up myself. . . .

"Then at one o'clock I went to the White House and had one of the most satisfactory conferences I have ever had with the President. He was very cordial and insisted on hearing about my trip. Then we plunged into the ROUNDHAMMER matter and, after recalling to his memory some of the matters which were in my memorandum and which as a whole he had very thoroughly in his mind, I produced my letter of conclusions and handed it over to him and told him that I thought that was better than my trying to explain verbally."

August 10, 1943.

Dear Mr. President:

In my memorandum of last week, which was intended to be as factual as possible, I did not include certain conclusions to which I was driven by the experiences of my trip. For a year and a half they have been looming more and more clearly through the fog of our successive conferences with the British. The personal contacts, talks, and observations of my visit made them very distinct.

First: We cannot now rationally hope to be able to cross the Channel and come to grips with our German enemy under a British commander. His Prime Minister and his Chief of the Imperial Staff are frankly at variance with such a proposal. The shadows of Passchendaele and Dunkerque still hang too heavily over the imagination of these leaders of his government. Though they have rendered lip service to the operation, their hearts are not in it and it will require more independence, more faith, and more vigor than it is reasonable to expect we can find in any British commander to overcome the natural difficulties of such an operation carried on in such an atmosphere of his government. There are too many natural obstacles to be overcome, too many possible side avenues of diversion which are capable of stalling and thus thwarting such an operation.

Second: The difference between us is a vital difference of faith. The American staff believes that only by massing the immense vigor and power of the American and British nations under the overwhelming mastery of the air, which they already exercise far into the north of France and which can be made to cover our subsequent advance in France just as it has in Tunis and Sicily, can Germany be really defeated and the war brought to a real victory.

On the other side, the British theory (which cropped out again and again in unguarded sentences of the British leaders with whom I have just been talking) is that Germany can be beaten by a series of attritions in northern Italy, in the eastern Mediterranean, in Greece, in the Balkans, in Rumania and other satellite countries. . . .

To me, in the light of the postwar problems which we shall face, that attitude . . . seems terribly dangerous. We are pledged quite as clearly as Great Britain to the opening of a real second front. None of these methods of pinprick warfare can be counted on by us to fool Stalin into the belief that we have kept that pledge.

Third: I believe therefore that the time has come for you to decide that your government must assume the responsibility of leadership in this great final movement of the European war which is now confronting us. We cannot afford to confer again and close with a lip tribute to BOLERO which we have tried twice and failed to carry out. We cannot afford to begin the most dangerous operation of the war under halfhearted leadership which will invite failure or at least disappointing results. Nearly two years ago the British offered us this command. I think that now it should be accepted—if necessary, insisted on.

We are facing a difficult year at home with timid and hostile hearts ready to seize and exploit any wavering on the part of our war leadership. A firm resolute leadership, on the other hand, will go far to silence such voices. The American people showed this in the terrible year of 1864, when the firm unfaltering tactics of the Virginia campaign were endorsed by the people of the United States in spite of the hideous losses of the Wilderness, Spottsylvania, and Cold Harbor.

Finally, I believe that the time has come when we must put our most commanding soldier in charge of this critical operation at this critical time. You are far more fortunate than was Mr. Lincoln or Mr. Wilson in the ease with which that selection can be made. Mr. Lincoln had to fumble through a process of trial and error with dreadful losses until he was able to discover the right choice. Mr. Wilson had to choose a man who was virtually unknown to the American people and to the foreign armies with which he was to serve. General Marshall already has a towering eminence of reputation as a tried soldier and as a broad-minded and skillful administrator. This was shown by the suggestion of him on the part of the British for this very post a year and a half ago. I believe that he is the man who most surely can now by his character and skill furnish the military leadership which is necessary to bring our two nations together in confident joint action in this great operation. No one knows better than I the loss in the problems of organization and world-wide strategy centered in Washington which such a solution would cause, but I see no other alternative to which we can turn in the great effort which confronts us.

Faithfully yours,
HENRY L. STIMSON
Secretary of War

The President,
The White House

The President "read it through with very apparent interest, approving each step after step and saying finally that I had announced the conclusions which he had just come to himself. We discussed the matter in its many aspects and then passed on to" other matters, among them current negotiations about the atomic bomb. By the time these matters were disposed of, "the time had come for a conference which he was going to have with the Joint Chiefs of Staff and he invited me to stay and sit in on the conference. Generals Marshall and Arnold and Admirals King and Leahy then came in together with Colonel Deane. We then had a very interesting conference on the subject of the coming conference with the Prime Minister and with the British Chiefs of Staff. The President went the whole hog on the subject of ROUNDHAMMER. He was more clear and definite than I have ever seen him since we have been in this war and he took the policy that the American staff have been fighting for fully. He was for going no further into Italy than Rome and then for the purpose of establishing bases. He was for setting up as rapidly as possible a larger force in Great Britain for the purpose of ROUNDHAMMER so that as soon as possible and before the actual time of landing we should have more soldiers in Britain dedicated to that purpose than the British. It then became evident what the purpose was and he announced it. He said he wanted to have an American commander and he thought that would make it easier if we had more men in the expedition at the beginning. I could see that the military and naval conferees were astonished and delighted at his definiteness. . . . . It was very interesting and satisfactory to me to find him going over with the Joint Chiefs of Staff the very matters which I had taken up with him and announcing his own support of the various positions which I had urged, and I came away with a very much lighter heart on the subject of our military policy than I have had for a long time. If he can only hold it through in the conferences which he is going to have with the Prime Minister, it will greatly clear up the situation."

The President held it through. The cross-Channel attack had at last become wholly his own, and it developed at Quebec two weeks later that the Prime Minister too was preparing to face the inevitable. Winston Churchill was as magnanimous in reconciliation as he was stubborn and eloquent in opposition, and when Stimson was called to Quebec from his vacation on August 22, he found that the President's scheme for moving troops to England had proved unnecessary. "He told me that Churchill had voluntarily come to him and offered to accept Marshall for the OVERLORD operation." In a later conversation Mr. Churchill "said he had done this in spite of the fact that he had previously promised the position to [Field Marshal] Brooke and that this would embarrass him somewhat, but he showed no evidence of retreating from his suggestion to the President. I was of course greatly cheered up. . . ." (Diary notes on vacation trip, August, 1943)

The decisions of Quebec were not quite final, but from this time onward OVERLORD held the inside track. There were further alarms from the Prime Minister during the Moscow Conference of Foreign Ministers in October, and in November at Teheran he made a last great effort to urge the importance of operations in the eastern Mediterranean, even at the cost of delay in OVERLORD. But at Teheran the President was reinforced by the blunt firmness of Marshal Stalin, whose comments on the doubts and diversionary suggestions of Mr.

Churchill Stimson followed in the minutes of the meetings with great interest. OVERLORD became at last a settled commitment, and in his press conference on December 9 Stimson allowed himself the following comment:

"The principal event of the past week has been the conference at Teheran. I have received and carefully studied the minutes of the military discussions and the records of the decisions at that conference. While, of course, the nature and details of those decisions cannot be made public, I can say that the presence of Premier Stalin and of his companion at the conference, Marshal Voroshilov, has contributed mightily to the success of the conference. Marshal Stalin's power of lucid analysis and the fairness of his attitude contributed strongly to the solution of several long-standing problems."

It was after Teheran, at Cairo, that the question of the supreme commander for OVERLORD was finally settled. It had been understood since Quebec that this commander should be an American, but objections had arisen in the United States to the selection of General Marshall. The news of his prospective appointment leaked to the press and persons eager to discredit the administration claimed that it was a British plot to remove his influence from the central direction of the war. Others dared to suggest that he was being sent away from Washington so that the President could replace him with General Somervell and insure the use of Army contracts to support his campaign for re-election. To this suggestion, an outrageous libel against all concerned, Stimson promptly gave a stern denial, but it was not so easy to quiet those who sincerely felt that Marshall was indispensable as Chief of Staff. None of this questioning would have been important if it had arisen *after* a definite announcement of Marshall's new position, for the enormous significance of his duties as supreme commander would then have been concrete and self-evident, not merely potential. But, as it was, Stimson could see that the President was disturbed.

Nor was the matter made easier by Marshall's own attitude. His sensitive personal integrity kept him completely silent about the question. Except on one occasion when Stimson drove him to a reluctant admission that 'any soldier would

prefer a field command,' he firmly refused to discuss the matter and the President was therefore cut off from the counsel
of the man whose advice he had learned to accept without
hesitation on all major Army appointments. Feeling himself
at least in part the originator of the move to make Marshall
supreme commander, Stimson did what he could to help the
President to a final conclusion. He even urged that Mr. Roosevelt might persuade the British to accept Marshall as commander of both the European and the Mediterranean theaters;
but the British, like the Americans, had public opinion to deal
with, and this plan proved impracticable. Furthermore,
Marshall's appointment would involve complex readjustments
of the command in other theaters and there remained the difficult problem of selecting a man to act in his place as Chief of
Staff. When the President departed for Teheran, the matter
was still unsettled.

Marshal Stalin emphatically stated at Teheran that he
could not consider the OVERLORD promise definite until a supreme commander had been appointed, and under this spur
the President reached his decision in a meeting with Marshall
at Cairo. Stimson learned from the cables what the President
finally decided, but he did not hear the full story until Mr.
Roosevelt returned to Washington. On December 18 he had
lunch with the President and received a detailed account of
the matter.

"He described his luncheon with Marshall after the conference was over and they had returned to Cairo. He let drop
the fact, which I had supposed to be true, that Churchill
wanted Marshall for the commander and had assumed that it
was settled as, in fact, it had been agreed on in Quebec. The
President described, however, how he reopened this matter
with Marshall at their solitary luncheon together and tried
to get Marshall to tell him whether he preferred to hold the
command of OVERLORD (now that a general supreme commander was not feasible) or whether he preferred to remain as
Chief of Staff. He was very explicit in telling me that he urged
Marshall to tell him which one of the two he personally preferred, intimating that he would be very glad to give him the
one that he did. He said that Marshall stubbornly refused,

saying that it was for the President to decide and that he, Marshall, would do with equal cheerfulness whichever one he was selected for. The President said that he got the impression that Marshall was not only impartial between the two but perhaps really preferred to remain as Chief of Staff. Finally, having been unable to get him to tell his preference, the President said that he decided on a mathematical basis that if Marshall took OVERLORD it would mean that Eisenhower would become Chief of Staff but, while Eisenhower was a very good soldier and familiar with the European Theater, he was unfamiliar with what had been going on in the Pacific and he also would be far less able than Marshall to handle the Congress; that, therefore, he, the President, decided that he would be more comfortable if he kept Marshall at his elbow in Washington and turned over OVERLORD to Eisenhower. I thanked him for his frank narration of the facts. I said that frankly I was staggered when I heard of the change for I thought that the other arrangement was thoroughly settled at Quebec. I said that I had chosen to recommend Marshall in my letter to the President last summer for two reasons: first, because I was confident that he was our best man for OVERLORD and he would be able to push through the operation in spite of the obstacles and delays which I felt certain it would meet in Great Britain on account of the attitude of the Prime Minister and the British Staff; but, secondly, I said that I knew that in the bottom of his heart it was Marshall's secret desire above all things to command this invasion force into Europe; that I had had very hard work to wring out of Marshall that this was so, but I had done so finally beyond the possibility of misunderstanding, and I said, laughingly, to the President: 'I wish I had been along with you in Cairo. I could have made that point clear.' And I told the President that, like him, I had had great difficulty in getting Marshall to speak on such a subject of his personal preference, but that I had finally accomplished it and that when he was on the point of leaving for this Teheran conference I had begged him not to sacrifice what I considered the interests of the country to the undue sensitiveness of his own conscience in seeking to seek a post." (Diary, December 18, 1943)

The appointment of Eisenhower was a disappointment to Stimson, but only in that it was not the appointment of Marshall. This feeling he promptly explained in a letter to the new supreme commander in order that there might be no shadow of misunderstanding; he assured Eisenhower of his confident and wholehearted support and received a reply of disarming sincerity:

"I have always agreed with you that General Marshall was the logical choice to do the OVERLORD job, but as long as it has been assigned to me you need have no fear but that I will do my best. It is heartening indeed to have your expression of confidence."

As for Marshall himself, never by any sign did he show that he was not wholly satisfied with the President's decision. It seemed indeed quite possible that Marshall had himself independently concluded that whatever his desires, his duty lay in Washington, and that he had refused to say so to the President or to Stimson because any such claim would have seemed immodest—it would have been as unlike Marshall as the contrary course of seeking field command. Many times in the war Stimson had cause to wonder at the quality of this American, but perhaps no other incident showed more clearly his utter selflessness. As Stimson had remarked in speaking of him a year before, the proverb truly applied: "He that ruleth his spirit is better than he that taketh a city."

Events confirmed the President's judgment. General Eisenhower fully justified the confidence placed in him, and General Marshall continued to serve in Washington as only he could do. By the middle of June, 1944, Stimson was happy to acknowledge to his diary that the two men were in the right place after all.

The decisions of Cairo and Teheran ended two years of discussion. At their meeting of December 18 the President had remarked to Stimson, "I have thus brought OVERLORD back to you safe and sound on the ways for accomplishment." And so it proved. Occasionally during the months that followed Stimson felt concern lest continued British caution might adversely affect the operation, but events belied his fears. When the time came in the following summer to mount the supporting invasion of southern France, there was one further contest with British advocates of a Balkan operation, but in this Stimson was only a satisfied observer of the firmness of the President and the Joint Chiefs of Staff. His major part in Operation OVERLORD had come to its victorious ending six months before the English Channel was crossed.

Through those six months the men in the War Department waited with a growing sense of tense anticipation. The game for them was now afoot, and they knew that OVERLORD would be a full test of their Army. They had argued for this campaign in the conviction that a properly equipped and well-trained Army could fight on equal terms with the best forces of an experienced enemy *in its first battle*—most of the divisions in the invasion would have no previous experience. More than that, the whole theory of victory by ground force superiority—supported by air mastery—was one in which the War Department had been a lonely advocate. The victories of North Africa and Italy had not dispelled the caution with which many Allied officers looked at the new American Army, nor were there many Americans outside the General Staff and the Ground Forces who wholeheartedly believed that the Army could produce explosive victories against the battle-tested Germans. In 1947, when the great American victories of the OVERLORD campaign were history, it seemed important to Stimson to recall that the Army which won those victories was born of George Marshall's faith, trained under Leslie McNair in the great maneuver grounds of the United States, and commanded by generals few of whom had commanded troops in battle anywhere before D-day.

It was no wonder, then, that as the eyes of all the world turned toward the English Channel in the spring of 1944, the senior officers of the War Department waited with especial anxiety for news from the Supreme Commander. What they heard needs no retelling here—the unprecedented sweep across France in the summer of 1944 is recognized as one of the great campaigns of all military history.

As the anxiety of the last days before the landing gave way to cautious satisfaction at its first success, and to full confidence after the first great victory at Cherbourg, Stimson realized that OVERLORD was destined to succeed, and he gave himself the satisfaction of going over to see it for himself. In a flying visit to England and Normandy in mid-July, he saw in action the magnificent forces of General Eisenhower and stood in wonder, like any private soldier, at the colossal scope of the undertaking, with its vast bases in Great Britain, its great fleets and beehive beaches on the other side, its overwhelming air support, its first-rate fighting troops, and above all its calm and supremely competent field leadership. At General Bradley's headquarters he heard the plan that later exploded the American Third Army through the enemy lines to clear the way for the liberation of all France, and, observing the troops and equipment which packed the narrow Cotentin Peninsula, he knew that Bradley had what he needed for the execution of this bold and brilliant plan. The brief visit with its sharply etched impressions was a clear demonstration to Stimson that in his unwearied assertion of the powers of the fresh and vigorous American Army he had, if anything, understated his case. It was not often that a man could see so clearly as a triumphant fact what he had argued as a theory not many months before. In England Stimson exchanged congratulations with his friend and former adversary, the Prime Minister. 'It is wonderful, a great triumph,' said the P.M., and Stimson did not see any need to quarrel when Mr. Churchill added, 'But we could never have done it last year.'

The foregoing account represents with complete frankness Stimson's part in the long deliberations which reached their climax in the final decisions of Cairo, and their fruition in the year of victories which began on the following sixth of June in Normandy. As an important part of Stimson's life this account has been a necessary chapter of our book, and it has seemed proper not to curb or moderate the story by any retrospective comment until it should be fully told. It is a story of persistent and deep-seated differences between partners in a great undertaking. Of Stimson's own share in it he found no reason later to be ashamed. If any advocacy of his had

been helpful in securing the adoption of the Operation OVER-
LORD he was proud.

But this accomplishment would become unimportant, and
it would be far better that it should not have been discussed,
if the reader should conclude from the foregoing that Stimson
considered these differences to be indicative of any basic cleavage between the British and the American leaders and peoples.
Still less would it be his wish that any small-minded conclusions should be drawn about the character or purposes of the
greathearted and brilliant Englishman who was the leader in
opposing the final decision. The great fact is not the differences but their settlement, and in the execution of OVERLORD
after Cairo there was no one more energetic or more determined than the Prime Minister, and no one more delighted
by its success.

The reluctance of British leaders to accept a cross-Channel
operation seemed far less remarkable to Stimson than the
courage with which they finally supported it. To the British
the Channel had been for centuries a barrier of special import,
and if it had protected them so long, might it not now protect
their enemies? Beyond the Channel lay France, where a generation before the British people had paid a ghastly price of
youth and strength in years of massive stalemate. From World
War II there were the further painful memories of Dunkirk
and Dieppe. The British Prime Minister had himself been a
farsighted and incisive opponent of the bloody futility of the
western front in 1915 and afterward; it was wholly natural
that he should be fearful lest there be a repetition of that
slaughter. If the Americans had suffered similar losses in the
First World War or faced similar succeeding dangers, would
they have felt differently? There was here no need for criticism. Americans could rest content with the fact that in their
freshness and their vast material strength they naturally
argued for the bold and forceful course, and in action justified
their argument.

After the war some writers plentifully endowed with misinformation chose to make capital out of "revelations" of disagreement between America and Great Britain; these men
demonstrated only their own special purposes. In America

some of these writings took the shape of personal attacks on Mr. Churchill. These could well be left to Mr. Churchill himself, for that doughty warrior had never yet required help in defending his policies. But this much it seemed proper for Stimson to say: It was his considered opinion that with the single exception of Franklin Roosevelt no man in any country had been a greater factor than Mr. Churchill in the construction of the grand alliance that destroyed the Nazis; no man had been quicker to leap the gulf of mutual suspicion and strike fellowship with Russia; none had more steadfastly sustained the allies of his nation while remaining frankly and explicitly "the King's first minister"; with no man at times had Stimson had sharper differences and for none had he higher admiration.

One of the postwar conclusions reached by some American writers was that the British opposition to OVERLORD was mainly guided by a desire to block Soviet Russia by an invasion farther east. This view seemed to Stimson wholly erroneous. Never in any of his long and frank discussions with the British leaders was any such argument advanced, and he saw no need whatever to assume any such grounds for the British position. Not only did the British have many good grounds to fear a cross-Channel undertaking, but Mr. Churchill had been for nearly thirty years a believer in what he called the "right hook." In 1943 he retained all his long-held strategic convictions, combined with a natural British concern for the Mediterranean theater, and in Stimson's view that was all there was to it.

Far more serious than any personal vilification, even of so great a man as Mr. Churchill, was the possibility that Americans of good will might be unduly affected by postwar discussion of differences and disagreements between their leaders and the leaders of Great Britain. Naturally and inevitably British and American interests had frequently diverged in specific areas of the world and disputes on these matters had frequently become warm. To draw broad and bitter conclusions from such disagreements would be mean and self-righteous folly.

Stimson's disagreement with Mr. Churchill over the cross-

Channel invasion was not his only difference with British leaders during the war. Sometimes he took issue with the British government and sometimes with individual Englishmen, and such differences of opinion were not new to him. As Secretary of State he had faced similar difficulties and as a private observer throughout his life he found points in British policy of which he could not approve. It would have been remarkable if it had been otherwise. But all of these differences were trivial compared to his underlying conviction that the final interests of both the United States and Great Britain required the two nations to live together in constantly closer association. The re-establishment of such cordial relations had been his first object as Secretary of State in 1929, and in World War II it was only on the basis of the solid mutual confidence established under the pressure of a common emergency that he was able to be bluntly frank in his disagreements with the British.

In the relationship between the British and American peoples Stimson found no place for pettiness. The true purposes and convictions of the two nations made it inevitable that they should be friends. On the basis of such friendship they might often frankly disagree, for it would be as unbecoming to avoid necessary disagreements as it would be foolish to rejoice in them. But in casting back through his thirty years of close relationship with the British nation it seemed to Stimson that the courage and honor of the Highland Division in 1918, the outstretched hand of Ramsay MacDonald in 1929, the invincible spirit of the whole nation under Churchill in World War II, and a score of other personal memories of Great Britain as a land of hope and glory and friendship— these things, and not specific disagreements, were of final importance.

The real lesson of World War II therefore was not to be found in any revelations of disagreement. Franklin Roosevelt and Winston Churchill established and sustained a wartime collaboration which grew ever stronger in the settlement of successive differences. When all the arguments have been forgotten, this central fact will remain. The two nations fought a single war, and their quarrels were the quarrels of brothers.

CHAPTER XVIII

The Wartime Army

IN LATE November, 1942, after the Joint and the Combined Chiefs of Staff had been created and had begun to function, one of the less tactful hangers-on of the administration asked Stimson how he liked being relegated to the position of housekeeper for the Army. The question was a foolish one, betraying a fundamental ignorance of the functions of a Secretary of War; in recording Stimson's work from Pearl Harbor to VJ-day, only this one chapter can be given to problems of War Department administration. A further foolishness lay in the assumption that Stimson did not like Army housekeeping, or thought it unimportant.

1. REORGANIZATION

The first and greatest wartime administrative achievement of the War Department was the reorganization made effective by Presidential order on March 9, 1942. In General Marshall's words, this reorganization "established three great commands under the direct supervision of the Chief of Staff—the Army Air Forces, the Army Ground Forces, and the Services of Supply (later designated as the Army Service Forces)."[1]

Decentralization of authority was an imperative requirement for effective war expansion. Whereas previously the chiefs of all the Army's arms and services had been largely autonomous officers, each with the right of direct appeal to the Chief of Staff, the Army inside the United States was now to be controlled by three officers, each clothed with full authority

[1] Biennial Report of the Chief of Staff, July 1, 1943, p. 33.

within his own field. This meant, for the Air Forces, a formal recognition of the increased measure of autonomy which had been agreed on in the previous summer, for the Ground Forces a centralized direction of the organization and training of the great new armies, and for the Service Forces, a more efficient co-ordination of the procurement and technical employment of the weapons and equipment of a technological war. But to Stimson the most important result of all was that the reorganization freed the General Staff for the broad duties of planning and supervision which were its proper assignment.

Since it is often argued that the Army is not capable of reforming itself, it is of some importance to note that Stimson's personal activity in this broad field of Army organization was more important in limiting change than in encouraging it. Twice he used his veto power to prevent suggested changes. During the preparation of the reorganization of 1942 he insisted on a rigorous adherence to the traditional conception of the duties and authority of the Chief of Staff, and in 1943 he prevented a further "streamlining" of the Army Service Forces. Both of these actions deserve attention; both originated in Stimson's memory of the issues involved in the great Root reorganization of 1903.

The title of Chief of Staff, borrowed by Root from Europe, was not lightly chosen; it was a deliberate statement of the fact that the highest military officer of the Army exercises his authority only by direction of the President. The name was designed by Root to implant a conception of military responsibility wholly different from that which had led "Commanding Generals" after the Civil War to believe that they were independent of the ignorant whims of presidents and secretaries of war. To Stimson it seemed vital that this reform should not be jeopardized, even unintentionally, by any change in the title and function of the Chief of Staff in 1942, and he accordingly vetoed the Staff's proposal to vest the Chief of Staff with the title of Commander. In the case of a man like General Marshall, fully alive to his responsibility both to the Secretary of War and to the President, the matter was quite unimportant, and Stimson certainly intended no disparagement of that great officer. It was further obvious that in the course of his duties, the Chief of Staff must inevitably exercise many of the functions of a commander, and Stimson was the first to insist that his authority must be unconditionally recognized by every other officer in the Army. But this authority must be that of the President's representative—under the Constitution there could be only one Commander in Chief, and to recognize any lesser officer with such a title was either insubordination or flagrant misuse of language. The Army was an instrument of the President; there must be no repetition of the state of mind which had led General Sherman, as "Commanding General" in 1874, to move his headquarters away from the wickedness of Washington to St. Louis.

The "streamlining" suggested for the Service Forces in 1943 was a brain child of General Somervell. The changes of 1942 had abolished the Chief of Infantry and the other chiefs of the arms, turning over their functions to the Commanding General of the Ground Forces, with a view to insuring the development of a fully co-ordinated training program for the combined arms. The chiefs of the administrative services, however—Ordnance, Quartermaster, Engineers, and so on—had survived with most of their traditional duties intact, under the direction of the Commanding General of the Service Forces. In September, 1943, General Somervell proposed that the functions and prerogatives of these branches be turned over to a set of new directors, mostly with new names, and with powers organized on more functional and less traditional lines. At the same time he proposed a redistricting of the Army's nine Service Commands. Stimson was prepared in general to accept Somervell's judgment that his proposed changes would in the end increase the efficiency of the Service Forces, but it was a grave question whether the improvement would outweigh its concomitant disadvantages in the creation of bad feeling. On September 21, Stimson discussed the matter with McCloy and Patterson. "We three had a very satisfactory talk about it. I have been tending to feel that this reorganization is ill advised . . . because it proposes to wipe out the existence of the administrative services such as the Engineers, the Ordnance, the Quartermaster's Department, and the Signal Corps. . . . This proposition brings up to me poignant memories of my experience in 1911-12 when I learned only too well how deeply imbedded in sentiment the services of the Engineers, Ordnance, and Quartermaster are in the memories of all the people that belonged to them, and the tremendous uproar that would be created if we tried to destroy all that sentiment by wiping out the distinction of the services with their insignia, etc. I found in this talk with Patterson that under the present organization the work of production and procurement is going satisfactorily. Whatever critics may say, we have done an almost miraculous job and I therefore am *prima facie* against stirring up a hornet's nest right in the middle of a war when things are going well. . . . Patterson and McCloy shared my views." (Diary, September 21, 1943)

The next day Stimson had the matter out in a conference with the soldiers, and the proposal was killed. Remembering his experiences in supporting Leonard Wood, "who was not unlike General Somervell in his temperament and other characteristics," Stimson saw no reason to create bitterness which could be avoided. Nor was it as if the service branches, like General Ainsworth in the olden time, had shown themselves insubordinate or un-co-operative. There had been slow and unimaginative work in the early days of the emergency, but Stimson had observed with satisfaction the high quality of the work done by such men as Campbell in Ordnance, and the Chief of Engineers and Quartermaster General were men of whom Somervell himself thought well enough to intend giving them new and enlarged responsibilities in his reorganization. General Somervell's driving energy was an enormous asset to the Army, but in this case it seemed better that it should be curbed. His plans were formally disapproved in a letter written by Stimson on October 5, and in succeeding weeks as belated rumors of the proposed changes began to produce a series of worried and disapproving questions from the President, Congress, and such knowing observers as Bernard Baruch, Stimson was confirmed in his belief that this decision against "reform" had been a wise one.

2. "DIPPING DOWN"

The reorganization of March, 1942, was the only major wartime change in the administrative setup of the War Department. The increased decentralization which it insured somewhat shifted the function of the Secretary of War, who retained direct control only over the Bureau of Public Relations and the administration of his own office. There remained, however, supervisory responsibilities which necessarily though occasionally involved Stimson in direct dealings with all the other branches. The principle on which he exercised these functions he explained to Somervell on May 27, 1943. "I gave him a long discourse on my views of the duties of the Secretary of War based on my experience with two great executives—Theodore Roosevelt and Franklin Roosevelt. I told him I did not intend to make the mistakes which Franklin had made of establishing a lot of independent agencies reporting only to himself; but on the other hand I did intend to do what Theodore Roosevelt did, which was to feel perfectly free to dip down into the lower echelons, so to speak, and interest myself keenly and directly with what is going on in exceptional cases." Giving as an example his work for the advancement of radar, Stimson assured the General, for whom he had the highest regard, that he had no intention of abusing this prerogative. Both Somervell and General Marshall fully understood this position, and there is no record of any significant cleavage between the Secretary's office and the chief military leaders of the War Department.

Most of the cases of such "dipping down" were of the kind that suggest themselves to a senior officer in a tour of inspection; either Stimson or someone whom he trusted would observe a failing or apparent failing, and the result would be a memorandum to General Marshall or a short inquiry directed straight to the officer in charge of the matter. Stimson had been on the receiving end of inspectorial comments often enough to know that in many cases they were based on an incomplete understanding of the problem, but he also knew the value of such criticisms in stimulating increased efforts to find a satisfactory solution.

In other cases, the activities of the Secretary were the result of some nonmilitary aspect of the matter. The appointment of a Surgeon General, or a Chief of Chaplains, for example, involved a decision in the Secretary's office because, especially in wartime, these offices attracted the close interest and attention of civilian doctors and clergymen, who felt that the normal methods of military selection could not be counted on to produce men with the desired standing as professionals. The Medical Department, furthermore, was a matter of special interest to Stimson on account of his personal experience in the tropics, and particularly after the appointment of Major General Norman T. Kirk, whom he had first known in the Philippines, he took an active part in supporting its labors.

Another department to which Stimson's attention was given, in accordance with the requirements of the law, was that of the Judge Advocate General. As wartime pressure increased, he was gradually released by new statutes from much of the labor of reviewing court-martial records, but throughout his years in the War Department he was forced from time to time to give his close attention to specific cases, particularly those involving the death sentence. In spite of the strong tendency of a humane reviewing authority to exercise leniency, Stimson fully understood the close relationship between military justice and military discipline; it was not easy, for example, to approve the dismissal of proved combat fliers who, returning from battle, insisted on disregarding the safety regulations of the continental United States, but he cheerfully accepted General Marshall's recommendation that mercy should be subordinated to justice—and the public safety.

Another section of the War Department to which his personal attention was frequently directed was Military Intelligence. By a curious irony, the matter of principal importance here was the development of the very operation of attacking foreign codes and ciphers which Stimson had banished from the State Department in 1929. In 1940 and after, the world was no longer in a condition to be able to act on the principle of mutual trust which had guided him as Secretary of State, and as Secretary of War he fully supported the extraordinary operations that were later revealed to have broken the Japanese codes. In early 1942, with McCloy's assistance, he established a special unit for the analysis and interpretation of this sort of material. This unit, under the direction of Alfred McCormack, a New York lawyer turned colonel, did its work with remarkable insight and skill. As investigation of the Pearl Harbor catastrophe later revealed, such a unit, if it had existed in 1941, might well have given warning of the degree of Japanese interest in the fleet at Hawaii. It was not Pearl Harbor, however, but the natural development of studies begun months before that led to the establishment of the unit, and if it came into existence too late to help in the prevention of that calamity, it made invaluable contributions in other matters of at least comparable significance during the war.

Stimson also did what he could to insure the effective exchange of military information among different branches of the Government and with America's allies, particularly the British. He backed General Marshall's efforts to break down American resistance to co-operation with the British, and he was insistent that no impatience with its occasional eccentricities should deprive the Army of the benefits of co-operation with General Donovan's Office of Strategic Services. Throughout the war the intelligence activities of the United States Government remained incompletely co-ordinated, but here again it was necessary to measure the benefits of reorganization against its dislocations, and on the whole Stimson felt that the American achievement in this field, measured against the conditions of 1940, was more than satisfactory. A full reorganization belonged to the postwar period.

3. THE PLACE OF SPECIALISTS

Stimson inherited, from the comments of his father on the subject of the "bombproof" officers of the Civil War, and from his own experience with 'the uniform-wearing civilians doing morale duty in the back areas' of World War I, a strong feeling that the dignity of the uniform should as far as possible be reserved for those who in fact did the fighting. It was true that this conviction flew in the face of the developing complexity of war; perhaps not half of the men who served usefully in the Army of World War II would have satisfied Dr. Lewis Stimson's definition of a genuine combatant. As one of those constantly urging the advantages of new weapons and techniques, his son was fully aware of the difference between Marshall's army and Grant's; but he was also, from his own experience, well aware of the constant pressure exerted by men anxious 'to obtain the kudos of having worn a combatant uniform without having performed combatant duty.' It was this experience that had made him lay down in 1940 a rigid set of requirements for appointments to commissioned rank.

In 1942, as he observed the increasing requirement for wholly noncombatant specialists in military operations, Stimson turned to the creation of an Army Specialist Corps, which should recruit for service with the Army the scientists and technical experts who were so much needed in all branches. The men of this corps were to be selected for nonmilitary qualifications and would serve as civilians but with military grades, in a uniform unlike that of the Army but designed to satisfy their self-respect and give them protection under the rules of war, if captured. Other armies, notably the German Army, had used and demonstrated the value of such an organized civilian corps.

But in the American Army the effort failed. Several months passed while the Specialist Corps was being formed, and before it was ready to carry out its assignment events had made that assignment impossible; civilians had already been commissioned in the Army of the United States in very large numbers, and the men of the Specialist Corps found themselves at a hopeless disadvantage in comparison with these other civilians who were already wearing the Army uniform.

Army commanders who needed high-class men for specialist civilian duty, and needed them in a hurry, 'found it so much easier to get them by pandering to the itch to wear the Army uniform that they threw their influence against the Specialist Corps and failed to support the effort to preserve the dignity of their own uniform.' In the face of this combination of disadvantages—the greatly increased complexity of civilian duties in the Army, the belated organization, and the reluctance of military commanders to run the risk of losing picked civilian aides—it was decided to abandon the new organization and to incorporate its recruits so far as possible in the Army itself.

Nevertheless the work which it had accomplished under the direction of a former Secretary of War, Dwight Davis, was far from wasted. The more than 200,000 applications it had processed became a useful part of the Army's file on available civilians. And from its experience came much of the knowledge and technique which made the Officer Procurement Service an outstanding success.

With the failure of the Specialist Corps—"an experiment noble in purpose"—Stimson ended his effort to distinguish between combat soldiers and rear-area troops; it was not that kind of war, and even a successful Specialist Corps would not have solved the problem. World War II saw the full development of the usual resentment of company for regiment, regiment for corps, corps for supply troops, and everyone overseas for everyone at home. But there was no denying that all of these resented echelons were necessary parts of the American Army.

4. STUDENT SOLDIERS

A wartime Secretary of War frequently finds himself the unhappy arbiter between the conflicting requirements of "military necessity" and "the long view." In no case during the war was this conflict more trying than in the complex task of adjusting the relationship of the Army to the colleges.

The basic decision of 1941 had been to find the bulk of the junior officers for the new army inside the Army itself. To this position the War Department adhered throughout the war; for a variety of reasons it was the only satisfactory general principle. But as the expanding demands of the growing Army remorselessly reduced the draft age in gradual stages from twenty-one to eighteen, it became apparent that special arrangements must be made to provide for a proper wartime employment of the nation's colleges. Without yielding to the extreme view of some educators that college training for general leadership was of such pressing importance as to justify wholesale deferment, Stimson fully accepted the more balanced view of most college presidents that the values of academic training must not be wholly disregarded in the general mobilization of American youth. He was irritated by the apparent willingness of the Navy to promise commissions to selected students without prior service and competition in the enlisted ranks, but part of this annoyance stemmed from his certainty that in the colleges of early 1942 there was a large reservoir of officer material from which the Army stood in danger of being cut off.

The first attempt at a solution to the problem was the establishment in the colleges of a program for students recruited into the Army Enlisted Reserve. Under this program college men were to be deferred as students to continue their studies, and upon their entry on active service they were to have an opportunity to *compete* for a commission. They were not, at Stimson's insistence, to be formally recognized cadets; they were potential, not designated, officer candidates.

The Army Enlisted Reserve lasted only a few months. As the demand for men increased, it became rapidly more difficult to justify the deferment of college students, either to the General Staff or to the general public. The program lacked justice in that it dealt kindly with men whose presence in college was the result largely of their happy choice of parents; there was no true answer to the charge that the deferment of such men was inconsistent with the Army's policy of democratic selection of officers. In August, 1942, Stimson announced that all members of the Enlisted Reserve would be called to active service as soon as they reached draft age.

There remained the colleges. Educators insisted that it was unwise to leave unemployed the nation's greatest engines for the instruction of young men of Army age, and Stimson and his advisers tried again. At the end of 1942 they established the Army Specialized Training Program (ASTP), under which selected younger soldiers of promise were to be sent, as soldiers, to continue at the colleges such studies as might be judged useful in their later military service. There was no connection between this training and a commission, except in so far as their added training might make these students more worthy of promotion, and the very small demand for new officers after 1943 in the end prevented all but a few from winning bars. Many ASTP students undoubtedly felt cheated at this result; they had however allowed their hopes to outrun the Army's promise. The novelty and breadth of this program made its organization and administration unusually difficult, but during 1943 it became gradually more and more effective. And then, in February, 1944, it was decided to end the program on the following April 1.

The ASTP was killed by the manpower shortage. At the end of 1943 the General Staff, finding itself in desperate need of additional troops for the great campaigns of the coming year, no longer accepted as controlling the argument that in the long run college training for selected men was a necessary investment in leadership. Although he took pains to make it entirely clear to the Staff that his interest in such training was personal and intense, Stimson himself felt unable to deny that the need for fighting soldiers must take precedence. The 140,000 men in the ASTP were needed more as present effective troops of ideal combat age than as future experts and officers.

Each step of this story tied in with ups and downs in the Army's estimates of its manpower requirements. In all such changes, the college training program, as a marginal undertaking, was very sharply affected. Factors to which we must give more attention in the next chapter limited the Army to a choice, in the end, between specialized training and an adequate combatant force. It would have been better to have both, but that would have meant fewer civilians, and a still heavier draft. The requirement of a sufficient fighting Army was overriding, but the true question for the Specialized Training Program was whether it should be continued at the expense of further drafts of fathers, deferred workers, and other civilians. Here the choice lay not with the War Department but with Congress, and the verdict of the people's representatives on this point was not a matter of doubt. The Army of early 1944 was forced to cannibalize itself, and the soldiers of the ASTP were among the first victims. Their consolation is to be found in the all but unanimous opinions of their new combat commanders— they made unusually fine troops.

Of all the dislocations of the war this one perhaps was the most disturbing to Stimson; on this issue of continuing college training he came very close to serious disagreement with his military staff. But there is no sensible answer to a professional decision on wartime troop requirements. If you trust your generals, you must give them the men they demand; Stimson had too often made that point to other citizens not to feel its force when applied to his own desires. When the President expressed his chagrin at the decision, Stimson explained "that General Marshall had made it clear to me that we faced the alternative of either making this immediate cut in ASTP or losing ten divisions from the forces which were necessary this summer."[2] In the face of such a warning there could be no hesitation.

Nor could Stimson sympathize with those who argued that a wartime suspension of academic activity would do irreparable damage to the long future of liberal education. He was content to rest in 1947 on a statement issued December 17, 1942, in defense of the military and "illiberal" curriculum of the ASTP:

"In reply to the question, 'Does not the Army Educational Plan go a long way to destroy liberal education in America?' the Honorable Henry L. Stimson, Secretary of War, today authorized the following statement:

"Temporarily, yes, so far as the able bodied men of college age are concerned, but in the long run, emphatically no. The immediate necessity is to win this war and unless we do that there is no hope for liberal education in this country. To win this war and win it as quickly as possible, we must have large numbers of young men in the Army. We must use every opportunity to train our soldiers for the immediate task ahead. The Army College Program is designed for that purpose and for that purpose alone. This training is of necessity primarily technical and other training must remain in abeyance.

"I am Chairman of the Trustees of one of the leading boys' schools and all my life I have been a devoted supporter of

[2] Notes after Cabinet meeting. February 18, 1944.

liberal education in school and college. So have my principal assistants, and the necessity of limiting such education in the colleges during the war is very painful. It has been accepted as a necessity. . . .

"It is of enormous importance to make plans ahead for the restoration of liberal education for the period after the war is won and during the period of demobilization. I should like to call your attention to the fact that this problem is already under careful consideration. . . . We hope and believe that many of the soldiers of today will return to become tomorrow the students and leaders in the field of liberal education."

So far as Stimson could see, in 1947, this was exactly what the soldiers were doing.

5. THE ARMY AND THE NEGRO

"We are suffering from the persistent legacy of the original crime of slavery." (Diary, January 17, 1942) There is no deeper or more difficult problem in America than that of the Negro, and the impact of this problem on the wartime Army (and vice versa) brought out its complexities in forms sometimes discouraging and sometimes hopeful.

Each man who comes in contact with "the Negro problem" brings to it his own deep-set beliefs. Stimson's convictions were those of a northern conservative born in the abolitionist tradition. He believed in full freedom, political and economic, for all men of all colors; he did not believe in the present desirability, for either race, of social intermixture. These two views were inconsistent, he believed, only in the opinion of those who *desired* them to be inconsistent. The man who would "keep the nigger in his place" and the man who wished to jump at one bound from complex reality to unattainable Utopia were in Stimson's opinion the twin devils of the situation. He had his troubles with both.

"The persistent legacy" as it came before the War Department in 1940 was a complex mixture of facts and attitudes. It was a fact that most white people would not sanction intermixture of whites and Negroes in the intimate association of military life; it was equally a fact that segregation was repellent to almost all educated Negroes and to an increasing number of the colored rank and file. It was a final fact that segregation was the tradition of the Army, and, in one form or another, of most of civilian America; it was the *modus vivendi*, and the Army followed it, except in its Officer Candidate Schools.

Negro troops had not in the main won glory for themselves in combat during World War I. Yet certain units, under particularly competent and sympathetic white leadership, had fought with distinction. Should the Army now have colored fighting troops? The War Department said it should, and the training given to Negroes in two infantry divisions and a number of other combatant units was more patient and careful and time-consuming than anything required by white units.

The Army contained Negroes in their due proportion to the rest of the nation's population. But wherever Negroes were trained or sent abroad, there was difficulty. Most training camps were in the South, and the South had feelings which seemed wholly wrong to the northern Secretary. Still more disturbing were its actions. A Negro in the Army was a United States soldier, and Stimson was deeply angered when it proved impossible to bring to justice southern police who murdered a colored M.P. Southern bus companies enforced the peculiar rules of the region in serving Army camps; as often happens under these rules, insufficient space was provided for Negroes. Stimson insisted to his deputies that this sort of blatant unfairness must be stopped.

More perplexing still was the problem of the Negro abroad. Theater commanders were co-operative but not enthusiastic in accepting Negro units; in each theater there were special considerations which made Negro troops a problem. To all alike the Negro was an additional complication in a full-time war. But fair-minded soldiers agreed that the Army must make full use of what Stimson called the "great asset of the colored men of the nation." The difficulties of the Negro were not, in the main, of his own making, and in neither justice nor policy could he be excluded from participation in the war.

As he wrestled with the problem Stimson found his own sympathies shifting. On three tours of inspection he saw Negro units in training; each time he was impressed by the progress achieved by intelligent white leaders and colored soldiers working together. In such an officer as Colonel Benjamin O. Davis, Jr., he found the direct refutation of the common belief that all colored officers were incompetent. Davis was exceptional, but in the development of more such exceptions lay the hope of the Negro people. Having at first opposed as unwise the training of colored officers, Stimson shifted his emphasis to an insistence that such officers should be selected and trained with the greatest care. He explained to the 99th Pursuit squadron, the first unit of colored combat fliers, "how the eyes of everybody were on them, and how their government and people of all races and colors were behind them." (Diary, October 5, 1942) In similar fashion, Stimson's early mistrust of the use of the Army as an agency of social reform dissolved under the impact of the manpower shortage, and was turned into enthusiasm by direct observation of the accomplishments of soldiers in attacking illiteracy among Negroes (and whites) at Fort Benning.

In the sharp tragedy of the Negro in America there was no place for bitterness in reply to bitterness, but Stimson occasionally lost patience with Negro leaders whose opinions he found radical and impractical. A further trial lay in the fact that at first the Communists and later both Japanese and Nazi agents made energetic efforts to use the race problem as an apple of discord. In Stimson's view the complaints of Negro leaders fell into three categories: the remediable, about which he was eager to hear, the trivial, rising generally from pride offended by the thoughtless slights of the ordinary white man, and the impossible—those which took no account of a heritage of injustice deeply imbedded in the mores of the nation. The deliberate use of the war emergency to stir unrest and force new policies for which the Negroes themselves were unprepared seemed to Stimson blind folly, and he felt that this hotheaded pressure was partly responsible for the rising racial tension which produced such ugly outbreaks as the Detroit riots of June, 1943. On the other hand, he was equally irritated by the "childishness" of his friends in the Navy, whose rigid restriction of Negroes to service as messboys was only modified on the personal insistence of the President. And Stimson himself pointed out to Army leaders that pictures of the Detroit outbreak showed young white thugs to be in almost every case the aggressors.

There could be no denial of the patriotism and the idealism of the "radical" Negro leaders, and their criticisms sometimes opened the eyes of the War Department, but their general attitude was hardly constructive. The attitudes and opinions advanced by most Negro newspapers, too, were shockingly biased and unreliable; as little as their white opponents would the Negro editors look for the mote in their own eye. It was more helpful to deal with such Negroes as Dr. Frederick Patterson of Tuskegee Institute, or Truman Gibson, Stimson's aide for Negro affairs after 1943. These men made suggestions and recommendations that were of great practical value to their people, and without the least disloyalty to their race they were prepared to face squarely the fact that oppression and injustice have left their mark on the bulk of American Negroes. For his honesty and courage Gibson was called bitter names by some other Negroes; to Stimson he was a trusted associate and a distinguished public servant.

The final reckoning on the Negro and the wartime Army was not clear when Stimson left the War Department. The performance of the only Negro infantry division sent into combat as a whole was disappointing, but smaller units (including elements of the same division) did better. The whole story was to be found only by a study of all the hundreds of Negro units—combatant, service, and training troops—and the man who generalized from a partial experience, even the experience of a Secretary of War, was on dangerous ground. Both the Army and the Negro, Stimson believed, did better than their respective enemies would admit, but from a thorough and dispassionate study of their work in all its aspects there would surely come ways for both to do still better in the future, and it was with great satisfaction that Stimson saw such studies promptly begun by his successor.

6. SCIENCE AND NEW WEAPONS

There was perhaps no more striking success in the American management of World War II than the marriage of science and the military, the basic outlines of which have now been recorded by James Phinney Baxter in *Scientists Against Time*.[3] The two principal agents of this triumph, in Stimson's view, were Vannevar Bush and James B. Conant, two distinguished scientists and administrators whose persuasive foresight had won the confidence of President Roosevelt at the beginning of the national emergency. These men and their associates from the beginning set a standard of effort which in its combination of soundness and daring left open for such officers as Stimson no intelligent course but full and hearty collaboration.

The service a Secretary of War could perform here was a triple one. The easiest, and at the same time perhaps the most important, was simply to make it clear to his Department and to scientific leaders that it was War Department policy to make the fullest possible use of scientific help in every part of the Army's work. This attitude, fully shared by General Marshall, did not always permeate to every level of the Army, and in occasional officers of otherwise outstanding ability there persisted a blind spot on the subject of "outside advice." But after one or two officers had been replaced, largely on account of their inability to make full use of modern techniques, the notion of fighting an up-to-date war began to spread, and it was a notable characteristic of the men whom General Marshall brought rapidly forward during the war that they were not frightened by new ideas.

There remained a real difficulty in establishing proper methods for the development of effective continuous contact between the Army and the scientists, and Stimson's second service was in choosing the men and establishing the organization which could do this job. His principal assistant in this work was Bundy, who was not a scientist but possessed the lawyer's talent for appreciation of the other man's problem. With Bundy and Bush, Stimson worked out in the spring of 1942 an organization, in which the Navy joined, whereby Bush and an officer from each service department became a committee of three for the education of the Joint Chiefs of Staff in scientific problem . To supplement this organization

[3] The Atlantic Monthly Press, Little, Brown & Co., 1946.

there was set up in November, 1942, a special section for new weapons in the G-4 division of the General Staff. Both of these moves were useful, but the latter particularly proved insufficient, and Stimson responded quickly to the suggestion of Bush and Bundy, in September, 1943, that new weapons must become an independent section of the Staff.

The work that followed is an excellent example of the proper functions of the Secretary of War, as Stimson understood that office. By constant but friendly pressure he and his friend Bush won Marshall's support for the new idea, an essential part of which was the selection for the new job of an officer with a solid reputation as a first-class soldier. When this officer had been selected, in the person of Major General Stephen G. Henry, Stimson provided him with a full-dress recital of the importance of his new assignment. The diary entry tells the story:

"I found that General Stephen Henry, whom I had selected for appointment to the new scientific weapons staff post, was here and he and McNarney [Marshall's deputy] came in and I tried to explain to him as well as I could what I wanted of him. I did this by telling him of my own experience with radar beginning with the time of my visit to Panama. Then Dr. Bush came in and joined the talk and gave him a talk on the new weapons which were being developed. Henry's job is to smooth the path of new weapons into use in the Army. It is pretty hard to define it because it is a new job. He is to do the work that it was intended that General Moses should do under G-4 but it has never been done because of interruption of other duties. While we were still talking, I called in Dr. Bowles to add his testimony of what was to be done and gradually the picture unfolded to General Henry and he became more and more interested. Of course he had come to Washington in a rather dejected and disappointed frame of mind because we were taking him away from his division— an armored division, to which he had recently been appointed, but gradually the picture of the greater importance of the new position I was offering him in the war effort had developed before him and he became more and more interested. He has had a very fine record for several years as head of the Armored

Force School at Fort Knox. I heard of him when I was there nearly two years ago and met him then and I had not forgotten the impression his work had made on me.

"Then while we were still talking we had another influx of people from Britain. This was a group headed by Sir Robert Renwick who has just come over to talk of the importance of radar to our Staff. . . . Renwick was a very forceful intelligent man who, although a civilian, holds a very high position in the actual war work in England in precisely the similar lines for which I am seeking Henry. Renwick launched into a vigorous talk about how far behind we were to the place where we ought to be if our effort was to be successful next year. I told him not to pull his punches but to let us have all he had in criticism and he did so, and when he painted the picture of the development that the British had already made in radar and how far we were behind that in our Air Forces, it made a profound impression on Henry. The whole job with Henry took from 10:25 until lunchtime at one o'clock. But it was a job well done for he has accepted his new post with vigor and enthusiasm." (Diary, October 11, 1943)

This process of indoctrination was one which Stimson frequently employed when advancing his favorite ideas. Occasionally, he feared, it left his auditors with the feeling that they had been subjected to an old man's lecturing, but in this case at least the results were thoroughly satisfactory.

Under General Henry, the new Developments Division of the Staff performed with outstanding success. The basic reasons for this success were two: first, the ready acceptance by the Army of such a division at the special staff level, and second, the selection of a director for that division out of the top drawer of the Army. Henry's success eventually priced him out of the market, and he was "stolen" by General Marshall a year later for the unconscionably difficult job of directing the redeployment and demobilization of Army personnel, but the standards he had set were maintained by his successor.

The third important service of the Secretary, and the most arduous, was his personal advocacy of specific new techniques and weapons. The most important single instance of this kind was the use of radar. Stimson's interest in the electronic eye was first kindled in 1940 by the enthusiasm of his relative, Alfred Loomis, and throughout the war it remained an object of his particular attention. In April, 1942, he selected Dr. Edward L. Bowles to serve as his special consultant "for the purpose of getting radar upon a thoroughly sound and competent basis as to installation, training, and maintenance." (Diary, April 1, 1942) Bowles possessed in high degree the knack of winning the confidence and arousing the interest of the military, and his services in the new and difficult business of co-ordinating electronics with tactics were of the first order.

Other matters in which Stimson's personal interest was keen were: artillery—Stimson and McCloy, indulging the inclination of two former artillerists, took a lively interest in all new developments, giving particular support to the development of self-propelled mounts and more powerful antitank guns; antiaircraft—an early slowness in this field drew Stimson's eye and he watched it carefully throughout the war, being personally responsible for a highly successful visit of British gunners from Malta in 1943; tanks—his own first inclination was in favor of heavier tanks than the General Sherman, but on the basis of reports from the party principally interested (General Patton) he stoutly defended the Sherman when it was attacked by critics in 1944 and after; aircraft— this was Lovett's field, and Stimson confined his labors mainly to the vigorous support of the Air Forces' theory of strategic bombing; bacteriological warfare—this purely defensive and precautionary undertaking required Stimson's personal attention in its organizational stages, but after the appointment of George Merck it ceased to give him concern, for Merck combined administrative skill with a keen appreciation of the peculiarly sensitive nature of his assignment; medical science —here Stimson's interest was keen and strong, and his direct contact with the Surgeon General, on the problems of wartime medicine, was probably greater than with any other single bureau chief (the subject, after all, had the strongest of human appeal to any civilian, and especially to a doctor's son) ; atomic energy—mentioned only in low voices behind closed doors for four years, this subject ceased to be an undertaking apart and became the center of Stimson's official life after March, 1945.

The close understanding which Stimson and Marshall maintained with their scientific advisers and the impressive achievements of wartime science combined in the end to produce a wholly new atmosphere in the Army. By March, 1944, it was clear to Stimson that scientists "are now thoroughly in vogue with our Army." For this result the main credit belonged to the scientific leaders who had constantly asserted and proved the value of their services; for his part Stimson was more than content with the generous encomium he later received from the scientists' historian: "It would be hard to exaggerate the role played by Secretary Stimson in ensuring effective cooperation between the civilian scientists and the huge organization over which he presided. No one in the War Department approached with keener zest the problem of extracting from scientific research the maximum contribution to the war effort. Again and again he provided the impetus which broke log jams and speeded major problems on their way to solution."[4]

[4] Baxter, *op. cit.*, pp. 32-33.

CHAPTER XIX

The Effort for Total Mobilization

IT MAY fairly be doubted whether anyone in America fully appreciated, in December, 1941, the size and scope of the war effort which would be necessary in the next four years. In every respect but one—the absence of fighting on American soil—the Second World War for Americans dwarfed all its predecessors, and the exception itself added to the magnitude of the task, for the distance of the front inevitably lent psychological support to those who wished to fight as easy a war as possible.

The extraordinary wartime accomplishment of the American nation left, in Stimson's view, no room for doubt as to the essential soundness and strength of American society. It had been his conviction, throughout his life, that there was no discernible limit to the power of the American people when they were firmly united in purpose. But the strength of Americans was only equaled by their ignorance, both of war and of high politics, and without the leadership of a firm and stouthearted President they could never have been mobilized for victory. The people themselves seemed often to have a willingness for sacrifice and effort which outpaced the actions of Washington, but they tolerated in their Congressmen an attitude of hesitation which frequently delayed and sometimes blocked the measures needed for an all-out prosecution of the war.

To Stimson the residents of wartime Washington broke down broadly into two classifications: those whose first and central object was to win the war, as quickly and thoroughly as a truly total effort would permit, and those who had other conflicting purposes to which they sometimes gave a prior allegiance. The men whose whole mind was on victory were always a minority, but fortunately this minority usually included the President. Yet it was from feelings for or against Mr. Roosevelt's own New Deal that much of the waste and suspicion of the war developed. Stimson would have found it hard to decide which angered him most, the congressional rear guard which looked at every wartime act through the distorted lenses of a rancorous mistrust, or the self-righteous ideologists who had multiplied around the President in the brave new years after 1933 and who now would not understand that the natural enemy was in Germany and Japan, not in Wall Street or among the brass hats. Why the right could not behave like Jim Wadsworth, and the left like Harry Hopkins, Stimson never understood. He had foreseen this sort of trouble in 1939 when he wrote, in supporting Mr. Roosevelt's firm stand against aggression, that "National unity is not . . . promoted by methods which tend to disrupt the patriotism of either party or the effective co-operation of the two."[1] Nevertheless he had hoped that war would produce a far greater degree of forbearance and unity than it did. Only in the first few months after Pearl Harbor was there any appreciable relief from the stale battles of a past age. Afterwards the New Deal "cherubs" returned with all their ancient zest to the struggle, and Stimson once estimated that antiadministration "troublemakers" in Congress added to his troubles about one-hundredfold.

Now no doubt some of Stimson's feeling was merely a healthy annoyance at the inevitable disagreements and difficulties of war; he was never, in his private feelings, a man of overwhelming patience. But he could not avoid the conclusion that in very large part his objections to the atmosphere of wartime Washington rose from two convictions which he deeply held and which were not generally shared. The first was his complete dedication, emotional and intellectual, to the proposition that the only way to fight a war is to fight it with your whole and undiluted strength. Discussion about what it would take to win seemed to him meaningless. Such considerations

[1] Letter to the New York *Times*, March 6, 1939.

might be appropriate in small campaigns like those of the Spanish-American War, but in the world conflicts of the twentieth century they were wholly out of place. The only way to minimize the final ghastly price of World War II was to shorten the struggle, and the only way to shorten it was to devote the entire strength of the nation to its relentless prosecution. Every sign of division was an encouragement to the enemy, and every concession to self-indulgence was a shot fired in folly at your own troops. The only important goal of the war was victory, and the only proper test of wartime action was whether it would help to win.

In the mind of a fanatic, of course, the convictions set out in the last paragraph might well have led to absurdity. But Stimson thought he understood that the best soldier is the balanced and healthy one, and neither for the troops nor for the nation did he advocate any ridiculous and unprofitable wearing of hair shirts—he continued to get his own rest and sport whenever possible, and his principal concern for his War Department friends was that they must do the same.

It was obvious, furthermore, that in the kind of war that America faced it would not do for every man to grab a rifle and start walking toward Berlin. Although critics sometimes seemed to doubt it, the War Department was fully aware of the degree to which World War II must be fought "in factory and farm." In the complex organization that was demanded of the United States, there must be balanced the demands of the Army and Navy, of allies in every continent, and of the American economy itself. All this Stimson understood—he had supported Lend-Lease on precisely this theory of America's role in the war. What he held was simply that every man and every dollar and every factory should be so employed as to contribute its maximum strength to the war.

Matched with his conviction that the war deserved the country's whole attention was a complete lack of apprehension lest war destroy any of the lasting values of American democracy. He could not share the fears of either right or left; from his knowledge of the country and its leaders, he was certain beyond doubt or fear that there would be no war-spawned dictatorship in America; nothing in his experience justified the laments of Mr. Roosevelt's opponents over the increased authority of the Executive. Even less was he alarmed by the bogy of "militarism." Only in the fantastic human and economic cost of war did he see important danger, and this cost could be cut down only by a policy of "war to the uttermost."

The general statement of these two convictions would probably have been accepted by most Americans throughout the war; but the application of principles to the terrain and the situation frequently brings to light major latent differences of emphasis, and in order to make Stimson's position wholly clear we shall have to study specific issues of his wartime years. The most fruitful field for such a study is the wartime use of manpower. Nothing touches more closely upon the opinions and interests of a man than the demands of his government with respect to the use of his person, and there is nothing more inextricably a part of modern war than the existence of such demands.

1. MILITARY MANPOWER

The American Army of December, 1941, was composed of those men who by inclination or availability had been most readily and painlessly detached from civilian life. Although the Selective Service Act of 1940 had given definite and conclusive recognition to the principle of the obligation of the citizen to serve as might be directed by his government, the limitations surrounding this principle were such that during the first year of the war Stimson and other administration leaders were involved in a series of moves to strengthen and broaden the Selective Service System. And after 1943, when the manpower requirements of the armed services had been mainly satisfied, these same leaders, by an extension of thinking as logical to them as it was fearsome to their opponents, became ardent advocates of a National Service Act for directing the assignment of the country's labor force, a measure which America alone of major fighting nations never enacted. At each of the different stages of this continuing struggle there were interesting episodes.

The first major improvement in Selective Service after Pearl Harbor was the reduction of the draft age from twenty to eighteen. In retrospect Stimson was astonished that it should have taken the nation almost a year to give legal recognition to the fact that war is a young man's game, but in the records there was ample evidence that this delay was forced not by a lack of foresight on the part of the Army and its leaders but by the reluctance of Congress to accept until absolutely necessary the drafting of younger men. Both before and after Pearl Harbor Army recommendations for a reduction in the draft age were ignored by Congress, and by April, 1942, the War Department had decided to wait until the pressure of events strengthened its case. The rising draft calls of the spring and summer finally provided the required pressure, and in October, 1942, explaining the Army's bitter needs to a House committee, Stimson emphasized the unpleasant fact that the draft was reaching the end of its present resources, and that it was now a choice between men under twenty and men palpably unfit for extended combat service (or else the family men who all agreed should come last). Such a choice was really no choice at all. The argument was unanswerable, although protests were heard from educators, clergymen, and others.

In November, after a month of delay and after the elections had safely passed, over the protests of many and with the reluctant support of others, the draft was at last extended to those who should by all the principles of effective warmaking have been the very first to be called. When General Marshall reported to the nation in 1945 that "men of eighteen, nineteen, and twenty make our finest soldiers" he was only re-emphasizing what troop leaders have known for generations. Yet throughout the war there was a considerable group of men in Congress who continued to be suspicious of the Army's use of younger men, and time after time Stimson was forced to re-emphasize that the War Department was not planning some sort of infant slaughter.

A somewhat contrasting problem was the issue of volunteer enlistments, which also reached its solution at the end of 1942. It was clear that no orderly manpower policy could be worked out while unrestricted volunteering was permitted, but here the advocates of control met strong opposition from the United States Navy, of whose many proud traditions not the least was its reliance upon volunteer sailors and marines. And one of the best-indoctrinated friends of the Navy was Franklin Roosevelt. The President supported with courage and force the reduction of the draft age, but throughout the early months of the war he backed the Navy in its insistence on maintaining a volunteer system. Stimson knew when he was outmatched; even late in 1942, when the question was urgent, he approached it gently. In a letter to the President on November 18 he asked for counsel as to the position he should take before Congress on manpower legislation: "My feeling, as you know, is that sooner or later we should come to a single selective process without any volunteering. But I have a vivid recollection of a letter written by yourself to the Navy painting an attractive picture of the superhuman character of a Navy built upon volunteering. . . ."

Circumstances caught up with the Navy and its friend, however, and on December 5, 1942, the President issued an Executive Order suspending all voluntary enlistments except for seventeen-year-olds. Later, after the usual interservice difficulties, an agreement was reached under which the Army and Navy shared in fair proportion the peaches and lemons produced by the draft. The change was overdue, for a year of delay had thrown the two services seriously out of balance in their relative average ages; figures for September, 1942, showed the average age of Navy enlisted men to be under twenty-three while the corresponding figure for the Army was over twenty-six. Whatever the reason—and the reasons given by Army and Navy supporters were as far apart as the poles— it was a fact that a disproportionate number of young volunteers preferred the naval service. Once more only the pressure of events had forced the correction of an essentially wasteful and inequitable policy. The Navy's desire for volunteers was natural—just as natural as the reluctance of matriarchal America to draft her eighteen-year-olds. But both were attitudes that insufficiently recognized the requirements of the war.

Reducing the draft age and ending volunteer enlistments were minor matters compared to the battle that ebbed and flowed throughout the war over the size of the Army. This was a subject upon which Stimson was more vehement than most of his military advisers; it seemed to him to involve very urgent questions as to the strength of America's wartime resolution.

Questions about the Army's size fell into two categories, one technical, the other almost entirely a matter of attitude. Technically, the problem was one of assessing the various components of the war effort so as to define their relative positions. The useful size of the Army depended upon the weapons and munitions that could be produced to arm it and the ships that could be built to transport and supply it, and the whole program of the Army in turn must be related to the undertakings of the Navy and the requirements of America's allies. A calculus so complex would have no undebatable answer, but some sort of conclusion was urgently required, if only as a basis for action. In this technical problem Stimson took no active part; the matter was one for professionals. The Army's projected strength, based on extended discussions in the Joint Chiefs of Staff and with administration leaders responsible for production and manpower, was fixed in 1942 at 8,200,000 officers and enlisted men. A downward revision in 1943 was offset in 1944 by rising casualty lists, and total strength of the Army on VE-day was approximately 8,300,000. The figure thus projected and defended against heavy opposition in 1942 proved to be both accurate and sufficient. For this Stimson could claim only the credit of never having lost confidence in General Marshall. His own feeling had been, throughout, that the cloth might well be cut too fine; in early 1944 and again a year later he urged Marshall to reconsider and if necessary expand his estimates. Both times the Chief of Staff rehearsed his thinking and stuck to his decision, and his judgment was vindicated in victory.

Stimson, believing that the projected army was perhaps too small, naturally plunged with considerable zest into the task of defending it against those who argued that it was too big. The facts and figures upon which the administration discussion was based were necessarily secret, and it was therefore not possible to undertake a detailed explanation of the situation. But in Stimson's view much of the national doubt about the size of the Army was due not to any difference on the facts but to a widespread misunderstanding of the nature of war. To this problem he addressed himself on March 9, 1943, in a radio speech which clearly demonstrated his broad view of the war, its prosecution, and the Army's critics.

First he addressed himself to a problem of "mental attitude." "Tonight I wish to speak to you about the subtle danger which, unless guarded against, may destroy our present bright hopes for a decisive victory. It arises out of a mental attitude which is quite prevalent among our people, including many of the best of them, and has danger of which most of them are quite unconscious. . . . It is hard to analyze the attitude to which I refer. . . . Very often it appears in patriotic people who do not realize what we are up against and who honestly do not understand the purpose and necessity of some of the war measures which their government is taking. But the attitude is just as dangerous even when it is innocent. I think it can accurately be called the attitude of trying to win the war—the most fierce and dangerous war which has ever confronted the United States—in some easy manner and without too much trouble and sacrifice. Abraham Lincoln met it in the Civil War even after that war had been going on for over a year and many bloody battles had been fought. He said to a caller at the White House in September 1862, 'The fact is the people have not made up their minds that we are at war with the South. They have not buckled down to the determination to fight this war through; or they have got the idea into their heads that we are going to get out of this fix somehow by strategy. . . . They have no idea that this war is to be carried on and put through by hard, tough fighting; that it will hurt somebody; and no headway is going to be made while this delusion lasts.'[2]

"Today this attitude which Lincoln described, manifests itself when we say: 'The Russians have destroyed so many Germans that Germany will not be able to carry on any more offensives'; or when we say: 'The German people are cracking'; or when we say: 'The best way to win the war is to give our Allies plenty of weapons to fight for us'; or when we say:

[2] Stimson had found this quotation in Carl Sandburg's *Abraham Lincoln, The War Years*, I, 553. This book was one in which Stimson found both consolation and instruction during 1943. It was good to know that many of the troubles of World War II had been faced and surmounted, in far more trying circumstances, eighty years before.

'If we make too big a military effort we shall so dislocate our economy that we shall never recover; we shall create a permanent dictatorship and lose our historic freedom'; or when we say other things which at bottom represent merely wishful thinking or the dread of personal sacrifices and the desire to find a better way out. I believe that this attitude towards hard fighting on our part really underlies much of the criticism which is being directed today against the proposed size of our Army."

Yet this attempt to dodge "tough fighting" was the surest way to lengthen the war and almost the only way to put victory in doubt. The people who held this attitude, and who questioned the need, in a time of rising success, for ever greater armies, "do not understand the psychology of combat. They do not realize that battles are won by continuous rapid blows upon an enemy and that when an enemy begins to show signs of demoralization these blows must be continued and, if possible, redoubled in order that he may not have time to re-form his forces. Once the enemy is checked or shaken on the field of battle, he must be constantly pursued and hammered until he is completely beaten or surrenders. The very fact that it is known that we have trained forces ready to do this tends towards his demoralization."

And Stimson cited the contrasting examples of Meade at Gettysburg and Foch in 1918. Hesitation in the one case had lengthened a war beyond expectation, while the remorseless aggressiveness of Foch, in the other, had brought victory months ahead of schedule.

Supporting the general tendency to think up easy ways to win the war were other misconceptions drawn from too hasty observation of the newfangled thing called total war. For if it was true that World War II was in scope and complexity unlike any previous struggle, placing demands upon all of society far exceeding those of simpler wars, it was emphatically not true that war had reduced the importance of armed forces. The lines of effort, for all their increased ramifications, still ended in regiments, ships, and aircraft manned by military men. It was not antediluvian to raise an army, and Stimson addressed himself cheerfully to his duty of explaining the

Army to the people. The first and most significant point was
its relatively small size, compared to the armies of its enemies.
Secondly, it was an Army of unprecedented variety and flexibility, with training problems of corresponding difficulty.
Third, it was an Army in which at least a year must separate a
major training program from the battlefield. "I speak with
careful consideration when I say that if we should halt this
great training establishment which we have now built and
timed according to the present timetable of the war, we should
deal a heavier blow to our hopes of a complete final victory
than by any loss which we are likely to sustain on the field of
battle."

The Army must be raised; more than that, the nation must
trust its leaders. It was possible of course that the Army and
the Navy were proceeding in pigheaded blindness on the basis
of wholly outdated concepts. Stimson could only rehearse the
nature of wartime planning and give his solemn assurance that
the figures for the size of the Army "have thus had the benefit
of all the brains, accumulated research, and judgment which
our governmental machinery provides for that purpose." Only
time could prove whether the decisions made were wise, but
all the advantages of study and experience lay with the administration and not its critics.

Another half-truth drawn from the concept of total war was
the theory that the projected army would too greatly strain the
nation's manpower resources. This theory in Stimson's view
embodied one of the most pertinacious fallacies of all, and he
jumped on it with both feet. For, however important the nonmilitary aspects of the war might be, it was wholly illogical to
support them at the expense of the Army until every other
means of industrial mobilization had been exhausted. "Only
those who believe that our industry and our farming and our
general civilian activity are really keyed to an all-out war are
entitled to make this argument. It is the duty of every citizen
to examine into his own life, and his own community and see
whether production in industry and on the farm cannot be
increased enormously in efficiency; whether absenteeism,
threatened strikes, general complacency, insistence on 'business
as usual,' or even insistence on hoped-for standards of living,

are not going a long way to prevent what could be accomplished by an all-out war effort."

To attack the size of the Army when the civilian economy was incompletely mobilized was absurd. "When you are driving a team of horses and one of them goes lame, you do not lame the other horse to equalize the team. You try to get two sound horses."

And then in his conclusion Stimson shifted from the defense of the Army to a note of personal challenge. "For myself, I have reached the conclusion that one of the reasons why industry and agriculture and the whole civilian population have not moved more rapidly towards an all-out effort is that we have relied almost entirely on voluntary co-operation. This voluntary co-operation would work with a large part of our population as soon as they clearly understood the need for it. But the effect of the recalcitrant or thoughtless few is so great upon the minds and efforts of others that I am convinced that the only way to accomplish the result which we must all reach, is through a General [National] Service Act. This has proved true in England and I believe it is now true here.

"The issue between the proponents of the Army program and its critics in my opinion largely narrows down to this difference: the leaders of the Army are trying, by shortening the war, to save the lives of thousands of young Americans— lives vital to the future of this country. The opponents of the Army program are trying to avoid present trouble—the inconveniences and relatively minor sacrifices which would be involved in a more thorough and drastic reorganization of our industrial and civilian life for the remaining period of this war."

This was Stimson's first public statement in favor of a principle to whose support a large proportion of his time was given in the following two years—without success.

2. NATIONAL SERVICE

Of all the shortages which complicated America's war effort, almost the last to appear was the shortage of manpower. At the beginning of the crisis, in 1940, there were more than nine million unemployed, and even at the time of Pearl Harbor there were still four million men out of work. It thus happened that as the manpower problem gradually became pressing in 1942, it was approached by most administration leaders with partial and specific remedies not based on any general policy for the mobilization of the nation's human resources. Later, when the general theory of national service was advanced, it was faced by the existence of commissions, policies, and attitudes based on the theory of voluntary or piecemeal arrangements. In December, 1942, the President had given to Paul McNutt, head of the War Manpower Commission, executive authority in the field of manpower which was loosely described at the time as dictatorial. But in point of fact McNutt's authority was extremely limited, nor was his commission so organized as to exercise any broadly effective leadership. Although Stimson's relations with McNutt were always personally friendly, it would be too much to say that the War Department and the War Manpower Commission approved of each other's views of the manpower problem. The War Department believed in drastic action; the Manpower Commission was committed to guidance and cajolery. And in between the two was Selective Service, a prize for the control of which both contended. This particular battle was decided against Stimson by the President late in 1942 when the former was away for a short rest. Mr. Roosevelt took the sting out of his decision in the first Cabinet meeting after Stimson's return. "He saw me, welcomed me back, and said 'Harry, I've been robbing your henroost while you were away.' I was ready for him and snapped right back, 'I won't go away again.' " (Diary, December 11, 1942)

But the Manpower Commission, the War Department, and Selective Service might be shuffled and reshuffled as often as the President chose, without changing the basic situation, for there was no law providing for genuine executive direction of the mobilization of civilian labor. Unlike Great Britain, Russia, and all the British dominions, the United States possessed no law in the area of civilian manpower matching its Selective Service Act for raising an army and a navy by compulsion. In other words, unlike her allies and enemies, she had no legislation which compelled a man to work for his country in the arsenals and factories and other activities which equipped and supplied American soldiers.

National service legislation was urged early in 1942 by such men as Grenville Clark; in July of that year a subcommittee of the War Manpower Commission, under Stimson's devoted assistant Goldthwaite Dorr, recommended such legislation in a comprehensive and compelling report; but the Dorr report was opposed by other elements of the administration, and the introduction of a national service bill in February, 1943, was left to Senator Warren Austin and Representative James Wadsworth, two men who as Republicans were wholly outside the administration and whose nonpartisan interest in the war effort was beyond challenge. Stimson promptly gave his support in principle to the proposals they had advanced, but in the absence of official backing from the White House the War Department refrained from active advocacy. Meanwhile, throughout 1943, Stimson continued to urge on the President the need for such legislation, pointing out that without active presidential support there was no possibility of its enactment. Mr. Roosevelt, alive as always to the political difficulties involved, and hopeful that his toothless War Manpower Commission might prove adequate to the emergency, held back; most of his administration, and particularly those members of it connected with labor and progressive circles, strongly supported his decision.

In December, 1943, the country was shaken by the imminent threat of a national railroad strike. Similar threatened tie-ups in coal and steel had already produced a strong wave of feeling against small groups who appeared to put their private interests above the wartime interests of the nation, and it seems certain that Mr. Roosevelt was himself deeply stirred by these events. Feeling that strikes and threatened strikes were merely surface evidence of the incompletely warlike attitude of the nation, Stimson joined with Secretary Knox and Admiral Land of the Maritime Commission in strongly urging that the President take the lead in advocating a National Service Act. Stimson further supported this appeal with a personal letter to "My dear Chief," pointing out that the President owed it to himself not to leave the nation in any doubt as to his support of a complete war effort.

As far as Stimson ever knew, the President's annual message of January 11, 1944, was prepared by him without the advice and consultation of either the advocates or the opponents of national service legislation, and Stimson was as surprised as he was delighted to find that in this message the President came out strongly and persuasively in favor of such an act, describing it as the only truly democratic method of organizing American manpower. Fortified by this pronouncement, the advocates of national service began a vigorous campaign for the enactment of a revised Austin-Wadsworth Bill. On January 19, 1944, Stimson appeared before the Senate Committee on Military Affairs as the first administration spokesman for this measure. The line of argument he there developed fairly depicts his general approach to the problem.

After stressing that 1944, as a year of extraordinary military operations, must also be a year of all-out production and unity at home, he pointed out the existence of labor unrest in some areas and labor shortages in others. Such a situation at home could hardly be viewed with understanding or approval by the men in the armed forces. "The evident remedy is for the nation to make clear in no uncertain terms the equality of obligation of its citizens. . . . The men in war production are not essentially different from the men who are proving themselves heroes in the South Pacific and on the Italian peninsula. They can be more accurately defined as the victims of the failure of the nation to develop a sense of responsibility in this gravest of all wars. . . . We must . . . bring home to each of these men the fact that his individual work is just as patriotic and important to the Government as any other cog in the great machine of victory. . . . The purpose of a National Service Law is to get at this basic evil which produces the irresponsibility out of which stem strikes, threats of strikes, excessive turnovers, absenteeism, and the other manifestations of irresponsibility with which we are now plagued. It is aimed to extend the principles of democracy and justice more evenly throughout our population. There is no difference between the patriotic obligations resting upon these two classes of men which I have described. Certainly the nation has no less right to require a man to make weapons than it has to require another man to fight with those weapons. Both processes should be so designed and carried out as to serve the interest of the country in winning the war. In a democracy they should also be so designed and executed as to serve the principles of justice between its citizens."

This was admittedly a principle new to the United States. Stimson rehearsed the historic reasons which had made such a move unnecessary in previous wars, pointing out that World War II was the first in which the nation had come anywhere near to a full mobilization. The dependence of the armed forces on the entire economy was obvious, and it was equally obvious that millions of civilian workers were not efficiently meshed into the war effort. An extremely heavy labor turnover in some war industries and severe labor shortages in others were seriously affecting war production. To meet this situation a new approach was needed.

The basic purpose behind Stimson's advocacy of a National Service Act was the same as his purpose in almost all other wartime affairs. "I have been discussing the logic of national service as an orderly, efficient process by which a democracy can give all-out effort in war. But more important now, national service will be the means of hastening the end of *this* war. . . . Every month the war is prolonged will be measured in the lives of thousands of young men, in billions of dollars. The attrition in manpower and in our national wealth will be felt for generations if this conflict is prolonged. National service is the one weapon we have neglected to use. Posterity will never forgive us if we sacrifice our plain duty to a desire for creature comfort or for private gain." Then as head of the War Department he emphasized the critical importance of giving full support at home to the troops abroad. "It will be tragic indeed if the discontent and resentment felt by our gallant soldiers on the fighting fronts burns deeply and festers in their hearts. . . . The voices of these soldiers speak out very clearly today in demanding that all Americans accept the same liability which a soldier must accept for service to country. . . . To me it appears to be the plain duty of the

Congress to give our troops this all-out necessary backing. It is time for all pledges to be redeemed in acts. . . . I remind this committee now of the solemn statement with which our Congress concluded its declaration of war against Japan and against Germany on December 11, 1941: 'to bring the conflict to a successful termination, all the resources of the country are hereby pledged by the Congress of the United States.' I ask no more than that you examine this proposed legislation in the light of that statement."

Stimson's support of the Austin-Wadsworth Bill was followed by similar statements from other leaders of the service departments. To these men their case seemed irrefutable, and they drew great hope for success from the fact that public opinion polls showed better than 70 per cent of the people to be in favor of their position. Yet the Austin-Wadsworth Bill was never even reported from committee, and a second great effort in 1945 produced a heavily diluted measure which was finally beaten by the Senate in April, one month before the end of the European war.

The idea of national service, for all its logic and its popular support, was roundly defeated by a combination of forces unlike any other in the war years. The first and most important factor in this combination was the violent opposition expressed by the leaders of organized labor. With complete unanimity, labor leaders denounced the President's proposal of January, 1944, and their opposition continued unabated throughout the war. Yet it was impossible for Stimson to believe that in the light of the British experience American union leaders were wholly honest in their claims that national service meant "slave labor." Stimson, like other advocates of national service, repeatedly emphasized that there was no intention of indicting labor as a whole. It was merely a matter of providing obviously needed leadership and direction in making full use of the nation's labor force. Nor did he believe that national service would operate against the rights of labor. "A National Service Act will not cause the evils which have been feared by its opponents. The man or woman who wants to do his or her part to win the war as quickly as possible has nothing to fear from a National Service Act. The act does not impair the rights of the worker in respect to wage scales, hours of labor, seniority rights, membership in unions, or other basic interests of the civilian workers. Wherever justified by considerations of family or health, deferment from service would be granted by the local Selective Service Board. I would not advocate any National Service Act which would not protect such elemental rights to the fullest. National Service Acts have been enacted by the great English-speaking democracies which are now fighting this war with us, namely Great Britain, Canada, Australia, New Zealand. With them the legislation has worked so successfully that the exercise of sanctions has become rare; the existence of the national service organization and the morale which it creates having proved that the people of a country want to do their duty when it is clearly pointed out to them by their government."[3]

But the leaders of American labor were not persuaded, and they were joined in opposition by spokesmen of industry in the National Association of Manufacturers, the Chamber of Commerce, and by industrial advisers within the Government itself. Both labor and management preferred the anarchy of a voluntary system to the imagined perils of Government direction.

Nor were matters made easier by division within the administration itself. The coolness of labor was reflected among many members of Congress who were ordinarily among the President's most ardent supporters, and in the War Manpower Commission, which should logically have been the principal proponent of national service legislation, there was deep-seated opposition not only to the general principle but to the specific form of the Austin-Wadsworth Bill, which would have by-passed McNutt's widely unpopular organization. Further, since only the leaders of the service departments and the Maritime Commission were explicitly on record in favor of the bill, there was a natural tendency to argue that national service was a militaristic proposal. How far this was from the truth, at least in Stimson's case, may be suggested by the fact that he constantly insisted that the director of any national service program must be a man commanding the support of labor and

[3] Statement at Senate hearing, January 19, 1944.

civilian groups; the only name which appears in his notes as a suggestion for this post is that of Henry A. Wallace. But the bulk of Mr. Roosevelt's New Deal supporters did not share the President's view of national service, and their opposition, though quiet, was consistent and strong.

In the face of this opposition the President himself did not until 1945 conduct any vigorous campaign for the legislation he had so eloquently advocated, and in one sense there was a justification for this reluctance which extended beyond a mere question of political prudence. In his message of January, 1944, Mr. Roosevelt had coupled his demand for national service legislation with requests for broader taxes and other powers of wartime control, and he had insisted that the message be considered as a whole. In the absence of congressional support for these other aspects of his program, he adhered through 1944 to his original pronouncement that it would be unfair to press for specific controls over manpower alone. Although Stimson could not share these conclusions, since manpower legislation was a matter of special importance from the standpoint of the War Department, he nevertheless agreed that the failure to obtain a National Service Act was essentially similar to the congressional failure in passing adequate tax legislation. Both were reflections of the national refusal to fight an all-out war.

Under different circumstances of timing, and with a different relationship between the executive and the legislative branches, a National Service Act, a strong tax program, and other measures adequately enforcing the austerity of effective war-making might perhaps have been passed even early in the war, but of this Stimson could not judge. National service was basically a matter not in his jurisdiction; he was drawn into it only by the pressure of events and by the default of those administration leaders directly responsible for the nation's manpower. Although the war was won without it, he was certain that an earlier, stronger policy would have brought a quicker and cheaper victory. And he was certain too that if for any reason the war had been prolonged, the absence of a National Service Act would have had most serious consequences. Stimson believed that in this field, as in many others, the American people were better judges than their representatives in Washington.

3. LABOR AND THE WAR

Through the early months of his service in Washington, Stimson had found his relations with labor leaders gratifyingly cordial. The question of labor relations was one on which he found the Roosevelt administration somewhat "tender," but fortunately Sidney Hillman, labor member of the National Defense Advisory Commission, was a man of breadth and character, and Stimson was quickly able to establish with him an enduring relationship of mutual confidence. Through Hillman he was able in the summer of 1940 to reverse a previous administration decision and shift the War Department's arsenals from a forty- to a forty-eight-hour week. The result of the longer hours, and higher wages, was increased morale and a 30-per-cent increase in production. Hillman was also cooperative in insuring approval of War Department arrangements for the movement of Jamaican laborers to Panama for work on the canal defenses. Both the increase of hours and the importation of labor were sensitive subjects in labor circles, and Hillman's assistance was proof of his stature.

Stimson's own view of the position of labor in the national crisis he expressed in a speech to the American Federation of Labor in convention assembled at New Orleans, on November 18, 1940. No group, he pointed out, was more directly concerned with the Nazi menace than labor. British labor was demonstrating that no group was more determined to defend its liberties. He expected a similar response from American labor, and thus far there was every evidence that his expectations were correct. In the coming struggle, labor, like everyone else, would have to make sacrifices; no responsible man could promise "business as usual." He *could* promise that "the practice and procedure of collective bargaining through freely chosen and independent unions will not be sacrificed." Within this policy the War Department was confident that all particular problems could be worked out.

These general views Stimson maintained throughout the

war. There were strikes and threats of strikes which did not
meet his concept of the proper obligations of labor in a national
emergency, and some of them involved energetic remedial
action by the War Department; and some few labor leaders,
with the administration's favorite enemy John L. Lewis in
the van, behaved with outrageous irresponsibility. But on balance he thought that the response of organized labor was as
patriotic as that of the rest of the nation.

Stimson always insisted that strikes affecting military production must be prevented. It followed that the rights of labor
must be protected and equitable conditions of work and pay
insured by the Government, for the strike is the one compelling
weapon of the worker. But there must be no strikes in defiance
of the Government's awards and decisions. A good example of
the kind of action Stimson approved in dealing with such
strikes occurred in June, 1941, when there was a strike at the
North American Aviation plant, in Inglewood, California.
The prompt and decisive handling of this affair was a matter
on which Stimson looked back with great pride, the more so
because it was an action of a united Government, in which
the President and Sidney Hillman were quite as firm as
Stimson and his assistants.

The North American plant was in 1941 one of the most
important and successful producers of military aircraft. In
defiance of an agreement to mediate, a strike was instigated
by men whom all competent observers believed to be Communists. The Government reacted quickly, taking over the
plant and bringing in troops to insure the undisturbed return
to work of those who wished to respond to the President's
appeal. Stimson himself ordered that Army patrols should
protect the homes of returning workers, which had been threatened by the strike leaders. With the President's explicit approval, Stimson co-operated with General Hershey in the
issuance of a directive to all local draft boards instructing
them to cancel the draft deferments of those who engaged in
such strikes. It is illustrative of the crosscurrents within the
administration that one of the President's administrative assistants later publicly announced that Hershey's statement had

been issued without Presidential authority. The strike quickly collapsed.

The North American strike was only one of a number on the west coast in early 1941 which the Government believed to be Communist-led. The party line at the time was of course that the imperialist Roosevelt was warmongering to hide the fatal weaknesses of his so-called New Deal. Whatever their other failings, the Communists were quite skillful in concentrating their operations in plants of major military importance; the issue sharply presented by the North American affair was whether the Government was strong enough to overcome such activities on the part of men whose primary allegiance was to a foreign (and at the time not friendly) power. The distinction between Communists and others in the labor movement was to Stimson one of vital importance. "I am drawing the line sharply between legitimate labor controversies and subversive action by men who have ulterior motives against our defense," he wrote in June 11, 1941; the same line was being drawn by the President, and by the Justice Department under Jackson. The issue was not decisively settled, because within two weeks of the end of the North American strike it vanished in the sharpest reversal on record of the Communist party line. The Nazi invasion of Russia thus had the incidental effect of postponing indefinitely a reckoning between the American Government and American Communists which would otherwise probably have occurred in the summer of 1941.

The use of the Army to break strikes is not pleasant; neither soldiers nor citizens like to see the armed forces employed against Americans. That it was necessary several times during the war Stimson regretted, but this was the result of a situation beyond his control or responsibility. His own duty was to protect the reputation of the Army, and he therefore insisted that in each case, when the Army was called in, it must have an opportunity for careful planning and energetic action. The outbreak of violence in such cases is usually the result of faulty preparation or imperfect leadership; in the record of the Army in its ventures into domestic conflict during the years 1940 to 1945 Stimson found another proof that the United

States Army deserved its reputation for versatility and tactful firmness. The decision to use troops of course never rested with the War Department, and in the case of the Montgomery-Ward strike Stimson strongly opposed the President's decision, for he was unable to see a connection between the war effort and a retail storekeeper, however intransigent.

In critical labor cases throughout the war Stimson found that he and the President were in broad agreement. On the other hand, Mr. Roosevelt's cautious approach to the general problem did not correspond with Stimson's thinking at all. He did not sympathize with the administration's unwillingness to take a flat stand against stoppages affecting war production. Here again Stimson believed that Mr. Roosevelt missed an opportunity for aggressive leadership; he could not believe that American labor was any different from other sections of the country, or that intransigent labor leaders should be solicitously treated by the administration. Labor's no-strike pledge was in the main loyally kept, but Stimson saw this loyalty as one reason the more for dealing sternly with those who chose to break the pledge. And there came a time, in 1943 and 1944, when Mr. Roosevelt's conciliatory methods in dealing with labor troubles became in Stimson's view a serious obstacle to all-out mobilization. Many a man in Congress—leaving aside the few who are always against labor—was reluctant to pass such drastic measures as a National Service Act or a stronger tax bill when the administration seemed to be unwilling to use its full existing strength to control irresponsible labor leaders.

4. THE ARMY AND WAR PRODUCTION—A NOTE ON ADMINISTRATION

We have seen that an important segment of the manpower problem as Stimson saw it was the relationship between the Army and civilian agencies of the Government; in the field of war production this relationship was the central difficulty. After Pearl Harbor there was never any doubt about the determination of the whole country to produce for war as it had never produced for peace, but disagreements on ways and means involved Stimson against his will in the resulting squabbles.

The question of organization for war production had faced the President since 1940, and by January, 1942, it was clear that the evolution from NDAC to OPM to SPAB was incomplete. As the President considered his next step Stimson wrote him a letter on January 7 which summarized his own broad view of the problem. In essence, two things were needed. First, there must be a reorganization giving adequate authority to a single man; this reorganization must not destroy the natural and traditional procurement functions of the Army and the Navy, but it must provide clear and sufficient authority for co-ordination at the top. Second, the President must find the right man for the job—and to Stimson this meant a man with real and demonstrated talent in production, or at least with a proved capacity for dealing with production executives. The post, furthermore, was of such importance that the President "should not move until you are dead sure of your man."

Mr. Roosevelt, on January 16, established the War Production Board with Donald M. Nelson as chairman. Both the form of the new organization and the man selected were satisfactory to the Secretary of War; Nelson had a good reputation, and he was now to have the priceless advantage of possessing genuine authority. Stimson, like most other members of SPAB, was a member of the new board, but his powers were merely advisory, and in the main he left his seat to Patterson. He was glad that the great abilities of William Knudsen were not lost in the shuffle; Knudsen moved to the War Department and for the rest of the war the Army had the assistance of his remarkable understanding of industrial management. His appointment as lieutenant general was a Presidential gesture which neither Stimson nor Knudsen considered very helpful but by sheer personal quality Knudsen gave distinction to his uniform and rank.

The War Production Board continued in operation throughout the war. During this period there occurred several sharp disagreements between WPB and the War Department; these matters were only of tangential importance in Stimson's life, since the procurement and production problems of the War

Department remained in the capable hands of Patterson. But there was current in the discussion of these widely publicized disagreements one misunderstanding which Stimson considered extremely dangerous. At the time he made no public comment on the question, adhering to his general view that it is never useful to indulge in public debate over intragovernmental problems, but his feelings on the matter were and remained strong.

Much of the comment on disagreement between the War Production Board and the military, both at this time and later, was based on the assumption that the underlying issue was a contest between civilians and the military for the control of the national economy. This view seemed to Stimson palpably preposterous. He was fully aware that in Patterson and Somervell he had two strong-minded associates, both of them fired by the single-minded purpose of meeting the Army's needs. But to assume that it was War Department doctrine that the Army should run the country's economy was arrant nonsense; this assumption, however, seemed to be accepted as gospel by a small group of men in WPB who were on cordial and communicative terms with the press, and who seem also to have converted Mr. Nelson. This was a conspicuous example of the sort of twisted thinking that Stimson met time after time among administration officials whose minds were fixed in the rigid grooves of self-styled "liberalism." These men had an ingrained distrust of military leaders which led them always to look for sinister militaristic motives in every Army action. That some irritation should be caused by the driving energy of General Somervell was not surprising, but there was no need to denounce the War Department—or Somervell himself—as "militaristic." Stimson and Patterson were themselves civilians, and they remained the chief officers of the War Department; what they wanted for the Army was not control, but supplies, and at no time did they believe that war production could be organized under other than civilian control.

The real issues between the Army and WPB were quite different. There was a difference of emotional value; there were men in WPB who felt that the Army failed to understand the needs of the civilian economy and men in the War Department who felt that WPB was not sufficiently aware of the needs of war. There was also an issue of administrative policy, centering on the desire of the service departments to supervise their own procurement. That these operations should in turn be supervised and co-ordinated by WPB was quite proper, and clearly there was room for disagreement on the exact manner in which this dual interest should be adjusted, but there was here no question of "militarism," and a compromise plan approved by Stimson in November, 1942, provided a clear basis for co-operation. All plans, however, depended on the quality of the head of WPB, and for his great task Nelson lacked the necessary stature as a man and talent as an administrator, or so Stimson was forced to believe. And he found an excellent proof that strong and able men were unfrightened by "militarism" in the relationship between the War Department and the War Shipping Administration, whose able deputy chief for operations was Lewis W. Douglas. Douglas had his troubles with overzealous Army officers, but by dealing openly with the War Department's civilian heads he was able to resolve his difficulties.

At first it was Stimson's hope that Nelson could be bolstered by the appointment of strong assistants, and he joined in the negotiations which brought Charles E. Wilson and Ferdinand Eberstadt into WPB in September, 1942. Although both men eventually broke with Nelson, they served with conspicuous skill while they lasted. In February, 1943, when Nelson proved unable to drive so spirited a team, Stimson and other administration leaders joined in asking the President to replace him with Bernard Baruch. No action was taken, however, until eighteen months later when in young Julius Krug the President found a man who was able to take over the WPB and run it without constant friction.

The history of war production showed the President's administrative technique at every stage. Having tinkered for nearly two years with boards and commissions he finally gave real power to the wrong man. Then when that man got into trouble, the President coasted along; he neither fully backed Mr. Nelson nor fired him. Stimson believed that it was Mr.

Roosevelt's irritated but indecisive tolerance of men lacking strength of character that lay behind many wartime administrative difficulties. Disagreements with men like Hull and Morgenthau were painful, but in these cases Stimson always knew where he stood; disagreements with men who backed and filled were extremely irritating.

In March, 1943, after several months of friction in the Government, Stimson took time out to register a summary complaint to his diary. After acquitting Mr. Roosevelt of the charge of playing politics with the war effort, he continued:

"But the President is the poorest administrator I have ever worked under in respect to the orderly procedure and routine of his performance. He is not a good chooser of men and he does not know how to use them in co-ordination.

"When I last held the post of Secretary of War under Mr. Taft, who was a very good administrator, there were only nine Cabinet officers or ten persons at the Cabinet table including the President. Barring the Interstate Commerce Commission and perhaps one or two other minor quasi-independent commissions, every administrative function headed up in one of the nine Cabinet officers and went to the President through the departmental head. Mr. Taft dealt with his departments through his Cabinet and that gave you a sense of responsibility and security that could not otherwise be obtained. Today the President has constituted an almost innumerable number of new administrative posts, putting at the head of them a lot of inexperienced men appointed largely for personal grounds and who report on their duties directly to the President and have constant and easy access to him. The result is that there are a lot of young men in Washington ambitious to increase the work of their agencies and having better access to the President than his Cabinet officers have. The lines of delimitation between these different agencies themselves and between them and the Departments [are] very nebulous. The inevitable result is that the Washington atmosphere is full of acrimonious disputes over matters of jurisdiction. In my own case, a very large percentage of my time and strength, particularly of recent months, has been taken up in trying to smooth out and settle the differences which have been thus created." (Diary, March 28, 1943)

Whatever his weaknesses as an administrator, however, the President had a firm understanding of the facts of war. His underlings might wish to give antitrust suits precedence over war production, but the President was not persuaded. Publicity-seeking officials might wish to turn a military trial of saboteurs into a public spectacle, in spite of the fact that these same officials had informed the War Department that much of the evidence would be valuable to the enemy; the President stood firm. In some of these matters, and notably in his impatience with irresponsible sections of the press, Mr. Roosevelt was indeed more vigorous than his Secretary of War.

5. PUBLIC RELATIONS

Stimson's relations with the press in World War II were easier than ever before in his public career. Although the War Department was a conspicuous target for criticism, its Secretary had learned many lessons in thickness of skin when he was Secretary of State, and only once in his last five years in Washington was he seriously annoyed by any personal attack. A national news magazine in 1941 portrayed him as unable to stay awake in conferences, and his lust for combat briefly stirred him to thoughts of a libel suit, but his friends calmed him in the same way that he later calmed subordinates. Life was too short for such irritations; in 1943, writing to a leading Republican who wanted confirmation or denial of a story by Drew Pearson, Stimson remarked that "I do not have the time to read the output of Drew Pearson and Company. Fortunately the work of running the Army keeps me so entirely occupied that I am spared these irritations which seem to be inherent in the American version of a free press." Except in the case of particularly vicious or sensational charges it was his policy not to try to catch up with irresponsible attacks. Nevertheless commentators (with a few conspicuous exceptions) remained a pet abomination; their lofty omniscience was a severe trial to a man who had always felt more sympathy with the actor than with the critic.

The central problem of the Army's public relations was to get and keep the confidence of the people. Basically, of course, the way to win this confidence was to earn it in action; no skill in public relations would offset failure in the Army's mission, while in a successful Army all problems of public relations would become minor. This principle came naturally to Stimson, whose eagerness for appealing to the public had always been limited by a rigid sense of what was fitting in a public servant.

The only enduring report on the Army furthermore would be that rendered to the people by the millions of citizen soldiers; in 1943 Stimson remarked to a friendly group of critics seeking improvement in the Army's public relations that "In general . . . our liaison agents to interpret the Army to the people of the United States are the five million young men who are in the Army and who can act as missionaries to their parents and families and who are doing so very successfully." (Diary, February 25, 1943) He saw nothing to be gained, and much to be lost, in flamboyant self-advertisement of the type that occasionally occurred in other parts of the armed forces and in the younger branches of the Army itself, and he sometimes became impatient with the irrepressible enthusiasms of the Air Forces. Especially while the Army remained largely untried there was no call for boastfulness; throughout the war Stimson avoided predictions of success and tried to guide himself by the counsel of the Old Testament: "Let not him that girdeth on his harness boast himself as he that putteth it off."[4]

The major difficulty in the Army's press relations was the necessity for military secrecy. While it was easy to agree in principle that nothing useful to the enemy should be made public, it was not always easy to determine in practice where the line should be drawn. Especially in the early months of the war there were many who felt that the War Department was unnecessarily niggardly in its release of information. But with both Archibald MacLeish and Elmer Davis, the two government officials who were successively concerned with this problem, Stimson found himself able to establish cordial relations, and although they did not always agree with his judgment, he

[4] I Kings 20:11, quoted to press conference, August 13, 1942.

found them open to persuasion. Stimson himself occasionally thought the professional rulings of his military advisers a trifle stern. Beyond a certain limit secrecy became self-defeating; especially in the case of units in combat the morale value of extensive and specific publicity seemed to outweigh any loss likely to result from telling the enemy about units he had probably already identified.

But criticism from within the Government was frequently caused by an incomplete appreciation of the problem. The War Department, for example, maintained a strict control over all information about Americans in Japanese hands and Japanese in American hands, not because it feared to tell the people the whole story, but rather because material incautiously made public might well give the Japanese authorities an excuse to suspend the exchange of prisoners or to cut off the supply of Red Cross packages to those remaining in their hands. Nor was it through any kindly feeling toward Francisco Franco that Stimson eliminated scenes accurately describing the Spanish dictator from an official War Department film in January, 1943; it was rather that early 1943 seemed a singularly poor time for official disparagement of a man whose armies lay on the flank of the whole North African enterprise.

The real fear of those who mistrusted the War Department's information policy was that material might be suppressed merely because it was unfavorable to the Army. There were certainly some instances of this kind of suppression in the war, but most of them occurred in areas far from Washington, and such suppression was no part of Stimson's or Marshall's policy. Stimson himself repeatedly described Army reverses in blunt and definite language for what they were, and he consistently approved release of photographs and motion pictures graphically portraying the horror of battle. Everything that would bring the war closer to those at home he thoroughly supported. Indeed, in his eagerness to see the American people fully aware of the war he sometimes found in military reverses a stimulation that was lacking in reports of success. Thus the battle of the Bulge, in December, 1944, and January, 1945, had a favorable effect on American determination, as Stimson saw it, while conversely the later rapid advances of General Patton so nourished public optimism that Stimson wrote to Patton in mock protest against his sabotage of the home front.

When suppression of news did occur in overseas theaters there was ordinarily much more involved than mere face-saving. Probably the most sensational such case in the war was the slapping by General Patton of two psychoneurotic soldiers under hospital treatment in Sicily. General Eisenhower had made a gentleman's agreement with the press in his theater not to report this affair; he had severely reproved Patton and had exacted an apology to the troops; he now wished to preserve the usefulness of a great combat leader. But Mr. Drew Pearson spilled the beans. In the ensuing hullabaloo Stimson firmly supported Eisenhower, meanwhile dispatching a personal letter to Patton in which he clearly expressed his disappointment that so brilliant an officer should so far have offended against his own traditions. The incident was not a pretty one, but Stimson fully agreed with Eisenhower's view that Patton's services must not be lost. When a further outburst from Patton again embarrassed Eisenhower in the spring of 1944, Stimson wrote another and much stronger letter to this "problem child," but once more he supported Eisenhower's courageous acceptance of such annoyances and his refusal to relieve Patton. Perhaps no decision of the war was more triumphantly vindicated by events than this one; in the summer of 1944 Patton became almost overnight the idol of many of the same newspapers and politicians who had most loudly demanded his removal in 1943.

Although criticism in such cases as the Patton affair was sharp, and although he was never able to satisfy certain sections of the press and some of the members of Congress that the War Department was not holding out on them, Stimson found that as the war progressed mutual understanding gradually developed. He considered it most regrettable that only in exceptional cases did congressional committees prove reliable guardians of secret information, for it would clearly have been well for the Army and Congress to understand each other better than they did. This weakness, like others in the Government, seemed to him deeply rooted in the mechanics and traditions of his ancient enemy, "Congressional Government." Whenever it proved possible to narrow the gap between legislators and administrators, the results were helpful to both parties. In 1943 the War and Navy Departments initiated a series of confidential meetings with Congress; whether because these meetings satisfied the ordinary human eagerness for "inside information" or because they truly served, as Stimson hoped, to give Congressmen a better understanding of the war, they certainly produced an improved relationship.

Both during the war and later Stimson regretted that he had not been able to do more of this sort of work himself. It was one of the disadvantages of his age that in conserving his strength he was forced to limit his own public activity as an interpreter of the Army. If he could have seen more of Congressmen and other Washington leaders, he could perhaps have prevented or limited some of the public misunderstandings and governmental squabbling that occurred. In general it seemed to him true throughout the war that the closer a civilian came to the Army, the more likely he was to give it his broad approval.

What he asked of critics, whether members of the Government or not, was that they start with some sympathy for the Army's problems and that their remarks be designed to help the War Department do a better job. When the rubber "czar" sneered at "Army and Navy loafers" he may have been referring to genuine weaknesses, but his approach was hardly helpful. In contrast, when James F. Byrnes quietly suggested that each agency of the Government investigate its own procurement work, the resulting Army report by General Frank McCoy was extremely useful. Stimson believed that the shrewd and skillful work done by Byrnes in his Office of War Mobilization was of vital importance in the operation of Mr. Roosevelt's fantastically complex administrative mechanism.

In his own press conferences Stimson tried to present at weekly intervals a balanced review of the war as he saw it. The factual material for these reports was written for him in the Bureau of Public Relations over which Major General Alexander Surles presided with great good sense throughout the war, executing without complaint a task which must have been distasteful to a soldier who had been in line for a corps command; Surles was much more than a "public relations man." His sound judgment and military knowledge were of frequent assistance to the Secretary of War in much broader fields. In his weekly summaries Stimson frequently added more personal comments, generally designed to set recent events in their broad focus. Against both optimism and undue gloom he waged a continuous battle, drawing from both victory and its absence the same lesson: there was much still to be done. Occasionally, at the year's end or at the close of a campaign, he would allow himself to point with pride at the work of the Army. Regularly he turned aside all questions relating to intragovernmental squabbles, until newsmen learned to ask them with hopeless and amused foreknowledge that they would get no answer. As the men who covered the Pentagon became old acquaintances, the atmosphere of the press conferences became more amiable than anything he had known in the past, and in his last press conference, on September 19, 1945, he spoke in a tone that was as sincere as it was unusual in him when he said, "In taking leave of you, I should like to tell you how greatly I have valued our association. In the midst of a war, there are many tensions. Tempers are apt to grow short. For my part, I feel that our differences have been unimportant during the five years I have been the subject of your scrutiny.

"You have always seemed to me to be carrying out your duty to the public with a high regard for the ethics of your profession and the safety of the Nation. . . . I should like to take this occasion to offer you my sincere thanks for the quality and understanding of your service and to give you my best wishes for your future success."

Throughout the war a heavy majority of the people remained satisfied that they were being adequately informed by the Government. Certainly there was never a war or an army more completely reported, and in the enormously difficult task of bridging the gulf fixed between soldier and civilian the press and the radio did distinguished work.

It was bridging this gulf—as far as it was possible to do so —that seemed to Stimson throughout the war to be the central task of war reporters and Army spokesmen. Evident and solid national unity seemed to him the greatest single moral force with which to crack the enemy's will to resist, and, finding himself constantly inspired by his own direct contacts with the troops, he regularly sought to give a similar directness of contact to other civilians. In public relations as in other matters where the Army touched on civilian life, it was his object so to spread the spirit he found in the armed forces that it might become the spirit of the nation as a whole. And while the failure to enact a national service law remained as proof that this unity of attitude was never fully achieved, it would not be fair to end this chapter on any note of failure. Taken as a whole the effort of Americans at home was more than sufficient, and if many sources of strength remained unused, Stimson was inclined to place the responsibility for waste more on the Government than on the people. His own greatest fear had been that in the different standards set for citizens and soldiers there might be bred a lasting bitterness between those who fought and those who stayed at home. But whether because so many at home made great and earnest efforts, or because so many in uniform "never had it so good," or because the citizen soldiers were always more civilian than military, no such cleavage seemed to develop in the early postwar years.

CHAPTER XX

The Army and the Navy

S O FAR as the United States was concerned the Second World War was an amphibious war. "No enemy forces reached our mainland, and five million American soldiers were required to be transported across various oceans in order to get at their enemies. Troop transport and assault landings are traditionally the most difficult and dangerous of all military operations. The American Navy, co-operating in some cases with the British Navy and the two national air forces, furnished the cover and protection for such transport and landings. It rendered this service with brilliant success. Practically no losses of men occurred in the transocean voyages, and remarkably few which could have been prevented by naval action occurred on the landings." (Memorandum, August 15, 1947)

As this quotation shows, Stimson thoroughly appreciated the help the Army received from the Navy. He had traveled as a soldier across waters infested by hostile submarines, and he knew from anxious study the extraordinary difficulty of landing attacks. Further, though he was not directly concerned with the purely naval campaigns of the American fleet, he was of course an admirer of the courage and skill with which the Navy wrote into military history the names of the Coral Sea, Midway, Guadalcanal, Leyte Gulf, and many other fleet actions.

This much said, we must proceed in this chapter to a discussion of Army-Navy relationships in which the less pleasant side of the story will be emphasized. In this field as in others, Stimson as Secretary of War was called in when there was friction and not when there was peace.

1. STIMSON AND THE ADMIRALS

The Army and the Navy fought the war together. After Pearl Harbor they fought in most areas under unified command. They fought well together, and they reached a level of co-operation and mutual trust unknown in earlier wars. But the fact remained that they were two separate services.

"Their leaders were not only separate but filled, ever since their cadet service at West Point and Annapolis, with a spirit of rivalry which reached into many phases of their lives. Not only had there been allowed between the two forces active competition for new personnel and equipment but even in sport the annual football game between the two academies had during the war reached a peak of rivalry where it became a national problem where and how the game should be located and managed." (Memorandum August 15, 1947)

When Stimson wrote that the problem of the Army-Navy football game was a national issue, he did not exaggerate. He had himself made it a subject of Cabinet discussion in 1943.

"At Cabinet meeting this afternoon I swung into a new line. Drew Pearson had had a recent article describing the present meetings of the Cabinet and their futility and how the Secretaries of War and Navy no longer tell the Cabinet anything but preserve that for private meetings with the President. Today when the President reached me in turn and asked the usual conventional question of whether I had anything, I said 'Yes, Mr. President, I have something of very grave importance.' I then in humorous oratorical fashion presented the charges that had been made that the Cabinet was decadent and that the Secretaries of War and Navy had felt unable to discuss their matters before the lady and gentlemen sitting in front of them and that in consequence of these serious charges I had gone through my files and picked out a matter which was of very serious importance to bring before the Cabinet. I then narrated how I had written a letter to the Secretary of the Navy, copy of which I had sent the President, asking that the Academies at Annapolis and West Point should take the lead in sacrifice in public opinion and give up their annual football game; that I had received a reply from the Secretary of the Navy to the effect that football was of such 'inspirational' value to the young men of the Academy that he did not feel able to give it up. I pointed out that these letters had lain unanswered on the President's desk ever since April 20th and I asked whether there were any matters of equal importance that had claimed his attention during this time. By that time I had the Cabinet in a roar of laughter. To my amusement, however, they took the subject of athletic sports up from my lead and debated it for over an hour and a quarter with such seriousness and diversity of opinion that the President suggested that he would appoint a committee to determine it. We all turned on him and said that this was a matter of such importance that he must decide it himself. This he was evidently afraid to do but he finally said he would give it very serious consideration and let us know later. But it was the first gleam of really vigorous and widely dispersed fun that we had had in the Cabinet for many months." (Diary, May 21, 1943)

The disagreement over the Army-Navy game was fit material for a joke, but it was nevertheless symbolic of a problem which was one of the most serious that Stimson faced. The Army and the Navy were called on in the Second World War to act with a co-operation and a mutual trust for which they had never been properly trained, and it required all the wisdom and self-restraint of which both sides were capable to achieve the astonishing success that was in general attained.

Although Army-Navy co-operation was close to Stimson's heart, the Army was closer still, and his wartime view of the relationship between the services cannot be taken as wholly dispassionate. Like everyone else involved, he occasionally lost his patience with the opposite service; still he always did so in private, and one Army Reserve officer who indulged in public squabbling with an admiral found himself summarily silenced by order of the Secretary of War. Stimson went out of his way to show his personal gratitude to naval officers who had served with distinction and good will in combined operations under Army command; cordial relations were conspicuously the rule in the European war, and he personally decorated both Admiral Hewitt, of Africa and the Mediterranean, and Admiral Kirk, of Normandy, with the Army's Distinguished Service Medal.

Stimson and his civilian staff maintained intimate and friendly contact with their colleagues of the Navy Department. Frank Knox was a man of robust integrity, without any trace of pettiness. He and Stimson became close friends whose mutual respect was not shaken by their occasional disagreement. A similar if somewhat more cautious friendship seemed to exist among most of the senior generals and flag officers. But on many issues friendship gave way to interest.

Differences between the Army and the Navy were frequent. Many of them were simply the inevitable clashes between two agencies of strong will; there were similar disagreements between the Ground Forces and the Air Forces, and between smaller subdivisions of the War Department. But some of the Army-Navy troubles, in Stimson's view, grew mainly from the peculiar psychology of the Navy Department, which frequently seemed to retire from the realm of logic into a dim religious world in which Neptune was God, Mahan his prophet, and the United States Navy the only true Church. The high priests of this Church were a group of men to whom Stimson always referred as "the Admirals." These gentlemen were to him both anonymous and continuous; he had met them in 1930 in discussions of the London Naval Treaty; in 1940 and afterwards he found them still active and still uncontrolled by either their Secretary or the President. This was not Knox's fault, or the President's, as Stimson saw it. It was simply that the Navy Department had never had an Elihu Root. "The Admirals" had never been given their comeuppance.

A striking illustration of this general situation was the Navy's refusal to share the Pentagon Building. Such a sharing was originally suggested by Admiral King; it was enthusiastically taken up by Marshall and Stimson, supported by the President and Knox, and finally blocked by resistance in the Navy Department. Since the suggestion was made at a time (October, 1942) when it would have provided a badly needed public demonstration of genuine Army-Navy solidarity, this naval obstinacy seemed particularly irresponsible. "The Admirals" wanted more of the Pentagon than the Army offered. Yet the Army offered space in the new building for as large a proportion of the Navy in Washington as it would keep for the Army itself. When it became apparent that the bright hope of October was to be smothered in November, Stimson noted in his diary (November 19) that "the Bureau admirals are holding Knox up and he is as helpless as a child in their hands. As a result, it seems as if this really important improvement of having the Navy come in to our building and share it with us in such a way as to assist united command will break down simply from the crusty selfishness of some Bureau officers . . ." and he continued with his central criticism of the Navy: "The Navy presents a situation very much like that which confronted Elihu Root [in the Army] in the first part of the century. The Navy has never had the benefit of the changes which Root made in the Army and which has removed from the Army the bureaucratic service officers who used to dominate the Department and defy the Secretary of War and the Commander in Chief of the Army." The Navy in World War II had in Knox, Forrestal, and King three strong men at its head; they accomplished much in moving their Department forward. But in Stimson's mind it was no discourtesy to remark of them that not one was another Elihu Root.

Other disagreements with the Navy revolved around somewhat different issues. The question of the Negro struck against strong Navy prejudice, and so did the ending of volunteer enlistments. General MacArthur was a constant bone of contention; Stimson was bound to admit that the extraordinary brilliance of that officer was not always matched by his tact, but the Navy's astonishing bitterness against him seemed childish. Another interservice difference was on the question of five-star rank. The whole idea of a new grade above that of general or admiral seemed absurd to Stimson and Marshall, who inclined to believe that a good officer would not need it, while a bad officer should not have it. But the Navy disagreed and eventually had its own way, even to taking half the new ranks while providing only a third of the armed forces.

But the bare rehearsal of all these disagreements is hardly

helpful. What seemed important to Stimson, in retrospect, was to look behind the disagreements toward their causes, in an effort to prevent or minimize their future occurrence. The best way to do it is to study one particular disagreement in some detail. And the one with which Stimson was most deeply concerned was the prolonged struggle over antisubmarine warfare.

2. LESSONS OF ANTISUBMARINE WAR

In the first sixteen months of American participation in the war, from December, 1941, through March, 1943, German submarines destroyed 7,000,000 tons of Allied shipping, a large majority in areas of American responsibility. The submarine was the only weapon with which the Germans could take aggressive advantage of American weakness, and they used it energetically. The complete history of the American defense against this attack will not here be told; the battle was a naval responsibility. But a combination of circumstances brought Stimson into closer contact with antisubmarine warfare than with any other single campaign of the war, and the story of his experience is instructive.

The battle of the Atlantic, whoever might be in charge of it, was a matter of vital interest to the War Department and its Secretary. The basic strategic purpose of Stimson and the General Staff, as we have seen, was to move American air and ground forces against the Germans as quickly and strongly as possible. Ship losses on the scale of those in 1942 and early 1943 were destructive of this purpose. However great the accomplishments of the shipbuilders, continued sinkings meant losses of both bottoms and equipment which seriously limited the effective deployment of American striking forces in Europe. Though submarine success might hurt naval pride, it was the Army which more seriously felt the pinch.

If its effect on the Army's grand strategy had been his only connection with the submarine, Stimson might have confined himself to proddings and complaints, but it happened that one branch of the Army was directly concerned with antisubmarine warfare, and the weapon which gave that branch new and vastly increased effectiveness was one in which his interest was personal and intense. The Army Air Forces, by ancient agreement, retained in 1941 and 1942 the general responsibility for all shore-based air operations, although late in 1941 General Marshall had granted a naval request to share in the use of long-range landplanes. And the development of radar, in particular of microwave, ten-centimeter air-borne radar, provided for aircraft a weapon of search at sea which in Stimson's view revolutionized the essential contest of submarine warfare, changing it from a battle between unseen U-boats and surface vessels into a battle between frequently surfaced submarines and far-ranging planes with superhuman powers of vision. For a long time this view was not shared by the naval officers directly responsible for antisubmarine operations, and in the resulting conflict many of the complexities of Army-Navy relations were clearly illustrated.

Stimson's interest in radar dated back to 1940. In that period, during the battle of Britain, the primary military use of the electronic eye was the detection of enemy aircraft from ground radar stations. Air-borne radar was a later development, the tactical importance of which was first brought home to him during his study of the defenses of Panama in early 1942. From the use of radar by aircraft to detect approaching enemy surface vessels it was an easy step to proceed to the idea of radar as an air-borne antisubmarine weapon, for submarines (until the annoying invention of the Schnorchel pipe in 1944) had to spend a substantial part of their lives on the surface.

This advance in Stimson's thinking roughly matched the development of radar sets suitable for this type of work. In the spring of 1942 ten pre-production sets of ten-centimeter radar were installed in Army bombers, B-18's with no other combat value, and in antisubmarine operations off the Atlantic coast these aircraft immediately demonstrated their power, catching their first submarine on April 1. (The first Army sinking confirmed in postwar analysis occurred on July 7.)

Stimson at once began to push for increased emphasis on this new weapon. He lectured the President and Secretary Knox; after having himself flown out over the Atlantic to observe the new radar set in action, he ordered Marshall and Arnold, on April 23, to follow his example. He put Lovett to work to make sure that radar production was at its maximum speed, and he ordered a reorganization of Army antisubmarine training along lines worked out by his radar consultant, Dr. Edward L. Bowles.

Under the combined pressure of air operations and increased escort protection, German submarines soon withdrew from the Atlantic coast, shifting their attack first to the Gulf of Mexico and then to the southeastern Caribbean. Meanwhile there came into the open a serious disagreement with the Navy over the tactics and control of antisubmarine aircraft.

For the War Department, the model of antisubmarine air operations was to be found in the work of the British Coastal Command, a division of the Royal Air Force which was charged with the primary responsibility for all British-controlled shore-based antisubmarine air operations. Coastal Command had been set up in early 1941 and had been increasingly successful in destroying submarines. Although it was under the "operational control" of the British Admiralty, it operated with a very high degree of autonomy, exercising direct and complete control over all its subordinate groups and wings. In the commands on each coast of the British Isles, air and naval officers operated as partners and friends in combined headquarters, but there was no attempt by the local Navy commander to guide and control the operations of the air. Thus autonomously organized, with no restrictions on its tactical doctrine, Coastal Command had developed and applied with striking success the theory of the antisubmarine offensive. Granting the essential function of the convoy, this theory assigned to aircraft the primary mission of searching out and killing submarines *wherever* they might be, and although it regularly responded to Admiralty requests for convoy cover in critical areas, Coastal Command devoted the weight of its effort to a direct offensive on U-boats.

The American setup in 1942, with all units, sea and air, Army and Navy, under naval command, was entirely different. It was the conviction of the Navy, forcefully expressed

by Admiral King, that "escort is not just *one* way of handling
the submarine menace; it is the *only* way that gives any promise of success."[1] It followed that the appropriate function of
aircraft was to provide additional convoy cover, supplementing the basically important labors of surface vessels. The
Navy, furthermore, was not persuaded that aircraft were effective submarine killers. As late as June, 1942, Secretary
Knox, apparently unconverted by Stimson's missionary work,
was reported in the New York *Times* as telling Congressmen
that no airplane had ever sunk a submarine; Knox corrected
himself when questioned on this statement, but that he could
make it at all was indicative of the blue-water attitude. (The
postwar records show that at the time Knox reportedly made
this statement two of the four kills of all United States forces
against German submarines had been made by Navy planes.)

Finally, the Navy wholly differed from the Army in its
view of the command and control of aircraft. Instead of permitting the concentration of Army aircraft under the direction of a single air officer, it insisted on assigning planes to the
command of individual sea frontier commanders, thus effectively preventing the concentrated use of air power against
the points particularly threatened by U-boats. Although Stimson pressed on Knox in July, 1942, the desirability of centralized control of both air and naval operations, his proposal
was rejected; the Navy preferred to place its trust in making
all areas independently strong, unconcerned by the waste of
force and delay in action which in the Army view this solution
necessarily involved. The result of this decision soon appeared
in the statistics of the antisubmarine battle. In November and
December, 1942, over thirty merchant vessels were sunk by
U-boats in the Caribbean area and none in the Gulf and Atlantic coast areas; during this period the Navy's own experts
estimated that ten German submarines, on the average, were
working in the Caribbean area and only one in the Atlantic
and Gulf areas combined. Yet during the same two months
Army and Navy aircraft flew 45,000 hours on patrol in the
almost unattacked northern areas, and only 9,000 hours in the

[1] Letter from King to Marshall, June 21, 1942. This letter is available in full in
Samuel E. Morison, *The Battle of the Atlantic*, Little, Brown, 1947, p. 310.

beleaguered Caribbean. In the entire month of December no aircraft in the northern areas made any contact with a submarine. And the shift of U-boats from the Gulf and Atlantic coasts had already been evident in September, two months earlier. With all allowance for the logistic difficulties of a shift in air strength to meet the U-boat move, Army officials contended that this sort of situation clearly demonstrated the need for integrated control over the relatively flexible air arm; sea frontier commanders were not likely to part with their aircraft, once allocated, nor could they be expected to visualize the "big picture."

Throughout 1942 Stimson continued to urge upon the Navy the advantages of a truly co-ordinated antisubmarine command and an aggressive attitude toward the submarine. The Army in the autumn of 1942 expanded its originally experimental organization into the Anti-Submarine Air Command, but this Command remained much less effective than Stimson had hoped; its aircraft under Navy direction continued to be assigned mainly to defensive operations. Not all of the difficulty in organizing the Army antisubmarine forces came from the Navy, by any means. If the Navy was enamored in single-minded fashion of convoy and escort, the Army Air Forces were at least equally devoted to the concept of strategic air power, and for many months their antisubmarine command remained a good deal of a stepchild.

In March, 1943, the whole problem was reopened in a big way. During the first three weeks of that month U-boats operating mainly in the North Atlantic southeast of Greenland, in an area not yet covered by air search, sank over three-quarters of a million tons of shipping. The President sent a sharp note of inquiry to Marshall and King as to the air dispositions planned to meet this threat. The War Department, fortified by a comprehensive and extremely able report prepared by Bowles, began a final effort to win for Army aircraft the autonomy and full naval co-operation needed for a prosecution of offensive operations.

This effort failed. Stimson suggested to Knox the establishment of an autonomous, offensive air task force for antisubmarine work; the suggestion was rejected. Then Marshall urged in the Joint Chiefs of Staff the creation of a new over-all anti-submarine command embracing all air and surface units, and responsible like a theater command directly to the Joint Chiefs. King rejected this solution, but he indicated his aware-ness of the problem by creating instead the Tenth Fleet, under his direct command, to co-ordinate all antisubmarine opera-tions in all the sea frontiers. Then Arnold urged the appoint-ment of an Army air officer to co-ordinate all shore-based air operations under this Tenth Fleet; King did not immediately reject this proposal, but in detailed negotiations it became ap-parent that the difference between the Navy and the Air Forces on the meaning of "operational control" was irrecon-cilable. The Air Forces, strongly supported by Stimson and Marshall, believed that antisubmarine air operations *must* be co-ordinated and directed by an aggressive air commander like Air Marshal Slessor of the British Coastal Command, subject only to the most general guidance of his naval superior. Admiral King believed this concept to be wholly mistaken and insisted that air operations must be directly controlled in each area by the local naval commander. The impasse was complete, and finally, in June, General Marshall reached the conclusion that there was no future for the Army concept so long as the Navy retained final control of antisubmarine op-erations. In return for certain concessions in other fields of conflict, he turned over to the Navy, with Stimson's approval, the entire responsibility for antisubmarine air activity. The Army squadrons assigned to this mission were gradually with-drawn, and in November, 1943, two months later than it had at first promised, the Navy assumed full responsibility for the work. Stimson shared the disappointment of his British friends Churchill and Slessor that so much training should be so arbitrarily discarded, but he agreed with Marshall that it was no use to fight a battle in which grudging naval conces-sions would be no concessions at all, since full co-operation was the necessary condition of success.

Meanwhile the crisis of the submarine war had passed; Allied air power, partly shore based and partly carrier based, had closed the North Atlantic gap in the spring, and had done such damage to the U-boat "wolf packs" that by June they had withdrawn almost entirely from the North Atlantic convoy route. After that time the submarine was reduced, in Admiral King's words, "from menace to problem."

In 1947, assessing the questions involved in this prolonged and mutually unsatisfactory conflict between the Army and the Navy, Stimson found himself convinced that on the tactical issues the Army was proved right and the Navy wrong. The record of Allied antisubmarine activity in all areas where the Germans operated clearly demonstrated the effectiveness of aggressively employed air power. From 1942 onward—and it was only in 1942 that air-borne radar began to be extensively used—aircraft operating at sea destroyed more German submarines than did surface vessels, and more than five-sixths of the submarines destroyed from the air were killed by shore-based aircraft. Moreover, the vast majority of these shore-based kills were accomplished by aircraft flying under the control of Slessor's Coastal Command in accordance with the principles of air autonomy and aggressive search so long and vainly urged by Stimson on the American Navy. The early Navy notion that convoy escort was the *only* way of fighting the submarine was in Stimson's view completely exploded by the brilliant operations of the Navy's own hunter-killer groups in 1943 and afterwards, not to mention the shore-based campaigns of Coastal Command first in the Bay of Biscay and later in Norwegian waters.

But the issue of tactics was not the most important matter to be reviewed. Far more important lessons were apparent to Stimson in the contest over antisubmarine warfare. The first was the importance of listening closely to the scientists. Scientific contributions to antisubmarine warfare were enormous, and they extended far beyond the merely technical. Scientists like Bowles and Bush proved themselves to be capable of sound strategic comment and of constructive proposals for the tactical control and use of antisubmarine weapons. They were far wiser than either naval or air officers who had become wedded to a limited strategic concept.

The second lesson of the antisubmarine campaign was the critical importance of the doctrine of command responsibility. Much of the continuing failure of both the Army and the

Navy in antisubmarine matters rose out of the absence of any central and clear-cut command. At least until 1943 the Navy Department was not organized as was the British Admiralty, with a vigorous and independent group of senior officers conducting antisubmarine warfare as a continuous campaign. There was no officer who could be held responsible for that mission and only that one; antisubmarine warfare, both in the Navy Department and in the Army's high command, was everyone's business and no one's. And if General Arnold's officers were thinking mainly of strategic air power, Admiral King's were primarily concerned with the Pacific. With rare exceptions, antisubmarine warfare received only the partial attention of the first-rate officers, while actual operations were left to commanders not always chosen from the top drawer. Comparing this arrangement with the method applied in Africa and Europe and the different theaters of the Pacific, Stimson concluded that it provided the proof, in failure, of the wisdom that set up the other theaters under single, strong, full-time commanders.

A third important lesson was that the Joint Chiefs of Staff was an imperfect instrument of top-level decision. Certainly it represented a vast improvement over anything that had existed before, and on the whole it was astonishingly successful, but it remained incapable of enforcing a decision against the will of any one of its members. It was an exact counterpart in military terms of the Security Council later established by the United Nations; any officer, in a minority of one, could employ a rigorous insistence on unanimity as a means of defending the interests of his own service. Quite aside from the question of which service was right as to antisubmarine tactics, there was no justification for a situation in which the Army and the Navy worked at cross-purposes for more than a year, each appearing to the other as an ignorant, presumptuous, interfering bungler. And if Marshall had been as narrow a man as some previous Army Chiefs of Staff, the impasse might have continued throughout the war; the right of the Army to operate antisubmarine aircraft was one on which he could have stood his ground forever. Only the President was in a position to settle disagreements by a definite and final ruling, and Mr. Roosevelt's general position was that dis-agreements should be adjusted without forcing him to act as judge. This seemed to Stimson a sensible attitude, since the President could hardly be expected to take time for a thorough study of dozens of differences, large and small. He remained as a court of last appeal, and fear of his displeasure frequently forced compromise agreement in the Joint Chiefs of Staff. But the absence of any constantly operating and truly decisive authority placed a heavy obligation of self-restraint on the Joint Chiefs, and the whole system might well have broken down completely if all its members, and Marshall particularly, had not been determined that it should reach and enforce decisions at least on points of primary importance. Stimson was appalled at the thought of what might have happened among the Joint Chiefs if Marshall had been replaced by any officer, however able, whose interests and attitudes were limited by a service viewpoint.

The fourth—and most important—feature of the antisubmarine affair was that it provided an almost perfect example of the destructive effect of the traditional mutual mistrust of the two services. Though the focus of the discussion was a question of tactics, it was surrounded by all sorts of interservice recriminations. It was unfortunate that the Army side of the question should have been mainly an Air Forces operation, for the Navy and the Air Forces had a mutual grudge of over twenty years' standing—the Navy feared that the Air Forces wished to gain control of all naval aviation, while the Air Forces saw in the Navy's rising interest in land-based planes a clear invasion of their prescriptive rights. The Air Forces considered the Navy a backward service with no proper understanding of air power; the Navy considered the Air Forces a loud-mouthed and ignorant branch which had not even mastered its own element. Thus it happened that many an incident which friendly commanders could have used as a signpost to improvement became instead a source of added bitterness. Although in many cases local and junior officers of both services established extremely friendly relations, what too often came to Army and Navy headquarters in Washington were emotionally embroidered reports of the incompetence of the other service. The simple fact of being under the Navy was no fun for the airmen, whose autonomy in action was their most jealously guarded principle of combat, and that the Air Forces should be sinking submarines at all was to some naval officers an affront. What should have been simply a question of tactics thus became at all echelons a question of feelings, and on neither side was much attention given to the vital task of seeing the other man's point of view.

This matter of attitude seemed to Stimson the fundamental issue in the Army-Navy relationship. On the whole the war marked a new high point in mutual good feeling. Especially in their great joint ventures in the complex art of amphibious warfare the Army and the Navy learned to respect and like each other; a similar if less intense good feeling developed among the men in Washington who were of necessity thrown together in planning and supplying these vast overseas undertakings. But a strong residue of mutual disapproval remained. Stimson himself was not exempt. On October 20, 1942, at a meeting with Knox and Hull, "After I had expatiated on the fruits of the bombers, . . . Knox . . . rather unnecessarily put in the remark that the Navy didn't think much of high-altitude bombing anyhow. I then rose in my wrath and tore him to pieces. In fact the debate was so hot I could see Hull pulling his legs in under his chair and generally gathering himself into a fighting position lest he be hit by the flying fragments!" The two Secretaries attacked each other's sore points, trading unpleasant opinions about bombers, MacArthur, Guadalcanal, and logistics. "But finally we wound up with a laugh and the smoke blew away." Though Stimson was by long training and predilection an Army man, Knox had no such background as a naval advocate; this mutual jealousy was the daily and insistent atmosphere of the separate Departments, and it sank imperceptibly into the minds of the most balanced of men.

In the first two years of the war Stimson strongly opposed the holding of public Army-Navy football games in large cities, on the grounds that such a major spectacle would eat up gasoline and other supplies better employed in warmaking. In 1944 he somewhat changed his tune, and although the main reason for this change was simply that a year of victories had

somewhat relaxed his insistence on austerity, there was a
further thought in his mind. "The President wanted my advice
as to whether or not he should shift the Army and Navy football game to New York. That comes a week from next Saturday. For two years we have been having semiprivate football
games at the homes of the two Academies . . . but now the pressure is for having it a public one. The fact that the Army has a
very good football team this year and has a darned good chance
of beating the Navy makes me a little more lenient towards it
than I was before." (Diary, November 13, 1944) The game
was held in New York, and the Army won, 23-7.

3. UNIFICATION AND THE FUTURE

The war was fought successfully without any important
revision of the separated status of the two services from
which all these troubles grew. The Joint Chiefs of Staff and
a number of other boards and committees were bridges across
the gap. Sometimes in the operating theaters these bridges
became so numerous and solid that the gap almost disappeared—and then incautiously someone would assume that it
did not exist and learn his mistake from a new outburst of feeling. To Stimson and others thinking of the future it seemed
evident that the primary objective of the postwar period in
military affairs must be to end this division of feeling.

The difficulty of attaining such an objective became brutally clear in the spring of 1944, when a Select Committee of
the House of Representatives began hearings on the controversial issue of "unification" of the armed forces. Stimson, like
most of his War Department colleagues, believed that the
consolidation of the armed forces into a single department
would be enormously helpful in reducing friction and dupli-
cation of effort. He saw it as a means of eliminating the waste
of time and money involved in the necessarily cumbersome
method of "co-operation," and as a way of insuring action
when and if "co-operation" ceased to exist. But knowing that
his friends "the well-known Admirals" were strongly opposed
to unification, he was at first reluctant to let his Department
be involved in public discussion of an issue on which feelings

would surely run high. Only the surprising discovery that
Knox strongly favored a single unified department overcame
this objection. Then just as the Army had completed a detailed statement of its position before the committee, Frank
Knox died. His views were not shared by his successor, James
V. Forrestal, who without directly opposing unification
argued strongly against jumping at conclusions. Agreement
between the Secretaries no longer existing, it was at once apparent that the hearings might become a free-for-all in which
nothing but bitterness would be produced. Although Stimson
and Forrestal agreed entirely that such a result must be
avoided if possible, it was too late to stop the hearings; Stimson duly testified, with caution and restraint, but in its later
stages the discussion before the House committee painfully
foreshadowed the remarkable shrillness of tone that for a time
dominated the debate when it was resumed in 1946.

But at last, in 1947, there was introduced in Congress a unification bill which had the firm support of both the Army and
the Navy. This successful reconciliation of divergent views
Stimson considered a triumph for all concerned and particularly for President Truman, and in a long letter to Senator
Chan Gurney he joined the battle for the bill's passage. This
letter presents in full Stimson's views on unification.

First he discussed the basic need as met by the new bill.

". . . I consider this measure to be one of the most important
peacetime forward steps ever proposed in our military history. . . .

". . . Like many things which have been carefully worked
out, the proposed measure is essentially quite simple. It
creates a new 'National Defense Establishment,' within
which the Army, the Navy, and the Air Force are to be included. For that Department it establishes a Secretary, and
the functions and powers of this new official are the heart of
the bill. 'Under the direction of the President, he shall establish policies and programs for the National Defense Establishment and for the departments and agencies therein; he
shall exercise direction, authority, and control over such departments and agencies.' And he is to supervise and control as
a co-ordinated whole the budgeted expenditures of the armed

forces—in this respect as in others the bill presents a striking parallel with the notable legislative reorganization achieved last year by the Congress.

"The Secretary of National Defense is provided with the necessary military and civilian assistants; he becomes Chairman of a War Council; he is given authority over the Joint Chiefs of Staff, which splendid engine of military skill and thinking is continued with its present general functions; he is given a Munitions Board and a Research and Development Board which will serve him as flexible instruments for the exercise of two critically important functions. . . .

"It is my considered opinion that the new Secretary of National Defense will have it in his power to integrate our armed forces as they have never been integrated before. In World War II we accomplished great things by co-operation between two separate Departments, but from that experience we learned that co-operation is not enough. I will not rehearse the unhappy list of duplications, or the instances of friction and disagreement which then hampered our work. But I would emphasize that each succeeding emergency in the last fifty years has made heavier demands on our armed services. The element of economy in our use of armed force might well be critical in any future contest. It came nearer to being critical towards the end of this last war than I had dreamed likely during the years preceding the war. I do not mean economy in dollar terms (though in the long run we should greatly gain in that respect too under this bill), but rather that strategic economy which exerts maximum force with limited national resources. Without increased unity we cannot get that kind of economy; we will continue instead to operate with the wasteful opulence that has characterized much of our work in the past. This new bill provides the framework for the increased unity we need."

Then he turned to the fears of its opponents.

"The Secretary of National Defense will be a powerful officer. That is entirely proper. He cannot successfully exercise his functions without adequate and flexible power. But it should be observed that he is given no powers which do not already belong to the President as Commander in Chief. What this bill does is to delegate to a recognized officer of the Government a part of the authority over the military establishment which in the end always belongs to the President. If it were possible today for any President to give his full attention to military affairs, this step would not be necessary. But we all know that the President even now is much overworked, and that he cannot permit himself to become entirely preoccupied by his duties as Commander in Chief. . . . Under this bill the President as Chief Executive retains his basic powers unchanged; he is provided with a suitable officer for the proper exercise of these powers; that officer remains under his entire control. This appears to me to be a wholly proper and natural step, entirely in keeping with our best administrative tradition.

"At the same time I see nothing in this bill that justifies any fear that tested and invaluable instruments of war like naval aviation—or specifically Army aviation for that matter—will be lightly and carelessly discarded. . . .

"In connection with this matter of specific fears and controversies, I can only repeat what I said to the Select Committee of the Congress three years ago: 'I would like to stress, as a major point, the importance of considering this organization of the armed forces from the standpoint of fundamentals rather than details. If the basic plan of centralization can be determined upon, hundreds of vexing problems will fall into proper perspective. They will lose much of their controversial aspect and be decided as matters of specific planning rather than of primary policy.' "

And finally he pointed out the fortunate circumstances in which the bill was presented and emphasized their importance, drawing on his own experience for illustrations.

"Not only is the bill a good one, but the time is ripe and the winds are fair for launching such a great reform. Political action is always in large measure a matter of time and circumstance, and in this case the time and circumstance seem so conspicuously right that I should like to emphasize them in detail." He recalled the painful atmosphere which had dominated the discussion in 1944 and again in 1946, remarking that "it began to appear that discussion of unification was serving merely to drive the services farther apart."

"With great wisdom and judgment, the President withdrew the matter from immediate consideration and referred it to the War and Navy Departments for thorough study, insisting that divergences be reconciled. As study and discussion proceeded . . . it became possible to reduce areas of disagreement until the great common objective again dominated, and, as I understand it, the present bill has the hearty endorsement of the responsible officers, civilian and military, of both of our present service departments.

"This fact is in itself of critical significance, as I think I can show by referring to a bit of War Department history with which I am personally familiar. When Elihu Root established the General Staff, integrating—unifying, if you please—the high command of the Army, he was faced by very decided military opposition from men in high administrative posts; but with the support of the top men of the Army and a majority of the Congress, he carried his work through successfully. Ten years later when the whole concept of the General Staff was violently challenged by an able administrative soldier of the old school, General Leonard Wood (as Chief of Staff) and I (as Secretary of War), as a team, were successful in defending the Root reforms. . . . When the civilians and the soldiers are in cordial and sympathetic agreement, each conscious of his proper function and his proper relation to the other, there are few limits to the advances that can be made. . . .

"With this sort of agreement and harmony existing, only one additional element is required to give life and meaning to the bill if enacted. That is, of course, the leadership and support of the President, now to be exerted in the first instance through his Secretary of National Defense. The Root reforms depended on the firm backing of Presidents McKinley and Theodore Roosevelt; in our battle to preserve them General Wood and I should have lost without the courageous and understanding help of President Taft; the extraordinary wartime co-operation of the Army and Navy in the recent world struggle depended in the end on the vision and courage of

President Franklin Roosevelt. Without understanding and firmness at the White House, no progress can be made in military organization. Most fortunately we have as President a man who has fully demonstrated his grasp of the problem this new reform is designed to solve, and who has been himself a leader in securing agreement within the services. We may be certain that President Truman will search out for service as our first Secretary of National Defense the best man he can find for the job, and when he has found that man he will give him strong and intelligent support."

Though it did not pass the congressional gantlet without some amendment, the Unification Bill was finally enacted in July, 1947, and James Forrestal, to Stimson's personal satisfaction, became on the following September 19 the country's first Secretary of Defense. The Army, the Navy and the Air Forces were thus at once separated and combined in a new organization for whose future Stimson had the highest hopes. The new act was not perfect, but it was an excellent first step. That it provided the framework for a better high command was certain. What was still more important, it provided a setting wherein, under firm and sympathetic leadership, the bitterness and misunderstanding of the past might be ended. Under a single leader, the Army, the Navy, and the Air Forces could now learn, and be taught, to live together. The great gains of World War II might thus be consolidated, while a repetition of its occasional failures could be prevented, and Stimson earnestly hoped that the time would quickly come when the struggles discussed in this chapter, both serious and comic, would find no echo of recognition among the soldiers, sailors, and airmen of the United States.

CHAPTER XXI

The Army and the Grand Alliance

WORLD WAR II was the first major experience of the United States in the political complexities of coalition warfare. In 1917 and 1918 the vast strength of America remained mainly potential. There was great importance in Pershing's stand for a united American Army, and there were lessons for naval officers in the relation between Sims and the British Admiralty, but neither of these experiences was adequate preparation for the extraordinary variety of problems presented to the Washington government in the years after Pearl Harbor—problems created by the simple fact that among all the nations fighting against the Axis the United States possessed incomparably the largest amount of flexible military and economic strength. The military power of the U.S.S.R. was necessarily committed almost wholly to the vast eastern front; the persistent and skillful effort of the British was by 1941 pinned down in major part to northwest Europe and Africa. Only the Americans had a free hand.

To Stimson the record achieved by his country in the resolution of the problems thus created seemed on the whole magnificent. The greatest single set of decisions were those leading to the Normandy landing, already discussed in an earlier chapter. But the OVERLORD decision was in the main one of military strategy, although in securing its adoption there was much political negotiation. Several other problems presented more clearly the ticklish interrelation of military and political aspects which is so difficult for the ordinary democratic statesman to grasp and act upon. The great flair here shown by Franklin Roosevelt seemed to Stimson a blessing of Providence upon the American people; by 1940 the President had already shown his deep comprehension of the menace of Nazism, but only under the test of actual war was his talent as a war leader revealed.

His success was triumphant, and it was substantially his own. In this chapter we shall deal with certain problems with which for one reason or another Stimson came into direct contact; in these cases he at times held views widely differing from those of the President—and indeed feared that the President was acting unwisely. But it would be wholly wrong to take these differences as illustrative of any basic difference over the political strategy of the war. In the main he was a loyal and sometimes surprised admirer of the force and skill with which Mr. Roosevelt—almost by himself, for this was his nature—laid out his course and led his countrymen along it.

The central political decision of World War II was that it must be fought in an alliance as close as possible with Great Britain and Soviet Russia. Not once during the war was this decision questioned or any modification of it seriously considered by Stimson or by any man whose views he knew among the leaders of the administration. The three nations, in American eyes, formed the indispensable team for victory over Germany. Together, with or without welcome and helpful accessions of strength from smaller nations, they could not lose. Apart, or at cross-purposes, or with any one of them defeated, they could hardly win. It was thus the constant purpose of the American Government to do all that would achieve and cherish a cordial unity of action—and so to reinforce its two great allies, from the vast American reservoir of material wealth, that each would press on with increasing power to a final combined victory.

There was of course a marked distinction in the degree of genuine understanding aimed at and achieved by Americans in dealing with their two major allies. Stimson's own contacts with the British and the Russians were illustrative of the distinction. With the British, from the first, he established the kind of close and wholly confident connection that he had maintained ten years before with Ramsay MacDonald. The vehemence and heat with which he fought against British opposition to the Channel invasion was understandable only in the light of his complete confidence that between such fast friends there could be no final falling out. Stimson argued with Mr. Churchill more bluntly than he ever did with Mr. Roosevelt; he could cut loose at the Englishman as he never felt free to do with his chief. And he talked with English officers as easily as with his own Army leaders—sometimes to get their advice and sometimes to give them his, in fairly vigorous terms.

The Russian question was different. Stimson's direct-contact with Russian matters was very slight until near the end of the war. In the earlier years, when the main American object was simply to help the Russians, his role was inconsiderable. In diplomatic negotiations he had no part; in Lend-Lease transactions he sometimes found himself the advocate of the Army's needs against those of the Russians; this was the necessary result of his duty to equip the Army, and implied no disagreement whatever with the policy of aid to Russia. Of course Russian visitors came to his office; ordinarily these were merely formal calls, but occasionally Stimson had a chance to put in a word—as in the following discussion of July 29, 1941: "At 11:18 I saw the Soviet Ambassador, Mr. Oumansky, a rather slick and unscrupulous gentleman I have been told, who used to belong to the OGPU—the secret police of Russia—and had had a rather brutal record. He came to pay his respects but, as I knew he would, brought in at the end a request for arms. He told me how important the battle in Russia was, and what great service the Russians were doing for the rest of the world. I told him I had no doubt that was so but I said, 'Mr. Ambassador, I have no eyes to see the things that you tell me. You have taken away my eyes and until I get my eyes back, I cannot take the responsibility of recommending giving away our weapons.' He said, 'You mean your Attaché should be allowed to go to the front?' I said, 'I mean just that.' That gave him a poser. . . ."

Such posers were more verbal than practical, however. Whatever the American annoyance at Russian secretiveness, it was not United States policy to squabble over details, and Oumansky and his successors got more than they gave. With this policy of one-sided generosity Stimson had little to do, but during the first years its objectionable features were quite obscured by the supreme importance of saving the Russians from defeat.

The real questions of American policy toward Russia went much deeper than such trivia. The great present goal was to help the Russians kill Germans. As they continued to fight effectively long beyond the most optimistic early estimates of most American intelligence officers, and as gradually a narrow but significant bridge of co-operation was constructed, it became clear that in their own strange way the Russians were magnificent allies. They fought as they promised, and they made no separate peace.

In 1943 and 1944 Stimson's concern for a proper second front led him to a certain sympathy with Russian suspicion of Western motives; not to open promptly a strong western front in France, he felt, would be to leave the real fighting to Russia. During the discussions at Washington in May, 1943, Stimson told the President "that the argument on the other side reminded me of the story of Lincoln with regard to General Franz Sigel who Lincoln said was a pretty poor general who, although he couldn't skin the deer could at least hold a leg. [Those who oppose invasion] are trying to arrange this matter so that Britain and America hold the leg for Stalin to skin the deer and I think that will be dangerous business for us at the end of the war. Stalin won't have much of an opinion of people who have done that and we will not be able to share much of the postwar world with him." (Diary, May 17, 1943)

But this fear was not realized; the alliance held together with each partner bearing a full load, and it was only in early 1945 that a cloud began to appear on the Russian horizon, as Stimson saw it. Nothing that happened in this later period seemed to him to bear against the wisdom and foresight of Mr. Roosevelt's decision to behave with complete friendliness and good will toward the Russians while the Allies were at war.

Thus on the central political issue of the war—alliance with Britain and Russia—Stimson was a wholehearted supporter of the President, without having any major part in the execution of policy. His principal activity in the field of wartime international policy, beyond the question of the Channel invasion, fell in three lesser fields into which he was brought by his Army responsibilities and by his special interest: China, France, and military government in Europe. In none of these cases did he have a continuous or determinant part, but his experience in each was illustrative of his own attitudes and of some of the difficulties faced by a necessarily inexperienced and unnecessarily personalized administration.

I. STILWELL AND CHINA

In Anglo-American grand strategy the war against Germany came first. Second came the great "triphibious" movement across the Pacific toward the Japanese island empire. The China-Burma-India theater was a poor third. Yet in its strategic and political significance this part of the world was of enormous importance; in a situation of extraordinary complexity it constantly offered the possibility of striking military and political success, at a remarkably low cost. For nearly three years Stimson and Marshall were leaders in an effort to achieve this success, and although their greatest hopes were not realized, the effort was not wholly barren, and in both its achievements and its failures it was extremely instructive.

Strategically, the object of American policy in this area was to keep China in the war, and so to strengthen her that she might exact a constantly growing price from the Japanese invader. The reinforcement of China depended on the maintenance of a line of supply through Burma, if necessary by air, if possible by land. But Burma was a part of the British Empire, and it was especially important to the British as the last buffer between India and Japanese aggression. There were thus three major Allied Nations whose respective interests came to a common point in Burma, and although all three were presumably agreed on the vital necessity of winning the Japanese war, only the United States, of the three, framed its policy in that area with military victory as its single object. And it was the peculiar difficulty of the American policy that it was dependent upon a British base and Chinese manpower. The situation was still further complicated by the traditional mutual distaste of the British and the Chinese, to both of whom any failure of the other was a source of racial satisfaction.

Long before Pearl Harbor the American Government established in Chungking a military mission. With American entry into the war, and the beginning of a Japanese campaign against Burma, it became evident that the American interest required in this theater a military representative of pre-eminent quality. Because of his intense interest in the Chinese situation, Stimson played a conspicuous part in the selection of this representative, and of few things was he more proud than of his share in the eventual choice of General Joseph W. Stilwell.

Stilwell's name was not the first suggested. The post was indeed offered, in January, 1942, to one of the Army's most senior generals. But after getting into a row with General Marshall, the officer under consideration submitted a memorandum of requirements which indicated a predominant interest in his own and not the national advantage. The response of the Secretary of War was definite.

"He had brought me a paper which he had drawn in which he virtually took the position that he did not think the role in China which I had offered him was big enough for his capabilities. The paper said a good deal more than that but that was what it boiled down to. I told him how much disappointed I was at the attitude that he had taken; that I myself had planned out the position which he was to take and that it seemed to me that it would lead to most important work for his country; that its sphere depended a good deal on his own abilities but that I had had confidence that he would be able to seize the opportunity to expand the importance of the place into a very important sphere. I showed him that he would have had the full support not only of myself but of Marshall and the General Staff. I told him I could not help contrasting the position he was taking with what I considered my own duty when I was offered a position in the Far East which I did not desire and which I felt constrained to

44

accept even in the nonemergent times of peace, because my government had selected me for it. I then closed the interview." (Diary, January 13, 1942)

Although the general took it all back the next day and said "he would do anything I wanted him to do," his mistake was not one which Stimson could readily forgive. The job in China and Burma would require a man who believed in it. And fortunately on the same evening Stimson found such a man.

"In the evening on my request General Stilwell came to see me. . . . Marshall had suggested that I had better see him with a view to China, and I had a long talk with him over the fire in my library about the Chinese situation. I was very favorably impressed with him. He is a very quick-witted and alert-minded man. He knows China thoroughly and for more than two years campaigned with the Chinese armies against Japan in 1937-8-9. In half an hour he gave me a better first-hand picture of the valor of the Chinese armies than I had ever received before. Of this valor he had a very high opinion. He said that practically the whole success of my Chinese proposition would depend on whether or not Chiang Kai-shek would, as Soong has promised, give command of any of his troops to an American. This he has always refused hitherto. With that permission Stilwell said that the possibilities of the Chinese proposition were unbounded and he was very enthusiastic about it. . . . So I went to bed with a rather relieved feeling that I had discovered a man who will be very useful." (Diary, January 14, 1942)

After checking his opinion with General Frank McCoy and of course with Marshall, Stimson determined that Stilwell was the man for China and cleared his appointment with the President. Within three weeks Stilwell was on his way to what Stimson later judged as the most difficult task assigned to any American in the entire war.

Stimson and Marshall did what they could to get Stilwell off to a good start. In negotiations with Chiang Kai-shek it was agreed that Stilwell should be Chiang's Chief of Staff, and the harmony of feeling and purpose which appeared to result from this agreement was heartening to the War Department's leaders in a time largely barren of encouragement.

On February 3, 1942, Stimson went before the House Foreign Affairs Committee in executive session to speak in favor of a 500-million-dollar loan to China. It was a time for advocacy, and the advocacy came easily to Stimson, for the Chinese venture was one in which he deeply believed.

"I worked pretty carefully over what I should say to the committee and it went off, I think, better than almost any hearing I have ever had in Congress. I outlined the difficult situation we were in in the southwestern Pacific, outnumbered in the air and sea and on the ground, and with immensely long lines of communication. I pointed out China's strategic position towards that area, including Indo-China, Thailand, Malaya, and Burma. I gave them a picture of the fighting character of the Chinese troops as it had been given me by General Stilwell. I told of China's unique relations with us and her unique attitude and confidence towards our government as demonstrated in many ways as I had observed it in the Philippines. I described the onslaught which was now being made by the Japanese to pull down Chiang Kai-shek upon whose character and influence rested the Chinese defense, and then I told what we were doing recently in our negotiations with Chiang and how he had promised to make our nominee chief of his staff. I told them that, while nobody could prophesy events in war, this represented to me a unique opportunity to play for the highest stakes for the Far East and that the success or failure of the war might depend upon this act; and in the light of the billions we had spent for less favorable opportunities, I thought that if America refused to take this chance, she would not deserve to win the war. The committee listened attentively throughout and, when I closed, there was a dead silence. No one asked me a question. The chairman turned to me and said that the committee was paying me the highest compliment it could pay, not even asking a single question on my report." (Diary, February 3, 1942)

If this statement had eloquence—and the response from those present indicated that it did—it was because this was a subject on which Stimson felt very strongly. The great tradition of American friendship with the people of China was one in which his personal part had not been small, and, as he faced the challenge of the Japanese warmakers, he saw that tradition as a basis from which a great military triumph might be created—and of course in such a triumph the tradition itself would be still further strengthened for service to both nations and the world after victory. Nothing that happened in the war was more disheartening to him than the gradual shrinking of these hopes.

This book is unfortunately not the place for a detailed study of the history of the China-Burma-India Theater. To Stimson that history unfolded principally as the saga of Joe Stilwell, fighting heroically against overwhelming odds. Stilwell's central military objective was to strengthen the Chinese armies and bring their force to bear on the Japanese in Asia. His enemies were of four kinds—Japanese, Chinese, British, and American.

The Japanese took Burma in early 1942, cutting off the only land route to China. The recapture of northern Burma thus became to Stilwell the goal of first priority. Without a road into China for the shipment of arms and supplies, the vast potential strength of the Chinese armies could never be developed into reality. But the recapture of Burma was not a primary goal of the Chinese and the British.

The Chinese Government of Generalissimo Chiang Kai-shek defies any brief analysis. Of its firm opposition to the Japanese there was never any doubt, and the administration in Washington was fully sensitive to the extraordinary sufferings which the Chinese had endured in five years of war before 1942. But even Stimson, who had studied as Secretary of State the twisted and personalized operations of Chinese nationalist politics, was astonished at the number of obstacles placed by Chinese leaders in the path of General Stilwell. Some of the obstacles were those typical of all personal government; others were rooted in the complexities of Kuomintang policy.

Stilwell, commanding Chinese troops in the first Burma campaign, found that his Chinese subordinates constantly received tactical instructions from the distant autocrat in Chungking, and Chiang's tactical skill was in Stilwell's view almost nonexistent. After the retreat from Burma, when he turned his energies to the creation of an effective Chinese force, Stilwell found his work constantly delayed or blocked by Chiang's inability to understand the meaning of modern training. Even after Stilwell had made a success of his training center for Chinese troops in Ramgahr, India, he found the Chinese still slow to co-operate in extending the new training methods to China proper. The entire Chinese war establishment was riddled with graft and personal power politics; these factors limited what Chiang could do if he would, and his intense preoccupation with the perpetuation of his own power was a still further limitation. To Stilwell the Chinese war ministry was "medieval" and the adjective was accurately used; balancing and rebalancing the semi-subordinate warlords, blind to the meaning of training and supply, innocent of any concern for its enlisted soldiers, squeezing and squeezed in the worst Chinese tradition, the war ministry, and Chiang Kai-shek too, adopted the attitude that China had already done her part. They passed their days and nights in pleading for clouds of airplanes and swarms of tanks, constantly insisting to the Western world that 'America must help her faithful ally.' But they would not help themselves.

The position and purpose of the British were very different, but their effect on Stilwell's work was much the same. The initial failure of British forces in Malaya and Burma was a shocking blow to the prestige of the Empire; the repair of this damaged prestige at once became a primary objective of British policy. But unfortunately the British were not agreed among themselves as to the best means for attaining this objective; few of them shared the conviction of such officers as Major-General Orde C. Wingate that the way to serve the British interest was to show first-class fighting quality against the Japanese, and do it quickly. The caution and defeatism which had led to the original debacle were never fully dissipated; even so gallant and dashing an officer as Lord Mountbatten, dispatched by Mr. Churchill with the specific purpose of putting in "some new punch to it" (Diary on conversation with Churchill, May 22, 1943), was not able to reverse this attitude entirely. Nor did the British agree with Stilwell on the importance of reopening the Burma Road, which after all led to a China they mistrusted, and not to Singapore. Stilwell's persistent faith in the potentialities of the Chinese soldier was not shared by most Englishmen in India.

But to Stimson the most trying of all Stilwell's problems was the constant undercutting to which he was subjected by Americans. Although the degree of their difficulty had not been correctly estimated, the British and Chinese obstacles to his mission had been foreseen when Stilwell was first sent out. Stimson could not share the disillusioned rancor of many Americans who faced these problems for the first time and reached hasty conclusions about the wickedness of their allies. The Chinese in China and the British in India were dealing with a situation whose complexity was far beyond anything in American experience, and while Stimson believed that both groups were false to their own interests in much of their opposition to Stilwell, he was prepared to face their failures without bitterness. Toward the Americans who hampered Stilwell he was less charitable.

American opposition to Stilwell was partly tactical and partly personal. Tactically, opposition came mainly from the Air Forces, whose commander in China was Major General Claire Chennault. It was the view of Chennault and his many American supporters that Stilwell's insistence on a first priority for the Burma campaign was not correct. They argued that the bulk of the supplies carried by air across the Hump into China should be used not for Stilwell's ground-force training center in Yunnan but rather for the operations of Chennault's Fourteenth Air Force. To Stilwell, Marshall, and Stimson this view appeared wholly wrong. They feared that much activity from unprotected air bases would merely stimulate a heavy Japanese land campaign against Chennault's airfields. But this possibility did not disturb the airmen; Chennault even argued that his aircraft would be able to repel any such attack. In spite of all opposition Chennault's view was approved by the Washington Conference of May, 1943. Stilwell himself was called to the conference to state his case, but his advocacy was unsuccessful. His build-up of Chinese land forces was once more delayed, this time by the decision of Franklin Roosevelt.

Tactical disagreements are inevitable in war. Stimson was to find his dire prophecies fully confirmed in the Japanese attack of 1944, which overran seven of the principal bases of the Fourteenth Air Force, but the tactical mistake of the Washington Conference was a minor matter compared to the political errors and personal activities which came before and after it.

More than any other American theater commander in the war, Stilwell required the constant and vigorous political support of his own government, and less than any other commander did he get it. Engaged as he was in a great effort to make China strong almost against her will, he was bound to find himself frequently in the disagreeable position of telling unpleasant truths to an autocrat. Americans like Chennault and some of his political-minded associates, on the other hand, were in the position of advocating tactics which suited the politics and strategic concepts of the Generalissimo; Chiang was happy to accept serenely the view that American air power would defeat the Japanese. Still other Americans, preoccupied with the intense poverty and economic weakness of China, tended to think largely in terms of loans and civilian supplies, and this too was a language which the Generalissimo understood and approved. What to Stimson seemed unforgivable was that many of these Americans allowed their differences with Stilwell over tactics or purpose so to weight their loyalty that they joined in and even encouraged the efforts of Chiang Kai-shek to undermine Stilwell's authority and weaken his support from Washington. And to Stimson it was not surprising, although terribly disappointing, that all this intrigue was in the end effective in the mind of President Roosevelt, although in defense of Stilwell General Marshall acted with even more than his usual wisdom and energy.

Stilwell, unfortunately, never really "made his number" with the President. Although Mr. Roosevelt was by no means blind to the weaknesses of the Chinese Government, he was unschooled in the details on which Stilwell's tactical and

political position was founded, and he was tied by personal
sympathy to the support of Chennault. For his information
on China he often depended on "personal representatives"
who were usually easy dupes of the wonderfully charming
circle around the throne at Chungking. He thus never gave to
Stilwell the freedom of action and automatic backing which
he so courageously accorded to his commanders in other
theaters. Stilwell to him remained a somewhat testy, if obviously loyal, soldier who had some strange attraction for
the War Department. It seemed doubtful to Stimson whether
the President ever realized how much his own personal
emissaries and his willingness to hear attacks on Stilwell contributed to the latter's difficulties. The only "emissary" to
China throughout the war whose work seemed to Stimson
truly helpful was Somervell, who happened on the scene in
October, 1943, during one of Chiang's most violent outbreaks
against Stilwell. With the aid of Mme. Chiang and some of
her remarkable family Somervell pulled the Generalissimo
round. Most of the other visitors, sometimes in ignorance,
sometimes on the basis of definite personal instructions from a
President playing by ear, only made matters worse. Stilwell
thus never was able to speak as the voice of the United States
war effort in Asia; he was only one side of it.

The last act in Stilwell's mission was played in October,
1944. By that time Stilwell had fully justified his insistence
on a Burma campaign by his brilliant advance in north
Burma, culminating in the capture of Myitkyina—this was
one of the great and insufficiently noticed military epics of
the war. But none of this satisfied Chiang, who had grown to
hate Stilwell—even as Stilwell had grown to hate him.

On October 3 Stimson summarized the matter as he saw it:
"After the daily conference with the Operations and Intelligence Staff, the morning was spent in preparing myself for
my luncheon with the President; also in discussing with General Marshall the crisis in China. This last is rapidly growing more and more serious. The Japanese are advancing and
have already made it necessary for us to evacuate two of our
advance bases for our airplanes. By this they have already
pushed us out of range of some of our important targets in

Japan. The Chinese Government of Chiang Kai-shek is getting more and more difficult to deal with. Not only has he failed to back Stilwell up but he has now again requested that we relieve him. Marshall and the Staff had prepared a sharp rejoinder for the President to send declining to do so, but the President has declined so far to send it. Stilwell has been the one successful element of the three forces that have been supposed to co-operate in Burma. The British dragged their feet, and Mountbatten last spring almost as soon as he got there sent us word that he wanted to have the campaign go over until after the monsoon. If we had accepted that, we would not yet have begun. On the other hand, Chiang Kai-shek has several times interfered with the Yunnan forces of Chinese whom he had promised to send and did send as far as the Salween River. In between these two hesitating and halting forces, Stilwell with his three American-trained Chinese divisions coming down the Ledo Road, and Wingate and Merrill with their air troops and raiders flying in to help, have brought victory out of hesitation and defeat. The British, stung by their example, have at last thrown the Japanese out of Imphal and our troops are well down near the Irrawaddy River. Stilwell has taken Myitkyina, and north Burma is virtually free of the Japanese. This campaign in all the difficulties of the monsoon has been a triumphant vindication of Stilwell's courage and sagacity. He had been pecked at from both sides, carped at by the British from India, and hamstrung at every moment by Chiang Kai-shek. Now the Japanese in China, stung by these defeats in Burma, have called their main forces into action in China and are closing in against the regular Chinese armies. If Chiang Kai-shek had supported Stilwell, we should have had a well-trained nucleus of these Chinese troops to meet them. As it is, they are still impotent Chinese, untrained and badly led. Incidentally, this result on both sides has shown the wisdom of Stilwell's diagnosis a year and a half or two years ago when he insisted that we must have ground bases and ground troops in China, well trained, to defeat just such an attack of Japanese; and on the other hand, at the same time Chennault was insisting that he could beat and drive off the Japanese attack by the use of air alone. Chennault has been given almost twice as much in the way of equipment over the Hump as he asked for and yet he is now failing abjectly to stop the Japanese. On the other hand, Stilwell fighting against all these obstacles, British incompetence and sluggishness, Chinese disloyalty, and the lack of supplies over the Hump line which Chennault's demands made necessary, has provided the only success in the whole horizon. One of our difficulties throughout has been the attitude of the President. He has insisted on sending his own people there . . . and (except Pat Hurley whom we suggested to him) they have all been disloyal to Stilwell and have all joined hands with his detractors. They have all joined in supporting Chennault's views and insisting that he be given a chance to save China in the air. Several times the President suggested that Stilwell should be relieved. Marshall and I have fought for him steadily and hard throughout. Now the issue is up again and the President again is siding against Stilwell. Marshall today said that if we had to remove Stilwell he would not allow another American general to be placed in the position of Chief of Staff and Commander of the Chinese armies, for it was so evident that no American would be loyally supported. I am inclined to go farther. The amount of effort which we have put into the 'Over the Hump' airline has been bleeding us white in transport airplanes—it has consumed so many. Today we are hamstrung in Holland and the mouth of the Scheldt River for lack of transport planes necessary to make new air-borne flights in that neighborhood. The same lack is crippling us in northern Italy. This effort over the mountains of Burma bids fair to cost us an extra winter in the main theater of the war. And, in spite of it all, we have been unable to save China from the present Japanese attack owing to the failure to support Stilwell in training adequate Chinese ground forces to protect Kunming."

All this was a summary of what Stimson was prepared to say to the President. He never said it, for Mr. Roosevelt was not well that day, and in a two-hour conference Stimson had quite enough to do in discussing eight other matters, of which one was pressingly important. (See p. 580.) This seemed an illustration in specific terms of the losses incurred through

Mr. Roosevelt's constant effort to keep all the threads in his own hands. One man simply could not do it all, and Franklin Roosevelt killed himself trying.

And by this time, too, the President's relation to Stilwell was water under the bridge. Chiang Kai-shek was prepared to insist on Stilwell's recall as a point of personal privilege, and to this position there could now be no answer. Mr. Roosevelt indeed felt more kindly to Stilwell at this time than he had ever felt previously, but it was too late. Greater than any single man or policy was the basic necessity for maintaining the wartime alliance with China, and it no longer seemed possible to keep both Stilwell and friendship with Chiang. Two weeks later Stilwell was recalled by Marshall and his great talents were put to other uses, first as chief of the Army Ground Forces, and then as commanding general of MacArthur's Tenth Army. Stimson surrendered for good his bright hopes for a real rejuvenation of the Chinese forces. China became to him a definitely limited commitment; in the later operations of General Wedemeyer he had no important part.

In assessing the Stimson-Marshall-Stilwell policy, it was not easy for Stimson to be dispassionate. It seemed clear that if Chinese and British leaders had shared the American view, the result could only have been to the advantage of all three nations. Had Chiang Kai-shek permitted Stilwell to carry out his training program on the scale and in the manner that Stilwell originally planned, he must surely have found himself, at the end of the war, with a vastly stronger army, of whose military reputation there could have been no doubt. Such support for Stilwell would have required a vigorous purge of the incompetent and the dishonest in Chiang's military entourage, but there were able young officers to take the place of those removed. It would also have required a shift in Chiang's whole attitude, which remained throughout the war what Stilwell had described in 1942 as that of an ignorant, suspicious, feudal autocrat with a profound but misconceived devotion to the integrity of China and to himself as her savior. But his failure to make this shift was stupid, for the strength of nationalist China could be measured in direct proportion to her escape from a corrupted feudalism.

As for the British, there was no real profit for them in a policy of constant delay and inaction, as many Englishmen clearly understood. Stimson would have liked to see his friend Churchill as theater commander in India; that rugged old champion of empire would hardly have countenanced the passive and Fabian attitudes that hung like a pall over his subordinates in the Far East. Mr. Churchill might not have shared Stimson's view that it was blind folly for the British to act as if China, Burma, and India had not changed since 1800, but he would never have permitted the imperial tradition to be tarnished by a stolid insistence that action was impossible.

Washington's failure to support Stilwell was to Stimson a clear example of badly co-ordinated policy, but he was forced to admit that for that failure Stilwell's own vigorous distaste for diplomacy was partly responsible.

Stilwell's mission was to train Chinese and fight Japan. For this function he was equipped as was no other general in any Allied army. On the other hand, he was no diplomat. It seemed to Stimson unsound to assume that "Vinegar Joe's" bluntness was the cause of his differences with Chiang and Chennault and the British; the differences were deeper than manners. Yet Stilwell could have done much to moderate feeling against him if he had possessed the endless patience and self-control of Marshall. And if he had been a careful and persuasive advocate, rather than a brilliant soldier with a passionate but inarticulate loyalty to his job, he would perhaps not have failed at Washington in May, 1943, in his greatest single chance to win the President's personal backing. But this was asking a great deal, and if Stimson had any regret about his support of Stilwell it was that his own work in explaining and defending the general to the President was not good enough.

And if, in the larger sense, Stilwell's mission was a failure, there were yet in it many redeeming points of success. China under Chiang *did* stay in the war; Stilwell *did* prove that Chinese troops well trained and led could match the valor of soldiers anywhere; he *did* clear the Ledo Road to China (rightly renamed the Stilwell Road); most of all, he left to the American Army a matchless record of devotion to duty and professional skill.

To Stimson the relief of Stilwell was a "terribly sad ending" to a great effort. His admiration and personal affection for Stilwell had constantly increased through nearly three years. Knowing the Secretary's personal interest in his mission, Stilwell had written to Stimson a series of letters (some of them in longhand) which gave the full measure of the man—his insight and understanding of the Orient, his imaginative grasp of warmaking, his modesty, and what General Marshall called his "amazing vigor." This was a man who could refer to his extraordinary retreat from Burma in 1942 with a single laconic sentence, "I then picked up my headquarters group and brought them out." This man's personal vision created a new army almost in spite of its own government, in the face of the skepticism and obstructionism of most Englishmen and many Americans; yet to him jungle fighting was "a heavenly relief" from planning and politics. Certainly, whatever else it was, Stilwell's record in Asia was the record of a great American soldier. On February 10, 1945, Stimson decorated Stilwell with the Legion of Merit and an oak-leaf cluster to the Distinguished Service Medal. "I was particularly happy to lay this encomium on Stilwell's hard and terrific work in Burma and in China and so I read the two citations myself and made a few comments to Stilwell which I think he appreciated. I said that I thought he had had the toughest job of any of our generals and that I had never conveyed one of these medals with such pleasure as I had in doing this."

2. FRANCE—DEFEAT, DARLAN, DE GAULLE, AND DELIVERANCE

The fall of France, in June, 1940, was to Stimson the most shocking single event of the war, and during the five years that followed, dealing with French affairs as they stood after this catastrophe, he was constantly aware of the essentially tragic character of the whole experience of a great and proud nation in defeat. Very little of his connection with the French in this period was wholly pleasant; in almost every problem there stood forth a painful choice of evils.

France after the armistice in 1940 became at once a battleground of wills, centering around the Vichy government of Marshal Pétain. The names and actions of the Frenchmen who were most conspicuous at Vichy were profoundly disappointing to Stimson. The apparent treachery of Pierre Laval astonished and deeply pained him—this was not what he would have expected from the practical and direct young Frenchman he had known nine years before. The position of Pétain he viewed with more sympathy; whatever his errors of policy and whatever his failings from simple senility, Pétain in Stimson's view was an honest servant of France. But Pétain became in 1940 the center of a two-year contest for the remaining strength of France; in this contest the whole effort of the American Government was to prevent France from joining the New Order, with the major specific objectives of blocking German expansion into French North Africa and German capture of the French Fleet.

With this policy Stimson wholly agreed. It was a policy in which he had no active part, but as he understood it Mr. Roosevelt and Hull, through Ambassador Leahy and others, were exerting all of their political and diplomatic skill to strengthen Pétain's will to resist German demands, while at the same time they were encouraging separate French agencies of defense in North Africa.

In the autumn of 1942, in preparation for the North African invasion, the American Government undertook a most complicated diplomatic and secret-service negotiation designed to produce a friendly French reception to the invaders. After pursuing a course so complex that Stimson, a highly interested observer, was never fully aware of all its ins and outs, this operation reached a quite unexpected climax three days after the landings, in the so-called "Darlan deal," which became one of the most violently controversial decisions of the war.

Stimson's view of the Darlan affair was throughout absolutely definite and clear, and in his view the outburst of criticism directed against it by his countrymen was a disturbing illustration of the political ignorance—and the ideological naïveté—of many kind-hearted Americans. That Darlan had an unsavory record Stimson fully understood. But the important fact in November, 1942, was that Darlan—and only Darlan—was able to issue an effective cease-fire order and to swing to the side of the invading armies the armed forces and the civil administration of French North Africa. In a vast and precarious military enterprise, squeamishness about the source of such considerable help was in Stimson's view absurd.

The number and quality of those who disagreed was astonishing, and Stimson promptly found it necessary to undertake an energetic campaign in support of General Eisenhower's decision. On November 16, at McCloy's suggestion, he argued the case at Woodley to a small group of doubtful administration leaders. "I gave them all a little talk, pointing out first the hazardous nature of our operation in North Africa and the perilous condition in which our troops would have been in case there had been any delay caused by the obstruction of the French, to say nothing of the loss of lives unnecessarily on both the American and the French sides. . . . I read them the telegram of Eisenhower in full, setting out admirably the reasons for the performance.[1] I pointed out to them that this was a temporary military arrangement, that the Army could not make foreign policy. . . . Finally after grunts and groans . . . I think I sent them home reconciled." (Diary, November 16, 1942) That same evening, hearing that Wendell Willkie was about to attack the agreement, Stimson telephoned to Willkie and did what he could to dissuade him; that a man of Willkie's stature should attack Eisenhower's stand seemed to Stimson very dangerous. "I . . . told him flatly that, if he criticized the Darlan agreement at this juncture, he would run the risk of jeopardizing the success of the United States Army in North Africa and would be rendering its task very much more difficult." Willkie reluctantly withheld his attack for the time being, expressing himself forcefully, however, a little later when the immediate crisis had passed.

With the firm support of the President, the Darlan agreement was maintained, and until his assassination in December

[1] This message is paraphrased in full in William L. Langer, *Our Vichy Gamble,* Knopf, 1947, pp. 357-360.

Admiral Darlan remained a very useful military support to General Eisenhower. Stimson was so placed as to see the importance of this military support more clearly than most Americans, and it was with real regret that he learned of Darlan's death. Whatever his sins, the Admiral in his last months did effective service in helping to fight the war.

Yet in looking back it can hardly be denied that Darlan's death was in some ways a relief to United States policy. Darlan had been taken up purely as a military expedient; there was no easy way of letting him down when he had served his purpose. His continued existence as the French leader in North Africa would almost surely have been a powerful embarrassment to the United States during the liberation of France; for his crime of collaboration with the Germans there could be no forgiveness by the French people, no matter what his achievements in Africa, or what the explanation he might give to Allied leaders.

But even this future embarrassment of a living Darlan would have been a light price for his services in Africa, as Stimson saw it. The North African venture was not a massive riskless attack by skilled and overwhelming forces; it was a daring and imaginative improvisation undertaken with full knowledge of its great risks and with high hopes for surprising success. The cutting of risks and the increase of hopes which came from Darlan's adherence might well have been the margin of success, and success for American arms in their first great venture against the Nazis was a military gain whose meaning could hardly be overestimated. And Darlan after all could never have become a Frankenstein's monster; even before his death the march of events had shifted the balance of bargaining strength to his disadvantage, and he was learning that he held his power only on sufferance. If he had lived, he would have been an embarrassment but not a danger.

No one in the American Government understood the Darlan affair more thoroughly than Franklin Roosevelt. On the night of his conversation with Willkie, Stimson telephoned the President to tell what he had done. "He was very nice about it; said he was glad I had done it, and told me of a Balkan quotation which he had found which had rather aptly fitted the present situation. It was somewhat to the effect that, if the devil offered to help you over a bridge, it was just as well to let him do so but not to continue to walk with him on the other side." (Diary, November 16, 1942) Later Stimson "thought up . . . a new analogy for the Darlan case, namely the story in the Bible of Joshua sending the spies to Jericho and their making a pact with Rahab the harlot which was ratified by Joshua, and I told the President of this analogy and he roared with delight over it." (Diary, December 11, 1942) It was in his warmhearted and unhesitating support of his soldiers on such trying issues as this one that Mr. Roosevelt earned the particular affection of his Secretary of War.

The death of Darlan led to a brief interregnum under General Henri Giraud, an officer whose chivalrous devotion to France was only matched by his lack of political skill. Giraud was soon succeeded in North Africa by General Charles de Gaulle, the man who had been first to raise the standard of French resistance in 1940. Increasingly, through 1943 and 1944, De Gaulle's Committee of National Liberation became the center of French anti-Nazi leadership, and its constantly growing stature among Frenchmen inside and outside France presented a serious problem to the American Government. In discussions of this problem Stimson, who had been a firm supporter of the President's Vichy policy and Eisenhower's Darlan decision, gradually found himself in the unexpected position, in some questions, of supporting De Gaulle against President Roosevelt and Secretary Hull.

During the winter of 1943-1944, as plans proceeded for the Normandy invasion, it became necessary to determine American policy toward liberated France, and it also became highly important to develop effective contact with the French resistance movement. The critical aspect of both of these questions was their relationship to De Gaulle's French Committee. To what degree should the Committee be recognized as the government of freed areas of France, and what part should it have in Allied dealings with the Resistance? To these questions there could be no easy answer, but Stimson was disappointed by the degree of feeling which seemed to enter into the thinking of Mr. Roosevelt and Mr. Hull, both of whom had been sorely tried, over a long period, by the personal peculiarities of the Free French leader.

Not that Stimson found De Gaulle personally charming. Since 1940 the General had consistently behaved with an arrogance and touchiness that were not pleasant to any of the Anglo-Americans. His abrupt seizure of St. Pierre and Miquelon in December, 1941, had been a typical example of his natural intransigence. In North Africa his behavior had been consistently annoying, and it was apparent that he had inextricably confused the cause of France with the cause of General de Gaulle as a latter-day Joan of Arc. To Secretary Hull, whose sensitive pride had been deeply aroused by unjustified and violent attacks on American policy toward Vichy, the very mention of De Gaulle was enough to produce an outburst of skillful Tennessee denunciation, and to the President, De Gaulle was a narrow-minded French zealot with too much ambition for his own good and some rather dubious views on democracy. The validity of these opinions Stimson did not deny.

A further factor in the President's mistrust of De Gaulle was Mr. Roosevelt's strong aversion, on principle, to any prejudgment by the United States on the government to be established in liberated France. This, he insisted, was a problem for Frenchmen, and he did not propose to confer the advantages of American recognition on any group whose position was unconfirmed by the French people. And with this position too Stimson agreed.

But admitting that De Gaulle was a difficult man to deal with, and admitting that the French Committee must not be recognized as the government of France until after it had been clearly approved by the French people, Stimson was nevertheless convinced of the military importance of effective working relations with De Gaulle and his supporters. In early January, 1944, Eisenhower emphasized to Stimson his view that closer dealings with the Committee would be a great contribution to the success of his forthcoming operations; Eisenhower was also hopeful that the Committee might be outgrowing some of its bad habits in dealing with Anglo-

Americans. On January 14, 1944, Stimson and McCloy went to see Secretary Hull and reported Eisenhower's views. Stimson there said that in his opinion the time had come for a change of heart toward De Gaulle. "I pointed out that for the past six weeks . . . ever since we received that telegram from the President when he was at Cairo [see p. 560], we were absolutely prevented from discussing with the Committee two important things—first, to get in touch through them with the Resistance, that is, the underground organization in France from which we hope to be able to get assistance. We want to get into communication with them from the very moment of the attack so that we will find friends on the shore waiting for us, so to speak. Secondly, we will also need to have their assistance when we are setting up the first regular organizations of government in the districts through which our Army will be operating and through which its lines of communication will run. I pointed out that time was running very short." Hull was not unsympathetic to Stimson's position. He strongly opposed the broader proposal of McCloy that the Committee should receive general recognition as the *de facto* government of the whole of France as soon as part of France was liberated. On the narrower questions Hull agreed that Stimson and McCloy should take their ideas to the President.

Mr. Roosevelt proved a tough customer. He deeply mistrusted De Gaulle and the French Committee, and his first draft of a directive to Eisenhower severely limited the Supreme Commander's authority to deal with the French Committee. All that Stimson was able to do is indicated by the following diary note: "The President granted me an interview . . . and I . . . put up to him my revised draft of his own draft of a directive to Eisenhower in respect to the French Committee. This was a ticklish matter which I, after much reflection, decided to handle lightly and personally. I told him I had committed the great sin of attempting to revise one of his papers; that I had tried not to change the aim of his paper but merely to put it in a form which I thought would go down more easily with the French Committee and also not to lay too much burden of detail on Eisenhower. He was very nice about it. He said his paper was only a draft and he had dictated it in a hurry. We went over my draft together, I pointing out the changes. He said he thought that was all right and that he would approve the paper though he wanted to look it over more carefully that evening. I told him that I had shown it to Stettinius [then Under Secretary of State] and that Stettinius had approved it, at which he expressed his approval." (Diary, March 3, 1944)

Mr. Roosevelt finally approved this draft, which permitted Eisenhower some freedom in treating with De Gaulle and his followers on military matters. But it was not enough. In June, 1944, there was a further demand on the President for more friendly treatment of De Gaulle.

The situation in this later negotiation was remarkably complex. On the one hand, the British Cabinet, led by Foreign Secretary Eden, were pressing for outright recognition of De Gaulle, to which both Secretary Hull and the President were sternly opposed. In the absence of agreement among his superiors, Eisenhower was seriously embarrassed in his choice of a policy. Meanwhile, De Gaulle, with his usual instinct for the wrong move, had outraged all and sundry by a denunciation just after D-day of the Allied military currency. As the French Committee had previously acquiesced in the issuance of this currency, De Gaulle's attack seemed particularly irresponsible. "It's as bad as if he were trying to steal our ammunition on the battlefield or turn our guns against us." (Diary, June 11, 1944)

This move did not improve the atmosphere in which Washington now reconsidered the issue of recognition. Stimson himself was extremely angry and for several days discarded his former stand in favor of increased cordiality to De Gaulle. But on June 14 he found himself back in his old position: De Gaulle was bad, but not to deal with him was worse. The diary record of his work and thinking on that day provides a full summary of the situation as he saw it:

"During the day I had been thinking carefully of the situation and I came to the conclusion that the President and the State Department were dealing a good deal in unrealities. Their policy is based upon giving the French people an opportunity to choose their own government by democratic methods which in substance means by a free election. That is the formula devised by the State Department for solving the various problems that come up in the different countries which have been enslaved, after we succeed in freeing them. But it is a very different thing to announce a formula on the one side and to put it into effect on the other. Very few countries outside the English-speaking countries know by experience what a fair election is. . . . I found this out some years ago in my experience in Tacna Arica and Nicaragua. . . .

"America cannot supervise the elections of a great country like France. Consequently we must eventually leave the execution of the State Department formula to the French themselves and I am deeply concerned lest in insisting upon this formula we get dragged into a situation where we ourselves will assume the responsibility in part or more for its execution according to Anglo-Saxon ideals. That would result in terrific dangers and would be likely to permanently alienate the friendship of France and the United States. Consequently I have been brought to the conclusion that all we can do is to insist upon a pledge of free elections from De Gaulle and his party, who apparently are the only available representatives of the French people at the present time, and that we should devote the rest of our time to winning the war instead of quarreling with De Gaulle's efforts to gradually inch himself forward into a position where he and his Committee will be the Provisional Government of France pending such an election. In other words, no matter what we do, if he tries to use his preferred position to win further rewards from the French people at the election, we really cannot stop it and it is better not to run the risk of bickerings now which will serve not only to divide us from De Gaulle but will divide us from the British who more and more are supporting De Gaulle. It is this latter situation, namely the cleft between us and the British, which most alarms me. We have been unable thus far to agree with them upon a directive to Eisenhower as to his conduct in setting up French authority in the operations of France which he is liberating. He is the General not of the United States but of the two allied governments, and he is in a dreadful position when those two governments differ and get deadlocked on such an important question.

"This morning a telegram came through from Marshall, King, and Arnold voicing in serious language Eisenhower's embarrassment and earnestly recommending that we and the British get together, but as yet nothing has been done to solve that deadlock. . . . On his part De Gaulle is doing his best to exploit this division and to rouse up feeling against us, which has serious danger. He has even denounced the provisional currency which we are introducing for temporary use in France until she establishes a government with new currency. This is a dangerous blow at our advancing troops. . . .

"Personally I have great distrust of De Gaulle and I think that the President's position is theoretically and logically correct, but as I said in the beginning, it is not realistic. The present situation I have come to believe requires for its solution an immediate reconciliation between the British and American Governments even if we provisionally recognize De Gaulle.

"Well, McCloy and I talked this over when I got back from my ride and he fully agrees with the position which I have just stated. In fact he has all along been anxious to recognize De Gaulle provisionally in order to bring to the aid of our war effort the uprisings of the Resistants with whom De Gaulle is in close touch. McCloy and I worked the thing out and I jotted down a memorandum for a talk with the President.

"But first I called up Hull and sought to make him see the difficulties of the situation. I read him the telegram above mentioned. . . . He didn't think it could be done unless the military forces did it. I pointed out to him that it was a political question into which the military forces could not be asked to enter, but I got nowhere. I had wanted to build up a foundation on which to approach the President with the consent of the State Department behind me. I failed.

"At nine o'clock I got a telephone connection with the White House and talked with the President. He had already received the telegram from Marshall, King, and Arnold but gave it scant attention. He was adamant in his refusal to depart from his position taken in the directive, that is now waiting in London, and considered it would be a departure from moral standards to do so. I patiently went over the different steps above enumerated in a talk which lasted on the telephone for nearly an hour, but I made very little advance. I pointed out the impossibility of actually supervising French elections and he fully agreed. But he believes that De Gaulle will crumple and that the British supporters of De Gaulle will be confounded by the progress of events. This is contrary to everything that I hear. I think De Gaulle is daily gaining strength as the invasion goes on and that is to be expected. He has become the symbol of deliverance to the French people. The President thinks that other parties will spring up as the liberation goes on and that De Gaulle will become a very little figure. He said that he already knew of some such parties. . . .

"Our conversation, while it was clear and the issue plainly stated on both sides, was perfectly friendly and . . . the President not only took no offense at my persistence but apparently wished himself to argue the matter out because he kept the conversation going even when I gave him several opportunities to stop."

This was almost Stimson's last effort on the recognition of De Gaulle, for from this time forward events pressed Mr. Roosevelt more effectively than his Secretary of War was able to do. De Gaulle himself calmed down considerably in the following weeks and carried through a visit to the United States without any particular outrages. During this visit his government was accorded "limited recognition." Still it was not until late August that Eisenhower finally received authority from the British and American Governments to deal with De Gaulle as the *de facto* authority in France, and not until October that the United States finally gave full diplomatic recognition to De Gaulle's French Provisional Government. Both of these moves were so grudging and late that relations between France and the United States were clouded for many months thereafter. What might have been a truly warm—and emotionally strong—relationship in the Lafayette tradition was on both sides marked by coolness.

It was hardly fair, in Stimson's view, to lay the major responsibility for this coolness on anyone but De Gaulle himself. A man of greater flexibility and judgment would surely have avoided the constant series of gratuitous obstructions and unilateral actions with which the general plagued American leaders, civil and military. On the other hand, Stimson could not believe that it was wise for the State Department to have so long a memory for such annoyances. Perhaps this was a counsel of perfection, but the disadvantage of Mr. Hull's— and Mr. Roosevelt's—feeling about De Gaulle was that it blinded them to the generally evident fact that De Gaulle *had* made himself the leader of all France. This was a miscalculation which cooler statesmanship might have avoided, and its result was that the American Government never had the advantages of a genuinely close relationship with the France of the liberation, although individual officers and diplomats on both sides did much to bring the two countries together in practical dealings.

The Vichy government, the Darlan episode, and dealings with De Gaulle were none of them hopeful signs to Stimson for the renaissance of France which he had anticipated as the first by-product of the great invasion. He had shared the aspirations of his old friend Herriot, who sent him by a neutral diplomat in 1942 his verbal assurance that the old France would rise again. But when a man he had trusted as he had Laval became "a mere Quisling," when Pétain, who had been a fine soldier, permitted in senility outrageous crimes against Frenchmen by Frenchmen, when French North Africa would join the Allies only on the word of a Darlan, when fighting France could find no greater leader than a man of twisted pride and out-of-date political ideas—then Stimson could say only that this was not the France that he had known.

Reluctant to judge—for who shall judge what peoples and their leaders do and feel under a defeat so shattering, and at such hands, as that of France in 1940?—Stimson could only trust that from her ruined cities and her damaged pride France might in time rebuild in strength and honor her own freedom and her self-respect. For seventy years, since his childhood days in the gardens of the Tuileries, he had been trained to love and honor France, and in 1945 and afterwards he was still hopeful that a new France would be reconstructed. The great achievements of the French Resistance were the best guerdon of such hopes. Frenchmen and Americans in the year after D-day had fought together with a common purpose, and in this fact, not in past differences—and still less in the envies of some Frenchmen or the ill-considered scorn of some Americans—he saw the true basis of enduring postwar Franco-American relations.

3. FDR AND MILITARY GOVERNMENT

World War II demonstrated with unprecedented clarity the close interconnection between military and civilian affairs; nowhere was this connection more evident than in military government. Yet no task undertaken by the Army produced more misunderstanding at high levels of the Government.

To the War Department and its Secretary the importance of adequate provision for government in the military theaters was obvious. It was a basic military principle, as General Marshall later wrote, that "Orderly civil administration must be maintained in support of military operations in liberated and occupied territories." It was obvious, furthermore, that such administration must at the beginning be under the control of the military commander, and even before Pearl Harbor the War Department began planning in anticipation of this sort of work. In May, 1942, the War Department established a school at Charlottesville, Virginia, for the training of military government officers. All these steps Stimson approved, but it was not until August, 1942, that a difference of opinion in the administration on the matter of military government brought the subject forcibly to his attention.

"Marshall and McCloy brought me news of a new tempest in a teapot raised by the jealous New Dealers around the throne, this time in respect to General Gullion. Gullion has started a school for the education of Army officers in their fiscal and economic duties in occupied territories, and this seems to have raised a storm among people who were anticipating such activities as an opportunity for themselves. As a result they made the most ridiculous attacks on Gullion and he is very much troubled. Apparently they have been to the President about it, so this brings the matter up to me. They accuse Gullion of being a Fascist and all other kinds of iniquity—a typical New Deal attack from the New Deal cherubs around the throne." (Diary, August 27, 1942)

Three months later this rumor of attack ripened into a sharp memorandum of inquiry from the President. Fortunately it proved easy to defend the Charlottesville school. Stimson was able to show the President that such preparation was absolutely essential, and Mr. Roosevelt was less easily frightened than the "cherubs." Stimson also found that he had a stanch ally in Secretary Hull, who agreed with his view that administration in foreign lands must initially be an Army responsibility, while Stimson in turn fully accepted the State Department's responsibility for the formulation of political policy. On the basis of this agreement in principle the two Departments were able to co-ordinate their work without major clashes.

But the trouble did not end there; indeed, this was only the beginning. The invasion of North Africa brought into the open latent differences between the White House and the War Department which were not wholly settled for more than a year; during part of that time Stimson found himself in the difficult position of acting without the real support of his chief. Luckily the President in the end was wholly converted, but at the beginning there was a significant divergence in principle.

The North African landings, in comparison with later Allied operations, were hastily improvised. Barely three months elapsed between the final decision to invade and the sailing of the invasion convoys. In this interval only sketchy preparation could be made for the handling of civil affairs after the landing, and no final decisions were reached as to organization and responsibility for such matters. As a result General Eisenhower was plagued in the early months of the operation by a series of problems that appeared to be of interest to nearly every Department of the American Government. As early as November 20, "The President opened up by a general scold of the Cabinet for trying to butt in and interfere with the civilian government of the occupied territories in North Africa. He said he addressed it to everybody except Frank Walker, the Postmaster . . . but I assume [perhaps rashly] that he did not mean either the Army or the Navy."

The scolding was not wholly effective. Nor was it sufficient merely to prevent conflicting agencies from interference in North Africa; what General Eisenhower needed was full authority and sufficient staff assistance, and from Casablanca, in January, Marshall cabled to Stimson that Eisenhower was getting neither. On his return Marshall recommended that McCloy be sent to help Eisenhower organize his civil affairs staff.

Stimson promptly recognized that the central difficulty in the situation was not in North Africa, and not in the War or State Department, nor even among the "cherubs." The central difficulty was in Mr. Roosevelt's way of handling things, and in a telephone conversation with Mr. Roosevelt on February 1 Stimson's worst fears were promptly confirmed. "He was very friendly but, as I expected, takes a different and thoroughly Rooseveltian view of what historic good administrative procedure has required in such a case as we have in North Africa. He wants to do it all himself. He says he did settle all the matters that were troubling Eisenhower when he was over there and that, if McCloy went over, there wouldn't be anything else to do; and as to Murphy he said that he was not there as a diplomat to report to Hull but as a special appointee of his own to handle special matters on which he reported to Roosevelt direct. This was a truly Rooseveltian position. I told him frankly over the telephone that it was bad administration and asked him what a Cabinet was for and what Departments were for except to have reports considered in that way, but I have small hopes of reforming him. The fault is Rooseveltian and deeply ingrained. Theodore Roosevelt had it to a certain extent but never anywhere nearly as much as this one. But I hammered out with him the proceedings that even in his opinion must be regarded as matters for the War Department. He admitted that in the handling of the railroads that were taken over and the lines of communication and the radios, such matters must be handled as military and as a part of the duties of the commanding general and be reported to the War Department. He says he wants to see me tomorrow or next day and at that [time] I shall have a real talk with him. It was hard to do it over the telephone. I think he realizes that he has transgressed the line of proper procedure in some matters, and I shall make him read my letter to get the historical viewpoint. I told him frankly that, if the process of whittling down the powers of the Secretary of War should continue, I would be in a very embarrassing position for I had no desire, in the words of Churchill, to go down in history as the person who consented to the liquidation of the great historic powers of my office."

The letter to which Stimson referred was one which he had prepared earlier the same day; it showed clearly how far his stand was from that of the President. To Mr. Roosevelt the whole concept of military government was both strange and somewhat abhorrent; to Stimson it was a natural and inevitable result of military operations in any area where there was not already a fully effective friendly government. Mr. Roosevelt argued that operations in World War II should be patterned on those of Pershing, but to Stimson the true parallel was rather with American experience in the Philippines, in Cuba and in Puerto Rico, for there would be no full-fledged central government in France or any of the other countries in which the American Army was going to have to fight. To Stimson the lessons of history were clear, and the tradition of military government was an honorable one. So in this letter, after rehearsing the facts of past experience—and they were facts which he knew at firsthand, facts which revolved around names like Elihu Root, Leonard Wood, and Frank R. McCoy —he summarized his conclusions in a form which showed why he felt strongly in the matter. This whole field of activity to him was one of the great and proper functions of an American Secretary of War.

"From the foregoing the following facts stand out as the historical policy of the United States Government in cases of military invasion and government:

"1. The authority of the military governor in each case has stemmed out from the military power of the United States exercised by the President as Commander in Chief.

"2. In each case the military governor has been compelled to employ agents for the solution of civil administrative problems of government. In each case these agents have been in the

first instance composed of Army officers although many of
them have been men of high civilian experience; for example,
Tasker Bliss who conducted the customs of Cuba with con-
summate skill and success; Gorgas and Walter Reed who
constructed its sanitary system; and many others like them.

"3. These Army officers continued until they were replaced
by competent local native administrators.

"4. The administrations thus set up have been so successful
as to constitute a bright page of American history, free from
scandal and, in such difficult communities as Cuba and the
Philippines, have laid the foundation of permanent good relations between those countries and the United States.

"5. In each case the President has used the Secretary of
War as the departmental officer who carried out this exercise
of the President's military power; who organized the plans
and systems under which the various governors general acted;
and whose Department served as the medium of record and
communication between the military governments and the
President.

"This necessarily followed from the fact that the War
Department from its connection with the military occupation
and its possession of a highly trained staff of military officers
was the normal, natural, and in fact only Department of the
government capable of rendering this service. I believe this
condition still exists today.

"6. There is ample opportunity in North Africa as there
was in the second intervention of Cuba for the exercise of the
functions of the American Department of State. But these
functions are not administrative. . . ."

The theory set forth in this letter was one which was very
dear to Stimson, but as he considered the nature of his problem
in the White House, he decided that no such blunt approach
would serve. Mr. Roosevelt was not going to be persuaded by
a lot of Republican history, nor were arguments about administrative procedure likely to hold his attention. So on February
3, Stimson took a different line. Arming himself with examples of the existing confusion, he set out simply to get his
camel's head McCloy into the President's tent of personal

government. The contrast between the undelivered letter and the actual conversation is striking:

"The President was in fine form and I had one of the best and most friendly talks with him I have ever had. He was full of his trip, naturally, and interspersed our whole talk with stories and anecdotes. But I had carefully prepared what I wanted to say and held him pretty well to the line. I had abandoned entirely the idea of bringing up the formal legal argument which I had made in the letter written last Monday, having come to the conclusion that the main thing was to get McCloy over there on a friendly basis and then work out from that. And so my object was just to show the President, in answer to his inquiries over the telephone Monday night, that there was a real problem of disorder there in which McCloy could be of help and in which we ought to support Eisenhower. In this I was perfectly successful. He cordially accepted the idea; asked to have an appointment made with McCloy for him to see him personally and this was done as I came out.

"But it was amusing, though to some degree discouraging, to see how he clung to the idea of doing all this sort of work himself. In the first place he thought he had practically wiped up the situation by his visit there and there was not much left to be done in the way of organization. But in this I pulled him down by the facts that I had gathered, showing that poor Eisenhower's first attempts to do the work with his 'Civil Affairs Section' of his General Staff, which is the usual annex of Army commanders for such work, were not successful; then how he had created as a part of his Staff the North African Economic Board as a more efficient engine for it, but that this was still incomplete; and then I swamped the President by showing him that none of these activities had been reported through any regular channels to me; the great difficulty I had had in finding even what had been done, the delays which necessarily occurred and the importance therefore of having a routine for this business. I showed him how neither Marshall nor I nor anybody in the Department had known of the vital papers which he, the President, had signed while on his conference there until I had dug them up this morning, getting one of them from the French mission that was here in Washington, and had a French copy of what they claimed was a contract the President himself had signed. This quite put him at my mercy. I gave him a translation which they had made for me in the Pentagon Building and he went off into an amusing story of how he had signed at least a part of the covenants in the paper and he could not deny the rest. The paper covered such important matters as the change in the ratio of exchange between the Morocco franc and the dollar which Roosevelt had made. He recollected this all right and told me a good story about it. I retaliated by telling him I knew all about this one because Hull had told me it was an agreement 'signed over a drink' by the President, at which he laughed and virtually admitted that the other covenants in the paper might have been accomplished the same way."

The permission given for McCloy's trip was a long step ahead. McCloy had already become Stimson's principal agent for all problems of civil affairs and all questions that affected the State Department; it was he who carried the main burden of work in these matters from this point forward. Mr. Roosevelt continued to believe that the administrative direction should be a function of the State Department and so ordered in early February. But Stimson was certain that experience would justify him, and carefully maintaining mutual understanding with Mr. Hull, he established in the War Department a Civil Affairs Division which soon became the province of Major General John Hilldring. In May, McCloy became Chairman of a Combined Civil Affairs Committee operating under the Combined Chiefs of Staff. This committee later extended its work to include such vital politico-military problems as terms of surrender, and it served as an invaluable bridge between military and political leaders. From this time onward the significance of and necessity for co-ordinated military government was not seriously questioned. Events once more taught the President what Stimson had tried to teach him by advocacy. Before the invasion of Sicily Mr. Roosevelt made one more effort to insure the dominance of civilian agencies in civil administration, but the experience gained in this operation and in the early stages of the Italian campaign appears to have convinced him that for good or ill the armed forces must have the administrative responsibility in all military theaters. Two actions in November, 1943, showed Stimson how far the President had moved. First, on November 10 he wrote a letter to Stimson declaring that the War Department must assume the responsibility for civilian relief in all liberated areas during the first six months after their liberation. Second, from Cairo he cabled to Stimson his view that all arrangements for civil administration and dealings with the French people and their leaders must initially be purely military; his main purpose in this second order was to minimize political contact with De Gaulle and so avoid any implied recognition of the Frenchman's status, but the cable was also proof that he had finally recognized the value and the inevitability of military government. That Mr. Roosevelt continued to be cautious in permitting the military to deal with the French (see p. 546) was to Stimson a minor matter compared with his conversion to sound principles of administration.[2] During the remainder of the war the Army was given a constantly increasing measure of the President's confidence in its work in civil affairs, and under McCloy and Hilldring the War Department organization became more and more effective in co-ordinating and administering a responsibility that in its eventual size and scope far exceeded anything that Stimson himself had anticipated. So clearly did the Army prove itself to be the proper agency for such work that more than two years after the end of the war, long after the military importance of the overseas theaters had been superseded by the dominance of economic and political problems, the War Department was still carrying on the administration of the American occupation in defeated countries. And this too Stimson held to be a proper assignment, notwithstanding the argument that the State Department

[2] The experience of Franklin Roosevelt in dealing with military government reminded Stimson very strongly of a similar lesson learned forty years earlier by his cousin Theodore. It was T.R. who tried civilian engineers in Panama before he turned to the Army and selected Goethals, remarking, as Stimson heard the story, that "the great thing about an Army officer is that he does what you tell him to do." Discipline without brains was of little value, but both Roosevelts learned to their cost the uselessness in administration of brains without discipline.

should handle such matters. From his experience in both Departments he was wholly convinced that the State Department by its nature was unequipped for major administrative chores, while administration was the War Department's normal, constant business. The State Department must frame the policies, but it could not hope to equal the Army in the task of carrying them out.

4. A WORD FROM HINDSIGHT

After the war, considering such problems as those just discussed Stimson was reinforced in his wartime belief that Mr. Roosevelt's personal virtuosity in high politics carried with it certain disadvantages which might have been limited if the President had been willing to provide himself with a War Cabinet for the co-ordinated execution of his policies—a body which might have done in war diplomacy what the Joint Chiefs of Staff did in military strategy.

Problems like those of China and France were not merely diplomatic—the State Department could not and would not assume the whole labor of determining policy in areas where the military interest was so significant. Yet the military interest could not of itself be wholly determinant; it was not proper that such questions should be decided by the Joint Chiefs of Staff, as the members of that body well understood.

Mr. Roosevelt therefore could not rely on his regularly constituted advisers—military or diplomatic—for final recommendation and co-ordinated execution in problems of war diplomacy. Nor were his regular Cabinet meetings a suitable place for such discussion and decision; there were nearly twenty men in Cabinet meetings, and during the war they became a formality; to Stimson they were useful principally as a way of getting into the White House to have a word with the President in private after the meetings were over; a typical diary entry describes a Cabinet meeting toward the end of the war as "the same old two-and-sixpence, no earthly good." Mr. Roosevelt's own view of Cabinet meetings was not wholly different: "The Cabinet meeting this afternoon was brief. The President opened it by saying humorously that he had just told his family that he wanted a short Cabinet meeting and they had said, 'Well, you know how you can get it. You can just stop your own talking.' There was a smile around the table because of the truth of the statement. The Roosevelt Cabinets are really a solo performance by the President interspersed with some questions and very few debates. When the President told this story, Hull broke in in his dry way. 'Yes,' he said, 'I found that when I was asked by the President to come over to lunch for a conference, I used to have to get a little bite to eat first myself so that I could talk while he was eating.' This met with great applause." (Diary, May 1, 1942)

The proper solution, Stimson believed, would have been for Mr. Roosevelt to provide himself with a War Cabinet like that upon which Winston Churchill relied in Great Britain. Cabinet responsibility of course is not the same in the United States as in Great Britain, but Stimson felt that Mr. Roosevelt would have found it helpful to have some such body for the handling of his war policies in foreign lands. Such a body would have included his most trusted personal adviser, Harry Hopkins, and perhaps the Secretaries of State, Treasury, War, and Navy. Organized like the Joint Chiefs of Staff, with a secretariat of top quality and a continuing record of the policy decisions made or approved by the President, such a body might have avoided some at least of the difficulties discussed above, and others not unlike them in other areas. Stimson would never have desired that the President's personal initiative and extraordinary talent should be limited by red tape, but he felt sure that such a body would have been a reinforcement to Mr. Roosevelt's less evident abilities as a co-ordinator and executive. Unfortunately the whole idea was foreign to the President's nature; only reluctantly had he accepted the notion of such an organization even in the purely military field, and he never showed the least disposition to alter his methods in diplomacy. Stimson himself never recommended a War Cabinet to Mr. Roosevelt; he had no desire to appear to push himself forward. But others made such a recommendation, and the President was not impressed.

To be useful, such a body would have had to be the President's own creation. No attempt to co-ordinate action on any lower level could have much value so long as the central threads of policy were personally managed in the White House. Back in 1940, in an effort to fill a gap which he felt at once on his arrival in Washington—and which he had noticed from the other side of the fence when he was Secretary of State—Stimson had been the leading spirit in setting up regular weekly meetings of Hull, Knox, and himself. These meetings were wholly unofficial and personal. They served a useful purpose in keeping the three Secretaries informed of one another's major problems. But they had no connection with Mr. Roosevelt's final determinations of policy, and in 1942 and 1943 they became less and less valuable. Reorganized late in 1944, with McCloy as recorder and with formal agenda and conclusions, this Committee of Three became more useful; Stimson, Stettinius, and Forrestal were able to use it for the solution of some important points and they were able to establish at a lower level, for routine co-ordination, the extremely useful State, War and Navy Co-ordinating Committee. But the Committee of Three, in considering major problems, always remained more of a clearing-house than an executive committee.

Another embryonic War Cabinet had existed before Pearl Harbor—the War Council, which met at frequent intervals in the White House. This group included Hull, Stimson, and Knox in addition to the senior military officers. But when Mr. Roosevelt learned to like the Joint Chiefs of Staff, in 1942, he allowed himself to dispense with any general meetings on war policy.

Stimson's belief in this notion of a War Cabinet was based partly on hindsight, and he knew that he might seem to be elevating his personal feelings into a theory of government. He hoped this was not the case. He had served in too many Cabinets to expect that all decisions would match his advice, and it was not his disagreements with the President on details of policy that bothered him, as he looked back in 1947; it was rather that Mr. Roosevelt's policy was so often either unknown or not clear to those who had to execute it, and worse yet, in some cases it seemed self-contradictory. In the case of

China, for example, all those who worked so energetically at cross-purposes in Chungking undoubtedly regarded themselves as possessors of a mandate from Washington—and even from the White House.

In summary, then, Stimson's experience of the diplomacy of coalition warfare in World War II left him with this conclusion: Franklin Roosevelt as a wartime international leader proved himself as good as one man could be—but one man was not enough to keep track of so vast an undertaking.

CHAPTER XXII

The Beginnings of Peace

1. A SHIFT IN EMPHASIS

THE main object of war is peace, and we have now to study Stimson's part in the framing of American policy for the establishment of a lasting peace after World War II. Not only as Secretary of War but as a man who had been forced to learn in 1931 and afterwards the consequences of bad peacemaking, he was deeply interested in the problems of the postwar settlement.

But it should be remembered that peace was an objective which depended first of all on victory, and, by reason of his official position as well as his natural inclination, Stimson's work until the latter part of 1944 was almost wholly concerned with winning the war. In this respect his attitude was little different from that of the President and most of the administration. Even in diplomatic questions like those discussed in the last chapter, the major consideration was almost always the advancement of military victory.

Some critics of American policy have judged it astonishingly naïve in this single-minded concentration on victory. Stimson could not agree. The general objectives of American policy had been clearly and eloquently stated by Mr. Roosevelt first in the Atlantic Charter and later in his assertion of the Four Freedoms. It was further clear that American policy envisaged the development of the wartime United Nations into a peacetime organization of friendly nations. So long as wartime policy did not directly and violently contravene these general principles, it seemed to Stimson wholly proper that detailed action should be governed by the overriding requirement of victory, in the confidence that as victory was the great common immediate objective, action which advanced victory must in general promote good international relations.

It was only in the summer of 1944 that high officials out-side the State Department began to give their close attention to postwar problems. The extraordinary success of the great invasion lifted from men's minds all fears and doubts about the basic strategy of victory; at the same time it created a pressing need for attention to new problems. The Normandy landing and the great Avranches break-through precipitated a situation in which victory was certain and apparently close, and as General Eisenhower's forces advanced toward the German border it became clear that the armies had outrun the policy makers. From this unsettled situation there developed in September the most violent single interdepartmental struggle of Stimson's career—the issue over the "Morgenthau plan" for the treatment of Germany. In order to set Stimson's part of this struggle in its proper focus, it will be useful to consider briefly his two most firmly held general views about the peace settlement.

His first and great commandment was the maintenance of friendship with Great Britain. Of itself, such friendship would not be sufficient to keep the peace—here Stimson differed somewhat from some who felt that an Anglo-American coalition could somehow assert its virtuous will throughout the world. But without the maintenance of close relationships with the British Stimson did not see how America could hope to be an effective member of world society. Division from the British would neutralize in mutual opposition two nations whose fundamental principles and purposes were so much alike that their opposition could only work to the disadvantage of both. Friendship with Great Britain had been cardinal in Stimson's policy as Secretary of State; in 1939 and 1940 his advocacy of "intervention" had been based on his belief in the fundamental unity of Anglo-American interests; it was a belief which he saw no reason to discard. Several times during the war he expressed forcibly to various groups of administration leaders "the conviction I am getting more strongly every day that our plan must be a plan to continue after the war the same controls as have saved us during the war, namely close association between the English-speaking countries." (Diary, May 11, 1943) This was a view which he found general among his colleagues; indeed much of his later disagreement with Mr. Roosevelt over the Morgenthau plan rose out of a misplaced Presidential eagerness to help the British.

Stimson's second great principle was that the essential basis of enduring peace must be economic, and here again his opinion was based on his own experience. The sermon preached by Keynes after Versailles had acquired deep and poignant meaning for Stimson when as Secretary of State he had wrestled with the results of that economically impossible treaty. Now he hoped for a settlement which would involve no burden of debts, no barriers to the internal trade of Central Europe, no politically independent and economically helpless group of "successor states." Evidence that these objectives were being ignored deeply disturbed him—when he learned of the pending three-power decision to restore an independent Austria his mind turned back to the financial collapse of Austria in 1931. "They haven't any grasp apparently of the underlying need of proper economic arrangements to make the peace stick. . . . If they restored Austria to her position in which she was left by the Versailles arrangement twenty-five years ago, why they would reduce her again to a non-self-sustaining state and they don't seem to have that thing in mind at all. Central Europe after the war has got to eat. She has got to be free from tariffs in order to eat." (Diary, October 28, 1943)

Although most of his time at meetings with Mr. Roosevelt in this period was devoted to more immediate questions like the OVERLORD command, he had a chance on December 18, 1943, to express his position briefly. "I got an occasion to tell him that I had seen proposals in regard to the division of Europe in case of victory and that I had only one general recommendation at present and that was not to divide Europe up into separate pieces which could not each of them feed itself on its own land." He went on to point out that in the case of Germany this policy must involve the retention of much German commerce and industry, for "unless this commerce was protected she could not probably feed her population by agriculture."

Until late in 1944 Stimson's thinking on the peace did not develop much beyond the two principles outlined above. While he of course accepted the general notion of an international organization to replace and if possible improve on the League of Nations, he did not regard any such organization as a proper point of focus for the peacemaking; he entirely agreed with the President that the problem of the peace settlement was necessarily one to be solved by the major victorious powers, a position explicitly stated by three of them in the Moscow Declaration of November, 1943. The question of future relations with Soviet Russia was one about which until early 1945 he was cautiously optimistic.

2. THE MORGENTHAU PLAN

It was with this general attitude that Stimson returned from Normandy in July, 1944, to find the administration belatedly but vigorously engaged in the construction of a policy for the treatment of Germany. At the same time, in anticipation of the Dumbarton Oaks Conference, the outlines of a postwar organization were being sketched in the State Department. It was a very different atmosphere from the one he had left a month before, and he at once recognized that he must shift his attention. In his own Department, officers responsible for civil affairs reported that they were face to face with a situation—the forthcoming occupation of Germany—for which they had no orders; it was not even settled which part of Germany United States forces should occupy. On July 31, after hearing from Harry Hopkins about "the postwar problems," Stimson remarked, "I myself am thinking along those lines now, and . . . as a result of all these thoughts, I had Jack McCloy and Ed Stettinius in to dinner and we talked over the pending negotiations. . . . The most pressing thing is to get the President to decide on which part of Germany will be occupied by the American troops. He is hell-bent to occupy the northern portion. We all think that

that is a mistake—that it will only get us into a head-on collision with the British." (Diary, July 31, 1944)

During the first weeks of August Stimson was on vacation in New York, leaving McCloy to act for him in these matters. Returning to Washington he found that no progress had been made. On August 25 he lunched with the President, and gave him five good reasons for a decision to occupy southwestern Germany; "I was inclined to think that I had made an impression on him but of course it was impossible to say." Then, after some discussion of the general nature of the German problem, "I made my main point—that we were running into a lack of preparedness. Our troops were going into Germany and they had no instruction on these vital points. . . . I pointed out that the President himself couldn't do the necessary study to decide these various points and suggested that he ought to appoint a Cabinet Committee who could assimilate the work that was already being done by men on a lower level and prepare it for the President himself. He took that point and accepted it and then we went into Cabinet and at the very beginning of Cabinet he . . . said that he would appoint Secretaries Hull, Morgenthau, and myself as the members of that committee, with the Secretary of the Navy acting on it whenever a Navy matter was involved." To this list Mr. Roosevelt later added Harry Hopkins.

The first meeting of the Cabinet Committee was called on September 5. In the meantime Stimson found that there was a strong divergence of view in Washington, between those who were in favor of a firm but discriminating treatment of Germany, looking toward her eventual reconstruction as a prosperous and peaceful nation, and those who frankly desired a Carthaginian peace. The night before the committee meeting Stimson and McCloy dined with Morgenthau and his assistant, Harry White. "We had a pleasant dinner but we were all aware of the feeling that a sharp issue is sure to arise over the question of the treatment of Germany. Morgenthau is, not unnaturally, very bitter and . . . it became very apparent that he would plunge out for a treatment of Germany which I feel sure would be unwise." (Diary, September 4, 1944)

The Cabinet Committee meeting confirmed Stimson's worst

fears. "Hull brought up a draft of agenda for the meeting. . . . This paper was all right on its face down to the last section which contained some extreme propositions and principles, and as soon as we got into a discussion of these I, to my tremendous surprise, found that Hull was as bitter as Morgenthau against the Germans and was ready to jump all the principles that he had been laboring for in regard to trade for the past twelve years.[1] He and Morgenthau wished to wreck completely the immense Ruhr-Saar area of Germany and turn it into second-rate agricultural land regardless of all that that area meant not only to Germany but to the welfare of the entire European continent. Hopkins went with them so far as to wish to prevent the manufacture of steel in the area, a prohibition which would pretty well sabotage everything else. I found myself a minority of one and I labored vigorously but entirely ineffectively against my colleagues. In all the four years that I have been here I have not had such a difficult and unpleasant meeting although of course there were no personalities. We all knew each other too well for that. But we were irreconcilably divided. In the end it was decided that Hull would send in his memorandum to the President while we should each of us send a memorandum of views in respect to it." (Diary, September 5, 1944)

It is worth noting the general nature of the parts of Hull's paper on which the Cabinet Committee was unanimous. These paragraphs provided for the complete demilitarization of Germany, the dissolution of the Nazi party and all affiliated organizations, with energetic punishment of war criminals, the institution of extensive controls over communications and education, and the acceptance of the principle of reparations to other states, though not to the United States. It was only on the issue of the destruction of German industry that Stimson was violently opposed to his colleagues.

His basic position on this issue was stated in the memorandum sent later the same day to his three colleagues, and forwarded by Hull to the President. This memorandum must be quoted nearly in full:

---

[1] This later seemed to Stimson an overstatement of Hull's position; in any event the Secretary of State soon took a quite different view.

"I have considered the [State Department] paper entitled 'Suggested Recommendations on Treatment of Germany from the Cabinet Committee for the President.' . . .

"With the exception of the last paragraph I find myself in agreement with the principles stated therein and they are in conformity with the lines upon which we have been proceeding in the War Department in our directives to the Armed Forces.

"The last paragraph, however, is as follows:

" 'h. The primary objectives of our economic policy are (1) the standard of living of the German population shall be held down to subsistence levels; (2) German economic position of power in Europe must be eliminated; (3) German economic capacity must be converted in such manner that it will be so dependent upon imports and exports that Germany cannot by its own devices reconvert to war production.'

"While certain of these statements by themselves may possibly be susceptible of a construction with which I would not be at variance, the construction put upon them at the discussion this morning certainly reached positions to which I am utterly opposed. The position frankly taken by some of my colleagues was that the great industrial regions of Germany known as the Saar and the Ruhr with their very important deposits of coal and ore should be totally transformed into a nonindustrialized area of agricultural land.

"I cannot conceive of such a proposition being either possible or effective and I can see enormous general evils coming from an attempt to so treat it. During the past eighty years of European history this portion of Germany was one of the most important sources of the raw materials upon which the industrial and economic livelihood of Europe was based. Upon the production which came from the raw materials of this region during those years, the commerce of Europe was very largely predicated. Upon that production Germany became the largest source of supply to no less than ten European countries, viz: Russia, Norway, Sweden, Denmark, Holland, Switzerland, Italy, Austria-Hungary, Rumania, and Bulgaria; and the second largest source of supply to Great Britain, Belgium, and France. By the same commerce, which in large part arose from this production, Germany also became the best buyer or customer of Russia, Norway, Holland, Belgium, Switzerland, Italy, and Austria-Hungary; and the second best customer of Great Britain, Sweden, and Denmark. The production of these materials from this region could not be sealed up and obliterated, as was proposed this morning, without manifestly causing a great dislocation to the trade upon which Europe has lived. In Germany itself this commerce has built up since 1870 a population of approximately thirty million more people than were ever supported upon the agricultural soil of Germany alone. Undoubtedly a similar growth of population took place in the nations which indirectly participated in the commerce based upon this production.

"I cannot treat as realistic the suggestion that such an area in the present economic condition of the world can be turned into a nonproductive 'ghost territory' when it has become the center of one of the most industrialized continents in the world, populated by peoples of energy, vigor, and progressiveness.

"I can conceive of endeavoring to meet the misuse which Germany has recently made of this production by wise systems of control or trusteeship or even transfers of ownership to other nations. But I cannot conceive of turning such a gift of nature into a dust heap.

"War is destruction. This war more than any previous war has caused gigantic destruction. The need for the recuperative benefits of productivity is more evident now than ever before throughout the world. Not to speak of Germany at all or even her satellites, our allies in Europe will feel the need of the benefit of such productivity if it should be destroyed. Moreover, speed of reconstruction is of great importance, if we hope to avoid dangerous convulsions in Europe.

"We contemplate the transfer from Germany of ownership of East Prussia, Upper Silesia, Alsace and Lorraine (each of them except the first containing raw materials of importance) together with the imposition of general economic controls. We also are considering the wisdom of a possible partition of Germany into north and south sections, as well as the creation of an internationalized state in the Ruhr. With such precautions, or indeed with only some of them, it certainly should not be necessary for us to obliterate all industrial productivity in the Ruhr area, in order to preclude its future misuse.

"Nor can I agree that it should be one of our purposes to hold the German population 'to a subsistence level' if this means the edge of poverty. This would mean condemning the German people to a condition of servitude in which, no matter how hard or how effectively a man worked, he could not materially increase his economic condition in the world. Such a program would, I believe, create tension and resentments far outweighing any immediate advantage of security and would tend to obscure the guilt of the Nazis and the viciousness of their doctrines and their acts.

"By such economic mistakes I cannot but feel that you would also be poisoning the springs out of which we hope that the future peace of the world can be maintained. . . .

"My basic objection to the proposed methods of treating Germany which were discussed this morning was that in addition to a system of preventive and educative punishment they would add the dangerous weapon of complete economic oppression. Such methods, in my opinion, do not prevent war; they tend to breed war."

On September 6 the President held a meeting with the Cabinet Committee. Stimson and Morgenthau submitted their new memoranda. The President addressed most of his comments to Stimson, "reverting to his proposition . . . that Germany could live happily and peacefully on soup from soup kitchens," but he appeared not to accept Morgenthau's view that the Ruhr should be dismantled, arguing rather "that Great Britain was going to be in sore straits after the war and . . . that the products of the Ruhr might be used to furnish raw material for British steel industry. I said that I had no objection certainly to assisting Britain in every way that we could but that this was very different from obliterating the Ruhr. . . . There was quite an easing up in the attitude of Hull, and the President certainly was not following Morgenthau. . . . I wound up by using the analogy of Charles Lamb's dissertation on roast pig. I begged the President to remember that this was a most complicated economic question and all that I was urging upon him was that he should not burn down his house of the world for the purpose of getting a meal of roast pig. He apparently caught the point." (Diary, September 6, 1944)

Stimson came away with the feeling that he had made some progress. Secretary Morgenthau apparently shared this feeling, for he promptly requested a rehearing before the President. A new meeting was set for September 9. Meanwhile both Morgenthau and Stimson prepared new papers expanding their views. The new Morgenthau paper, submitted on September 9, asserted that it was a fallacy that Europe needed a strong industrial Germany, that the mines and mills of the Ruhr had indeed been a depressing competitor of Great Britain particularly, and "it contained a specious appeal to the President's expressed desire to help England by . . . the proposal that by sealing up the Ruhr we would give England the chance to jump into Germany's business of supplying Europe industrially and thus curing the alleged English depression in coal mining. It asserted that England had coal enough to supply its present output for five hundred years! This certainly is contrary to everything I have heard about the mines of Great Britain which have been constantly asserted to have been dug so deep as to become almost uneconomic." (Diary, September 9, 1944)

In Stimson's memorandum of the same date he summarized again the basic difference between his position and Morgenthau's. The latter had expressed in writing (in his paper of September 6) the proposals made orally before the Cabinet Committee. Speaking of the Ruhr "and surrounding industrial areas" to a total of over 30,000 square miles, Morgenthau had written: "This area should not only be stripped of all presently existing industries but so weakened and controlled that it cannot in the foreseeable future become an industrial area. . . . All industrial plants and equipment not destroyed by military action shall either be completely dismantled or removed from the area or completely destroyed, all equipment shall be removed from the mines and the mines shall be thoroughly wrecked." Stimson reiterated his unalterable opposition to any such program. It would breed war, not peace; it would arouse sympathy for Germany all over the world; it would destroy resources desperately needed for the reconstruction of Europe. Asking that no hasty decisions be made, he urged the President to accept for the time being a slightly revised version of Secretary Hull's original memorandum, leaving the controversial economic issue for future discussion.

Without making any decision on any of these papers, Mr. Roosevelt went to Quebec, where on September 11 the Octagon Conference with Mr. Churchill began. One of the principal issues on the agenda for this meeting was the German problem, and Stimson was not happy about the President's state of body and mind. "I have been much troubled by the President's physical condition. He was distinctly not himself Saturday [September 9]. He had a cold and seemed tired out. I rather fear for the effects of this hard conference upon him. I am particularly troubled . . . that he is going up there without any real preparation for the solution of the underlying and fundamental problem of how to treat Germany. So far as he had evidenced it in his talks with us, he has had absolutely no study or training in the very difficult problem which we have to decide, namely of how far we can introduce preventive measures to protect the world from Germany running amuck again and how far we must refrain from measures which will simply provoke the wrong reaction. I hope the British have brought better trained men with them than we are likely to have to meet them." (Diary, September 11, 1944)

The President seemed to Stimson to be further hampered by his obsession with the notion of a coming revolution in France. "I have argued the question with him already several times. He has been warned by Leahy that he may expect a revolution in France. . . . Although [Leahy] has had the advantage of being stationed in Vichy for several years, I don't think his advice is good. I think it is very doubtful whether there will be a revolution. But as I have pointed out to the President, the revolution can hardly possibly occur until Germany is conquered. Pending that time the danger of a common enemy, Germany, will keep the French factions together. Therefore by the time such a revolution can come, in all likelihood our forces will be in Germany and will have lines of communication not running across France. Therefore there is no reason why we should accept any call to occupy France. In fact it seems entirely farfetched that any of the Allies should occupy France. She has had many revolutions before now which she has been left to settle herself and that ought to be done now. But the President has worked himself up into an apprehension of this. . . . At that meeting on Saturday morning whenever any question came up as to our duties in Germany, he would say: 'I want somebody to be sure and keep a buttress between us and France'." (Diary, September 11, 1944)

His preoccupation with France seemed to be preventing the President, not only from making a decision on the zone of occupation, but even from any balanced consideration of the German problem as a whole. And although he finally accepted the southwestern zone at Quebec, he did not so quickly master the German question as a whole. As the Quebec Conference proceeded Stimson began to hear disturbing reports. On the thirteenth he learned that Morgenthau had been called to the conference; on the sixteenth he heard that the President and the Prime Minister had accepted the Morgenthau plan. But it was not until the twentieth, when Morgenthau had returned victorious to Washington, that he learned the whole story.

It appeared that the President had called Morgenthau to Quebec, where he had argued the case for his plan, that Morgenthau had found the British at first entirely opposed to him, that Mr. Churchill had been converted by the argument that the elimination of the Ruhr would create new markets for Great Britain, and that finally the President and the Prime Minister had initialed the following agreement:

"At a conference between the President and the Prime Minister upon the best measures to prevent renewed rearmament by Germany, it was felt that an essential feature was the future disposition of the Ruhr and the Saar.

"The ease with which the metallurgical, chemical, and

electric industries in Germany can be converted from peace
to war has already been impressed upon us by bitter experience. It must also be remembered that the Germans have
devastated a large portion of the industries of Russia and of
other neighboring Allies, and it is only in accordance with
justice that these injured countries should be entitled to remove the machinery they require in order to repair the losses
they have suffered. The industries referred to in the Ruhr
and in the Saar would therefore be necessarily put out of
action and closed down. It was felt that the two districts
should be put under some body under the world organization
which would supervise the dismantling of these industries
and make sure that they were not started up again by some
subterfuge.

"This programme for eliminating the war-making industries in the Ruhr and in the Saar is looking forward to
converting Germany into a country primarily agricultural
and pastoral in its character.

"The Prime Minister and the President were in agreement
upon this programme.

O.K.

F.D.R.

W.S.C.

15 9.

"September 16, 1944"

Morgenthau told this story "modestly and without rubbing
it in, but it was the narration of a pretty heavy defeat for
everything that we had fought for." The extraordinary document initialed by the two leaders marked a remarkable shift
from another document signed by the same two men three
years before. As McCloy pointed out to Stimson, it was the
Atlantic Charter which had pronounced that the United
States and the United Kingdom would "endeavor, with due
respect for their existing obligation, to further the enjoyment
by all States, great or small, victor or vanquished, of access,
on equal terms, to the trade and to the raw materials of the
world which are needed for their economic prosperity."

Fortunately for all concerned, the Quebec memorandum did not long remain official United States policy.

When he first heard of the President's decision, Stimson was about to sign a third memorandum to Mr. Roosevelt on the Morgenthau plan. Although it seemed a waste of time to submit a further paper when the decision was already made, he decided to keep the record straight. "It will undoubtedly irritate him for he dislikes opposition when he has made up his mind. But I have thought the thing over and decided to do it. I should not keep my self-respect if I did not." (Diary, September 17, 1944)

This third memorandum (drafted in large part by McCloy) pitched the argument on a higher level than anything that had before been written. The paper was designed to appeal from FDR., the hasty signer of ill-considered memoranda, to Franklin Roosevelt, the farsighted and greatly humanitarian President of the United States. Its critical paragraphs follow:

"The question is not whether we want Germans to suffer for their sins. Many of us would like to see them suffer the tortures they have inflicted on others. The only question is whether over the years a group of seventy million educated, efficient and imaginative people can be kept within bounds on such a low level of subsistence as the Treasury proposals contemplate. I do not believe that is humanly possible. A subordinate question is whether even if you could do this it is good for the rest of the world either economically or spiritually. Sound thinking teaches that . . . poverty in one part of the world usually induces poverty in other parts. Enforced poverty is even worse, for it destroys the spirit not only of the victim but debases the victor. It would be just such a crime as the Germans themselves hoped to perpetrate upon their victims—it would be a crime against civilization itself.

"This country since its very beginning has maintained the fundamental belief that all men, in the long run, have the right to be free human beings and to live in the pursuit of happiness. Under the Atlantic Charter victors and vanquished alike are entitled to freedom from economic want. But the proposed treatment of Germany would, if successful, deliberately deprive many millions of people of the right to freedom from want and freedom from fear. Other peoples all over the world would suspect the validity of our spiritual tenets and question the long-range effectiveness of our economic and political principles as applied to the vanquished.

"The proposals would mean a forcible revolution in all of the basic methods of life of a vast section of the population as well as a disruption of many accustomed geographical associations and communications. Such an operation would naturally and necessarily involve a chaotic upheaval in the people's lives which would inevitably be productive of the deepest resentment and bitterness towards the authorities which had imposed such revolutionary changes upon them. Physically, considering the fact that their present enlarged population has been developed and supported under an entirely different geography and economy, it would doubtless cause tremendous suffering involving virtual starvation and death for many, and migrations and changes for others. It would be very difficult, if not impossible, for them to understand any purpose or cause for such revolutionary changes other than mere vengeance of their enemies and this alone would strongly tend towards the most bitter reactions.

"I am prepared to accede to the argument that even if German resources were wiped off the map, the European economy would somehow readjust itself, perhaps with the help of Great Britain and this country. And the world would go on. The benefit to England by the suppression of German competition is greatly stressed in the Treasury memorandum. But this is an argument addressed to a shortsighted cupidity of the victors and the negation of all that Secretary Hull has been trying to accomplish since 1933. I am aware of England's need, but I do not and cannot believe that she wishes this kind of remedy. I feel certain that in her own interest she could not afford to follow this path. The total elimination of a competitor (who is always also a potential purchaser) is rarely a satisfactory solution of a commercial problem.

"The sum total of the drastic political and economic steps proposed by the Treasury is an open confession of the bankruptcy of hope for a reasonable economic and political settlement of the causes of war."

This paper was sent to Mr. Roosevelt at Hyde Park via Harry Hopkins. At the end of the week Stimson received word that the President had read it and would like to talk with him about it. "I hope this is a good symptom but I dare not be too sure." (Diary, September 23, 24, 1944) Then on Sunday the twenty-fourth, to Stimson's annoyance, but not surprise, a report of the Cabinet disagreement (but not including the documents) was published in the newspapers. Three days earlier a pro-Treasury version had been put out by Drew Pearson. The immediate press reaction was strongly in favor of Hull and Stimson (the Secretary of State had completely reversed his initial and tentative position); the bulk of the press strongly attacked Morgenthau, and the President too for reportedly backing him. On Wednesday the twenty-seventh Mr. Roosevelt telephoned to Stimson, who was at Highhold. "He . . . was evidently under the influence of the impact of criticism which has followed his decision to follow Morgenthau's advice. The papers have taken it up violently and almost unanimously against Morgenthau and the President himself, and the impact has been such that he had already evidently reached the conclusion that he had made a false step and was trying to work out of it. . . . He told me that he didn't really intend to try to make Germany a purely agricultural country but said that his underlying motive was the very confidential one that England was broke; that something must be done to give her more business to pull out of the depression after the war, and he evidently hoped that by something like the Morgenthau plan Britain might inherit Germany's Ruhr business. I had already treated that argument in one of my memoranda sent to the President while the controversy was on, so I said nothing further about it." The two men agreed to discuss the matter further on Stimson's return to Washington.

On October 3 Stimson had lunch with the President. Mr. Roosevelt was apparently very tired and unwell, but "he was very friendly, although in evident discomfort, and I put my propositions to him with all the friendliness and tact possible —and after all I feel a very real and deep friendship for him. So the program went through as follows:

". . . I reminded him that he had asked me to talk with him when we next met about our issue over the treatment of Germany. He grinned and looked naughty and said 'Henry Morgenthau pulled a boner' or an equivalent expression, and said that we really were not apart on that; that he had no intention of turning Germany into an agrarian state and that all he wanted was to save a portion of the proceeds of the Ruhr for use by Great Britain (which was 'broke') . . . leaving some of the products of the Ruhr for Germany. This he considered to be the only method of achieving a very desirable end which he could think of or which had been suggested. He got so affirmative to this effect that I warned him that the paper which Churchill had drawn and which he had initialed did contain the proposition of converting Germany 'into a country primarily agricultural and pastoral in its character,' and I read him the three sentences beginning with the one saying that 'the industries referred to in the Ruhr and in the Saar would therefore be necessarily put out of action and closed down' down to the last sentence saying that 'this programme for eliminating the warmaking industries in the Ruhr and in the Saar is looking forward to converting Germany into a country primarily agricultural and pastoral in its character.' He was frankly staggered by this and said he had no idea how he could have initialed this; that he had evidently done it without much thought.

"I told him that in my opinion the most serious danger of the situation was the getting abroad of the idea of vengeance instead of preventive punishment and that it was the language in the Treasury paper which had alarmed me on this subject. I told him that, knowing his liking for brevity and slogans, I had tried to think of a brief crystallization of the way I looked at it. I said I thought that our problem was analogous to the problem of an operation for cancer where it is necessary to cut deeply to get out the malignant tissue even at the expense of much sound tissue in the process, but not to the extent of cutting out any vital organs which by killing the patient would frustrate the benefit of the operation. I said in the same way that what we were after was preventive punishment, even educative punishment, but not vengeance. I told him that I had throughout had in mind his postwar leadership in which he would represent America. I said throughout the war his leadership had been on a high moral plane and he had fought for the highest moral objectives. Now during the postwar readjustment 'You must not poison this position,' which he and our country held, with anything like mere hatred or vengeance. In the course of the talk I told him of my personal friendship for Henry Morgenthau who had been so kind to me when I first came into the Cabinet and that I had shuddered when he took the leadership in such a campaign against Germany. . . ."

Stimson never discussed the "pastoral Germany" issue again with the President; it was clear that Mr. Roosevelt had never really intended to carry out the Morgenthau plan, and that the Quebec memorandum did not represent his matured opinions. Governmental discussions of policy toward Germany were resumed at a lower level, and McCloy carried the burden for the War Department.

But if Secretary Morgenthau's plan was discarded, the attitude which it represented remained, and continuous pressure was exerted throughout the winter before VE-day for a stern directive to General Eisenhower on the treatment of Germany. The eventual product of the debate was the directive known as J.C.S. 1067;[2] rereading this order two years later, Stimson found it a painfully negative document. Although it contained no orders for economic destruction, it certainly was not designed to make the rebuilding of Germany an easy task, and indeed it explicitly ordered the American military governor to "take no steps (a) looking toward the economic rehabilitation of Germany or (b) designed to maintain or strengthen the German economy"—with the exception that he might act to insure reparation payments and to prevent starvation or rebellion. Yet in the spring of 1945 J.C.S. 1067 seemed so much less punitive and destructive than earlier proposals that Stimson found its final draft "a fairly good paper." (Diary, March 29, 1945)

The question remained essentially one of attitude, and during the remaining months of his service Stimson constantly urged that there was no place for clumsy economic vengeance in American policy toward Germany. On May 16 he wrote at Mr. Truman's request a memorandum summarizing views already orally expressed to the new President. "Early pro-

[2] Published in Dept. of State *Bulletin*, Vol. XIII (1945) pp. 596-607.

posals for the treatment of Germany provided for keeping Germany near the margin of hunger as a means of punishment for past misdeeds. I have felt that this was a grave mistake. Punish her war criminals in full measure. Deprive her permanently of her weapons, her General Staff, and perhaps her entire army. Guard her governmental action until the Nazi-educated generation has passed from the stage—admittedly a long job. But do not deprive her of the means of building up ultimately a contented Germany interested in following non-militaristic methods of civilization. This must necessarily involve some industrialization, for Germany today has approximately thirty million excess population beyond what can be supported by agriculture alone. The eighty million Germans and Austrians in Central Europe today necessarily swing the balance of that continent. A solution must be found for their future peaceful existence and it is to the interest of the whole world that they should not be driven by stress of hardship into a nondemocratic and necessarily predatory habit of life." (Memorandum for the President, May 16, 1945)

In a further conversation with Mr. Truman on July 3, just before both men left for Potsdam, Stimson found that his views were fully shared by the White House. From this time forward American policy was more and more directed toward reconstruction of a denazified, demilitarized, but economically sound Germany. Unfortunately vestiges of the old attitude remained at lower levels. Still more unfortunately, the execution of American policy was necessarily dependent upon inter-Allied agreement, and in the two years that followed the Potsdam Conference of 1945 the difficulty of securing effective agreement became even more clear. The German question became part of a still larger and more complicated subject—American policy toward Soviet Russia.

NOTE: In 1948, when the issue over the Morgenthau plan had given way to a very different debate over the *control* and *use* of the resources of the Ruhr, it seemed important to remark that Stimson's position in 1944 and 1945 did not in any way commit him to support the reconstruction of Germany *as against* the reconstruction of France and other liberated countries. His general sympathies, indeed, ran in exactly the opposite direction. During his debate with Morgenthau and afterward he repeatedly made clear his belief that French claims upon Ruhr production deserved a most sympathetic hearing, and he believed too that France should share in the international control of the Ruhr. But he could not believe that the French interest, or any humane interest, would be served by a policy of deliberate destruction or by an attempt to make of Germany a land of permanent paupers.

3. THE CRIME OF AGGRESSIVE WAR

Concurrent with the struggle over the Morgenthau plan, and intertwined with it, was a debate over the proper treatment of the Nazi leaders. In this debate too Stimson was active, and because in his view the eventual result was a striking triumph for the cause of law and peace, his share in the matter deserves detailed attention.

One of the proposals in the Morgenthau memorandum of September 6 was that a list should be made of German archcriminals—men whose obvious guilt was generally recognized by the United Nations—and that upon capture and identification these men should be shot at once. Commenting on this proposal in his paper of September 9, Stimson wrote:

"The other fundamental point upon which I feel we differ is the matter of the trial and punishment of those Germans who are responsible for crimes and depredations. Under the plan proposed by Mr. Morgenthau, the so-called archcriminals shall be put to death by the military without provision for any trial and upon mere identification after apprehension. The method of dealing with these and other criminals requires careful thought and a well-defined procedure. Such procedure must embody, in my judgment, at least the rudimentary aspects of the Bill of Rights, namely, notification to the accused of the charge, the right to be heard and, within reasonable limits, to call witnesses in his defense. I do not mean to favor the institution of state trials or to introduce any cumbersome machinery but the very punishment of these men in a dignified manner consistent with the advance of civilization, will have all the greater effect upon posterity. Furthermore, it will afford the most effective way of making a record of the Nazi system of terrorism and of the effort of the Allies to terminate the system and prevent its recurrence.

"I am disposed to believe that at least as to the chief Nazi officials, we should participate in an international tribunal constituted to try them. They should be charged with offenses against the laws of the Rules of War in that they have com-

mitted wanton and unnecessary cruelties in connection with
the prosecution of the war. This law of the Rules of War has
been upheld by our own Supreme Court and will be the basis
of judicial action against the Nazis.

"Even though these offenses have not been committed
against our troops, I feel that our moral position is better if
we take our share in their conviction. Other war criminals
who have committed crimes in subjugated territory should be
returned in accordance with the Moscow Declaration to those
territories for trial by national military commissions having
jurisdiction of the offense under the same Rules of War. I
have great difficulty in finding any means whereby military
commissions may try and convict those responsible for excesses
committed within Germany both before and during the war
which have no relation to the conduct of the war. I would be
prepared to construe broadly what constituted a violation of
the Rules of War but there is a certain field in which I fear
that external courts cannot move. Such courts would be without jurisdiction in precisely the same way that any foreign
court would be without jurisdiction to try those who were
guilty of, or condoned, lynching in our own country."

The question of trial as against shooting was not decided at
Quebec, but Stimson heard from McCloy reports that the
President had there expressed himself as definitely in favor of
execution without trial. It seemed probable that this was only
a curbstone opinion, but it was deeply disturbing to the War
Department, and Stimson and McCloy promptly set up a
group of military lawyers to study in detail the possibilities
for a trial. After a month of study these lawyers reported to
the Secretary.

"Our meeting lasted for an hour and a half and was deeply
interesting. These men had reached the conclusion that besides
local tribunals to punish war crimes against the international
Rules of War, we could for the same purpose establish an
international tribunal if we wished it or mixed tribunals, the
latter to prosecute criminals whose criminal activities had
extended over several jurisdictions. . . . Colonel Bernays of
the JAGD gave an interesting talk on the possibility of bring-

ing charges against the whole scheme of Nazi totalitarian war, using for the promotion of its end methods of warfare which were in conflict with the established Rules of War. This was virtually upon the theory of a conspiracy and I then told them of my experience as United States Attorney in finding that only by [charging] conspiracy could we properly cope with the evils which arose under our complicated development of big business. In many respects the task which we have to cope with now in the development of the Nazi scheme of terrorism is much like the development of big business. It was a very interesting talk and carried my mind farther along the line which it has been following in connection with dealing with the German secret police and the forms of secret police itself among other nations." (Diary, October 24, 1944)

The concept of conspiracy became more and more, in Stimson's mind, the guide to a proper course in trying Nazi leaders. The advantages of showing the whole gigantic wickedness for what it was quite outweighed his initial distaste for a complex state trial, and he made his point not long after to the President. "I told him the story of the seventeen holes—the case which I tried against the American Sugar Refining Company. He was greatly interested in this and gave his very frank approval to my suggestion when I said that conspiracy with all of the actors brought in from the top to the bottom, or rather with representatives of all classes of actors brought in from top to bottom, would be the best way to try it and would give us a record and also a trial which would certainly persuade any onlooker of the evil of the Nazi system. In fact he was very nice about it." (Diary, November 21, 1944)

Meanwhile the War Department committee worked on, and in January its report was completed. In January, too, the President, shifting somewhat from his earlier view, appointed Judge Samuel Rosenman to study the question for him. Meeting with Rosenman, Joseph P. Davies, Attorney General Biddle, and others on January 18, "I was glad to find they were all in favor of legal action rather than political action against the head Nazis, and secondly, that in their study of the proper kind of legal action they were coming to the view which I have held from the first[3] that we had better stage up a big trial in which we can prove the whole Nazi conspiracy to wage a totalitarian war of aggression violating in its progress all of the regular rules which limit needless cruelty and destruction."

This was the tenor of the War Department's own recommendations, which Stimson signed "with great satisfaction" on January 21. Two days before, he had argued his position once more with Mr. Roosevelt, hoping to keep the President from any hasty decision at the forthcoming Yalta Conference. Stimson rehearsed to the President the views he shared with his committee and with Judge Rosenman and the Attorney General's office. He emphasized again the advantage of a trial as against political action. Mr. Roosevelt "assented to what I said but in the hurry of the situation I am not sure whether it registered." (Diary, January 19, 1945)

The last view of Mr. Roosevelt Stimson never knew, for when the final decision was taken in May another man was President, but after these meetings and recommendations of January there was never any serious question that the American Government favored a state trial. To Stimson's great surprise the principal opposition to legal proceedings came from the British, who for a long time urged direct military executions instead. But with firm French and Russian support, the American view prevailed, and in August, 1945, there was signed at London a four-power agreement chartering the International Tribunal which met at Nuremberg the following November. In the international negotiations which led to the London Charter Stimson had no part, but he watched with great admiration the work done for his country at London and later at Nuremberg by Mr. Justice Jackson.

Both during and after the Nuremberg trial there was a considerable debate in the United States and elsewhere over its legality. To Stimson it was not merely legal but so clearly

---

[3] "From the first" is not quite accurate; as a matter of fact Stimson was skeptical about the trying of war criminals on the charge of aggressive war when it was first suggested to him by his law partner, William Chanler. He thought it "a little in advance of international thought" (Memorandum to McCloy, November 28, 1944) and it was only after further consideration that he became an ardent advocate of the principle.

so that any other course would have been crassly illegal. From his retirement he wrote for *Foreign Affairs* a careful explanation of his view. The central argument of the article[4] represents so plainly his general attitude toward the international law of war that it is here quoted in part.

The principal complaint leveled against Nuremberg was that its charter dared to name aggressive war as a punishable crime. In Stimson's view this was its greatest glory, and to this point he addressed the bulk of his argument:

"The defendants at Nuremberg were leaders of the most highly organized and extensive wickedness in history. It was not a trick of law which brought them to the bar; it was the 'massed angered forces of common humanity.' . . .

"The Charter of the Tribunal recognizes three kinds of crime, all of which were charged in the indictment: crimes against peace, war crimes, and crimes against humanity. There was a fourth charge, of conspiracy to commit one or all of these crimes. To me personally this fourth charge is the most realistic of them all, for the Nazi crime is in the end indivisible. Each of the myriad transgressions was an interlocking part of the whole gigantic barbarity. But basically it is the first three that we must consider. The fourth is built on them.

"Of the three charges, only one has been seriously criticized. . . . The charge of crimes against peace . . . has been the chief target of most of the honest critics of Nuremberg. It is under this charge that a penalty has been asked, for the first time, against the individual leaders in a war of aggression. It is this that well-intentioned critics have called '*ex post facto* law'."

The charge of *ex post facto* law rested on the indubitable fact that the Nuremberg proceeding was unprecedented. But Stimson argued that the climate of opinion in which the Nazis launched their war of aggression was also unprecedented. In the years after the First World War the community of nations had repeatedly denounced aggression as criminal, most conspicuously in the Kellogg-Briand Pact of 1928. "In the judgment of the peoples of the world the once proud title of 'conqueror' was replaced by the criminal epithet 'aggressor'."

It was of course quite true, as critics of Nuremberg argued,

[4] "The Nuremberg Trial: Landmark in Law," *Foreign Affairs*, January, 1947.

that before 1945 there was little to indicate that the "peoples of the world" were prepared to accept the capture and conviction of such aggressors as a legal duty. "But it is vitally important to remember that a legal right is not lost merely because temporarily it is not used. . . . Our offense was thus that of the man who passed by on the other side. That we have finally recognized our negligence and named the criminals for what they are is a piece of righteousness too long delayed by fear."

Then Stimson came to the heart of the matter.

"We did not ask ourselves, in 1939 or 1940, or even in 1941, what punishment, if any, Hitler and his chief assistants deserved. We asked simply two questions: How do we avoid war, and how do we keep this wickedness from overwhelming us? These seemed larger questions to us than the guilt or innocence of individuals. In the end we found an answer to the second question, but none to the first. The crime of the Nazis, against *us*, lay in this very fact: that their making of aggressive war made peace here impossible. We have now seen again, in hard and deadly terms, what had been proved in 1917—that 'peace is indivisible.' The man who makes aggressive war at all makes war against mankind. That is an exact, not a rhetorical description of the crime of aggressive war.

"Thus the Second World War brought it home to us that our repugnance to aggressive war was incomplete without a judgment of its leaders. What we had called a crime demanded punishment; we must bring our law in balance with the universal moral judgment of mankind. The wickedness of aggression must be punished by a trial and judgment. This is what has been done at Nuremberg.

"Now this is a new judicial process, but it is not *ex post facto* law. It is the enforcement of a moral judgment which dates back a generation. It is a growth in the application of law that any student of our common law should recognize as natural and proper, for it is in just this manner that the common law grew up. There was, somewhere in our distant past, a first case of murder, a first case where the tribe replaced the victim's family as judge of the offender. The tribe had learned that the deliberate and malicious killing of any human being was, and must be treated as, an offense against the whole community. The analogy is exact. All case law grows by new decisions, and where those new decisions match the conscience of the community, they are law as truly as the law of murder. They do not become *ex post facto* law merely because until the first decision and punishment comes, a man's only warning that he offends is in the general sense and feeling of his fellow men.

"The charge of aggressive war is unsound, therefore, only if the community of nations did not believe in 1939 that aggressive war was an offense. Merely to make such a suggestion, however, is to discard it. Aggression is an offense, and we all know it; we have known it for a generation. It is an offense so deep and heinous that we cannot endure its repetition.

"The law made effective by the trial at Nuremberg is righteous law long overdue. It is in just such cases as this one that the law becomes more nearly what Mr. Justice Holmes called it: 'the witness and external deposit of our moral life.'

"With the judgment of Nuremberg we at last reach to the very core of international strife, and we set a penalty not merely for war crimes, but for the very act of war itself, except in self-defense."

This was to Stimson the great accomplishment of Nuremberg, and after devoting some attention to other lesser aspects of its achievement, he returned to the same point, from a slightly different angle, in his concluding paragraphs. Not merely was aggression now a crime, but in a sense it was the only important crime connected with war. For in World War II it had been shown that there is not much restraint or humanity left in modern warfare, once the bloody contest has begun.

"We as well as our enemies have contributed to the proof that the central moral problem is war and not its methods, and that a continuance of war will in all probability end with the destruction of our civilization.

"International law is still limited by international politics, and we must not pretend that either can live and grow without the other. But in the judgment of Nuremberg there is affirmed the central principle of peace—that the man who makes or plans to make aggressive war is a criminal. A standard has been raised to which Americans, at least, must repair; for it is only as this standard is accepted, supported, and enforced that we can move onward to a world of law and peace."

4. PLANNING FOR RECONSTRUCTION

The treatment of Germany and her leaders was important, but still more important was the general framework of American policy toward the postwar world. In this larger framework, as in the matter of Germany itself, Stimson's work was that of an adviser representing the War Department in the nation's councils; he had of course no authority and no responsibility in the larger task of advancing the American position among divergent Allied views. But the interest of the War Department and his own deep concern with foreign affairs combined to lead him during 1945 to the framing of a fairly comprehensive position on American policy. This position, constantly including as basic elements his long-standing insistence on friendship with Great Britain and recognition of economic reality, involved three additional general principles: America must participate in world affairs; America must be strong and secure; and America must get along with her wartime allies. Illustrations of his interpretation of each of these three principles were not lacking in 1944 and 1945.

As Secretary Hull again and again emphasized in his regular meetings with Stimson, the critical question of the postwar period was whether or not the United States would truly become a participating and effective member of the world community. Uncertain as the path to peace might be, it seemed clear that the decision of 1920 had led up a blind alley; the bankruptcy of isolationism was evident.

Upon the proper nature and extent of future American participation in world affairs there was less agreement. Stimson inclined to agree with Hull that here, as in the peace treaties, economics was central. America must so organize her trade and her foreign finance that the world might achieve the economic stability which had never been approached after 1918. In long-range terms, this meant a constant effort to expand American foreign trade, and especially American imports, by the kind of policy so valiantly begun by Mr. Hull twelve years before. When the Reciprocal Trade Agreements Act was extended in May, 1945, Stimson warmly congratulated President Truman. "I told him that I had always regarded these treaties as the fundamental basis for our postwar condition and that I thoroughly shared his views and was greatly relieved at the good size of the vote." (Diary, May 27, 1945)

Though proper long-range trade policy seemed the fundamental requirement, Stimson's thinking during the last year of the war was largely directed toward the more pressing immediate problems of reconstruction and rehabilitation. The relief operations directed by Army civil affairs officers in some areas and UNRRA officials in others he thoroughly approved in principle, but in looking ahead he believed the main difficulty to lie nearer home—in American unawareness of the scale of help required by the prostrated nations in war areas. In his approach to this difficulty Stimson found himself once again differing somewhat from other administration leaders.

Mr. Roosevelt and his advisers were thoroughly alive to the bitter need for American assistance existing in Allied countries, and particularly in the case of Great Britain they were determined that this help must be provided. British needs, eloquently explained by Prime Minister Churchill, were a major subject of discussion at Quebec in September, 1944, and Mr. Roosevelt returned to Washington determined to plan for and furnish further American assistance. But to Stimson's alarm he appeared to intend using the Lend-Lease Act for this purpose. Although possibly legal, such a course seemed to Stimson most unwise, and at the Cabinet meeting on October 13 he explained his position:

"I got involved enough to say that the only point that I thought came my way in that was that, as one of the members in the debate before the congressional committee for the original Lend-Lease, I was a witness of the representations made to Congress and that I knew perfectly well that Congress had made the lend-lease appropriations on the representations that it was in aid of an actual war effort to help an ally who was actually fighting for us and not for the purpose of rehabilitating a nation which was not fighting or appropriations which were not, in other words, an aid to our own war effort. I therefore thought that if we were going to go into making use of lend-lease appropriations in the postwar period or when there was no longer any connection between them and the actual fighting of the recipient, we ought to consult Congress. I did not at all oppose the purpose but I thought it would be very dangerous to go ahead under the original authority which was aimed at another objective." (Diary, October 13, 1944)

In the end no significant postwar assistance was given under the alleged authority of Lend-Lease, but in Stimson's opinion the discussions looking toward this goal had the unfortunate effect of preventing adequate consideration of and preparation for a more forthright and farsighted approach to the same general goal. He would have preferred "a great act of statesmanship on the part of the President" (Diary, November 22, 1944) to close out the British lend-lease account, with its enormous balance in favor of the Americans, followed by a further act of statesmanship to provide help on a similar basis after the war. Such a course would obviously have required "a great effort of education," but it would have had the advantage of proceeding in an atmosphere of war, instead of in the cooler and more cautious time of 1946, when a somewhat cold-blooded British loan was with great difficulty passed through Congress. But Stimson was forced to admit that in part this was hindsight, for it was not until well after 1944 that he came to a full appreciation of the desperate nature of the British economic position.

That not only Britain but all of Europe would need large-scale American help was wholly clear to Stimson by July, 1945, however, after he had seen, on his way to Potsdam, the devastation left by the war. This was a challenge larger than that of Germany, or even Great Britain—it involved the very survival of Europe. In a memorandum submitted to the President on July 22 he summarized his view of American responsibility in the situation. In this paper he tied the German question in with the problem of Europe as a whole.

"I am impressed with the great loss in economic values on

the Continent, but even more with the loss in widespread moral values which destruction and war conditions have caused in Europe.

"We have immediate interests in a return to stable conditions—the elimination of distress conditions to ease our problems of administration and the speed and success of our redeployment. But our long-range interests are far greater and much more significant.

"One hope for the future is the restoration of stable conditions in Europe, for only thus can concepts of individual liberty, free thought, and free speech be nurtured. Under famine, disease, and distress conditions, no territory or people will be concerned about concepts of free speech, individual liberty, and free political action. All the opposite concepts flourish in such an atmosphere. If democratic interests are not given an opportunity to grow in western and middle Europe, there is little possibility they will ever be planted in Russian minds.

"I therefore urge . . . that Germany shall be given an opportunity to live and work; that controls be exercised over the German people only in so far as our basic objectives absolutely require, and that the ethnological *and economic* groupings of Germany should be disturbed only where considerations make it inescapable. We cannot be misled by the thought that because many plants, at least on our side of the line, exist in relative integrity, that German economy can readily be restored. I am satisfied that it cannot be unless there is a flow of commerce, establishment of transportation systems, and stable currency. The Russian policy on booty in eastern Germany, if it is as I have heard it reported, is rather oriental. It is bound to force us to preserve the economy in western Germany in close co-operation with the British, so as to avoid conditions in our areas which, in the last analysis, neither British nor American public opinion would long tolerate.

"Secondly, I urge that a completely co-ordinated plan be adopted for the economic rehabilitation of Europe as a whole; that in doing this, all the economic benefits which the United States can bestow, such as war surplus disposal, Export-Import Bank credits, etc., be channeled through one man and one agency. Our means must be concentrated in one agency in order to use all our power to achieve our ends. Diverse policy and diverse methods of distribution lead to competition in bestowal of favors and interfere with the carrying out of the only effective and politically supportable program, namely, one of helping Europe to help herself.

"There are large food, fuel, and industrial sources in Europe, and, if all resources are marshaled, much can be done to achieve stability in Europe with the promptitude and in the degree necessary to preserve democratic governments. It does require a period of management in which I am convinced we have to take a part. I would recommend one United States agency as I have indicated, and I would feel that an Economic Council for Europe should be set up. The chairman should be an American, in whose hands, subject to the authority of the President and pursuant to the directions of the central United States agency just recommended, would be vested the disposition in Europe of all benefits flowing from the United States. Other members of the Council would consist of the representatives of other contributing powers who would be similarly authorized. They should act in close liaison with the Control Council for Germany, and their duties should be, over a limited period, to assist the governments of Europe *to help themselves* in the restoration of stable conditions."

In the two years that followed his submission of this memorandum Stimson saw no reason to alter the essentials of the recommendations it contained. The surface aspect of the situation changed as the immediate postwar period passed and American war assets on the spot were largely liquidated. But the need for American assistance continued—and his estimate of the quantity of assistance needed was if anything increased by the passage of time.

5. A STRONG AMERICA

The difficulty of achieving popular understanding of America's place in the modern world was a favorite subject for Stimson's meetings with Secretary Hull, and sometimes when they had exhausted their stock of epithets for isolationism, they would shift their fire through a wide arc and take aim at the "fuzzy-minded idealists." To both men the world in which the United States was called to participate was the real world, fully equipped with problems and difficulties, and not an abstraction waiting for Good Will to give it life in a New Age of Lasting Peace. To Stimson as Secretary of War it was especially disturbing to note that very often the people who talked most persuasively about American responsibility for peace were the ones who seemed least aware of any connection between this responsibility and the maintenance of American strength. His own view was entirely different; he could not conceive of an effective United States except as a nation equipped with the military establishment required for a leading power. Twice in 1945 there arose questions which drew from him clear statements of this position.

On June 15, 1945, Stimson appeared before the Committee on Postwar Military Policy of the House of Representatives to testify in favor of peacetime universal military training. The argument he there developed was his final judgment on a subject to which he had given thirty years of study. Much of his statement was of course devoted to the specific advantages of universal training as a method of maintaining effective national defense, and another large section was given over to an attack on the notion that military training would lead to militarism. He also explained in some detail the incidental advantages which he had found for himself in military service and which he believed were found by most men. But the core of the argument was in a few paragraphs in the beginning; here he connected military preparedness with the maintenance of peace.

"I believe that a necessary foundation on which to build the security of the United States is a system of universal military training. And in saying this I intend the broadest meaning of the term 'security.' I mean not merely protection against the physical invasion of our territory. I mean the security which goes with the strong and tested character of the citizenship of a nation, giving to that nation a leadership among the peoples of the world and a well-founded respect for it on their part which swells its power and influence. . . .

"In the first place, let me speak of universal military training as necessary for the physical protection of our country and its people. Never in my long life have we lived in a world where the very civilization of humanity has become so broken and unsettled; where the methods of war have become so brutal and so far-reaching in their peril as today; and where the respect of civilized man for those constitutional safeguards of government, not to say even the traditions of religious and humanitarian regard of one group of human beings for another, have become so shaken. . . .

". . . And no matter how dearly we may desire to preserve our way of life by peaceful persuasion alone, no matter how earnestly we may deplore the resort by other nations to aggressive force to gain their ends, these attitudes of peaceful persuasion can never be a substitute for the physical means of our own self-preservation—certainly not in such a world as that we now live in. No nation is fit to assume responsibility for others unless it is capable of being responsible for itself.

"Universal military training is the fundamental basis of such security. No matter how complicated the weapons of war may become, no matter how necessary to the nation's future security are programs for scientific research and industrial mobilization, the disciplined, trained, and patriotic citizenry of a nation remain the bricks of the foundation upon which the other methods and means of security rest.

"But in the second place, beyond and above any responsibility attending her own sovereignty, there now attaches to the United States as a great world power a further duty. In a short span of years we have seen our nation emerge as a leading power of the world. It is worse than idle to blink the responsibility which goes with this position. Already in almost every international emergency which arises, the eyes of the other nations turn to us for leadership. Our country's retention in the years to come of a stature befitting such a position will depend in my judgment upon her possession of the balanced elements of greatness which now support her responsible position in the family of nations. Particularly she must retain her capacity effectively to discharge her obligations under the world peace organizations which are now in process of being formed. The ideals which inspired the world plan now being framed in San Francisco must be supported and made to work by methods of known efficacy—by the use of force in the last analysis if necessary to prevent the depredations of an aggressor.

"Again I speak from personal experience. From my service as Secretary of State during a period of national isolationism and irresponsibility for world affairs, I realize only too well the futility of what the Chinese call 'spears of straw' and 'swords of ice' when the first steps of a new war are seen approaching. In this disordered world, for decades to come, the success of a program for peace will depend upon the maintenance of sufficient strength by those who are responsible for that peace. To advocate any Dumbarton plan and then to shear ourselves of the power to carry it out would be even worse than our refusal to join the attempt at world organization in 1919. Although the objectives of a program for collective peace are loftier and more idealistic than the mere defense of national sovereignty, they take root in the same soil of national self-interest. The goal of each peace-loving nation is still its individual security, a goal now sought to be attained through the collective security of all nations.

"Thus to meet our obligation of bearing our full share in preserving world peace, a part of America's present military readiness should be retained."

At the end of his statement, he was asked a question by the committee chairman, Congressman Woodrum, which brought out a still stronger statement. Would he comment "in regard to the suggestion that has been made, that for the United States now, while the San Francisco Convention is laboring in the cause of setting up a world organization, to take any step of this kind would be not only an evidence of our lack of faith in their efforts, but would be construed as an overt act by our present allies and other nations."

Stimson replied that "to know that we are taking such a precautionary and preventive step against war . . . would have just the opposite effect; . . . it would show that we were in earnest. . . . The people who for a long time have got to preserve the peace are the people who have brought about the peace by the victories in this war. The fact that those people keep their armor girded on will be the best deterrent in the world against any one aggressor in the future, and such an aggressor would know, at the same time, that we had shared in forming this new organization at San Francisco and we were prepared to defend it and to make it work. The worst thing we did to break the chance of peace after the last war, and to tempt willful nations toward aggression, was to keep out.

"We did two things: We kept out of all efforts to organize, and we dissolved all our armies and took no precautions against a future war.

"It was those two things which made America—in quite a large share, in my opinion—responsible for what came afterward."

6. BASES AND BIG POWERS

More complex, and perhaps more significant, than his feelings on military training was Stimson's attitude on the vexed issue of American policy toward certain Pacific islands won from Japan during the Pacific war. In what way, if any, should American authority for these islands be subjected to the new systems of trusteeship under the United Nations? During the first months of 1945 there developed within the Government a considerable debate over this question.

The State Department, in preparing for the San Francisco Conference, wished to formulate a general American policy toward areas of the kind which under the League of Nations had been "mandates"—areas in which colonial people not ready for self-government were governed by member nations accountable for their stewardship to the League. It was the hope of President Roosevelt that the mandate principle, exercised by the League only in a limited number of places, most of them territories formerly owned by Imperial Germany, might now be extended so far as possible to all colonial territories, *whether or not* these territories had been held by the enemy before the war.

Since most such territories were the legal property of other nations behind whose ownership rested all the national pride and self-interest associated with colonialism, it was evident that such a hope could hardly be effectively expressed by the United States unless she too were prepared to submit to the new principle. Accordingly it was planned that any islands retained by the United States in the Pacific should be held by her only in trusteeship from the United Nations.

In principle this proposal was unobjectionable, but to Stimson it seemed dangerously unrealistic; his own immediate object was to protect American interests in the Pacific islands, and he did not believe that any useful purpose was served by classing such islands with colonial areas containing large populations and considerable economic resources. "They [the Pacific islands] do not really belong in such a classification. Acquisition of them by the United States does not represent an attempt at colonization or exploitation. Instead it is merely the acquisition by the United States of the necessary bases for the defense of the security of the Pacific for the future world. To serve such a purpose they must belong to the United States with absolute power to rule and fortify them. They are not colonies; they are outposts, and their acquisition is appropriate under the general doctrine of self-defense by the power which guarantees the safety of that area of the world."[5] To Stimson this proposition seemed beyond debate; World War II had made wholly evident the fact that the United States must be the principal guarantor of the peace of the Pacific, and it had also demonstrated the outstanding strategic significance of the scores of small atolls held before 1941 by the Japanese in the western Pacific. After World War I, ignoring the warnings of Army and Navy leaders, the American Government had permitted the western Pacific islands to be mandated to Japan, on assurances that they would not be fortified. The folly of this decision was written in blood. An equal error had been committed in the Four-Power Treaty of 1921, under which the United States had agreed not to add to the fortifications of the Philippines, and Stimson was insistent that there should this time be no such mistake. He had not himself understood in 1921 the dangers of such agreements; like the men who made the agreements, he had placed his faith in the sanctity of treaties. But as he explained to the American dele-

[5] Memorandum for the Secretary of State, January 23, 1945.

gates to San Francisco, in a meeting on April 17, he had had to learn of these errors at firsthand. "I pointed out that as Governor in 1928 it had been my unhappy position to go over the plans for the defense of Corregidor and to realize that the brave men on that island were deliberately being left there to a glorious but hopeless defense of the island. . . . We . . . shackled ourselves and placed our reliance upon treaties which the Japanese promptly broke, and I earnestly begged them [the delegates] never again to repeat that error. I then told them how in 1941 I was in office again and in the position where I could see the errors which I had pointed out ripen into their inevitable disaster. I stood in Washington helpless to reinforce and defend the Philippines and had to simply watch their glorious but hopeless defense. I said that I believed that we could under proper conditions introduce the trustee system even into these bases, but it must give us full control and full strategic rights for the protection of them." So long as the United States retained its vital interest in the western Pacific, and so long as American strength was the principal safeguard against aggression in that area, that strength must not be hamstrung by unconsidered idealism. The policemen must be armed.

A curious aspect of the debate within the Government was that no one seemed to deny that American interests in the islands under discussion must be protected. President Roosevelt was "just as keen as anybody else to take the full power of arming them and using them to protect the peace and ourselves during any war that may come, and for that reason his people at San Francisco will be trying to form a definition of trusteeships or mandates which will permit that to be done." (Diary, March 18, 1945) The difficulty with this approach, as Stimson saw it, was that it camouflaged the realities of the situation. "The State Department proposals were meticulously building up a world organization which was to be the trustee and were proposing that we should turn over these bases to this trustee and then take back the management of them and try to make the powers of management big enough to give us the power which we now hold from our efforts in the war." (Diary, March 30, 1945) Such a procedure seemed to Stimson pointlessly roundabout. He would have preferred to state plainly that the defense of strategic islands was essential to the United States and a definite advantage to all Pacific powers. "With that attitude properly demonstrated I feel sure that we could have met with no objection to retaining enough bases to secure our position in the Pacific. My point was that we had always stood for freedom and peace in the Pacific and we had waged this war to throw out an aggressor and to restore peace and freedom and everybody knew it; that these bases had been stolen by the aggressor, who had used them to attack us and destroy our power; that we had fought this war with much cost of life and treasure to capture these bases and to free from the threat of aggression all of the peace-loving nations of the Pacific. We had actually thus saved from threat Australia and the Philippines and we were engaged in the process of doing it to the East Indies and to China; that if we had called attention to all of this and then said that we proposed to hold the bases which we now had gained in this painful struggle as a means and for the purpose of protecting freedom and peace in the Pacific, no one would have objected. In other words, we should have announced our possession with a declaration of trust in which all peace-loving nations were the beneficiaries." (Diary, March 30, 1945)

The intragovernmental differences on trusteeships were safely resolved before the San Francisco Conference. It was agreed that no particular territories should be discussed, and in return the War and Navy Departments agreed that it would be practicable to devise a trusteeship system which would provide for the maintenance of United States military and strategic rights in the Pacific and elsewhere. As finally signed, the United Nations Charter contained only a general framework for the handling of trust territories; specific agreements on specific areas were left for later negotiation. In 1947 an agreement was signed which adequately safeguarded the American interest.

The real issue in the trusteeship question was one of attitude; both sides in the Government wanted the same results. They differed about the way of getting it. This same difference persisted in the much larger question of securing a successful peace settlement. However attractive it might be to think in terms of a world organization, the real guarantee of peace could only come from agreement among the major powers, and such agreement would be much more readily achieved if attention were not diverted from it to blueprints which must remain without effect unless guaranteed by the three great nations. On January 23, in a memorandum to Secretary Stettinius, Stimson explained this view in some detail.

"1. The Moscow Conference of November 1, 1943, contemplated two organizations: (a) 'A General International Organization based on the principle of the sovereign equality of all peace-loving states and open to membership by all such states, large and small' etc. (b) An interim consultative organization of the four large powers for 'maintaining international peace and security pending the re-establishment of law and order and the inauguration of a system of general security.'

"2. This recognized the self-evident fact that these large powers who have won the war for law and justice will be obliged to maintain the security of the world which they have saved during the time necessary to establish a permanent organization of the whole world, and for that purpose they will have to consult and decide on many questions necessary to the security of the world and primarily their own safety in establishing that security. I have always thought that this interim organization should be formal, subject to rules of consultation similar to Article XI of the old League, and actively at work until the world had gotten stabilized enough to establish and turn loose the large world organization which includes the small nations.

"3. The job of the four big nations is principally to establish a guarantee of peace in the atmosphere of which the world organization can be set going.

"This will necessarily include the settlement of all territorial acquisitions in the shape of defense posts which each of these four powers may deem to be necessary for their own safety in carrying out such a guarantee of world peace.

"4. For substantially this purpose, at the end of the last war President Wilson proposed a joint covenant of guarantee by

Britain and America of the security of France as the pillar of western Europe. But the mistake was made of not securing that guarantee before the second step of creating the League of Nations whose safety was in large part to be dependent upon such a guarantee. As a result the League of Nations lacked a foundation of security which ultimately proved fatal to it.

"5. I think we are in danger of making a similar mistake by attempting to formulate the Dumbarton organization before we have discussed and ironed out the realities which may exist to enable the four powers to carry out their mission, and I was much interested to read Senator Vandenberg's recent speech [of January 10, 1945] in which he took practically the same ground.

"6. Any attempt to finally organize a Dumbarton organization will necessarily take place in an atmosphere of unreality until these preliminary foundations are established. The attitude of the numerous minor nations who have no real responsibility but plenty of vocal power and logical arguments will necessarily be different from that of the large powers who have to furnish the real security. . . ."

The memorandum continued with specific references to the trusteeship problem, and then with a passage pointing out that Russian ideas and interests must also be considered. "She will claim that, in the light of her bitter experience with Germany, her own self-defense as a guarantor of the peace of the world will depend on relations with buffer countries like Poland, Bulgaria, and Rumania, which will be quite different from complete independence on the part of those countries."

And then Stimson re-emphasized his main point.

"For all these reasons I think we should not put the cart before the horse. We should by thorough discussion between the three or four great powers endeavor to settle, so far as we can, an accord upon the general area of these fundamental problems. We should endeavor to secure a covenant of guarantee of peace or at least an understanding of the conditions upon which such a general undertaking of mutual guarantee could be based.

"If there is a general understanding reached among the larger powers I do not fear any lack of enthusiasm on the part of the lesser fry to follow through with the world organization whenever a general meeting may be called.

"The foregoing constitutes a consideration which I believe to be fundamental yet it is no more than the common prudence one would exercise in preparing for the success of any general assembly or meeting in business or political life."

This insistence on the vital importance of achieving big-power agreement before entrusting the peace to an infant organization remained throughout 1945 and even afterward a cardinal point in Stimson's attitude toward world affairs. He believed that in general it was shared by President Roosevelt, although perhaps the President was less fearful than Stimson of the effects of too early a start with the United Nations Organization. Certainly this principle lay behind the President's constant and devoted effort to establish enduring friendship with Soviet Russia. And equally certainly the main block to Stimson's policy, as to the world of the United Nations later, lay in the peculiar difficulty of dealing with the Russians.

7. THE EMERGENT RUSSIAN PROBLEM

During the war two facts became quite apparent to Stimson from the American Army's dealings with Russia. One was that the Russians were, consciously or unconsciously, bad-mannered and irritating beyond the normal degree of permissible international effrontery. Trustfulness and courtesy in whatever quantity seemed to inspire little if any reciprocity in official dealings, however merry the receptions, dinners, and vodka parties. The balance of effort was strikingly illustrated when President Roosevelt hastened his death by traveling to the Crimea in order to meet with Stalin, who reported himself forbidden by his doctor to make a long voyage.

The second evident fact about Soviet Russia was her strength. The colossal achievement of the Soviet armies and the skill and energy of the Russian leaders were perfectly apparent to men like Stimson and Marshall who had spent many anxious hours in contemplation of the awful task of beating Nazi Germany if the Russians should go under. A nation which could do what the Russians did, after suffering the losses and the devastation inflicted by the invader in the first eighteen months of his attack, was a nation of whose strength and heart there could be no serious question.

Neither of these two facts particularly disturbed Stimson, for he was used to international bad manners, and he saw no reason for the United States to be upset by the fact of Russian strength. Diplomatic reports of 1943 and early 1944 gave reason to hope that in the future as in the past Russians and Americans could pursue their respective policies without clashing. Stimson was not disposed to contest the Russian claim that there must be no anti-Russian states along the Soviet borders, and pending their disproof he chose to accept as hopeful signs the constant Soviet assertions that the independence and integrity of states like Poland were a fundamental principle of Russian foreign policy.

Only one aspect of Soviet Russia gave him any deep concern. This was the absence of individual political freedom. The historic danger of authoritarian government, not only to its own citizens but also in any major power to other peoples as well, was a subject with which he was painfully familiar, and in the iron dictatorship of Russia he saw the greatest single threat to an effective postwar settlement. Still more disturbing was evidence that the secret police followed the flag and operated wherever the Russian Army penetrated. "Averell Harriman [then United States Ambassador to Russia] came in this morning and . . . as I listened to his account about the way in which the Russians were trying to dominate the countries which they are 'liberating' and the use which they are making of secret police in the process, my mind was cleared up a good deal on the necessity of beginning a campaign of education on the problem of the secret police in the postwar world. It very evidently is a problem upon the proper solution of which the success of our relations with Russia ultimately will largely depend. Freedom cannot exist in countries where the government uses a secret police to dominate its citizens, and there is nothing to choose between the Gestapo which the Germans have used and the OGPU which the Russians have historically used. Stalin recently promised his people a constitution with a bill of rights like our own, but he has not yet put it into execution. It seems to me now that . . . getting him to carry out this promised reform, which will necessarily mean the abolition of the secret police, lies at the foundation of our success. Harriman says that it will be practically impossible to get the Russians to do it for themselves just at present but that we ought certainly to prevent them from introducing [the secret police] into the countries which they are now invading, particularly Hungary. Hungary has not a Slavic population and I do not believe would willingly accept the methods of the OGPU. We should not allow them to be driven by the Russians into doing it. . . . The two agencies by which liberty and freedom have been destroyed in nations which grant too much power to their government now seem to me clearly to be (1) the control of the press and (2) the control of the liberty of the citizens through the secret police. The latter is the most abhorrent of the two." (Diary, October 23, 1944)

Although the question of freedom in Russia and freedom in nations surrounding her seemed steadily more significant to Stimson in the months that followed, he continued to believe that Mr. Roosevelt was wholly correct in trying to handle the postwar settlement on the basis of Big Three agreement. There seemed to him no doubt that such agreement was the essential prerequisite to true stability in the peace settlement, and he looked with favor on the President's method of direct bargaining. Hearing about Yalta from Stettinius, the new Secretary of State, Stimson was particularly pleased by "the increase in cordiality that has appeared between Stalin and the rest of us. This is lucky because we will need it. There are so many sources of friction between the three great nations now that there are liberated countries for them all to wiggle around in and rub up against each other." (Diary, March 13, 1945)

But in March and April, 1945, a series of episodes showed both Stalin's good humor and Russian "bad manners" in a striking light. None of these incidents was important in itself but messages arrived during each of them indicating "a spirit in Russia which bodes evil in the coming difficulties of the postwar scene." (Diary, March 17, 1945) First, the Russians showed suspicion and mistrust over Anglo-American negotiations for the surrender of the German forces in northern Italy. To Stimson it appeared that this as a strictly military surrender was a matter in which Russia had no more business than the United States would have had at Stalingrad, and President Roosevelt strongly agreed, but there was some disagreement in Anglo-American circles, Mr. Churchill particularly preferring to lean over backwards in correctness. The matter was finally settled on a compromise basis, but the tone and feeling on both sides were sharp. A similar sharpness developed in negotiations over prisoners, both Americans in the Russian lines and persons from Russian or Russian-occupied territory in American hands. Although there seemed to be little doubt that the ordinary Russian soldier and officer were friendly to liberated Americans, official obstructionism to American efforts to care for Americans was extremely irritating and finally led to a sharp telegram from the President to Stalin. At the same time the Russians indicated a keen interest in the "repatriation" of many men in American hands who showed no desire whatever to be handed over to Russian control, and the Americans were faced with the unpleasant alternative of offending a great ally or abandoning the great principle of political asylum.

In all these lesser matters Stimson was in favor of firmness. For a long time he had felt that the Americans tended to give way too easily on these smaller questions, leaving the Russians with the impression that they had only to be disagreeable to get what they wanted. Small-minded haggling was no part of Mr. Roosevelt's nature, and in the larger sense this was most fortunate, but it left lesser officials at a considerable disadvantage in trying to make co-operation mutual. This difficulty was by no means peculiar to dealings with the Russians, but there was a discernible tendency among the Russians to build their whole policy on the other fellow's good nature, and Stimson thought that toleration of such nonsense was foolish —he inclined to believe that Stalin was the sort of man with whom it was useful to speak bluntly.

Stimson, however, did not share the attitude of general impatience which came over the administration in the last

weeks of President Roosevelt's life and in the early days of
the Truman administration. Perhaps because he had not been
closely connected with any of the negotiations with Russia,
he did not feel the personal pique at unkept agreements and
efforts to overreach which affected the thinking of so many
who had dealings with the Soviets. Shortly after Mr. Roosevelt died it appeared that on two matters at least he had in his
last weeks wholly lost sympathy with the Russians and had
begun to follow a somewhat altered, 'firmer,' American
policy. The failure of the Russians to carry out the Yalta
provisions for a genuinely reconstructed Polish government
and the aggressive attitude of the Yugoslavs toward Trieste
had struck Mr. Roosevelt as wholly unjustified and deeply
disquieting; he had outlined policies designed to make clear
American disapproval of the Lublin Polish government and
American opposition to any Yugoslav coup in Trieste. Both
of these policies were inherited by Mr. Truman, and both
soon came before his advisers. In a meeting on April 23 the
question of Poland was discussed and the general sentiment
was strongly in favor of vigorous protest against the Soviet
failure to keep the Yalta agreement. Stimson's own reaction
was different; although he admitted that he was not fully
informed, he was very doubtful about the wisdom of too
'strong' a policy. "So I . . . told the President that I was very
much troubled by it. . . . I said that in my opinion we ought
to be very careful and see whether we couldn't get ironed
out on the situation without getting into a head-on collision. . . .
I . . . pointed out that I believed in firmness on the minor
matters where we had been yielding in the past and have said
so frequently, but I said that this [Polish problem] was too
big a question to take chances on; and so it went on. . . ."

On the question of Trieste Stimson took a similar position.
The core of his feeling here was that the Balkans and their
troubles were beyond the sphere of proper United States
action.[6] This had been the American position throughout the
war, and he saw no reason for any present change, although he

[6] This view Stimson revised in 1947; by then the whole international situation had
so changed that the Balkans were very much a United States problem; no longer able
to limit their participation to traditional areas, the Americans had inherited a new
responsibility from a weakened Great Britain.

relished as little as anyone else the proposal of Yugoslavian domination of Trieste. Fortunately it proved possible to take and hold Trieste without any important clash of arms.

Occurring as they did during the period of the San Francisco Conference, which was drawing up a charter for the permanent organization of the United Nations, such incidents as these were extremely unpleasant. To Stimson they seemed a further confirmation of his long-held belief that basic agreement among the major powers should be achieved *before* any new world organization was set up. Contemplating the embarrassment of the State Department as it faced the problem of excluding the Lublin government from San Francisco, together with the possibility that this exclusion might seriously damage Russo-American relations, he wrote in his diary: "Contrary to what I thought was the wise course, they have not settled the problems that lie between the United States and Russia and Great Britain and France, the main powers, by wise negotiations before this public meeting in San Francisco, but they have gone ahead and called this great public meeting of all the United Nations, and they have got public opinion all churned up over it and now they feel compelled to bull the thing through. Why, to me, it seems that they might make trouble between us and Russia in comparison with which the whole possibilities of the San Francisco meeting amount to nothing. . . . I have very grave anxiety as a result since then as to what will happen. I am very sorry for the President because he is new on his job and he has been brought into a situation which ought not to have been allowed to come in this way." (Diary, April 23, 1945)

And a further difficulty was that in those cases in which there *had* been prior negotiations, the American negotiator had not been sufficiently hard-boiled. "I think the meeting at Yalta was primarily responsible for it because it dealt a good deal in altruism and idealism instead of stark realities on which Russia is strong and now they have got tied up in this mess." And again: "Although at Yalta she [Russia] apparently agreed to a free and independent ballot for the ultimate choice of the representatives of Poland, yet I know very well from my experience with other nations that there are no nations[7] in the world except the U. S. and the U. K. which have a real idea of what an independent free ballot is." (Diary, April 23, 1945)

Stimson's own notion of the proper general policy was to reverse these two earlier tendencies: first, to aim at agreement between the major powers before placing any emphasis on the United Nations as a whole, and second, to negotiate carefully and in good temper, on facts and not theories, with the difficult Russians. "It seems to me that it is a time for me to use all the restraint I can on these other people who have been apparently getting a little more irritated. I have myself been in the various crises enough to feel the importance of firm dealing with the Russians but . . . what we want is to state our facts with perfectly cold-blooded firmness and not show any temper." (Diary, April 3, 1945)

This remained Stimson's attitude throughout the spring of 1945. But as the days passed, a new and important element entered into his thinking about Russia, and by midsummer it had become almost dominant, dwarfing lesser aspects of the problem.

---

[7] The phrase "no nations" was an evident exaggeration. Stimson had no intention of excluding the democracies of western Europe, for example, from his list of nations that understood the free ballot.

CHAPTER XXIII

The Atomic Bomb and the
Surrender of Japan

1. MAKING A BOMB

ON AUGUST 6, 1945, an atomic bomb was dropped by
an American Army airplane on the Japanese city of
Hiroshima. There was thus awfully announced to the world
man's mastery of a force vastly more deadly, and potentially
more beneficial too, than any other in human history. In the
months that followed, as Americans considered in mingled
pride and fear the extraordinary achievement of the free
world's scientists in combination with American engineers and
industry, there was much discussion of the Hiroshima attack.
As one of those largely concerned in this decision, Stimson at
length concluded that it would be useful "to record for all
who may be interested my understanding of the events which
led up to the attack." The paper which he published in February, 1947, in *Harper's Magazine*, contains a careful record of
his personal connection with this issue to which only occasional
comments need be added.

"It was in the fall of 1941 that the question of atomic energy
was first brought directly to my attention. At that time President Roosevelt appointed a committee consisting of Vice
President Wallace, General Marshall, Dr. Vannevar Bush,
Dr. James B. Conant, and myself. The function of this committee was to advise the President on questions of policy relating to the study of nuclear fission which was then proceeding
both in this country and in Great Britain. For nearly four years
thereafter I was directly connected with all major decisions of
policy on the development and use of atomic energy, and from

May 1, 1943, until my resignation as Secretary of War on September 21, 1945, I was directly responsible to the President for the administration of the entire undertaking; my chief advisers in this period were General Marshall, Dr. Bush, Dr. Conant, and Major General Leslie R. Groves, the officer in charge of the project. At the same time I was the President's senior adviser on the military employment of atomic energy.

"The policy adopted and steadily pursued by President Roosevelt and his advisers was a simple one. It was to spare no effort in securing the earliest possible successful development of an atomic weapon. The reasons for this policy were equally simple. The original experimental achievement of atomic fission had occurred in Germany in 1938, and it was known that the Germans had continued their experiments. In 1941 and 1942 they were believed to be ahead of us, and it was vital that they should not be the first to bring atomic weapons into the field of battle. Furthermore, if we should be the first to develop the weapon, we should have a great new instrument for shortening the war and minimizing destruction. At no time, from 1941 to 1945, did I ever hear it suggested by the President, or by any other responsible member of the government, that atomic energy should not be used in the war. All of us of course understood the terrible responsibility involved in our attempt to unlock the doors to such a devastating weapon; President Roosevelt particularly spoke to me many times of his own awareness of the catastrophic potentialities of our work. But we were at war, and the work must be done. I therefore emphasize that it was our common objective, throughout the war, to be the first to produce an atomic weapon and use it. The possible atomic weapon was considered to be a new and tremendously powerful explosive, as legitimate as any other of the deadly explosive weapons of modern war. The entire purpose was the production of a military weapon; on no other ground could the wartime expenditure of so much time and money have been justified. The exact circumstances in which that weapon might be used were unknown to any of us until the middle of 1945, and when that time came, as we shall presently see, the military use of atomic energy was connected with larger questions of national policy."

During these years, from 1941 to 1945, the atomic project occupied a gradually increasing proportion of Stimson's time. In addition to his duties in general supervision of the brilliant work of General Groves, he became chairman of a Combined Policy Committee, composed of British and American officials and responsible directly to the President and Prime Minister Churchill. The atomic undertaking was not solely American, although the managerial direction was exercised through American leaders working mainly with American resources. It was rather another and conspicuous example of co-operation between the United States and the British Commonwealth, in this instance represented by Great Britain and Canada, the latter being a critically important source of the necessary raw materials. In all these matters Stimson's direct agent was Bundy, who maintained constant contact with the work of General Groves and served as American secretary of the Combined Policy Committee.

A further responsibility faced by Stimson and his associates was that of securing the necessary appropriations from Congress. Until 1944 work on the atom was financed from funds elastically available from other appropriations, but as the expenditure increased, and the size of the gamble too, it was decided that direct appropriation would be necessary and that congressional leaders should be informed. Accordingly, in February, 1944, Stimson, Marshall, and Bush made their case before Speaker Rayburn and the two party leaders of the House of Representatives, Congressmen McCormack and Martin. With great courage and co-operation these leaders piloted the necessary appropriation through the House without public discussion. A meeting in June with Senators Barkley, White, Bridges, and Thomas of Oklahoma produced similar results in the Senate. Again in 1945 further large appropriations were obtained in the same manner. Although one or two members of Congress desired to investigate the enormous construction work in Tennessee and Washington, they were successfully held off, sometimes by their own colleagues and at least once by Stimson's direct refusal to permit such investigation. Similar difficulties were surmounted in arranging for Treasury handling of atomic funds and forestalling antitrust action against the Du Pont Company, whose executives must not be disturbed in their great labors for the construction of plants at Clinton and Hanford for a profit of one dollar.

"As time went on it became clear that the weapon would not be available in time for use in the European theater, and the war against Germany was successfully ended by the use of what are now called conventional means. But in the spring of 1945 it became evident that the climax of our prolonged atomic effort was at hand. By the nature of atomic chain reactions, it was impossible to state with certainty that we had succeeded until a bomb had actually exploded in a full-scale experiment; nevertheless it was considered exceedingly probable that we should by midsummer have successfully detonated the first atomic bomb. This was to be done at the Alamogordo Reservation in New Mexico. It was thus time for detailed consideration of our future plans. What had begun as a wellfounded hope was now developing into a reality.

"On March 15, 1945, I had my last talk with President Roosevelt. My diary record of this conversation gives a fairly clear picture of the state of our thinking at that time. I have removed the name of the distinguished public servant who was fearful lest the Manhattan (atomic) project 'be a lemon'; it was an opinion common among those not fully informed.

" 'The President . . . had suggested that I come over to lunch today. . . . First I took up with him a memorandum which he sent to me from ———— who had been alarmed at the rumors of extravagance in the Manhattan project. ———— suggested that it might become disastrous and he suggested that we get a body of 'outside' scientists to pass upon the project because rumors are going around that Vannevar Bush and Jim Conant have sold the President a lemon on the subject and ought to be checked up on. It was rather a jittery and nervous memorandum and rather silly, and I was prepared for it and I gave the President a list of the scientists who were actually engaged on it to show the very high standing of them and it comprised four Nobel Prize men, and also how practically every physicist of standing was engaged with us in the project. Then I outlined to him the future of it and when it was likely to come off and told him how important it was to get ready. I went over with him the two schools of thought that exist in respect to the future control after the war of this project, in case it is successful, one of them being the secret close-in attempted control of the project by those who control it now, and the other being the international control based upon freedom both of science and of access. I told him that those things must be settled before the first projectile is used and that he must be ready with a statement to come out to the people on it just as soon as that is done. He agreed to that. . . .'

"This conversation covered the three aspects of the question which were then uppermost in our minds. First, it was always necessary to suppress a lingering doubt that any such titanic undertaking could be successful. Second, we must consider the implications of success in terms of its long-range postwar effect. Third, we must face the problem that would be presented at the time of our first use of the weapon, for with that first use there must be some public statement."

In order to insure careful consideration of the extraordinary problems now presented, Stimson set up in April a committee "charged with the function of advising the President on the various questions raised by our apparently imminent success in developing an atomic weapon." This committee, known as the Interim Committee,[1] held discussions which "ranged over the whole field of atomic energy, in its political, military, and scientific aspects. . . . The committee's work included the drafting of the statements which were published immediately after the first bombs were dropped, the drafting of a bill for the domestic control of atomic energy, and recommendations looking toward the international control of atomic energy."

[1] "I was its chairman, but the principal labor of guiding its extended deliberations fell to George L. Harrison, who acted as chairman in my absence. . . . Its members were the following, in addition to Mr. Harrison and myself:

"James F. Byrnes (then a private citizen) as personal representative of the President.

"Ralph A. Bard, Under Secretary of the Navy.

"William L. Clayton, Assistant Secretary of State.

"Dr. Vannevar Bush, Director, Office of Scientific Research and Development, and president of the Carnegie Institution of Washington.

"Dr. Karl T. Compton, Chief of the Office of Field Service in the Office of Scientific Research and Development, and president of the Massachusetts Institute of Technology.

"Dr. James B. Conant, Chairman of the National Defense Research Committee, and president of Harvard University."

But the first and greatest problem was the decision on the use of the bomb—should it be used against the Japanese, and if so, in what manner?

The Interim Committee, on June 1, recommended that the bomb should be used against Japan, without specific warning, as soon as possible, and against such a target as to make clear its devastating strength. Any other course, in the opinion of the committee, involved serious danger to the major objective of obtaining a prompt surrender from the Japanese. An advisory panel of distinguished atomic physicists reported that "We can propose no technical demonstration likely to bring an end to the war; we see no acceptable alternative to direct military use."

"The committee's function was, of course, entirely advisory. The ultimate responsibility for the recommendation to the President rested upon me, and I have no desire to veil it. The conclusions of the committee were similar to my own, although I reached mine independently. I felt that to extract a genuine surrender from the Emperor and his military advisers, there must be administered a tremendous shock which would carry convincing proof of our power to destroy the Empire. Such an effective shock would save many times the number of lives, both American and Japanese, that it would cost.

"The facts upon which my reasoning was based and steps taken to carry it out now follow." The argument which follows represents the opinion held not only by Stimson but by all his senior military advisers. General Marshall particularly was emphatic in his insistence on the shock value of the new weapon.

2. THE ACHIEVEMENT OF SURRENDER

"The principal political, social, and military objective of the United States in the summer of 1945 was the prompt and complete surrender of Japan. Only the complete destruction of her military power could open the way to lasting peace.

"Japan, in July, 1945, had been seriously weakened by our increasingly violent attacks. It was known to us that she had gone so far as to make tentative proposals to the Soviet

Government, hoping to use the Russians as mediators in a negotiated peace. These vague proposals contemplated the retention by Japan of important conquered areas and were therefore not considered seriously. There was as yet no indication of any weakening in the Japanese determination to fight rather than accept unconditional surrender. If she should persist in her fight to the end, she had still a great military force.

"In the middle of July, 1945, the intelligence section of the War Department General Staff estimated Japanese military strength as follows: in the home islands, slightly under 2,000,-000; in Korea, Manchuria, China proper, and Formosa, slightly over 2,000,000; in French Indo-China, Thailand, and Burma, over 200,000; in the East Indies area, including the Philippines, over 500,000; in the by-passed Pacific islands, over 100,000. The total strength of the Japanese Army was estimated at about 5,000,000 men. These estimates later proved to be in very close agreement with official Japanese figures.

"The Japanese Army was in much better condition than the Japanese Navy and Air Force. The Navy had practically ceased to exist except as a harrying force against an invasion fleet. The Air Force had been reduced mainly to reliance upon Kamikaze, or suicide, attacks. These latter, however, had already inflicted serious damage on our seagoing forces, and their possible effectiveness in a last ditch fight was a matter of real concern to our naval leaders.

"As we understood it in July, there was a very strong possibility that the Japanese Government might determine upon resistance to the end, in all the areas of the Far East under its control. In such an event the Allies would be faced with the enormous task of destroying an armed force of five million men and five thousand suicide aircraft, belonging to a race which had already amply demonstrated its ability to fight literally to the death.

"The strategic plans of our armed forces for the defeat of Japan, as they stood in July, had been prepared without reliance upon the atomic bomb, which had not yet been tested in New Mexico. We were planning an intensified sea and air blockade, and greatly intensified strategic air bombing, through the summer and early fall, to be followed on November 1 by an invasion of the southern island of Kyushu. This would be followed in turn by an invasion of the main island of Honshu in the spring of 1946. The total U. S. military and naval force involved in this grand design was of the order of 5,000,000 men; if all those indirectly concerned are included, it was larger still."

(These plans did not bear any significant impress from Stimson, who was never directly concerned in the handling of Pacific strategy. In his view, however, they were wholly sound; he had been throughout 1944 and early 1945 an opponent of the contrary plan for a preliminary invasion of China, holding in the Pacific to the same general theory of the straight and heavy blow, with no diversions, which he had advocated for the European war.)

"We estimated that if we should be forced to carry this plan to its conclusion, the major fighting would not end until the latter part of 1946, at the earliest. I was informed that such operations might be expected to cost over a million casualties, to American forces alone. Additional large losses might be expected among our allies and, of course, if our campaign were successful and if we could judge by previous experience, enemy casualties would be much larger than our own.

"It was already clear in July that even before the invasion we should be able to inflict enormously severe damage on the Japanese homeland by the combined application of 'conventional' sea and air power. The critical question was whether this kind of action would induce surrender. It therefore became necessary to consider very carefully the probable state of mind of the enemy, and to assess with accuracy the line of conduct which might end his will to resist.

"With these considerations in mind, I wrote a memorandum for the President, on July 2, which I believe fairly represents the thinking of the American Government as it finally took shape in action. This memorandum was prepared after discussion and general agreement with Joseph C. Grew, Acting Secretary of State, and Secretary of the Navy Forrestal, and when I discussed it with the President, he expressed his general approval."

This memorandum was originally prompted not by the problem of atomic energy but by the American desire to achieve a Japanese surrender without invading the home islands. The distinction is an important one, and Stimson thought it worth noting that the germ of the memorandum, from which the Potsdam ultimatum later developed, was in a meeting at the White House on June 18 at which final plans for the invasion of Japan were approved. The inclusion of civilian advisers at this meeting was a return to the procedure which Franklin Roosevelt had abandoned in 1942, and the presence of Stimson and McCloy, combined with President Truman's insistent desire to be sure that there was no alternative to invasion, was the beginning of the political actions which so greatly assisted in obtaining surrender.

"July 2, 1945

"Memorandum for the President.

PROPOSED PROGRAM FOR JAPAN

"1. The plans of operation up to and including the first landing have been authorized and the preparations for the operation are now actually going on. This situation was accepted by all members of your conference on Monday, June 18.

"2. There is reason to believe that the operation for the occupation of Japan following the landing may be a very long, costly, and arduous struggle on our part. The terrain, much of which I have visited several times, has left the impression on my memory of being one which would be susceptible to a last ditch defense such as has been made on Iwo Jima and Okinawa and which of course is very much larger than either of those two areas. According to my recollection it will be much more unfavorable with regard to tank maneuvering than either the Philippines or Germany.

"3. If we once land on one of the main islands and begin a forceful occupation of Japan, we shall probably have cast the die of last ditch resistance. The Japanese are highly patriotic and certainly susceptible to calls for fanatical resistance to repel an invasion. Once started in actual invasion, we shall in my opinion have to go through with an even more bitter finish fight than in Germany. We shall incur the losses incident to such a war and we shall have to leave the Japanese islands even more thoroughly destroyed than was the case with Germany. This would be due both to the difference in the Japanese and German personal character and the differences in the size and character of the terrain through which the operations will take place.

"4. A question then comes: Is there any alternative to such a forceful occupation of Japan which will secure for us the equivalent of an unconditional surrender of her forces and a permanent destruction of her power again to strike an aggressive blow at the 'peace of the Pacific'? I am inclined to think that there is enough such chance to make it well worth while our giving them a warning of what is to come and definite opportunity to capitulate. As above suggested, it should be tried before the actual forceful occupation of the homeland islands is begun and furthermore the warning should be given in ample time to permit a national reaction to set in.

"We have the following enormously favorable factors on our side—factors much weightier than those we had against Germany:

"Japan has no allies.

"Her navy is nearly destroyed and she is vulnerable to a surface and underwater blockade which can deprive her of sufficient food and supplies for her population.

"She is terribly vulnerable to our concentrated air attack upon her crowded cities, industrial and food resources.

"She has against her not only the Anglo-American forces but the rising forces of China and the ominous threat of Russia.

"We have inexhaustible and untouched industrial resources to bring to bear against her diminishing potential.

"We have great moral superiority through being the victim of her first sneak attack.

"The problem is to translate these advantages into prompt and economical achievement of our objectives. I believe Japan *is* susceptible to reason in such a crisis to a much greater extent than is indicated by our current press and other current comment. Japan is not a nation composed wholly of mad fanatics of an entirely different mentality from ours. On the contrary, she has within the past century shown herself to possess extremely intelligent people, capable in an unprecedentedly short time of adopting not only the complicated technique of Occidental civilization but to a substantial extent their culture and their political and social ideas. Her advance in all these respects during the short period of sixty or seventy years has been one of the most astounding feats of national progress in history—a leap from the isolated feudalism of centuries into the position of one of six or seven great powers of the world. She has not only built up powerful armies and navies. She has maintained an honest and effective national finance and respected position in many of the sciences in which we pride ourselves. Prior to the forcible seizure of power over her government by the fanatical military group in 1931, she had for ten years lived a reasonably responsible and respectable international life.

"My own opinion is in her favor on the two points involved in this question:

"a. I think the Japanese nation has the mental intelligence and versatile capacity in such a crisis to recognize the folly of a fight to the finish and to accept the proffer of what will amount to an unconditional surrender; and

"b. I think she has within her population enough liberal leaders (although now submerged by the terrorists) to be depended upon for her reconstruction as a responsible member of the family of nations. I think she is better in this last respect than Germany was. Her liberals yielded only at the point of the pistol and, so far as I am aware, their liberal attitude has not been personally subverted in the way which was so general in Germany.

"On the other hand, I think that the attempt to exterminate her armies and her population by gunfire or other means will tend to produce a fusion of race solidity and antipathy which has no analogy in the case of Germany. We have a national interest in creating, if possible, a condition wherein the Japanese nation may live as a peaceful and useful member of the future Pacific community.

"5. It is therefore my conclusion that a carefully timed

warning be given to Japan by the chief representatives of the United States, Great Britain, China, and, if then a belligerent, Russia, by calling upon Japan to surrender and permit the occupation of her country in order to insure its complete demilitarization for the sake of the future peace.

"This warning should contain the following elements:

"The varied and overwhelming character of the force we are about to bring to bear on the islands.

"The inevitability and completeness of the destruction which the full application of this force will entail.

"The determination of the Allies to destroy permanently all authority and influence of those who have deceived and misled the country into embarking on world conquest.

"The determination of the Allies to limit Japanese sovereignty to her main islands and to render them powerless to mount and support another war.

"The disavowal of any attempt to extirpate the Japanese as a race or to destroy them as a nation.

"A statement of our readiness, once her economy is purged of its militaristic influence, to permit the Japanese to maintain such industries, particularly of a light consumer character, as offer no threat of aggression against their neighbors, but which can produce a sustaining economy, and provide a reasonable standard of living. The statement should indicate our willingness, for this purpose, to give Japan trade access to external raw materials, but not longer any control over the sources of supply outside her main islands. It should also indicate our willingness, in accordance with our now established foreign trade policy, in due course to enter into mutually advantageous trade relations with her.

"The withdrawal from their country as soon as the above objectives of the Allies are accomplished, and as soon as there has been established a peacefully inclined government, of a character representative of the masses of the Japanese people. I personally think that if in saying this we should add that we do not exclude a constitutional monarchy under her present dynasty, it would substantially add to the chances of acceptance.

"6. Success of course will depend on the potency of the

warning which we give her. She has an extremely sensitive national pride, and, as we are now seeing every day, when actually locked with the enemy will fight to the very death. For that reason the warning must be tendered before the actual invasion has occurred and while the impending destruction, though clear beyond peradventure, has not yet reduced her to fanatical despair. If Russia is a part of the threat, the Russian attack, if actual, must not have progressed too far. Our own bombing should be confined to military objectives as far as possible."

HENRY L. STIMSON
Secretary of War.

Stimson's *Harper's* account went on:

"It is important to emphasize the double character of the suggested warning. It was designed to promise destruction if Japan resisted, and hope, if she surrendered.

"It will be noted that the atomic bomb is not mentioned in this memorandum. On grounds of secrecy the bomb was never mentioned except when absolutely necessary, and furthermore, it had not yet been tested. It was of course well forward in our minds, as the memorandum was written and discussed, that the bomb would be the best possible sanction if our warning were rejected.

"The adoption of the policy outlined in the memorandum of July 2 was a decision of high politics; once it was accepted by the President, the position of the atomic bomb in our planning became quite clear. I find that I stated in my diary, as early as June 19, that 'the last chance warning . . . must be given before an actual landing of the ground forces in Japan, and fortunately the plans provide for enough time to bring in the sanctions to our warning in the shape of heavy ordinary bombing attack and an attack of S-1.' S-1 was a code name for the atomic bomb.

"There was much discussion in Washington about the timing of the warning to Japan. The controlling factor in the end was the date already set for the Potsdam meeting of the Big Three. It was President Truman's decision that such a warning should be solemnly issued by the U. S. and the U. K. from this meeting, with the concurrence of the head of the Chinese Government, so that it would be plain that *all* of Japan's principal enemies were in entire unity. This was done, in the Potsdam ultimatum of July 26, which very closely followed the above memorandum of July 2, with the exception that it made no mention of the Japanese Emperor.

"On July 28 the Premier of Japan, Suzuki, rejected the Potsdam ultimatum by announcing that it was 'unworthy of public notice.' In the face of this rejection we could only proceed to demonstrate that the ultimatum had meant exactly what it said when it stated that if the Japanese continued the war, 'the full application of our military power, backed by our resolve, will mean the inevitable and complete destruction of the Japanese armed forces and just as inevitably the utter devastation of the Japanese homeland.'

"For such a purpose the atomic bomb was an eminently suitable weapon. The New Mexico test occurred while we were at Potsdam, on July 16. It was immediately clear that the power of the bomb measured up to our highest estimates. We had developed a weapon of such a revolutionary character that its use against the enemy might well be expected to produce exactly the kind of shock on the Japanese ruling oligarchy which we desired, strengthening the position of those who wished peace, and weakening that of the military party.

"Because of the importance of the atomic mission against Japan, the detailed plans were brought to me by the military staff for approval. With President Truman's warm support I struck off the list of suggested targets the city of Kyoto. Although it was a target of considerable military importance, it had been the ancient capital of Japan and was a shrine of Japanese art and culture. We determined that it should be spared. I approved four other targets including the cities of Hiroshima and Nagasaki.

"Hiroshima was bombed on August 6, and Nagasaki on August 9. These two cities were active working parts of the Japanese war effort. One was an army center; the other was naval and industrial. Hiroshima was the headquarters of the Japanese Army defending southern Japan and was a major military storage and assembly point. Nagasaki was a major seaport and it contained several large industrial plants of great wartime importance. We believed that our attacks had struck cities which must certainly be important to the Japanese military leaders, both Army and Navy, and we waited for a result. We waited one day.

"Many accounts have been written about the Japanese surrender. After a prolonged Japanese Cabinet session in which the deadlock was broken by the Emperor himself, the offer to surrender was made on August 10. It was based on the Potsdam terms, with a reservation concerning the sovereignty of the Emperor."

This Japanese reservation precipitated a final discussion in Washington. For months there had been disagreement at high levels over the proper policy toward the Emperor. Some maintained that the Emperor must go, along with all the other trappings of Japanese militarism. Others urged that the war could be ended much more cheaply by openly revising the formula of "unconditional surrender" to assure the Japanese that there was no intention of removing the Emperor if it should be the desire of the Japanese people that he remain as a constitutional monarch. This latter view had been urged with particular force and skill by Joseph C. Grew, the Under Secretary of State, a man with profound insight into the Japanese character. For their pains Grew and those who agreed with him were roundly abused as appeasers.

Stimson wholly agreed with Grew's general argument, as the July 2 memorandum shows. He had hoped that a specific assurance on the Emperor might be included in the Potsdam ultimatum. Unfortunately during the war years high American officials had made some fairly blunt and unpleasant remarks about the Emperor, and it did not seem wise to Mr. Truman and Secretary of State Byrnes that the Government should reverse its field too sharply; too many people were likely to cry shame. Now, in August, the Americans were face to face with the issue they had dodged in previous months. The Japanese were ready to surrender, but, even after seeing in dreadful reality the fulfillment of Potsdam's threats, they required some assurance that the Potsdam Declaration "does not comprise any demand which prejudices the prerogatives of His Majesty as a Sovereign Ruler."

August 10 was hectic in Washington. Radio reports from Japan announced the surrender offer before official notification reached Washington by way of Switzerland. At nine o'clock Stimson was called to the White House where the President was holding a conference on the surrender terms. All those present seemed eager to make the most of this great opportunity to end the war, but there was some doubt as to the propriety of accepting the Japanese condition.

"The President then asked me what my opinion was and I told him that I thought that even if the question hadn't been raised by the Japanese we would have to continue the Emperor ourselves under our command and supervision in order to get into surrender the many scattered armies of the Japanese who would own no other authority and that something like this use of the Emperor must be made in order to save us from a score of bloody Iwo Jimas and Okinawas all over China and the New Netherlands. He was the only source of authority in Japan under the Japanese theory of the State." (Diary, August 10, 1945)

The meeting at the White House soon adjourned to await the official surrender terms. Meanwhile Secretary Byrnes drafted a reply to which Stimson gave his prompt approval. In a later meeting this masterful paper was accepted by the President; it avoided any direct acceptance of the Japanese condition, but accomplished the desired purpose of reassuring the Japanese.

The *Harper's* article continued:

"While the Allied reply made no promises other than those already given, it implicitly recognized the Emperor's position by prescribing that his power must be subject to the orders of the Allied supreme commander. These terms were accepted on August 14 by the Japanese, and the instrument of surrender was formally signed on September 2, in Tokyo Bay. Our great objective was thus achieved, and all the evidence I have seen indicates that the controlling factor in the final Japanese decision to accept our terms of surrender was the atomic bomb."

After the *Harper's* article was published, Stimson found

that some of his friends retained certain doubts about the atomic decision, believing that it was based on an incorrect appreciation of the Japanese attitude. They asked whether the use of the bomb might not have been avoided if the American Government had been fully aware in the spring and early summer of the strength of the Japanese will to surrender.

This question, in Stimson's view, was based on a double misunderstanding—first, of the meaning of war, and second, of the basic purpose of the American Government during this period.

The true question, as he saw it, was not whether surrender could have been achieved without the use of the bomb but whether a different diplomatic and military course would have led to an earlier surrender. Here the question of intelligence became significant. Interviews after the war indicated clearly that a large element of the Japanese Cabinet was ready in the spring to accept substantially the same terms as those finally agreed on. Information of this general attitude was available to the American Government, but as Stimson's own paper of July 2 clearly shows, it was certainly not the view of American leaders that the Japanese already considered themselves beaten. It is possible, in the light of the final surrender, that a clearer and earlier exposition of American willingness to retain the Emperor would have produced an earlier ending to the war; this course was earnestly advocated by Grew and his immediate associates during May, 1945. But in the view of Stimson and his military advisers, it was always necessary to bear in mind that at least some of Japan's leaders would seize on any conciliatory offer as an indication of weakness. For this reason they did not support Grew in urging an immediate statement on the Emperor in May. The battle for Okinawa was proceeding slowly and with heavy losses, and they feared lest Japanese militarists argue that such a statement was the first proof of that American fatigue which they had been predicting since 1941. It seemed possible to Stimson, in 1947, that these fears had been based on a misreading of the situation.

Yet he did not believe that any intelligence reports, short of a direct report that the Japanese were fully ready to surrender, would have changed the basic American attitude. No such report was made, and none could have been made, for it was emphatically not the fact that Japan had decided on surrender before August 6; forces in the Japanese government for and against surrender continued in balance until the tenth of August. There were reports of a weakening will to resist and of "feelers" for peace terms. But such reports merely stimulated the American leaders in their desire to press home on *all* Japanese leaders the hopelessness of their cause; this was the nature of warmaking. In war, as in a boxing match, it is seldom sound for the stronger combatant to moderate his blows whenever his opponent shows signs of weakening. To Stimson, at least, the only road to early victory was to exert maximum force with maximum speed. It was not the American responsibility to throw in the sponge for the Japanese; that was one thing they must do for themselves. Only on the question of the Emperor did Stimson take, in 1945, a conciliatory view; only on this question did he later believe that history might find that the United States, by its delay in stating its position, had prolonged the war.

The second error made by critics after the war, in Stimson's view, was their assumption that American policy was, or should have been, controlled or at least influenced by a desire to avoid the use of the atomic bomb. In Stimson's view this would have been as irresponsible as the contrary course of guiding policy by a desire to insure the use of the bomb. Stimson believed, both at the time and later, that the dominant fact of 1945 was war, and that therefore, necessarily, the dominant objective was victory. If victory could be speeded by using the bomb, it should be used; if victory must be delayed in order to use the bomb, it should *not* be used. So far as he knew, this general view was fully shared by the President and all his associates. The bomb was thus not treated as a separate subject, except to determine whether it should be used at all; once that decision had been made, the timing and method of the use of the bomb were wholly subordinated to the objective of victory; no effort was made, and none was seriously considered, to achieve surrender merely in order not to have to use the bomb. Surrender was a goal sufficient in itself, wholly transcending the use or nonuse of the bomb. And as it turned out, the use of the bomb, in accelerating the surrender, saved many more lives than it cost.

In concluding his *Harper's* article, Stimson considered briefly the question whether the atomic bombs had caused more damage than they prevented.

"The two atomic bombs which we had dropped were the only ones we had ready, and our rate of production at the time was very small. Had the war continued until the projected invasion on November 1, additional fire raids of B-29's would have been more destructive of life and property than the very limited number of atomic raids which we could have executed in the same period. But the atomic bomb was more than a weapon of terrible destruction; it was a psychological weapon. In March, 1945, our Air Forces had launched the first great incendiary raid on the Tokyo area. In this raid more damage was done and more casualties were inflicted than was the case at Hiroshima. Hundreds of bombers took part and hundreds of tons of incendiaries were dropped. Similar successive raids burned out a great part of the urban area of Japan, but the Japanese fought on. On August 6 one B-29 dropped a single atomic bomb on Hiroshima. Three days later a second bomb was dropped on Nagasaki and the war was over. So far as the Japanese could know, our ability to execute atomic attacks, if necessary by many planes at a time, was unlimited. As Dr. Karl Compton has said, 'it was not one atomic bomb, or two, which brought surrender; it was the experience of what an atomic bomb will actually do to a community, *plus the dread of many more*, that was effective.'[2]

"The bomb thus served exactly the purpose we intended. The peace party was able to take the path of surrender, and the whole weight of the Emperor's prestige was exerted in favor of peace. When the Emperor ordered surrender, and the small but dangerous group of fanatics who opposed him were brought under control, the Japanese became so subdued that the great undertaking of occupation and disarmament was completed with unprecedented ease."

[2] K. T. Compton, "The Atomic Bomb and the Surrender of Japan," *Atlantic Monthly*, January, 1947.

And then, in a "personal summary," Stimson reviewed the whole question as he had seen it in 1945.

"Two great nations were approaching contact in a fight to a finish which would begin on November 1, 1945. Our enemy, Japan, commanded forces of somewhat over 5,000,000 armed men. Men of these armies had already inflicted upon us, in our break-through of the outer perimeter of their defenses, over 300,000 battle casualties. Enemy armies still unbeaten had the strength to cost us a million more. *As long as the Japanese Government refused to surrender*, we should be forced to take and hold the ground, and smash the Japanese ground armies, by close-in fighting of the same desperate and costly kind that we had faced in the Pacific islands for nearly four years.

"In the light of the formidable problem which thus confronted us, I felt that every possible step should be taken to compel a surrender of the homelands, and a withdrawal of all Japanese troops from the Asiatic mainland and from other positions, before we had commenced an invasion. We held two cards to assist us in such an effort. One was the traditional veneration in which the Japanese Emperor was held by his subjects and the power which was thus vested in him over his loyal troops. It was for this reason that I suggested in my memorandum of July 2 that his dynasty should be continued. The second card was the use of the atomic bomb in the manner best calculated to persuade that Emperor and the counselors about him to submit to our demand for what was essentially unconditional surrender, placing his immense power over his people and his troops subject to our orders.

"In order to end the war in the shortest possible time and to avoid the enormous losses of human life which otherwise confronted us, I felt that we must use the Emperor as our instrument to command and compel his people to cease fighting and subject themselves to our authority through him, and that to accomplish this we must give him and his controlling advisers a compelling reason to accede to our demands. This reason furthermore must be of such a nature that his people could understand his decision. The bomb seemed to me to furnish a unique instrument for that purpose.

"My chief purpose was to end the war in victory with the

least possible cost in the lives of the men in the armies which I had helped to raise. In the light of the alternatives which, on a fair estimate, were open to us I believe that no man, in our position and subject to our responsibilities, holding in his hands a weapon of such possibilities for accomplishing this purpose and saving those lives, could have failed to use it and afterwards looked his countrymen in the face."

He might have added here a still more personal comment. In March he visited an Air Forces redistribution center in Florida. There he met and talked with men on their way to the Pacific after completing a term of duty in Europe. The impression he received was profound. These men were weary in a way that no one merely reading reports could readily understand. They would go to the Pacific, and they would fight well again, but after this meeting Stimson realized more clearly than ever that the primary obligation of any man responsible for and to these Americans was to end the war as quickly as possible. To discard or fail to use effectively any weapon that might spare them further sacrifice would be irresponsibility so flagrant as to deserve condign punishment. Paraphrasing Shakespeare (but with life and not death as his end), Stimson could have said, as he felt, that "He hates them who would upon the rack of this tough war stretch them out longer."

And yet to use the atomic bomb against cities populated mainly by civilians was to assume another and scarcely less terrible responsibility. For thirty years Stimson had been a champion of international law and morality. As soldier and Cabinet officer he had repeatedly argued that war itself must be restrained within the bounds of humanity. As recently as June 1 he had sternly questioned his Air Forces leader, wanting to know whether the apparently indiscriminate bombings of Tokyo were absolutely necessary. Perhaps, as he later said, he was misled by the constant talk of "precision bombing," but he had believed that even air power could be limited in its use by the old concept of "legitimate military targets." Now in the conflagration bombings by massed B-29's he was permitting a kind of total war he had always hated, and in recommending the use of the atomic bomb he was implicitly confessing that there could be no significant limits to the horror of modern war. The decision was not difficult, in 1945, for peace with victory was a prize that outweighed the payment demanded. But Stimson could not dodge the meaning of his action. The following were the last two paragraphs of his article:

"As I read over what I have written, I am aware that much of it, in this year of peace, may have a harsh and unfeeling sound. It would perhaps be possible to say the same things and say them more gently. But I do not think it would be wise. As I look back over the five years of my service as Secretary of War, I see too many stern and heart-rending decisions to be willing to pretend that war is anything else than what it is. The face of war is the face of death; death is an inevitable part of every order that a wartime leader gives. The decision to use the atomic bomb was a decision that brought death to over a hundred thousand Japanese. No explanation can change that fact and I do not wish to gloss it over. But this deliberate, premeditated destruction was our least abhorrent choice. The destruction of Hiroshima and Nagasaki put an end to the Japanese war. It stopped the fire raids, and the strangling blockade; it ended the ghastly specter of a clash of great land armies.

"In this last great action of the Second World War we were given final proof that war is death. War in the twentieth century has grown steadily more barbarous, more destructive, more debased in all its aspects. Now, with the release of atomic energy, man's ability to destroy himself is very nearly complete. The bombs dropped on Hiroshima and Nagasaki ended a war. They also made it wholly clear that we must never have another war. This is the lesson men and leaders everywhere must learn, and I believe that when they learn it they will find a way to lasting peace. There is no other choice."

CHAPTER XXIV

The Bomb and Peace with Russia

THE first reaction of the American people to the advent of atomic energy was a great feeling of pride and satisfaction in a colossal wartime achievement. The bomb which exploded over Hiroshima made it clear that the victory was at hand. But this reaction was quickly succeeded by others relating to the disquieting future. As Stimson put it on August 9:

"Great events have happened. The world is changed and it is time for sober thought. It is natural that we should take satisfaction in the achievement of our science, our industry, and our Army in creating the atomic bomb, but any satisfaction we may feel must be overshadowed by deeper emotions.

"The result of the bomb is so terrific that the responsibility of its possession and its use must weigh heavily on our minds and on our hearts. We believe that its use will save the lives of American soldiers and bring more quickly to an end the horror of this war which the Japanese leaders deliberately started. Therefore, the bomb is being used.

"No American can contemplate what Mr. Churchill has referred to as 'this terrible means of maintaining the rule of law in the world' without a determination that after this war is over this great force shall be used for the welfare and not the destruction of mankind."

This statement was the public expression of thoughts which had been for many months heavily on the minds of those familiar with the atomic project. When Stimson went to the White House on April 25, 1945, to discuss the atomic bomb with a President from whom the matter had hitherto been

kept secret, he took with him a memorandum which dealt
not so much with the military use of the bomb as with its
long-range political meaning.

MEMORANDUM DISCUSSED WITH THE PRESIDENT

April 25, 1945

"1. Within four months we shall in all probability have
completed the most terrible weapon ever known in human
history, one bomb of which could destroy a whole city.

"2. Although we have shared its development with the U.
K., physically the U. S. is at present in the position of controlling the resources with which to construct and use it and
no other nation could reach this position for some years.

"3. Nevertheless it is practically certain that we could not
remain in this position indefinitely.

"a. Various segments of its discovery and production are
widely known among many scientists in many countries, although few scientists are now acquainted with the whole
process which we have developed.

"b. Although its construction under present methods requires great scientific and industrial effort and raw materials,
which are temporarily mainly within the possession and knowledge of U. S. and U. K., it is extremely probable that much
easier and cheaper methods of production will be discovered
by scientists in the future, together with the use of materials
of much wider distribution. As a result, it is extremely probable that the future will make it possible to be constructed
by smaller nations or even groups, or at least by a large nation
in a much shorter time.

"4. As a result, it is indicated that the future may see a
time when such a weapon may be constructed in secret and
used suddenly and effectively with devastating power by a
willful nation or group against an unsuspecting nation or group
of much greater size and material power. With its aid even a
very powerful unsuspecting nation might be conquered within
a very few days by a very much smaller one. . . .

"5. The world in its present state of moral advancement

compared with its technical development would be eventually at the mercy of such a weapon. In other words, modern civilization might be completely destroyed.

"6. To approach any world peace organization of any pattern now likely to be considered, without an appreciation by the leaders of our country of the power of this new weapon, would seem to be unrealistic. No system of control heretofore considered would be adequate to control this menace. Both inside any particular country and between the nations of the world, the control of this weapon will undoubtedly be a matter of the greatest difficulty and would involve such thorough-going rights of inspection and internal controls as we have never heretofore contemplated.

"7. Furthermore, in the light of our present position with reference to this weapon, the question of sharing it with other nations and, if so shared, upon what terms, becomes a primary question of our foreign relations. Also our leadership in the war and in the development of this weapon has placed a certain moral responsibility upon us which we cannot shirk without very serious responsibility for any disaster to civilization which it would further.

"8. On the other hand, if the problem of the proper use of this weapon can be solved, we would have the opportunity to bring the world into a pattern in which the peace of the world and our civilization can be saved. . . ."

And it was already apparent that the critical questions in American policy toward atomic energy would be directly connected with Soviet Russia. Whatever might be the complications of domestic atomic policy, and whatever difficulties might arise in negotiations with noncommunist Allied nations, it seemed reasonable to believe that the overwhelming menace of uncontrolled atomic power would in these areas compel satisfactory agreement and effective controls. But in the case of Russia matters were wholly different. There was no assurance that the Russians would hasten to agree on controls, nor could any agreement including Russia be regarded with any great confidence unless it contained such far-reaching rights of inspection as to counterbalance (and perhaps, in Russian eyes, to undermine) the protective and fearsome secrecy of a police state.

Even the immediate tactical discussion about the bomb involved the Russians. Much of the policy of the United States toward Russia, from Teheran to Potsdam, was dominated by the eagerness of the Americans to secure a firm Russian commitment to enter the Pacific war. And at Potsdam there were Americans who thought still in terms of securing Russian help in the Pacific war. Stimson himself had always hoped that the Russians would come into the Japanese war, but he had had no part in the negotiations by which Franklin Roosevelt tried to insure this result, and in June, 1945, he was disturbed to find that a part of the Russian price was a Soviet lease of Port Arthur and Soviet participation with the Chinese in the control of the Manchurian railways. This agreement was accompanied by a Russian promise to leave the Chinese in full control of Manchuria, but in the light of the Polish situation Russian promises of this character no longer seemed reliable. Such an agreement was perhaps better than nothing, but it would be an irony indeed if a new Manchurian crisis should one day develop because of arrangements made during a war whose origins were in that very area.

The news from Alamogordo, arriving at Potsdam on July 16, made it clear to the Americans that further diplomatic efforts to bring the Russians into the Pacific war were largely pointless. The bomb as a merely probable weapon had seemed a weak reed on which to rely, but the bomb as a colossal reality was very different. The Russians may well have been disturbed to find that President Truman was rather losing his interest in knowing the exact date on which they would come into the war.

The Russians at Potsdam were not acting in a manner calculated to increase the confidence of the Americans or the British in their future intentions. Stalin expressed a vigorous and disturbing interest in securing bases in the Mediterranean and other areas wholly outside the sphere of normal Russian national interest, while Russian insistence on *de facto* control of Central Europe hardly squared with the principles of the Atlantic Charter to which the Russians had so firmly announced their adherence in early 1942. These extravagant demands were backed by the Red Army, which was daily increasing in its relative strength in Europe, as the Americans began their redeployment for the Pacific attack. Naturally, therefore, news of the atomic bomb was received in Potsdam with great and unconcealed satisfaction by Anglo-American leaders. At first blush it appeared to give democratic diplomacy a badly needed "equalizer."

Stimson personally was deeply disturbed, at Potsdam, by his first direct observation of the Russian police state in action. The courtesy and hospitality of the Russians was unfailing, but there was evident nonetheless, palpable and omnipresent, the atmosphere of dictatorial repression. Nothing in his previous life matched this experience, and it was not particularly heartening to know that the Soviet machine for the time being was operating to insure the comfort and safety of the Allied visitors. Partly at firsthand and partly through the reports of Army officers who had observed the Russians closely during the first months of the occupation, Stimson now saw clearly the massive brutality of the Soviet system and the total suppression of freedom inflicted by the Russian leaders first on their own people and then on those whose lands they occupied. The words "police state" acquired for him a direct and terrible meaning. What manner of men were these with whom to build a peace in the atomic age?

For the problem of lasting peace remained the central question. Any "equalizing" value of the atomic bomb could only be of short-range and limited value, however natural it might be for democratic leaders to be cheered and heartened by the knowledge of their present possession of this final arbiter of force. As Stimson well knew, this advantage was temporary.

But could atomic energy be controlled, he asked himself, if one of the partners in control was a state dictatorially and repressively governed by a single inscrutable character? Could there be *any* settlement of lasting value with the Soviet Russia of Stalin? With these questions and others crowding his mind, he wrote in Potsdam for the President a paper headed, "Reflections on the Basic Problems Which Confront

Us." It was a tentative and, as he later thought, an incomplete piece of work, presenting only one side of a many-sided question. But it was all right as far as it went.

The central concern of this paper was the Russian police state, and only secondly the atomic bomb. Stimson's first main point was that the present state of Russia, if continued without change, would very possibly in the end produce a war.

"1. With each international conference that passes and, in fact, with each month that passes between conferences, it becomes clearer that the great basic problem of the future is the stability of the relations of the Western democracies with Russia.

"2. With each such time that passes it also becomes clear that that problem arises out of the fundamental differences between a nation of free thought, free speech, free elections, in fact, a really free people, [and] a nation which is not basically free but which is systematically controlled from above by secret police and in which free speech is not permitted.

"3. It also becomes clear that no permanently safe international relations can be established between two such fundamentally different national systems. With the best of efforts we cannot understand each other. Furthermore, in an autocratically controlled system, policy cannot be permanent. It is tied up with the life of one man. Even if a measure of mental accord is established with one head the resulting agreement is liable to be succeeded by an entirely different policy coming from a different successor.

"4. Daily we find our best efforts for co-ordination and sympathetic understanding with Russia thwarted by the suspicion which basically and necessarily must exist in any controlled organization of men.

"5. Thus every effort we make at permanent organization of such a world composed of two such radically different systems is subject to frustration by misunderstandings arising out of mutual suspicion.

"6. The great problem ahead is how to deal with this basic difference which exists as a flaw in our desired accord. I believe we must not accept the present situation as permanent for the result will then almost inevitably be a new war and the destruction of our civilization."

It was easier to state the problem and insist that it be solved than to suggest any course likely to be effective. Stimson found some hope in the brave words of the Soviet Constitution of 1936. They were an indication that Stalin knew at least what freedom *ought* to mean. But they did not suggest any clear answer to the questions he then posed. "(a) When can we take any steps without doing more harm than good? (b) By what means can we proceed? (1) by private diplomatic discussion of the reasons for our distrust? (2) by encouraging open public discussions? (3) by setting conditions for any concessions which Russia may ask in respect to territorial concessions, loans, bases, or any other concessions?

"How far these conditions can extend is a serious problem. At the start it may be possible to effect only some amelioration of the local results of Russia's secret police state."

All these aspects of the Russian problem paled in meaning before the question of Russia and atomic energy. And in the last paragraph of his Potsdam reflections Stimson came to a gloomy conclusion.

"7. The foregoing has a vital bearing upon the control of the vast and revolutionary discovery of X [atomic energy] which is now confronting us. Upon the successful control of that energy depends the future successful development or destruction of the modern civilized world. The committee appointed by the War Department which has been considering that control has pointed this out in no uncertain terms and has called for an international organization for that purpose. After careful reflection I am of the belief that *no* world organization containing as one of its dominant members a nation whose people are not possessed of free speech, but whose governmental action is controlled by the autocratic machinery of a secret political police, can give effective control of this new agency with its devastating possibilities.

"I therefore believe that before we share our new discovery with Russia we should consider carefully whether we can do so safely under any system of control until Russia puts into effective action the proposed constitution which I have mentioned. If this is a necessary condition, we must go slowly in any disclosures or agreeing to any Russian participation whatsoever and constantly explore the question how our head-start in X and the Russian desire to participate can be used to bring us nearer to the removal of the basic difficulties which I have emphasized."

Returning from Potsdam Stimson found himself nearing the limits of his strength, and after two weeks made crowded by the atomic attacks and their announcement, followed by the surrender negotiations, he retreated from Washington for three weeks of rest. In the quiet of the Adirondacks he thought again about the atom and Russia. Twice McCloy came from Washington to talk with him, and at the other end of the secret telephone were Harrison and Bundy; the War Department civilian staff was thinking long and painful thoughts about the atomic triumph.

Stimson was worried. Granting all that could be said about the wickedness of Russia, was it not perhaps true that the atom itself, not the Russians, was the central problem? Could civilization survive with atomic energy uncontrolled? And was it practical to hope that the atomic "secret"—so fragile and short-lived—could be used to win concessions from the Russian leaders as to their cherished, if frightful, police state? A long talk with Ambassador Harriman persuaded Stimson that such a hope was unfounded; the Russians, said Harriman, would regard any American effort to bargain for freedom in Russia as a plainly hostile move. Might it not then be better to reverse the process, to meet Russian suspicion with American candor, to discuss the bomb directly with them and try to reach agreement on control? Might not trust beget trust; as Russian confidence was earned, might not the repressive— and aggressive—tendencies of Stalinism be abated? As he pondered these questions—and above all as he pondered a world of atomic competition—Stimson modified his earlier opinion and on September 11 he sent to the President a memorandum urging immediate and direct negotiations with the Russians looking toward a "covenant" for the control of the atom. With its covering letter, the memorandum is self-explanatory.

September 11, 1945

Dear Mr. President:

In handing you today my memorandum about our relations with Russia in respect to the atomic bomb, I am not unmindful of the fact that when in Potsdam I talked with you about the question whether we could be safe in sharing the atomic bomb with Russia while she was still a police state and before she put into effect provisions assuring personal rights of liberty to the individual citizen.

I still recognize the difficulty and am still convinced of the ultimate importance of a change in Russian attitude toward individual liberty but I have come to the conclusion that it would not be possible to use our possession of the atomic bomb as a direct lever to produce the change. I have become convinced that any demand by us for an internal change in Russia as a condition of sharing in the atomic weapon would be so resented that it would make the objective we have in view less probable.

I believe that the change in attitude toward the individual in Russia will come slowly and gradually and I am satisfied that we should not delay our approach to Russia in the matter of the atomic bomb until that process has been completed. My reasons are set forth in the memorandum I am handing you today. Furthermore, I believe that this long process of change in Russia is more likely to be expedited by the closer relationship in the matter of the atomic bomb which I suggest and the trust and confidence that I believe would be inspired by the method of approach which I have outlined.

Faithfully yours,
HENRY L. STIMSON
Secretary of War.

The President,
The White House.

MEMORANDUM FOR THE PRESIDENT

11 September 1945

Subject: Proposed Action for Control of Atomic Bombs.
"The advent of the atomic bomb has stimulated great mili-

tary and probably even greater political interest throughout the civilized world. In a world atmosphere already extremely sensitive to power, the introduction of this weapon has profoundly affected political considerations in all sections of the globe.

"In many quarters it has been interpreted as a substantial offset to the growth of Russian influence on the continent. We can be certain that the Soviet Government has sensed this tendency and the temptation will be strong for the Soviet political and military leaders to acquire this weapon in the shortest possible time. Britain in effect already has the status of a partner with us in the development of this weapon. Accordingly, unless the Soviets are voluntarily invited into the partnership upon a basis of co-operation and trust, we are going to maintain the Anglo-Saxon bloc over against the Soviet in the possession of this weapon. Such a condition will almost certainly stimulate feverish activity on the part of the Soviet toward the development of this bomb in what will in effect be a secret armament race of a rather desperate character. There is evidence to indicate that such activity may have already commenced.

"If we feel, as I assume we must, that civilization demands that some day we shall arrive at a satisfactory international arrangement respecting the control of this new force, the question then is how long we can afford to enjoy our momentary superiority in the hope of achieving our immediate peace council objectives.

"Whether Russia gets control of the necessary secrets of production in a minimum of say four years or a maximum of twenty years is not nearly as important to the world and civilization as to make sure that when they do get it they are willing and co-operative partners among the peace-loving nations of the world. It is true if we approach them now, as I would propose, we may be gambling on their good faith and risk their getting into production of bombs a little sooner than they would otherwise.

"To put the matter concisely, I consider the problem of our satisfactory relations with Russia as not merely connected with but as virtually dominated by the problem of the atomic bomb. Except for the problem of the control of that bomb, those relations, while vitally important, might not be immediately pressing. The establishment of relations of mutual confidence between her and us could afford to await the slow progress of time. But with the discovery of the bomb, they became immediately emergent. *Those relations may be perhaps irretrievably embittered by the way in which we approach the solution of the bomb with Russia. For if we fail to approach them now and merely continue to negotiate with them, having this weapon rather ostentatiously on our hip, their suspicions and their distrust of our purposes and motives will increase.*[1] It will inspire them to greater efforts in an all-out effort to solve the problem. If the solution is achieved in that spirit, it is much less likely that we will ever get the kind of covenant we may desperately need in the future. This risk is, I believe, greater than the other, inasmuch as our objective must be to get the best kind of international bargain we can—one that has some chance of being kept and saving civilization not for five or for twenty years, but forever.

"The chief lesson I have learned in a long life is that the only way you can make a man trustworthy is to trust him; and the surest way to make him untrustworthy is to distrust him and show your distrust.

"If the atomic bomb were merely another though more devastating military weapon to be assimilated into our pattern of international relations, it would be one thing. We could then follow the old custom of secrecy and nationalistic military superiority relying on international caution to prescribe the future use of the weapon as we did with gas. But I think the bomb instead constitutes merely a first step in a new control by man over the forces of nature too revolutionary and dangerous to fit into the old concepts. I think it really caps the climax of the race between man's growing technical power for destructiveness and his psychological power of self-control and group control—his moral power. If so, our method of approach to the Russians is a question of the most vital importance in the evolution of human progress.

"Since the crux of the problem is Russia, any contemplated action leading to the control of this weapon should be

[1] Italics added. Stimson later considered those sentences and one later passage to be the heart of the memorandum.

primarily directed *to* Russia. It is my judgment that the Soviet would be more apt to respond sincerely to a direct and forthright approach made by the United States on this subject than would be the case if the approach were made as a part of a general international scheme, or if the approach were made after a succession of express or implied threats or near threats in our peace negotiations.

"My idea of an approach to the Soviets would be a direct proposal after discussion with the British that we would be prepared in effect to enter an arrangement with the Russians, the general purpose of which would be to control and limit the use of the atomic bomb as an instrument of war and so far as possible to direct and encourage the development of atomic power for peaceful and humanitarian purposes. Such an approach might more specifically lead to the proposal that we would stop work on the further improvement in, or manufacture of, the bomb as a military weapon, provided the Russians and the British would agree to do likewise. It might also provide that we would be willing to impound what bombs we now have in the United States provided the Russians and the British would agree with us that in no event will they or we use a bomb as an instrument of war unless all three Governments agree to that use. We might also consider including in the arrangement a covenant with the U. K. and the Soviets providing for the exchange of benefits of future developments whereby atomic energy may be applied on a mutually satisfactory basis for commercial or humanitarian purposes.

"I would make such an approach just as soon as our immediate political considerations make it appropriate.

"*I emphasize perhaps beyond all other considerations the importance of taking this action with Russia as a proposal of the United States—backed by Great Britain but peculiarly the proposal of the United States. Action of any international group of nations, including many small nations who have not demonstrated their potential power or responsibility in this war would not, in my opinion, be taken seriously by the Soviets.*[2] The loose debates which would surround such proposal, if put before a conference of nations, would provoke

[2] Italics added; this was the most important point of all.

but scant favor from the Soviet. As I say, I think this is the most important point in the program.

"After the nations which have won this war have agreed to it, there will be ample time to introduce France and China into the covenants and finally to incorporate the agreement into the scheme of the United Nations. The use of this bomb has been accepted by the world as the result of the initiative and productive capacity of the United States, and I think this factor is a most potent lever toward having our proposals accepted by the Soviets, whereas I am most skeptical of obtaining any tangible results by way of any international debate. I urge this method as the most realistic means of accomplishing this vitally important step in the history of the world.

> "HENRY L. STIMSON
> "Secretary of War."

These opinions, which he urgently expressed again to the President and the Cabinet on the day of his retirement, were the ones with which Stimson left office. As an expression of his views in 1947, they were seriously incomplete. A major point of his September memorandum was that the best way to make a man trustworthy was to trust him. This point he publicly re-emphasized in his last press conference. But what if the man whose trust you sought was a cynical "realist" who did not choose to be your friend? What if Stalin and his lieutenants were in this final and essential test of purpose no different from Hitler? What if the police state were no transitional revolutionary device but a fixed and inevitable accompaniment of nationalistic aggression? Would trust and candor by themselves break down or even modify the menace to the world in such a case?

These questions and others like them acquired for Stimson new and pregnant meaning in the two years that followed his presentation of the September memorandum. The behavior of the Russians during this period filled him with astonishment and regret. Like many other Americans, he had met and talked with Stalin during the years of effective wartime alliance (at Potsdam in July, 1945). Like other Americans, he had received Stalin's cordial acquiescence in his general statement that Russia and the United States were natural friends and allies. But in the two years after Potsdam Russian policy everywhere was based on broken pledges, and the United States replaced Nazi Germany as the target of Communist abuse. Russian hostility to the Western democracies was not in the main a reaction to antecedent Western wickedness. It was the Russians who ended the wartime friendship.

Soviet threats against Greece and Turkey, Soviet aggression in Iran, and the maneuvers of Russian-dominated Communists everywhere raised deep and serious questions about the basic intentions of the Kremlin. It was a daring and imaginative democrat indeed who could ignore in 1947 the mountain of evidence supporting the hypothesis that Stalin and his associates were committed to a policy of expansion and dictatorial repression. In so far as it insufficiently emphasized this aspect of the Russian problem, Stimson's September memorandum was dangerously one-sided.

Yet that memorandum was not designed to present a complete policy, but only to urge a certain tactical procedure. Presented at a time when some Americans were eager for their country to browbeat the Russians with the atomic bomb "held rather ostentatiously on our hip," it was designed to present an alternative line, aiming at a great effort to persuade the Russians that, in a choice between two worlds and one, they could find more profit in the latter. Stimson had no desire to criticize the course actually followed by the United States between September and December, 1945, but he did not believe that this course represented precisely the policy and method he had in mind in presenting his September memorandum. This was not by any means the result of a purely American decision; the Russians continued to make it extremely difficult for any American negotiator to conduct the sort of bed-rock discussion of fundamental problems which Stimson was advocating. The good faith and honorable intentions of those charged with American policy in this period seemed to Stimson unquestionable. If he had a difference with them, it was in method and emphasis, and not in basic purpose. Nor could he claim with any certainty that his own policy would have been more successful. If there had been an immediate and direct effort, in September, 1945, to reach agreement with Russia on the control of atomic energy, would it have been successful? Stimson could not say. Much would have depended on the manner in which the attempt was made; there would have been required a clear understanding, detailed and definitive, of what was meant by the "covenant" Stimson proposed; such a covenant would surely have involved more than the mutual assurances that had been so quickly violated by the Russians after Yalta and Potsdam. In talking with the Russians about the atom it would have been necessary to "talk turkey." If these points were not clearly stated in the September memorandum, it was because at that time it was Stimson's primary object to turn the thoughts of his colleagues back to the great principle of direct negotiation on basic issues which had been so long pursued by Franklin Roosevelt, and upon which Stimson's whole experience in forty years of public service had led him to rely. If the Americans and the Russians could reach real agreement, face to face, on atomic energy, then the world could breathe more easily and turn back with renewed optimism to lesser questions. In 1947 Stimson was inclined to think the chances of a successful direct approach in 1945 had been smaller than he thought at the time; but the existence of any chance at all would have justified the attempt, so great was the objective at stake.

And even two years later he still believed that there was every reason to keep open wide the door to Russian-American agreement. The detailed plan for international control of atomic energy developed and advocated by the American Government he thoroughly approved. Yet he could not believe that in the United Nations Commission, in an atmosphere of charge and countercharge, with a dozen nations free to comment and amend, there was available to the United States the best means of winning Russian adherence to those proposals. The way to agreement was still in direct action.

But in 1947 he was no longer able to believe that American policy could be based solely on a desire for agreement with

Russia, and writing in the summer of 1947[3] he saw the proper line of policy as a sort of synthesis of his two memoranda of 1945. He dismissed as "naïve and dangerous" any refusal "to recognize the strong probability that one of our great and powerful neighbor nations is at present controlled by men who are convinced that the very course of history is set against democracy and freedom, as we understand those words."

He continued with an explanation of his unhappy conclusions: "We have been very patient with the Soviet Government, and very hopeful of its good intentions. I have been among those who shared in these hopes and counseled this patience. The magnificent and loyal war effort of the Russian people, and the great successful efforts at friendliness made during the war by President Roosevelt, gave us good reason for hope. I have believed—and I still believe—that we must show good faith in all our dealings with the Russians, and that only by so doing can we leave the door open for Russian good faith toward us. I cannot too strongly express my regret that since the early spring of 1945—even before the death of Mr. Roosevelt—the Soviet Government has steadily pursued an obstructive and unfriendly course. It has been our hope that the Russians would choose to be our friends; it was and is our conviction that such a choice would be to their advantage. But, for the time being, at least, those who determine Russian policy have chosen otherwise, and their choice has been slavishly followed by Communists everywhere.

"No sensible American can now ignore this fact, and those who now choose to travel in company with American Communists are very clearly either knaves or fools. This is a judgment which I make reluctantly, but there is no help for it. I have often said that the surest way to make a man trustworthy is to trust him. But I must add that this does not always apply to a man who is determined to make you his dupe. Before we can make friends with the Russians, their leaders will have to be convinced that they have nothing to gain, and everything to lose, by acting on the assumption

[3] "The Challenge to Americans," *Foreign Affairs*, October, 1947.

that our society is dying and that our principles are outworn. Americans who think they can make common cause with present-day communism are living in a world that does not exist."

But Stimson was not willing to accept the argument of extreme anti-Russians that only force would stop communism. "An equal and opposite error is made by those who argue that Americans by strong-arm methods, perhaps even by a 'preventive war,' can and should rid the world of the Communist menace. I cannot believe that this view is widely held. For it is worse than nonsense; it results from a hopeless misunderstanding of the geographical and military situation, and a cynical incomprehension of what the people of the world will tolerate from *any* nation. Worst of all, this theory indicates a totally wrong assessment of the basic attitudes and motives of the American people. Even if it were true that the United States now had the opportunity to establish forceful hegemony throughout the world, we could not possibly take that opportunity without deserting our true inheritance. Americans as conquerors would be tragically miscast."

He preferred a middle course. "In dealing with the Russians, both uncritical trust and unmitigated belligerence are impossible. There is a middle course. We do not yet know surely in what proportion unreasonable fears and twisted hopes are at the root of the perverted policy now followed by the Kremlin. Assuming both to be involved, we must disarm the fears and disappoint the hopes. We must no longer let the tide of Soviet expansion cheaply roll into the empty places left by war, and yet we must make it perfectly clear that we are not ourselves expansionist. Our task is to help threatened peoples to help themselves. . . .

"Soviet intransigence is based in very large part on the hope and belief that all noncommunist systems are doomed. Soviet policy aims to help them die. We must hope that time and the success of freedom and democracy in the Western world will convince both the Soviet leaders and the Russian people now behind them that our system is here to stay. This may not be possible; dictators do not easily change their hearts, and the modern armaments they possess may make it

hard for their people to force such a change. Rather than
be persuaded of their error, the Soviet leaders might in
desperation resort to war, and against that possibility we have
to guard by maintaining our present military advantages. We
must never forget that while peace is a joint responsibility,
the decision for war can be made by a single power; our
military strength must be maintained as a standing discouragement to aggression.

"I do not, however, expect the Russians to make war. I do
not share the gloomy fear of some that we are now engaged
in the preliminaries of an inevitable conflict. Even the most
repressive dictatorship is not perfectly unassailable from
within, and the most frenzied fanaticism is never unopposed.
Whatever the ideological bases of Soviet policy, it seems clear
that some at least of the leaders of Russia are men who have
a marked respect for facts. We must make it wholly evident
that a nonaggressive Russia will have nothing to fear from
us. We must make it clear, too, that the Western noncommunist world is going to survive in growing economic and
political stability. If we can do this, then slowly—but perhaps
less slowly than we now believe—the Russian leaders may
either change their minds or lose their jobs."

In such a policy atomic control must wait for a change of
attitude in Russia. Stimson continued to believe that "the riven
atom uncontrolled can only be a growing menace to us all,"
and that "upon us, as the people who first harnessed and made
use of this force, there rests a grave and continuing responsibility for leadership, turning it toward life, not death." He was
further convinced that "lasting peace and freedom cannot be
achieved until the world finds a way toward the necessary
government of the whole." But he was forced to the conclusion
also that these goals were dependent on Russian agreement.
"We cannot have world government or atomic control by
wishing for them, and we cannot have them, in any meaning-
ful sense, without Russia. If in response to our best effort there
comes no answer but an everlasting 'NO,' then we must go to
work in other fields to change the frame of mind that caused
that answer. We cannot ignore it."

But the core of this statement, published on Stimson's

eightieth birthday, was not his opinion of Russia, though that was what the press mainly noted. His central argument was directed once again, in hope and challenge, to the American people. Drawing on his unhappy knowledge of past failures as well as his experience of success, he summarized his understanding of the central issues of American foreign policy. And he found the final question to be "one of will and understanding." The following excerpts may stand as a better summary of his position than any restatement would be.

"Americans must now understand that the United States has become, for better or worse, a wholly committed member of the world community. This has not happened by conscious choice; but it is a plain fact, and our only choice is whether or not to face it. For more than a generation the increasing interrelation of American life with the life of the world has outpaced our thinking and our policy; our refusal to catch up with reality during these years was the major source of our considerable share of the responsibility for the catastrophe of World War II.

"It is the first condition of effective foreign policy that this nation put away forever any thought that America can again be an island to herself. No private program and no public policy, in any sector of our national life, can now escape from the compelling fact that if it is not framed with reference to the world, it is framed with perfect futility. This would be true if there were no such thing as nuclear fission, and if all the land eastward from Poland to the Pacific were under water. Atomic energy and Soviet Russia are merely the two most conspicuous present demonstrations of what we have at stake in world affairs. The attitude of isolationism—political or economic—must die; in all its many forms the vain hope that we can live alone must be abandoned.

"As a corollary to this first great principle, it follows that we shall be wholly wrong if we attempt to set a maximum or margin to our activity as members of the world. The only question we can safely ask today is whether in any of our actions on the world stage we are doing enough. In American policy toward the world there is no place for grudging or limited participation, and any attempt to cut our losses by setting bounds to our policy can only turn us backward onto the deadly road toward self-defeating isolation.

"Our stake in the peace and freedom of the world is not a limited liability. Time after time in other years we have tried to solve our foreign problems with halfway measures, acting under the illusion that we could be partly in the world and partly irresponsible. Time after time our Presidents and Secretaries of State have been restrained, by their own fears or by public opinion, from effective action. It should by now be wholly clear that only failure, and its follower, war, can result from such efforts at a cheap solution.

"We have fresh before us the contrary example of our magnificent success in wartime, when we have not stopped to count the cost. I have served as Secretary of State in a time of frightened isolationism, and as Secretary of War in a time of brave and generous action. I know the withering effect of limited commitments, and I know the regenerative power of full action. I know, too, that America can afford it—as who does not know it, in the face of our record in the last seven years? . . .

"The essential question is one which we should have to answer if there were not a Communist alive. Can we make freedom and prosperity real in the present world? If we can, communism is no threat. If not, with or without communism, our own civilization would ultimately fail.

"The immediate and pressing challenge to our belief in freedom and prosperity is in western Europe. Here are people who have traditionally shared our faith in human dignity. These are the nations by whose citizens our land was settled and in whose tradition our civilization is rooted. They are threatened by communism—but only because of the dark shadows cast by the hopelessness, hunger, and fear that have been the aftermath of the Nazi war. Communism or no communism, menace or no menace, it is our simple duty as neighbors to take a generous part in helping these great peoples to help themselves.

"The reconstruction of western Europe is a task from which Americans can decide to stand apart only if they wish to desert every principle by which they claim to live. And, as a decision of policy, it would be the most tragic mistake in our history. We must take part in this work; we must take our full part; we must be sure that we do enough.

"I must add that I believe we should act quickly. The penalty of delay in reconstruction is to increase the size of the job and to multiply difficulties. We require a prompt and large-scale program. The Government must lead the way, but we who are private citizens must support that leadership as men in all parties supported help to our allies in 1941. The sooner we act, the surer our success—and the less it will cost us. . . .

"As we take part in the rebuilding of Europe, we must remember that we are building world peace, not an American peace. Freedom demands tolerance, and many Americans have much to learn about the variety of forms which free societies may take. There are Europeans, just as there are Americans, who do not believe in freedom, but they are in a minority, and . . . we shall not be able to separate the sheep from the goats merely by asking whether they believe in our particular economic and political system. Our co-operation with the free men of Europe must be founded on the basic principles of human dignity, and not on any theory that their way to freedom must be exactly the same as ours. We cannot ask that Europe be rebuilt in the American image. If we join in the task of reconstruction with courage, confidence, and good will, we shall learn—and teach—a lot. But we must start with a willingness to understand.

"The reconstruction of western Europe is the immediate task. With it we have, of course, a job at home. We must maintain freedom and prosperity here. This is a demanding task in itself, and its success or failure will largely determine all our other efforts. If it is true that our prosperity depends on that of the world, it is true also that the whole world's economic future hangs on our success at home. We must go forward to new levels of peacetime production, and to do this we must all of us avoid the pitfalls of laziness, fear, and irresponsibility. Neither real profits nor real wages can be permanently sustained—and still less increased—by anything but rising production.

"But I see no reason for any man to face the American future with any other feeling than one of confident hope. However grave our problems, and however difficult their solution, I do not believe that this country is ready to acknowledge that failure is foreordained. It is our task to disprove and render laughable that utterly insulting theory. Our future does not depend on the tattered forecasts of Karl Marx. It depends on us. . . .

"We need not suppose that the task we face is easy, or that all our undertakings will be quickly successful. The construction of a stable peace is a longer, more complex, and greater task than the relatively simple work of warmaking. But the nature of the challenge is the same. The issue before us today is at least as significant as the one which we finally faced in 1941. By a long series of mistakes and failures, dating back over a span of more than twenty years, we had in 1941 let it become too late to save ourselves by peaceful methods; in the end we had to fight. This is not true today. If we act now, with vigor and understanding, with steadiness and without fear, we can peacefully safeguard our freedom. It is only if we turn our backs, in mistaken complacence or mistrusting timidity, that war may again become inevitable.

"How soon this nation will fully understand the size and nature of its present mission, I do not dare to say. But I venture to assert that in very large degree the future of mankind depends on the answer to this question. And I am confident that if the issues are clearly presented, the American people will give the right answer. Surely there is here a fair and tempting challenge to all Americans, and especially to the nation's leaders, in and out of office."

CHAPTER XXV

The Last Month

WHEN Franklin Roosevelt died and Harry Truman succeeded him, Stimson like other members of the Cabinet submitted his resignation to the new President. Mr. Truman promptly and earnestly assured his Secretary of War that he was wanted not just temporarily but as long as he could stay, and Stimson and the War Department continued to receive from the White House the firm and understanding support to which they had become accustomed in the previous five years.

But already, in April, 1945, Stimson knew that he was in a race. Humanly, he wanted to stay at his job until victory was achieved. Just as humanly, he was beginning to tire. He was now nearly seventy-eight, and the accumulated strain of five years in Washington had begun to affect his heart. More and more he was forced to limit his effort, concentrating after April mainly on the policy questions presented by the atomic bomb. His personal staff and General Marshall combined to save him work wherever possible, but neither they nor he himself could desire that he should remain beyond the time when he could usefully serve.

The European war ended in May. In July Stimson went to Potsdam. On August 6 the first atomic bomb was dropped. The Japanese war seemed almost over. But on August 8 Stimson prepared to face retirement; his doctors had told him that he needed a complete rest and he went again to the White House to suggest his resignation. Mr. Truman told him to take his rest at once for a month if necessary, and then to report back for duty if he could. The war was almost over, he said, and he wanted Stimson with him at its end. Then on August

10 the surrender message came through. Stimson went away for a rest, but it was already clear that he was resting for the final ordeal of winding up his affairs in office, and not for further active service. On his return he formally requested that his resignation be accepted, and President Truman and he fixed September 21 as a suitable date. It would be his seventy-eighth birthday.

1. JUDGMENT ON THE ARMY

Between the tenth of August and the twenty-first of September Stimson was mainly occupied with two subjects: the future of the atomic bomb, which has been discussed in the last chapter, and the recognition by appropriate awards of his associates in the War Department. It was a time for casting up the balance and weighing the achievement of men who had served the Army in the war. Naturally too it was a time for looking over the achievement of the Army as a whole.

The Army of the United States in World War II was a triumphant compound of many elements—troops, commanders, staff, and high command. All of them, of course, were sustained and equipped by the unflagging spirit and the unparalleled productive strength of their countrymen at home, but as his mind turned back over five years of service it was not the weapons or the supplies that Stimson mainly pondered—it was the men. He would not admit that anything they had shown themselves to be had surprised him, but he was proud to say that they had measured fully up to his highest expectations.

The troops had been mobilized as if from nowhere, until in five crowded years a skeleton force of a quarter-million men became a fully armed and battle-trained victorious host of over eight million. This was America in arms—not four men in a hundred had been professional soldiers before. And the Army had been America's finest, losing nothing in comparison with its three great predecessors of the Revolution, the Civil War, and World War I.

The spirit and quality of these troops defied description, for as the war was unexampled in complexity, so the activities and accomplishments of American soldiers were of unnumbered variety. Yet everywhere that Stimson saw them certain things remained constant. They were young in heart and innocent, though they might have laughed with soldiers' oaths to hear themselves so called. They were technically skillful and self-confident. They were good in attack, brilliant in pursuit, and best of all, surprised, angry, and magnificent in defense. They hated the whole ghastly business of war, and sometimes they were sorry for themselves, yet they paid out their strength to the limit in a war which they imperfectly understood. On his visits abroad, a civilian from home, Stimson learned from every man he met that they were the most homesick troops in the world, and he knew how they felt, for twenty-five years before, with all the advantage in spirit of a volunteer catching up with twenty years of military hopes, he had felt exactly the same way.

For if there was one conviction deeper than another in the hearts of these soldiers, it was the belief behind each soldier's uniform that he was an individual to whom life offered special values. Thoughtless or thoughtful, ignorant or profoundly aware, schooled to the discipline of war and its terror or let off easily with work far from the enemy and free from danger, these men were individuals, and they knew it.

And the Army knew it, too. When first sergeants groaned about paper work and critics jeered at the administrative overhead of the Army, did they remember how much this burden was the product of the Army's recognition of the soldier as a unique man and a citizen? Allotments and insurance, point scores and specialties, mail service and the Red Cross, courts-martial, and inspectors general, chaplains and psychiatrists, all were the Army's instruments for wrestling with its colossal problem—to build and maintain a fighting machine composed of individuals.

In this task, of course, the most important tool was leadership. It was one of the regrets of Stimson's service as Secretary of War that he did not see more of the junior officers of the Army, the men from second lieutenant to colonel who led the troops in the field. Their record spoke for itself, and having served one war earlier in this echelon, Stimson knew well the magnitude of their accomplishment. These leaders, targets for the hasty abuse of all who disliked military authority, had successfully faced the great and challenging task of commanding men whom they could and should know as individuals.

The men whom Stimson was able to meet personally were mainly at a higher rank, starting with commanders of divisions and corps. This was the critical level of professional competence. Here it was required that the Army find men in considerable numbers equipped to handle arms and services in effective combination. More than that, it was necessary that these men be able to operate under constantly changing higher commanders—and, in the case of corps commanders, with constantly shifting subordinate formations—for it was a major element of the high commander's strength that he should be able to regroup his forces rapidly in accordance with a changing situation. This required a uniformly first-rate set of commanders. And such commanders were found. Stimson knew well how stern and trying had been the continuing problem of command at these middle levels in previous wars. No part of the Army's achievement in World War II impressed him more than its success in producing fighting major generals. On the leadership and professional skill of these men, of whom few received the public attention they deserved, rested much of the achievement of still higher commanders.

Yet the high command in the field well deserved such subordinates, and Stimson fully shared the nation's pride in MacArthur, Eisenhower, Devers, Bradley, Hodges, Patton, Clark, Krueger, Patch, Eichelberger, Simpson, and Stilwell. All of them he knew; he might have written for each one a personal citation of assessment and honor. But the important thing about these men was not their quality as individuals but rather that the Army met its greatest test with such a group of leaders. As individuals they needed no praise from Stimson. As a group they were proud proof that the American Army could produce field leaders of the highest caliber.

Supporting the field forces were supply commanders overseas and at home. The accomplishments of these men were of particular interest to Stimson. A Secretary of War could only watch in delighted admiration while General Patton set his tanks to run around in France "like bedbugs in a Georgetown kitchen." The problems of supply he could see more directly, for many of them came right back to him and to his immediate subordinates. From General Somervell downward, the supply officers of the Army seemed to him the worthy teammates of the field command; it was they who translated the prodigious economic strength of America into a new way of war which combined mobility with matériel so effectively that field campaigns were regularly and decisively won without troop superiority.

At all echelons was the staff. The staff work of the American Army came of age in World War II. What brilliant individuals had done in earlier wars was done this time by thousands of officers trained in the maturing tradition of Leavenworth. Nearly half a century before, Stimson had heard about staff work when it was only a bright idea in the minds of a few farsighted men led by Elihu Root. In World War I he had himself taken staff training at a time when many senior officers were still skeptical. The Army of his last five years in office had mastered the concept. Stimson felt safe in leaving the record of staff officers to the commanders; rare was the general who had been successful without superior staff work.

His own thoughts turned particularly to the staff in Washington. On the day before he retired he called three hundred of them together in order that he might pay his personal tribute to their work. Their vision, their insistence on teamwork, their ability to merge the individual interests of all arms and services in the great over-all mission of furnishing maximum fighting power to the front—these talents, applied with superior devotion to duty, in the face of the natural eagerness of the soldier for field assignment, had combined to produce staff work far better than that of the German and Japanese high commands.

And then there was his own civilian staff. Stimson himself wrote the citation for awards of the Distinguished Service Medal to Patterson, McCloy, Lovett, and Bundy. Their services to the Army and the nation were clear without further comment from him; so was the accomplishment of other close associates—Dorr, Harrison, Martyn, and Bowles. But again it was as a group that he thought these men important. These were men who put the job ahead of themselves and the common interest ahead of special pleading. What they had meant to Stimson himself he could not trust himself to put on paper. Whatever he had been able to do he had done with their devoted help.

Yet he knew that they joined with him in the firm conviction that the work of the Army in the war was essentially a record of the quality of the American Army officer. On September 20 he called to his office his civilian staff and a dozen of the senior War Department general officers, and he spoke informally in tribute to them all; his remarks to the soldiers were remembered and later reported by McCloy in a form that Stimson was proud to take as his own:

"Through these years I have heavily depended upon my civilian staff, but they and I know that it is to the work, thought, and devotion to duty you men have displayed that we owe the victory. You have lived up to the exacting standards of personal integrity and constant application which I first came to know and appreciate when I was formerly Secretary of War. You and those whom you represent have shown yourselves brave but not brutal, self-confident but not arrogant, and above all, you have prepared, guided, and wielded the mighty power of this great country to another victory without the loss of our liberties or the usurpation of any power."[1]

Though his own training and fighting had been as a ground soldier, the Army for which Stimson was Secretary was an Army which included the Air Forces, and he did not forget it. Had he been minded to take part in the pointless discussion as to who won the war, he could have argued as heartily for the fliers as for any single group. It seemed wiser to say simply that the Air Forces performed with magnificent courage and skill, under the imaginative and forceful direction of a splendid group of officers. Their commanding general, Henry H. Arnold, was a man for whom Stimson felt a special regard. He had shown vision combined with loyalty, force combined with tact, and a comprehension of the larger issues of strategy which gave his word great weight in the

[1] John J. McCloy, "In Defense of the Army Mind," *Harper's Magazine*, April, 1947.

councils of the War Department, and in the Joint and Combined Chiefs of Staff. In 1947 the Air Forces, full grown and eager for autonomy, separated from the Army. Stimson believed that under Lovett and Arnold this strapping young giant had learned well to fly alone.

2. THE CHIEF OF STAFF

The civilians might bow to the soldiers, and the soldiers to the civilians, the commanders might give honor to their troops, and the nation might give rousing greeting to returning generals, but to Stimson the greatness of the American Army of World War II was the projection of the greatness of George C. Marshall, and in the last weeks of his service he did what he could to make this opinion clear.

Marshall's professional skill was written in history. "His mind has guided the grand strategy of our campaigns. . . . It was his mind and character that carried through the trans-Channel campaign against Germany. . . . Similarly his views have controlled the Pacific campaign although there he has been most modest and careful in recognizing the role of the Navy. His views guided Mr. Roosevelt throughout.

"The construction of the American Army has been entirely the fruit of his initiative and supervision. Likewise its training. As a result we have had an army unparalleled in our history with a high command of supreme and uniform excellence. . . . With this Army we have won a most difficult dual war with practically no serious setbacks and astonishingly 'according to plan.' The estimate of our forces required has been adequate and yet not excessive. For instance, Marshall estimated against the larger estimates of others [including Stimson] that eighty-nine American divisions would suffice. On the successful close of the war, all but two of these divisions had been committed to action in the field. His timetables of the successive operations have been accurate and the close of the war has been ultimately achieved far sooner than most of us had anticipated.

"Show me any war in history which has produced a general

with such a surprisingly perfect record as his in this greatest
and most difficult war of all history."[2]

But mere professional skill would hardly have won General
Marshall his outstanding position. He had in addition shown
the greatest of force in advocacy, combined with a continual
insistence on unity.

"From the very beginning, he insisted on unity between the
services and among our allies. He realized that only by this
means could our combined resources be employed to the fullest advantage against the enemy. To achieve wholehearted co-
operation, he was always willing to sacrifice his own personal
prestige. To him agreement was more important than any
consideration of where the credit belonged. His firm belief
that unity could be preserved in the face of divergent opinions
was a decisive factor in planning throughout the war."

And the whole had been founded on the rock of character.

"General Marshall's leadership takes its authority directly
from his great strength of character. I have never known a
man who seemed so surely to breathe the democratic American spirit. He is a soldier, and yet he has a profound distaste
for anything that savors of militarism. He believes that every
able-bodied citizen has a personal responsibility for the nation's security and should be prepared to assume that responsibility whenever an emergency arises. But he is opposed to a
large standing Army as un-American.

"His trust in his commanders is almost legendary. During
the critical period of the Ardennes break-through no messages
went from the War Department to General Eisenhower
which would require his personal decision and reply. This is
standard practice with General Marshall. When one of his
commanders is in a tight spot, he does everything possible to
back him up. But he leaves the man free to accomplish his
purpose unhampered.

"He is likewise the most generous of men, keeping himself
in the background so that his subordinates may receive all
credit for duties well done.

"His courtesy and consideration for his associates, of whatever rank, are remarked by all who know him. His devotion

[2] Letter to President Truman, September 18, 1945.

to the nation he serves is a vital quality which infuses every-thing he does. During the course of a long lifetime, much of it spent in positions of public trust, I have had considerable ex-perience with men in Government. General Marshall has given me a new gauge of what such service should be. The destiny of America at the most critical time of its national existence has been in the hands of a great and good citizen. Let no man forget it."[3]

What it meant to Stimson personally to serve with such a man he had tried to express before a small gathering of War Department leaders on VE-day.

"I want to acknowledge my great personal debt to you, sir, in common with the whole country. No one who is thinking of himself can rise to true heights. You have never thought of yourself. Seldom can a man put aside such a thing as being the commanding general of the greatest field army in our history. This decision was made by you for wholly unselfish reasons. But you have made your position as Chief of Staff a greater one. I have never seen a task of such magnitude performed by man.

"It is rare in late life to make new friends; at my age it is a slow process but there is no one for whom I have such deep respect and I think greater affection.

"I have seen a great many soldiers in my lifetime and you, sir, are the finest soldier I have ever known."

3. THE COMMANDER IN CHIEF

One other name must be remembered in the Army's roll of honor for superb achievement in World War II. Stimson could not pretend to give a final judgment on the total labor of Franklin D. Roosevelt, but he was wholly certain that the Army had never had a finer Commander in Chief. In the tur-bulence of the war years there were many incidents on which Stimson and his President disagreed; the significant ones have been recorded in previous chapters. But throughout that period Stimson never wavered in his admiration for Mr. Roosevelt's great qualities, and his affection for the man who

---

[3] Press conference, September 19, 1945.

carried his burdens with such buoyant courage constantly increased. Against the great human leadership of the President minor differences and difficulties became insignificant, and Stimson, who did not hesitate to disagree with the President, never concealed his contempt for those who had allowed years of disagreement to ripen into general bitterness. Speaking at a Harvard commencement on June 11, 1942, he went out of his way to speak of Mr. Roosevelt to an audience which he suspected might contain a number of full-blown Roosevelt-haters.

"I think it is appropriate that here at the home of his Alma Mater I should say a word as to the leadership of that Harvard man who is the Commander in Chief of this great Army. It has been my privilege to observe him in time of conference and of crisis and of incessant strain and burden, of which he has cheerfully borne by far the heaviest share. His clarity of foresight and his unfailing grasp of the essential strategic factors of a world-wide struggle, you have all been able to follow. But only those who have been his lieutenants in the struggle can know the close personal attention with which he has vitalized every important decision. And only they can fully appreciate the courage and determination he has shown in time of threatened disaster, or the loyalty and consideration by which he has won the support of all of his war associates. Out of these characteristics comes the leadership which will achieve the final victory."

This opinion was reinforced during the next three years, and as he wrote for his diary on April 15, 1945, a summary of his feelings about Mr. Roosevelt, Stimson found that in the retrospect of nearly five years, "the importance of his leadership and the strong sides of his character loom up into their rightful proportions. He has never been a good administrator and the consequence of this has made service under him as a Cabinet officer difficult and often harassing for he has allowed himself to become surrounded by a good many men of small caliber who were constantly making irritating and usually selfish emergencies. But his vision over the broad reaches of events during the crises of the war has always been vigorous and quick and clear and guided by a very strong faith in the future of our country and of freedom, democracy, and humanitarianism throughout the world. Furthermore, on matters of military grand strategy, he has nearly always been sound and he has followed substantially throughout with great fidelity the views of his military and naval advisers. In the Army on no important occasion has he ever intervened with personal or political desires in the appointment of commanders. He has always been guided in this respect by the views of the Staff and myself. The Staff has recommended to him many thousands of general officers and he has accepted their selections practically without exception. I can only remember one or two where he has insisted upon appointments according to his own views and those were of minor importance. In these last respects I think he had been without exception the best war President the United States has ever had. . . . On the whole he has been a superb war President—far more so than any other President of our history. His role has not at all been merely a negative one. He has pushed for decisions of sound strategy and carried them through against strong opposition from Churchill, for example, and others. The most notable instance was where he accepted the views of our Staff in regard to the final blow at Germany across the Channel. . . . That was a great decision."

To Stimson personally the President's kindness and courtesy were unfailing. The two men had always been friendly, but Stimson knew that on his side at least the years of crisis and war had produced a feeling that far exceeded anything based merely on the official relations of a Cabinet officer to his chief. It might be irritating that Mr. Roosevelt was so good a talker that his Secretary of War was proud when he could claim to have been given 40 per cent of the time of their meetings for his own pearls of wisdom—but the President's talk was almost always heart-warming. And in dozens of little ways, with messages and personal notes, and Cabinet badinage, the two men, so different in many ways, showed each other their mutual respect and affection.

On the whole, Stimson was content to stand, in his judgment of President Roosevelt, on a letter written just after his death:

April 16, 1945

My dear Mrs. Roosevelt:

The sudden breaking off of the official ties which I have enjoyed with your husband and with you is a very great shock and grief to me. In the midst of it I find it very difficult to adequately express the affection and honor which I have held for you both. I have never received from any chief, under whom I have served, more consideration and kindness than I did from him, even when he was laboring under the terrific strain of a great war and in spite of the fact that I was a newcomer in his Cabinet and a member of another party. He thus made natural and easy relations which might otherwise have been difficult. Out of these his characteristics grew the very real and deep affection which I came to have for him.

He was an ideal war Commander in Chief. His vision of the broad problems of the strategy of the war was sound and accurate, and his relations to his military advisers and commanders were admirably correct. In the execution of their duties he gave them freedom, backed them up, and held them responsible. In all these particulars he seems to me to have been our greatest war President. And his courage and cheeriness in times of great emergency won for him the loyalty and affection of all who served under him.

Lastly and most important, his vision and interpretations of the mission of our country to help establish a rule of freedom and justice in this world raised a standard which put the United States in the unique position of world leadership which she now holds. Such facts must constitute priceless memories to you now in your sad bereavement. You may well hold your head high to have been his worthy helpmate at such a time and in such a task.

With very deep respect and affection, I am

Very sincerely yours,
HENRY L. STIMSON

4. THE END

With such memories of the men with whom he had served, Stimson prepared to leave Washington. Twice before he had left Cabinet office, each time convinced that he would not return. This was the third strike, and he was surely out now. But where before he had left with defeated administrations, to be sure with few regrets and no bitterness, now he was leaving at the triumphant climax of five years which had been "the high point of my experience, not only because of the heavy responsibility of guiding the nation's military establishment, but because of the opportunity they offered me to serve the nation in a great war. I shall always be grateful to Mr. Roosevelt for giving me that opportunity."[4]

On the twenty-first of September he went as usual to the War Department. There were still one or two letters to be signed and a few appointments to be kept. In the middle of the morning the members of his civilian staff came in to give him a silver tray in token of farewell. A little later he had a last talk with General Marshall. At twelve-thirty he went to lunch as usual in the General Officers' Mess and was there greeted by an enormous birthday cake—the Army had always remembered his birthdays. After lunch he went to keep an appointment at the White House and found that the President had sent for him to present him with the Distinguished Service Medal—"as Secretary of War from the beginning of the actual mobilization of the Army to the final victory over Japan, Henry Lewis Stimson gave the United States of America a measure of distinguished service exceptional in the history of the nation. . . ."

Then he attended his last Cabinet meeting.

"Immediately after the Cabinet meeting I said good-by to the President and to the Cabinet and hurried away to the Pentagon Building where I picked up Mabel and Colonel Kyle [his aide] who were waiting for me there and went to the Washington Airport. There to my surprise was a huge meeting of apparently all the general officers in Washington, lined up in two rows, together with my immediate personal civilian staff. It was a very impressive sight and a complete surprise to me. These men had been standing there for an hour because the time of my departure was supposed to have been at three o'clock, and the Cabinet meeting had lasted so long that I did

---

[4] Press conference, September 19, 1945.

not get there until four o'clock. The nineteen-gun salute was given as Mabel and I reached the two lines of generals and the band played 'Happy Birthday' and 'Auld Lang Syne.' Then after waving a general good-by and salute to the whole lines that we passed, I shook hands with Marshall and the top commanders at the end of the line and with my own civilian staff, and Mabel and I entered the plane together and took off for home."

AFTERWORD

THIS book has recorded forty years spent largely in public life; from this record others may draw their own conclusions, but it seems not unreasonable that I should myself set down in a few words my own summing up.

Since 1906 the problems of our national life have expanded in scope and difficulties beyond anything we ever dreamed of in those early times. It is a far cry from the problems of a young district attorney to the awesome questions of the atomic age.

Yet I do not wish that the clock could be turned back. Neither a man nor a nation can live in the past. We can go only once along a given path of time and we can only face in one direction, forward.

No one can dispute the progress made by the man of today from the prehistoric man—mentally, morally, and spiritually. No one can dispute the humanitarian progress made more recently, since those times before the age of steam and electricity, when man's growth was limited by sheer starvation, and the law of Malthus was an immediate reality.

It is true that the record of my own activity inevitably includes my conviction that in the last forty years the peoples and nations of the world have made many terrible mistakes; it is a sad thing that more than half of such a book as this should have to be devoted to the problem of warmaking. Yet even so, it is well also to reflect how much worse the state of mankind would be if the victorious peoples in each of the two world wars had not been willing to undergo the sacrifices which were the price of victory. I have always believed that the long view of man's history will show that his destiny on earth is progress toward the good life, even though that progress is based on sacrifices and sufferings which taken by themselves seem to constitute a hideous mélange of evils.

This is an act of faith. We must not let ourselves be engulfed in the passing waves which obscure the current of progress. The sinfulness and weakness of man are evident to anyone who lives in the active world. But men are also good and great, kind and wise. Honor begets honor; trust begets trust; faith begets faith; and hope is the mainspring of life. I have lived with the reality of war, and I have praised soldiers; but the hope of honorable faithful peace is a greater thing and I have lived with that, too. That a man must live with both together is inherent in the nature of our present stormy stage of human progress, but it has also many times been the nature of progress in the past, and it is not reason for despair.

I think the record of this book also shows my deep conviction that the people of the world and particularly our own American people are strong and sound in heart. We have been late in meeting danger, but not too late. We have been wrong but not basically wicked. And today with that strength and soundness of heart we can meet and master the future.

Those who read this book will mostly be younger than I, men of the generations who must bear the active part in the work ahead. Let them learn from our adventures what they can. Let them charge us with our failures and do better in their turn. But let them not turn aside from what they have to do, nor think that criticism excuses inaction. Let them have hope, and virtue, and let them believe in mankind and its future, for there is good as well as evil, and the man who tries to work for the good, believing in its eventual victory, while he may suffer setback and even disaster, will never know defeat. The only deadly sin I know is cynicism.

HENRY L. STIMSON

A NOTE OF EXPLANATION AND ACKNOWLEDGMENT

SINCE this book is rather unusual in its form, some explanation of the method of its construction may be of value to careful readers and students.

Although it is written in the third person, the book has no other aim than to present the record of Mr. Stimson's public life as he himself sees it. It is an attempt to substitute a joint effort for the singlehanded autobiography he might have undertaken if he were a little younger. It follows that we have made no effort at an external assessment, and in the writing I have sought not to intrude any views of my own, but rather to present Mr. Stimson's actions as he himself understands them. Thus objective praise and blame are equally absent; and for the latter, I fear, another student altogether will be necessary.

The major sources of the book are two: Mr. Stimson himself and his records. If I have held the laboring oar, Mr. Stimson has held the tiller rope, and the judgments and opinions expressed are always his. We have however tried to make a clear distinction between his views as they were during any given period and his present opinions, and wherever memory or desire has conflicted with the written record, we have followed the record.

The most important written record of Mr. Stimson's public life is his diary. It begins in 1910, but until 1930 it was not kept from day to day; entries were made only as time and inclination permitted. The first passages are a short undated description of the Saratoga Convention of 1910 and a long account of the period May, 1911 to March, 1913, written in the spring of the latter year. The diary continues with sporadic entries between 1915 and 1926. There is a separate manuscript volume containing entries made by Lieutenant Colonel Stimson overseas in 1918. The Nicaraguan episode and the Philippine year are both covered by separate volumes of almost daily notes and comment. But the first eighteen months of Mr. Stimson's term as Secretary of State have unfortunately no diary, though a short summary of this period was written in August, 1930.

It is in September, 1930 that the daily diary begins. In that month Mr. Stimson acquired a dictaphone which he kept at his home in Washington, and the diary contains an entry for very nearly every day in which he held public office from that time forward, whether he was in Washington or traveling abroad. In most cases these entries were made the same day or early the following morning. Very occasionally a period of two or three days passed before the entry could be dictated. The average daily entry is two or three typewritten pages in length, but on important occasions there are as many as ten. The diary for the last thirty months of the State Department years fills eleven bound volumes; that of the period 1940 to 1945 fills twenty. There are three volumes of occasional entries covering the period 1933 to 1940.

For the periods it fully covers, the diary is the basic document; it shows what was really in Mr. Stimson's mind at any given time as no files or correspondence can do. In studying the work of a modern public servant, whose signature must appear on thousands of documents each year, it is often important to know what he merely approved and what was a part of his own personal activity. The diary serves as an invaluable check on this point. It also contains expressions of opinion which did not find their way into any official documents or public statements.

The diary has been liberally quoted, and wherever the date of an entry is of any significance, it is given. Omissions are indicated by the usual dots; in most cases the omissions are merely for brevity; in a few, they involve comments or expressions which Mr. Stimson does not now wish to publish, either because he no longer agrees with himself or because they might cause unnecessary pain to men who were his associates and are his friends. One or two alterations have been made in order to clarify confusing entries, and these are noted with the usual brackets. And since the diary was typed from a dictaphone record, we have felt free to make occasional changes in punctuation and spelling. But in general, the diary text is astonishingly clean and clear, and the changes we have made are no more than elementary copyreading. We have made no effort to edit away the informal and conversational style of the usual entry.

Supplementing the diary, and serving as a substitute in those periods which are not covered by a daily record, are Mr. Stimson's papers—reports, speeches, books, memoranda, and correspondence. These have been extensively studied but I cannot claim to have "exhausted the material"; lawyers do not throw things away, and only the intelligent and sympathetic help of Miss Elizabeth Neary, Mr. Stimson's personal secretary, has made it possible for me to find my way in reasonable order through his papers. These materials too have been freely quoted in the text, and the source given wherever it seemed relevant.

In addition to the personal records, I have of course made extensive use of published materials dealing with events in which Mr. Stimson had a part. No bibliography is given, since these volumes usually have been consulted only to give me a working familiarity with matters with which Mr. Stimson was already intimately acquainted. But where these books, magazines, and newspapers are quoted, due acknowledgment is made, and we are indebted to all the publishers who have permitted quotation, both of other writings and of Mr. Stimson's own published work.

An even more important source of help has been the advice and comment of many of Mr. Stimson's intimate associates and colleagues. These men have had the kindness to read parts of the manuscript, and to their comments we owe many a correction and addition. Since most of them are men whose work is praised by Mr. Stimson in the text, I will not embarrass them by listing their names; it is fair to note, however, that almost without exception they have asked to have their own work minimized.

We owe a particular debt to the Department of the Army, whose officers have read and cleared Part III as free from violations of military security. We are still more in the debt of Dr. Rudolph A. Winnacker, without whose generous help this part of the book could hardly have been written at all. Dr. Winnacker's basic historical studies of the work of the Office of the Secretary of War broke the back of the job of getting a connected record of Mr. Stimson's activities between 1940 and 1945. His rounded study of the whole wartime work of the War Department's civilian leaders will contain much about Mr. Stimson which lack of space has forced us to omit, and a great deal more of the work of associates, which has not come within the scope of this book.

The making of a book involves many problems with which neither Mr. Stimson nor I was familiar when we began to work, and we have been greatly assisted by the sympathetic counsel of Mr. Stimson's old friend, associate, and neighbor Arthur W. Page. We have also had the constant co-operation of Mr. Cass Canfield and the experienced staff of Harper and Brothers. And there are many others who will note that in one place or another the book has taken a shape that marks our effort to follow their advice.

The final and fundamental source of the book, however, is Mr. Stimson himself. I have spent most of the last eighteen months as his guest, and daily we have met to work together. At first we simply talked for hours on end. Later, as I began to work with the written records, each point of interest was referred to Mr. Stimson, and all questions of meaning and emphasis were worked out together. The outline of each chapter was the product of joint consideration, and every section of the book, in its several drafts, has been read by Mr. Stimson and revised to meet his criticisms. From our discussions have come many observations and recollections which I have quoted, but in order to set off these remembered comments from passages found in contemporary written records, I have in these cases used the single and not the double quotation mark.

In every important sense, then, this is Mr. Stimson's book. It is his experience and his reflections which have informed its every page. In the nature of things, the responsibility for errors of fact and deficiencies of style is mine, but even in these areas his close attention to detail and his mastery of clear English have prevented many mistakes.

I must take this opportunity of expressing my indebtedness to the Senior Fellows of the Society of Fellows of Harvard University, who encouraged me to undertake this work under my appointment as a Junior Fellow. I have a special obligation also to Mr. John Finley, the Master of Eliot House, for his kindness in giving me "a room of one's own" when I have been in Cambridge. To be a Junior Fellow and a member of Eliot House is to enjoy an opportunity for undisturbed work and enlightening company which is not, in these postwar days, the general lot of students.

But of course my principal personal indebtedness is to Mr. and Mrs. Stimson, whose kindness and generosity, added to the intrinsic and absorbing interest of the task, have made this year and a half a landmark in my life.

McGEORGE BUNDY

BRIEF CHRONOLOGY OF
WORLD WAR II

This brief chronological listing of outstanding events is included as a guide for those readers who may be interested in checking Mr. Stimson's war service against the progress of the war at any given time. The listing makes no pretense of completeness and aims rather to reconstruct something of the headline atmosphere of those years.

1939	September	1	Germany invades Poland
		3	France and Great Britain declare war on Germany
	November	4	United States modifies Neutrality Act to permit cash-and-carry trade with belligerents
		30	Russia invades Finland
1940	March	12	Russo-Finnish war ends
	April	9	Germany invades Denmark and Norway
	May	10	Germany invades Holland, Belgium, and Luxembourg
		11	Winston Churchill becomes Prime Minister of the United Kingdom
		14–16	Germans break through French lines at Sedan
		28	Belgian King surrenders
		29	Retreat from Dunkirk begins
	June	10	Italy declares war on France and Great Britain
		14	Paris falls to Germans
		17	Petain asks for an armistice
		22	France surrenders
		24	Opening of Republican Convention which nominates Wendell Willkie for President
	September	3	Destroyer Deal announced
		15	British shoot down 175 German planes in Battle of Britain
		16	Selective Service Act of 1940 is signed
		27	Japan, Germany, and Italy sign Tri-Partite Pact aimed at United States
	October	28	Italy invades Greece
	November	5	Franklin Roosevelt re-elected President
	December	14	British victory over Italians in Egypt
1941	March	11	Lend-Lease Act signed
	April	3	Axis forces defeat British in North Africa

1941	April	6	Germany attacks Yugoslavia and joins in war on Greece
		18	Yugoslavian Army surrenders
		27	Athens falls
		29	British withdraw from Greece
	May	20	Germans execute air-borne invasion of Crete
		27	German battleship *Bismarck* sunk
	June	1	Crete conquered
		22	Germany attacks Russia
	July	7	United States troops land in Iceland
		24	Japan occupies southern Indo-China
		26	United States freezes Japanese assets
	August	9–12	Atlantic Charter meeting
		12	House extends Selective Service, 203–202
	September	11	President announces shoot-on-sight order to Atlantic naval forces
	October	19	Moscow in state of siege
	November	17	Neutrality Act amended to permit American merchant ships to carry arms to Allies
		19	Second British offensive in Libya begins
		26	Secretary Hull restates American position to Japanese emissaries
		27	War and Navy Departments send warnings of imminent war to Pacific commanders
	December	7	Japan attacks Pearl Harbor, declaring war on United States and Great Britain
		8	United States and Great Britain declare war on Japan
		11	Germany and Italy declare war on the United States and United States recognizes state of war with these countries
		11	Japanese land in the Philippines
		22	Winston Churchill arrives in Washington for first allied war council
1942	January	2	Japanese enter Manila
		2	"Declaration by United Nations" signed at White House
	February	15	Singapore falls
	March	6	Batavia, Java, falls
		17	General MacArthur arrives in Australia
	April	8	Second Axis offensive begins in Libya
		9	Bataan falls
		18	Carrier-based Army bombers raid Tokyo
	May	6	General Wainwright surrenders on Corregidor
		6–8	Battle of the Coral Sea
		8	Germans begin second Russian campaign
		30	First British 1000-bomber raid on Germany

1942	June	4–7	Battle of Midway
		18	Winston Churchill arrives in Washington for second allied war council
		21	Tobruk falls to Axis; Rommel enters Egypt
	July	1	Germans capture Sevastopol
	August	7	Marines land at Guadalcanal
		9	Battle of Savo Island
		17	First independent United States bombing attack in Europe
		18	Canadians and British raid Dieppe
	November	4	British victory at Alamein in Egypt
		7	Anglo-American forces land in North Africa
		12–15	Battle of Guadalcanal
		21	Russians begin great counteroffensive in Caucasus
	December	24	Darlan assassinated
1943	January	24	President Roosevelt and Prime Minister Churchill announce ten-day meeting of third allied war council at Casablanca—the "unconditional surrender" meeting
		31	Battle of Stalingrad ends in surrender of German Sixth Army
	February	14	Americans suffer setback at Kasserine Pass
	March	1–3	Battle of the Bismarck Sea
		29	British break through the Mareth line in Tunisia
	May	11	Prime Minister Churchill in Washington for fourth allied war council
		11	Americans land on Attu
		12	North African campaign concluded in great allied victory
	June	30	Americans land on Rendova
	July	10	Anglo-American forces land in Sicily
		25	Mussolini falls
	August	15	Allies land at Kiska and find no Japanese
		17	Prime Minister Churchill and President Roosevelt meet in Quebec for fifth allied war council
		17	Sicilian campaign completed
		17	Eighth Air Force anniversary raid on Schweinfurt and Regensburg
	September	3	Allies invade Italy
		8	Italy surrenders
		9	Amphibious landing at Salerno, Italy
		16	Americans take Lae in New Guinea
	October	1	Naples falls
		19	Moscow Conference of Foreign Secretaries begins
	November	1	Marines land at Bougainville
		6	Red Army retakes Kiev

1943	November	21	Americans land on Tarawa and Makin in the Gilbert Islands
		22	President Roosevelt, Prime Minister Churchill, and Generalissimo Chiang-kai-shek meet at Cairo
		28	President Roosevelt, Prime Minister Churchill, and Marshal Stalin meet at Teheran
	December	15	Americans land at Arawe in New Britain
		21	Stilwell begins second Burma campaign
		29	Russians break through west of Kiev, entering Poland
1944	January	11	Pre-invasion strategic air offensive from Britain begins
		22	Allies land at Nettuno-Anzio beachhead south of Rome
		31	Americans land in Marshall Islands
	March	28	Allies admit failure at Cassino in Italy
	April	10	Russians recapture Odessa
		22	Americans land at Hollandia in Dutch New Guinea
	May	10	Russians recapture Sevastopol
		11	Allies renew Italian offensive
		17	Myitkyina airstrip captured
	June	4	Rome liberated
		6	Anglo-American forces land in Normandy
		15	Americans land in Saipan, in the Mariana Islands
		25	Cherbourg liberated
	July	3	Russians take Minsk
		9	British take Caen
		20	Hitler survives attempted assassination and coup d'état
		21	Americans land on Guam
		25	American offensive begins at Avranches, Normandy
	August	2	Russians reach the Baltic Sea in Latvia
		3	Myitkyina falls
		15	Franco-American forces land in Southern France
		25	Paris liberated
	September	4	British free Brussels
		11	Americans free Luxembourg
		12	Americans enter Germany
		13	Prime Minister Churchill and President Roosevelt meet at Quebec for seventh allied war council
		15	Marines land at Peleliu
		17–28	Battle of Arnhem
	October	7	Dumbarton Oaks Conference ends
		20	Americans return to the Philippines
		20	Red Army enters East Prussia
		23–26	Battle of Leyte Gulf
		28	General Stilwell recalled

1944	November	7	Franklin Roosevelt re-elected President
		20	Americans enter Metz
		24	Tokyo bombed by B-29 bombers from Saipan
	December	3	Civil war in Greece
		16	German counteroffensive launched in the Ardennes
		27	Bastogne relieved
		31	Russian-sponsored Polish government set up in Lublin
1945	January	9	Americans land on Luzon
		17	Russians take Warsaw
	February	4–10	President Roosevelt, Generalissimo Stalin, and Prime Minister Churchill meet at Yalta in eighth war council
		19	Marines land on Iwo Jima
	March	7	At Remagen Americans capture bridgehead across Rhine
		21	British retake Mandalay
		27	Americans take Frankfurt
	April	1	Americans land at Okinawa
		1	Double envelopment of Ruhr completed
		9	Russians take Vienna
		11	Americans reach the Elbe
		12	Franklin D. Roosevelt dies
		17	Americans take Nuremberg
		22	Red Army fighting in Berlin
		25	Russian and American troops meet at Torgau, Germany
		25	San Francisco Conference opens
	May	1	Death of Adolf Hitler
		2	Berlin falls
		8	V–E day
	June	21	Okinawa taken
		26	United Nations Charter signed at San Francisco
	July	16	Atomic bomb exploded in New Mexico
		17	President Truman, Prime Minister Churchill and Generalissimo Stalin meet at Potsdam in final war council
		26	The Potsdam Ultimatum issued to Japan
		26	Clement Attlee becomes British Prime Minister
	August	6	Atomic bomb dropped on Hiroshima
		8	Russia declares war on Japan
		9	Atomic bomb dropped on Nagasaki
		10	Japan sues for peace
		14	Japan accepts Allied terms
		15	V–J day
	September	2	Japanese surrender signed on U.S.S. Missouri in Tokyo Bay

INDEX

Adams, General Charles F., 92
Adams, Charles Francis, 166
Aggressive war, crime of, 584-591
Ainsworth, General Fred C., 33-37, 452
American Sugar Refining Co., prosecution of, 8, 9-14
Andrews, General Frank M., 407
Andrews, Walter G., 377-378
Antisubmarine war, lessons of, 508-518
Argentina, 174, 178
Army. *See* U. S. Army
Army Specialized Training Program (ASTP), 457-461
Army-Navy football game, 504-505, 517-518
Arnold, General Henry H., 415, 416, 425, 510, 515, 550, 661, 662
Atlantic, battle of, 367-376
Atlantic Charter, 565
Atomic bomb, effect on Japanese surrender, 628; making of, 612-617; New Mexico test, 625, 637; political meaning of, 635-638; use of in World War II, 629-633; use of in future, 634-636. *See also* names of countries
Atomic energy, 468-469
Austin, Warren, 482
Austin-Wadsworth Bill, efforts in behalf of, 482-488
Austria, 201, 567
AVALANCHE (landing at Salerno), 431, 432

Bacon, Robert, 91
Balfour, Lord Arthur James, 251-252

Balkans, invasion of contemplated, 430, 434
Ball, William S., 7
Ballinger, Richard A., 19-21, 29
Ballinger-Pinchot controversy, 19-21
Baker, Newton D., 91, 93, 94, 130, 246
Bard, Ralph A., 616
Barker, Major General Ray W., 430, 432
Barkley, Alben W., 614
Barnes, William, Jr., 63, 68-69, 75
Baruch, Bernard, 354, 452, 494
Baxter, James Phinney, 465
Bennett, James Gordon, 14
Bernays, Colonel, 585
Biddle, Francis, 587
Bird, Francis W., 7
Bliss, Tasker, 557
Bolivia, 174, 178
BOLERO (building up American strength in England), 418-428, 437
Bonaparte, Charles J., 18
Borah, William E., 104, 213, 214, 217, 273; letter to, 246, 248-255, 256-257, 263
Bowers, John M., 15
Bowles, Dr. Edward L., 466, 468, 510, 514, 660
Brackett, Edgar, 69-71, 72, 75, 77
Bradley, General Omar, 445
Brandegee, Frank B., 104, 159
Brandeis, Louis D., 20
Brazil, 178, 179, 180, 187
Brent, Charles H., 138
Briand, Aristide, 170, 265, 273, 275
Bridges, Styles, 614
British Army, Stimson attached to, 96
British Fleet, 318

Brooke, Field Marshal Sir Alan Francis, 417, 439

Bruening, Heinrich, 212, 270, 271, 272, 277, 279

Buckner, Emory R., 7

Bundy, Harvey H., 193, 295, 343-344, 396, 465, 466, 641, 660

Bundy, McGeorge, xi, 100, 673-677

Burma, Stilwell's campaign in, 528-541 *passim*

Bush, Dr. Vannevar, 465, 466, 514, 612, 613, 614, 615, 616

British Eighth Army, 427

Byrnes, James F., 500, 616, 626, 627

Cairo, conference at, 440, 443, 445, 446

California, evacuation of Japanese from, 405-406

Campbell, General, 452

Canada, and destroyer deal with Great Britain, 358-359; vacations in, xvi; work on atomic bomb, 614

Canfield, Cass, 676

Carr, Wilbur J., 193

Casablanca, conference at, 428

"Case of the Seventeen Holes," 10-14

Castle, William R., 192, 193, 210

Cement makers, defended against antitrust suit, 108, 109

Chang, General, 232

Chamberlain, Neville, 387

Chamorro, President, 112

Chanler, William, 587

Chennault, General Claire, 534, 535, 536, 537-538, 540

Chiang Kai-shek, opposed to Stilwell, 530, 531, 532, 533, 535, 536, 537, 539, 540

Chiang, Kai-shek, Madame, 536

Chicago *Tribune*, publishes secret war plans, 393

Chile, 182

China, dispute with Russia, 188-189; Japanese attack, 311-312, 384; Japanese invade Manchuria, 220-263;

Shanghai incident, 239-243; and Stilwell, 528-541 *passim*; visit to, 157

Choate, Joseph H., 15, 16, 44

Churchill, Winston, 166, 357, 513, 533-534, 540, 556, 592, 608, 614; and Anglo-American strategy, 1941-1944, 413, 416, 419-420, 423-425, 428-430, 436, 438-442, 446-448; on atomic bomb, 634; and controversy over using Great Britain as base of operations, 413-448; and destroyer deal, 358; and Morgenthau plan, 575, 576-577, 581; visit to, 431-433

Clark, Grenville, 323, 346, 348, 410, 482

Clark, J. Reuben, 184

Clark, General Mark, 659

Clarke, Mr., xviii

Claudel, Paul, 206, 207, 256

Clemenceau, Georges, 276

Cleveland, Grover, xviii-xix, 298

Coal operators, defended in law suit, 108-109

Colombia, 176, 182, 185

Combined Chiefs of Staff, establishment of, 413-414, 417

Communism, 653 ff.

Compton, Dr. Karl T., 616

Conant, Dr. James B., 465, 612, 613, 615, 616

Constitutional Convention. *See* New York

Coolidge, Calvin, 124, 127, 129, 184; appoints Stimson Governor General of the Philippines, 116, 128; sends Stimson to Nicaragua, 111; Stimson meets, 110-111

Coral Sea, battle of, 407

Corregidor, surrender at, 405

Cotton, Joseph P., 161, 174, 177, 191-192, 193

Coudert, Frederic R., 89

Cox, James M., 105

Craig, General Malin, 350

Credit-Anstalt, collapse of, 201-202
Crim, John W. H., 7
Croly, Herbert, 59, 62, 76
Crowder, General Enoch, 34-35, 92, 347
Cuba, 181, 183, 185
Customs service, report on, 12-14
Cutler, Robert, 340

Darlan, Admiral, 542-545, 552
Davies, Joseph P., 586
Davis, Governor General, 149
Davis, Colonel Benjamin O., Jr., 463
Davis, Dwight, 457
Davis, Elmer, 497
Davis, Norman, 310
Dawes, Charles G., 165, 167, 202, 229, 233, 234
De Gaulle, Charles, 545-553, 560
Deane, Colonel, 438
Debuchi, Katsugi, 228
Deming, Harold S., 7
Denison, Winfred, 7
Devers, General Jacob L., 431, 659
Diaz, President, 112, 113, 114
Dickinson, Jacob, 28
Dill, Field Marshal Sir John, 414
Disarmament, problem of in 1931 and 1932, 265-281
Dix, John A., 26, 28
Dominican Republic, 184
Donovan, General William, 455
Doolittle raid, 405
Dorr, Goldthwaite H., 7, 482, 660
Douglas, Lewis W., 25
Draft. See Selective Service System
Draft Extension Act, battle over, 377-379. See also Selective Service System
Dykstra, Clarence, 347, 348

Eberstadt, Ferdinand, 494
Eden, Anthony, 257, 430, 433, 434, 548
Eichelberger, General Robert L., 659
Eisenhower, General Dwight D., 416, 431, 433, 442, 443, 499, 543, 544, 545, 566, 582, 659, 663; and De Gaulle, 549-550, 547-548, 551; and military government in North Africa, 554, 555, 558
Elections, of 1912, 48-55, 62; of 1916, 88; of 1920, 104-107; of 1932, 282-288; of 1932, aftermath of, 288-296; of 1940, 335-336; of 1944, 340; in liberated France, 548-549
Ethiopia, betrayal of, 307; invasion of, 310-311
Europe, 310, postwar need of help, 590-595; plan for reconstruction of, 593-595, 653-654
Executive budget, efforts in behalf of, 72-73, 74, 107

Far Eastern Crisis, 220-263
Far Eastern Crisis, The, 220, 222, 227, 229, 234, 237, 239, 247, 297
Fascism, 314-316
Feis, Herbert, 193, 291
Finland, Russian attack on, 317
Finley, John, 677
Fisher, Walter L., 29, 44
Foch, General Ferdinand, 478
Forbes, Cameron, 41, 122, 128, 149, 184, 228
Ford, Henry Jones, 62
Foreign Affairs, articles in, 588-591, 649-655
Forrestal, James V., 354, 507, 519, 523, 563
Four-Power Treaty, 600
Fox, Austen, 15
France, Darlan affair, 542-545; dealings with De Gaulle, 545-553; fall, 541-544; fear of revolution in, 575-576; invasion of, and Anglo-American strategy, 413-448; invasion of, 1940, 317-318; liberated, 545-553; London Naval Conference, 166, 169-172; Manchurian crisis, 238; Nine-Power Treaty, 237; problem of disarmament, 265-281 passim;

problem of war debts, 202-219 *passim*; three-power military understanding proposed, 314-316; residence in, 83; as soldier in, 95-99. *See also* Elections

Franco, Francisco, 498

Frankfurter, Felix, 7, 26, 161, 195, 334; intermediary between Franklin D. Roosevelt and Stimson, 289-292

Gallup Poll, on America's attitude toward war, April, 1941, 374-375

Gann, Mrs., 159-160

Garfield, James, 20, 31

Garrison, Lindley, 54-55, 87, 88

General Staff, battle for protection of, 32-37, 38-39

Geneva, Stimson at, 257

George V, 167

Germany, attacks Russia, 371, 383; attitude toward, 83-84; experiments on atomic weapon, 613; invasion of France, 1940, 317-318; pact with Russia, 316; postwar need of help, 593, 594; problem of disarmament, 265-281 *passim*; problem of war debts, 201-219 *passim*; urges program of resistance to, 318-320; visit to, 270-272; war guilt of, World War I, 89-90; in World War I, 82-100 *passim*. *See also* Morgenthau plan, War criminals

Gibson, Hugh, 167

Gibson, Truman, 464

Giraud, General Henri, 545

Goethals, George W., 41

Gompers, Samuel, 77

Gorgas, William C., 557

Govern, Hugh, Jr., 7

Government, responsible, efforts in behalf of, 56-81

Government service, dearth of first-rate men, 194-195

Grandi, Count Dino, 268-269

Great Britain, anti-submarine air operations of, 510; and atomic bomb, 614, 645; and Burma, 528-529, 533-534, 538, 539, 540, 541; and China, 528, 529, 533-534, 538, 539, 540; destroyer deal, 355-360; Morgenthau plan, 573, 574, 575, 576-577, 579, 580, 581; passage of Lend-Lease Act, 360-363; postwar need of help, 592, 593; problem of disarmament, 265-281 *passim*; problem of war debts, 202-219 *passim*; Stimson urges U. S. support of, 1940, 318-320; three-power military understanding proposed, 314-316; U. S. aid to, 355-363; and U. S. war strategy, 1941-1944, 413-420, 423-426, 428-433, 436-441, 445, 446-448. *See also* Atlantic, battle of; BOLERO; London Naval Conference

Green, William, 354

Grew, Joseph C., 619, 626

Grey, Sir Edward, 306

Grinnell, George Bird, xvi

Groves, General Leslie R., 613, 614

Guadalcanal, 407

Gullion, General, 553-554

Gurney, Chan, 519

Guthrie, William D., 16

GYMNAST. *See* TORCH

Haiti, 182, 183, 184, 186

Hamaguchi, Premier, 225

Hammond, Lyman P., 141

Harding, Warren G., 105-106, 107, 122, 158, 353

Harper's Magazine, article on atomic bomb, 612-613, 620-626, 627, 630, 631-632, 633

Harriman, Averell, 606, 641

Harrison, Francis Burton, 121, 123, 130, 133, 135

Harrison, George L., 209, 616, 641, 660

Harrison, Pat, 337

Harvard Law School, xv-xvi

Harvey, George, 200
Hawaii, attack on, 382-394
Hay, John, 234, 237, 249-250, 254, 256
Hays, Will, 103
Hearst, William Randolph, 8
Hedges, Job, 27
Henry, General Stephen G., 466-467
Herriot, Edouard, 211-212, 217, 273, 279, 552
Hershey, General Lewis B., 347, 348, 489
Hewitt, Admiral Henry K., 505-506
"Highhold," establishment of residence at, xxii
Hilldring, General John, 559, 560
Hilles, Mr., 29, 30
Hillman, Sidney, 354, 355, 488, 489
Hindenburg, Paul von, 270
Hiroshima, 625, 630
Hitler, Adolf, 264, 270, 305, 306, 589
Hodges, General Courtney H., Jr., 659
Holmes, Oliver Wendell, 92, 590; visits to, 197-199
Hoover, Herbert, 19, 110, 191; aftermath of election of 1932, 288-296; appoints Stimson Secretary of State, 143, 155-158, 160; election of 1932, 282-288; Finnish relief, 317; and Latin America, 177, 181-183, 185-187; London Naval Conference, 164, 165, 166, 167, 172, 173, 174; Ramsay MacDonald visits, 166; moratorium, 202-219, 273; and Philippines, 149; problem of disarmament, 275, 276; Stimson guest of in White House, 161-162; temperament of, 195-197, 199-200
Hopkins, Harry, 333-334, 373, 381, 416, 417, 418, 424, 425, 434-435, 471, 562, 568, 569, 570, 580
Hornbeck, Stanley, 249
Howard, Mr., xviii

Hughes, Charles Evans, 21, 26, 61, 66, 88, 109-110, 158-159, 177, 179, 237, 254, 256
Hull, Cordell, 256, 310, 360, 382, 399, 495, 517, 559, 595; aided by Stimson at London, 298; appointed Secretary of State, 294-295; at Cabinet meetings, 562, 563; friendship with 332, 333; liberation of France, 541-553 passim; and military government, 554, 555; Morgenthau plan, 569, 570, 575; Stimson supports trade policy of, 298-301, 591; and strategy in Pacific before Pearl Harbor, 382-390 passim; on Supreme Court Bill of 1937, 303-304
Hurley, Patrick, 243, 244, 245, 247, 538
HUSKY (invasion of Sicily), 428, 429

Iceland, occupation of, 372, 373
Ickes, Harold, 333, 371
India, Stilwell's campaign in, 528-541 passim
Isolationism, battle against, 307-309, 312
Italy, and disarmament, 266-270, 274; invaded, and Anglo-American strategy, 428, 429, 430, 431-432, 433, 434, 436, 437; invades Ethiopia, 310-311; London Naval Conference, 166, 169-172; Manchuria crisis, 238; visit to, 268-270
Iwo Jima, 620

Jackson, Robert H., 333, 371, 490, 587
James, William, xv
Japan, and atomic bomb, 618, 625-626; attack on China, 311-312; attack on Pearl Harbor, 382-394; conquest of Philippines, 395-405; embargo against, 384-385, 387; Emperor, 242, 626, 627, 628, 630, 631; invasion of Manchuria, 220-

263; and League of Nations, 306; London Naval Treaty, 162-174; proposed program for, 620-624; Franklin D. Roosevelt in 1902 hears tale of ambitions of, 301-302; Stimson foresees threat of, 306-307, 311-312, 314; surrender of, 617, 619, 627-629; visit to, 157; westernalization of, 222-223

Japanese-Americans, evacuation of, 405-406; troops, 406

Jefferson, Thomas, 59, 60, 61, 178

Johnson, Hiram, 104, 172, 236

Joint Chiefs of Staff, organization of, 414-415, 438, 515

Jones Act, 118, 121, 122, 123, 125, 129, 133-134, 149

Jones, Jesse, 354

Kamikaze, 618

Kellogg, Frank B., 110, 158

Kellogg-Briand Pact, 158, 164, 188, 189, 226, 227, 235, 238, 253, 259, 260, 262, 275, 588; speech on, 278-279

Keynes, Lord John Maynard, 567

Kimmel, Admiral Husband E., 391

King, Admiral Ernest J., 396, 399, 416, 425, 438, 506, 507, 511-512, 513, 514, 515, 550

King, Mackenzie, 358

Kirk, Admiral Alan G., 506

Kirk, General Norman T., 454

Klots, Allen T., 192, 195, 249

Knox, Frank, 388, 389, 396, 416, 482, 563; and appointment of Stimson as Secretary of War, 323, 324, 332, 333; Army-Navy relations, 506, 507, 509, 511, 512, 517, 519; and battle of Atlantic, 66, 367, 368, 371, 386; and mobilization, 354, 355, 356

Knudsen, William S., 354, 355, 380, 492

Korea, Japanese conquest of, 261

Krueger, General Walter, 659

Krug, Julius, 494

Kyle, Colonel, 668

Labor, before Pearl Harbor, 381: and war, 488-491

Lamarr, Hedy, 412

Lamb, Charles, 573

Land, Emery S., Admiral, 340

Landis, Kenesaw Mountain, 9

Latin America, 157; in 1931, 174-187; peace of Tipitapa, 110-116; mission to Nicaragua, 110-116; relations with, as Secretary of State, 174-187

Lausanne agreement, 211-214, 215-216

Laval, Pierre, 207, 211, 212, 273-274, 275, 542

Law, profession of, attitude toward, xxi-xxii; practice of, 1918-1927, 107-116

League of Nations, 159, 264, 276, 568, 599, 604; fight for, 101-107; Germany joins, 270; invasion of Ethiopia, 310; and Manchurian crisis, 227, 228, 229-236, 239, 244, 246, 248, 249, 259, 260-261, 263; belief in success of, 306; U. S. assurance to, 310

Leahy, Admiral William D., 438, 542, 575

Lee, John C. H., 41

Lend-Lease Act, 360-363

Lend-Lease supplies, 367-376

Lewis, John L., 109, 381, 489

Lincoln, Abraham, 437, 477

Lindbergh, Charles A., 116

Lindsay, Sir Ronald, 293

Littlefield, Congressman, 15

Lloyd, D. Frank, 7

Loomis, Alfred, 468

Locarno Pact, 270, 277

Lodge, Henry Cabot, 20, 104, 159

London Economic Conference, 298

London Naval Conference, 162-174, 187, 192, 210, 224, 266-267

London Naval Treaty. *See* London Naval Conference

Longworth, Nicholas, 20

Longworth, Mrs., 160

Lovett, Robert A., 343, 344, 396, 468, 510, 660, 662

Low, Seth, 66

Lowell, A. Lawrence, 246

Ludlow Resolution, 313

Lytton Commission, 231, 236, 259, 260-261

MacArthur, General Douglas, 388, 407-408, 507, 517, 539, 659; Roosevelt's message to, 400-401, 404-405; and question of Philippine withdrawal from war, 397-404

McCloy, John J., 342-343, 344, 396, 406, 451-452, 455, 468, 543, 550, 553, 555, 557-559, 560, 563, 568, 569, 577, 578, 582, 585, 587, 620, 641, 660, 661

McCormack, Alfred, 455

McCormack, John W., 614

McCoy, General Frank.R., 40, 115, 149, 261, 350-351, 500, 530, 556

MacDonald, Ramsay, 205, 206, 209, 211-212, 257, 265, 448, 525; and London Naval Treaty, 165-166, 167, 170, 171; visits Washington, 166

Macfarlane, Wallace, 15

Machado, President, 183

McKinley, xviii, 118, 127, 375, 522

MacLeish, Archibald, 497

McNair, General Leslie, 444

McNarney, General Joseph T., 466

McNutt, Paul, 481, 486

Mahan, Alfred T., 506

Manchuria, dispute between China and Russia in, 188-189; Japanese invasion of, 220-263

Marshall, General George C., and Anglo-American strategy, 1941-1944, 413-420, 423-425, 428, 431, 433, 435; and antisubmarine war,

510-516 *passim*; army of, compared to Grant's army, 456; on army reorganization, 449; on ASTP, 460; and atomic bomb, 612, 613, 614, 617; aware of Russian strength, 605; and battle of Atlantic, 366, 367, 386; and controversy over General Gullion, 553; co-operation with British, 455; and defense of Philippines, 388, 396, 398, 399, 404, 405; and De Gaulle, 550; establishment of unified Allied high command, 413-414; establishes unity of command in Army outposts, 407; explains Draft Extension Act, 377; grants naval request, 509; helpful influence on War Department, 409, 410, 656; and Lend-lease, 356, 359; and military discipline, 454; on military government, 553; and military government in North Africa, 555, 558; and officer training program, 348-349, 350, 351; and Pearl Harbor probe, 391; and problem of size of Army, 476; and public relations, 498; and question of change in title of the Chief of Staff, 450; and question of supreme commander for invasion of France, 437-443; and reorganization of War Department, 453; and scientists, 469; and Selective Service Act, 346; "steals" services of General Henry, 467; and Stilwell, 528-541 *passim*; Stimson bids farewell to, 668, 669; Stimson's estimate of, 330-331, 662-664; suggests Navy share Pentagon Building, 506; and use of radar, 510; on use of scientific help, 465; on young men as soldiers, 474. *See also* AVALANCHE, BOLERO

Martin, Joseph, 614

Martyn, John W., 410-411, 660

Marx, Karl, 655

Matsudaira, Tsuneo, 257

Maynard, Isaac, xix
Meade, General George, 478
Mellon, Andrew W., 204
Merck, George, 468
Merrill's Marauders, 537
Mexico, 178, 179, 181, 183, 186-187
Meyer, George von L., 49
Midway, battle of, 407
Milburn, John G., 15
Military government, 553-561
Military training. *See* Universal military training
Mills, Ogden, 200, 204, 205, 211, 290
Minseito Cabinet, 169, 231
Mobilization, industrial, 351-355; military, *see* Selective Service System, U. S. Army
Moley, Raymond, 293, 298
Moncada, General, 114
Monroe Doctrine, 175, 184, 185
Montana, exploring in, xvi
Moody, W. H., 3, 18
Moratorium, on intergovernmental debts, 202-219
Morgan, General Frederick Edgworth, 430, 431-432
Morgenthau, Henry, Jr., 332, 354, 356, 359, 360, 495; and Morgenthau plan, 568-570, 573-574, 576-577, 580-581, 582, 583
Morgenthau plan, 570, 574, 576, 577, 584; estimate of, 566-568, 571-573, 578, 580-582; *See also* Roosevelt, F. D.
Morrow, Dwight, 167, 178, 181, 183
Morse, Charles W., 10, 56
Moses, General, 466
Mountbatten, Admiral Lord Louis, 423, 424, 533
Murphy, Charles Francis, 68
Murphy, Frank, 150
Murphy, Robert, 555
Mussolini, Benito, 172; visit to, 268-270

Nagasaki, 625
National Service Act, 473; efforts in behalf of, 480-491
Naval Treaty. *See* London Naval Treaty
Nazis, estimate of threat of, 1933-1940, 305, 306, 307, 314. *See also* War criminals
Neary, Elizabeth, 411, 675
Negro, and the Army, 461-464; Navy prejudice against, 507
Nelson, Donald M., 380, 492, 494
Neutrality acts, attack on, 1935-1940, 309-320
New Deal, attitude toward, 297, 302-303
New Haven, speech at, 1940, 318-320, 324, 326-327, 328, 329
New York Bar Association, elected president of, 297
New York City, boyhood in, xii-xiii
New York Constitutional Convention (1915), 65-81
Newfoundland, visit of inspection to, 411-412
Nicaragua, 183, 185, 186; efforts to remove marines from, 183-184; refuses to use American forces in, 181-182; special emissary to, 111-116
Nichols, J. Osgood, 7
Nicoll, Delancey, 15, 67, 70
Nine-Power Treaty, 226, 227, 237, 238, 239, 244, 247, 248, 249, 255, 257; letter to Borah on, 249-255
Nonrecognition, doctrine of, 257-258; and Manchurian crisis, 226-239, 243, 244
North Africa, invasion of, decision on arrived at, 425-426; Franklin Delano Roosevelt on, 419; Stimson on, 422-423, 426; success of, 427-428
North Africa, military government of, 554-559
Nuremburg trial, 583-590

O'Brian, John Lord, 65, 66, 71, 304, 355
O'Brien, Morgan J., 67
Officer Candidate Schools, 349-350
Okinawa, 620
Osborn, Frederick, 379
Osmeña, Sergio, 124, 125, 127, 129, 131, 134, 135, 136, 138-139, 144, 149, 151
OVERLORD (invasion of France), 429-448, 524, 567

Pacific bases, attitude on, 599-605
"Pact of Paris," speech on, 259-260
Page, Arthur W., 676
Palmer, Arthur E., 341
Palmer, George M., xv
Panama, 178
Panama Canal, defense of, 406-407
Papen, Franz von, 212, 270, 279
Paraguay, 185
Parker, Judge, 15
Parkman, Henry, Jr., 337-339
Parr, Richard, 11-12
Parsons, Herbert, 65, 66, 71, 96, 99, 105, 106
Parsons, John E., 15
Patch, General Alexander M., 659
Patterson, Dr. Frederick, 464
Patterson, Robert P., 323, 324, 337, 338, 339, 341-342, 343, 344, 351, 354, 362, 451-452, 492, 493, 660
Patton, General George S., 41, 96, 351, 427, 468, 499, 659-660
Payne-Aldrich tariff, 19, 20
Peace, Stimson's principles for maintenance, of, 566-568
Pearl Harbor, attack on, 382, 389; effect on national morale, 393-394; responsibility for, 391-393; Stimson learns of, 390-391
Pearson, Drew, 496, 499, 504, 580
Pepper, George W., 20
Pershing, General John J., 37, 97, 99, 524, 556

Peru, 174, 178, 185
Pétain, Marshal, 542
Philippines, 157, 158; efforts to defend before Pearl Harbor, 388-389; efforts at independence, 148-152; inadequate defenses of, 600-601; Japanese conquest of, 395-405; Roosevelt's attitude toward, 298; Stimson as Governor General of, 117-148; Stimson's differences with Navy over defense of, 395-397; tariff agitation in, 146-150; visit to, 110-111
Phillips Academy, Stimson at, xiii-xiv
Pinchot, Gifford, 19-21, 28, 29, 30, 31, 42, 43
Pitkin, Walcott H., Jr., 7
Platt, Tom, 4
Poincaré, Raymond, 272
Poland, and Yalta agreement, 609
Portal, Air Chief Marshal Sir Charles, 417
Potsdam, Stimson at, 656
Pound, Admiral Sir Dudley, 417
Pratt, Admiral William V., 168
Press, relations with, 210-211, 496-502
Proctor, Robert, 354
Production, effect of national indecision on, 380-381
Progressive movement, speech on, 58-62
Prohibition, 286-287
Public relations, 210-211, 496-502
Pulitzer, Joseph, 14
Putnam, Mr., xviii

Quebec, decisions at, 439, 440
Quezon, Manuel, 124-125, 127, 129, 134, 137-138, 141, 143, 144, 147, 148, 149, 150, 151; Roosevelt's message to, 401-403; and Philippine withdrawal from war, 397-405.

Railroads, prosecution of, 8-10
Rayburn, Sam, 614

Reconstruction, planning for, 591-595. *See also* Europe
Reed, David, 166-167, 168, 169, 172
Reed, Walter, 557
Regnier, Captain Eugene, 193
Renwick, Sir Robert, 467
Reparations, problem of, 202-219
Roberts, George, 155, 156, 161, 195, 323
Robinson, Joseph T., 166, 167, 172
Rogers, James Grafton, 192-193, 249, 291, 295
Roosevelt, Franklin Delano, 279, 338, 352, 406, 453, 465, 648, 668; administrative technique, 494-496; and advisers, 333-334, 620; aftermath election 1932, 288-296; and Anglo-American strategy, 413-418, 419, 423-427, 435, 437-439, 441, 443, 444, 447-448; and antisubmarine war, 509, 512, 515-516; and Army-Navy game, 504-505, 518; and Army-Navy relations, 522-523; as Commander in Chief, 524-525, 565-566, 664-667; and Atlantic Charter, 565; and atomic bomb, 611-612; Cabinet meetings of, 561-564; and crime of aggressive war, 586-587; and Darlan affair, 542-544; and dealings with Russia, 297, 608-609, 637, 649; death, 656; and De Gaulle, 545-552, 560; and destroyer deal, 355-360; election of 1932, 282-288; fears revolution in France, 575-576; first meeting with Stimson, 292-293; foreign and domestic policy 1934, 301-302, 310; guided by Marshall's views, 662; and Haiti, 184; handling of visitors, 411; hears in 1902 tale of Japanese ambition, 301-302; and Italy, 310-311; and Lend-Lease, 360-363, 592-593; and London Economic Conference, 298; and London Naval Treaty, 173; and military government, 553-561; and Morgenthau

plan, 567, 573, 574, 576-578, 580-582; and National Defense Advisory Commission, 354-355; and Negroes, 463; and New Deal, 302-304; offers Stimson position of Secretary of War, 323-324; and Pearl Harbor, 382-393; and Philippine withdrawal from war, 397-405; physical condition, 575, 605; and postwar Allies, 592-593; prepares U. S. for war, 364-381; "quarantine speech," 312.; and Selective Service, 345-348; and Stilwell, 530, 535-536, 537, 538-539, 540; Stimson's conferences with, 335; and Stimson's views on Philippines, 298, 395-396; and Supreme Court, 80, 303-304; and total mobilization, 470-502 *passim*; and Trade Agreements Act, 300, 301; understands Nazism, 524-525; and U. S. in Pacific, 601, 602; and use of radar, 509; and war debts, 217-218
Roosevelt, Mrs. Franklin D., letter to, 667
Roosevelt, Theodore, 6, 61, 78, 107, 170, 195, 245, 312, 331, 332, 374, 453, 522, 555, 560; appoints Stimson U. S. Attorney, 3-4; attitude toward Woodrow Wilson, 91; and customs reforms, 12, 18; and customs service reforms, 14; death of, 91; and election of 1916, 88; final break with William Howard Taft, 48-55; generation of, 82-83; and Latin American policy, 184; and Orient, 244; and Panama Canal, 176; Herbert Parsons a political adviser of, 66; and party split, 62; plans to raise division, 92, 93; praises Stimson's speech, 62; relations with William Howard Taft, 18-55 *passim*; requests Stimson to make speech, 58; Stimson meets, xx; Stimson's campaign for governor of New York, 21-28; Stimson's recon-

ciliation with, 91; use of open letter, 249; Wickersham's mistrust of,
65; and World War I, 91, 92, 93
Root, Elihu, 3-4, 41, 172, 180, 450,
506, 507, 522, 556, 660; Ainsworth
dismissal, 35, 36; on class reunions,
198; and election of 1916, 88; and
fight against rebates, 9; and fight
for League of Nations, 102-106;
Latin American policy, 177; and
New York Constitutional Convention of 1915, 63, 65, 66, 68, 71,
75; and Panama Canal tolls, 41;
and Philippines, 118, 127; on Platt
Amendment, 183; on problem of
disarmament, 276-277; and Roose-
velt-Taft split, 20, 49-50, 52, 53;
as Secretary of War creates general
staff, 32-33, 39; and Sherman Act,
45-46; Stimson assistant to in law
cases of, xxi; Stimson enters 'law
firm of, xviii; and Stimson's appointment as Secretary of War, 29,
30; and Stimson's campaign for
Governor, 24, 25; as U. S. Attorney, 5; on use of government troops
to protect private interests, 181
Rosenman, Judge Samuel, 586, 587
ROUNDHAMMER. See OVERLORD
Roxas, Manuel, 125, 129, 131, 134,
144
Royce, Josiah, xv, 198-199
Russia, 226; alliance with, 525, 526-
527; and Anglo-American strategy
in 1942, 416, 418, 419, 420, 421,
422, 423, 426, 427; and atomic
bomb, 642-647, 651; attack on Finland, 317; dispute with China, 188-
189; German attack on, 371, 383;
Japan makes peace proposals to,
617-618; and Manchuria, 222,
233; nonrecognition of, 159; pact
with Germany, 1939, 316; and
problem of disarmament, 266, 268;
relations with, 568, 583, 605-611,
637-642, 648-651; Stmison's contact with, 525, 526-527; as threat
to Japan, 624; and trusteeship
problem, 604; Russo-Japanese war,
224

Sacasa, 112
Salisbury, Lord, 250
Sandino, General, 114-115, 181
Santo Domingo, 185, 186
Sayre, Joel, 398, 399
Scotland, visit to, 297
Scott, General Hugh L., 93-94
Secretary of War, effect of state of
war on functions of, 408-409
Seiyukai Cabinet, 231
Selective Service System, battle over
extension of, 377-379; efforts to
broaden, 473-480; efforts to re-
duce draft age, 473-476; introduc-
tion of, 345-348
Senate, confirms Stimson as Secretary
of War, 325-331
Shaler, Professor, 198-199
Shanghai incident, 239-242, 243, 246,
253
Sherman Act, attitude toward, 44-48
Sherman, John, 417
Sherman, James S., 23
Sherman, General William T., 451,
468
Shidehara, Baron, 223, 225, 226,
227, 228, 230, 231, 252
Shiozawa, Admiral Koichi, 239, 240
Shiratori (Jap spokesman), 229
Short, General Walter C., 391
Sicily, invasion of, 428, 429
Simon, Sir John, 237, 242, 247-248,
257, 263
Simpson, General William H., 659
Sims, Admiral, 524
SLEDGEHAMMER ("beachhead" inva-
sion of France), 418, 426
Slessor, Air Marshal, 513, 514
Smith, Alfred E., 67-68, 78, 107
Smuts, General Jan, 434
Socialists, 107-108

Somervell, General Brehon, 354, 440, 451, 452, 453, 492, 536, 660
Soong, T. V., 530
Spain, war in, 307, 313-314
Spanish-American war, xx-xxi
Spooner, Senator, 15
Stalin, Joseph, 439-440, 607, 608, 637, 638, 640, 646, 647
Stark, Admiral Harold R., 357, 366, 386, 399
Stassen, Harold, 325
State Department, 154-296 *passim*; reorganization of, 1931, 191-195
Stephenson, Robert P., 7
Stettinius, Edward R., Jr., 548, 563, 568, 603, 607
Stilwell, Joseph W., and China, 528-541, 659
Stimson, Henry L., ancestry, xii; education, xii-xvi; love of outdoor life, xvi; joins law firm, xviii; marriage, xviii; early work as Republican, xix-xx; enlists Spanish-American war, xx; appointed U. S. Attorney for N. Y. Southern District (1906), 4; runs for Governor of N. Y., 21-28; appointed Secretary of War (1911), 29-31; officer in World War I, 91-100; private law practice (1918-1927), 107-109; special emissary to Nicaragua, 111-116; appointed Governor General of Philippines, 116-117; appointed Secretary of State (1929), 143, 156; return to private life (1933), 297; appointed Secretary of War 1940), 323-331; working routine World War II, 411; resigns as Secretary of War (1945), 656-657
Stimson, Mrs. Henry L., xviii, xxii, 14, 16, 30-31, 95-96, 98, 111, 113, 117, 128, 138-139, 155, 199, 268, 296, 297, 323, 344, 411, 668, 669, 677
Stimson, Lewis (father), 30, 83, 95, 455-456; career of, xvii-xviii

Straight, Willard, 96
Stresemann, Gustav, 212, 265
Submarine warfare, 84-86, 89, 508-518
Sumner, "Billy," xiv
Supply, Priorities, and Allocations Board, 380
Supreme Court, 80, 303-304
Surles, General Alexander, 500-501
Suzuki, 625

Tacna-Arica affair, 110, 157, 185, 187
Taft, Robert A., 327, 328-330
Taft, William Howard, 283, 329, 495, 522; executive budget, 72; final break with Theodore Roosevelt, 48-55; and Philippines, 118, 119, 127, 129, 138; relations with Theodore Roosevelt, 18-55 *passim*; Stimson as Secretary of War under, 28-55; and Stimson's campaign for governor of New York, 21-28; swears Stimson in as Secretary of State, 157-158
Tanaka, Baron, 224
Tanner, Frederick, C., 66
Tardieu, André 257, 272
Teheran, conference at, 439-440, 441, 443
Thatcher, Thomas D., 7
Thomas, Elmer D., 614
Timberlake Resolution, 145, 146, 148
Tipitapa, Peace of, 110-116
TORCH (invasion of North Africa), 419, 422, 423, 424, 425-428
Toynbee, Arnold, 190, 191, 238
Trade Agreements Act, 591; speech in behalf of, 299-301; support of, 298-301
Trieste, question of, 609-610
Truman, Harry S., 44, 107, 519, 523, 583, 592, 609, 610, 617, 656, 657, 663, 668; and atomic bomb, 619-624, 625, 626, 629, 634-636, 637, 638-640, 642-646; and surrender of Japan, 627

TVA, attitude toward, 43-44, 303
Tweed Ring, 58-59
Tydings-McDuffie Act, 149-150, 151

United Nations, 515, 584, 597, 600, 648; and question of Pacific bases for U. S., 599-605; and Russo-American relations, 610, 611
U. S., as world power, 308, 310, 629, 652-655
U. S. Air Forces, 661-662
U. S. Army, controversy over size of, 475-480; and controversy over unification of armed forces, 518-523; defends west coast, 405; and the Grand Alliance, 524-564; mobilizes, 345-351; morale of, 1941, 379-380; and the Negro, 461-464; and war production, 491-496; providing supplies for, 350-355; reorganization of, 31-41; Stimson as officer in, 91-100; Stimson's judgment on, 657-662; Stimson's work for preparedness, World War I, 86-91; wartime organization of, 449-469
U. S. Army-Navy relationships, 503-523
U. S. Navy, and controversy over unification of the armed forces, 518-523; difference of opinion on movement of U. S. Fleet before Pearl Harbor, 386-387; differences with Stimson over defense of Philippines, 395-397; effect of Pearl Harbor attack on morale of, 396; and London Naval Treaty, 162-174; and Negroes, 463, 507; opinion of, 506; voluntary enlistments suspended, 475
Universal military training, 318-320, 596-600

Vandenberg, Arthur H., 327, 328, 604
Versailles treaty, 264, 265, 271, 272, 273-274, 275, 277, 567

Villabos, Ruy López de, 118
Visitors, method of handling, 411
Vitetti (translator), 268
Voroshilov, General, 440

Wadsworth, James, 27, 471, 482
Wagner Act, 303, 304
Wagner, Robert, 67, 304
Wainwright, General Jonathan M., 405
Walcott, Frederick W., 89
Walker, Frank, 554
Wallace, Henry A., 487, 612, Stimson impressed by book of, 299
Walsh, David I., 337-339
Walton, Daniel D., 7
War criminals, 584-590
War debts, problem of, 202-219
War Department, effect of state of war on functions of, 408-409; organization of, 331, 340-344; protects West Coast and Panama, 405-408; reorganization of, 449-453; staff of, 409-412
War production, and the Army, 491-496
War Production Board, 492-494
Warren, Senator, 35-36, 37-38
Washington, D. C., climate of, 411
Washington, George, xii
Water power, federal regulation of, 41-44
Watson, Edwin M. ("Pa"), 334
Wedemeyer, General Albert C., 539
Welles, Sumner, 356, 399
Wheeler, Burton K., 378
White, Charles A., xviii
White, Francis, 177, 193
White, Harry, 569
White, Miss Mabel Wellington. See Stimson, Mrs. Henry L.
White, Wallace H., Jr., 614
White, William Allen, 184, 327, 357
Wickersham, George W., 18, 45, 65-66, 71
Willkie, Wendell, 140, 329, 357, 543, 544

Wilson, Charles E., 494

Wilson, Hugh, 229

Wilson, Woodrow, 41, 61, 62, 71, 78, 80, 159, 247, 283, 353, 375, 437, 603; and Clayton Act, 48; declares war on Germany, 88-89; and fight for League of Nations, 101-107; on neutrality, 90; notes to Germany, 1915, 84-85; Latin American policy, 177-178, 179; and League of Nations, 264; and Philippines, 120-121; Theodore Roosevelt's hatred of, 91; Stimson opposes lack of preparedness, 86-88

Wingate, General Orde C., 533, 537

Winnacker, Dr. Rudolph A., 675-676

Winthrop, Bronson, xviii, 30, 324

Wise, Henry A., 7

Wood, General Leonard, 452, 522, 556; and battle for General Staff, 33-39; death of, 127; and election of 1920, 104-105; as Governor General of Philippines, 122-126, 133, 134, 135, 136; and reorganization in Army, 33-41; Stimson visits Philippines with, 110-111; and work for preparedness, World War I, 86-87

Woodley, purchase of, 160-161

Woodring, Harry H., 323, 327

Woodrum, Clifton A., 598

World Court, 276, 278

World Disarmament Conference, 265-268, 279

World War I, 82-100; Stimson as officer in, 91-100

Yale, Stimson at, xiv-xv

Young, Owen D., 202, 205